# The Analytical Writer

## A COLLEGE RHETORIC

# The Analytical Writer

## A COLLEGE RHETORIC

### 2ND EDITION

*Adrienne Robins*

*Director of Writing Programs*
*Occidental College*

COLLEGIATE PRESS

Collegiate Press
San Diego, California

Executive Editor: Christopher Stanford
Senior Editor: Steven Barta
Senior Developmental Editor: Arlyne Lazerson
Design and Typography: John Odam Design Associates
Cover Art: Paul Slick

Telephone (619) 697-4182

Library of Congress Card Number 95-69716

ISBN : 0-939693-35-6

# CONTENTS

## PART 2 Drafting 91

## PART 3 Revising 141

## PART H  The Handbook 361

# TO THE STUDENT

I n the first edition of this book, I wrote essentially the following note to students; as I review it on the completion of the new edition, I feel strongly that it still says what I want to say to you: Some textbooks reduce the teaching of writing to a few absolutes about "good writing." Those books do have a virtue: they are short. That is also why I think they are dangerous. You might read the entire book and think you now know how to write. These books are at best placebos; the concepts they profess do not apply to much of the effective writing you read, much less to what you write. They are far too general on the one hand and too specific on the other. They leave writers out of control because they do not teach students how to analyze, only to conform.

Writing in college requires more than conformity: you must channel your existing writing abilities and continue to develop them, particularly your ability to analyze. It is my hope, then, that you will look at essay assignments as more than an obstacle or a direct path to a good grade and instead as opportunities for learning about a subject. Through writing, you can identify how much you already know about a subject and how much you will need to discover about it in order to convey a worthwhile point to another person. Writing becomes part of your thinking process.

When you adopt an attitude that permits free exploration of ideas, the act of writing will help you generate thoughts. In this book I explain college writing as a process of discovery, as a strategy or series of strategies that any college student can learn to apply.

I will quickly admit to you that not all people write the same way or at the same pace. Nor does every assignment have the same requirements for "good" writing. But these facts shouldn't concern you. Although on the surface it can at times seem frustrating to decide what constitutes effective writing for each situation, rest assured that you make similar decisions whenever you talk with someone. You would most likely not use profanity to communicate with a child; you would "edit" your talk to make your best impression on a first date; and you would incorporate the kind of humor your friends enjoy hearing if you were telling them a story.

These are issues of rhetoric, the effective use of language to communicate a point. Theories of rhetoric are predicated on the notion that nobody communicates without a context. Understanding the contexts of college writing will help you write well.

Another key to writing effectively is understanding the characteristics that make up a writing process. As you study this book, you will discover various strategies that can work well for you, and you will gradually incorporate them into a process or various optional processes that will help you to understand how you write best. With that goal in mind, you may want to scan the following overview of the chapters in this text:

Chapter 1 introduces some of the key considerations of college writers—what college writing is like, how a writer sounds, what approach writers take to their material, and how audience influences this approach. The last part of the chapter is an overview of the writing process that is taken up in the next seven chapters.

Chapter 2 poses various solutions to the problem "What should I write about?" It quickly moves into methods for developing a topic into a thesis that will help generate and focus the essay.

Reinforcing the sense of purpose the writer defines in the preceding chapter, Chapter 3 describes creative outlines and the major patterns of organization writers use.

Chapter 4 presents ways to develop, divide, and connect paragraphs. The chapter shows structural similarities and differences between paragraphs and essays and between journalistic paragraphs and those in college writing. Development of thoughtful, coherent paragraphs is emphasized through establishing clear boundaries for each paragraph and creating careful play between explanation and illustration of ideas.

Chapter 5 stimulates the imagination of the writer to entice the reader with appropriate and eye-catching beginnings and provocative endings that flow with the rest of the essay. Throughout, excerpts from students' essays provide patterns to imitate.

Chapter 6 takes writers from the rough draft to the polished paper, offering a three-step method for identifying and correcting common writing flaws, among them deadwood, trite phrases, faulty repetition, and excessive reliance on *to be*.

Chapter 7 shows the writer how to direct emphasis and meaning through varied sentence structure, by combining related ideas, using deliberate marks of punctuation, and imitating the styles of established writers.

Chapter 8 encourages writers to make concrete and direct word choices, make good use of the dictionary, build a solid but natural vocabulary, avoid wordiness, and recognize levels of language use appropriate to various audiences, purposes, and occasions. The chapter includes strategies for vocabulary development and avoiding trite expressions or jargon.

Chapter 9 is a comprehensive guide to library use written by Ann Perkins, chair of public services at the Oviatt Library at California State University, Northridge. Arranged by subject areas, the guide is easy to use. Its lively conversational tone makes it appropriate for a one-sitting reading, but its design by subject makes it a handy reference as well.

Chapter 10 takes the writer through ten effective steps for writing a research paper. A sample complete research paper, annotated with helpful information illustrates MLA style documentation. Electronic citation is included in the section on bibliography format.

Chapter 11 explains and gives samples of various special assignments or writing tasks: book reviews, annotated bibliographies, business letters and resumes, the personal statement, and both social science and scientific papers.

The last four chapters of the text make up a handbook of writing mechanics. Chapter A provides the basics of grammar, with descriptions of the parts of speech, sentence structures, and dialects, followed by a brief discussion of common interdialectical and interlanguage confusions. A final section explains in easy-to-use flow charts the principles of spelling and provides a list of commonly misspelled words.

Chapter B explains how to correct common errors. The chapter explains alternative practices for freeing writing of such prevalent errors as subject and verb disagreements, faulty predication, faulty pronoun reference and agreement, and so forth. The chapter can be used as a helpful step-by-step method of revising a paper or as a handy reference for specific information.

Chapter C is a comprehensive glossary of effective punctuation and mechanics. It presents examples for each rule and suggests revisions for common weak or incorrect usages.

Chapter D is the usage guide, a glossary of commonly misused and confused expressions. Suggested rewordings for the entries are all in context. Written with the awareness that language is not static, the usage glossary indicates which usages are controversial.

All strategies explained in this text are based on sound theories of teaching writing and on the patterns of successful writers. Writing and thinking should not be separated, and presenting only the steps without the accompanying explanation of how they influence your thinking would be of little more help than having no method at all. By using this text you will see as you plan, draft, and revise how your writing helps clarify your thoughts.

*Adrienne Robins*

# TO THE INSTRUCTOR

In developing this revision of *The Analytical Writer*, I have kept in the back of my mind that so many of my colleagues charged with teaching writing respond the same way at the end of the semester: "Teaching writing takes so much time." It's a legitimate complaint. This sense of being overwhelmed by the paper load, the conferencing, and the necessary integration of subject matter with the teaching of strategy is often compounded by students' finding their textbook "boring," lowering the classroom morale and placing the full burden of instruction on the teacher. I have done my best to make the text nonthreatening and engaging by giving real examples of student writing, popping in appropriate cartoons here and there, and speaking informally. At the same time I refuse to "dummy down" the complexity of learning about writing, for I believe that in understanding the many choices and criteria for them, students take control of their writing and eventually succeed. Even with the best of texts, it is a reality that writing instruction is sometimes intense and time consuming. Moreover, although we initially invest so much of ourselves, we often later redouble our efforts, feeling that we have to do all we can to assure that real results materialize in our students' writing. Most of us recognize ultimately, however, that the effort has been worthwhile— that teaching writing energizes us and gratifies us more than can other subjects because we do see sweeping changes in our students' thinking, their speaking, and even their living.

The cognitive growth of student writers goes far beyond the correction of surface features of writing to the ability to analyze, synthesize, and extrapolate, in school and beyond. My challenge has been to create a textbook worthy of the kind of teacher who both recognizes and accepts the cognitive issues in writing instruction. I have consistently asked myself how to make the book readable and teachable in that context. I have asked myself, "How does one help students learn to construct an argument; to create authentic, not just structural, introductions and conclusions; to garner and test support; and to present all this to an audience? Avoiding formulas and simplistic explanations, I have tried to get to the heart of thinking, not just of idea presentation, to treat ideation, language, and communication as interactive partners. I indeed have questioned myself about how to write a book that students find accessible (not boring) and at the same time that enthusiastic new teachers and T.A.'s who want to engender in their students a love of deep thinking find challenging to their students. Part of the solution for me has been to pay attention to learning style. That ambiguous term "thinking" my colleagues and I speak so heatedly about needs a broad—not a narrow—definition; learning styles vary greatly within every classroom. Thus I have tried to appeal in varied ways to students who need to work on their writing: each chapter offers various strategies for reaching similar goals.

Occasionally another teacher will ask whether the book is process or product oriented. Because I see writing as both the product of thinking and the generator of thoughts, I am eclectic. If in actuality the former question really means "Don't you grade grammar?" I answer yes, of course, but that I try to put such corrections in context, recognize the inherent logic in the student's error, and help the student (either in conferences or by commenting on the paper) reconstruct his or her thinking. Out of my approach grows the process-oriented approach in chapter B, through which students learn to edit by turning their essays into "exercises." Such a tactic helps to accomplish a fuller understanding than can a handbook organized by related grammatical topics alone or even worse, arranged alphabetically.

If you are an experienced user of *The Analytical Writer*, you will find some of the book familiar. I thank all the professors and students who devoted their time to completing the large-scale evaluation of the first edition. I was pleased to see that some of my favorite parts were also yours. My revisions to a great extent represent the directions of composition research, influenced by the suggestions of students and professors who have used the first edition. The new edition reflects four essential values: recognizing the diversity of writing processes, the necessity of peer and teacher interaction with the writer on drafts, the integration of writing and reading, and the appropriate uses of technology. Specific features of this second edition include

new writing samples

electronic citation formats

updated library use chapter with technological guidance

concise paragraph chapter

revised introduction and conclusion chapter

rhetorical as well as grammatical explanations for punctuation usage

new cartoons

exercises drawn from students' papers

a condensed chapter on research papers

and an expanded, and clearer, chapter on special assignments and other writing tasks

I hope you will be pleased with this new work.

*A.R.*

# ACKNOWLEDGMENTS

I want to thank my colleagues at Occidental College who have offered me sound advice on the writing in their disciplines. They include professors Norman Cohen and Wellington Chan in history, Louise Yuhas in art history, Dan Fineman in Literary Studies, Benedict Freedman in math, Tom Somerville in music, Tom Walsh in classics, Diana Linden in biology, Linda Lasater in chemistry, and Nancy Dess in psychology. Their suggestions for the text and descriptions of student writing have inspired me over the years to derive a unified, yet flexible approach to teaching composition. Ann Perkins, director of public services at the Oviatt Library at CSUN, has been a dedicated and patient colleague and co-author in scrutinizing chapter 9 to bring it up to date. I thank Debby Martinson of the Department of English Writing for sharing her resources on electronic citation, and Tom Burkdall of the same department for the times he has listened patiently to my computer woes. The students who permitted me to make use of their papers or passages from papers deserve my gratitude. I cannot acknowledge enough the humane and intelligent feedback of my editor, Arlyne Lazerson, of Collegiate Press. My thanks to Esiquio Gustavo Casillas for his help with the index. I wish, finally, to give thanks to my wonderful family. For the hours he devoted to helping me proofread the manuscript, I want to express appreciation to Morley Robins. For the opportunity to revise my work in peace, I wish also to recognize my husband, Steven Robins, who not only patiently and professionally advised me on the sticky parts of the manuscript but also looked after our son hour after hour while I needed quiet time. I thank my son, too, for his tolerance of my intermittent distractedness when he had something "important" to tell me.

# EDITORIAL ADVISORY BOARD

Professor Ray Clines
Department of Humanities
Jacksonville University
Jacksonville, FL 32211

Professor Gerald Concannon
Department of Humanities
Massachusetts Maritime Academy
Bourne, MA 02532

Professor Jessan Dunn DeCredico
Department of Humanities and
    English
Bryant College
1150 Douglas Pike
Smithfield, RI 02917

Professor Kathleen De Grave
Department of English
Pittsburg State University
Pittsburg, KS 66762

Professor Richard A. Dennison
Department of Humanities
Saint Josephs College
North Windham, ME 04062

Professor David De Vries
Department of Rhetoric
Hobart Wm. Smith Colleges
300 Pulteney Street
Geneva, NY 14456

Professor Mary DeWane-Lander
Department of English
University of North Carolina
Wilmington, NC 28403

Professor E. Sue Doss
Department of English and Languages
Arkansas Tech University
Russellville, AR 72801

Professor Dixie Durham
Department of English
Chapman University
333 North Glassell Street
Orange, CA 92666

Professor Barb Egeler
Humanities Division Head
Jordan College
1925 Breton
Grand Rapids, MI 49506

Professor Carol J. Falk
Department of English
Concordia College at Moorhead
Moorhead, MN 56560

Professor Chuck Fisher
Department of Humanities
Aims Community College
5401 20th Street
Greeley, CO 80634

Professor Carol Galbus
Department of English
Winona State University
151 West 8th Street
Winona, MN 55987

Professor Paul Gatschet
Department of English
Fort Hays State University
600 Park Street
Hays, KS 67601

Professor William Gilbert
Department of English
University of Houston Downtown
1 Main Street
Houston, TX 77002

Professor Thomas M. Gilligan
Department of General Education
Pennsylvania State University
    Allentown Campus
6090 Mohr Lane
Fogelsville, PA 18051

Professor Donald Glover
Department of English
Mary Washington College
1301 College Avenue
Fredericksburg, VA 22401-4666

Professor Jean M. Gonzalez
Department of Humanities
Inter American University
Arecibo, PR 00612

Professor Madeline Gorga, Ph.D.
Department of Humanities
Union County College
12 West Jersey Street
Elizabeth, NJ 07202

Professor Esther Gormley
Department of Humanities
Highland Community College
Highland, KS 66035

Professor Virginia Grant
Department of Arts and Sciences
Southside Virginia Community
    College
Daniel Campus
Keysville, VA 23947

Professor Katherine M. Gray
Department of English
Lynchburg College
Lynchburg, VA 24501

Professor Teresa Griffis
Department of Language Arts
Savannah College of Art
Savannah, GA 31402

Professor Holly Gritsch de Cordova
Department of Humanities
Contra Costa College
2600 Mission Bell Drive
San Pablo, CA 94806

Professor Donna L. Halford
Department of Language and
    Literature
Texas A and I University
Santa Gertrudis
Kingsville, TX 78363

Professor Lynda Hall
Department of English
Chapman University
333 North Glassell Street
Orange, CA 92666-1031

Professor Suzanne Hart
Department of English
Eastern Montana College
Billings, MT 59101

Professor Bruce C. Henricksen
Department of English
Loyola University
6363 Saint Charles Avenue
New Orleans, LA 70118

Professor Roberta Henson
Department of Language and
    Literature
Indiana Wesleyan University
4201 South Washington Street
Marion, IN 46953

Professor Susan Henthorne
Department of English
Buffalo State College
1300 Elmwood Avenue
Buffalo, NY 14222

Professor Mary Hicks
Department of Arts and Sciences
University of Alaska Juneau Campus
11120 Glacier Highway
Juneau, AK 99801-8625

Professor Gervase Hittle
Department of English
University of South Dakota
Vermillion, SD 57069

Professor Allison D. Holland
Department of Rhetoric and Writing
University of Arkansas at Little Rock
2801 South University
Little Rock, AR 72204-1000

Professor Anna M. Holloway
Department of Humanities
Ford Valley State College
Fort Valley, GA 31030

Professor Thomasita Homan
Department of English
Benedictine College
Atchison, KS 66002-1499

Professor Clarence Hooker
Department of American Thought
Michigan State University
229 Bessey Hall
East Lansing, MI 48824

Professor Laurie J. Hoskin
Department of English
University of Michigan at Flint
Flint, MI 48502

Professor Catherine Houser
Department of English
Southeastern Massachusetts University
North Dartmouth, MA 02747

Professor Pamela R. Howell, Ph.D.
Department of Language and Fine Arts
Midland College
3600 North Garfield Street
Midland, TX 79705

Professor Marie Hughes
Department of Arts and Sciences
New Hampshire Technical College
2020 Riverside Drive
Berlin, NH 03570

Professor Donald E. Hubele
Department of Communications
Liberty University
Lynchburg, VA 24506

Professor Marie Hubert
Department of English
Immaculata College
Immaculata, PA 19345

Professor Maribeth Impson
Department of English
Southwest Missouri State University
901 South National
Springfield, MO 65804

Professor Tommie L. Jackson
Department of English
Saint Cloud State University
Saint Cloud, MN 56301

Professor Eleanor J. James
Department of English
Georgia Southern College
Statesboro, GA 30460

Professor Susan Johnson
Department of General Education
South College-Savannah Campus
709 Mall Boulevard
Savannah, GA 31406

Professor Rosalyn J. Jones
Department of English and Philosophy
Johnson C. Smith University
100 Beatties Ford Road
Charlotte, NC 28216

Professor Gillian M. Jordan
Department of Liberal Arts
University of Maine at Bangor
Bangor, ME 04401

Professor Joseph Keefe
Department of Humanities and Social
    Science
Ulster County Community College
Stone Ridge, NY 12484

Professor George Kerrick
Department of English
Middle Tennessee State University
Murfreesboro, TN 37132

Professor Susan Kissel
Department Language and Literature
Northern Kentucky University
Highlands Heights, KY 41076

Professor Niaz A. Khan
Department of Language and
    Literature
University of West Alabama
Livingston, AL 35470

Professor Nicholas Knight
Department of English
University of Missouri at Rolla
Rolla, MO 65401

Professor Regina P. Krummel
Department of Liberal Arts
Bridgeport Engineering Institute
785 Unquowa Road
Fairfield, CT 06430

Professor Mary Theresa Kyne
Department of English
Seton Hill College
Greensburg, PA 15601

Professor Elmer Lange
Department of language and Literature
Northern Kentucky University
Newport, KY 41099

Professor David Layton
Department of Humanities
South Puget Sound Community
    College
2011 Mottman Road Southwest
Olympia, WA 98512

Professor Mary Libertin
Department of English
Shippensburg University
Shippensburg, PA 17257

Professor Ronald Link
Department of English
Miami Dade Community College
    Kendall
11011 Southwest 104 Street
Miami, FL 33176-3330

Professor Lockett
Department of Language Arts
San Jose City College
2100 Moorpark Avenue
San Jose, CA 95128-2799

Professor Loren Logsdon
Department of Humanities
Eureka College
Eureka, IL 61530

Professor Janis S. Londraville
Department of English
SUNY College at Potsdam
Potsdam, NY 13676

Professor Theresa R. Love
Department of English
Southern Illinois University
Edwardsville, IL 62026

Professor Carol Lowe
Department of English
McLennan Community College
1400 College Drive
Waco, TX 76708

Professor Fred R. Mac Fadden
Department of Language
Coppin State College
2500 West North Avenue
Baltimore, MD 21216

Professor Karen Malcolm
Department of English
University of Calgary
2500 University Drive
Calgary, AB T2N1N4
CANADA

Professor Sandra Manderson, Ph.D.
Department of Language and
  Literature
Armstrong State College
11935 Abercorn Street
Savannah, GA 31419

Professor Alexander J. Marshall
Department of English
Randolph Macon College
Ashland, VA 23005-1697

Professor Lynn S. Martin
Department of English
Saint Johns University
Grand Central and Utopia
Jamaica, NY 11439

Professor S. Allison Mc Cormack
Department of Humanities and
  English
Miami University, Hamilton Branch
Hamilton, OH 45011

Professor Bernadette Mc Coy
Department of English
Adelphi University
Garden City, NY 11530

Professor Clare Mc Donnell
Department of Humanities
Springfield Technical Community
  College
Armory Square
Springfield, MA 01150

Professor Linda Mc Ginley
Department of Humanities
West Liberty State College
West Liberty, WV 26074

Professor Helen Mc Kinnon
Department of Communications
Saint Petersburg Junior College
6605 5th Avenue North
Saint Petersburg, FL 33733

Professor Richard Mc Nally
Department of General Education
Northern Nevada Community College
901 Elm Street
Elko, NV 89801

Professor Ronald Meyers
Department of English
East Stroudsburg University
East Stroudsburg, PA 18301

Professor Mary T. Miritello
Department of English
Depaul University
802 West Belden
Chicago, IL 60614

Professor Gary Morgan
Department of Language Arts
Oxnard College
4000 South Rose Avenue
Oxnard, CA 93033

Professor Trevor J. Morgan  Ph.D.
Department of English
Howard Payne University
Brownwood, TX 76801

Professor Carole Murphy
Department of Theology
Bangor Theological Seminary
300 Union Street
Bangor, ME 04401

Professor Linda M. Nassar
Department of Humanities and
  English
Oakland Community College
  Highland Lakes
7350 Cooley Lake Road
Union Lake, MI 48085

Professor Kathy Mosdal O'Brien
Communication Arts Department
Miles Community College
2715 Dickinson
Miles City, MT 59301

Professor Paul A. Orlov
Department of English
Pennsylvania State University
  Delaware Campus
25 Yearsley Mill Road
Media, PA 19063-5522

Professor Christopher C. O'Hearn
Department of Communication Arts
  and Sciences
Los Angeles Harbor College
1111 Figueroa Place
Wilmington, CA 90744

Professor Ollie Oviedo
Department of English
Eastern New Mexico University
Portales, NM 88130

Professor Randi Pahlau
Department of Language and
  Literature
Malone College
515 25th Street Northwest
Canton, OH 44709

Professor Nancy B. Palmer
Department of English
Western Maryland College
Westminster, MD 21157

Professor Carl R. Perrin
Department of General Education
Casco Bay College
477 Congress Street
Portland, ME 04101

Professor Carole C. Pfeffer
Department of English
Bellarmine College
2001 Newburg Road
Louisville, KY 40205

Professor Robert Pfingstler
Department of English
Edinboro University of Pennsylvania
Edinboro, PA 16444

Professor June J. Phillips
Department of Humanities
Southern University Shreveport
3050 M. L. King Jr. Drive
Shreveport, LA 71107-4795

Professor Barbara Pitz
Department of English
Saint Ambrose University
518 West Locust Street
Davenport, IA 52803

Professor Vincent B. Puzick
Department of English
University of Colorado
1420 Austin Bluffs
Colorado Springs, CO 80918

Professor William E. Rand
Department of Humanities and Social
  Science
Cosumnes River College
8401 Center Parkway
Sacramento, CA 95823

Professor Bruce Reid
Department of Humanities and Social
  Sciences
Edmonds Community College
20000 68th Avenue West
Lynnwood, WA 98036

Professor Alden Reimonenq
Department of English
Saint Marys College
Moraga, CA 94575

Professor Rose Reynoldson
Department of Humanities
Seattle Pacific University
3307 3rd Avenue West
Seattle, WA 98119

Professor Donald J. Richardson
Department of English
Phoenix College
1202 West Thomas Road
Phoenix, AZ 85013

Professor Oscar Rodriguez
Department of English
University of Puerto Rico
Barrio Tejas
Humacao, PR 00661

Professor Matthew C. Roudane
Department of English
Georgia State University
Atlanta, GA 30303

Professor Mary Rundell-Holmes
Department of Communications
Moody Bible Institute
820 North Lasalle Street
Chicago, IL 60610-3276

Professor Erlinda Rustia
Department of English
Seattle University
12th and East Columbia
Seattle, WA 98122

Professor Sabah Salih
Department of Communication Arts
    and Science
Ashland Community College
1400 College Road
Ashland, KY 41101

Professor William San Giacomo
Department of Humanities and
    English
Tri State University
Angola, IN 46703

Professor Michael W. Schaefer
Department of English
University of Central Arkansas
Conway, AR 72032

Professor Anne K. Schinbeckler
Department of English
Tennessee Technological University
Cookeville, TN 38505

Professor Melvin Seesholtz
Department of English
Pennsylvania State University
Ogontz Campus
Abington, PA 19001

Professor Alton Seidl
Department of English
Southern Connecticut State University
501 Crescent Street
New Haven, CT 06515

Professor Margaret Senatore
Department of English and Languages
University of Southern Colorado
2200 Bonforte Boulevard
Pueblo, CO 81001

Professor David Shevin
Department of Arts and Sciences
Tiffin University
155 Miami Street
Tiffin, OH 44883

Professor Margaret C. Sims
Mississippi Delta Community College
Cleveland, MS 38732

Professor Mary B. Smith
Department of Humanities
Lee's College
Jackson, KY 41339

Professor Maura Snyder
Department of Humanities
Saint Leo College
Saint Leo, FL 33574

Professor William Snyder
Department of English
Saint Vincent College and Seminary
Latrobe, PA 15650

Professor Bes Spangler
Department of Language and Fine Arts
Peace College
15 East Peace Street
Raleigh, NC 27604-1194

Professor Hartley S. Spatt
Department of Humanities
SUNY - Maritime College
Fort Schuyler
New York, NY 10465

Professor Mary Spoto
Department of English
Saint Leo College
Saint Leo, FL 33574

Professor Robert Stafford
Department of Liberal Arts
Cuyamaca College
2950 Jamacha Road
El Cajon, CA 92019

Professor Gabriele Stauf
Associate Academic Dean
Texas Lutheran College
1000 West Court
Seguin, TX 78155

Professor Leroy Sterling
Department of English and Languages
Alabama A and M University
Normal, AL 35762

Professor E. Kate Stewart
Department of Communication Arts
University of Arkansas Monticello
Monticello, AR 71655

Professor J. T. Stewart
Department of Humanities and Social
    Science
Seattle Central Community College
1701 Broadway
Seattle, WA 98122

Professor Juanita Stock
Department of General Education
Haywood Community College
Freedlander Drive
Clyde, NC 28721

Professor Sharon Stockton
Department of English
Dickinson College
Carlisle, PA 17013-2846

Professor Pina Sturdivant
Department of Fine Arts
Arkansas College
Batesville, AR 72501

Professor Dolly M. Tarver
Department of Humanities and Social
    Science
Virginia Highlands Community
    College
Abingdon, VA 24210

Professor Chezia B. Thompson  Ph.D.
Department of Language and
    Literature
Maryland Institute College of Art
1300 West Mount Royal Avenue
Baltimore, Maryland 21217

Professor Marty Trammell
Department of Liberal Arts
Western Baptist College
5000 Deer Park South East
Salem, OR 97301

Professor Veryl Walter
Department of Humanities and Fine
    Arts
Lincoln College
300 Keokuk Street
Lincoln, IL 62656

Professor Susan H. Warren
Department of Humanities
Widener University
700 East 14th Street
Chester, PA 19013

Professor Elaine Whitaker
Department of English
University of Alabama, Birmingham
University Station
Birmingham, AL 35294

Professor Angela W. Williams
Department of English
The Citadel
Citadel Station
Charleston, SC 29409-0001

Professor Kristi Williams
Department of English
Lewis and Clark College
0615 Southwest Palatine Hill
Portland, OR 97219

Professor Meredith Wilson
Department of Language Arts
Solano Community College
4000 Suisun Valley Road
Suisun City, CA 94585

Professor J. A. Worman
Department of English
Dartmouth College
Hanover, NH 03755

Professor Helen M. Yanko
Department of English-Humanities
  Building
California State University
Room 715F
Fullerton, CA 92634

Professor Anne Ysunza
Department of Language Arts
Solano Community College
4000 Suisun Valley Road
Suisun City, CA 94585

# PLANNING

# HOW DO YOU WRITE AN ESSAY?

You have already done a lot of writing in your life. Much of that writing has probably had a rather simple and immediate purpose. You wrote a letter to a friend, you dropped a note to your boss asking for next Friday off, or you wrote to the local department store to point out a mistake in your bill. In these instances, your purpose was to get your point across to your reader quickly and clearly, and your writing probably flowed without much effort on your part.

You wrote more or less the way you would speak, "Mom, be home at 7:30" and didn't find the need to revise. Your mother would know the complete context in which you were writing, that you had a soccer game that afternoon, and would realize that the message meant that *you* would be home, not that you were requesting that *she* come home at 7:30.

But in other situations, when your topic is more complex than a personal note, and your reader potentially an authority on the subject about which you are writing, examining the subject and editing the spoken language become more important. Consider the level of analysis and revision required even in a note to a bank officer questioning an unclear policy. Compare this simple statement you might make were you speaking to him or her in person at the bank, "Please refund my money for the bounced check. I deposited the money the same day I wrote the check," with what you might have to write in a letter to the same person. The spoken version presumes the opportunity to elaborate by answering questions face to face. It could provide a good first draft attempt at a letter to the bank, but you would need to revise that draft to include a more complex description of the context for writing and a stronger explanation of your case: "As a customer of Seattle Trust for four years, I have never received a notice for insufficient funds, so you can imagine that last Monday when my statement came I felt confused. Here is the situation. The check apparently bounced because the deposit, although made on Wednesday when I wrote the check, did not get posted until Thursday. Since you have never informed me that checks deposited after 2 P.M. are posted the following day, I think you should not charge me for a bounced check." The expression "here is the situation" could as easily be spoken as written, and the language is not excessively formal. Yet there are complex combinations of ideas in the third sentence that might have taken two or three sentences if spoken. The deliberate inclusion of "apparently" reinforces the earlier reference to "confused" and raises suspicion in the reader's mind about the efficiency of the bank's handling of the situation.

These are clues that a writer planned and revised. She knew her readers and sized up the situation in order to manipulate them to her position. Chances are great that if she had sent her first version of the letter, her request would not have been granted, at least not without necessary, and probably irritating, follow-up phone calls and letters to gather information and evidence. The readers only know in this situation what they have read, and so the case must be established clearly and completely.

So, too, how precisely you write in college essays conveys exactly how you have grasped and interpreted what you have studied; the content and the writing become virtually inseparable. Since you would not want to risk your reputation or your grade, it becomes important to plan and revise every college essay.

Writing assignments in college, however, serve a more important purpose than proving to your professors that you have done your homework. They afford you the opportunity to sort out your thinking and learn more about a subject. The fiction writer and essayist E. M. Forster once said, "How do I know what I think until I see what I say?" Analytical writing gives you an opportunity to see what you have to say or think about a topic. Unlike conversation, in which thoughts often whiz by unquestioned and unchallenged, the written word summons you to look and think again. As you look back through your writing, you may realize that you have not explained a concept carefully enough or that you have not grouped your ideas effectively. When you rewrite, you clarify your thinking as well. These realizations occur when you keep in mind your audience and your purpose for writing.

Many of the essays that you will write in college will focus on material studied in class. You may be asked to explain a concept or to defend an idea. No matter what the assignment, you will first have to consider your purpose and the needs and interests of your audience. You must then design what you intend to say so that it will accomplish the intended purpose for that particular audience.

## AUDIENCE AND ACADEMIC COMMUNITIES

The people you talk to are "listeners," and those you write to are your "readers." Both of these groups come under the broad heading of audience. In everyday writing and speaking, you relate to a specific person or a certain group. To a great extent, what you say or write and how you do so depend on who is to receive your words. For example, you might describe the party you went to last night in one way for your roommate and in another way for your parents. You would certainly explain your concept of marriage differently to a six-year-old than to another adult. In talking to members of your immediate family or friends, you might even use a different dialect (see Chapter A) than in talking to your math professor. Although talking provides a more immediate audience than writing does, writing also has an audience. In writing, you would be likely to present the concept of love differently in a philosophy paper and in a psychology paper because each academic field has special conventions for writing and thinking about subjects in that field. Each discipline has conventional ways of organizing, explaining, and citing information. These conventions suit the audiences in the respective fields because they grow out of the unique way a philosopher or a psychologist thinks about her subject matter.

It is true that certain writing tasks have more clear-cut audiences than others. When you write a journal, unless it is written for a class assignment, you are writing only for yourself and can include pet phrases without explaining them, or you can leave out steps in a sequence of events because you know what happened. When you write a personal letter to someone, you know exactly to whom you must appeal. You usually know something about the tastes and interests of the person, so you try to refer to them. You wouldn't deliberately use words far above or below the level of your reader's vocabulary.

When you write a paper for a class, your instructor is part of the audience. But to assume that only your teacher is the audience would seem to defeat the purpose of the writing assignment. Writing the essay exposes you to a body of information and ideas that stimulate you to think in a new way. Your essay sets forth these ideas, clarifying them for you and for your reader. But if the gap between you and your reader is great, as it can be if your teacher is a specialist in the field you're writing about, you can run into difficulty by trying to communicate above your own level. Therefore, teachers shouldn't be your only audience. The most practical decision, unless your instructor suggests otherwise, is to write to an audience of your peers. Consider yourself a part of their academic community; whether they be students of science, literature, sociology, or history, you will share academic interests and a context for the paper. If you write to your classmates, you have a common ground, the course work, to build on. You needn't talk up or down to them. You can assume they are a group of intelligent people who will be convinced by a logical argument. On this same level you will no doubt appeal to your teacher as well.

### Audience Considerations

Here is an example of the kinds of decisions you might make if you were writing to your classmates as your audience. Suppose you are asked to write a paper on F. Scott Fitzgerald's novel *The Great Gatsby* for your freshman English class and you know that all your classmates have read the book. It would be unnecessary to retell the plot of the novel. When you must refer to the plot, you need only mention some main event that will identify for your audience the part of the story you mean. You might say something like "The failure of Gatsby's dream of success is further illustrated by the fact that only Gatsby's father and the drunk from the library show up at Gatsby's funeral." You don't need to explain the scene in which the drunk appears earlier in the book, since your audience is already familiar with the plot. Neither do you need to explain how Gatsby's father came to town or how Gatsby died. On the other hand, you do need to discuss in detail your point about the dream of success. You need to point out the implications of what you have said about the failure of the American dream. The explanation may involve an interpretation of why the drunk appears at the graveyard, but your explanation should not require a plot summary.

You might wonder whether constructing an audience in one's mind by appealing to a known group seems reasonable. Professional writers, not just students, do so, as you can observe by skimming any popular magazine or technical journal. Articles in any magazine are written for a certain sector of the public—those who would buy the magazine. One way of evaluating the audience for a particular magazine is to study the advertisements. The companies that advertise in the magazine want to sell their products to that audience, so their ads are specifically designed to take into account the likes, dislikes, interests, values, and buying habits of this particular segment, whether they are working mothers, affluent business people, or teenage rock fans.

Technical journals, too, have definite audiences. Most journal articles include specialized language that the ordinary person would not understand. Advertisements, if there are any, appeal to a group familiar with specifications and uses of the advertised equipment or materials. Unless a reader knows the field, he or she may find the articles and advertisements confusing. Some time, try to read part of a journal article on a technical topic. Then, just for fun, pick up a copy of *Highlights for Children*. What is your response to reading matter obviously designed for a different audience than you? Confusion? Anger? Laughter?

You can often determine an intended audience's educational level and interests by taking note of several characteristics of the writing itself. Is the language very formal? Very informal? Do specialized terms abound? Are there many undefined terms or concepts that assume prior knowledge of the topic? Does it seem that the readers and writer share certain unstated assumptions? Are the paragraphs long, like those in formal writing, or especially brief—just a few sentences—like those in popular magazines and newspapers? Are many of the sentences complicated? Even word length might be considered a mark of formality and of the audience's educational level, or at least of their concentration span. Finally, the writer might directly address the readers, as in "Now listen, freshmen and sophomores" or "Perk up your ears, my fellow Americans." As a writer you can use similar techniques to appeal to your target audience.

### An Audience Survey

To properly gear your writing to the right level, you will need to assess the character of your audience. One way to make such a judgment is to do an audience survey in which you ask yourself several key questions about the tastes, values, and experiences of your readers. Here are some guidelines for questions you might wish to ask:

Why would the readers be interested in my essay?

What is the average educational level of my readers?

Do the readers have specialized knowledge in the field? How
   much?

Will any of my evidence for the essay seem strange to the audience
   and thus require special explanation?

Will the readers be likely to accept my main point? If not, what
   might they think instead?

Do the readers expect me to follow a certain structure in this paper?

Are the readers generally of any one age, sex, or ethnic background?
   If not, what diversity should I keep in mind?

For a particular essay, you might think of even more specific questions pertaining to the assignment that will help you to know your readers. You can see that asking yourself these kinds of questions will keep
the concept of audience in the back of your mind as you write, helping
you make decisions about what to include and what not to include in
your essay.

The value of adapting your writing to a particular audience is evident at every stage of the writing process. From the first step—picking a subject—you will want to appeal to the group you have defined
as readers in your audience survey. Pick a subject that suits you both;
then decide on a main point to focus the essay, making sure that it is
something both you and the readers are likely to find interesting. Should
your approach be formal or informal?

Next, as you select evidence for the body of the essay, consider what
the readers already know, what they want to know, and what they need
to know. Do they need elaboration on a given point to understand it?
If you take a stand on a subject, you will want to recognize the possible opposing views your readers might hold. Finally, throughout the
paper, you will want your writing to be easy to read.

This close connection with your readers should not confine you so
that you write only to please your audience, as Linus does in the "Pea-
nuts" cartoon on page 8. Writing should grow out of the relationship
between the readers and the subject, the writer and the readers, and the
writer and the subject. Otherwise, the writing will probably mean little
to the readers or to the writer, even if it "sells," as it does in the cartoon.
You can see how writing that reflects something important to the writer,
in the writer's personal style, differs from writing made only of compro-
mises to a reader—the writing that merely "sells." Good writers express
themselves while appealing to their audiences.

## DEVELOPMENT OF IDEAS

The point of view from which any writer perceives the subject influences him or her to develop a central idea, or thesis. An essay is never

just a stringing together of facts. Instead, it develops a subject area into a focused topic—makes a statement about a subject, adds an "aboutness" to it. The subject "gangs in the city" becomes "a plan for creating truces between rival urban gangs" and the subject "rap and heavy metal lyrics" becomes "whether pornographic or vicious song lyrics should be censored." The point is developed and expanded in the paper; although the original topic may have been conceived because it interests the writer, information and ideas are selected for the essay because they develop the point.

Evidence is needed for an essay. Opinion alone or bright ideas that do not back up the thesis, no matter how sincere, are inappropriate and best saved for a journal, a letter to a friend, or a different paper. Even the most heartfelt ideas must bear examination and development. In college you will have few assignments that call for your feelings alone. Note how the following short paper seems full of incidental remarks and how it fails to hold together because it skips around in a few different directions, spending so little time on each point under consideration that the reader comes away with little understanding of any significant point about love.

```
                          Love

     Love is a human behavior that is the most misunder-
stood. It is said to be the strongest feeling possible
for a human to feel. I agree with this saying because
love forms a bond that stays with you. I am not saying
that love remains the same forever; I am saying that it
remains in you forever. There are many types of love. I
```

have experienced three types: the love of family members, the love for friends, and affectionate love.

Love for your family members is an unconditional love. It is the feeling that a person feels for their children: a feeling so strong that they will not allow anything to happen to them.

This is the type of love I have for my cousin Jevon. He and I have been best cousins since I could remember. He lives in Alabama and whenever he comes to town we take care of each other. If one of us was short on money, we would spend our last dime on the other.

The second kind of love I have experienced is the love for a friend. This love usually is shared between best friends. These two people have a lot in common and spend a lot of time together. In this time they spend together they become very close; they start to know each other pretty well and they become very much alike. They start to dress alike and even talk alike and soon it becomes like the two are almost the same person. When I was young, my best friend Ronnie and I were inseparable. He lived next door to me and we were together every day. On the weekends he was spending the night at my house or I was spending the night at his. We would dress up in the same types of clothes when we went out. We were together so much that we had people believing we were brothers. Until this day I sometimes refer to him as my brother. Still today, when we each are living different lives (he is a father and I am in college), nothing has changed between us. We even still buy some of the same clothes. Even if we were to be apart for years, my memory of him would still remain. As long as I remember him, I will love him.

The third type of love I have experienced is affectionate love. This is the type of love that a person feels for another male or female. It is a feeling much stronger than lust or infatuation. It is sometimes even hard to explain. This type of love is probably the most emotional love out of the three I explained. I say this because the way of expressing this type of love is based so much on the emotions felt for each other.

This love causes a person to act funny also. A person will find themselves doing things for or because of that person that they would not do for any other. Things like staying up all night by the telephone waiting for their call because they haven't heard from them all day and they are worried. Or taking time to run errands for that person when there is hardly time to take care of their own business. Sacrifices are common.

When I was in high school I had a girlfriend who I had
been with for three years. I was crazy over this girl. I
wanted to be with this girl at all times. I loved her so
much I wanted to marry her. There was no telling what I
would have done for that girl. But she was fooling me.
One day I found out that she was fooling around with my
friend. When I found this out, I cried like a baby. Her
cheating on me devastated me and I suffered academi-
cally. My performance in sports slackened. Even now I
occasionally think about her but if she wanted me back I
would have to think twice. Still the love I have for her
remains the same today. It will never totally disappear.

   Love is a human behavior that people feel in many
different forms. The forms I feel it in are love for
family, love for a friend, and affectionate love. In
these forms a bond has been formed between me and the
person who I shared it with; the bond will last forever.

This paper lacks direction and development. The writer starts out
with too broad a thesis, one that promises no more than a description
of the types of love. A better thesis might have made a statement about
the significance of identifying and separating them or might have nar-
rowed the topic to one of the types and settled on a controversial issue
related to it. Many heartfelt ideas, even potential topics for analysis,
are raised in the paper, but none is explored in detail.

   The writer relies on a structure that is workaday, the five-paragraph
essay, which sets out the thesis (the main point of the essay), describes
what is in the thesis, gives an example of each point, and restates the
thesis in the conclusion. This pattern of saying what you are going to
say, saying it in a little more detail, and repeating it in the conclusion
is boring and predictable—too much so for an academic audience. It's
one thing if your essay just happens to have a five-paragraph structure
and is a well developed piece of writing with an analytical thesis, but
it's another to pick a general and mundane topic and drive it into the
ground.

   Although the essay on love is not well written and could not serve
as the final draft, it could serve as a starting point from which the writer
could sort out his ideas on the subject before beginning to write the
real paper. It could serve as preparation for writing the paper, a way of
collecting ideas. After scratching down these thoughts, the writer of
this particular piece was ready to come to a thesis and write a real essay. Drawing the best ideas from the preparatory writing, the student
composed an essay with the thesis "There would be far fewer divorces
if more people realized that partners in affectionate love are in a constantly changing relationship requiring perpetual negotiation about
power and love—unlike the notion of romance in T. V. and movies."
Some of the ideas in the original essay were thrown out because they
did not fit the point the writer is trying to make. The writer found

himself going to the library to investigate current perceptions of romantic love in the media and theories of love in psychological literature. Writing the first draft made him realize that he needed even more information if he wanted to write on this subject. After feeling more "grounded" in the subject, he could more easily explain the psychological concepts that apply to current love themes in movies and on television.

## TONE

Tone reflects the writer's attitude about the subject—and more. It may be formal or informal, straightforward or subtle and cunning, comical or somber. The word choice, type of evidence, and structure of each paragraph and sentence can affect tone. You may want to experiment with all three types of tone, but in most of the writing done for term papers and essays, your goal should be a serious tone, neither too formal nor too informal. In college papers, most of the words will be in the vocabulary of an educated reader; the evidence will be drawn from reliable sources and tested; and the paragraphs and sentences will be well developed, longer than those characteristic of an article in a popular magazine. Writers should watch for consistency and appropriateness in tone at every step of writing.

Problems can arise with tone, especially when a writer deals with a subject about which he or she tends to become impassioned. Writing can be intensely personal. You write from your own experiences—physical, emotional, intellectual, and spiritual. Your writing may be designed to share your experiences with your readers or to convince them to accept some view. However, one of the basic rules of writing essays is to avoid emotionalism or sarcasm. In the following passage, the writer loses control of feelings, relying on hysterical judgments instead of on solid evidence. How might the passage be rewritten to make it more objective?

> Violence in the cinema is very dangerous. It motivates people in the worst possible ways. Violence seduces children more than adults into its horrible grips. And these are the very children who will be tomorrow's adults and leaders. If children go on being corrupted by movies our future will be unavoidable misery.

The writer of this passage uses an array of highly emotional words and phrases—"the worst possible ways," "seduces," "its horrible grips," and so forth. The ideas are often vague and dogmatic—what is meant by "unavoidable misery"?

When you are committed to a particular political or social cause and find yourself writing an essay on it, take a deep breath and step back from your intense involvement. The danger otherwise is to adopt a preaching tone that will only alienate your readers. If you allow yourself to think that you can pressure others into accepting your view, you are forgetting that college-level persuasive writing is based on logical argument. The following passage is marred by the writer's ineffective preaching tone in his conclusion to a philosophy paper on the good life. If you were to discuss with this student what he or she might do to remove the preaching tone, what would you say?

> We always want to explain, express everything, to verbalize instead of being absorbed in thought. Some feelings are too full, too deep to be expressed. We are too wordy, let silence be thy guide. Many times our individuality makes us stand apart from what is close to us. We become very objective about the things around us, instead of just absorbing them. We have a deep tendency to advocate the logos doctrine too readily. We subject our experience to the intellect, instead of to the heart. We become too analytical, individualistic, intellectual; instead we should be more spiritually individualistic, socially group minded, intuitive, totalizing, etc.

The writer is too close to the material, as evidenced by the use of first person in a kind of sermonizing way. The writer wants to show people the ills of their ways and to convert them. Instead, it would be better to present the subject more as a reporter would. The writer should also try to make concrete some of the abstractions and try to give examples of what he or she means by "our individuality makes us stand apart from what is close to us." As written, this argument is hard to understand. The writer should remove old-fashioned language like "let silence be thy guide" and replace it with a statement instead of a command. Finally, the writer should remove the "etc." at the end of the passage and explain what he or she means.

Another kind of emotionalism is flowery writing—writing that seems inflated and false. Treating your subject with sensitivity does not call for exaggerating your feelings. For instance, it is a bit much to say that your mother "wept piteously" instead of that she cried or to say that you "chanced to set your gaze on the sky and its billows of radiant and varied colors" instead of that you looked at the sunset—or even at the colorful sunset. This overly poetic tone, often called "purple prose," can be confusing, insincere, and ultimately offensive to an academic audience.

While an emotional tone is often the accidental byproduct of an author's attitude, an ironic tone is usually created deliberately by mixing formal vocabulary with slang or by writing about a common subject (like frying an egg) in an inflated, formal way. In either case it would be clear that the tone was deliberately ironic because the author intended to be humorous. The cartoon on page 13 is funny *because* of the mixture of tone.

It is best for the writer of academic papers to stick to an appropriate and consistent tone. Sometimes a student, in trying to develop her vocabulary or in trying to impress a reader, will rely on the thesaurus,

*Dearly beloved, we are gathered here . . . to join this gal and this guy in holy matrimony.*

selecting words that are unfamiliar to her. Or a student will try to achieve an authentic voice by writing exactly how he would speak in conversation. Probably either approach will result in an undesirable, though unintentional, mixture. Mixing formal with informal "conversational" tone confuses readers about the writer's attitude on the subject, making it unclear how they are to piece together the ideas in the essay. Moreover, an unintentionally mixed tone always sounds unnatural. Most writers can look back over what they've written and judge whether it sounds natural. They notice sudden shifts to a pretentious, sarcastic, or humorous voice. An adjustment needs to be made if the writing is uneven or unnatural in spots. Take a look at the following passage. What would you suggest that the writer do to even out the mixed tone?

Each female in the correctional facility recounted her story. They all felt at loss for their children. They had lives before this, even if their lives were not going their way. The incarcerant who had killed her kid had told us, in so many words, to believe in God. But what was she thinking? And where was her godliness before she sinned? And the woman who fatally punished her husband for abusing their kids, where did she ever get the idea that it was up to her and not the authorities? They each made choices and were struggling to be in control of their lives; however they were going nowhere because the Man in the tower is always on duty.

The passage contains mixed tones. At the same time the writer uses formal words like "incarcerant" and "correctional facility," she uses slang like "kids." She introduces an inappropriate sarcastic tone in her questions "but what was she thinking? And where was her godliness before she sinned?" The pun at the end on the words "going nowhere" is clever but has a sarcastic ring to it as well. For a personal letter or journal entry, such writing might be very effective; after all, it contains a good deal of personal voice. But for academic writing, a serious and straightforward tone would permit this student to convey less bias; it might also help her recognize the need for more evidence.

---

### Exercises

A. Describe the tone of the following short passage from published sources. Would the tone of each be appropriate as well to a college essay? Why or why not?

1. Rachel House, Union Station, Homeboy Bakery and school lunches for Haitian youth were the causes that received the strongest support at Occidental's eighth annual Alternative Holiday Mart held last Wednesday in Samuelson Pavilion. Better than 300 participants from campus and the community donated in excess of $3,500 to 13 different charitable endeavors in Southern California and around the world. . . . Mart attendants were entertained during lunch by a Cuban drum group led by Carlos Gomez. The Afro-Cuban rhythms, accompanied by intricate interpretive dance movements, sparked enthusiastic audience participation. Hands wiggled, toes tapped, and eager voices joined in the throbbing chants. (From *Quadrangle Newsletter*, Dec. 7, 1994.)

2. In defense of the autonomic nervous system, it must be said that it is uncrippled by the intellect or the force of the will. Intuition governs here. Here is one's flesh wholly trustworthy, for it speaks with honesty all the attractions and repulsions of our lives. Consciousness here would be an intruder, justly driven away from the realm of the transcendent. One *feels;* therefore one is. No opinion but spontaneous feeling prevails. Is tomorrow's love expected? Yesterday's recalled? Instantly, the thought is captured by the autonomic nervous system. And alchemy turns wish and dream to ruddy reality. The billion capillaries of the face dilate and fill with blood. You blush. You are prettier. Is love spurned? Again the rippling, the dance of energy, and the bed of capillaries constricts, squeezing the blood from the surface to some more central pool. Now you blanch. The pallor of death is upon you. Icy are your own fingertips. It is the flesh responding to the death of love with its own facsimile. (From *Confessions of a Knife,* 113.)

3. The class expressiveness of a car doesn't stop with the kind and condition of car it is, or with the way you drive it. It involves also the things you display on or in it, all the way from the rack holding three rifles,

shotguns, or carbines in the rear window of the pickup with the Southern Methodist University sticker to the upper-middle-class rear window announcement "I'd Rather Be Sailing." Proles (the proletariat) love to decorate their cars, not just with mock-leopard upholstery and things like dice and baby shoes dangling from front and rear windows but with bumper stickers (AUSABLE CHASM; SOUTH OF THE BORDER; AYATOLLAH—PIG'S ASSHOLAH; HONK IF YOU LOVE JESUS), and of course little plastic Saint Christophers and the like on the dashboard. The middle class likes bumper stickers too, but is more likely to go in for self-congratulatory messages like CAUTION: I BRAKE FOR SMALL ANIMALS. (From Paul Fussell's *About the House.*)

4. I just spent two days with Edward T. Hall, an anthropologist, watching thousands of my fellow New Yorkers short-circuiting themselves into hot little twitching death balls with jolts of their own adrenalin. Dr. Hall says it is overcrowding that does it. Overcrowding gets the adrenalin going, and the adrenalin gets them queer, autistic, sadistic, barren, batty, sloppy, hot-in-the-pants, chancred-on-the-flankers, leering puling, numb—the usual in New York, in other words, and God knows what else. (From Tom Wolfe's "O Rotten Gotham.")

5. If God had given the individual prime responsibility for his own spiritual destiny, it followed that he must have made this possible by signifying his intentions to the individual in the events of daily life. The Puritan therefore tended to see every item in his personal experience as potentially rich in moral and spiritual meaning; and Defoe's hero is acting according to this tradition when he tries to interpret so many of the mundane events of the narrative as divine pointers which may help him to find his own place in the eternal scheme of redemption and reprobation. (From *The Rise of the Novel,* by Ian Watt.)

B. What specifically contributes to the tone of each of the following passages? Which are appropriate for academic writing? Why? How could the others be made appropriate?

1. Possibly Wilson's most important message to his audience can be found in the chapter "The Conservation Ethic," where he clearly states that the extinction of any species "takes with it millions of bits of genetic information, a history ages long, and potential benefits to humanity left forever unmeasured" (138). If human beings are to succeed as participants in the cycle of all life, it is vital that we recognize the importance of letting other organisms thrive as well. This is not only for the sake of animals' and plants' own right to life but also from what Wilson refers to as a purely "selfish" standpoint, the economic stability and growth of the world. Hence, by "raising the status of nonhuman creatures" we are better able to embrace the role of humans in relation to all forms of life.

2. It is like being the only one in a foreign country whose language you do not know. The person addressing you speaks, and from the gestures and voice fluctuation you conclude he or she is commenting on something of importance; but you simply don't have a clue about what's be-

ing said. The notion that American schools leave many American students similarly alienated, even those who consider themselves English speakers, is beyond doubt. These students simply have not lived in an environment that exposes them to the linguistic complexity that they find in school; they have nontraditional backgrounds. Excluding this background, educators ignore their only reference point, not incorporating into the classroom their interests, history, or culture, and the students not unlike being in a foreign country are alienated by their educational environment. Consequently, the effectiveness of Eurocentric education in serving all American students is doubtful when the demographics reflect increasing minority presence (From *Education Digest,* 92).

## THE WRITING PROCESS: PLANNING, DRAFTING, REVISING

Considerations of tone and of such incidentals as accurate spelling and punctuation lie in the back of the mind during most of the writing process. More immediate concerns are the structure of the essay, the direction in which the evidence seems to be developing, and the level of explanation of your ideas. It is true that attending to the details of mechanics and spelling can save you time in the long run—when it comes time to revise the essay. However, when you write the essay, try not to become preoccupied with these less important considerations and instead try to concentrate on the steps you can use to achieve a good thesis, support, and flow. Good writing is first well reasoned, honest, and purposeful; these are qualities any writer needs practice to develop.

Because you cannot be expected to know how to write effective essays without understanding how to use the necessary strategies, writing classes and writing textbooks emphasize a system you can practice whenever you write. There are basic guidelines for composing essays that writers commonly agree on. Most successful writers divide their task into three broad stages: planning, drafting, and revising.

### Planning

Planning, sometimes called "prewriting" because it precedes writing the essay itself, is necessary to good writing. It provides the time to develop, try out, and reject a number of possible topics and theses until you settle on the one that feels right for you. It also allows you the time to map out your paper before you sit down to write it out. Actually setting aside time for this stage gives you a chance to engage yourself in a dialogue of choices, a process that can make a big difference in the next step, writing the rough draft. Once the entire paper has been planned, in the drafting stage you can focus your attention on supporting your ideas with examples and explanations, linking your ideas to one another, and defending your thesis. Finally, the rewriting stage gives you a chance to polish words, sentences, grammar, punctuation, and spelling.

It is important to note that this is not a lock-step system. There will be times when your process gets bogged down in one stage and you must return to an earlier stage. For example, it is not unusual to have to return to planning as you are writing a paper from an outline because the drafting stage makes you remember a point you would like to include and you must reconsider your outline to fit the idea into the paper. Likewise you might want to redraft a paragraph or a string of sentences when you are editing for word choice; it may not be until then that you realize your point could be made clearer if you offer an example. This is no failure on your part. In reality the writing process described here is recursive—it spirals—rather than linear.

### Flexibility—Different Approaches for Different Writers and Topics

Some subjects seem to have a built-in natural order that develops as you write. You may find yourself describing a process and then analyzing its link to another similar process, or you—by luck or logic—may divide up your subject into parts that follow in a sequence. Students sometimes find these are the simplest essays to write, the ones that just seem to flow out of their keyboards. But most writing assignments require people to adopt a basic strategy (planning, drafting, revising) to avoid writing essays with practically no form. Writing an essay requires a great deal of decision making and mind changing. These take time. Using the writing process described in this section gives your essays direction as you write and assures a finished product with a clear beginning, middle, and ending.

Each person naturally develops individual habits the more he or she writes. But remaining flexible is the key to successful writing. A particular assignment may raise questions that require you to revert to planning during the rough draft or even during revision. There is no one way to write, and there is no one set of guidelines that cannot be adjusted when the need arises. But the overall strategy presented here offers structure for beginners or for those who wish to improve the clarity of their presentation.

### A Chronicle of One Student's Essay

Just how does the writing process work? You can get a sense of its effectiveness by following a sample essay through the various stages and putting yourself in the writer's place. Try to concentrate on how each stage contributes toward the whole and toward the final version of the essay.

#### Write Freely

The student's assignment was to write a short paper on an experience that changed her thinking on the subject of the American family. First the student jotted down some notes. Speeding along as fast as the ideas occurred to her, trying to record them, she jotted down ideas on what her family and friends always led her to believe the ideal family was—on single mothers, particularly on her friend Bonnie's life with her daughter, and whatever else she could think of. The point of recording whatever comes to mind is to force a confrontation with the subject, to put down as many ideas in as short a time as possible, no matter how unrefined the thoughts may seem. In this prewriting exercise, sometimes called automatic writing, the writer need not discriminate among ideas—just get them down, even if they seem irrelevant. You can see that the prewriting in Figure 1-1 is far from a perfect piece of writing, but it still is good because it helped the writer to come up with an idea for an essay. Prewriting is for your eyes only, so you can be free to say just what you are thinking at the moment. After reading through the prewriting below, you may wish to try an automatic writing exercise on your own.

---

**Figure 1-1.**

I always grew up with the belief that the ideal family had a mother and a father, happily married for life, and 2 children who lived with them in a relative safe and secure family life. I am sure that I never thought about the hardships people in lesser economic situations felt or of high school kids who got pregnant or god knows what else, which is really a normal life event. I was over protected and naive. I didn't realize I was also a horrible bigot out of my own ignorance and tunnelvision, I judged anyone who wasn't like me or my friends. I used to laugh at the guy on the bus who said he was the first one to detect the Watergate scandal—he was nuts but I shouldn't have dismissed him so quickly. Well, let's see—I'm supposed to write about the American family. What can I say? The American family is not necessarily as screwed up as the people I grew up with made me think it is. After reading about it I see that there are many types of family situations, not that they are all equally hard or secure for the kids. But I shouldn't judge them morally and can see them as part of the complexity of family life in the 90's. Actually my first taste of all this was Bonnie, who I went to school with. I was terrible to her at first, but when I got to know her and her daughter and all they went through because of people like me I changed my tune. The ballgame on a rainy day when I took Alexandra to the gift shop and got stares really made me think twice. I was ashamed of my Irish background and how I was sheltered by my family.

---

From the automatic writing, the student decided on a limited subject: the change in my thinking about single mothers

### Devise the Thesis

The student's next step was to develop a tentative thesis statement. She systematically revised the point she wished to make and checked over the statement to assure that it said what she had set out to say.

```
Subject: single mothers
Focused subject from the automatic writing: The change
    in my thinking about Bonnie after the ballgame
Question: How did I feel about Bonnie as a result of
    going to the ballgame with her and Alexandra?
Tentative Thesis: After going to the ballgame with
    Bonnie and Alexandra, and walking in their shoes, I
    came to realize how my sheltered life in our Irish
    community had influenced me not to respect anyone whose
    family situation did not fit the standard definition I
    had grown up with.
```

### Write a Scratch Outline

Next the student wrote a scratch outline. Because the subject was not involved and the student felt familiar with the ideas for the paper, she did not write out a formal outline. A set of basic notes was enough to keep her writing in the order she wished to present her ideas.

```
Bonnie's history
How our friendship began
The ballgame
    Intensity of crowd
    Rain
    Alcohol
    Taking Alex to bathroom
    Souvenir shop
    New ability to look at crowds
Getting beyond stereotypes
```

### Write the Rough Draft

Using the scratch outline to map her course, the student wrote an initial draft of the essay. As she wrote, it seemed only natural to cross out and rephrase several expressions, but mainly she concentrated on getting down her ideas.

### Revise the Rough Draft

Once the rough draft was complete, the student set it aside for a day and worked on other assignments. When she came back to the essay the next day, she felt better able to criticize her work than right after its completion. Now she found many words, phrases, and sentences she wanted to change as well as several spelling errors, grammatical errors, and sexist language.

The rough draft along with revisions is reproduced in Figure 1-2. The typed portion of the paper is the first draft. Any crossed out or written-in words are changes the student made as she wrote the draft or during the revision stage.

---

**Figure 1-2. Rough draft with workshop revisions.**

Lessons from the Ballpark

~~In high school I hung around with a fairly popular crowd. I didn't realize the negative effect our togetherness in everything from cultural background to the clothing we bought had on me.~~ My friends and I set standards for what was cool and normal, and we felt perfectly justified in ignoring or outcasting those people who didn't strictly adhere to these standards. This is probably one reason that explains why even though I went to high school with Bonnie for almost four years, it wasn't until over two years after my graduation that we first met.

*Add analogy of homeless man?*

Bonnie dropped out of high school during the fall semester of her senior year. That same year she also gave birth to her daughter Alexandra. The only time I paid much attention to young mothers was to gossip with my friends about the father's identity or to assume the girls slept around. I imagined their lives must be filled with hardships and while this stereotype led to some occasional feelings of compassion, for the most part, I felt removed from their worlds and therefore ignored their situations.

My friendship with Bonnie began when we worked together as corps members in a community service program in Boston. The corp's diversity ~~made it impossible for me to~~ find*ing* that circle of friends I'd always been comfortable with, friends who walked, talked and dressed like me. ~~As a result~~, my unlikely relationship with Bonnie developed ~~easily~~. Monday mornings we'd share stories about our weekends. While Bonnie told me about taking Alex to the playground, I detailed the bar my friends and I, all newly twenty-one, had discovered that Saturday night. As I was making plans to head off to college in September, Bonnie was deciding whether to send Alex to kindergarten in the fall, or to wait another year.

*① & ②*  *was striking*  *-would be impossible*

*① Our first week in the program was spent on a retreat at a camp in W. Mass. Standing outside at orientation, waiting impatiently to be assigned to the team I would work closely with for the next year,*

*② I looked around nervously at all the other participants.*

## Produce the Final Draft

After the student reviewed all the changes and felt sure that they made her paper sound just as she wanted it to, she went ahead and produced the final draft, as shown in Figure 1-3. Even as she incorporated all the revisions into the rough draft, she made additional changes that improved the flow of the final essay. She added a whole new sentence, for instance, to the beginning of the fourth paragraph. She also added transi-

**Figure 1-2 (continued).**

One unusually cool night in August, Bonnie and Alex and I, along with some other friends, attended a Red Sox game. Minutes after struggling through the typical drunk and rowdy Fenway Park crowd to our seats, the rain began streaming down. Fortunately our seats were covered because it was pouring so hard it reminded me of the unrealistic rain I'd only seen on television or in movies. Like any almost five year old, Alex wasn't well suited to this rain delay and lasted only ten minutes before complaining she was hungry and declaring just how badly she needed to use the bathroom. Sean and I, who were heading for the snackbar anyhow, agreed to escort. We each reached for one of her tiny hands and led Alex back through the frenzied mob.

There was an intensity in the crowd under the stands, where the stench of stale alcohol and popcorn is permanently trapped. The Red Sox were in the middle of another losing streak and the rain delay could mean the fans, who were very anxious for a win, would have to wait yet another day. The rain delay also meant more time for drinking, which was made clear by the scattered beer lines ~~that consumed~~ filling most of the hallway. A group of young men who had obviously just emerged from these lines was standing outside the entrance to the women's restroom. They resembled the guys who had made up my "in" crowd in high school: handsome jocks with short hair, baseball caps and designer jeans. They watched Alex and me intently as we entered the restroom, and because they were good looking I was initially flattered. When they resumed staring at us a few minutes later, as we exited and walked towards ~~Shawn,~~ Sean I realized their gazes signaled anything but admiration. Clearly assuming we were Alex's young parents, they were looking on with obvious disgust. I imagine this disgust was fueled further by the simple fact that ~~Shawn~~ Sean is African-American and I am white.

**Figure 1-2 (continued).**

Caught between embarrassment that anyone would believe I had a child, and outrage that anyone would judge me if I did, I turned away silently in the direction of the snackbar, following ~~Shawn~~ Sean and Alex. I felt the disapproving eyes of the grouchy old Irish woman as we passed. Stopping at a souvenir shop, I noticed the suburban family noticing us with disbelief. I wasn't sure if my face, now as red as it used to become when I was called upon to speak aloud during class, was a result of extreme shame or an uncontrollable and mounting rage.¶ It was now at least a half hour since the game had been scheduled to start. The fans were becoming louder and along with the sound of cash registers and occasional music, their voices began to resound like a collective hum. To me, this hum echoes like a deep and ominous voice uttering the word "no" over and over again. Fully convinced I was the center of everyone's attention, I imagined the "no" was directed towards me. Waiting at the souvenir stand, all I wanted was to escape this unbearable and punishing hum. However, watching ~~Shawn~~ Sean and Alex leaning over the display case, trying to decide which pin to buy, both oblivious to the millions of eyes upon us, I realized escape was not in the too-near future.

Turning my back to the stand, hoping if I was facing the other direction people would think I was waiting for someone else, I began to observe the passersby. An overweight couple, laden with greasy food, passed, followed by a teenager with green hair. Some local college students walked by next to two men in business suits who had probably walked to the ball park from their offices. Not everyone who passed was necessarily attractive, successful, or content. ~~or fit in to the norms of society.~~ A mother passed, steps ahead of her young daughter, whom she glanced at occasionally to scold. Not ~~was~~ everyone there was as wonderful a parent as Bonnie had been for the last four years. Realizing these were all conclusions that shouldn't surprise me, I turned back to the counter to help ~~Shawn~~ Sean and Alex select a pin. Finally, walking back to our seats, I grabbed one of Alex's hands, while ~~Shawn~~ Sean took the other. People's gazes no longer felt menacing or even seemed focused on us. The menacing hum disappeared and I recognized ~~again heard~~ the distinct sounds of ~~people's voices, distant music, and the busy cash registers.~~ distant music, and people having fun.

tional words and phrases and refined some of the wording. It is usual for a writer to add finishing touches to the essay as he or she retypes it or reviews it on the computer screen, and by no means should you feel that it is too late to make minor changes.

---

**Figure 1-3. Revised version of "Lessons from the Ballpark"**

Lessons from the Ballpark

Riding the bus downtown, I used to stare at the homeless man, who, when he wasn't talking to himself, was telling other passengers he was the one responsible for uncovering the Watergate scandal. I had viewed Susan, a sixth grade classmate, with this same distaste; her hideous brown corduroy pants would've been too tight and too short for even my eight-year old sister. Setting standards for what was "cool" and "normal," my friends and I felt perfectly justified in ignoring or outcasting those people who didn't strictly adhere to these standards. This explains why even though I went to high school with Bonnie for almost four years, it wasn't until over two years after my graduation that we first met.

Bonnie dropped out of high school during the fall semester of her senior year. That same year she also gave birth to her daughter Alexandra. The only time I paid much attention to young mothers was to gossip with my friends about the father's identity or to assume the girls slept around. I imagined their lives must be filled with hardships and while this stereotype which led to some occasional feelings of compassion, for the most part, I felt removed from their worlds and therefore ignored their situations.

My friendship with Bonnie began when we worked together as corps members in a community service program in Boston. Our first week in the program was spent on a retreat at a camp in western Massachusetts. Standing outside at orientation, waiting impatiently to be assigned to the team I would work closely with for the next year, I looked around nervously at all the other participants. The corp's diversity was striking. Finding that circle of friends with whom I'd always been comfortable—friends who walked, talked and dressed like me—would be impossible. Thus, my unlikely relationship with Bonnie developed. Monday mornings we'd share stories about our weekends. While Bonnie told me about taking Alex to the playground, I detailed the bar my friends and I, all newly twenty-one, had discovered

Note that the final product presented in Figure 1-3 has a few pen-
ciled-in corrections on it. If, when you are proofreading the final draft,

---

**Figure 1.3 (continued)**

that Saturday night. As I was making plans to head off to college in
September, Bonnie was decide-deciding whether to send Alex to kindergarten
in the fall, or to wait another year.

One unusually cool night in August, Bonnie and Alex and I, along with some
other friends, attended a Red Sox game. Minutes after struggling through the
typical drunk and rowdy Fenway Park crowd to our seats, the rain began
streaming down. Fortunately our seats were covered because it was pouring so
hard it reminded me of the unrealistic rain I'd only seen on television or in
movies. Like any almost five year old, Alex wasn't well suited to this rain
delay and lasted only ten minutes before complaining she was hungry and
declaring just how badly she needed to use the bathroom. Sean and I, who were
heading for the snackbar anyhow, agreed to escort her. Each reaching for one
of her tiny hands, we led Alex back through the frenzied mob.

There was an intensity in the crowd under the stands, where the stench
of stale alcohol and popcorn is permanently trapped. The Red Sox were in
the middle of another losing streak and the rain delay could mean the fans,
who were very anxious for a win, would have to wait yet another day. The
rain delay also meant more time for drinking, which was made clear by the
scattered beer lines filling most of the hallway. A group of young men who
had obviously just emerged from these lines was standing outside the
entrance to the women's restroom. They resembled the guys who had made up
my "in" crowd in high school: handsome jocks with short hair, baseball caps
and designer jeans. They watched Alex and me intently as we entered the
restroom, and because they were good looking I was initially flattered. When
they resumed staring at us a few minutes later, as we exited and walked
towards Sean, I realized their gazes signaled anything but admiration.
Clearly assuming we were Alex's young parents, they were looking on with
obvious disgust. I imagine this disgust was fueled further by the simple
fact that Sean is African-American and I am white.

Caught between embarrassment that anyone would believe I had a child,
and outrage that anyone would judge me if I did, I turned away silently in

a few errors should come to your attention, as they did in this student's case, it is perfectly acceptable to pencil in corrections. Most readers would rather see a few pencil marks than read an incorrect copy. How-

**Figure 1.3 (continued)**

the direction of the snackbar, following Sean and Alex. I sensed the disapproving glance of a grouchy woman as we passed. Stopping at a souvenir shop, I noticed the suburban family looking on with disbelief. I wasn't sure if my face, now as red as it used to become when I was called upon to speak aloud during class, was a result of extreme shame or an uncontrollable and mounting rage.

It was now at least a half hour since the game had been scheduled to start. The fans were becoming louder and along with the sound of cash registers and occasional music, their voices began to resound like a collective hum. To me, this hum echoes like a deep and ominous voice uttering the word "no" over and over again. Fully convinced I was the center of everyone's attention, I imagined the "no" was directed towards me. Waiting at the souvenir stand, all I wanted was to escape this unbearable and punishing hum. However, watching Sean and Alex leaning over the display case, trying to decide which pin to buy, both oblivious to the millions of eyes upon us, I realized escape was not in the too-near future.

Turning my back to the stand, hoping if I was facing the other direction people would think I was waiting for someone else, I began to observe the passersby. An overweight couple, laden with greasy food, passed, followed by a teenager with green hair. Some local college students walked by next to two men in business suits who had probably walked to the ball park from their offices. Not everyone was attractive, successful, or content. A mother passed, steps ahead of her young daughter, whom she glanced at occasionally to scold. Not everyone there was as wonderful a parent as Bonnie had been for the last four years. Realizing these were all conclusions that shouldn't surprise me, I turned back to the counter to help Sean and Alex select a pin. Finally, walking back to our seats, I grabbed one of Alex's hands, while Sean took the other. People's gazes no longer seemed focused on us. The menacing hum disappeared and I recognized the distinct sounds of busy cash registers, distant music, and people having fun.

ever, if many corrections are needed, it is better to reprint the paper; a sloppy paper should always be redone, even if it takes a little longer than you had planned.

By using a step-by-step strategy to write your essays, you will be able to perfect each stage of the process, making the final essay your best possible effort. To help you develop your abilities by using an effective writing process, each step is taken up in depth in the following chapters.

## WRITING ON A COMPUTER

Most writers today prefer to use a computer for preparing their papers, for the obvious advantages of being able to correct errors easily and make last-minute changes in text without retyping. A great many writers prefer to write the entire paper on the computer (except for certain prewriting activities) because the computer affords a kind of freedom that longhand does not. First of all, it is easy to see what one has written since it is typed on the screen. Because moving around text and other major changes are a simple matter, many writers feel that the computer encourages them to write multiple drafts. Most programs for word processing allow writers to compare drafts with a split screen, a procedure that seems a great deal easier than shuffling a stack of papers with crossouts and arrows. Writers find that spelling checkers allow them to concentrate on the important matters of support and development of ideas without the distractions of maintaining a hypercorrect attitude about surface features like spelling and grammar. They know that eventually the computer will help them make those corrections and that the early drafts need not be perfect in these details.

Prewriting activities such as automatic writing lend themselves readily to the computer. Most writers can adopt a rather carefree approach to pouring out words onto a screen since they know that the text is so easily changed. They are less likely to become as preoccupied with correcting errors as they would if handwriting or typing their prewriting, and they are therefore less likely to experience writer's block or to procrastinate about starting an assignment. Somehow, writing on a computer is less intimidating than other methods. For most writers, computers foster a healthy experimental attitude throughout the writing process.

The fact that one has limited space and is writing on a screen can produce some temporary inconveniences, but hard copy is always available to solve the problems. For example, some writers complain that they find proofreading difficult on the screen. The simple solution is to proofread from hard copy. Perhaps a more legitimate complaint about writing on the computer is that with some programs it is difficult to tell the exact dimensions of the paragraph you're working on, especially if your text is double spaced. Moving around in the file can be inconvenient, and if you don't do so, you sometimes wind up with very long paragraphs. A solution is to consider paragraph division as a feature of revision. Because paragraphing is largely for the convenience of the audience anyway, you can paragraph as well as you can while composing the rough draft and then redivide the paragraphs once you print out a hard copy, which will reveal paragraph proportions.

Although writing on the computer may seem a bit daunting or strained at first, the majority of writers have found that practice with the word processor eliminates most of their worries and in fact creates an environment that motivates them to write.

# WHAT SHOULD YOU WRITE ABOUT?

Many writers have trouble getting started. When asked what they plan to write about, they answer that they need more time to think. They may not realize that a good way to resolve their confusion is to take a pen in hand and think the subject through on paper, right away. There is no need for you as a writer to fear the tyrannical white page or blank screen if you become familiar with a few structured ways to sort out your thoughts. With a few techniques at your fingertips, you will find yourself able to arrive, rather simply, at an interesting and sufficiently focused topic for a paper. This chapter gives you those techniques.

Few people sit down at a desk or a keyboard without first putting off the task for a few hours—there's always the laundry to wash or phone calls to make or some important checks to write. Did you ever notice how hungry you get the minute you think of sitting down to write? The fact is that writing often frightens people because it requires so much integration of feelings and ideas, so much personal evaluation, so much commitment to a subject. Writing is not merely a mechanical skill—it engages the whole person.

Every day we express many feelings and thoughts orally. In fact, we are so used to dropping ideas and attitudes in casual conversation that we feel alarmed by the permanence and concreteness of academic assignments. We feel that once our ideas are expressed on paper we cannot retract them or alter them even slightly; and we fear that once down on paper, our ideas are not the only things that will be judged—we ourselves will be personally evaluated.

Thus, either we do not write until we have formulated our ideas with a degree of precision, or we get so tense in our alarm over a required written assignment that we temporarily block the flow and spontaneity of our thoughts. What all professional writers know—and what you, too, should remember if you tend to feel blocked—is that writing an essay for a class assignment is the second step of the process. The first step is prewriting, or planning.

## WHY PLANNING?

The first step should be merely the scratches and scrawls of a working mind: a valuable if imperfect beginning. At this point, your thoughts need not be polished, or even clear. Just keep your mind rolling. You should no more begin with rigid expectations of yourself in writing than you would, for instance, if you were buying a car. You wouldn't just drive home in the first one you saw; you'd consider the various levels of quality, options, safety records, engineering, good looks, and costs. In fact, you might write a list of comparisons so that you wouldn't forget about any important advantage or disadvantage. For the car buyer, the first step is to record raw ideas, sort through them, and adjust them. This step is important for the writer, too.

As you recall from Chapter 1, the step before drafting an essay is planning, or prewriting: everything you put down on paper before you actually start the draft. The following steps are all part of planning:

1. Inventing the subject: in this step you pick a general subject area that interests you.
2. Focusing the subject: in this step you explore the limits and the possible options that your subject offers; then you settle on one focused subject.
3. Writing a thesis: in this step you develop the limited subject into an assertion that will direct your whole essay.
4. Outlining the paper: in this step you create a set of detailed notes that you can use as a map for writing out the first draft of the paper.

How each writer goes about the steps involved in planning is largely a matter of personal taste. For example, you may find, after trying several methods of inventing and exploring subjects, that one method sticks with you—you feel at home with it. Because the technique works well for you, you use it whenever you write, over and over. Or the methods you choose may depend on how familiar you are with the subject of an assigned paper, or on the amount of time you have to spend on an essay.

Whatever prewriting method you use, you will save yourself much time and worry in the long run. There are two good reasons for this: you will have the chance to look over your options and select a topic you want to write about, and you will feel in control of your presentation—you will not discover when writing page seven that page six contains three irrelevant ideas and that page four has five ideas that belong to page one. Essays written without recorded preparation are likely to be diffuse, unfocused, underdeveloped, boring, and illogical despite all your efforts to think your topic through before beginning to write. As you saw in Chapter 1 with the essay called "Love" the chances are that an essay handed in without planning would serve as a good example of prewriting, but not of the final written product.

You can view the planning stage as a written conversation with yourself rather than as a formal writing assignment. It is free writing in the early stages, without any demands for proper grammar or spelling. As long as you can decipher what you have put down, it will do the job. Planning is also generative and positive—it can help you see how many ideas you really do have, how many views you can come up with that give an interesting slant to your topic.

## INVENTING THE SUBJECT

It's fine to say you should find an interesting subject, and it's a good first step, but how do you begin? Where do good topics come from? You can begin by writing rough notes, really just words and phrases, as they strike you. The specific sources of these ideas can be class readings or library sources, personal experiences, the experiences of people you know, discussions with friends, television watching, class discussions and lectures, indexes in the library (see Chapter 9), suggestions from teachers and friends, daily casual reading of newspapers and magazines, and so forth. To invent a general subject for a paper, you only need to tap your recent experiences or responses to what you have read, seen, discussed, and heard. One possible way to approach several experiences at once is to make a list of ideas and events that have stirred your emotions—whether positively or negatively—over the past few weeks. You might even divide a sheet of paper in half and let your mind roam free:

Editorial on political correctness
TV coverage of "national" health care in U.S.
Read "Allegory of the Cave"—liked the idea of truth
Carole's wedding (costs)
Dodgers won
Linda's medical school interview

Now, this list may not at first appear to offer many possible topics, but it actually does. You could single out the most annoying qualities of TV specials on the national health care plan or the roadblocks to eventually solving the problems in medically underserved communities, the Dodgers, or Plato. These topics are at least possibilities, starting points. If the assignment is more specific, of course, you would have to find a subject within the restrictions. Still, listing your initial inspirations

within the subject area assigned will be likely to engage you in something you can commit time and energy to.

## FOCUSING THE SUBJECT

When you are given an assignment to write an essay of 500 words, you are expected to focus your subject to an appropriate size for the paper. It is true that you could, in effect, write a few pages on any topic, and encyclopedias do just that. Turn to the entry on China, and you find only a few pages. But you can see that the kind of information in encyclopedias is far less specific than that required in most college papers. Even if your assignment is to write a paper of about fifteen pages, you probably need to limit the original conception of your topic. As you research or explore your own ideas, you will repeatedly find reason to narrow your subject. You can't elaborate on all the symptoms and treatments of autism in five pages, but you may be able to discuss the role of one psychologist's theory in changing the current treatment models. You cannot write about educational equity for the disabled in ten pages, except in a very general way—whole volumes are devoted to the subject. However, you can discuss the need to teach both lipreading and sign language to young deaf children.

You may wonder whether it is possible to focus your subject too much. The fact is that most college writers have little difficulty settling on a broad subject; rather, they struggle to cut down the scope of their topic to manageable size. A good college essay usually says a lot about a few things, not a little about many things. If you do prewriting every time you write, you should be able to limit your subject systematically and adequately. Generally, you need not worry about making your subject too narrow. Writers who feel that they have limited their topics too much (and as a consequence have little to say) have more likely failed to expand adequately on the separate subdivisions of a good limited subject. But how do you narrow a broad topic like South Africa to the question of whether the "new freedom" in South Africa means a new way of life or just a political stance? Or how do you take a topic from your readings and test it for focus?

### Exploring the Subject

Writers have found certain planning techniques especially helpful in focusing their subject, among them, keeping a writer's notebook, using a copy book, and brainstorming. These techniques, explained here, have structures, but they are very flexible. They aim only at getting you to explore the limits of your subject and helping you to determine what view and which parts of your broad topic you are most committed to investigating and writing about. Naturally, the process will be somewhat different for each individual. You may find that you use one pattern exclusively because it works best for you or that you concoct a version of your own by combining the prewriting techniques explained in this chapter. Try each pattern and choose the ones that work best for you.

### Keeping a Writer's Notebook

'The writer's notebook is a sourcebook of collected insights and a testing ground for ideas. An entry may provide you with a general subject, but more important, it can free you to express your important feelings about an idea. However, before you try this technique, it's important to know the differences between this sort of notebook and a diary, so that you avoid making entries that will not help you. A diary is a daily record of events. It is for recording everything that happens. A writer's notebook, on the other hand, is for recording only special perceptions that might serve as the core statements of essays. These insights may arise from the particular way in which you view something that occurred during the day, from your response to some book, or simply from an unsummoned idea that pops into your head. To illustrate:

> *Diary:* Finished reading Norman Mailer's book about Gary Gilmore.
> *Writer's Notebook:* Mailer ennobles the killer Gary Gilmore in his book. This shows how naif Mailer is.

The most satisfying part of maintaining a writer's notebook is that it becomes a record of how your perceptions change and grow over time. When you begin to read a novel, for instance, you may identify with a certain situation between two lovers in the book, but by the middle of the work you may find that the characters act in predictable and unrealistic ways that make the writing cheap and sentimental. The series of entries in your writer's notebook could provide you with specific critical points that you might turn into an essay on the shallowness of character development. In a writer's notebook your first impressions often combine to become a generalization about the work you are dealing with or the aspect of your life you are exploring. Such generalizations are at the heart of all essays.

The writer's notebook serves a dual purpose in prewriting: it helps you hold onto the ideas that flow so quickly through your mind, and it helps you explore those ideas beyond their rough beginnings as they become more developed and more clearly formed thoughts.

Many professional writers keep a notebook of this type. In fact, the term "writer's notebook" was borrowed from the title of W. Somerset Maugham's journals. Figure 2-1 presents samples from a student's notebook. You will notice many writing errors, but these, you will recall, do not matter in prewriting, which is done only to collect ideas. Notice also that the three entries are cumulative, each showing different thinking patterns that eventually lead to the generalization (in the third entry). What essay topics might this student have developed from this germinal idea?

### Using a Copy Book

A pleasurable way to build a storehouse of ideas—and, as a byproduct, to improve your writing style—is to keep a copy book. It is an old literary practice to keep a notebook in which you copy favorite

---

**Figure 2-1. Samples from a writer's notebook**

**Journal Entry #1**

Richard Rodriguez, in "A Memoir of a Bilingual Childhood" states that living in a white neighborhood caused them to feel tremendous social pressure to conform to American ways, meaning "white" ways. His family felt like the foreigners on the block (80). As the son of ambitious Mexican immigrants who earned relatively higher salaries than other immigrants of the same nationality, Rodriguez speaks of being sent to catholic school where he is the only Mexican among Caucasian children. According to Rodriguez, the alienation he felt—and his family felt—caused him to assimilate quickly, to learn English, change their dress, and not to speak publically of his "home" life. He learned to separate the two parts of himself, the "private" and the "public" selves, and Spanish became a "private" language. Based on what we have been reading Rodriguez is the exception. I would go so far as to question whether one can really overcome the marginalization one feels when one is outcast by the community for ethnic differences. No matter how "white" he tried to act outside his home, didn't people in his neighborhood still see him as different from them, as the "foreigner"? He makes it all seem so pat and simple, just decide to fit in and you will. Racism and classism make this harder than it looks. Though one big thing in Rodriguez's favor was that he was better off financially than most Mexican immigrants. He had to (in another chapter of the book) get a construction job in the summer to find out what other Mexicans experienced daily as a matter of course. Rodriguez was on a scholarship at college but his family was not really poor and oppressed economically.

---

passages from works you are reading. You simply record direct quotations whenever you come upon them; they may be as short as a sentence or as long as two or three paragraphs. You will note subconsciously how the author phrases ideas, uses punctuation, and structures sentences. Before long you may find yourself naturally using some of the same strategies. Many writers say that this is the best way to influence your style and thinking because it calls upon the writer's intuition for language—what rhetoricians refer to as "linguistic imagination." Whether or not that is the case, you will benefit from collecting interesting passages for your copy book.

### Brainstorming

The process of freely associating ideas is called brainstorming. To brainstorm, as the word suggests, is to write down everything that comes into your mind—words, phrases, or sentences. You usually begin with some stimulus (a concept, a film, a photograph, a painting) and, writing as fast as your mind works, come up with a list of related thoughts. The very act of writing under pressure without a set structure produces new ideas. There are two slightly different approaches to

**Figure 2-1 (continued)**

**Journal Entry #2**

I keep wondering if Rodriguez is someone I should like or hate. Is he a sell-out? But doesn't he have a right to upward social mobility? He had to work hard to learn English? Even his family thought he was selling out, though. But then again that kind of anti-intellectualism and lack of support from the family can lead to a less than easy life. I'm confused.

**Journal Entry #3**

I'm beginning to see what an exception Rodriguez is. Neidert and Farley (1985) say that the relative lack of education of Mexican-Americans assigns them specific positions in the work force. They also found correlations with education, prestige and income. Carlos Arce found salaries and education connected to prestige and assimilation (Rodriguez's family). Most of what I am reading about Mexican immigrants makes it clear they are the poorest of immigrants and thus the least empowered to be educated, have high status in the work force, or earn good incomes. Therefore, it is likely they would assimilate less because they would not have the incentives. The argument can be made that if they assimilate less, they are more marginalized. That makes sense to someone like Rodriguez who thinks that the route toward success is assimilation. Retaining culture is not a sometimes thing, though. Is it? How could he really be one person in private and one in public? I think he changed and gave up parts of his culture. Therefore, he (or his kids) would be more like the second- and third generation Asians and Europeans, who have few cultural constraints because they operate nearly totally in the mainstream. This has its costs too.

brainstorming: automatic writing and word lists. Remember that in neither case should you concern yourself with grammar and spelling. Never go back to cross out a word or think twice of what to say.

### Automatic Writing

Automatic writing is particularly useful when you feel blocked on a given subject, whether you write by hand or on the computer. The technique of automatic writing is to write as fast as possible, without stopping, for some prescribed time limit—say, five minutes. If you are using the computer, you may wish to adjust the light on the screen so that what you write isn't readable and thus isn't distracting. It's invisible writing! Write freely, in complete sentences or phrases, whatever comes into your head. Don't lift your pen from the paper or your hands from the keyboard. If your mind is blank, write your last phrase again and again until a different thought replaces that one. After completing the automatic writing, examine each line closely for interesting ideas on which you might like to write. Your product won't be the world's greatest writing, but for planning it will be fine. Here is an example of one student's automatic writing:

The consequences of lax enforcement of water policy is horrendous pollution that negatively affects human and marine life. The trickle-down effect starts from the $3 billion fishing industry and then to the consumers since fishermen depend on the ocean's livelihood and abundance in healthy marine life. Many fishermen lose their jobs and the consumers must pay more for seafood consumption. Furthermore, the waste washed ashore on beaches nationwide prevents any type of recreation, as a result, businesses and resorts suffer. While one may argue that the human quality of life is inconsequential or that we can survive without the luxury of sporting the beaches, the overriding issue remains that the wastes, compounded with toxic dumping annihilate our ecosystem. In June 1987 scientists discovered 150 dead dolphins lining the Atlantic Coast. They discovered their blistered and cratered snouts, flippers and tails, in addition scientists found that harbor seals in the Gulf of Maine have the highest level of radiation of any U.S. mammal. Lobsters and crabs have holes in their shells and fish have rolled fins—just a few of the mutations. Just a few of the mutations Just a few of the mutations Sea birds and marine animals die yearly as a result of the water's toxicity levels. This includes nonbiodegradable plastics that could ensnare a sea turtle or sea lions. The misconception that the vast ocean, covering 70% of the world's surface, can neutralize itself by decomposing contaminants or allowing them to settle harmlessly below the surface is dead wrong. So is the belief that the ocean's resources are inexhaustible. Such premises are put forth by politicians with other motivations and lead to laws that reflect short-term solutions.

When you finish the automatic writing, you should read over what you have written and list the interesting subjects. Here's the list compiled by the writer of our sample:

    political motivations for keeping laws lax
    misperceptions about resources
    economic effects
    humanistic argument

If the writer felt a need to further focus these subjects, he or she could do an automatic writing on each one of them, finally selecting the best ideas. You can use a similar expanding, limiting, and selecting process to eventually arrive at a topic sufficiently limited for an essay.

Another way you might want to focus your automatic writing is by centering. To center you simply ask yourself about your five-minute writing, "What have I said, in essence?" You then put the answer to that question into a sentence or two. If the point you have arrived at is not sufficiently focused, you can begin another five-minute automatic writing, using the centered sentence as the first sentence. Then you center this second five-minute writing.

This technique is excellent for getting started on all sorts of projects. Try it some time on a letter you have been putting off. Rarely will you need to repeat the process of automatic writing and centering more than three or four times (a total of twenty minutes). And the results will certainly be worth the time investment. Here is an example of automatic writing and centering that a student used to focus a subject from the assignment "Write on anything you want to from the reading of 'Momma and the Dentist' by Maya Angelou." Note that the student did not pay attention to spelling or structure. Her goal was to capture the thoughts racing through her head.

First five-minute automatic writing:

"Momma and the Dentist" is a very touching story and one that I can relate to because I have felt the sting of prejudice from time to time in my life. My immigrant family moved to a small town when I was about ten and that is when the problems began. It reminds me of what Angelou says about Stamps and everybody having to keep up an impression for the richer people in town. The poor people can't help there feeling of inferiority and it just gets worst when they expect it to. This ties in with the idea of self-respect, which is what I believe this story is about. Momma had a lot of self-respect and her grandchild was too young to have it herself but she was a fighter and would probably get it when she grew up. I guess she did since the grandchild in the story is the author. Maybe writing is the way she got it. Anyway, what can I say . . . what can I say . . . OK the grandmother was the symbol of self-respect in the story because she did not let the dentist get his own way—not entirely. She showed him that she was a person too and that he had to admit that by giving her the extra money to get to a dentist and have her grandbaby treated. Even if she wasn't as dramatic as the child imagined her to be, the grandmother was a pretty strong woman. She did not let feelings of inferiority get to her when it mattered.

Centered sentence:

```
    Self-respect in the face of inferiority is the main
theme of "Momma and the Dentist."
```

After the student centered, she asked, "Is this subject focused enough?" She concluded that it wasn't, so she completed another five-minute writing and centered once again. Then she repeated these steps until a suitable focused topic arose in the centered sentence.

Second five-minute automatic writing:

```
    Self-respect in the face of inferiority is the main
theme of "Momma and the Dentist."
    Momma must feel some sort of inferiority because the
society all around her at the time was extremely preju-
dice. She didn't really have the right to be asking a
white dentist for his services, according to the soci-
ety. Wait a minute, maybe she didn't feel inferior. Let
me see what I can come up with to back this up.
    She is very clean—cleanliness is close to godliness.
She is bold—goes to white side of segregated town. She
makes sure her grandbaby is properly washed and dressed
to face the whites.
    Well, maybe she is, sort of because she is putting up
a face to impress the whites and prove to them she is
equal. Could her inferiority be the cause of her self-
respect. I mean could it make her mad? Maybe she knows
she is equal to the whites but she also doesn't want to
give them anything to stereotype her with so she cleans
up extra special when she goes to see them. That doesn't
mean she is feeling less of a person. In fact, she may
be pretty crafty, playing their game their way.
```

Second centered sentence:

```
    Momma in "Momma and the Dentist" has self-respect
because she does not feel inferior to whites and she
knows how to play their game.
```

Third automatic writing:

```
    Momma in "Momma and the Dentist" has self-respect
because she does not feel inferior to whites and she
knows how to play their game. Does she play their game?
Well, maybe not exactly. She plays her own game. She is
naturally a proper woman who is very clean and wants to
look her best. And she expects anyone, including the
dentist to pay proper attention to her—treat her as a
```

person like she treats people (when she loaned the
dentist money she did it for that reason). Can't think
of anything new. Can't think of anything new. Oh, yes,
when the dentist says that he would rather put his hand
in a dog's mouth than in a black's she just keeps on
talking with him, others might have gotten scared or
shown their anger but she wasn't threatened at all. She
definitely doesn't feel inferior to the dentist because
she knows who she is and she is spurred on by the des-
perate need to take care of her grandchild. Maybe it is
wrong for her to collect interest from the dentist when
he doesn't owe her any money, but she is just playing by
the rules of inequality. At that time blacks had to get
back in any way they could. The whole story is about
personal power.

Centered sentence:

In "Momma and the Dentist," Maya Angelou depicts that
through self-respect blacks were able to establish
themselves as powerful in the white society that oppressed them.

This final focus point is practically a thesis statement. After approximately fifteen minutes of automatic writing and centering, the student
decided to write her essay on the connections between power, trickery,
and self-respect. Tracing these issues through the previous five-minute
writings, you can see how arriving at the final statement was a cumulative process.

Note also that in the course of her brainstorming the author occasionally flipped her arguments, sometimes arguing the opposite of what
she had just said. Doing so is a good way of generating ideas. Another
good method she used was to ask questions when she felt stuck. Questions seemed to generate speculations that kept her writing moving.
By keeping herself engaged in the act of brainstorming, this writer was
able to sort out—and eventually to synthesize—several of her ideas
about the story.

### Word Lists

When you have an idea for a paper or have discovered an interesting subject but you are wondering whether it is worth pursuing, you
might try the word list technique. Many people prefer this technique
to automatic writing because it is not timed and because it requires
only listing key words. The first step in writing a word list is to write
down at least twenty to thirty words quickly, without stopping if possible, and without hesitating to select the most appropriate word. One
student's word list on the American jail system looked like this:

| | |
|---|---|
| jobs in jail | killers |
| cures | suicide |
| punishment | bitterness |
| cruelty—guards | macho |
| life terms | rehabilitation |
| money gets you off | initiation |
| probation arrangement | time |
| condition of cells | toilets |
| social hierarchy | showers |
| sexual harassment | theft |
| public defenders | drugs |
| rapists | smuggling |
| murderers | plan future crime |
| dehumanization | no real behavior change |
| loss of privacy | underdogs |
| loss of hope | muggings |
| crowded | bugs |
| church | rats |
| school | beds on floor |
| occupational therapy | recidivism |

The next step is to review your list and cross out any word that repeats another. Here the writer could cross out *killers* and leave *murderers* and could delete *jobs in jail* in favor of *occupational therapy*. Step three is to go through the list and group similar ideas. This is often a subjective process that begins to direct you toward the main point of your paper. Another student might group the same words in a different way to achieve a different set of ideas. No one way is right—it's entirely up to the writer. Following is the student's grouping for the words in the preceding list. Note how the writer developed a category to cover each main idea. He found labels within the word list—or else made them up, as with "Crime Within Jail" and "Jail Sentences."

| Crime Within Jail | Jail Sentences |
|---|---|
| drugs | life terms |
| muggings | money gets you off |
| macho | public defenders |
| future crime plans | probation arrangement |
| rapists | time |
| murderers | |
| suicide | Condition of Cells |
| | crowded |
| Punishment | beds on floor |
| cruelty—guards | bugs |
| social hierarchy | rats |
| initiation | toilets |
| | showers |

| Psychological Adjustment | Rehabilitation |
|---|---|
| loss of privacy | cures |
| social hierarchy | church |
| initiation | school |
| underdogs | occupational therapy |
| loss of hope | no real behavior change |
| bitterness | recidivism |
| suicide | |

The pattern that emerges from a word list should tell you at a glance which subjects offer you the most material. It is easy enough to know what you are sufficiently knowledgeable about, and your interest in a subject will cause you to pursue it. After completing the word list and the grouping, you can select one or two word groups, the most interesting ones, as a list of potential limited subjects.

### Using a Subject Chart

The most structured and most graphic of the prewriting techniques for limiting the subject is the subject chart. To develop a subject chart, begin at the middle of a clean sheet of paper. Draw a circle and write your broad subject in it. You may start out very broad, as in the example of the chart in Figure 2-2, or more focused as in the following example. Where you begin will depend on your assignment and on how much you know about the subject.

Then, turning the subject over in your mind, ask yourself what aspects of the subject you can name. Remember, you want to look at some interesting and possibly controversial aspects of your subject. For example, if your subject is advertising as socialization, you might break it down according to the different themes you have considered or would like to know more about. Next you might ask yourself what smaller units you can break down each of the second-level topics into. You might decide on categories such as cosmetics, food, clothing, and services. Or you might approach controversial issues, such as the ethics of advertising aimed at children on Saturday morning television or sexual themes in magazine ads. Topics like these really add focus to your subject.

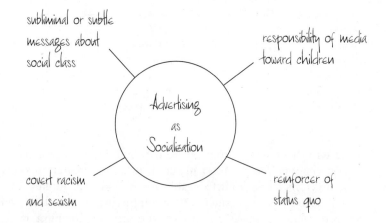

You could then break down each of the second-level topics even further. The point of this exercise is to allow you to subdivide your subject into many of its focused categories, presenting all your ideas for topics in a logical order. You can see in Figure 2-2 how one student used this method to develop a rather extensive subject chart on the general topic of bilingual education. After drawing up a subject chart, you can pick potential topics for a short or detailed paper from the areas farthest from the center of the chart. The more general the assignment is intended to be, the closer to the center your topic is likely to be.

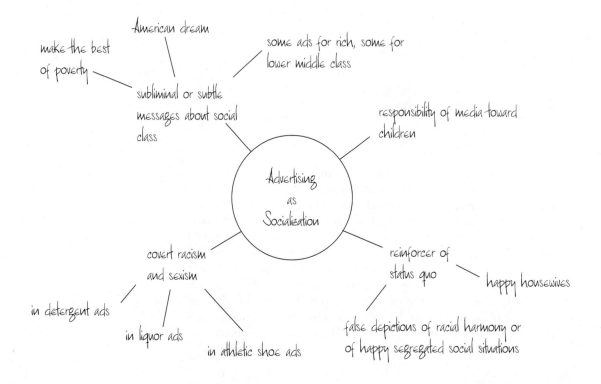

The subject chart in Figure 2-2 is very well developed and no doubt took quite some time to complete. Your charts need not always be so developed. You may include certain categories that you do not wish to explore, so you leave those less developed than others. You may quickly decide on a variety of interesting topics and feel no need to expand the chart so completely.

If you trace some of the topics in Figure 2-2, you can see how the writer's mind worked, focusing the topic more and more narrowly:

**Figure 2-2. Example of a subject chart.**

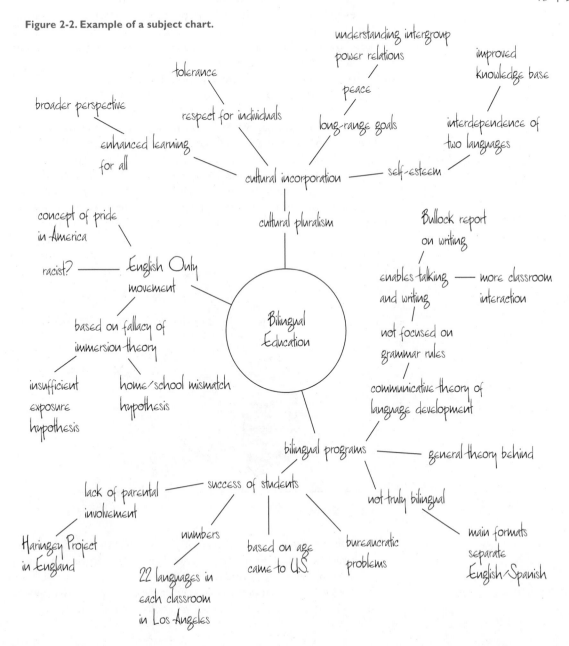

### Selecting the Best Subject

Once you have explored the limits of the general subject in which you're interested, you are ready to decide which aspect of the subject you wish to write about. From your exploring, you have various choices. Your decision should be made with a few things in mind. What sort of interest do you have in the subject? What information is available on your subject? Who is your audience?

Remember, you are going to devote some time and quite a bit of energy to the subject, so you want it to be one that is meaningful to you. Nevertheless, the topic, no matter how interesting, must invite further development. For you to investigate it, information must be available to you. If it is a subject requiring research but also very current (you heard about it on the news two days ago), you may experience difficulty finding up-to-date information in the library (see Chapter 9). You should find out before you go a step further. The same goes for a topic requiring no library research. Do you know enough about it to expand it into a good paper? Are you full of good ideas at this point?

Then, of course, there is the matter of whether your audience (the teacher and your classmates) will find the subject interesting, valuable, and appropriate to the assignment (see Chapter 1). Whatever focused subject you select should be appealing from the vantage points of writer, subject, and audience. The appropriate subject for a paper would fall, ideally, where these considerations meet, as diagrammed in Figure 2-3.

**Figure 2-3. Your choice of essay topic must take three factors into account.**

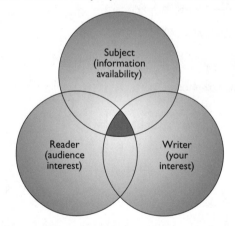

### Exercises

A. Discuss with a classmate and explain your resulting view on the following: whether you believe it easier to write about subjects that are interesting to you than subjects that you have no opinion about. Is it possible to develop an interest in any subject? Offer one example from your personal experience as concrete support of your opinion on the matter.

B. For two weeks, keep a writer's notebook of your reactions to ideas encountered in classes and readings. Before you write each new entry, read the one before it. After the two weeks are up, sift through the notebook and make a list of ten possible topics for essays.

C. On your own, begin a copy book, aiming for three or four entries per week. After a month's worth of entries, review what you have recorded to locate possible topics for essays.

D. Make a subject chart on one of the following topics and identify three limited subjects for essays from the chart: violence in schools, morality in the media, Americans' (or anyone's) perception of the family.

E. Write a word list on one of the following subjects: sports in college, salaries of teachers, AIDS education in elementary school.

F. Develop three four-minute automatic writings on this subject: the value of first impressions. Be sure to center the free writing each time before starting the next automatic writing.

G. Deliberately pick a very broad subject and write a page-long essay about it. What characteristics stand out about the information?

H. Look up China in the encyclopedia. How long is the article? Why do you suppose authors of encyclopedia articles are able to write on broad subjects in such a short space? Can you think of any other type of writing that does the same thing?

I. Spend five minutes doing an automatic writing about a movie you have seen recently. How many topics for essays can you derive?

J. Write a word list on the subject of parental responsibility. Derive four possible essay topics from your efforts.

K. Select any object you would like to examine and look at it for ten minutes without writing anything down. Then for ten minutes (try not to stop) record any associations that occur to you. Can you think of anything to compare the object with that will clarify for your reader what it looks like, feels like? Did this sort of "meditation" suggest any issues to your mind? Might your ten-minute writing sample serve as the beginnings of an essay?

L. Write a sequence of two writer's notebook entries on a subject from a reading you have done for a course. Can you derive any topics for essays?

## DEVELOPING A THESIS

Since writing ought to be a series of promises to the reader and responses to those promises, the first part of your essay should include a thesis: a sentence or group of sentences that presents what the essay aims to prove, define, describe, or illustrate. The chances are that you do not have the point of your paper clear in your own mind if, early in the paper (but not necessarily early in your process of writing), you cannot commit yourself to a concise statement of it. Papers without focus lose the readers' interest. Why pay attention to someone if that person doesn't know what he or she wants to say?

Your thesis should be stated concisely and directly—it should prepare the readers in a few words for what is to come. Compare these two introductory statements for a simple informative essay:

This paper will examine the relationships between the roles of ancient Japanese goddesses and current-day geisha.

Since Elizabethan times, comedies have been designated as three types: romantic, critical, and rogue.

Writers in some fields, such as the social sciences and sciences, favor intention statements like the first. Others, notably in the humanities, more commonly incorporate thesis sentences into critical essays. Whether you use an intention statement or a thesis is a matter of personal taste (readers' and writers') and a matter of convention in the discipline you are writing for.

In any case, most effective thesis statements have three parts that you should learn to recognize. Because the thesis is a complete sentence, it has a subject and a predicate; these are the first two of the three parts. Naturally the predicate part of the sentence makes a statement about the subject. The predicate part often contains the third part you should look for: a controlling idea. A controlling idea indicates your main idea for support and is always a clue to the development of the essay. A clear controlling idea shows the readers what to expect in the body of the paper and commits the writer to the information that supports the main point. The controlling idea says, "Here is what evidence supports my point." Of course, not every thesis you read contains a stated controlling idea. A writer who chooses to leave out the controlling idea is deliberately leaving more to the readers' imagination.

Here is an example of a thesis statement:

*Thesis:* Smoking in public buildings should be outlawed because inhaled smoke is dangerous to the health of all people and often offensive to nonsmokers.

The subject is "smoking." The predicate part is "should be outlawed because inhaled smoke is dangerous to the health of all people and often offensive to nonsmokers." The controlling idea is "dangerous to the health of all people and often offensive to nonsmokers." You can see that while the predicate tells the readers a great deal, it is necessarily long and complex. Leaving out the because clause would simplify matters, but the readers would find the argument less clear from the start of the paper and therefore would have to work harder at reading.

Making the thesis no longer than one complete sentence is usually not too difficult, but there may be times when, for clarity, you will need more than one sentence. Your goal is to state your main idea as directly and clearly as possible. Therefore, when you can fit the point into a sentence you should do so.

### Steps in Developing a Thesis

The following steps will help you write a direct—but complex—one-sentence thesis. As you progress through the steps, you get closer and closer to developing the whole thesis. In the final step, you add up the work in the previous steps and create the thesis. Try not to digress or take shortcuts at first when following the steps—always remember in each step to write out your subject completely, as it is an integral part of the final step and should not be lost.

1. *Name your focused subject.* Assume for a moment you are assigned a five-page essay in your American Cultures class. You can write about anything you have been studying in the broad area of immigration, but you must show evidence of your reading and the issues raised in class. You have already done a journal as you were reading for the class (see pp. 34-35 for a few sample entries), and the journal has revealed to you your interest in Mexican assimilation to the United States. Still you realize that the topic is rather broad.

For Step One you need to check the scope of your subject against the goal of the assignment.

Since the class has been studying the issue of acculturation vs. assimilation among many different groups immigrating to the United States, you decide to write about the following focused topic:

Step One: the degree to which Mexicans assimilate to American culture

2. *Ask a question about the focused subject.* Here you decide on what you want to investigate in your paper. Devising an interesting question, you can see that in effect you are adding a predicate or "aboutness" to the focused subject. On your topic of Mexican assimilation, you've read in class that Mexicans assimilate slowly, and so you wish to explore the reasons for this slowness as well as why other ethnic groups assimilate faster. So you ask:

Step Two: Why do many Mexicans assimilate more slowly to American culture than do members of other ethnic groups?

3. *Revise your question into an assertion.* Since most thesis statements are not in question form, you will want to revise your question into a statement. As you do so, you will want to make it even more pointed or elaborated. Suppose you wish to add to the concept you are working with that there is a positive aspect to the fact that these immigrants adjust slowly to the new culture.

You try the following:

Step Three: Many Mexicans assimilate to American culture more slowly than do other ethnicities, but they retain their culture more effectively in subsequent generations.

You read over that statement and aren't happy with it. You think the first half still has an unintentional negative connotation. It will take some revision later, but now you want to move on so as not to lose ideas. You decide to polish it up later.

4. *Add a group of words in which you set forth your key supporting ideas.* You may be able to use words such as *because, by,* or *in that* to introduce the controlling idea, linking it to the rest of the sentence. In Step Four you are listing or summarizing your main ideas, which you will take up in turn in the essay.

For the paper on Mexican assimilation you start out with *because:*

Step Four: because of socioeconomic, political, and cultural realities

5. *Recognize the opposing view.* If your topic is controversial, it is sound argumentative practice to state your opponents' claims. There may be members of your audience who would disagree with you. Assume there are. A good place to insert these claims is in an *although* clause, perhaps at the beginning of your assertion, or, if the claim is long, in a complete sentence preceding the thesis. Ask yourself what someone arguing for quick assimilation would say, and recognize the validity of that person's argument by placing that idea right in your thesis, where the reader will get a fair view of the issue. For Step Five you summarize the valid points on the other side:

Step Five: although some Mexicans assimilate quickly in response to extreme social pressures and those who do not often are frustrated by being marginalized

There were two considerations: how fast Mexicans assimilate and whether slow assimilation is positive or negative.

6. *Put it all together and refine wording.* Combine the last three steps in the following order: Step Five, Step Three, and Step Four. As a finishing touch, polish up any wordiness or awkwardness in the thesis sentence. If the controlling idea forms an unwieldy list that overwhelms the reader, try to condense it by using fewer words or revise into several consecutive sentences. In this case the writer has some work to do with the precision of the original sentence in Step Three and a long, complex statement of opposition to contend with. It's best to experiment with a few possible

versions and pick the clearest. Keep in mind that this is the tentative thesis—you might still change it as a result of drafting the essay or coming upon a new bit of research.

Version One: Although some Mexicans assimilate quickly in response to extreme social pressures and those who do not are often frustrated by being marginalized, the majority of Mexican immigrants do not incorporate themselves swiftly into mainstream American culture because of socioeconomic, political, and cultural realities not shared by Asians and Europeans.

Version Two: It is true that not all Mexicans assimilate slowly to American mainstream culture. However the majority find that socioeconomic, political, and cultural realities not faced by Asians or Europeans are responsible for what has been called "delayed" assimilation. Contrary to popular opinion, this "delay" becomes positive for subsequent generations of Mexican-Americans.

Version Three: Few Mexicans assimilate quickly to American mainstream society because of socioeconomic, political, and cultural realities not shared by Asians and Europeans. Despite the marginalization immigrant Mexicans experience as a result of slow assimilation, the delay is positive in that the original culture is retained and reinforced over several generations of Mexican-Americans.

The third version is the best because related points are placed in the same sentence. Note that the idea of social pressure has been deleted since it is a subpoint that can easily be covered in the body of the essay.

The key to developing a good thesis, as you can see, is learning how to ask a good question. After practicing the six steps to an effective thesis for a while, you will probably find yourself able to compose good thesis statements just by asking a question and stating a complete answer to it. The answer will be the thesis.

You have many opportunities during the day to practice the development of a good thesis statement; you don't have to wait until a paper is due. As you walk out of a lecture with the ideas fresh in your mind, ask yourself the central question of the lecture and then turn it into a statement that sums up the whole lecture. You not only will be reinforcing the classwork in your own mind, a good study habit, but also will be practicing the most crucial step in effective writing: forming a thesis.

### The Clustering Approach

Do you think of yourself as a rather intuitive person? Do you respond better to more free-flowing methods than to structured ones? Then you will probably prefer clustering to the six-step method of developing a thesis. Clustering is a technique that helps you to synthesize information quickly. If you feel as if you have a lot of ideas on a subject but no actual direction for the thesis, clustering may be the best method to try.

The first step in clustering is to develop a cluster of ideas. Allow nine minutes for this step. This technique may seem similar to the subject chart method on pages 41-43, but there are important differences. Whereas in the subject chart you develop each idea into structured subsets, in the clustering technique you simply free associate, writing down your ideas along a single strand, like this:

Male friendships

active
do things together
play sports
compete
prove maleness
dominance games

Then, when you complete the first string of ideas, you start another from the center of the circle. After nine minutes you should have a drawing that looks something like a spider or a child's picture of the sun:

than others
some more open
individual character
pick friends for
friends
a few close
college friends
fraternities
false bravado
values about women—bad
good & bad male roles
learn to be "strong"
learn to fear vulnerability
fear revealing weakness to male friends

hang out in groups
safe
impersonal
intellectual

Male friendships

father/son
father as mentor
teach son to be a "man"
patriarchal society
diverging views on this: father/son

active
do things together
play sports
compete
prove maleness
dominance games

The second step of clustering is to write about one of the strands, using your cluster as an outline. Again, you will devote nine minutes to this task. This writing should be completed in the same spirit as automatic writing, but you should make an effort to connect your ideas. Each time you move from one idea on the strand to another, make a connection between what you just wrote and what you are about to write. Write a couple of sentences about each element on the strand, keeping your ideas in the same order as you originally recorded them. If you complete your writing on one strand within the nine-minute allotment, don't stop writing. Simply pick up the first element from another of your strands, connecting that idea to what you just wrote (don't start a new paragraph—just let everything blend together). Continue writing on that strand in the same manner as you did for the first until the nine minutes are up. Figure 2-4 provides an example of a nine-minute writing on two of the strands from the cluster on the topic of male friendships.

The final step of clustering takes only a minute or two. You simply read over your nine-minute writing and ask yourself what you have said. Try to bring together the various ideas into what the creator of the concept of clustering, Gabrielle Rico, calls "a coherent whole." Write a sentence or two that explains your point. For our example, it might be:

Fraternities can foster superficial relationships between men based on bravado rather than true feelings.

---

**Figure 2-4. Example of nine-minute writing in the clustering approach.**

Male Friendships

It would seem that some of the most significant male friendships develop in college. There are a lot of opportunities to meet other men and many chances to get to know them well because of all the available social, athletic, and academic activities. Fraternities are a prime place for social interaction between men. But what happens in most of these relationships? In my opinion, fraternities encourage men to have superficial relationships. I belong to a fraternity, and I do think it has its value. Sure the men develop relationships and act like "brothers" are supposed to—help each other out of some things and go out together. There's a feeling of "community" among frat brothers. But it's not really very deep friendship. A lot of the conversation between brothers, especially when more than two get together, is false bravado and competition. A key subject is women, who conquered whom and how many times, and I think that's just disgusting, but I have to participate to be one of the guys. Most of the guys are just making up stuff, so I guess it does no harm—besides we only pretend to take it all so seriously. And it gives us a good time. But from all this don't our true values about women get kind of twisted? All this macho stuff is based on our constantly being strong, never vulnerable. If we keep talking this way, won't we begin to believe it? Won't we begin to feel it's never ok to be vulnerable? Maybe not. In our hearts we know what's right and wrong, but at least in front of our friends—we don't talk about it. So, does that make us true friends? I don't think so. Emerson once said, "A friend is one in front of whom you can think aloud." He didn't say that about a fraternity brother.

In most cases the sentence you come up with could serve as the thesis for your paper.

### Discovery Drafts

Some writers need more than a brief automatic writing to arrive at a thesis. They need to explore a subject by rehearsing a draft of their essay. By the time they write out a few pages, they've arrived at a thesis. Writing such discovery drafts is, perhaps, not new to you. However, the attitude that helps you to learn most from them may be new. The technique of writing discovery drafts is not complicated. Spend no more than forty minutes on the task. You simply begin your paper from scratch, without any previous planning, knowing all the while that this draft—which will certainly be weak in content and style—is for your eyes only. Write a very rough draft of an essay, keeping your audience in the back of your mind. When you feel a gap in needed information or when a question arises that you need to think more about, simply put a question mark in the margin or jot down a phrase that will remind you to check out the details. Your attitude should be cavalier, not hypercorrect.

Don't be discouraged if your idea fizzles as a result of writing the discovery draft. Part of the purpose of the paper is to discover the thesis you wish to propose in your actual essay.

Because this draft is something between a paper and automatic writing, don't expect to produce a uniformly good piece of writing. In fact, you are unlikely to even use any of the sentences from this draft. Essentially, your purpose is to find out what you already know about the subject and discover what you need to learn. After writing the discovery draft, you will also have a clearer sense of the parameters of your subject. You can read over the draft and ask yourself what direction would be the best one for the essay. You will usually discover a refined thesis in the process, and you will have some good ideas to help you proceed with planning your essay.

### Exercises

A. The following four theses are appropriate to essays of different lengths because of their various levels of specificity. Rate the specificity of the theses from least to most specific.
  1. Capital punishment should be discontinued because it is inhumane and without value to society.
  2. Capital punishment should be discontinued because it is inhumane and because it does not deter criminals from committing crimes.
  3. Hanging as capital punishment should be discontinued because it is inhumane.
  4. Capital punishment should be discontinued because it denies those punished the rights guaranteed by the Constitution.

B. For three of the following questions write two theses, one appropriate for a two- or three-page essay and one better suited to a ten-page essay.
1. Why has the United States undergone changes in its view of health care for teens?
2. In what way has the increase in minority graduates from colleges and universities affected racial relations in urban areas?
3. In what way is the recent focus on multiculturalism in the United States an outgrowth of former social movements?
4. Why do Disney characters present poor role models?

C. Practice the six-step process to form a thesis for three of the following topics. Because the topics are broad, you will first need to focus them, using one of the techniques described earlier in this chapter.
1. How an event changed your thinking about a subject
2. The rights of adopted children to find their birthparents
3. A campus problem and solution
4. An economic issue

D. For the following theses, identify the controlling idea and suggest at least one likely supporting idea.
1. The design of most modern suburban developments encourages social interaction among neighbors.
2. The alarmingly great increase in dog and cat populations makes necessary the mandatory sterilization of all pets found straying.
3. Modern law—the result of a nation's unrealistic attempts to be humane, to understand the psychology of criminal behavior, and to attack the cause of antisocial acts rather than to punish the actors—has resulted in a system of "justice" by which criminals are protected against punishment for their crimes so that they can go out and commit more illegal acts.
4. Natural disasters, more than wars and habitual propagandizing, have the effect of solidifying national interests and involving people in the concerns of others.

E. Which of the following are good thesis statements for a five-page essay?
1. The doctor-patient relationship must be a partnership in which decisions are made mutually and open communication is accepted.
2. Antique collecting is popular because it allows collectors to feel that they can regain the past and postpone the change and uncertainty of the future.
3. Artistic creations are invariably the products of deeply felt longing and an immature sense of self-worth.
4. The peacock, a recurring image in Flannery O'Connor's stories, functions as a gauge of spirituality.
5. Air travel has become more convenient since the early days of commercial flight.
6. Peasant revolutions that are run by social or intellectual elites will not result in improved living conditions for the masses.

F. Complete all three steps of clustering on one of the following subjects.
1. Symbolism in a novel of your choice.
2. AIDS disclosure laws/practices.

3. Stress in college life.

4. A campus issue of your choice.

G. Write a discovery draft in response to an assertion in a piece of nonfiction prose of your choice. Develop a thesis that could be used in a three-page essay on the topic.

## INCUBATING VERSUS PROCRASTINATING

After developing the thesis, some writers need a break from the project. In this case, putting off a writing assignment isn't just laziness or apprehensiveness. Many well-known writers find that a certain amount of delay is necessary to their writing processes. Various writers report incubation periods of anywhere from an hour to three days. And the periods seem to follow the same pattern whenever the writer is working on a project.

You, and most writers, recognize the feeling of incubation: it is a resistance caused by a lack of readiness to put pen to paper. You sense that the ideas have yet to form, though the basic idea is there in mind. Or you have questions about the way you have begun to pursue an argument. You need more time for things to fall into place.

Doing a pleasurable activity for an hour, perhaps going for a walk, is often the best option at such times. Some writers report that they need to jog around the block. When they return, everything suddenly comes together, seems clear, and the resistance is gone. During your idea's incubation period, you can deliberately turn your attention to another subject so that your unconscious mind will work on the problem you have presented to it. Incubation is constructive, not destructive like procrastination. Procrastinators simply delay the whole project, never getting a handle on it early enough to grapple with the subject matter.

Naturally, writers who need time for incubation must figure this period into their schedule so that they complete assignments on time. This fact is precisely why it is important to start early on an essay assignment.

The most effective strategy is to develop a focused subject and tentative thesis before allowing yourself the luxury of incubation. In order to incubate an idea, you must pose one to yourself! On this point, the line between incubators and procrastinators is clear: incubators are in the process of writing, whereas procrastinators have failed to engage in the process altogether.

## CHOOSING A PLANNING STRATEGY

The various forms of planning, singly or combined, can help you not only to begin and complete projects on time but to develop confidence in your ability to write a good essay. It takes a lot less emotional effort to sit down at the computer and brainstorm than to attempt an actual essay introduction when you have only ill-formed ideas and an uncertain goal. Planners tend to begin assignments earlier and with less anxiety than nonplanners.

Many college writers do not make a habit of planning. As a result, their first draft becomes their planning, and if the deadline is near, they usually have no choice but to edit that draft and hand it in, knowing they could have done better. Occasionally, such a strategy will work; an "as is" paper will hold up well. But most of the time, using any of the planning techniques described in this chapter would have produced a more interesting and better-thought-out essay, with more opportunity to learn about the subject.

In considering the variety of methods available to you for planning, you may feel temporarily overwhelmed. But the wealth of planning strategies need not be confusing. Clearly, you can make this first step in your writing process suit your personality and the needs of a particular assignment by varying your technique. Figure 2-5 presents an overview of the choices discussed in this chapter.

**Figure 2-5. Strategies for planning.**

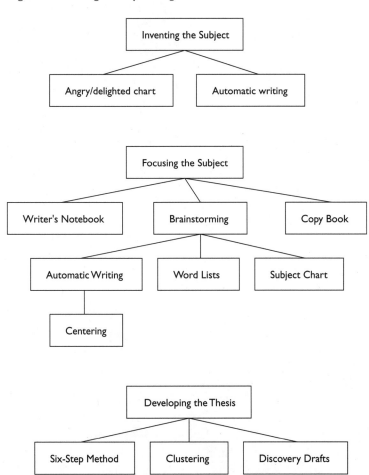

Students who tend to perceive themselves as intuitive rather than linear thinkers may prefer the "organic" nature of automatic writing, clustering, or discovery drafts to the more structured subject chart or the six-step sequence for developing the thesis. Whatever strategies you choose, and whether you stick to one strategy throughout your college years or vary your techniques, the eventual benefit of having planned your work will convince you that this stage in writing holds great value.

# HOW CAN YOU ORGANIZE YOUR THOUGHTS?

You have now explored your subject to the point of arriving at a tentative thesis and several rough ideas for supporting that thesis. The next step is to impose some order on your ideas and to develop them more fully. At this point you actually begin to visualize a paper taking shape. You consider the placement of ideas in relation to one another and ask yourself how much information your audience will need to understand and accept the ideas you are proposing. As you expand your thoughts, you will automatically test them against your tentative thesis, adding enhancements to your argument or sometimes changing your original conceptions to form a stronger argument.

Most writers find that a plan—a set of notes such as a scratch outline or a formal outline—rapidly organizes their thoughts and helps them build on their previous prewriting. It also gives them the confidence to go forward with writing a draft of the essay. The outline provides a sort of road map to the essay's terrain.

Outlining is a natural outgrowth of earlier prewriting activities. Those who have used the word list technique to build a thesis (described in Chapter 2) may find it helpful to expand on their word lists, adding details such as examples they would like to use or key points that occur to them as they continue to visualize the paper taking shape. Those working with a discovery draft may wish to make a "descriptive" outline, one summarizing the content of the discovery draft, which they can then use as the basis of the rough draft for a more developed essay.

Some students have had bad experiences with outlines, finding them restrictive rather than productive. Most likely these students learned a rigid method of formal outlining that failed to mesh with their creative learning styles. If you are such a student, do not despair. Outlining does not have to be laborious and painful. Many kinds of nontraditional outlines—among them graphic outlines and computer outlines—serve the same useful purpose as formal outlines. Outlines can look like pictures or trees or lists. Moreover, formal outlines need not take shape in a rigid manner—in fact, taking an informal approach generally produces a more workable plan. Keep your mind open to all the possible strategies as you plan your essays.

## METHODS FOR GENERATING IDEAS THROUGH OUTLINES

In this section you'll learn about a variety of approaches to outlining that can help you organize your thoughts about a thesis.

### Scratch Outlines

When the subject is familiar, when the time for writing is short, or when you need to do further research but want to get down a skeleton for your paper, a scratch outline will serve your purposes well. It is essentially just a set of notes, often showing various levels of indentation to signify which ideas belong to others. Actually, it is a spewing out of all the information you currently have on your thesis. You can see why it is an important part of planning for most writers: it is important to review what you already know so you can identify what more you will need to know.

A good method for developing a scratch outline is to pretend you are talking to a friend, professor, or other interested party, but record your ideas on paper, using an indented format like the one most students use for note taking in class. Your goal is to explain all you can about how you will prove your thesis in your paper. You can also include questions you might have, points that need checking at the library, and conjectures about conclusions you might like to draw. It's a good idea to use the computer to build the outline but then to print out a hard copy on which you mark these questions and conjectures with a different color ink or a notation in the margin. Then you will know at a glance whether the idea is solid or needs more work before you can include it in your paper. In the following example, the student used question marks to indicate that more information was needed. Once you get some ideas down on paper, you may also wish to change their order or omit some of them; feel free to make changes as you build the outline or to mark changes with arrows.

Here is an example of a student's scratch outline:

*Thesis:* Increasing handgun violence has led to volatile debates about private ownership and use of firearms. Personal protection from handgun violence is a complicated issue which demands consideration of many factors; consequently, possible gun-control solutions cannot be reduced to either/or propositions of outright banning of private firearm ownership or facile application of the right to bear arms according to the Second Amendment. Both fail to consider the complexity of urban America and the urban American. Firearms in America are an unfortunate inevitability, but it is possible to generate an acceptable compromise which allows for responsible, trained and safe, private use of defensive firearms.

—Contexts
  Global-Bureau of Alcohol, Tobacco and Firearms lists
      about 211 million guns in U.S. in 1994
      —inappropriateness of forming U.S. policies upon
          comparisons to other countries' policies
        —U.S. has very different social strains than e.g.
            Switzerland, U.S. culture is not homogeneous

—U.S. has a long history of firearm availability
and use
—tied to issues of liberty for Am., not so in most
other countries
National—urban versus suburban, rural contexts
—private use of firearms
—recreation, self-defense, illegal activities
—not many opportunities for sport (eg. hunting) in
urban environment
—restricting discussion solely to defensive firearms
—social strains
—high crime rates, overcrowding, racial tensions,
drug dealing

—Los Angeles, CA, an urban America
—police cannot effectively prevent random handgun violence
(need to flesh out, research why)
—some maintain that a responsibly trained and armed
citizenry could deter random violence
—1991 to 1994 crime rates in L.A. fell in nearly
every category as gun ownership increased
—(caveat about statistics: easy to conceal invalid
arguments by "playing with numbers," how
accurately do statistics convey reality of
illegal firearm use? and consider how statistics
oversimplify to strict causal relationships)
—the Los Angeleno, an urban American—rising number of
citizens are arming themselves (give change in stats)
—profile of a defensive firearm owner
—firearm owners' attitudes toward defensive firearms
—guns as equalizer
—all women should have a gun
—(Paxton Quigley, *Armed & Female*)
—firearms lend a sense of reassurance

—political/social issues
—2nd Amendment to the Constitution
—debatable interpretation does it specify right to
maintain an armed and regulated militia or any
individual
—favorite NRA argument "guns don't kill people,
people kill people"
—guns are tools and not inherently good or evil
—but guns are designed to destroy and must be
strictly regulated as opposed to, for instance, cars, which also can be deadly
—balancing test

—private rights versus public safety
—politics
    —easy issue for politicians to grandstand on,
      everyone is against crime
    —lobbyists
—concerns about the criteria of acceptable, effective
  restrictions
    —those who can prove the ability to be responsible
      in owning/carrying a gun should be allowed to
    —who decides the criteria for "ability" (seems an
      easily abused system)
—regulations addressing handgun violence
 —current regulations
   —Brady law
 —proposed
   —Federal licensing of gun owners
   —making firearms manufacturers, dealers, parents,
     employers, landlords more subject to civil
     lawsuits resulting from gun-related crimes in
     order to make this list of people change their
     behavior in light of potential liability to tort
     actions
   —Schumer-Bradley Handgun Control and Violence
     Protection Act
—my suggestions
  —restrict access to firearms
  —only licensed for self-defense, emphasize for use
    only as a last resort in the face of threat to
    personal safety
  —require extended training, proficiency and yearly
    relicensing
  —submit each applicant to rigorous background check
    for any unsuitability—criminal activity, mental
    instability, drug use, medical problems

The student felt that this broad outline put her on the right path toward writing the essay. She could tell which details she needed to investigate further and which already provided strong support for the thesis. Also, she felt that the order of the ideas in the outline would lead her to write an essay that readers could understand. After getting this scratch outline down on paper, she decided to develop it further and then to annotate the resulting outline so she would know which points to think about more and find more sources on before writing the essay. Her improved version is shown in Figure 3-1.

For some papers, the scratch outline will provide a sufficient guide for writing the rough draft. For others, you will find it inadequate. If your thesis is unfamiliar or complex, you may wish first to write a scratch outline and later to embellish it, turning it into one with more detail and structure.

**Figure 3-1. Example of an expanded scratch outline.**

1. context—urban versus suburban or rural contexts
   • private use of firearms
      — recreation, self-defense, illegal activities
      — not many opportunities for sport (eg. hunting) in urban environment
      — I am restricting my discussion solely to defensive firearms
   • social strains in urban environment
      — high crime rates, overcrowding, racial tensions, drug dealing
         eg., Albuquerque and Chicago have very different needs
      — conclude that we need localized regulations based on specific
         context and its associated social strains, *tailor the regulations*
2. Los Angeles, CA, an urban America
   • police cannot effectively prevent random handgun violence
      — in L.A. only 800 or so on the street at any one time
      — many have little or no training in shooting
      — labor disputes has led to low morale which worries citizens
      — some officers speak of confusion about proper use of force in
         wake of King verdicts
   • some maintain that a responsibly trained and armed citizenry could
      deter random violence—1991 to 1994 crime rates in L.A. fell in
      nearly every category as gun ownership increased not necessarily a
      direct relationship between falling crime rates and increasing gun
      ownership, could be a coincidence (note: I need a caveat about
      statistics: easy to conceal invalid arguments by "playing with
      numbers," how accurately do statistics convey reality of illegal
      firearm use? and consider how statistics oversimplify situations.
      Where does the caveat fit?)
3. the Los Angeleno, an urban American (rising number of citizens are
   arming themselves, give change in stats over the years)
   • profile of a defensive firearm owner (is the profile actually changing
      or only public perception?)
      — not the stereotypes not "rednecks," paramilitary freaks, etc.
      — are ordinary, gentle, literate citizens from grey-haired piano
         teachers to cardiologists to homemakers
   • firearm owners' attitudes toward defensive firearms
      — guns as equalizer
         all women should have a gun (Paxton Quigley, *Armed & Female*)
         women seen as easy marks, specificity of gender-based crime
            (rape) evens out physical advantage of assailant
      — firearms lend a sense of reassurance

## Graphic Outlines

Graphic outlines are simple, clear diagrams of the proposed support
for the thesis. They look similar to the subject chart used earlier in the
prewriting process (see Chapter 2). However, a major difference is that
they grow out of a statement of thesis instead of just a topic. Graphic

**Figure 3-1 (continued).**

4. political/social issues (seems safest to operate according to a
   "hermeneutic of suspicion," i. e., who do gun control laws target/
   protect?)
   • 2nd Amendment to the Constitution
       —debatable interpretation, does it specify only a well-regulated
          militia, or any private individual has the right to bear arms?
       —favorite NRA argument "guns don't kill people, people kill
          people"
             guns are tools and not inherently good or evil but guns are
                designed to destroy and must be strictly regulated as
                   opposed to, for instance, cars, which also can be deadly
       —balancing test
             private rights versus public safety
   •  politics
       —easy issue for politicians to grandstand on, everyone is against
          crime
       —lobbyists
   • concerns about the criteria of acceptable, effective restrictions
       —those who can prove the ability to be responsible of owning/
          carrying a gun should be allowed
       —but who decides the criteria for "ability"?
             this could be easily abused where biased legislation and
                implementation could lead to, for instance, racist judg-
                ments ("more African-Americans than whites are in prison,
                so they should not be allowed to carry a gun"), homophobic
                discrimination ("homosexuality is a sign of instability and
                consequently gays cannot be armed"), or classist biases if
                applicants are required to pay for extensive background
                checks (probably a burden to poor or working class citi-
                zens)
5. regulations addressing handgun violence
   • current regulations
       —Brady law requires a five-day waiting period and background check
             early surveys show that some 2,000 have been stopped from
                legally purchasing handguns because of information from
                background checks

outlines can help a writer—at a glance—get ideas and evaluate the arguments he or she is developing for the paper. And many writers feel
more comfortable with them: they do not look as intimidating as a formal outline with all its roman numerals and levels of indentation.

Begin a graphic outline by drawing a rectangle at the top of the page
and writing the tentative thesis in it. Then create a strand for each

**Figure 3-1 (continued).**

•proposed
- —Federal licensing of gun owners
- —making firearms manufacturers, dealers, parents, employers, landlords more subject to civil lawsuits resulting from gun-related crimes (makes this list of people change their behavior in light of potential liability to tort actions)
- —Schumer-Bradley Handgun Control and Violence Protection Act
    - all handgun purchasers would be licensed with an i.d. card
    - handguns would have to be registered with local law enforcement
    - prevents "clean" individuals from buying from criminals (transfer of ownership would require registration transfer similar to selling a used car)
    - handgun purchasers limited to one gun a month (prevents gunrunners from buying in bulk and reselling on illegal market)
    - uniform standards for legal gun dealers imposed (with tough security measures)
    - expensive dealer's licenses
- —my suggestions
    - restrict access to firearms
    - only licensed for self-defense, emphasize for use only as a last resort in the face of threat to personal safety
    - submit each applicant to rigorous background check for any unsuitability—criminal activity, mental unstability, drug use, medical problems
    - require extended training, proficiency and yearly re-licensing
6. conclusion (reassert the importance of tailoring gun-control regulations to specific contexts and of instituting some manner of checks to prevent abuses of the criteria for suitability,) Handgun violence is an indicator of deeply rooted social ills, and these suggestions are merely an immediate band-aid to an urgent problem. Adequate solutions to handgun violence lie less with appropriate firearm regulations than with addressing the source of such violence. Until long-term policies are formulated and begin to have an effect, carrying a defensive firearm is one realistic, albeit depressing, response to urban crime.

supporting idea. As you proceed to draw the outline, feel free to skip from one support to another, to cross out, to make changes, and to write down half-baked thoughts. Remember, the outlining stage is formative—that is, it helps you develop and evaluate your thoughts about the thesis you have proposed. You are not attempting to produce a final paper, only to draw up a plan, and when ideas are in this process of taking shape, a good deal of guesswork and redefinition is expected. Figure 3-2 presents one student's graphic outline on the subject of Watson and Rayner's 1920 experiments on emotional conditioning of children. The same outline might have been drawn in a tree fashion, with the thesis statement at the far left of the page or at the top of the page—see Figure 3-3.

### Formal Outlines

The two types of formal outlines that offer writers the most help are the topic outline and the sentence outline. The difference between

**Figure 3-2. Example of a graphic outline.**

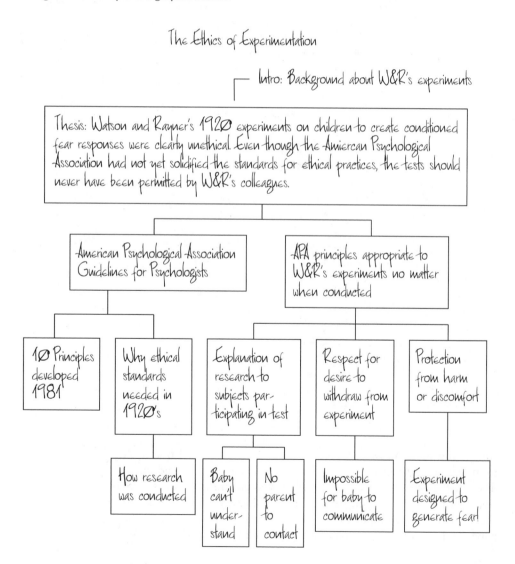

the two is in the form of the entries. In the topic outline, main ideas expressed in a few words or even a single word are used as entries. In the sentence outline, each entry is a complete sentence. Which type of outline to use, or whether to use a combination of the two, is up to the individual writer. Some writers feel that the sentence outline is too restrictive, while others feel that the topic outline is too relaxed. Many writers choose the type of outline that works best for each particular paper, preferring a sentence outline for abstract or complex subjects and a topic outline for subjects that are more straightforward. Once you have learned the basic forms for these outlines, you will be in a position to choose the type that works best for you.

**Figure 3-3. Example of a graphic outline using a tree format.**

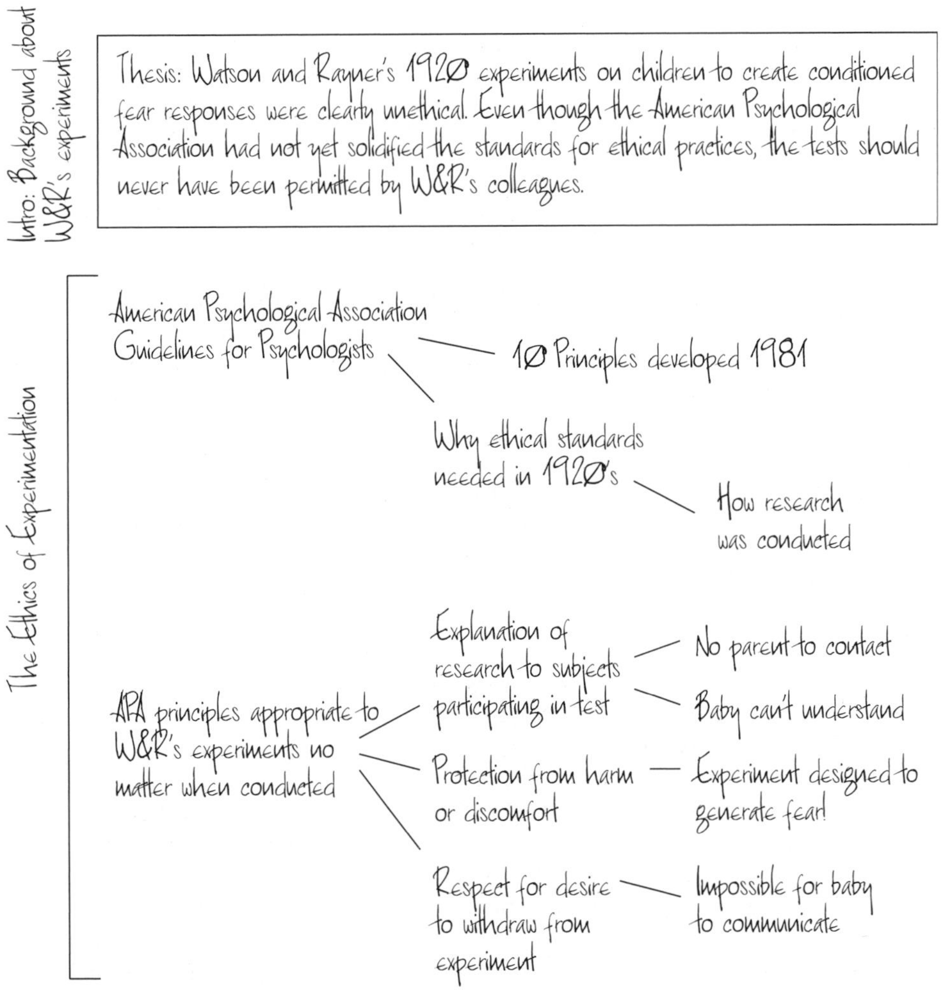

### CONVENTIONS OF THE FORMAL OUTLINE

The conventions of formal outlining are easy to remember. A typical outline has the following basic format:

*Thesis:*
I.
  A.
  B.
    1.
      a.
      b.
    2.
  C.
    1.
    2.
II.
  A.
    1.
    2.
      a.
      b.
  B.

The numerals and letters that head each entry stand for a progression of ideas in the entries themselves from general to specific. Thus, roman-numeral entries are the most general; capital-letter entries are more specific than roman-numeral entries; arabic-numeral entries are more specific than capital-letter entries; and small-letter entries are more specific than arabic-numeral entries. Note that there must be at least two parts for each division of a formal outline. If there is a roman numeral I, there must be a roman numeral II; an A requires at least a B, a 1 a 2, and so on.

Three other conventions are usually kept in mind by careful outliners: (1) All letters or numbers that serve as headings are followed by periods. (2) Each entry begins with a capital letter. (3) Each entry in a sentence outline takes a period at the end, while entries in the topic outline take no punctuation at the end.

### AN INFORMAL METHOD FOR DEVELOPING YOUR FORMAL OUTLINE

When you are ready to develop your outline, write your thesis statement at the top of a piece of paper. The thesis should stand out so that you can check your outline against it as you work. The clearer the thesis statement is, the easier the development of the outline will be. To begin, it is a good idea to set down all your roman-numeral entries. Perhaps the easiest way to do this is to put each on a separate piece of paper so that you have plenty of room to develop ideas under each. You will use these various entries like folders in a file cabinet—to store your ideas. You will file your ideas as they occur to you, putting each in its appropriate "folder." Place each of your main supports for your thesis under the heading of a roman numeral.

Because you are outlining the body of the paper, do not include any ideas you may have for an introduction or conclusion. The introduction and conclusion do not back up the thesis but are, instead, at least as general as the thesis. Therefore, it's best to leave them out of the outline altogether.

When you have made all your roman-numeral entries, check them over to ensure that they indeed prove your point. Have you left anything out or included anything unnecessary? Once you are satisfied with all the roman-numeral entries, go back to the roman-numeral item for which you have the most information. Under it, list whatever supports come to mind. These will be your capital-letter entries: A, B, C, and so forth. As you list your supports, look them over. Have you included everything you wish to? List all the points about A that you want to discuss. These will be your arabic-numeral entries: 1, 2, 3, and so forth. Then go on to list the points under those entries, if you have any, heading them with small letters. Although your outline can be subdivided even further, you will seldom need to go beyond small-letter entries. If you wish to go further, however, the process is the same. Subsequent entries would be made first by arabic numerals enclosed in parentheses and then by small letters enclosed in parentheses.

### KEY REQUIREMENTS OF A FORMAL OUTLINE

Setting down your ideas in a formal outline is basically a process of carefully arranging your general and specific ideas in a logical sequence. The completed outline provides you with a clear picture of how your essay will develop. For the plan to be effective, however, you should keep three important ideas in mind as you develop your outline:

1. The development of your outline should progress logically.
2. Your entries should be parallel in their generality.
3. Your outline should be balanced.

The thoughts presented in your outline should flow logically. One idea should clearly lead to the next, and each subdivision should logically expand the entry it is under. Therefore, you should watch what you are saying and make sure that when you promise something, you deliver it. Suppose you are writing an oral history of your family's Quaker background, and your capital letter A is "The progression of religious fervor in the 20th century." What you are, in fact promising is a chronological arrangement of these stages:

    A. The progression of religious fervor
      1. Grandmother in the 1930's—strict
      2. Mother in the 1950's—stricter
      3. Me today—strictest

Although you might decide that the reverse order is more suited to your discussion, some sort of chronological order is needed. If there is logical progression in your outline and you follow the outline, your paper should be logical, and the development of your thesis will be easy to follow.

Also important to an effective outline are parallel levels of generality. More simply stated, all of the supports for your thesis should be similar in their complexity. The topic for roman numeral III should not be any more specific than that for roman numeral I or II. Similarly, all of the capital-letter entries under a roman numeral should be of the same complexity, as should the items for arabic numerals, for small letters, and so on.

The best way to ensure that your entries are parallel in their generality is to make them parallel grammatically. Similar wording of entries of like scope helps you to keep your thoughts parallel. Although not an infallible rule, this practice at least keeps you thinking on the same track for each entry on the same level. Let's look at another example of a portion of an outline:

> B. Influential schools of philosophic thought
>     1. Thomism
>     2. Idealism
>     3. Neoplatonism
>     4. Positivism

Notice that all the arabic-numeral entries are phrased in a similar way. Suppose, instead, that one of the entries were worded differently—say, the entry for 2 were "the impact of linguistics on philosophy." Or suppose the entry for 1 were "Wittgenstein." Either of these entries would cause problems when you began to write the paper; the lack of parallelism would reveal a shift in thinking that would distract the reader. Even before you start to write, however, you should notice any differences in phrasing, which should alert you to potential problems and the need to restructure your approach.

Finally, after you develop your outline you should make sure that you have balance in your supports; allow roughly the same amount of information to each point. You do not want your paper to be lopsided. One of the big advantages of a formal outline is that you can detect lack of balance before you begin to write the paper. If, for instance, you have seventeen entries under B but only two under C, you probably need to reconsider the entries. Perhaps you have made entries under B that are similar and should be combined. Maybe you have included some ideas that really aren't very important and could be left out. It could be that your B category needs to be split into two or more divisions. On the other hand, you might not have enough material to develop point C fully. In that case, you should do some more research and rethinking before coming back to your outline. It is true that each part of the outline need not contain the same number of entries, but preparing an outline with a measure of balance will help you ensure that your essay is adequately developed. An unbalanced essay is sketchy and generally unconvincing.

### THE COMPLETED OUTLINE

Figures 3-4 and 3-5 present two versions of an outline a student developed for a research paper. The first version is not effective. It contains flaws in logical progression, in levels of generality, and in balance. In the second version these errors have been corrected. Both versions have been annotated, the first to point out the flaws and the second to show you how the student corrected them.

---

**Figure 3-4. A faulty outline.**

*Thesis:* Since 1947 both lay people and scientists have engaged in an important controversy about the existence of unidentified flying objects.

  I. Since 1947 there have been many famous reports of UFO sightings.
    A. 1947, Kenneth Arnold
       1.   Arnold's statement
       2.   Newspaper's description
    B. After 1947 reports increased
      1. Everyone saw UFOs—hysteria
      2. Staged pranks deceived people
        a. Eat at Joe's
        b. Set up pictures
    C. Exeter
      1. Norman Muscarello's story
      2. Police reports
      3. Exeter townspeople's stories of similar sightings
    D. The hills
      1. Abduction by astronauts
      2. Dr. Benjamin Simon's report
      3. Spaceship psychotherapy
 II. Details of sightings vary, but certain patterns occur frequently
    A. Shapes
    B. Colors
    C. Electromagnetic effects
    D. Movement
III. Cynical interest by official agencies
    A. Report on reaction to Mt. Rainier
    B. Project Blue Book
    C. University of Colorado Scientific Study of Unidentified Flying Objects

*Sentence and topic formats are mixed.*

*A through D have various levels of generality, causing illogical subdivisions.*

*The capital letters under I, II, III, and IV lack balance of details. More details needed.*

**Figure 3.4 (continued).**

       D. Formation of support organizations
         1. APRO
         2. NICAP
   IV. Explanations for UFOs
       A. Unscheduled flights in an area
       B. Weather conditions
       C. Electrical corona
       D. Insufficient data
       E. Unknown cases still existing
    V. Conclusion: Value of continuing investigations
       A. Diminished fear of space exploration
       B. If theory of UFOs accepted, human's role in
          universe upset—will change

The conclusion of the paper should not be part of the outline.

**Figure 3-5. The corrected outline.**

*Thesis:* Since 1947 both lay people and scientists have engaged in an important controversy about the existence of unidentified flying objects.

    I. Famous reports since 1947
       A. Kenneth Arnold's experience
         1. Arnold's statement
         2. Newspaper's description
       B. Norman Muscarello's experience
         1. Muscarello's story
         2. Exeter townspeople's stories of similar
           sightings
         3. Police reports
       C. Dr. Benjamin Simon's experience
         1. Abduction of Simon by astronauts
         2. Spaceship psychotherapy
         3. Holes in Simon's report
   II. Patterns that reoccur in reports
       A. Shapes
         1. Saucerlike
         2. Cigar shape
         3. Pointed ovals
       B. Colors
         1. Green
         2. Blue
         3. White
       C. Electromagnetic effects
       D. Movement

Only topic format is used.

A through C are now parallel because they have one pattern of arrangement.

## COMPUTER OUTLINES

Computer outlining can motivate you to plan your paper because it helps you to arrange ideas relatively quickly and efficiently. Most programs permit you to shift from a view of the paper to a view of the outline and then back again to the paper you are composing. They even permit you to copy passages and headings from the outline to the composition without retyping them. However, when you use a computer outlining program, it is also wise to keep a hard copy of the full outline next to you while you write your essay. That way you will not be restricted by the size of the computer screen.

**Figure 3-5 (continued).**

```
        1. Jumping in air
        2. Floating
        3. Spinning
III. Cynical interest by official agencies
     A. Report on reaction to Mt. Rainier
     B. Project Blue Book
        1. Duration of study
        2. Findings
     C. University of Colorado Scientific Study of Uniden-
        tified Flying Objects
     D. Formation of support organizations
        1. APRO
        2. NICAP
 IV. Typical scientific explanations of UFOs
     A. Human error
        1. Unscheduled flights in an area
        2. Conclusions from insufficient data
     B. Natural conditions
        1. Weather conditions
        2. Electrical corona
        3. Previously undiscovered heavenly bodies
  V. Typical nonscientific justification that UFOs exist
     A. Lack of scientific explanation for 2 to 3 percent
        of sightings
     B. Lack of scientific explanation for people and
        vessels who suddenly disappear
        1. Bermuda Triangle
        2. Black holes
     C. Presence of Biblical explanations
     D. Presence of aerial landing strips
        1. "Chariots of the gods" mentality
        2. Assumptions about space travel
```

I through IV are now balanced and elaborated through the analysis of sightings.

I through IV have been expanded and logically subdivided.

Previous IV has been split into two major topics, IV and V.

The conclusion has been deleted.

An important advantage of a computer outline is that most programs allow you to look at one level of headings at a time so that you can check whether your points are parallel and well ordered. Also, once you have arranged your outline, most programs will number them for you automatically. You do need to be careful with this tool. Because the computer cannot discriminate between a logical outline and an illogical one, it will number any outline you produce as if it were logical. Such an outline may look good, but it will be difficult to write from. Another advantage of computer outlines is that they are easily changed as you work. They are definitely worth investigating if your word processing program offers the feature.

---

**Exercises**

A. Make the unparallel entries of the following outline parallel and logical in progression. Consider whether all sections are consistent in form and are in the best order.

Treating anemia.

*Thesis*: Treating anemia is a 4-step process.

   I. The patient's symptoms
      A. Complaints of fatigue and shortness of breath
      B. Facial pallor and weakness is manifested
      C. Draw blood and do a smear
  II. Hypotheses and testing and diagnosing
      A. Consider possibilities
         i. Iron deficiency
        ii. Test for chronic disease deficiency
       iii. Could be thalassemia
       iv. Atypical blood cells
      B. Tests
         i. Serum iron
        ii. TIBC (total iron binding capacity)
       iii. Percent saturation
       iv. Take a bone marrow iron stain
      C. Diagnose the patient's ailment
         i. Read results of tests
        ii. Results show low serum iron, high TIBC, low saturation, absent iron in marrow
       iii. Consult
       iv. Determine iron deficiency
 III. Determine cause of iron deficiency
      A. Sex—if female, probably due to menstruation or pregnancy
      B. Elderly people sometimes suffer loss of blood from hemorrhoids or colon cancer
      C. Is the patient a vegetarian, poor, or anorexic, which might lead to an inadequate diet

D. Internal complication—malabsorption syndromes (e.g. intestinal bypass) can prevent iron absorption

IV. Treatment of cause of iron deficiency

    A. Prescribe iron supplements

    B. Treatment of hemorrhoids

    C. Nutritional advice and diet

    D. Surgery

B. Arrange each of the following groups of words according to their most general to most specific entries.

| 1. | 2. | 3. |
|---|---|---|
| Periods of literature | Impressionism | Foreign languages |
| Novels | Painting | Romance languages |
| Realism | Baroque | Spanish |
| Literature | Art history | Dialects |
| Plays | Visual arts | College requirements |
| Romanticism | Sculpting | Italian |
| Essays | Art | Latin |
| Genres of literature | Movements in art | |
| *Beloved* | Printmaking | |
| | Cubism | |
| | Neo-classicism | |

C. Write both a scratch outline and a formal outline for the same assignment (choose your own topic or use one assigned by your professor). What are the advantages and disadvantages of each method?

D. Reoutline the plan in Exercise A using a tree diagram.

## COMMON PATTERNS FOR ORGANIZING YOUR ESSAYS

Whether you decide to construct a scratch outline or a more elaborate one, you will find it useful to follow one of the common organizational patterns used by essayists. Why reinvent the wheel? The most common organizational orders are two-part, process, chronological, spatial, classification, illustration/ division, and comparison. An entire essay, especially if it is short, may be structured around just one of these patterns. Longer essays usually use a combination of patterns but with a definite emphasis on one. The emphasized pattern should be apparent from the roman-numeral entries in your formal outline or the main entries in your scratch outline.

### Two-Part Structure

Three types of two-part essay structures are common to academic writing: description-analysis, problem-solution, and comparison-contrast, with the last being the predominant one. In *description-analysis* essays, the first half of the body of the paper defines in detail an idea, practice, event, or character and the second half launches into a deep analysis of the ideas mentioned in the description. A writer might, for instance, describe the concept of personal space (how far people stand from one another when conversing) as it is manifested in each of several different cultures, then analyze the implications for cross-cultural communication.

In *problem-solution* papers, the first half of the body of the paper is devoted to describing (defining) a problem, while the second half is devoted to posing various solutions and evaluating their efficacy.

*Comparison-contrast* papers afford an opportunity to synthesize a great deal of information, which is no doubt the reason that teachers so often ask for them on examinations; to compare and contrast, the writer has to know the subject extremely well. In a two-part comparison-contrast paper, half of the body of the paper is devoted to an integrated discussion of comparisons and about the same space is given to contrasts.

It is not necessary to divide two-part essays precisely in half. Most likely, you will have more to say in the most analytical half of the paper. For instance, if the subject you are discussing has more contrasts than comparisons, you will make the contrast section longer. Most problem-solution papers require greater depth in the solution section. Similarly, a description-analysis paper would probably require more writing in the analysis part.

### Process Order

Process order is structured around the steps necessary to do something. This order is most appropriate for narrative or descriptive writing, but it is also used in many other instances. The "how to do it" essay is a process essay that develops its points in the exact sequence necessary for accomplishing the activity. Sequence is the most important item in the process paper. Your task is to arrange your material in the proper order and then to provide appropriate connections between the parts so that your reader will see the movement from step to step and the logical connection between the steps. Here is an example of notes for a process essay:

> *Thesis:* Preparing a wall for painting is an important task that must be carefully done if the finished paint job is to be attractive and permanent.
>
> Step 1: Clean the wall of any grease or oil marks.
> Step 2: Use a scraper to remove any peeling paint or plaster.
> Step 3: Patch and sand any cracks.
> Step 4: Wipe entire wall once with dust cloth to remove all particles before painting.

### Chronological Order

Your topic may lend itself to a chronological, or time-ordered, treatment. You might be describing a series of historical events or explaining the development of some theory or belief. Here is an example of notes for a chronological essay:

*Thesis:* Chemical warfare, the morality of which should be questioned, has actually been practiced in wars throughout history and continues in the present.

Use of Greek fire in ancient times

Use of poison gas in trenches during World War I

Flame throwers and atomic bombs in World War II

Napalm in the Vietnam War

Chemicals by Sadaam Hussein against ethnic groups in Iraq

## Spatial Order

It may be appropriate to arrange the body paragraphs of the essay according to a spatial pattern or relationship. For instance, when you discuss the ravages of a hurricane, it might be effective to trace the destruction from the point along the coast where the hurricane first hit, then further inland through the city, then to the farms nestled in the valley. Spatial patterns are like maps, whether they chart the course over land, through a painting, from one end of a car to the other, or from a person's feet to forehead. But there must be a defined pattern, such as left to right or near to far, in your scheme. Such spatial patterns need not be merely descriptive. For instance, a paper on cars that traces the spatial arrangement from rear fender to front fender may discuss not so much the appearance of the automotive parts as the function of each part in relation to the whole mechanism. Although spatially treated subjects are frequently descriptive, many analytic topics can be arranged effectively according to their physical space. Your notes for a spatial essay might look like the following:

*Thesis:* The architecture of the Hagia Sophia reflects and reinforces the dogma of the eastern orthodox church, and inspires a spiritual awe in the viewer.

Three doors lead to outer vestibule, five more open from outer vestibule to vestibule proper, and nine doors lead from there to the aisles and the nave

Numerological significance of number of doors

Feeling of transition with each threshold crossed

Proliferation of doors and increasing height of ceiling as each threshold is crossed begins to dwarf the viewer

Entering the heart of the church, one's sight is blocked by columns, walls, screens

As gaze rises, however, obstacles and clutter slip away

Eye traverses curves of arches and light-filled windows, leading to open brightness of the dome's great ceiling

Nothing mediates between the viewer and the divine

The ceiling center of the dome, not the altar, becomes the focus of the church

The construction of windows which ring the bottom of the dome heightens the viewer's feeling of awe and insignificance

Bright sunlight from through these windows pierces where the
dome rests upon its supporting walls
The dome appears to float above the church, a miracle sus-
pended by faith

### Classification Order

Classification is dividing and labeling the various parts of a subject
into logical classes or groups. This method of organizing is often used to
explain or define a term or concept, but it is appropriate to any subject
that can be broken down into types. To classify a subject, you simply
need to ask yourself, "What are the broad types?" Classifying is an everyday process. Restaurants have smoking and nonsmoking sections. You
identify yourself as a member of a college class: freshman, sophomore,
junior, senior. You view yourself and others as part of the above-thirties
group or part of the below-thirties group. You rarely think about these
common sorts of classification, but when you do, you realize that the act
of classifying provides a definite order to your thinking process.

Everyday experience with classifying makes the method relatively
easy. For instance, if you want to classify the types of approaches to social activism, you might come up with the following groups:

Reformist: working within the system legally
Separatist: refusing to work within the system, and establishing an
    alternative system
Terrorist: attacking the system or its representatives violently and
    illegally

This classification of activism is effective because it upholds the three
requirements of a good classification:

1. The parts must be divided by a single principle.
2. The parts must be parallel.
3. The parts should add up to the whole subject.

When you choose to classify something, you should first settle on a
rationale for the grouping. In the activism example, the rationale is the
degree of cooperation with the system. Each type of activism represents
a relationship with the system and none overlaps with the others. For
instance, a reformist cannot be also a separatist. Less obviously, a terrorist cannot also be a separatist, though neither agrees to interact with
the system. The classifications are also parallel grammatically: each is
described by an adjective. Finally, the total of the three groups covers
all possible interactions that might be termed activist. Any example of
activism you can think of should fit into one of the categories. The following thesis, based on classification of activist types of intervention,
would be useful in analyzing whether the Egyptian Sheik Abdel
Rahman, charged with "seditious conspiracy," is in fact terrorist.

*Thesis:* In multiple attempts to undermine United States' support of Israel, Sheik Abdel Rahman and his nine co-defendents used terrorist tactics to wage war against the U.S. military, identifying them as "seditious" conspirators rather than separatists or reformists.

### Illustration/Division Order

Illustration is arrangement by use of examples. You could, for instance, write an essay about the stress of examinations in the life of the typical Japanese student in which the body of your essay is composed of two or three examples (case studies) that you proceed to analyze. You could also write the same essay using division as an organizing principle. Division is separation of a whole into several parts. Using this strategy, you could focus on the causes of stress for Japanese students undergoing examination "hell": the hierarchy of Japanese lifestyles, parental pressure, and the competitiveness of an educational system that measures people only in terms of what they produce.

Both kinds of essays, frequently assigned in college, require a bit of ingenuity on the part of the writer setting them up. It often seems that the separate points or examples could be arranged in any order: one idea is not necessarily the foundation for another and various arrangements make sense. However, you can better manipulate your readers' acceptance of your thesis by arranging your points according to what you wish to emphasize. In most of your papers you will find that your evidence for one of your points is stronger than the evidence for others. One supporting point can be so moving or convincing that it heightens the effect of the idea that follows it, or it may seem a perfect note to end on.

If you were writing a paper for an abnormal psychology course, you could divide the personality disorder known as borderline personality into several parts. Here is what your scratch outline might look like:

*Thesis:* Borderline personality disorder, bordering psychosis and neurosis, has five main characteristics.

Separation anxiety
Lack of controls
Poor ego boundaries
The inability to express feelings
The use of borderline defense mechanisms

## Comparison Order

Drawing a comparison means showing the similarities and differences between two or more parts of a subject. If only the differences are pointed out, the essay contrasts rather than compares. Before a comparison or contrast can be made, some similarity must exist between the parts of the subject. For instance, the pictograph systems of ancient Sumeria and China might serve as a subject for a comparison. Both are writing systems of ancient cultures. But there would not be much point in writing a serious comparison of the physical exertion of watching television and that of playing racquetball. All you could say is that the activities are completely different, that one requires no exertion and the other a great deal of exertion. Your essay would probably turn out to be a one-sided discussion of playing racquetball. A significant point must arise from a comparison; thus, it is useless to compare thoughts, concepts, or things that have nothing significant in common. A sound thesis must come from the comparison, and the paper should not have a great deal to say about one point and little to say about another. The comparison may show only similarities, only differences, or a combination of the two, but all pertinent parts of the subject should be discussed.

The comparative essay may be structured in one of three ways: alternating between the parts of the subject, dividing the subject, or combining such alternation and division.

### ALTERNATING COMPARISONS

Alternating comparisons make a point-by-point examination of similarities, differences, or both. When specific comparisons come readily to mind, the alternating format, which makes for an easily read and coherent essay, should be used. For example, if you were comparing the mating behavior of two types of birds, you might isolate typical behavioral patterns as your points for comparison (courtship dances, calls, physical changes) and then discuss those characteristics as they appear in the two types of birds you are examining. The final essay might alternate either whole paragraphs or sentences, depending on how much there is to say about each half of the subject for a particular point.

To help you draw comparisons clearly, you should start by making a list of items to compare. You can use the list to test each comparison and include notes for your more detailed outline, which will most often simply follow the development of the list. Here is an example of such a list for the comparison of bird mating habits:

| Characteristic | Nordic Pigeon | Southwest Robin |
| --- | --- | --- |
| Courtship dances | Three types: square, circle, triangle | Two types: straight line back and forth, circle |
| Number of calls | Has around thirty different calls, one for mate selection | Only calls to select mate |
| Physical changes during nesting | Beak becomes dark brown when nesting | Color of feathers changes but beak remains the same when nesting |

You can see that an essay developed from this list would include differences but would emphasize similarities between the mating and nesting habits of the two birds. Here is a possible thesis for the essay:

*Thesis:* Although the Nordic pigeon and the southwest robin live in quite different climates, one warm and one polar, their mating habits are surprisingly similar in courtship and in nesting.

### DIVIDED COMPARISONS

A divided order, rather than comparing the same topics point by point, presents one complete topic and then another. Divided comparisons, used widely in journalism, work best when the subject you are writing about does not break up neatly into specific subpoints. That is, you are making a statement about the overall similarity or difference between topics. There are two main approaches to the divided comparison. It is clearer to divide your information in half if you have two topics to compare, or in thirds if you have three. In the body of the essay you would simply detail each topic, in turn. Then, in the conclusion of the essay, you can try to draw more specific comparisons. Or, if you prefer, you may use the second and subsequent paragraphs where you introduce the second topic to compare and contrast the second topic with what you have said about the first, then create a conclusion that is more general.

Let's look at an example of a paper topic. Comparing the way teachers and police officers interact with the people they serve in order to argue the need for community support of the police in the inner city is a good subject for a paper—but one that does not easily break down into point-by-point analysis. Your audience may think that many of the qualities of a good teacher are also those of a good police officer but that their duties differ too much to allow an analogy. Your job is to convince the audience that good police should portray to the community a spirit similar to that of the excellent teacher. The most effective way to make your statement might be to discuss the role of a teacher in the first half and that of a police officer in the second. Then, in the conclusion, you could name the parallels that you have discovered and why they are significant in developing support for the police in the community.

*Tentative thesis:* To improve relations in the inner city between residents and police, one can look for a model at the role a teacher plays in relation to her students.

Problem:
    Problems with inner-city disrespect for police officers
    Problems with police officers' attitudes toward the city
    Problems police have with marketing themselves

Solution:
    Role of teacher
        Nurturer
        Provider of information
        Counselor
        Judge
        Model American
    Police Officer
        Knows the law
        Enforces the law
        Possesses high moral standards
        Holds concern for protection of the public
        Has good judgment
        Is a model American
        Acts as a reliable friend

---

**Figure 3-6.**

Two Aspects of the River
Mark Twain

Now when I had mastered the language of this water, and had come to know every trifling feature that bordered the great river as familiarly as I knew the letters of the alphabet, I had made a valuable acquisition. But I had lost something, too. I had lost something which could never be restored to me while I lived. All the grace, the beauty, the poetry, had gone out of the majestic river! I still keep in mind a certain wonderful sunset which I witnessed when steamboating was new to me. A broad expanse of the river was turned to blood; in the middle distance the red hue brightened into gold, through which a solitary log came floating black and conspicuous; in one place a long, slanting mark lay sparkling upon the water; in another the surface was broken by boiling, tumbling rings, that were as many-tinted as an opal; where the ruddy flush was faintest, was a smooth spot that was covered with graceful circles and radiating lines, ever so delicately traced; the shore on our left was densely wooded, and the somber shadow that fell from this

To grasp how the evidence could be set up in a divided comparison, look at how Mark Twain organized the comparison of his view of the Mississippi River before and after he became a riverboat captain (Figure 3-6). Note how he has kept all his observations about the river before he became a captain (first topic) in his first paragraph, then moved

**Figure 3-6 (continued).**

forest was broken in one place by a long, ruffled trail that shone like silver; and high above the forest wall a clean-stemmed dead tree waved a single leafy bough that glowed like a flame in the unobstructed splendor that was flowing from the sun. There were graceful curves, reflected images, woody heights, soft distances; and over the whole scene, far and near, the dissolving lights drifted steadily, enriching it every passing moment with new marvels of coloring.

I stood like one bewitched. I drank it in, in a speechless rapture. The world was new to me, and I had never seen anything like this at home. But as I have said, a day came when I began to cease from noting the glories and the charms which the moon and the sun and the twilight wrought upon the river's face; another day came when I ceased altogether to note them. Then, if that sunset scene had been repeated, I should have looked upon it without rapture, and should have commented upon it, inwardly, after this fashion: "This sun means that we are going to have wind to-morrow; that floating log means that the river is rising, small thanks to it; that slanting mark on the water refers to a bluff reef which is going to kill somebody's steamboat one of these nights, if it keeps on stretching out like that; those tumbling 'boils' show a dissolving bar and a changing channel there; the lines and circles in the slick water over yonder are a warning that that troublesome place is shoaling up dangerously; that silver streak in the shadow of the forest is the 'break' from a new snag, and he has located himself in the very best place he could have found to fish for steamboats; that tall dead tree, with a single living branch, is not going to last long, and then how is a body ever going to get through this blind place at night without the friendly old landmark?"

No, the romance and beauty were all gone from the river. All the value any feature of it had for me now was the amount of usefulness it could furnish toward compassing the safe piloting of a steamboat. Since those days, I have pitied doctors from my heart. What does the lovely flush in a beauty's cheek mean to a doctor but a "break" that ripples above some deadly disease? Are not all her visible charms sown thick with what are to him the signs and symbols of hidden decay? Does he ever see her beauty at all, or doesn't he simply view her professionally, and comment upon her unwholesome condition all to himself? And doesn't he sometimes wonder whether he has gained most or lost most by learning his trade?

on to the second paragraph with a transitional statement "But as I have said, a day came when I began to cease from noting the glories and the charms which the moon and the sun and the twilight wrought on the river's face. . . ." This statement is also the topic sentence that introduces his second topic.

After reading all three paragraphs, you will marvel at the level of detail in each of the first two. Note that the last paragraph goes into very little detail as to the distinctions. The main reason is that Twain has used the second paragraph to show the contrasts with the first. What becomes most appropriate for the conclusion then is a more general statement. For deeper comprehension of it he adds an apt analogy.

This type of comparison seems easy to write, but it fools a lot of people. Most important to the success of this structure, you may have guessed, are the strong thesis that makes an important connection between the compared items and, of course, the detailed conclusion. The middle of the essay should also be closely geared to the controlling idea in the thesis (see page 45). Each point you make in the paper must be there for a purpose. You should not talk about the home life of the police officer in one part and about the convenient schedules of teachers in the other unless you show some logical connection between the points. If you exercise control over your material, keeping in sight that the purpose of the paper is to compare, you will avoid the snare of producing vague, disconnected descriptions of two things.

### COMBINING PATTERNS

If you write essays longer than a few pages, you may wish to integrate the divided pattern with the alternating pattern. Many readers feel that used alone, the alternating format creates an undesirable ping-pong effect, yet they do not like the lack of specific information early in the essay in the divided pattern. They would prefer that comparative papers offer the variety of the combined form. Considerations of subject and audience and your own personal preferences will dictate your choice.

The beginning of an essay in the combined format might include one or more points fixed in an alternating pattern, discussing a certain trait of one part of the subject, then describing that trait in relation to the other half of the subject. After the two parts of the subject have been treated in this way, the essay may develop into a divided structure in which various traits of half of the subject are treated together. In such an essay, the first section would naturally discuss specific points of comparison, while the second half would discuss general points. Of course, any combination of divided and alternating patterns can be effective if it suits the nature of the subject.

An example of an essay developed in the combined form might be a comparison of contemporary public high schools and an ideal public high school. Here is how the notes would look:

*Thesis:* The contemporary rural public high school's programs and atmosphere are more regimented and limited than they should be given the resources and personnel.

   I. Strategic Planning
      Ideal schools
      Public schools
  II. Intent of Curriculum
      Ideal schools
      Public schools
 III. Faculty Roles
      Ideal schools
      Public schools
  IV. Student Roles
      Ideal schools
      Public schools
   V. Public School Conditions
      Tensions because of social class stereotyping
      Standardized testing
      Alcohol, drugs
      Cliques
      Rote learning
      Required classes
      Large classes/combined grades
  VI. Ideal schools
      Individualized instructional opportunities
      Supplemental education
      Liberal arts approach
      Self-paced studies
      Safe and supportive drug-free atmosphere
      Many electives

You can see that the combined method is by far the most complex type of comparison. In the above notes, a point-by-point comparison is used to convey specific similarities, and then a divided comparison is used to give an overall impression of each school system.

Choosing the best arrangement for a paper is a creative and engaging task that will ultimately be worth any effort you put into the decision. You could have all the interesting content available on a subject, but if that content is not pieced together so that the reader can grasp it, the ideas will be lost. The pattern you choose will make the writing yours, allowing you to convey just what you mean to say.

Outlining and using common patterns of thought development help you understand the scope of your essay. And they can help you get new ideas to develop your argument. Most professional writers rely heavily on these organizing strategies, and most students like the idea of using this sort of planning to keep track of where they are in their paper at a given moment and where they are going.

---

### Exercises

A. Write notes for a chronological process essay on one of the following topics:
   An event that changed your thinking on some matter of personal importance
   The best way to ask for (or refuse) a date
   The emotional changes a person experiences between ages fifteen and eighteen
B. Develop notes for a comparative essay on a topic of your choice.
C. In the following draft, the student uses primarily a chronological arrangement. Might the author have made the same point by using a different pattern of organization? Why?

The Phenomenon of Death

When I was a child there was never any reason to think about death. I knew what it was, knew man was not immortal and I didn't have any fears. Then one day, unexpectedly, a man whom I loved was erased from my life. He was my maternal grandfather, and I can never forget the day he died. It was the second night of Chanuka in the year of 1980. We were just getting ready to open our presents when the telephone rang. Suddenly, I heard my mother screaming and crying. I was extremely horrified to hear her in such a state, so I too began to cry. I had sensed something was dreadfully wrong but had no idea what it was. Within a short time, I found my mother, father, and sister at my side. With a quivering voice and tears in her eyes, my mother said, "Dad isn't with us anymore." I began to cry and we all embraced for a few minutes. We began the long drive to San Diego about a half hour later because we wanted to be with my maternal grandmother in her time of need.

During the drive and for weeks thereafter a whole world of thoughts and confusion opened up for me. No matter how hard I tried to think things out, I couldn't accept the fact that my grandfather was gone forever. I became very inquisitive and asked my parents so many questions with the idea in mind to possibly acquire an understanding of the death of my grandfather in particular and of death in general. What happens to the soul? Does he live in another world? Does he know we will always love him? My parents tried to answer. I was still not satisfied because there was so much more I had to think about than they could respond to. Within a week of the time he died, I found myself feeling angry toward grandpa for no longer being near me, for abandoning me. As the youngest grandchild in the family, I had the least number of years in which to love and be with my grandfather. I felt cheated and wanted him to come back to me. For a while my faith in God diminished to the point that I blocked all religious beliefs from my mind. What good was religion? I couldn't see why God would deprive such a fine man of the happiest years of his life, when he could enjoy his children and the material things he had worked so hard for all his life. These thoughts and others plagued me for years after my grandfather's death.

Now nine years have passed since grandpa died. I have begun to think more about the strange phenomenon of death. No longer do I question death, as I did when I was a child, but I realize that the confusion I felt right after my grandfather's death is a confusion that will always be on my mind—the living cannot know what death really is, not in all its strange aspects. I now can actually accept the possibility of my own death, that at some point my time will come. But accepting that death happens to everyone, I still have not overcome the sorrow of that occasion nine years ago enough to live without a fear of my last moments. Perhaps when I am older and have put more of my life into a fixed perspective, I will be able to face the subject of death with a bit less diffidence. I wonder how my grandfather felt.

D. Write a miniessay about a piece of art or a place. Open with a description by spatial arrangement in the first paragraph and then in another paragraph or two analyze the artwork or scene through division.

E. Write a brief divided comparison of how a certain quality that two of your friends have is manifested differently in each of them. Make the first paragraph your thesis. Devote the next paragraph to one friend and a separate paragraph to the other friend. In the conclusion draw together the similarities and differences.

F. Explain how two particular patterns of development—two-part, process, chronological, spatial, classification, illustration, or comparison—might suit each of the following topics; justify your answers.

Periods of architecture

Day-to-day life in a foreign country

Oral hygiene

The enjoyment of popular movies

G. If you were writing an essay with the thesis and supports given below, in what order would you place the supports to achieve the best emphasis? Why?

*Thesis:* Arguments against homosexuality based upon claims that the practice is "unnatural" are not tenable.

There are instances (exemplified by the whip tailed lizard and Benobos monkeys) of homosexual practices in the wild.

Whatever becomes habit or custom is labelled "natural" though there is no essential basis for such a claim.

Many celebrated technological advances are unnatural and yet accepted and welcome facets of everyday life.

What is considered "natural" seems to be culturally specific.

H. Draw a comparison chart for an essay on the subject of horror films. Focus the topic and develop a thesis that interests you before doing the chart.

I. Take notes on a comparison of two articles or books you read recently on similar subjects or by the same author. Is the essay most adaptive to supports arranged in a divided, alternating, or combined pattern?

J. Revise the Twain essay in Figure 3.6 so that the second paragraph is merely descriptive of Twain's second topic and the conclusion is a deep analysis of the similarities and differences in the two topics covered in the essay.

K. Read an essay in a magazine and write a one-paragraph analysis of the pattern or patterns of development used in the essay.

L. Be as specific as possible about which pattern of organization might best suit the following topics:

Similarities and differences between the radical right and the radical left wings in politics

Advantages of living in the city instead of in a small town (or vice versa)

The diverse duties of a congressperson

The dreams of a child and the dreams of an adult

The failure of youthful marriages

M. Write a question that you think one of your teachers might ask on an essay assignment. Choose some topic you have just been studying in one of your classes. What patterns might you use in writing the essay based on the question? Why?

N. Draw a scratch outline for a two-part essay, using the following steps. Write for five minutes without stopping on a solution to a problem (global, national, local, or personal). Then draw a single-sentence thesis from this automatic writing. Your final step is to develop a scratch outline for this two-part, problem-solution essay.

## ARGUMENTATIVE EDGE

Any structure mentioned in this chapter may call for an argumentative approach to the subject—one in which you take a stand on a subject.

The major skill needed here is developing an awareness of your audience's opposition to your proposal or stance. Some of their objections may be worthy of consideration, and if you do take them up in your essay and give credit to them, you will be more likely to keep all of your audience with you than if you do not. One of the best ways to convince an audience of your position is to consider the arguments of those who disagree with your view and to present a fair description of the strengths, not just the weaknesses, of that opposing view.

It's just common-sense communication we're speaking about here. A simple, everyday example will illustrate the point. Say you want to borrow the car from one of your parents. Just asserting your position ("I need the car to go somewhere because the bus takes too long") will not convince a parent in many cases. Especially if there is an "issue" to be discussed—suppose you forgot to fill up the car with gasoline the last time you borrowed it and your mother was late to work because she did not leave in time to stop for gas on the following morning when she drove the car again. Chances are that empty gas tank is what flashes into your mother's mind at your request to borrow the car now.

So if you take the time to consider her position and you approach the situation by telling her up front that you regret you did not return the car refueled the last time you used it (a valid argument against lending the car to you again), you weaken the opposition's resistance. The opposition begins to think that maybe you have seen the error of your ways. Besides, common sense tells you that not everything the opposition argues is wrong. There must be some viable arguments. If you present these in a positive way, you are less likely to alienate readers who disagree with you from the outset; since you have considered their

view, perhaps they will listen attentively to yours. Many times arguments that demonstrate broad-mindedness win over readers with views different from your own. The question is how to present such views without seeming insincere and wishy-washy.

One key to making your own argument clear and forceful at the same time you recognize the opposition is structure; the other is appropriate transitions. Sheridan Baker first described the following patterns of argumentation in a college writing textbook, *The Practical Stylist,* in the 1970's. Consider using them, for you will want to structure the argument so that your points take precedence over the opposition's. Often, placing the opposition before your argument creates just the right balance; it's just enough recognition to hook your reader, but your argument will be the part that changes the reader's mind. Depending on how much you know about your opposition, you may wish to keep it all together or break it up into separate points that parallel your own. Note how the first two structures given here clump the opposing views together whereas the last breaks them up.

*Strategy Number 1*
Cite Opposition
Transition
Thesis
Support
Support
Conclusion

*Strategy Number 2*
Lead-in (see Chapter 5 for suggestions)
Thesis
Transition
Cite opposition
Transition
Support
Support
Conclusion

*Strategy Number 3*
Lead-in
Thesis
Cite opposition first point
Respond first point
Cite opposition second point
Respond second point
Conclusion

In a short essay, the patterns given in the first and second options could consist of a paragraph or more of discussion. The discussion would generally present the opposing views that offered some validity despite your position overall on the subject. You would not find the need to refute the opposition, for only evidence for your argument—not evidence against the opposition's—will support your position. In the first option the introduction acknowledges the opposition, offers a transition to your argument, and then spends the rest of the essay backing up your thesis. It is not necessary to mention the opposition again. In the second structure, the introduction and the thesis strike the reader immediately and the opposition is delayed. This structure is particularly useful if you need to define a key term before using it in the thesis or must offer important background before proceeding to the point of the essay. Also, it is a bit more complex in structure than the first option, which dispenses with opposition right away. (The first option is easiest too.)

Because the second option is more complex, the transitions may pose more of a challenge than in the first structure, where often a "however" or an "on the other hand" will suffice. First you will need a transition into the opposition from the thesis. Then you will need a transition out of the opposition back to the argument that supports the thesis. These twists and turns may seem difficult, but with practice and with considering your audience, you will master them. In fact, it's likely you already perform such mental machinations as you speak with friends; you probably don't give it any thought since the context is informal and nonthreatening.

*You:* I want to go to Burger Continental for lunch. I'm craving one of their pita burgers. But I know you said yesterday you were in the mood for fish. We really shouldn't eat so much red meat, I admit.

*Joe:* Yeah, there's that fish and chips place on the corner of Colorado and Rose. I've been wanting to try it, but it's no big thing. You sound really hungry for the burger, and it's beginning to sound good to me too, especially since we know that place is good and the fish place is a gamble.

*You:* Although I know I shouldn't eat red meat often, I do like it once in a while, and my cholesterol count has been good. So, let's try the fish place next week and that way we won't have red meat two weeks in a row.

You have considered the opposition's valid point and incorporated it into your argument. You have used informal transitions that help the conversational shifts between your and Joe's positions. In writing you will find that transitions such as the following are extremely helpful in moving between positions: *no one can deny that . . . but . . .* ; *however, to some degree*; *frequently that is the case, but . . .* ; *we must take into account . . .* ; and *however*. Of course, each has its own special meaning, and you must apply it to your own argument.

Strategy 3 looks like a debate, but it's not really. Note that the opposition precedes a full discussion of your point, but your point is not a rebuttal of the opposition. More than that, you will want to expand your view of the opposition. So if your position is anti-abortion and you have just acknowledged the opposing view that bringing unwanted children into the world is irresponsible because so many of them lead miserable lives, you can expand your view by discussing options (such as adoption) for raising the children so that they would not suffer from abuse or neglect. The argument on the topic of responsibility that would emerge could create a new humanistic impression on the reader of a position he or she formerly believed morally wrong.

Now let's take a look at an essay with an argumentative edge, the topic being how to rid inner-city schools of weapons. Here is the set of notes one writer made for comparing the "I tip" programs with "weapons buy-back" programs.

*Tentative thesis:* Although neither "I tip" nor "weapons buy-back" programs are foolproof, anonymous "I tip" programs reporting potential sources of violence in public schools work more successfully than "weapons buy-back" programs because the "I tip" program appeals more to ethics than to greed.

*Transition:* No one can deny that "weapons buy-back" programs, when well publicized, do collect many weapons that could conceivably find their way into the schools,

*Opposition:* but they are theoretical and generic rather than concrete and specific, not targeting emergent violence. It is also true that some "I tip" programs do

give financial rewards, suggesting that some people may
report for money, but the records indicate that rarely
are the reporters interested enough in receiving the
money to call back and give their names.

    *Transition:* A look at the key characteristics of each
program will reveal the key motivations of participants.

```
Weapons buy-back
    characteristics of program
    presumed morality
    Texas, Chicago programs' results
I tip
    characteristics of program
    civic responsibility
    fear
    California, Georgia's programs' results
Appeal to Ethics
    weapons buy-back
    I tip
Appeal to Greed
    weapons buy-back (garage sales)
    I tip
Efficiency
    weapons buy-back
    I tip
Control
    weapons buy-back
    I tip
```

You will note that the writer has chosen to dispense with opposition after the thesis, chunking it all together. The rest of the essay has the form of a combined comparison, with the first two points looking like a divided comparison and the last four points being in the form of an alternating comparison.

Why do I not suggest that you place your opposition at the end of your essay before the conclusion—where we often hear it in speeches? The answer is simple. It seems lip service, and no more. You will find such strategies used in some essays, and you will have to form your own judgment of them, but my belief is that it's too little and too late for the reader to be impressed by your empathy for his or her contrary position. Your readers do not get the chance early in the paper to see your broadmindedness and may likely prejudge you for not knowing your subject. The point of using all the strategies in this chapter is to bring your readers, no matter what may be their predispositions, into the heart of your essay. Giving the readers a guided tour of your thinking and showing empathy for all positions will communicate your ideas fully and clearly.

# DRAFTING

Whatever planning strategies you have used, they are bound to save you time in the next stage of the writing process: writing the rough draft. Planning consumes about 30 percent of the time you need to produce your essay. Revision will take a good forty percent of the time. So you can see that the actual writing of the first draft is relatively easy when you've done sufficient planning.

# HOW DOES THE BODY TAKE SHAPE?

Drafting an essay is much like explaining an idea to a friend. You need not worry about precision in grammar, mechanics, or even word choice. At this point you simply want to concentrate on idea formation. Your main focus should be the construction and development of paragraphs. You will be addressing your paragraphs to an audience, not just writing for yourself, so it is important to think of who your readers will be and how you can best set forth your concepts and information for them. How much information do they already have? How intimate should your tone be? How much information can they tolerate in a short space? These are all questions you ask yourself automatically when you speak with people, and the process is no different if you are to communicate well on paper. Simply picture your readers as you write to them.

Along the way, you will no doubt discover a few new ideas—ideas you may not have realized you had—for that is the generative quality of drafting. As you write, you are not just recording prefabricated information; you are actively generating and synthesizing concepts. You have probably experienced this when writing a personal letter—you started out thinking you had only a little to say and discovered that the more you wrote, the more the ideas kept coming.

Although you will follow the plan set forth in your outline, you may see a need to restructure parts of the original plan as you write the draft. You will want to move freely between the outline and the working draft. Not only will you add and subtract ideas to and from the outline, but you will probably alter the order of the ideas from that in the original outline. It is important to remain flexible during the drafting stage and to see your paper as a piece of work still in its formative stages, evolving as you work on it. Rarely does a draft look exactly like the outline that inspired it.

## DRAFTING TECHNIQUES

### Using Discovery Drafts

Strategies that help you to generate ideas may take a different form from what you have previously learned about writing, especially if your teachers have strongly reinforced a pattern of outlining before you write. No one strategy works for everyone, and therefore you will want to consider the more "natural" techniques explained in this chapter and the next. They emphasize the value of composing in a "noncritical" frame of mind, following the mind's intuitive ways of thinking to arrive at a complex treatment of your subject.

As mentioned in Chapter 2, discovery drafts can help in planning—in discovering and developing a thesis statement and supporting ideas. Discovery drafts do not replace rough drafts, which are developed after the formation of the tentative thesis and some sort of plan, but they may give you a good start on a rough draft since they help you see the parameters of your subject. You may wish to write a discovery draft, take a break from it for an hour or so, come back to it and read it closely (perhaps outlining it), and then write a new "rough" draft from the outline or just from memory—without looking again at the discovery draft. Each time you redraft in this fashion your thinking evolves and the essay improves, because the focus and evidence become clearer to you. Once you feel satisfied that your argument is solid, you can move on to revising (see Chapters 6–8).

### Drafting the Body Before the Introduction and Conclusion

Introductions are "word stoppers"—that is, they often cause writers to block since they demand so much creativity and precision. Thus, it is usually a good idea to skip them when you begin the drafting stage. You already have a strong tentative thesis and an outline of the body of your paper. Why not start on a positive note by writing what you have already planned? Simply place your thesis as your first sentence and launch into the body of the paper, following the general guidelines set down by the outline.

Now, some writers say that they cannot do without the introduction, that the introduction is the place where their ideas take shape. Some say, "I can't go on until I get my introduction down on paper." If you are one of these people, you probably need to look more closely at your claim. In effect, you are using the introduction as prewriting. What this choice probably indicates is that you have started the rough draft too early and have not remained flexible about errors in the earlier stages of the writing process. Students locked into writing and rewriting the introduction until it is perfect do get started, but they usually cause themselves a great deal of unnecessary anguish and frustration in the early stages of their writing process. It is a good idea to reconsider this approach if you use it consistently. Skipping the introduction and experimenting with various prewriting strategies instead of sitting down to write your first draft cold will save you time and help you feel more confident about what you write.

Drafting the body first will give your introduction time to incubate. Moreover, the chances are great that you will devise a better introduction this way. First, you will be less likely to give away material needed for the body of the paper. And, since you will know exactly what the body of the essay contains, you can tailor the introduction to the paper using one of the strategies outlined in Chapter 5. After drafting the body and then the introduction, you will find it useful to reread the whole essay and then add an effective conclusion.

## PARAGRAPH AND ESSAY: SOME SIMILARITIES

Have you ever wondered where to begin or end your paragraphs? why paragraphs are important in essay writing? how to organize your thoughts in the proper sequence for a paragraph? The answers to these and other questions often asked by student writers are not so difficult when you see the paragraph as a miniature unit of composition designed to fit into the total pattern of the essay.

Three types of paragraphs are most common in essay writing. The introductory paragraph often has an attention-getting lead-in and contains the thesis. The middle paragraphs each clarify one or another part of the controlling idea in the thesis. The concluding paragraphs may summarize the points in the essay and add to that summary an implication or recommendation derived from your argument. Introductory and concluding paragraphs are discussed in the next chapter. This chapter is concerned with the structure of body paragraphs. A striking similarity exists between a body paragraph and an essay—a similarity that can make learning to write a bit easier than you might suppose. In fact, some scholars suggest that if you can master the structure of the paragraph, you can write a good essay, and vice versa. You can see why if you take a look at the shape of each:

| Essay | Paragraph |
|---|---|
| Introduction—thesis | Topic or top sentence |
| Support | Support |
| Support | Support |
| Support | Support |
| Conclusion | Transition or concluding comment |

### Thesis Statement and Topic Sentence

The thesis statement and the paragraph topic sentence perform the same function: they are primary focal points for the reader. Each serves as the place where writers commit themselves to their material—for the paragraph or the essay—by clearly setting out the point.

### Supports

Supports for the paragraph and essay serve the same purpose. Thus, paragraph supports may be arranged in the same ways as supports within the body of an essay (see Chapter 3). Usually, however, it is not necessary to compose your paragraphs according to strict arrangements, since they develop intuitively, depending on what you need to say to explain the point you are making.

### Conclusion

Writing a conclusion for a paragraph is a bit more difficult than writing one for an essay because it requires a more subtle choice of words; however, the concepts are parallel. Whereas the essay may have several sentences of summarized information in its conclusion, the paragraph may end with a lighter, less obvious, concluding comment, or it may wind up with a transition leading into the next support.

## CHARACTERISTICS OF A GOOD PARAGRAPH

Body paragraphs have four characteristics: (1) a main idea expressed in a topic sentence, or a top sentence that begins the sequence of ideas; (2) unity of purpose; (3) coherence, or flow, from one sentence to the next; and (4) adequate development through explanations and examples.

### The Topic Sentence

It is not necessary to fit a topic sentence into every paragraph; topic sentences that set forth exactly what you want to say in the paragraph are more suitable for some paragraphs than for others. To make the point of a paragraph clear, however, you may wish to control the ideas in it and your readers' perception of the ideas by including a topic sentence. When you do, it is important to create topic sentences that are clear summaries of the point set forth in the paragraph. You want your topic sentence to be specific enough to allow you to cite essential details as supports. It should also serve the purpose of the paragraph as a whole in driving home the controlling idea of the thesis.

Not every paragraph is written at the same level of generality, so there is no one rule for how specific a topic sentence should be. As you write, you will develop skill in using your thesis sentence as a guide to determining the specificity of topic sentences. Here are a few examples of the relative levels of generality between a thesis statement and a topic sentence for papers on the same topic:

> TV shows are more controversial, and some would say more politically correct, than ever this year.

You can see that the level of generality of the previous statement is broader than that of the following sentence, which could serve as a topic sentence for a paragraph in the body of the same essay:

This season several television shows are permitting same-sex kisses on the air.

Here are some more pairs to consider:

> *Thesis:* The aims of multiculturalism and the sometimes unavoidable pressures of political correctness have become incendiary topics on already beleaguered American college and university campuses.
> *Topic Sentence:* Some conservatives, fearing the erosion of Judeo-Christian traditional values in our society, have called for businesses to withdraw funding from colleges and universities now endorsing a multicultural curriculum.
> *Thesis:* Most of the dreams of a child around the age of five, according to many psychologists, are wish-fulfillment dreams.
> *Topic Sentence:* Freud maintained that children at the age of five often get their way in their dreams when they have been frustrated in fulfilling a desire during the day.
> *Thesis:* By studying Latin, one can gain a better awareness of the workings of the English language.
> *Topic Sentence:* Many of the words a college student should know are based on Latin roots.

If you decide to write a topic sentence, you also need to decide where it might best be placed in the paragraph. Some writers like to place topic sentences first, where they really stand out. But topic sentences may work just as well anywhere in the paragraph as long as the paragraph remains focused on the central idea in the predicate. For instance, some writers like to bring in the topic sentence after an introductory sentence or two. The introductory sentences might be a pertinent analogy, a transition from the previous paragraph, or information needed for a full understanding of the topic sentence. In the following paragraph beginning, an analogy opens the paragraph, and the topic sentence (in italics) comes next:

> When the Santa Ana winds blow in southern California, it is as if the gods have loosed their rage. *The winds cause massive destruction and evoke in people their most vitriolic humors.* Trees fall. People rush about with frayed tempers. Fires spread unchecked throughout the Southland.

Placing the topic sentence at the end of the paragraph can have the effect of building up your ideas to a climax. The climactic topic sentence lends an air of surprise or finality to the paragraph. This technique of reserving the main idea of the paragraph is not one to use often, because it can become gimmicky rather than logical and sincere. But you might have an idea that would function best when placed at the end of your paragraph. For instance, if you were writing a paper on the technique of flashbacks in Alfred Hitchcock's classic film *Marnie,* you might open a paragraph with a description of a flashback and a detailed explanation of the technique, only then concluding the paragraph with the topic sentence tying in the film. Another type of paragraph that works effectively with the climactic topic sentence lists a number of examples, only clarifying the connection between them in the final sentence (the topic sentence) of the paragraph:

> A woman with a master's degree in English finds a job as a salesclerk in a large department store after a six-month search for a position in her field. She earns $1,000 a month. A man with a double B.A. in philosophy and history accepts a $1,300-a-month position as a beginning file clerk for an insurance company. Thousands of other college graduates register for unemployment; in their desperate quest for work, they are repeatedly turned away because their education is counted as a strike against them. College no longer brings the rewards, financial or professional, that it once promised. *"Overqualified and underpaid" describes the average college graduate in the United States.*

Sometimes the precise topic sentence will be clearer to you once you have written the whole paragraph. It is a good strategy to reread paragraphs to check their topic sentences against the newly evolved support in the body of your paragraph. Often a simple phrase added to or deleted from the original topic sentence will greatly clarify your ideas.

### The Top Sentence

Topic sentences can lend considerable clarity to paragraphs, making them easy to read and keeping you on track. A more difficult type of paragraph to write, but one that sounds less mechanical, does not come right out and state a topic sentence. Nonetheless, the paragraph is organized around an unstated central idea or has as its first or second sentence the beginning to a sequence of thoughts that is played out in the rest of the paragraph. In such cases, this first sentence is simply called the "top" sentence. Here is an example:

> Many of the self-help books on the market today have not been clinically tested (Rosen 50). That fact does not stop publishers from making exaggerated claims as to their worth. For example, on the back cover of *How to Raise Your Self-Esteem,* the best-seller by Nathaniel Branden, readers are told that this book will help them "break free of negative self-concepts and self-defeating behavior, dissolve internal barriers to success in work and love, conquer the fear of intimacy and success, and find—and keep—the courage to love oneself" (Branden). The emotional language of the statement attracts readers who feel desperate. In addition, the book's front cover states that Branden is taking "the proven action-oriented approach to greater self-respect and self-confidence."

The combination of emotive language and sweeping claims temporarily empowers the readers who probably know deep inside that no single book could possibly accomplish such a task. Anyone who reads the book soon learns that the meaning of the word "proven" refers to highly unscientific and self-congratulatory anecdotes from Branden's professional life. These "come-on's" violate the standards set forth by the American Psychological Association's Ethical Guidelines for self-help therapies, the key to which is "responsibility" on the part of the writer-therapist (Rosen 49).

### Unity

The points made in a paragraph should all relate to the same statement or idea. Unity—the consistency of ideas—seems as if it should come automatically if you have organized the paper with a clear thesis and outline. But at the same time a writer is not a slave to the outline, since new ideas will come as the writing progresses. How you fit those ideas into your overall plan makes a difference to your reader. If irrelevant or tangentially related ideas are just stuck into your body paragraphs, your reader can get lost. Therefore, you must be vigilant not to include extraneous information or ideas in a paragraph, at least not by the time of the final draft. You are trying to convey something definite. Digressions, as interesting as they may seem, will confuse your readers. Avoid them. In a well-handled paragraph every point relates to the predicate of the topic sentence or to the intention, even if there is no topic sentence.

Following is an example of a paragraph that lacks unity. The sentences that throw off the paragraph do not stick to the point of the predicate in the topic sentence. They take up side issues. Most likely, the points being made (a concession to the clear-cut notion that there are two separate worlds) belong in the essay, but they belong in a separate paragraph. The writer could have improved the paragraph by taking out these sentences, which do not flow with the established sequence of ideas.

Once in college, a student is faced with a difficult decision. Does he or she give up all his or her friends from the "community" who decided not to go to college or acquire new friends at school as a kind of second string of relationships that represent a different type of interest sharing? If one returns home for weekends while living on campus during the school week, the split can feel as if one is living a double life. *It's not that the students never realized this would happen. In fact, it was already happening before they "left" for college, when they decided to go to a good school as opposed to the local community college for a course or two or a technical or business school. They have already gone through many emotions, but they get forgotten until the weekend when the conflict re-emerges.* Community friends will have different life styles that could lead to trouble for the college student who has to spend part of the week-end, at least, studying seriously. Going out "cruising" and participating in risky behaviors have more than ever lost their appeal to the student, but lest he look like a snob, he feels compelled to fit in with the old crowd. After all, aren't they his true friends? Isn't this really who he is? There is a certain comfort level at home that entices the student to regress to old behaviors and denounce the new world he or she has entered as artificial or pompous. When he is at school, on the other hand, it seems easy to be serious about classes, and going to the library to study at night helps avoid the social pressure projected by a few students who prefer to just watch television with friends or hang out in a neighboring room playing cards. That isn't what he came to college for, and it all seems clear. He is succeeding through hard work, just like the majority of his classmates. Few students have an anti-intellectual mindset, and there is little negative effect from them on the new approach the college student has had to adopt to succeed in his or her new environment. It doesn't seem like he could be the same person. He feels caught between two worlds.

This student began the paragraph by proposing a question and then narrowing its focus to a description of the "double life" he is experiencing, having moved from a community with values different from those of his new college community. The predicate of the topic sentence, which comes three sentences into the paragraph is *can feel as if he is living a double life.* But then the student interrupts the flow of that idea with his previous feelings about the subject. Although he spends three sentences on the subject, not enough information is given to support the point. For instance, what emotions is the student referring to? Then the student returns to the subject of the life of the community and does a good job of describing the social forces that drive his desire to be at one with his old friends. Finally, he describes the same kinds of forces at school. Although the ideas in the italicized sentences are related to the whole subject, they would be better handled in a separate paragraph with more support for them. As is, they intrude on the unity of the paragraph, bringing up a different point. That straying from the point distracts and confuses readers.

### Coherence

At both the essay and paragraph levels, coherence means that the ideas flow from one to the next and make sense together. Note in the paragraph that follows how lost you feel as a reader; although there are several interesting thoughts, it's hard to tie them together as you read.

Most studies reveal that abusers were once abused by their own parents. A fourteen-year-old child was tied to a pole and beaten with a bucket by his mother and boyfriend for stealing money from the boyfriend. The child chose not to prosecute his attack-ers pointing out that the mother had had a hard life, with a very strict father and that was why she tended to beat him. It was not the first time, and speculation tells us that it will not be the last. Did the young boy really feel empathy for the mother's position, or was he afraid of further reprisals if he pursued arrest? We cannot know. The doctor who treated the child for his injuries reported the case to the police after he also noted several scars on the boy's body and limbs. Does this mean that by recognizing the origin of a problem (abuse), we automatically should ignore its consequences and excuse the perpetrator? The answer is "no." We must require the perpetrator to seek professional help by using the strong arm of the legal system, and we must prevent the child from facing further abuse.

Now look at a more connected version of the same paragraph. Note that the order of ideas has become easier to follow; there are now transitional words where the preceding paragraph left gaping holes; and a final sentence has been added to reinforce the point made early in the paragraph and tie it all together.

Most studies reveal that child abusers were once abused by their own parents. Does this mean that by recognizing the origin of a problem (abuse), we automatically should ignore its consequences and excuse the perpetrators? The answer is "no." In fact, we must require the perpetrators to seek professional help by using the strong arm of the legal system, and we must at the same time prevent the child from facing further abuse. A case in point is that a fourteen-year old boy recently was tied to a pole and beaten with a bucket by his mother and her boyfriend for stealing money from the boyfriend. The doctor who treated the child for injuries reported the case to police after he also noted several scars on the boy's body and limbs. It had not been the first time this boy had been abused, and speculation tells us it will not be the last. However, when the case came to court, the child withdrew the charges, citing his mother's "hard" life and "strict" father as the reasons she tended to beat him. Was this child really feeling empathetic towards his mother, or did he just fear further reprisals if he pursued arrest? We cannot know. Nevertheless, we can see that nobody is served by dismissing such cases. We have to push for prosecution.

*Annotations: repeated word; repeated word; pronoun reference; repeated word; repeated word; (abuse); repeated word; transitional word; logical order: question and answer format; transitional word; repetition of key idea; repetition of key idea*

Specifically, three devices help sentences and paragraphs cohere grace-fully: natural order, word choice, and transitions. Using the most natural order for your subject is usually intuitive, so don't strain for coherence; instead, arrange your paper in the order that seems the most logical and is the easiest to understand. Here are a few tips. It is important always to state the background before you make the points based on that background. And never place step three of a process before step two (unless you are using reverse order on purpose). In less analytic pa-pers, like descriptive-narrative essays, use chronological or process ar-rangements (see Chapter 3) whenever appropriate because they auto-matically provide smooth shifts between ideas. Remember: you want to be understood, and you want your reader to be able to anticipate the order of the ideas in your essay.

Your choice of words also keeps your ideas flowing. Repetition of a key word that reinforces the controlling idea or the use of a synonym for a key idea within the essay or paragraph reminds the reader of a main point. But be careful to select important words when you use this technique. Following are two paragraphs, one that effectively uses rep-etition of a key word and synonyms and another that tediously repeats and repeats and repeats.

*Paragraph 1*

The real American Dream is the fantasy that we can be as un-marked as those models in magazines, movies, and television com-mercials appear to be. This quest of the modern American woman is never realized, however, for unerasable are the wrinkles, the blemishes, and scars of aging. These are the wrinkles that cannot be removed with magical creams. These are the blemishes that must heal slowly and cannot be prevented with layers of pomades and packs and gels. These are the scars that come from living, and no "beauty plan" can cause them not to happen. But the dream perpetuates the great cover-up.

Note how the synonyms and repeated words make the paragraph flow.

*Paragraph 2*

Most Americans would find the lifestyles of Hell's Angels re-pugnant. The Hell's Angels seem to engage in the most distaste-ful activities. They engage in communal sex orgies that would humiliate a "normal" American. The Hell's Angels engage in more aggressively violent activities than most people. The Hell's An-gels fight with other Hell's Angels as often as they threaten or attack others. The bodies of the Hell's Angels and the clothes of the Hell's Angels seem dirty, their dirty hair is matted, and the stench exuded from a gang of Hell's Angels would repulse most "normal" Americans. The Hell's Angels disdain the stable life that most Americans work to achieve.

You can see that the writer practically hits the readers over the head with repetition of *Hell's Angels, most Americans,* and the deadly verb phrase *engage in.* None of these words is significant to the point about lifestyles; thus such repetition breaks down the flow of the paragraph rather than lends coherence.

Another way to control flow in your essay is by using transitions. These connective words have three functions: to point out an addition to what has been said, to signal a contrast or a concession to the opposition, or to show a result. Here is a list of transitions you might want to select from:

| | |
|---|---|
| *Addition or expansion:* | moreover, furthermore, finally, first, last, also, in fact, for instance, in particular, in addition, besides, another, actually |
| *Contrast or concession:* | yet, though, nevertheless, despite this, but, however, although, on the other hand, on the contrary, still, whereas, otherwise, now, in the past, instead, the truth is |
| *Results:* | thus, in any case, finally, therefore, consequently, hence, on the whole, in other words, as a result, then, predictably, now, all in all |

This list should be helpful when you're writing, but keep something in mind when you use it: If a paragraph is brief, transitions can stick out awkwardly, defeating their purpose, unless they are placed and chosen cautiously. You don't want them to seem merely mechanical. This problem, which is not as common in the essay as in the paragraph, can be avoided without too much trouble. Here's how.

First, never weigh down a paragraph with too many transitions. Don't forget that a logical sequence of ideas or natural repetition of a key word can do the same trick. It is easy to tell whether you have overdone transitions if you read what you have written aloud. If there are too many, they will call attention to themselves. Second, try not to place the transitions in the same position in each sentence. Many people fall into a habit of making the transition the first word of the sentence; they consequently fail to write interesting, varied sentences. Try instead to insert the transition after the first word—or include it in the middle or at the end of a sentence to achieve a less blatant link between ideas. Then, too, you should avoid the obvious. Don't use the same transition over and over. And avoid "in conclusion," for it says outright to the reader, "Hey, you dummy—this is the ending, get it?"

Note how effectively transitions are used in the following paragraph from a student's essay:

Though it may sound strange, working in the dishroom at the college cafeteria has improved my study habits. First of all, this experience has shown me how to be a more organized worker. Actually, I used to pretend, in the past, that I was organized. But the truth is that I could never find what I was looking for. In a corner of my room I stacked up all of my papers, mail, books, anything that came into my hands. Now, instead, I have established a filing system for each of my classes and extracurricular activities. In the dishroom, since I have to work fast, I must keep my stacks of dishes perfectly in order. The dishroom has also taught me to be a doer, not a procrastinator. There one job gets done at a time, before the worker moves on to the next. I have used this method in studying during the last six months, and it has made a difference in my grades. Another habit I have carried over from the dishroom is careful scheduling. Now, I plan my homework according to the class test schedule—no more cramming for me. It's surprising how parallel the work in the dishroom is with homework, and it's a pleasure to find myself with such expeditious study habits.

Similar strategies can be used between paragraphs. Note the effective use of coherence devices in the following paragraphs from a student's essay:

> The screenwriter, when writing his or her scenario, knows that he or she will work not only with the producer but also with the director. As a matter of fact, the latter will be chosen by the producer to execute the script. The most recognized job is, axiomatically, the director's. He or she is the one giving atmosphere to the movie by adding many elements to the mere script, such as the music, the photography, and the directing. Putting his or her own interpretation of the script into the film, the director often betrays the screenwriter's intentions.
>
> In order to protect their own scripts, some scenarists, such as Woody Allen, become their own producers and directors. By being both producer and director—not to mention actor . . .

The writer has drawn connections between the last sentence of the first paragraph and the first sentence of the second paragraph: If direc-

tors might "betray" a writer's intention, it is logical that writers will want to protect and preserve their intended messages from such betrayal.

### Paragraph Development

One of the most common flaws in college writing is inadequate development of paragraphs. A reader's eye can pick up this problem immediately because the paragraphs look too short. The presence of many paragraph breaks on a page is called overdifferentiation of paragraphs. It is true that overdifferentiated paragraphs are commonly found in print; journalists and advertisers often write paragraphs of just one, two, or three sentences. Does this fact mean that some professional writers do not accept the principles of paragraphing discussed in this chapter? Yes and no.

Your paragraphs will be longer, in most cases, than those found in newspapers and magazines. The audience for a news article is not as homogeneous as that for your college essays, so the writer must appeal to a broad group with wide variations in interests, education, and experience. To accommodate this range of readers, most writers try to keep their material fairly simple and brief. Another consideration in newspapers and magazines is layout: brief paragraphs look more attractive on the printed page. Finally, advertisers and textbook writers often use short paragraphs to set off important material for emphasis. So do journalists. The point is that overdifferentiated paragraphing in these cases is deliberate and effective.

If you combined several of the paragraphs from a news item into one, they would probably work into unified and coherent units that fit the standards of regular college essays. It's not that journalists have left out any elements of good paragraphs. They simply have broken up their paragraphs into smaller logical units in order to suit the needs of their audience. Doing so fits their purpose.

You may have guessed that the paragraphs you will be writing for most essays will be, on the average, a third or half of a page, typed and double spaced. This is by no means an ironclad rule—no rule could be expected to govern the length of every paragraph you write—it is only a guideline so that your paragraphs will not be grossly underdeveloped. One source of poor development is overgeneralizing your ideas. You cannot discuss, in more than a very general way, the duties of a high school math teacher in a single paragraph, but you could describe in one detailed paragraph the audiovisual aids used by the teacher of an algebra class. So the first step in good development is framing a topic you can say something about for each paragraph. Then develop your paragraph so that it fully covers your topic sentence, or fulfills your intention, one point after the other without leaving any blanks.

Essentially, begin a new paragraph where it is logical to do so as you write from your outline or notes. You can easily readjust paragraphs during revision, especially if you are writing on a computer. You may find that covering the point of a paragraph takes three supporting ideas about the point, which produces a paragraph of about nine sentences. Other ideas may take only one sentence each. Paragraphing is rarely predictable from the outline. You need to start writing, letting your ideas flow from the ideas suggested in the outline, before you can decide exactly where to divide paragraphs. Even then, changes are usually needed. In fact, it is a good idea to look over your rough draft to evaluate and change your paragraph divisions. The structure of the paper and of the paragraph, of course, help you generate ideas along the way, but you should be careful not to allow yourself to be too fixed into a prescription for paragraphs. Your writing could lose its sparkle. Good writers are flexible so that their writing doesn't become mechanical, repetitious, or lifeless.

---

## Exercises

A. Write a possible topic sentence for each of the following groups of details. Underline the predicate in the topic sentence.

1. The Chicana *mestiza* is a blend of Native American, Mexican, and Anglo-American heritages.

   She calls the *mestiza* consciousness a consciousness of the borderlands.

   The borderlands is fraught with struggle from negotiating three cultures, languages, and value systems.

   Gloria Anzaldúa describes her Chicana identity as formed from living on the Mexican-American border.

2. To contrast the amount of money paid versus amount of benefit invested in society, some people point to the discrepancy between the salaries of teachers and the astronomical amount of money professional sports figures receive from their contract and endorsements.

   The portion of the California public education K-12 budget which is spent on the salaries of those who never see the inside of a classroom (i.e., bureaucrats) is over 65 percent.

   A California public-school teacher's average annual salary as of 1994 exceeds that of a state prison guard by only $1,000.

3. Snow covers Wisconsin for two-thirds of the year.

   It is difficult to buy fresh vegetables there in the winter.

   Travel is not easy during the winter in Wisconsin.

   Temperatures get so low that walls of the houses can crack, and car engines must be warmed with electrical devices.

B. The following paragraph from a student's paper appears to have no topic sentence. Devise a topic sentence that will work and underline the predicate.

It is necessary to make the rights and privileges of being Americans known to the Chinese people here in Los Angeles's Chinatown. It is also important to inform the general public of the problems confronting the Chinese community. There should be development of facilities in the areas of employment, physical and mental health, education, housing, and recreation. The city should establish a daycare center. An old age home and a youth community center should be available in Chinatown. On-the-job training should be provided for new immigrants through vocational guidance centers. Bilingual education should be the method used in the schools of Chinatown.

C. Here is a paragraph from *Science and Human Values* by J. Bronowski. Identify the transitional words and phrases.

> The discoveries of science, the works of art are explorations—more, are explosions, of a hidden likeness. The discoverer or the artist presents in them two aspects of nature and fuses them into one. This is the act of creation, in which an original thought is born, and it is the same act in original science and original art. But it is not therefore the monopoly of the man who wrote the poem or who made the discovery. On the contrary, I believe this view of the creative act to be right because it alone gives a meaning to the act of appreciation. The poem or the discovery exists in two moments of vision: the moment of appreciation as much as that of creation; for the appreciator must see the movement, wake to the echo which was started in the creation of the work. In the moment of appreciation we live again the moment when the creator saw and held the hidden likeness. When a simile takes us aback and persuades us together, when we find a juxtaposition in a picture both odd and intriguing, when a theory is at once fresh and convincing, we do not merely nod over someone else's work. We re-enact the creative act, and we ourselves make the discovery again. At bottom, there is no unifying likeness there until we too have seized it, we too have made it for ourselves.

D. The following excerpt from a student's essay does not hold together. Provide transitions that will make it flow better.

> Christianity became popular in Japan because of the wave of Westernization. The Meiji Restoration aimed to make Japan into a modern country in order to seek equality with the West in the eyes of the rest of the world. The international world of the nineteenth century was completely dominated by the West. Since the Western countries believed themselves to be culturally superior to the East, the Japanese assumed that they had no chance to be considered equal unless they adopted Western ways. The adoption of many superficial aspects of Western culture was encouraged by the government. The people started to practice the Western style of life, adopting whatever they could of Western clothing, hairstyles, and eating habits. Western dress was prescribed for all court and official ceremonies in 1872. In 1873 the ban on Christianity was removed.

## BUILDING PARAGRAPHS

Covering a point thoroughly seems to require a delicate balance of examples and elaboration. If a writer does not develop a point, the paragraph may look short, and he or she may think the best thing to do is to combine paragraphs. The resulting paragraph may be too general to support the argument or too difficult for the reader to follow. Some writers struggle to develop their ideas but find it hard to know when to explain something and when to let it stand without elaboration or examples. The key to covering a point fully but not overwriting is to remember that one is communicating with readers. Several questions are useful: Do my readers know the definition of my key terms? Do I need to fill in the readers on the details of the case or example I just gave? Will doing so strengthen their understanding of my position? These are all issues of communication. By familiarizing yourself with how successful academic paragraphs communicate and by adapting this logical sequencing to your personal writing style, you will find the answers.

A good method of analyzing the sequencing within paragraphs is based on the discovery of Francis Christensen some thirty-five years ago that both sentences and paragraphs in twentieth-century American writing seem to be cumulative. Christensen also proposed a numbering system that you can use in two helpful ways—constructing and revising paragraphs. You can apply his numbering system in your rough draft to construct paragraphs when the development of ideas is difficult, or to revise paragraphs when you reach the stage of deciding which paragraphs are adequately developed and which need more elaboration.

### Sequencing of Sentences

Christensen realized that sentences and paragraphs are cumulative; that is, they begin with a base to which the rest of the sentence or the rest of the paragraph is added. What is added to the base can be viewed as a "sequence of structurally related ideas" that detail, expand, and emphasize what is set forth in the first part. Christensen described these two sequences as either coordination or subordination.

Coordination adds an idea at the same level of generality as a previous one. Subordination develops an idea one step further based on another idea already given in the paragraph, often in the previous sentence. Let's look at an example of how these concepts work in the paragraph. Note that the first sentence is the topic sentence. The two subsequent sentences give different illustrations of the hidden criticism mentioned in the first sentence. Neither is more specific than the other, making them coordinate with each other. And both develop or subordinate the first idea.

*Paragraph One*

Praise can pack a wallop if it's hiding criticism in its pockets. For example, "Your new beau is fabulous—he's not boring, like the last one" seems to be praising your new beau, yet you walk away smarting from the slap to your old one. Similarly, the compliment, "Your presentation was excellent. It was much easier to follow than your last one," leaves you with a vision of your audience scratching their heads over your last presentation. (From *You Just Don't Understand,* by Deborah Tannen)

Now let's look at another type of sequence. This one is strictly subordinate.

*Paragraph Two*
Offering suggestions can also indirectly imply criticism. For example, a woman named Sarah suggested to her friend Phyllis that Phyllis might ease her parents' next visit by having them stay in a hotel instead of in Phyllis's one-bedroom apartment. Instead of appreciating the advice, Phyllis correctly perceived that Sarah thought she was too involved with her parents. (Also from *You Just Don't Understand,* by Deborah Tannen)

Once again the topic sentence comes first, followed by subordination in the form of an example. But in the third sentence the example is further explored, making not just the second sentence subordinate to the first sentence but the last sentence subordinate to the second one. Each sentence in the sequence takes the previous idea a step further. We could not reverse the order of the second and third sentences because the third is dependent on the second's having been already stated. In the previous example about the hidden criticisms, however, either of the examples could have been stated first because neither was dependent on the other; they both depended on the topic sentence. Therefore, one helpful trick in checking your own paragraphs for coordination and subordination is trying to switch the order of sentences to see if the meaning is retained. If they are interchangeable, they are likely to be coordinate with one another. If not, subordination is present.

The most common sequence in academic writing is the mixed sequence, blending coordination and subordination. Here's an example. Note that essentially there are three coordinate sentences, all supporting the predicate of the topic sentence—in this case, the second sentence. Each of these coordinate sentences is introduced by a transitional word or phrase (*One is, We also know*, and *Finally*) . The author, Gordon Allport, a famous psychologist, follows each of these "facts" with an explanatory subordinate sentence.

*Paragraph Three*
No subject within the psychology of religion has been more extensively studied than conversion. Various facts are fairly well established. One is that the average age for conversion, like that for the rejection of parental systems of belief, is sixteen, although there is evidence that in recent years the trend is toward an earlier age. One suspects that the impact of movies and radio has sharpened the emotional susceptibilities of children, so that the blandishments of evangelists, if responded to at all, are effective at an earlier age than formerly. We also know that the frequency of conversion experiences varies with cultural conditions. Children in rural areas and in families holding a stern theology are more susceptible than are city children, especially those associated with churches that practice confirmation. Finally, the frequency of abrupt conversions is certainly less today than it was fifty years ago. In the time of our grandparents it was not un-

common for whole families to attend revival camp-meetings and to return home with the adolescents formally converted. (From *Religion and Skepticism,* by Gordon Allport)

You can see that much of the reading and writing you do includes developed sequences like the preceding one from Allport's book.

Christensen had to develop a means of identifying the varying ways that coordination and subordination could evolve, so he created a numbering system to reflect the levels of subordination and coordination in any one paragraph. Using these numbers to identify the patterns in your rough draft can help you detect flaws in development of your ideas. Here is how the numbering works:

The first sentence of the paragraph is usually a 1 (unless it is a transition or an introductory remark).

Ideas that are coordinate with one another are assigned the same number as each other.

An idea that is subordinate to a previous idea in the paragraph takes the next number to the sentence it subordinates. Thus 3 subordinates 2 and 4 subordinates 3. Let's look at the same paragraphs now with the levels of coordination and subordination numbered and indented to show subordination.

### Paragraph One
1 Praise can pack a wallop it it's hiding criticism in its pockets.
  2 For example, "Your new beau is fabulous—he's not boring, like the last one" seems to be praising your new beau, yet you walk away smarting from the slap to the old one.
  2 Similarly, the compliment, "Your presentation was excellent. It was much easier to follow than your last one," leaves you with a vision of your audience scratching their heads over your last presentation.

### Paragraph Two
1 Offering helpful suggestions can also indirectly imply criticism.
  2 For example, a woman named Sarah suggested to her friend Phyllis that Phyllis might ease her parents' next visit by having them stay in a hotel instead of in Phyllis's one-bedroom apartment.
    3 Instead of appreciating the advice, Phyllis correctly perceived that Sarah thought she was too involved with her parents.

### Paragraph Three
1 No subject within the psychology of religion has been more extensively studied than conversion.

2 Various facts are fairly well established.

  3 One is that the average age for conversion, like that for the rejection of parental systems of belief, is sixteen, although there is evidence that in recent years the trend is toward an earlier age.

    4 One suspects that the impact of movies and radio has sharpened the emotional susceptibilities of children, so that the blandishments of evangelists, if responded to at all, are effective at an earlier age than formerly.

  3 We also know that the frequency of conversion experiences varies with cultural conditions.

    4 Children in rural areas and in families holding a stern theology are more susceptible than are city children, especially those associated with churches that practice confirmation.

  3 Finally, the frequency of abrupt conversions is certainly less today than it was fifty years ago.

    4 In the time of our grandparents it was not uncommon for whole families to attend revival camp-meetings and to return home with the adolescents formally converted.

---

### Exercises

Number and indent the following paragraphs as in the preceding examples.

1. *Topic sentence:* The English royal legacy seems to be eroding in public opinion in light of recent royal hypocrisies and criticisms that it perpetuates an unjust class-system.

    Public scandals lead some English citizens to view the Royal Family as morally equal to or worse than most common citizens.

    Popular conception of Prince Charles as a whining wimp undermines the image of royalty as ruling by divine right.

    The Queen's acquiescence to being taxed like all British citizens and her agreement in the face of public outcry to pay for palace repairs signal public questioning of royal privilege

2. The English royal legacy seems to be eroding in public opinion in light of recent royal hypocrisies and criticisms that it perpetuates an unjust class-system.

    Public scandals lead some English citizens to view the Royal Family as morally equal to or worse than most common citizens.

    Prince Charles' awkward indiscretions with a married woman have seriously tarnished the royal image as a noble tradition.

As mentioned earlier, the Christensen method is useful both in revision of existing paragraphs in your rough draft and in actually writing your first draft. Depending on your personal preference, you can use Christensen's numbering system to keep track of your evolving coordinate and subordinate sentences. By using this numbering system in your rough draft, as you develop each body paragraph, you can determine which of your paragraphs need further development and which are sufficiently elaborated.

Here's how the numbering pattern works. Remember, coordinate elements take the same number as sentences with which they are coordinate; subordinate sentences take the next number to the sentence they subordinate. That is, if you begin your paragraph numbering by calling the first sentence a one, you would quite likely number the second sentence a two, since it would usually add detail to the concept in the first sentence. Now the following sentence could be either coordinate with the level-two sentence, making it another two, or subordinate to it, in which case it would be a three.

Explaining the numbering system is much like teaching someone to ride a bicycle: it's easier to show someone than to give instruction verbally. So, as you continue to read about coordinate and subordinate sequences, the basic principles of numbering should become clearer to you. You will soon find it easy and practical to number your own paragraphs. Keep in mind that ideas directly referring to the previous sentence usually have a subordinate relationship to it. It is ideas that are on the same level of generality that are coordinate, and such ideas are usually about *different* concepts or are different examples of a single point.

Some people find that numbering paragraphs during the rough draft—the actual writing of the paper—helps them focus on their audience and evaluate how much to develop each idea. Many students say that the strategy suggested in the following models helps them to think clearly. Such a practice can be slow at first, but it is nearly foolproof and saves time in revision. Also, after numbering a few paragraphs as you write, you will become proficient and faster.

Another way to use the numbering system is to write your rough draft and then number your body paragraphs. After numbering them, you can approach their revision with a certain amount of suspicion as to whether your paragraphs are adequately developed. For instance, what would you conclude if your sequence turned out to have the following numbers?

1
   2
   2
   2
   2

Most likely, you would conclude that the paragraph is too general. You would need to include some 3s and 4s and perhaps take out some of the 2s if they did not contribute substantially to your point. Remaining general and giving various examples of a point is not as appealing to most academic readers as a more focused statement that goes into depth on fewer examples.

What if you arrived at the following sequence?

1
  2
    3
      4
        5
          6
            7

You may have the opposite problem here. Perhaps you have gone into too much detail and created a veritable free association, failing to substantiate what you had set out to say in your first two sentences. To rectify this problem, you could introduce some coordinate sentences, where needed.

What if you came across a sequence that looks like this?

1
  2
    3
      4
  2
  2
    3
      4

The potential problem appears to be that the second two is not as elaborated as the other twos. The paragraph lacks balance. Perhaps the two is misplaced; it may well belong in another paragraph. Perhaps once you elaborate on the second number two, you will need to start a new paragraph for the third number two.

There are no hard and fast rules about what sequences to follow. Even the previous three sequences could be effective in a given context. You may be able to cover a great deal in one well-developed sentence and yet need two or three sentences to achieve the same degree of development elsewhere in the paragraph. Thus, the numbers alone cannot form your judgment. Nevertheless, the Christensen method of paragraph numbering gives you an opportunity to look objectively at what you have written and to get some ideas about what might need improvement in your paragraphs. This sort of consciousness is badly needed when you have just spent a good deal of time writing a rough draft and you feel saturated with your own material.

Infinite combinations of coordination and subordination are possible. Your combinations will result from your thinking through a specific topic as you write. You will subordinate when you feel your readers need further explanation or more details; you will coordinate when you feel your readers need another example or another idea to reinforce a point you have just explained. Every sentence you add to the topic or top sentence should fit into one of the two sequences, and you can determine just what to write next by keeping your readers' needs in mind, then subordinating or coordinating as necessary.

Sometimes coordination will dominate the paragraph; sometimes subordination will. Here is an example of a coordinate sequence:

1 My apartment is disorderly around midterms because I am stressed.
  2 Books are stacked up on tables, on top of cabinets, and even on the floor—wherever I last read them or set them before bedtime at 2 A.M.
  2 Also, the kitchen table generally has notebook paper, pens, clips, and used staples spread across it, leftovers from the papers I've been writing or the notes I've been recopying to meet last-minute deadlines or to study for tests.
  2 My bed remains unmade each morning as I dash out of the house barely in time to make it to class after only a few hours sleep.
  2 The kitchen sink is half full of dishes when I wake up because by the time I get to bed I'm too sleepy to wash them.
  2 Worst of all, the trash is lined up in three or four bags next to the kitchen door because it can't be my priority.

Here is an example of a subordinate sequence:

1 Preschool teachers across the nation are concerned about the surge of pretend "violent" behavior they are witnessing on playgrounds as result of the newest Power Ranger blitz.
  2 Three-year-olds don't seem to recognize that they can hurt each other by performing Power Ranger kicks and hits.
    3 Injuries occur more frequently than they have over previous superhero stunts, partly because unlike Superman and Batman, these are animated superheroes who are also "regular teenagers" (actors) during part of the show.
      4 What appeals to the children most is this ability to "transform" into figures who can do only what animated heroes can do.
        5 The resulting confusion between reality and fantasy when children think they can be animated characters is dangerous because real children cry and bleed.

Most often, you will want to mix coordination with subordination, as is done in the examples in the following sections. These examples are practice for applying Christensen's numbering method to construct and to revise paragraphs. You may wish to study these paragraphs to reinforce your understanding of how coordination and subordination can help your paragraphs.

### Constructing Paragraphs

You may number as you write the body of your essay, thinking always in terms of what you have just said and what the audience needs to have explained. So you would start off writing a sentence Christensen would call a 1, then think as you write about the sequence of coordination and subordination that fits what you would like to say. Here is an example of how you might think through a sequence. Suppose you are writing a paper comparing two essays on education, one written by Steffens and one by Simpson.

*Step One: The Topic Sentence*

Set forth exactly what you wish to compare in a clear topic sentence derived from the controlling idea of your thesis. Remember that the predicate of the topic sentence focuses the rest of the paragraph. Suppose you are comparing the ideas of two writers on the subject of what makes someone truly educated. Your first sentence might look like this:

Both Lincoln Steffens and Alan Simpson, in their articles on education, believe that to be educated in the true sense of the word means to be actively skeptical and intellectually aggressive.

*Step Two: Subordinate*

Explain what you mean by offering an example. If the predicate seems clear, you want to begin to develop your first point, about Steffens:

Steffens states that "everything in the world remains to be done or done over," that "everything is still in the air waiting to be researched and rewritten."

*Step Three: Subordinate*

Explain your first main idea. Your readers will want to know the relationship between the quotation and the point of the paragraph. What makes someone truly educated? Therefore, you need to expand— add detail to—the second sentence:

He implies that no real student just sits back and absorbs what he or she is taught.

*Step Four: Subordinate*

Expand on the explanation. It's still not entirely clear how you are backing up the predicate of the topic sentence. The readers will be interested in what a student does with the learning other than "absorb."

The application of what he or she is learning is important, and the student should recognize that this learning can be demonstrated only by upgrading something he or she learns about.

*Step Five: Coordinate*

Now that the first point is clear, the second part of the point in the predicate come forth:

> In agreement with this view, Simpson talks about looking deeper, past the "sham."

*Step Six: Subordinate*

Explain the second point: "What does it mean?" the readers wonder.

> One should be able, according to Simpson—and Steffens would agree—to listen to and detect a false argument, to assess its inaccuracy.

*Step Seven: Subordinate*

Expand on the point. The readers would want you to take this last point a step further. What's the difference between a "sham" and a fact? What does the real student do that the less involved student fails to do?

> According to Simpson, taking notes from a lecturer and accepting tradition is a sham, but to argue with the lecturer or to challenge the tradition is a sign of education.

*Step Eight: Subordinate*

Directly compare by expanding the last point. Now that the points of each writer are clear, show the similarity:

> This assertion can be compared to Steffens' demand that the educated revise the intellectual world.

*Step Nine: Subordinate*

Expand the last point, one notch more, and wind up the paragraph. The readers need a key concept to take away from the paragraph and to remember:

> The key word for both writers seems to be "action."

Although the process of numbering and identifying the pattern of each sentence in your paragraphs may be a bit tedious or slow at first, you will not have to do it for long before the method becomes so second nature that you will not even have to think about the numbers.

**Revising Paragraphs**

Many writers find using the Christensen method more practical as a revision strategy. They can write quickly and then assess their work for revisions. In numbering paragraphs writers can determine whether a point requires more explanation, is misplaced, needs deleting—or even whether an assumption has been made without stating it. Take a look at the following numbered paragraph. As you will see, the student could not get very far with the numbering before realizing that irrelevant material had been included, ideas had not been explained, and the organization needed reworking:

1 I developed my cynical distaste for Jewish ritual at a fairly young age.

  2 I grew up in a "Jewish" home, which meant that my three siblings and I were sent to religious school to learn about Judaism.

  2 However, the only Jewish rituals we practiced in the home were Chanukah—a minor holiday—and Passover, at my aunt and uncle's house.

  2 Our family did not keep kosher (observe dietary laws).

    3 In fact, our mother would feed us pork sausage (not kosher) in the morning before sending us to religious school.

  2 I learned about a Jewish way of life in religious school that I never experienced at home.

    3 The hypocrisy of the situation was beyond my parents' understanding.

      ? My father was involved in the Reform movement, when Reform meant that you were basically just like a Christian except you didn't believe that Jesus was the Messiah.

      ? My mother was born into a Protestant family and did not convert until I was eighteen.

        ? Except when she occasionally helped us with religious school homework, she had no Jewish education.

    4 Eating pork did not create a moral dilemma for either of my parents.

The sentences with questions marks are impossible to number, given the rest of the paragraph—probably they should be placed elsewhere in the paper, maybe even in the introduction since they are so general. The 4 sentence at the end of the paragraph clearly needs to be moved up. Perhaps it would be better placed as a 3 with the current first 3 in the paragraph as a 4. Such decisions become clearer to a writer in revision than in drafting the first time, and that is precisely why numbering existing paragraphs can be so helpful.

Each writer will settle on a style of his or her own; whether numbering during writing or after a draft is on paper, use of the Christensen method will pay off.

## Exercises

A. Place the sentences in this paragraph in the best possible order and add transitions.

Thieves, though, can get into any place they wish to enter, no matter what safeguards there may be. I am certain I would protect my family and myself if someone entered my house, and that is all there is to the matter. I would use any weapon I could. Because I care for my family, I try always to protect them as well as I am able. My house is equipped with deadbolts on the door and locks on all windows. We have a trained dog who barks at any strangers who come to the house. And often thieves have knives and guns with them when they burglarize homes. They can, despite what everyone would hope, pick locks and trick even the most loyal dogs. It would grieve me terribly to see my little girl hurt by a burglar.

B. Describe the pattern or patterns of the following paragraphs. Explain the subordinate and coordinate sequences in them by writing out the paragraphs in the indented form with numbers.

1. The primary fault with most bilingual programs is that they are based on the assumption that the best way to produce an English-speaking population is to make immigrants give up their native languages. Although this assumption seems logical, it is incorrect. In fact, the majority of the studies over the past fifty years have shown that children who are taught in their native language learn English more quickly than those who are taught in English. This fact could be due to what Cummins calls "the interdependence hypothesis," which is that there are a few basic concepts which children must learn in order to speak, read, and write any language. Once these concepts are mastered, they can easily be reapplied to any other language. Therefore, the acquisition of English literacy should be much easier when Spanish-speaking children have first learned to read and write in Spanish. (from a student's paper)

2. The loudspeaker in the East Los Angeles Stadium screamed first call for the Bee one-hundred-yard dash. I put my warmup shoes on and began to jog my warmup laps. In the middle of my warmup, the speaker again cried out second call for the one-hundred-yard dash. I hurried and put on my new track shoes that my mother had purchased the day before and walked slowly over to the starting line. I looked at the now nine empty lanes and wondered which lane would be filled by the one who was really best. For months I had worked to get where I stood now, and in about ten seconds or less my worries and possibly my dreams would come true. (from a student's paper)

3. Not only industrial production is ruled by the principle of continuous and limitless acceleration. The educational system has the same criterion: the more college graduates, the better. The same in sports: every

new record is looked upon as progress. Even the attitude toward the weather seems to be determined by the same principle. It is emphasized that this is "the hottest day in the decade," or the coldest, as the case may be, and I suppose some people are comforted for the inconvenience by the proud feeling that they are witnesses to the record temperature. One could go on endlessly giving examples of the concept that consistent increase of quantity constitutes the goal of our life; in fact, that it is what is meant by "progress." (from Erich Fromm, The Revolution of Hope, p. 37)

C. Name four or five details that might support each of the following possible topic sentences.

1. A garage at a gas station is not a comforting place to spend the afternoon.
2. Library reading rooms can be too comfortable.
3. New cars are not built to last for many years.
4. Animals have some of the same physical expressions as humans.
5. What is "reliable" to me is not the same thing as it is to my employer.

D. Name at least three details that might support each of the following potential topic sentences and suggest which of them might be subordinated further.

1. Letters of recommendation can be misleading when one is hiring a candidate.
2. Reforms in health care should not apply to those with emergencies.
3. Border patrols should be handled differently than they are.

E. Explain why it is difficult to number the following paragraph. How do you suggest the author clear up the confusion?

In Johnstone's study, not only did men more often tell about experiences in which they had acted alone, but when men and women told about acting alone the outcomes tended to be different. The vast majority of men who reported acting alone also reported a happy outcome. The majority of women who reported acting alone portrayed themselves as suffering as a result. Only a very small number of stories told by men (four out of twenty-one) had the protagonist receiving help or advice from someone. In a much larger proportion of the women's stories (eleven of twenty-six), the protagonist received help or advice from others. (From *You Just Don't Understand,* by Deborah Tannen)

Y ou have already drafted the body of your essay around the outline or notes you developed to support your tentative thesis statement. Writing the body of the paper has permitted you to examine your subject in a way that allows you to ask, "Now, what have I said?" This is a good time to adjust the tentative thesis so that it covers everything you have said in your essay. Then, your next step is to turn your attention to developing the rest of the introduction and, later, your conclusion.

# HOW SHOULD YOU BEGIN AND END THE ESSAY?

## WRITING GOOD INTRODUCTIONS

The introduction of your essay, although not as long as the body, is certainly important to the worth of the total project. The introduction is much like the display window at a department store—it suggests to your readers what is inside. It gives your readers an indication of your subject and of your attitude toward it (see the discussion of tone in Chapter 1). If the beginning is not interestingly written, they may not read any farther or, at best, will read with little attention. Writing good introductions is a skill that you will develop with practice. Introductions, not having a prescribed form, have to be thought out for each paper individually and therefore can be time consuming. The idea for the introduction may come to you more easily for some essays than for others. Many writers find that drafting the introduction in conjunction with the conclusion produces the needed originality. Written at the same time, the beginning and ending balance each other, not only in content but in length. There is no one "right" length for a beginning or ending. You have to use good judgment on the matter by considering the length of the essay, the complexity of the thesis, and the familiarity of the readers with the point you are making.

The introduction to an essay accomplishes three things in a relatively small space: (1) It sets the tone of the paper, whether humorous, satiric, serious, or prophetic; (2) it engages the readers, making them want to read on; and (3) it states the main point of the essay, the thesis. For a short paper (three to five pages) the introduction may be only a brief paragraph. However, longer essays such as research papers sometimes require a great deal of background information before the major proposition can be stated. For such papers (often ten pages or more) the introduction often requires several paragraphs and may run as long as one-fifth of the essay.

Many people think that they should write the introduction to an essay first. Yet the opening is often the hardest part of the paper to write. It is difficult for most people to focus the beginning of the paper from just a thesis statement or even from an outline of the body of the essay. The act of writing the body of the paper from the outline makes you think about and clarify exactly what you want to say; it is not until you have written the body of the paper that you feel completely comfortable with your material, in many cases.

Staring at a blank paper and worrying about how to begin will most likely lead to stiff writing, and you will probably need to rewrite the introduction later anyway. Instead of facing what has been called "the tyranny of the blank page," why not try the following process?

*Step one:* Devise and focus your subject (see Chapter 2).

*Step two:* Develop a tentative thesis statement (see Chapter 2).

*Step three:* Set down an arrangement for the middle in notes (see Chapter 3).

*Step four:* Write out your tentative thesis statement as the first sentence of your rough draft.

*Step five:* Use your notes, or a fuller outline (see Chapter 3), as a guide to writing your middle.

*Step six:* Now return to the thesis and write the introduction.

*Step seven:* Reread the whole rough draft and write a conclusion that grows out of the rest of the essay.

You will usually arrive at a good beginning before you write the final draft of the essay. Rehearse introductions in your spare moments—when you take a break, while you eat dinner—as good ideas often come when you least expect them. Remember that the idea you decide to place before the thesis should be generated by the point in the thesis; in other words, it should clearly pave the way for the main part of the essay. Modeling yours after the effective introductions provided in this chapter will help you make this connection.

Equally important is consistency of tone between the introduction and the rest of the essay. For example, before you settle on a dramatic opening, you should consider the point you are making—how serious you want to sound. It is quite possible that a straightforward opening would be as suitable or even better than a dramatic one. Each essay should be judged separately. If, say, your essay explores the flaws in the proposed system of national health care in the United States and is written for an economics class, it would be inappropriate to the tone of your essay to begin your economic analysis with a personal story about your family's struggle with an HMO to get proper care for your grandmother. In this example, the use of background, a significant statistic, or just the thesis would be more authoritative than a dramatic opening.

### Basic Patterns for Introductions

One of two basic patterns effectively introduces most essays. The first is the thesis paragraph. In short essays of three to five pages, you may wish to have your thesis sentence stand as the thesis paragraph. This method is direct. It also saves you time on in-class essays. But to many readers, this one-sentence opening is too abrupt. A second type of thesis paragraph is the thesis sentence followed by several sentences that elaborate on it. A third type of thesis paragraph is one in which the thesis statement is made up of several sentences that add up to the main point of the paper. But unless the thesis is complicated and the point would be missed by condensing all the information in one sentence, you should probably restrict the thesis to the one sentence Chapter 2 suggests. You can see from the following example that the second kind of thesis paragraph provides a clean statement of the point of the paper:

> Bilingualism benefits, rather than impairs, ethnic minorities in the United States. Critics of bilingual education strongly believe hastened assimilation helps students become social individuals; however, the literature on first-language retention does not support this view. Most recent studies, in fact, suggest that first language retention facilitates learning English and does not negatively affect one's social mobility. Additionally, rejecting one's native language not only limits opportunities for communication but also contributes to a loss of identity.

The first sentence gives the thesis. The writer is going to argue for the benefits of bilingualism. In this case, the writer has gone on to examine the opposition and to dispute it. The introduction becomes an overview of the essay's main points.

However, since starting right off with the thesis can be too abrupt for some papers, many writers use a second kind of basic pattern for certain essays: they provide a few lead-in sentences to prepare the way for the reader. The content of the lead-in should always be interesting to the audience and should add something to the understanding of the thesis, which normally follows it in the same paragraph. The lead-in is, in some cases, more general than the thesis, but in other cases it draws on a specific detail that might have been included elsewhere in the paper but that has been reserved instead for the introduction. The following introduction includes a lead-in:

> Biology's increasing sophistication has been accompanied by an expansion of its uses and its power. Through the practical applications of biological knowledge, human beings have gained a great amount of control over their lives. They can, for instance, now manipulate the environment, change their lifestyles, and alter themselves permanently both mentally and physically. Beyond the awe most people feel toward these accomplishments, there must be questioning of the uses of this knowledge. Other issues must be raised besides whether something can or cannot be done. The question is whether some of it *should* be done and whether scientists should restrict their research and experimentation if the morality of a particular part of their work is questionable. Scien-

tists must be forced to face up to the moral and ethical implications of their research and experimentation.

The introduction moves from general background on applications of biology (the lead-in) to the specific statement in the thesis about the moral consequences of scientific freedom.

### Effective Strategies for Introductions

Here are eleven effective strategies you can use for beginning an essay.

1. Make a clean statement of the thesis.

> "Everything That Rises Must Converge" by Flannery O'Connor and "Boxes" by Raymond Carver both illustrate the discontent of mothers in their old age and the son's frustration and anger towards his parent for her feelings.

2. Explain your personal interest in or involvement with the subject.

> Between the ages of ten and nineteen, I was a television addict. There was rarely a free moment when I did not have the set on. And, come to think of it, there were busy moments when I had it on, too—cooking dinner, washing my hair, getting dressed. Of course, now being cured, I wonder how I ever watched so often, or more accurately, what made me addicted to television. According to many psychologists who have studied the television habits of children, the television addict shares many of the problems of those with other common forms of addiction, such as excessive drinking and overeating.

3. Explain the divisions and proportions of your topic.

> After living in a small town for five years, I am a changed person from the typical alienated urban person I once was. Many qualities of small-town life have contributed to these changes, which I view as favorable. The key influences on my life here have been political, cultural, and social. But the social influences have been most telling. Small-town life has shown me the human need for solidarity with one's neighbors and the personal value of viewing myself as an integral part of a town.

4. Offer some important background.

> The social and economic conditions in England during the sixteenth century influenced Sir Thomas More to develop his theory of punishment. Farmers had been forced from their homes because their lands were needed for grazing.

They wandered until their funds were depleted; without jobs, they then had no alternative for survival but stealing. The state tried to deter these vagabonds by inflicting a death penalty—hanging—as punishment for theft. It felt obligated to destroy the very thieves it had produced. More, however, suggested an approach which, although it required a restructuring of the economic system, was far more practical and humane.

5. Define your subject.

> Euthanasia is a heatedly debated topic because it involves moral, medical, legal, and social issues. The term "euthanasia" literally means "good death." It entails the deliberate taking of life by injection, overdose prescriptions given by a physician, abatement of life support systems, and withholding of intravenous feeding. The more gruesome acts of euthanasia include self-hanging, gunshot wounds, and overdose on illegal or over-the-counter drugs.
>
> Although I cannot support all these types of euthanasia, given certain qualifications, certain types of euthanasia can prevent the destruction of a family and the interminable pain, both moral and physical, that a suffering terminally ill patient faces.

6. Give an anecdote that raises the issues in your thesis.

> An eighteen-year-old girl goes to the chemistry laboratory of her college, mixes together a few chemicals, and drinks the solution. She is dead on arrival at the community hospital. A twenty-year-old man who attends a prominent East Coast college returns to the dormitory from a late party and slits his wrists. He is found dead in his room on the following morning. Such horrifying events occur more often than we would like to think. The number of youthful suicides has almost doubled in the last ten years. Several psychologists are currently investigating the kinds of personalities that fall victim to this behavior and how much the pressures of college life play a role in the tragedies.

7. Offer an interesting reliable fact or statistic that pertains to your topic.

> After research on 101 HIV-positive hispanic men in Los Angeles, researchers recently found that 75 percent would reveal their status to heterosexual friends whereas 95 percent would do so if the male friend was either homosexual or bisexual. Similarly, there was a higher tendency to reveal their status to family members who already knew about their

sexual orientation, and more reservation when they were unaware of it. Even within families, cultural values such as machismo, simpatico (not causing conflict), and a general disrespect for nonheterosexuals makes the disclosure of this medical condition extremely difficult (Marks, Bundek, Richardson, et al., 1992).

The relevance of this research can be seen when one takes into account the degree of disapproval of nonheterosexual relationships in a given cultural group and the subsequent lack of support that gays and bisexuals may face in that culture. If we are to take an honest look at why AIDS education is not working well in certain communities, we need to include the aspect of culture. The next step in AIDS awareness is for schools to develop a multicultural approach to AIDS education rather than one that avoids culture and tries to present AIDS as strictly a medical issue.

8. Make an analogy that would interest your reader.

Picture a man who plans to move to a foreign city. He imagines that by studying a street map he can learn all about the place. The man is obviously naive. No doubt, the information he has absorbed from the map will help him when he actually arrives at the city, for he will have at least a "book" knowledge of the street layout. But far more than this characterizes a city. The man certainly cannot "know" the landscape, the architecture, or the attitudes of the people until he lives there. Biology students are in a similar situation when they study only textbooks. Although they can learn a certain amount from written descriptions and diagrams, to "know," biology students must actually work with organisms. Laboratory work is therefore an important experience for the biology student because it provides the active and practical scientific investigation that "book" learning alone cannot give.

9. Begin with a quotation that supports or contradicts your main point. Be careful to connect the quotation to your ideas.

According to Mike Rose in *Lives on the Boundary,* the vocational track of schooling places you in a curriculum "that isn't designed to liberate you, but to occupy you." His searing yet insightful autobiographical narrative graphically portrays the attitudes and subsequent behavior patterns that vocational students often adopt for survival. "Students will float to the mark you set," Rose advises teachers. For him, that mark was barely above drowning. Although to some degree, Rose may be unfair in his caricature of vocational education programs, the grim reality is that they often do not challenge their students. Rose's and others' commentary and the available information about the current curriculum in my home town school point out the immediate need to recharacterize public vocational education in this country.

10. Contrast or explain two views.

When one thinks about the art of movie making, one is more likely to think, not of that which is entertaining, but of that which has a purpose, direction, and meaning beyond entertainment. This is what is often called "high art" in movies. The lower art or "popular art" of movies is sheer entertainment. Neither deserves more credibility or praise. However, many critics take an elitist stance, asserting that the only true art is high art. They would not even refer to popular movies as art. This last view needs reevaluation for two reasons: the division between the two is not so clearcut, and each type of art requires a careful analysis of purpose and whether the artists have fulfilled it.

11. Cite your opposition and refute it.

Stress is often associated with the onset of disease. The assumption made by the general public and promoted by some physicians is that the presence of stress is responsible for a weakened (and therefore vulnerable) immune system. In reality, although it appears clear that the existence of stress correlates minimally with disease onset, the exact role of stress in the process is highly controversial. In fact, it appears likely, based on recent medical research, that it is not the avoidance of stress but the development of "hardiness" which should be the medical doctors' focal point; many immunological studies have shown that certain hardy personality types can resist illness despite the presence of intense stress.

12. Quickly describe a position and critique it.

Lindsey, in "Friends as Family," refutes the idea of the family necessarily being of a biological nature, resulting from marriage, and concludes that a family is "chosen" by each person based on the people one chooses to identify and associate with. In coming to this conclusion Lindsey discusses the three myths of marriage: protection and economic security, the promise of permanence, and the spouse as the chosen relative. Lindsey believes that these myths have drawn women to marriage and given them an idealized view of the family. She suggests that women base their choice to marry on these dispensable expectations. Although one could certainly find examples of contemporary women who would fill the mold Lindsey has prepared, Lindsey overgeneralizes and jumps to the conclusion that marriage is unnecessary because of the diverse ways that family can be formed. She misses the point by confusing the issue of family with the issue of marriage.

### Ineffective Strategies for Introductions

Here are some examples of strategies to avoid when beginning an essay.

1. Avoid beginning your paper with a complaint or an apology or a summary of the assignment. This kind of opening produces strikes against the writer right away. It gives readers the impression that one has nothing to say about the subject and causes them to question the value of reading on.

> After reading the three assigned articles on advertising, I am convinced that nobody agrees with anybody else when it comes to morality. Anybody can have a valid argument if they twist the facts right.

2. Avoid beginning your paper with information that is too general, obvious, or irrelevant. Chop off the irrelevant or overly general first sentence. Stay away from the "throughout time," "in our society," and "since the beginning of recorded history" openers, which usually signal a huge generalization. Get right to the point instead.

> The topic of free will has fascinated writers and philosophers for centuries. Boethius discussed free will in the context of attaining happiness. He states that the essence of self-determination is choice over one's state of mind: "Nothing is miserable unless you think it so." In *Troillus and Criseyde* and *The Parliament of Fowls* Geoffrey Chaucer agrees with Boethius that people should take responsibility for their feelings, and in addition comments on the limitations of free will. But overall, Chaucer believes that humans must make their own choices in order to survive.

3. Avoid beginning with too obvious a statement.

> Slavery was one of the main issues of the Civil War.

This kind of beginning not only offends readers but causes them to worry about the writer's authority on the subject. They may utter under their breath, "So what else is new?"

4. Avoid beginning your paper with a literal question that you answer in the next sentence.

> What are the symptoms of diabetes? The symptoms of diabetes are extreme thirst, sudden weight change, and frequent urination.

This type of introduction is repetitive. Leave out the question and state the answer instead. In this example, a question such as "Why are the symptoms of diabetes often overlooked?" might work better.

5. Avoid starting out with a dictionary definition.

> "Hearing" as defined in *Webster's New Collegiate Dictionary* is "the process, function, or power of perceiving sound; the special sense by which noise and tones are received as stimuli." Hearing requires no voluntary thought. Because the process is involuntary, it goes on all the time, and people and other animals always hear what goes on around them. But listening is quite a different thing. It requires voluntary thought; when people listen, they analyze what they hear. While people hear many things, they sort out what is important or interesting and listen only to those things.

A dictionary definition provides a stiff, uninteresting, trite opening for a paper. In addition, the definition is often not helpful to the readers because it is general, worded very formally, and, in most cases, abbreviated. Your own words would flow more naturally and fit the context of your discussion much better than words from the dictionary. In the example, the dictionary definition does not really fit the discussion about voluntary and involuntary listening and hearing. The writer would have done better to begin with the second sentence.

6. Avoid beginning with an introduction that merely repeats the assignment.

> The two essays I will be comparing and contrasting for this paper are "I Become a Student" by Lincoln Steffens on page 81 and "The Marks of an Educated Man" by Alan Simpson on page 117. The underlying theme in both of these essays is the struggle to get an education and to succeed in a profession. Both writers discuss the value of education, the difficulty of getting one in a university, and the true meaning of a liberal arts education.

This sort of introduction is boring and unnecessary. When an assignment is made, there is an understanding between the students and the teacher that it will be carried out, so there is no need to make any reference to it in the essay. The essay should stand on its own. In the example, if the student had left off the first sentence and placed the names of the two authors and the titles of their essays in the second sentence, the introductory paragraph would have been greatly improved.

7. Avoid introducing your paper with an obvious platitude.

> Today in modern America there are issues that are similar yet quite different once the issue has been analyzed. The role of women is a good example.

Platitudes are unimaginative statements empty of meaning that are treated as if they were profound. They are especially harmful in an introduction because readers are likely to put the essay aside, deciding that it has nothing much to say. In the example, the first sentence doesn't say anything. Whoever reads this beginning will probably mutter an annoyed, "So what?"

8. Avoid starting your essay with a reference to the title.

> As the title of this paper indicates, this essay is about the needs of senior citizens. They are a much ignored minority. In actuality, senior citizens could contribute a great deal to the communities they live in. If community leaders would only give senior citizens a chance, senior citizens could make valuable contributions, which at the same time would fulfill their own individual, social, and financial needs.

Because the title of the essay is not part of the essay, it should not be referred to in the introduction. Readers would normally expect the title to refer to the point of the paper, so why bother to say so? They are only put off by such comments. In the example, the writer could have offered some interesting background on the current roles of senior citizens or, if the tone permitted, might have given an anecdote from the life of a typical senior citizen.

---

### Exercises

A. Read an article in a popular magazine. What makes the introduction effective or ineffective? Is there a lead-in introduction? Now look at an introduction from a journal in an academic field. What differences do you note in tone?

B. What are the advantages of placing the thesis at the end of an introduction? What are the disadvantages?

C. What is your reaction to speakers or writers who start their presentations with *"Webster's Dictionary* defines . . ."?

D. Read the following introductions from student essays. Describe the strategy used by referring to points made in this chapter. What specifically makes them poor or good beginnings?

1. What is in a name? An interesting pair of words is "pro-life" and "pro-choice." Each one puts itself in a positive light and simultaneously makes the other appear entirely undesirable. All of this is due to the names the groups have chosen for themselves. They pick names that appeal to emotions.

2. A quite heated and rather strange debate over "political correctness" is raging on college campuses across the country. Someone attending a faculty meeting at the University of Texas might possibly hear an English professor say "Don't use the term classic. It makes me feel oppressed." Meanwhile the student handbook at Connecticut College threatens students with disciplinary measures for "inappropriately directed laughter." How far to go to develop a measure of fairness without interfering with First Amendment rights is the issue at hand.

3. One of the primary means by which popular culture is created in America is through television. The general goal of these popular television programs is light entertainment. Their purpose is more to reinforce a popular ideology than to challenge it. Reinforcing an ideology many times means avoiding the real issues at hand. Television's limited view of the world tends to create a superficial reality that prevents citizens from thinking deeply about complex social issues.

4. Many similarities and differences can be found between European and American celebrations. What are some of the similarities between the European celebration of Christmas and the American celebration? Some of the main similarities include the festive atmosphere, the sharing of gifts, and the eating of special goodies.

E. Which types of introductions might best appeal to the groups of people named for each of the following thesis statements? Why?

1. People living in the inner city should form renters' unions to protect themselves from infringements of their rights by absentee landlords and to inform themselves of their responsibilities.
   a. In-residence owners of apartment buildings
   b. A group of renters from an inner-city neighborhood

2. Legalized gambling in our state offers more advantages than disadvantages.
   a. A group of business people
   b. A group of homemakers

3. No matter how much money a family has to spend, planning a budget for a vacation will ultimately save time, money, and anxiety.
   a. Families
   b. Members of a singles' tour group

F. Go to a dictionary of quotations or other source and find appropriate quotations that could be used as lead-ins for two of the following assertions.

1. There should be a required college course entitled "identity crises."
2. Speech codes on college campuses are unethical.
3. Selfishness can be either constructive or destructive.
4. Teaching assistants should not be permitted to grade students' work.

G. How would you characterize the writer's attitude toward the subject based on the following introductions? Does the writer intend to be serious, sarcastic, humorous? What tone might readers expect in the essay?

1. "I'm going to take your blood," she said as though that was something someone says to me every day. I'm not a character in a Count Dracula movie, and on the average day I'm far too busy with my social life to be running to the doctor. I'm sure, however, she said it to people every day. In any case, I wasn't very thrilled to hear it. So I closed my eyes, held my breath, then screeeeeeeeeeamed! A few minutes later she stuck the needle in me. It wasn't so bad. She told me to return in a few days for the results. I didn't really care what the results were; I now had a name for this emerging disease: mononucleosis. Convinced in the past three minutes that I had become almost deathly ill, I hobbled back to my residence hall, holding my medicine feebly in one hand. I made sure everyone who passed me noticed the medicine, and my frail walk. Although this was an act, as time progressed it became a more accurate depiction, transporting me from an energetic, independent college woman back to the dependent little girl who needed her mommy. It was a journey that is humorous in retrospect but one that helped me take myself seriously, ultimately forcing me to reassess my goals and my image.

2. The gavel determined my fate as it struck the oak podium. The next two years of my life would be spent far away from my home, and I was still numb. As I turned to gather my belongings, I looked up to see my mother and found her crying. I remembered, after nine years of forgetting, that she loved me. Feeling my mother's warmth made me recall the accident. I thought of the night that a man lay on the ground, a product of my vengeance on the world. Victim to the anger I unleashed upon society resulting from the death of a sister and grandfather, and the disappearance of a father, here I was, but I was not alone. I took an oath to change my life. To this day, I hold that morning in court as a turning point away from an unstable past.

H. For each of the following introductions, excerpted from professional essays, try to identify the strategy. Is it successful? Do you want to read on?

1. You can get a hint concerning the higher purposes of communication by looking at the word itself. "Communication" is much more closely related to the word "community" than it is to any of the instruments of communication which man has created, such as language, radio, and pictorial or dramatic art. This point suggests that you will miss the deeper meaning of communication if you allow yourself to think only of the machinery of communication. You might get a further hint if you really examine the meaning of the word "community." (Lyle L. Miller and Alice Z. Seeman, "Concepts of Communication," *Guidebook for Prospective Teachers*)

2. The six-year-old child who succeeds in repairing his broken bicycle bell has a creative experience, New York University psychologist Morris I. Stein is fond of pointing out, but no one would claim that the repaired bell constitutes a "creative product" in the generally accepted meaning

of the term. It is possible, in other words, to differentiate roughly between individual creativity and social creativity. If you have an idea, it may be creative in comparison to all the other ideas you have ever had, which certainly represents individual creativity, or it may be creative in comparison to all the ideas everyone has ever had; this represents social creativity of the highest order. (Helen Rowan, "How to Produce an Idea," *IBM Corporation Magazine*)

3. Scientists, above all, are supposed to be honest. Politicians and advertising copywriters are expected to distort facts, but if a scientist falsifies a single record, he commits an unforgivable crime. Yet the sad fact is that the history of science teems with cases of outright fakery and instances of scientists who saw their data only through the distorting lenses of passionately held beliefs. (Martin Gardner, "Great Fakes of Science," *Esquire*)

## WRITING GOOD CONCLUSIONS

With the introduction out of the way, the draft is nearly complete. Why is it that so often writers feel stumped at this point? It's common to hear students facing a deadline say about their papers, "It's done—I just need a conclusion." One possible explanation for delaying the conclusion is that the writer might need some time for incubation on the question "What exactly do I conclude from what I have written?" Another is that perhaps nothing more really needs to be said. The paper feels complete to the student, but he or she feels a certain anxiety, having been trained to include a conclusion. Whatever the reasons, the conclusion, at least for some writers, is the most difficult part of the essay to write well. But that need not be the case if you consider the purpose of your conclusion for a particular essay and take advantage of the strategies often used by writers to form effective conclusions, which are described later in this chapter.

The conclusion conveys a sense of completion to your readers, reinforces your central point, and ties together the different parts of the paper. Therefore, most of the time your papers will benefit from a conclusion. Every essay should have a smooth and finished feeling about it; it should never just come to a halt. But not every paper requires an elaborate ending. If you have written an essay, especially a brief one that seems complete, you probably would not add a formal conclusion. Moreover, your conclusion should not just be tacked on to whatever point comes last in the paper. Unless the paper is arranged in a logical order and each point is fully developed to the advantage of the thesis, the end of the paper will seem abrupt, no matter how you conclude. For the best possible ending, with or without a conclusion, the body of the essay itself has to be well formed.

You will want to evaluate whether each essay you write requires a conclusion. One clue is length. Very short papers with complete thesis statements that set out the controlling ideas specifically and with clear paragraph divisions may seem boring if a summary conclusion is added. However, if you have something to add, even to a short paper, and you think that the idea naturally grows out of the previous discussion, the conclusion will probably be effective.

The best way to write a conclusion is to reread your paper before you compose the ending. This process will freshen your awareness of the points in the essay and allow you to fit your conclusion to your purpose. Having a good idea of what you have written can help you avoid tacking on a mechanical and unenthusiastic ending that seems to say, "Let's get this assignment over with."

Just how long should your conclusion be? In a short paper of no more than five pages, a single paragraph can suffice; in a longer essay, you might want to write up to a whole page. Unless the essay is lengthy, you probably do not want to write much more than a page conclusion because you risk digressing from your main subject; you may, in effect, find yourself beginning a new essay. One way of judging the length of the conclusion is to make it proportionate with the introduction.

Exactly what you say at the end of the paper will depend on such things as your original purpose, conventions for conclusions in your discipline (your sense of what your audience expects), and the quantity and variety of information brought together in the essay. Keep in mind two hints when you choose a strategy for writing a particular conclusion:

You want your audience to be stimulated by the conclusion.
You want your paper to seem complete

### Basic Patterns for Conclusions

One of two basic patterns is suitable for most conclusions: the summary or the lead-out. In the *summary,* you simply restate the thesis in other words or summarize your main points. Whether you will need only one sentence, a group of sentences, or several paragraphs depends on the complexity of the summary. However, summaries often seem forced and unnecessary. They should be avoided in most short papers and used only in papers where a restatement or summary contributes to your audience's understanding of the paper as a whole.

The *lead-out* begins with a point that acts as a transition between the body of the paper and an interesting related idea, anecdote, quotation, analogy, or question. The main point of using the lead-out pattern is to make a connection between your thesis and some other idea that will stimulate the readers to continue to think about the paper after they have finished it. Whether the information in the lead-out conclusion is arranged from the general to the specific or the specific to the general depends on how general or specific your related idea is compared to your essay's main point.

An example of a typical lead-out conclusion from an essay follows. The thesis of the essay is that using leisure time well is an important ingredient in everyone's life. This student explains various productive ways of using leisure time and shows the need for leisure. After tying up the main points in the essay, the student continues with an implication of what has been discussed in the paper:

> Leisure time, then, is more than just time with nothing to do. In fact, there are many things to be done during this so-called free time. There are no set rules, of course, for what qualifies as leisure because what might be leisure for one person might not be for another. In any case, leisure is never what one considers "work." For instance, many people would consider a game of tennis to be leisure, but to the professional tennis player, it would be work. The tennis player would probably find leisure in something else. The many ways to spend leisure time are up to each person to discover, and they all share the same rewards: a healthy, clear mind and a strong, refreshed body.

The student draws on the suggestions from the essay and mentions what they all have in common in the last sentence. You can feel how the paragraph gradually leads out of the body of the essay and deals generally with the value of leisure for each person.

### Effective Strategies for Conclusions

Here are some basic strategies you can use in concluding your essay.

1. Restate the thesis in new words. An essay with the thesis that "television sitcom coverage of social problems is counterproductive to awareness building in the public" ended this way.

> Many social problems in the United States never become clear to the television viewing public because the shows' purpose is more to entertain than to present the nuances of complex social problems so that the society will respond with an answer.

2. Summarize the main points of the essay. An essay with the thesis "The new optimism for Jews in Poland seems to imply a bright future where Poles and Jews recognize their shared history" concluded:

> The Jewish community in Poland barely survived the devastation and repression of the past twenty years. But now, rather than focus on divisiveness, the Poles and Jews are rebuilding their mutual history. Jewish community centers and schools have sprung up as well as libraries, student unions, and recreational organizations, and with these the constant reawakening of Polish Jews who are discovering their hidden roots. The new focus is on the joy of Jewish life rather than on oppression, but the degree of suffering the entire society witnessed in the 80's stands as a constant reminder to families not to repeat the horror. Therefore, optimism is warranted.

3. Offer an analogy that reinforces your main point. An essay on "the blend of inspiration and knowledge needed by the poet" had the following conclusion:

> Writing poetry, then, takes more than imagination. It takes some knowledge of form. You could no more expect someone to write a good poem solely on the basis of inspiration than you could expect someone to build a house because he or she had a good idea for one. Of course, you realize that building a house is a technical matter. The builder needs to know the subtle interworkings of the materials at every phase of the process. So too, poets are deliberate about what they build with words, and they must work from a broad foundation of knowledge.

4. Add a final quotation that sums up your point well.

An essay on "obscenity in rap" reminds us in the conclusion that the influences on youth by this sort of violence to the mind may not be simply free artistic expression.

> "Whether you call it *decadent art* is not the issue," points out Philip Lehmer, a psychologist at the Center for the Child, a nonprofit counseling center for family problems in the inner city. "Intellectuals become sidetracked by what to name this social phenomenon and forget that their kids are out tonight blasting their radios and singing along—these are the same kids they have been trying to teach respect at home. Parents need to look beyond their own interactions with their children to see the center of the budding immorality. It's not like in the old days when such lessons began and ended at home. The center cannot hold when the heros, the guys who make it, are smut dealers." Arguing that the right to self-expression should not be violated can go only so far. It is time to create some limits.

5. Suggest possible solutions, alternatives, or policies. An essay with the thesis "Noxious noise pollution in prisons should be controlled because it creates an anxiety-ridden environment similar to that in overcrowding, promoting anger, violence, and rioting" ended this way.

> Prison life is traumatic and rigorous. Overstimulation of the senses is a major cause of depression and violent disturbance. One possible solution is inmate group rotation, whereby individuals are placed together based on psychological profiles. If inmates are categorized in groups according to interests and sleeping patterns, it might cut down on the amount

of noxious stimuli for that certain group, and individual in-mates might be better able to cope within their environment. Large-scale testing is costly, however, and for many prisons would be unrealistic; perhaps beginning programs on a small scale would be the answer to arriving at a less costly adapta-tion of the complex procedure now being proposed by prison administrators. Ultimately the cost must be weighed against the consequences of the current level of inaction.

6. Predict the outcome of a situation or warn the readers of possible effects of a situation under discussion in the essay. An essay on "the danger of antidepressant use in the society at large" ended with a warning:

> Although to some degree the onslaught of public criti-cism of Prozac and other antidepressant drugs as responsible for violent and suicidal behaviors is not well founded, we must look at the social control that prevalent use of such drugs suggests. We must ask ourselves whether we want to desensitize and normalize the public to the degree that id-iosyncratic character traits begin to disappear from the treated population. Who will be the Van Goghs, the Billie Holidays of our future generations if we produce chemically a society that is happy and homogeneous? We must deter-mine the social costs and benefits of such a society, includ-ing an investigation of the link between intense emotion and creative impulse.

7. Offer a reminder of the context of your argument. Reminding the reader of the larger problem from which you extracted your ar-gument drives home the importance of your ideas. Placing your ideas in perspective shows that your point develops one of the many directions implied by your topic. In this kind of conclu-sion you explain the relationship between the problem at hand and other related problems. Be careful not to get off the track and onto a new subject.

8. Refer to the introduction. Bringing your argument full circle gives the readers a satisfied feeling, a sense that the point of the essay has been brought around to its natural completion with all the loose ends tied up neatly. If you have, for instance, begun the es-say with an anecdote that leads into the thesis, you might con-clude by referring to the anecdote, noting how much it reflects your conclusions on the matter under discussion. If you have be-gun the essay with a question or have from the start posed a prob-lem, the most appropriate conclusion might include a quick ref-erence to the question or problem and a direct statement of your

answer or a possible solution. An essay that began with several quotations from a survey by Hirsch on "the one quality that characterizes a good marriage" had the thesis that a successful marriage requires a lot more than just love. In the conclusion the writer returned to the quotations noted in the introduction of the essay and used them to tie up the paper:

> Love is not enough, it would seem, to sustain a relationship. Hirsch is accurate in his findings, then, that many characteristics, not one—and certainly not just love—keep a relationship going. With love the relationship is set in force: with "friendship" and "security" and "shared values" the relationship keeps spinning.

### Ineffective Strategies for Conclusions

Here are some examples of strategies *not* to use when writing a conclusion.

1. Avoid conclusions that telegraph what they are:

> In conclusion . . .

This one is permissible in a formal speech, but in most college essays such overt signals are obtrusive.

> This paper has attempted to show that . . .

Any reader knows that the point of a paper is to show something.

> My paper has discussed . . .

The readers say, "We know, we know."

2. Avoid conclusions that open up a whole new topic. Your conclusion should tie up your ideas and may possibly offer an implication from them, but you should not introduce any points that are far removed from the discussion in the body of the essay and that would be, in effect, theses of new essays. Because you do not have the space for elaboration on new ideas in the conclusion, any related thoughts you present must be understandable to your readers without elaboration. For instance, if the essay you have written shows that "self-defense for women requires more than physical strategy," you should not conclude with "Every college campus should offer a series of classes on the emotional and physical aspects of self-defense." A whole new paper would be needed to substantiate that point, and there is no information in the body of the essay that logically leads the readers to the conclusion. A

better conclusion might be derived from one of the other strategies—perhaps, for example, you might quote an expert in Karate on the spiritual and psychological aspects of the discipline.

3. Avoid conclusions that apologize. Apologies are inappropriate conclusions because they diminish the authority of the writer. Readers should have confidence in the writer. Therefore, apologizing for a lack of information, for a rushed presentation, or for poor typing undermines the effectiveness of the essay.

4. Avoid conclusions that offer platitudes or panaceas. Pat answers to complicated problems and trite overgeneralizing should be avoided in all writing. If you slip a cliché into the conclusion, your readers will probably think all the writing is insincere. A conclusion should be tailored to the point of the paper. Tacking on an obviously held belief or a sweeping generalization to cover the end of your essay is ineffective; it does not deal honestly with the material and comes to terms with nothing. Instead, it substitutes something that could fit any number of essays. Thus the conclusion is valueless. For an example of what to avoid, take a look at the following conclusions:

> The country ought to look into this problem seriously because it represents a threat to the American way.
> But we're all human, aren't we? What will the future bring?

Of course, neither conclusion means very much; both should be avoided.

---

### Exercises

A. How might the conclusion of a paper written by a team of students reflect the tone of the various sections of the paper?
B. What is wrong with the conclusions below? Rewrite each of them so that it is effective.
   1. In conclusion, the only way of thinking in which we are not concerned with ourselves is "creative thinking." This way of thinking might enable us to learn. At least we should admit the value of objective thinking so that we might be able to separate our own opinions and prejudices from the evidence before us.
   2. This essay has attempted to show the insignificance of Corben's argument that water shortages are inevitable.
   3. Marx's definition of a rebel is as valid as any other definition, in my opinion.

C. Take the conclusion from an essay you have already written and rewrite it using a different strategy.

D. Describe some of the ways you might create a transition between the body of the essay and the conclusion. To answer this question, you may wish to review some of the discussion on transitions on page 103. Is there anything special you would have to keep in mind when developing a transition between the body and the conclusion?

E. Read an article in a popular magazine. How does it end? Would its strategy for the conclusion be effective for a research paper? Why or why not?

# 3

# REVISING

# HOW MUCH SHOULD YOU REVISE?

Good writing, even for most professional writers, seldom happens the first time a piece is developed. When you are preparing the initial draft of your essay, you are probably so concerned with proving or developing your ideas that you pay little attention to some of the finer points of writing. There is nothing wrong with this attitude; that is exactly what you should be doing during the first draft. But if you want your essay to be more polished, more professional, you need to take the next step of addressing yourself to the serious activity of revision.

You have probably heard someone say that there is no good writing, only good rewriting. And you have probably wondered just why you have to rewrite something that has already demanded so much time and thought. Carefully planned rewriting need not be a difficult task; in fact, it can be exciting to see just how much you can improve what you have already done. If you approach the task correctly, you will almost certainly turn an ordinary piece of writing into something that is much more effective.

## USING THE COMPUTER FOR REVISION

Most writers agree that writing on the computer promotes revision. Students report that they complete many more drafts when they write on the computer because manipulating text is so much less laborious than with typing. Capabilities such as split screens to compare versions of paragraphs and "save" options that permit you to return to your earlier draft if you prefer it to the revised one dramatically facilitate the process. Electronic mail systems have even made it possible for students to generate rough drafts, mail them to a professor or another student for feedback, have the evaluator insert his or her comments right into the text of the paper on the screen, and receive the commentary back in time to revise the paper before handing in the final draft. Many word-processing programs offer revision aids, including tools that flag repeated words and phrases, wordiness, lack of sentence variety, and so on. However, these tools must be applied carefully. The computer can flag a suspicious word, sentence, or paragraph, but it is the writer who must use judgment in evaluating the offending item and deciding whether to change it.

Except for minor changes, the most effective method for making revisions on the computer is to print out a hard copy, make your changes on it, enter the changes into the computer, and then evaluate the effectiveness of the revisions. Reading on the computer screen is difficult for most writers because of its limited size. Writers tend to lose their place and spend an inordinate amount of time hunting for text to be revised, added, or deleted. Scrolling up and down and trying to remember various versions of a sentence in the process of revision can be truly frustrating. The advantage of printing a hard copy is that you can check one version against the next and check all the pages of your paper at a glance.

## SHARING YOUR WRITING WITH OTHERS—PEER EVALUATION

An important part of revising is showing a rough draft to a classmate, to your writing center, or perhaps to your professor before preparing your final draft. On your own you can identify many needed revisions but not all. It is easier for someone else to identify unclear statements, inaccurate evidence, and confusing structure. By the time that you as the writer get to revising, you may simply be too close to the material and too comfortable with your own style to identify certain problems with the text.

It makes perfect sense for someone else to read what you write; after all, writing is communication, so someone other than the author needs

to test whether the paper communicates effectively. Why wait until it is graded to find out? Readers can make suggestions in a supportive and unintimidating fashion. And by making the required revisions, you not only produce a better essay but learn something about writing in the process. You can also learn about what succeeds in your piece of writing. Most learners gain a great deal more from knowing what they did well than from having only their errors pointed out.

The idea of sharing writing with a classmate or teacher can be momentarily threatening. But when an evaluator adopts the proper attitude, most writers get hooked—they find that sharing their drafts becomes a natural part of the writing process. In fact, most writers feel that they intuitively learn about writing by observing how others write. When two students complete the same assignment a bit differently, they can compare approaches. You might need to be the one to initiate an informal sharing of papers among friends in a particular class. If you provide a positive role model, commenting in a helpful way and supporting the positive features of what you read, others are likely to follow your lead when they evaluate your paper.

Descriptive outlines are an extremely helpful aspect of an evaluator's commentary. In this technique, the evaluator writes in the margin what amounts to a brief summary of your essay as he or she reads. It is a good idea for the evaluator to number these points and to label the thesis statement so that the descriptive outline can be differentiated from marginal suggestions. Note how Ben creates a descriptive outline by numbering the main points of Chris's paper in the margin (see Figure 6-1 on page 163). His description of the points Chris makes in her first draft lead him to conclude that there is not enough compelling evidence for her thesis—see his final remarks at the end of the first draft on p. 164. From the descriptive outline, you can feel sure that you and the evaluator share a common interpretation of the essay's content. Where ideas are unclear or your interpretations differ, a change to the text—or at least scrutiny of it—is probably in order. Once you are sure that you fundamentally agree on the thesis and support pattern established in the paper, you can discuss in greater depth whatever criticisms have arisen in the evaluator's mind.

When a classmate evaluates your writing, you do not want him or her to get sidetracked by surface errors such as spelling, punctuation, or picayune word choice. Ask your evaluator instead to concentrate on structure and development of ideas, feeling free to refer to particular confusing words and statements.

Several important structural and logical concepts will be the heart of the evaluation. Request that the evaluator keep in mind the following eleven questions that introduce the following sections.

### 1. Is the Thesis Reasonable?

The paper cannot be logical unless the thesis is reasonable. First, make sure the assertion is not, in itself, so obvious that it is not worth expanding. Something that people already take for granted should not be the basis of a college paper because it would not interest an academic reader. Nor would there be any purpose in writing a paper on an obvious point.

*Too obvious: Alice in Wonderland* is more than a children's story.

This is a simple fact. Just giving examples of it would not make for a good paper. A better approach might be to analyze the symbol of the looking glass as a "reflection" of the politics of the day.

The evaluator should also check the wording of the thesis. Even though the statement contains an opinion, it should be expressed unemotionally, and it should not be all-inclusive. An all-inclusive thesis is often tipped off by such words as *all, every, always,* and *must.* As alternatives, the evaluator can suggest such moderating words as *many, some, often,* and *could.* Here is an example of how an all-inclusive thesis could be modified:

> *Ineffective:* Participating in medical research studies never directly benefits the patient because the studies are based on the profit motives of drug companies rather than on good will. The patient gets no real information about the treatment, and the treatments are often dangerous or even deadly.

> *Effective:* Participating in medical research studies generally does not benefit the patient because the studies are based on the profit motives of drug companies rather than on good will. The patient therefore gets little information about the treatment, and treatments can even be dangerous or even deadly.

### 2. Does Each Support Defend the Thesis?

Any support that does not defend the thesis or clarify some point needed to defend the thesis should be thrown out. As you check your partner's essay and he or she checks yours, you should be on the lookout for three major types of support problems: supports that merely restate the thesis, supports that contradict the thesis or another support, and supports that extend beyond the scope of the thesis instead of defending it. The first problem is often called circular reasoning because it gets the reader nowhere. Notice how the problem occurs in the following supports extracted from one student evaluator's descriptive outline:

> *Thesis:* Bicycle paths should be provided in all major cities to help reduce pollution.
>    1. Bicycle paths would encourage more people to ride bicycles instead of drive cars.
>    2. Bicycle paths would be a part of an effort to reduce pollution levels.

The first support is good. Point 2, however, merely restates the thesis. Instead, it should give another example of how bicycle paths could help reduce pollution. Let's look at one more example of circular reasoning:

> *Thesis:* Life in the barrio teaches young children to survive by using their wits to size up and handle social situations.
>    1. Learning to get respect from peers
>    2. Learning how to get what they need from their families
>    3. Learning how to deal with police and bill collectors
>    4. Analyzing social situations to help them survive

In this example, the first three points are effective. The fourth, however, merely repeats the thesis. The fact that it is more general than the other supports is a good clue that it does not belong.

Contradictory statements are fairly easy for an evaluator to notice when completing a descriptive outline, yet buried in a paragraph they may "sound" just fine to the writer. Uncovering such contradictions can be extremely important to the success of a paper.

Sometimes writers make statements that extend beyond the scope of the thesis. Because they believe in the ideas they set forth, they may assume too much. Even though a writer may wholeheartedly believe in a thesis, he or she should not draw implications from the thesis statement, or from any other statement for that matter, before it has been fully explained and supported. An evaluator can catch this problem in the rough draft. Here is the basic descriptive outline for one student's essay. Can you see where the implications extend beyond the thesis?

*Thesis:* Vocational education programs will continue to succeed because they are more practical than liberal arts programs, are open to anyone, and provide a variety of opportunities for people who once thought they had none.
1. More practical than liberal arts
   Emphasize skills, not ideas
   Skills produce more job offers than ideas do
   Good opportunity for someone who already has a liberal arts education and wants something else
2. Open to anyone
   Anyone who is eighteen years old or older and applies for the program gets in
   No educational prerequisites
   No cutoff age
3. Success of vocational education may eventually diminish the interest in liberal arts programs
4. Success of vocational programs will call for tremendous expansion in the programs
   New programs to fit the needs of the future
   Expansion of current programs
   Government funds to be increased for purpose of expansion

The first two main ideas bear out the controlling idea of the thesis statement. The last two, however, expand on the assertion in the thesis rather than support it. They assume that the thesis has already been proven. Only in the conclusion of the essay is there room for the sort of speculation called for in the last two points. You might also have noticed that although the first two supports are based on the first two parts of the controlling idea of the thesis, the third Part—that vocational educational programs "provide a variety of opportunities for people who once thought they had none"—is not treated at all. It should be included in place of the unacceptable supports.

### 3. Has the Thesis Been Proven Step by Step?

Has the writer included all the points necessary to logically prove the thesis? Something that the writer thinks is obvious may not be so obvious to the readers. Look at the following passage from the rough draft of an essay:

"A ghetto star is a neighborhood celebrity known for gang-banging, drug selling, and so on," says Shakur (4). These stars, as well as the promise of material wealth, serve young people with a way to gain all that they feel is lacking in their lives. The riches that children see in the media, especially when they live in low-income environments, appear to be untouchable dreams that can only become available to them through gangs. Islands points out that those who became involved with gangs "most often gave as their reason the belief that it [sic] would provide them with an environment that would increase their chances of securing money (40)." The quote supports the idea that temptation is too much for youths to bear. My friend David 2 explained this to me with this example, "My mom worked every day to put food on the table and dress us. I could do what she did in two weeks, in two days. How are you going to tell me what I'm doing is wrong? Isn't living in a neighborhood where most of us die young doing me and my family wrong?" The dream of a better life consumes us all, and in David 2's case consumed him with three shots from a .45. The reality of it all is that the chances for advancement are more realistic to these men through dealing than through education.

A reader may not automatically make all the connections that Richard is implying in his paper. His thesis, contrary to that of many sociologists, is that fear of death and inner conflict are not deterrents to gang involvement. He raises several points here that could support the thesis, including the desperation of inner city youths faced with poverty and overworked parents, the limited options they will consider—including the failure to see education as a link to success and money, and, underlying all, the hopelessness and devaluing of their own lives since youthful death is common. Each of these topics makes an important contribution to the thesis, but only if it is discussed fully and linked to the others. In Richard's paper, the readers have to make the jump from hopeless devaluing of life back to being willing to take risks with their own lives that will bring them money so they can take care of their family. The connection between the delayed gratification that comes of education and the devalued life is also not established. These are excellent perceptions, and if the writer had provided all the necessary links in his thought process, the reader would have been impressed with the depth and complexity of the argument. However, without the links, the gaps in the argument confuse the reader.

With your peer evaluator reviewing the rough draft of your essay as a preliminary reader, you can receive information on how clear you have been in your paper; it is easier for someone other than the writer to find gaps in development of an argument.

### 4. Are Underlying Assumptions Clear?

Many of the statements writers make in essays are based on certain assumptions. Those assumptions that the audience accepts as obvious do not need to be stated. However, any other assumptions must be substantiated. It can be difficult for the writer to spot certain underlying assumptions because they may be firmly held opinions, but an evaluator can better realize that readers may not hold the same views.

Two problems can arise if you do not clarify your underlying assumptions. First, your readers might miss your point because they would not understand how you arrived at it. Second, even if they could infer what you mean, they might so disagree with what you imply that they would refuse to read on. Take the following statement, for example:

> Children forced to go to day care do not thrive as well as those remaining under a mother's care.

The statement implies that mothers alone care for children (leaving out fathers and extended family altogether) and also that no one would *choose* to send a child to day care—that the parent is "forced" to do so. This prejudice against day care would stand in the way of looking at the subject fully; it's almost as if the writer presumes he or she has proven the argument simply by asserting it. This case is relatively mild in terms of bias, however, in comparison with the next example, which illustrates what can happen if one chooses to write about a highly charged subject about which one holds deep and unyielding convictions. Take a look at the following sentence from a student's essay on AIDS:

> AIDS is more than a physical disease; it is a moral scourge on humanity for its recklessness and perversity.

This sentence implies a value judgment that is not explained or supported. The underlying assumption is that those who get AIDS are necessarily sexually promiscuous and deviant. The sentence also suggests that diseases are imposed by a supernatural force as retribution for sins. Both these ideas would require careful discussion because the writer and readers could have different definitions of promiscuity and deviance and different moral/intellectual foundations. The writer would have to show why he or she thinks it is immoral to make certain kinds of sexual choices. If the writer is taking a religious stand, and the audience would be likely to accept it as well, the writer can simply state openly that he or she is writing "from a religious standpoint." But if the audience is not likely to accept such a stance, the writer would have to show a cause-and-effect connection between "immoral" behavior and the disease. Underlying assumptions can be tested by asking, "What do readers who disagree think, and to what extent is their stance valid as well?" Because readers may not share every aspect of the writer's opinion, he or she would need to develop the argument carefully and cite opposition along the way—or write on some other aspect of the topic about which he or she is less biased.

### 5. Are All the Points Within Reason?

Have you ever noticed that a person may be socially undesirable—a car thief, for instance—yet still be an honest and caring parent? Most people are not either angelic or devilish, happy or unhappy, energetic or lazy. Instead, they generally fall into categories somewhere between the extremes. The same is true of ideas. Because there is usually more than one explanation for a problem and more than one way to see an issue, a writer should avoid making statements that are either-or judgments. A dogmatic stand can undermine the proof of a thesis. For instance, in a paper on the possibility of socialized medicine in the United States, a student might write that we can have either socialized medicine and communism or our present medical system and democracy, but not socialized medicine and democracy. Such a statement is not within reason; it sets up two extremes and connects them with the word *or*. Most readers would realize that the alternatives are not so rigidly opposed and that some sort of coexistence is possible; the Canadian system gives evidence of this.

Those who think in either-or patterns tend to press the panic button immediately. Their language becomes overly emotional and the readers tend to discredit what they have to say. Notice the unfortunate effects of the following statements:

> When we acquitted O. J. Simpson, we proved there is no justice in America.
>
> If we see Vietnam as a partner in trade, we forget about the horrors of the Vietnam War.

Such exaggerated assertions are difficult to defend. At best they oversimplify the intended point, and at worst they falsify it. As your evaluator checks over your paper, make sure that he or she considers your points from as many angles as possible so that the ones you present are reasonable.

### 6. Do the Abstractions Reveal the Writer's Meaning?

An abstraction is a quality or concept that does not directly correspond with any physical object. However, abstractions may be illustrated by concrete or specific examples. You cannot conjure up in your mind a picture of rage, the abstraction itself, although you could certainly think of an instance in which you were enraged. You might see the look on your face at the moment or picture the circumstances surrounding your anger, but those pictures are not rage.

*Love, reality, freedom, identity, sense of community, beautiful, bad, politically correct, successful,* and *powerful* are a few of the abstract words common in college essays. Nothing is wrong with using such words; in fact, they are usually necessary in all but the simplest discussions. But logical problems can occur if readers do not have the same definition of the abstractions as the writer or if the writer has not settled on one meaning for an abstraction. And this is where an evaluator can help.

Suppose you come up with the following statement: Although I was born in Spain, *mentally and spiritually* I am an American. Because this topic is close to your heart, you understand just what you mean by the italicized phrase. But your readers may not. Do you mean by *mentally* that you are éducated in an American fashion that stresses participation in the classroom? That you think about the same things most Americans tend to think about? Or even that you believe yourself (in your mind) to be an American? What is the distinction between that definition and *spiritually*? Does *spiritually* refer to one of the major American religions? Does it mean that you are very patriotic? Could it refer to what some consider a lack of spirituality? Could it mean that you like to eat hot dogs and drink beer on July 4? Obviously, the sentence has been taken out of the context of a whole student essay, and reading the paper would provide some contextual clues to help define these abstractions. However, it's still safe to say that your reader should not be lost, even momentarily, in your essay. It would improve the essay to define the terms by stating exactly which mental processes were being referred to, what spiritual affiliations were suggested, and what the differences were between them.

An evaluator can quickly determine whether the context of an abstraction causes the word to mean only one possible thing. If so, it probably need not be defined. Also, if the piece is for a particular audience who shares the writer's definitions, the abstractions will probably be clear enough. However, if an abstraction does require clarification, the writer can take one of three courses: replace the abstraction with concrete words, replace the abstraction with specifics, or keep the abstraction but explain it so that the audience knows the definition being used.

There is a subtle distinction between concrete words and specific words. Specifics often help define abstractions. For example, the abstraction "sexual harassment" has received a great deal of attention lately. Colleges and universities have developed policies concerning it. In finding the need to clarify the abstraction, committees at these schools inevitably list in their policy statements the specific behaviors that constitute harassment. One statement lists, among other behaviors, "subtle pressure for sexual activity, including flirtation, invitations, and sexual suggestions." Similarly, student handbooks often call for "academic honesty." This abstraction is then followed by a list of specific behaviors such as "acknowledging and identifying the sources of borrowed material."

Concrete language is often more specific than the language in abstractions, but that's not what makes it concrete. The quality of concreteness belongs to language that directly corresponds to physical objects and is expressed by reference to the senses. "As warm as a motor revving up," "icy," and "blinding light" are all concrete images. Thus, the abstraction *beautiful* as in "a beautiful day" might be clarified by describing the day with the more concrete words "sunny and crisp."

Frequently, the unqualified use of abstract words is accompanied by highly emotional language. Such a combination, of course, is no substitute for reason and can destroy the consistency of an essay's tone. But emotional language and abstractions are all around us, in the advertising we read and the political rhetoric we hear. Worse, the combination seems to convince some people. You can see how members of an audience might attach whatever personal meaning they want to abstractions; they can, in essence, hear what they want to hear rather than listen closely to what is said. And the emotionalism in the language seems to carry it. For example, in the sentence, "The justice, humanity, and natural greatness of the American people is never to be denied," there are three abstractions composing the main part of the sentence. Each is emotionally charged, not to mention excessive (note the use of *never* and the strong word *denied*). What does the writer or speaker really mean? Is he or she merely playing a trick on the audience, intending only to move the emotions? It's hard to tell for sure.

In a well-known essay, "Politics and the English Language," George Orwell points out that language can be used in many ways to hide rather than reveal the writer's true meaning. But trickery is not the goal of the academic writer, who does all he or she can to explain, as honestly and clearly as possible, what is on his or her mind. College writing appeals, furthermore, to a rational audience, and few in that group would settle for straight emotionalism. Academic writers are more likely to lose control over their emotional reactions to the paper's subject matter. An alert evaluator can point out this problem and help the writer revise.

### 7. Has the Writer Acknowledged Opposing Viewpoints?

Either-or thinking often goes along with a failure to recognize the views of the opposition. You should be aware of ideas concerning your topic that disagree with your own. In Chapter 2 citing the claims of the opposition was mentioned in developing the thesis. But if the claims are important, you should also remember to discuss them in the body of the essay. Deliberately leaving out mention of opposing viewpoints is likely to cause your readers to think that you are not familiar enough with your subject to fully defend your ideas.

If, upon suggesting the validity of opposing ideas not included in your paper, an evaluator does find weaknesses in your argument, you should not be afraid to adjust it and even to alter your thesis. Your efforts up to this point will not have been wasted, because you will have gained greater insight into your topic, which can serve as the basis for a new paper. Fortunately, your evaluator will not usually identify a need for such a complete revision. More often, you and the evaluator will feel that most of the opposing ideas are indefensible. It is likely, though, that while you do not agree with some of the opposing ideas, others— whether you have mentioned them or not in the draft the evaluator has reviewed—are worth validating. In this case, your paper may be restructured so that although you point out the value of certain opposing viewpoints, you demonstrate the equal or greater value of your own thesis. Frequently, opposing statements are found in subordinate clauses in the actual paper because, as you will see in Chapter 7, such structures deemphasize the points contained in them. You would want to emphasize your point and de-emphasize your opposition's in most cases. Here are some statements from students' essays. Notice how they effectively treat opposing viewpoints.

> Despite traditional role playing in some heterosexual relationships, more men and women report that they feel more autonomous and that their relationships are more equal than couples studied twenty years ago.
>
> Although most gangs participate in actions that put the members at odds with society, many values are learned that reinforce community identity and help the members to survive hardships.

When your evaluator checks over your essay, make sure he or she is satisfied with your treatment of the opposition.

### 8. Are All Causes and Effects Accurate?

A cause is something that brings about a result. An effect is something that is directly produced by an action or agent. Many papers you will write will contain causes and effects, signaled by a variety of expressions, including *because of*, *due to*, *the reason for*, and *the result of*. When you name the causes of an effect or the effects of a cause, you should keep in mind that only certain information can qualify as a cause or an effect. First, the fact that one event preceded another is not sufficient reason to believe that the first caused the second, even though causes do always precede effects. If it rains just before an earthquake, the rain did not cause the quake. If someone takes a vitamin C tablet in the morning and comes down later with a miserable cold, the vitamin did not cause the cold. This connecting of mere coincidences, which is the reasoning that pervades superstition, is not appropriate for college papers.

There is, however, an easy test your evaluator can use in looking for sound cause-and-effect reasoning. In true causal relationships, one should be able to say what links the cause to the effect. The *why* of the connection is important. For instance, you might say your father's dedication was the main reason for his success as a teacher. In giving this cause, you are basing the relationship between dedication and success on more than just the sequence in which the two occurred. True, the dedication came before the success, but you also realize that the dedication led to certain behaviors or practices, and these were more directly responsible for his success. Unless your readers are familiar with the details of your father's success, all the links in the cause-effect sequence should be explained. An evaluator, who is less close to the subject than you are, can help you judge how much detail to present in the final draft.

Also, be careful not to conclude, just because you have found one cause for an effect or vice versa, that the cause or effect is the only one. Be aware that most effects do not have just one cause, and most causes have more than one effect. Most likely you will need to deal only with the important or primary causes and effects. However, your evaluator can help here with wording to show that there are other unmentioned causes or effects. For instance, you may need to revise the current draft to say "one cause" or "an effect" instead of using the too-inclusive "the cause" or "the effect." Let's return now to the example of your father. You realize, of course, that other causes—his understanding nature, his ability to communicate well, his grasp of his subject—contributed to his success as a teacher. Thus, you will notice that the statement does not attempt to imply that dedication was the only cause; it appropriately says "the main reason."

### 9. Do All Analogies Serve to Clarify Points?

An *analogy* is a comparison of two like ideas, events, or situations. Analogies are frequently used for clarification. An idea that might otherwise be strange to readers can click in their minds if the writer can describe it in terms of a similar, familiar situation. But analogies must be used with caution, because most ideas or situations that are analogous also have easily overlooked but distinctive differences. Thus, by going about proving one point through reasoning out the analogy to it, a writer may dangerously ignore important differences between the original and the analogous points. The differences may throw off the reasoning.

If, for instance, you were to argue in an essay that moderators on television news programs should not make their personal views known because moderators need to maintain an image of objectivity, you might compare moderators with judges, who should also remain impartial. Despite the similarity, the analogy actually clouds the issue instead of clarifying it, since the purpose of objectivity for the two is not the same. If, assuming moderators are no different than judges, you were to defend the point about moderators by accounting for all the reasons a judge would need to remain objective during a trial, your argument would be illogical.

Naturally, before you use an analogy, you should pick out any differences between the point you have in mind and the analogy. But because analogy is a form of creativity, it's easy to be so entranced with your idea that you cannot recognize its flaws. This is why your evaluator should also try to approach your analogies with suspicion; he or she can mention any differences that might undermine your argument. If the differences are not relevant to the point, the analogy will probably be effective.

WHEN YOU THINK HOW WELL BASIC APPLIANCES WORK, IT'S HARD TO BELIEVE ANYONE EVER GETS ON AN AIRPLANE.

### 10. Is the Thinking Free of Stereotypes?

The technical term *stereotype* refers to metal plates used by printers to reproduce many exact copies. Thinking can also be stereotyped in the sense of applying a fixed notion about something to all the members of a particular group and not allowing for individual differences. Inherent in stereotyping is the belief that all members of a group are exact copies of one another who will act predictably. Some familiar stereotypes include the all-brawn, no-brain athlete; the dumb, sexy blonde; and the unscrupulous lawyer. Other stereotypes are more subtle and perhaps for that reason more insidious: the lazy homeless person, the effeminate gay man, the poor black, the smart Asian student, the rowdy and dangerous rock concert, or the flat and boring midwest.

No matter how subtle, stereotypes are inaccurate and trite. Although some members of a given group may seem to fit their stereotype, not all, or even most, do. Yet stereotyped thinking remains all too common. People who stereotype others may observe one characteristic of the stereotype and incorrectly assume that all the other characteristics automatically fit the person. For instance, a person who thinks in stereotypes would see an athletic male student and assume that he is stupid, is a stud, and is more concerned with sports than with academics.

You can see that the underlying assumption of any stereotype is either-or thinking: people are one way or another. You should keep an eye open for stereotypes you hold. You should look for exceptions to the "rule." If there is one intelligent athlete, one honest lawyer, the stereotype cannot hold since it assumes all athletes to be alike, all lawyers to be the same. Like the cliches discussed in Chapter 8, stereotypes reveal a failure to evaluate on the part of those who use them. Passive and automatic acceptance of them is far too easy. Any hint of stereotyping picked up by your evaluator should be removed from your essay and replaced with thoughtful examination of your subject.

### 11. Is the Information Representative?

The information in an essay should be as representative as possible of the knowledge in your field. Representative statements are typical and true; they are quite different from stereotypes. Your evaluator can point out the possibility that you have cited an exceptional case as if it were

typical. One example of something is not usually enough for drawing a generalization. The instance could be an exception to the rule. If, for example, you were writing an essay about the abuses of prescription drugs, you might discuss the seeming casualness with which some doctors administer powerful prescriptions. To cite an instance in which a friend of yours went to the campus doctor for sore muscles and came home with five prescriptions for symptoms from anxiety to cold sores would be a poor example, because the case is certainly not usual. Most doctors do not treat any symptoms that they have not verified. To assume they do so from this example would be unreasonable. Attempting to sensationalize your argument by offering extremes and exceptional examples can only undermine the effectiveness of your point. Even if you found a second example, you would have to look further, into more cases, to be sure that the information is representative. Otherwise the rare incidence of the problem would probably require your abandoning the point altogether.

The preceding guidelines have been provided to help you explain to your evaluator the kinds of concerns you have about your paper and to help you evaluate your partner's paper. An evaluator who uses these questions to identify key problem areas in your essay can save your argument—and your grade. Similar questions are listed inside the front cover of this textbook for your convenience during draft-sharing sessions. Your teacher will no doubt hold you responsible for writing the best-reasoned essay you can; therefore, when you work with a partner, you must insist that the person offer you adequate criticism, not just say, "I like your paper"—which will do little to help you revise.

While discussing your rough draft essay with a classmate or with your professor, you will no doubt come away with several valuable suggestions. It is a good idea to take notes during the sharing session, then to organize the notes into a list that shows the order in which you will pursue the suggestions for revision. Drawing up such a plan for revising the rough draft will help you decide which suggestions you consider the most valuable and which suggestions you will take less seriously.

## POLISHING THE DRAFT: SELF-EVALUATION

After the initial revision based on the comments of your peers or professor (or even if you have no opportunity to share a particular piece of writing), you will want to review the paper to make polishing touches. The following three-step strategy is used by many writers, professional and amateur, to evaluate their writing and provide the finishing touches that will make for an effective essay. The strategy is summarized on page 161.

### Let Your Writing "Cool"

Only when you are alert and able to concentrate fully on your words can you revise your writing effectively. Before you start, let your paper "cool." Set it aside—a day or two is ideal but even an hour or two will help—and try to forget about it. The time spent away from your writing will help to freshen your perceptions. You will then be able to return to the paper with new eyes and greater objectivity.

### Check What You Have Written

An important part of polishing is to make sure that the paper gives a clear and complete impression. Read your thesis sentence and identify the controlling idea. What type of arrangement does it promise: spatial, chronological, cause and effect, comparison? Is the arrangement promised the one you actually use? Does all of the information in the paper support the thesis, or do irrelevant ideas, no matter how interesting, somehow slip in?

To check the overall impression of what you have written, complete each of the following steps.

*Step One*

Read the introduction and ask yourself these questions:

1. Is there an attention-getting device? Is it effective?
2. Is the material in the introduction pertinent to the thesis?
3. Is the thesis controversial? If so, is the opposition cited and effectively dealt with?

*Step Two*

Identify the topic sentence of each paragraph and put it to the following tests:

1. Does each topic sentence either support the thesis directly or further the case of a principal support of the thesis?
2. Do the topic sentences follow the order promised by the controlling idea of the thesis, or are there gaps in the development of the essay?

*Step Three*

Read the conclusion and ask yourself the following questions:

1. Is the conclusion effective?
2. Does it leave the reader with something to think about?

3. Does the ending round out the essay, or does the essay come to an abrupt halt?

*Step Four*
Examine the title.
1. Is it short and eye catching?
2. Does it convey your main idea in an original way?

**Refine What You Have Written**
This stage takes you through a careful reading of the essay so that you can make what you have written clearer and less awkward.

*Examine Your Sentences*
Let your eyes glide over the paper, paying particular attention to the sentence structure. Is passive voice used only where effective? Are the sentences of varied lengths and structures? If not, recombine the sentences (see Chapter 7).

*Remove Unnecessary Words*
Read the paper aloud. As you read, listen for ineffective word use—deadwood, pileups, overuse of *to be* verbs, trite phrases, and inappropriate repetition.

Deadwood
Deadwood refers to a word or phrase that serves no purpose. Writing full of deadwood is heavy and boring. Some common examples of deadwood are phrases such as *the fact that*, *my point is*, and *the reason is*. Following are examples of how deadwood should be removed from your writing:

His association                                           damaged
~~The fact that he associated~~ with members of the Mafia ~~proved damaging to~~ his testimony.

~~My point is that~~ we are isolated from any sort of real culture when we live on a college campus.

~~The fact is that~~ the majority of high school students in a large Eastern city voted for nongraded classes.

Pileups
The use of excessive prepositional phrases is a major cause of wordiness. They have a tendency to pile up in sentences and bog down your writing. Phrases beginning with *of*, *by*, *to*, and *on* are frequent troublemakers. As you read your paper aloud, see whether you have used any unnecessary prepositional phrases. Some, such as *in terms of*, *of the fact*, and *in regard to*, seldom add to the effect of your writing and might

simply be deleted. If a sentence is still wordy, you can remove other prepositional phrases in either of two ways. You can often convert the noun of the prepositional phrase to a verb:

> *Original:* By morning, most of the prisoners in the camp had undergone the process of interrogation by a group of government agents.
> *Revised:* By morning, government agents had interrogated most of the prisoners in the camp.

Or you can convert the noun of a prepositional phrase to an adjective:

> *Original:* The needs of the students for cultural activities were not met by my high school because the budget of the school was too small.
> *Revised:* The students' needs for cultural activities were not met by my high school because the school's budget was too small.

This is a particularly effective way to eliminate *of* phrases.

Here are additional examples of ways sentences can be revised to eliminate pileups:

One member of the ~~consumer-action~~ committee ~~of consumers~~ from the state of New Jersey admitted that consumer groups were not able to help about 45 percent of the people who brought complaints to them.

Two ~~of the~~ magicians in the Kansas City Hilton's "Forty-Niner's Club" ~~in the~~ cocktail lounge ~~of the Kansas City Hilton~~ gave my friend a magic lesson.

The final act, which has as its highlights the king's murder ~~of the king~~, the queen's remarriage ~~of the Queen~~, and the prince's suicide ~~of the prince, is one of~~ excites ~~excitement for~~ the audience.

### *To Be* Verbs

*To be* verb forms lead to deadwood and pileups and in themselves have little spunk. Overuse of *to be* forms can make your writing tedious. Instead of writing *is* or *are,* use more descriptive verbs as often as possible. Note how the following sentences have been revised:

Weitz believes ~~is of the belief~~ that historical mistreatment of lesbians is socially conditioned and not "from some universal biological or ethical law."

shows
The need for companionship ∧ ~~is quite apparent~~ in her behavior.

are often confused
~~There is a prevailing confusion among many~~ students of literature ∧
about the differences between a narrator and an author.

### Trite Phrases and Concepts

State more directly any cliches you identify as you read along. Be alert too for any worn-out concepts that seem clever on the surface but to most academic readers are superficial, too cute, and all too familiar. Examples are Friday the 13 being unlucky, professors being absent minded, and the ubiquitous "learning experience." After all, anybody can use a cliche, and readers will expect your essay to be more than a pastiche of worn words. (See pages 206-208 for a full discussion of cliches.)

### Repetition

Check your paper for unnecessary repetition of words. Such repetition can ruin the flow of your paper and cause your readers to lose interest. Repetition of words can also tip you off to lack of development. Look at what repetition does to the following paragraph:

> Natives are usually prejudiced against immigrants. The natives think the immigrants are a danger to society and the natives do not think the immigrants can be trusted. The natives think the immigrants are spies infringing on the natives' traditions and politics. Furthermore, the immigrants become thought of as lower-class people, possibly because the natives have stereotyped images of immigrants. In fact, the natives' stereotyping may be the root of much of the anti-immigrant thinking.

Awkward isn't it? Most of the sentences begin with *the*, and the repetition of *natives* and *immigrants* wears out the reader. Now see how much better the paragraph sounds without the unnecessary repetition:

> Natives are usually prejudiced against immigrants, considering them untrustworthy and dangerous to society. Immigrants seem to be spies infringing on native traditions and politics. Furthermore, natives misperceive the immigrants as lower-class people, possibly because the natives know only their own stereotypes and have no idea of the standard of living of the other people. In fact, the stereotyping may be the root of much of the anti-immigrant thinking.

### *Check for Transitions*

Look for transitions between the sentences and between the paragraphs of your paper. Remember that readers will need to be helped along from point to point in your paper. (See pages 100-104 for a complete discussion of transitions. )

To summarize the final polishing phase, here are the steps you should follow:

1. Let your writing cool.
2. Check what you have written.
   Evaluate the introduction.
   Evaluate the topic sentences.
   Evaluate the conclusion.
   Examine the title.
3. Refine what you have written.
   Check for sentence variety.
   Remove unnecessary words.
   Eliminate deadwood and pileups.
   Omit excessive *to be* verbs.
   Rewrite trite phrases.
   Eliminate repetition.
   Check for transitions between ideas.

---

**Exercises**

A. Remove or revise any wordiness or unnecessary repetition in the following sentences taken from student essays.

1. Malcolm X lived a difficult and hard life.
2. Contrary to stereotypes, many Asian women wish that they could be more recognized and visible in society.
3. My mother's reaction to the loud noise of the siren and the sudden movement of the car, which was making a right turn, happened simultaneously.
4. Despite the wide variation in their labor market potential which shows they have skills for performing a variety of jobs, a large proportion of criminal offenders are faced with employment problems and are actively in need of help.
5. Writing to one's congressperson has a minimal effect on changing laws.
6. Prior to commitment to state prisons, most criminal offenders have jobs that involve them in a variety of labor-type vocational experiences.
7. In the Weitz article, the approach is taken from an angle which shows the theoretical causes of nonacceptance of lesbians in society.
8. Pinball machines can have a hypnotizing type of effect on people.
9. The fact that some ex-criminals cannot adapt to the real world can be attributed to the basic fact that the cultures in which they have been living have been of an emotionally nonsupportive nature.
10. The inmate's training needs should take first precedence over the utilization of the inmate's potential skills and talents in terms of the prison's needs for staff.
11. But not only do white women often not fit the model of beauty shown on television and in magazines, but women from other racial backgrounds do not either.

12. The main problem with school is academics versus social life, basically not which is of more importance but which has a more attractive force to draw the student.

B. Evaluate the following passive constructions and convert any sentences that should emphasize the doer of the action into active constructions.

1. In the United States, nearly 75 percent of waste materials could be converted into energy.

2. The conclusion of *A Farewell to Arms* was rewritten thirty times by Ernest Hemingway.

3. Madonna was launched to stardom by the *Live Aid* show of 1985, where she made her first public splash.

4. Next year a freeway to Westridge will be opened if the voters demand it.

5. Ivory, a rarity at home, could be found at every African vendor's stand, carved into intricate jewelry and animal shapes.

6. Robert Bly's *Iron John* is known as a radical text even by those who deem themselves feminists.

7. Emotion-packed speeches were delivered by three members of the Senate.

8. Was it right that a New York woman and her three small children were refused medical treatment last year by a doctor who did not feel they could pay the fees?

9. When four of the most popular teachers on campus were sued by a fraternity last year, much of the student newspaper was devoted to the event and its various moral implications.

10. Gonzo journalism is typified by the work of Hunter Thompson.

## REVISION IN ACTION—A SAMPLE ESSAY

To see how a paper improves through the revision process, examine the stages of the sample essay in Figures 6-1 through 6-4. Here is how the writer, Chris, revised the essay. First, she shared her original draft with a classmate, Ben, who wrote several suggestions in the margin (Figure 6-1). As you read through this initial draft, pretend that it is your own essay. Can you detect any weak spots that the evaluator missed?

Next, Chris read over her classmate's suggestions and prepared the following plan from them. Putting the ideas in order and in her own words helped Chris visualize the new draft and gave her the confidence to begin rewriting.

```
Plan for Revision of Discrimination in the Corporate
Environment
   Ben's suggestions:
   1. Reword thesis. Focus on examples of discrimination.
   2. Parag 2: Explain Equal Opportunity Employment.
   3. Parag 3: Shift argument from effects on employees
      to back up discrimination idea. Elaborate on idea.
   4. Dump transition parag.
   5. Explain cornrows hairstyle argument better—focus on
```

all cultures being part of business community
(discrimination).

Chris was writing this essay on the computer. She found, to her surprise, that it was easy to transform the evaluator's suggestions into a

---

**Figure 6-1. Peer revisions from a rough-draft sharing session.**

Descriptive Outline

Thesis: "Discrimination is still very much alive in the corporate
atmosphere and it's disturbing."

1. Categories stereotype and pressure individuals—judged as member of
group

2. Laws protect unequal salary and sexual harassment but not expressions
of culture that deviate from mainstream

   —dress and hairstyle

3. Not talked about but social pressure to look a certain way

Chris Schabow
English 15
September 27, 1995

Discrimination in the Corporate Environment

In today's economic world, opting for a career in the corporate environment can be a wise decision. Employment by a corporation offers financial
security and the work is challenging and rewarding. But a word of caution
before running off to sign any contracts or agreements. [Despite—or perhaps
because of—existing rules and regulations to protect individuals and groups
from harassment, discrimination is still very much alive in the corporate
atmosphere and encountering it unawares can be a disturbing experience.]

*Thesis* →     ①

Large posters displayed in personnel offices across the continent attest
*explain this phrase?* to equal opportunity employment; but a closer look reveals a different
picture. Management is still very much aware of ethnic or gender differences and this knowledge goes into the formation of corporate policy.
Specific groups, for instance women, the handicapped and minorities, are
"targeted" in order to assure equal treatment for them.

But the classification of individuals into groups in order [to statistically prevent discrimination is a more subtle form of discrimination.] *Good point!*

substantially revised draft (Figure 6-2). Ideas came readily because she focused on the plan she had drawn up.

Once Chris had developed the new draft, she printed out a hard copy and proceeded to polish that draft according to the suggested three-

**Figure 6-1 (continued).**

*Not clear how this supports discrim. argument. Expand and explain more*

Women, the handicapped, and minorities are relegated into categories and then as individuals must strive to overcome the barriers built categorically around them. This creates a sense of being continually assessed and continually assessing the surrounding environment. Am I meeting up to standards, is this what is expected of me? Not only as an employee of this corporation but also as a member of this particular group? [Additional psychological burdens are placed on individuals by these categories.]

*← Not sure what you mean here.*

The media have proved helpful in making the public aware of discrimination in the workforce based on issues such as unequal salary compensation between men and women and sexual harassment. These issues are more evident and hence more easily detectable. Subtler issues such as the manner of dress are more difficult to define.

*Need a better transition from last idea*

*Is media idea pertinent?*

*②*

Some corporations dictate the dress of their employees. Appearance and professionalism are of utmost importance in the corporate world, and demanding appropriate dress is acceptable. But requiring permission for an employee to wear a particular hairstyle demands questioning. A hairstyle of "ethnic origin" such as the braids favorable among African American men and women should not require permission of the employer. If a hairstyle does not detract from the business atmosphere, in a distracting manner, then it should be deemed appropriate.

*Define this abstract term?*

*Good citing opposing views here*

*③*

*Doesn't this assume some kind of conformity?*

*Why discrimination? Explain why it does or doesn't detract. Give ex.*

The corporate world can offer much to our society. The number of people corporations employ as well as the wealth they amass make them powerful influences in America. But management should learn to channel its energies into truly efficient ways of preventing discrimination by respecting the differences among people and not trying to demand an unhealthy conformity to an unspoken but demanding norm.

*Chris-*
*I found the idea that discrimination is common (despite laws and raised consciousness) really interesting! I also liked how fair you tried to be to both sides. But I would suggest you re-word your thesis to match the support better. The thesis doesn't seem to progress step by step. Maybe you could focus on a few well-explained examples of discrimination.*

*Ben*

step process described earlier in this chapter. Figure 6-3 shows her third draft. The annotations reflect stages two and three of the polishing process to help guide her in producing the final draft, which she later handed in to her teacher for grading (Figure 6-4).

---

**Figure 6-2. Second draft of essay.**

Chris Schabow
English 15
September 28, 1989

Discrimination in the Workplace

   In today's economic world, opting for a career in a corporate environment can be a wise decision. Not only does it offer security, but employment by a corporation can be challenging and rewarding for social and personal reasons as well, such as the opportunity to travel and live in other parts of the country, if not the world. But a word of caution before running off to sign any contracts or agreements. For despite existing rules and regulations to protect individuals and groups from harassment, discrimination is still alive in the corporate atmosphere, and can have devastating effects on whoever encounters it unawares.

   Large posters displayed in personnel offices across America attest to equal opportunity employment (EOE). EOE has played a powerful role in U.S. labor history. It arose out of the racial battles of the 1960s, a turbulent period of strife and tension as blacks demanded and received recognition from white America. Employment hiring policy came under scrutiny at this time, and, as a result, federal regulations were set down governing hiring procedures. These rulings, commonly referred to today as EOE regulations, state that an individual cannot be denied employment because of "race, color, religion, sex, or national origin." My involvement in the corporate world reveals that while EOE addresses the issue on one level, these regulations are not the complete answer. They often create another type of discrimination or, through their very existence, create a kind of complacency that will fuel the fires of segregation, assuring powerlessness and disrespect for some groups.

   The Civil Rights Act of 1964 established a special board, the Equal Employment Opportunity Commission (EEOC) to ensure that employers subscribe to EOE regulations. The EEOC requires employers to document hiring proce-

---

By revising, the writer has clarified her own grasp of the subject: she has put her ideas into a structure that contributes to the precise thesis she wishes to defend, and she has polished her use of words to suit her purpose and meanings. Although by the time she finished the revision, even she could not say that the essay was perfect (and she did decide to change a few things while typing), she felt that the revision was an improvement—that it said basically what she had set out to say, in the least possible words and in an interesting way. She was ready to receive criticism from her professor.

**Figure 6-2 (continued).**

dures and, as a result, management is put in an awkward position: subject to fine or imprisonment if convicted of EOE violations, they have responded by forming "target" groups. This amounts to tracking employees into these categories. This method, while statistically "preventing" discrimination, intensifies it psychologically for those in the targeted groups. Women, minorities, and the handicapped are isolated: notably absent from the target groups are nonminority males. In the 1980s this absence is a statement of dominance: either they are superior and above categorization or should be the "accepted norm," the standard of measurement for all others. Those placed in special categories—women, minorities, and the handicapped—are made to feel that it is against this norm that they must be measured and must prove themselves capable. Worse yet, they must prove their whole group worthy by their performance. Executive women have a reputation for being hard nosed. Perhaps their attitude arises from the tremendous psychological pressure they feel to act strong in a stereotypical "man's world."

The pressure is due largely to the fact that management is still in the hands of nonminority males, whose experience represents only one of the many groups employed by the corporate world. There is no denying that minorities, for instance, are more common in the lower ranks of corporations than they were ten years ago, but why haven't they, on the whole, moved up to the top of the corporate ladder? That EOE regulations exist has perhaps quelled the storm. The government offices are appeased by statistics, and the general public has little knowledge of what progress has—or should we say hasn't—been made since the 1960s.

It is a good assumption that a rough draft is just that—rough. Critical revision develops that rough vision into a fully expanded and polished statement. Really, then, good writing is usually only good revision. Very few persons can set down what they want to say, as they wish to express it, the first time around. The point of revising is to look again at what you've created, checking to see whether you have conveyed to your reader just what you set out to say. Revision is usually the natural follow-up to the rough draft, the point at which you give your approval before the final presentation to your reader.

**Figure 6-2 (continued).**

    Unheard on the executive level, minorities form organizations to speak

for them. This trend is developing among professional accountants, for

instance, the National Association of Black Accountants or the Latino

CPA's. This forced polarization can actually create racial tension because

it is based on racial differences rather than the occupation itself; black

accountants do not work any differently than any other accountant. This is

another case in which the discrimination occurring in the workplace has

been responded to with more discrimination.

    Even on a daily basis, discrimination can "pass" for "corporate policy."

A recent example in a firm I am familiar with occurred one day when one

African American woman showed up for work with a cornrow hairstyle, only to

be called in to personnel and informed that such a style reflected "ethnic

origin," and hence was unsuitable for office attire. What is most revealing

about this corporate claim is that personnel failed to recognize that

America's white culture is as much an ethnic group as is black America's.

Any hairstyle, a perm or long straight hair, reflects ethnic origin. Once

again the assumption was that the white style was the "norm."

    In this case, personnel, by requiring this conformity, acted against

EOE; but unless the employee reports the instance, such abuses will recur.

Most employees assume that we have laws to protect us against discrimina-

tion and therefore that it does not exist in the workplace. Few employees

question the firm's right to determine rules of so-called corporate "profes-

sionalism."

    It is time that corporate America began to respect the differences among

people rather than demand an unhealthy conformity to an unspoken norm.

Most often you will revise before handing in the essay, and that will be that. You will receive the paper back with comments and an evaluation so that next time you write a paper you may take into account some general suggestions. But sometimes there is an opportunity to

*Check What You Have Written*

(1) Change title to liven up.

(2–11) Delete current intro: not as pertinent to thesis as paragraph 2. Also, attention-getting device does not fit tone of rest of paper.

(12) Addition of "corporate" makes paragraph 2 into suitable introduction.

(19) Topic sentence indicates need for new paragraph.

*Refine What You Have Written*

(24) Remove deadwood.

*Check What You Have Written*

---

**Figure 6-3. Third draft of essay, annotated by writer.**

Chris Schabow
English 15
September 28, 1989

1          Discrimination ^Legal in the Workplace ?

2      In today's economic world, opting for a career in corporate

3   environment can be a wise decision. Not only does it offer

4   security but employment by a corporation can be challenging and

5   rewarding for social and personal reasons as well, such as the

6   opportunity to travel and live in other parts of the country,

7   if not the world. But a word caution before running off to sign

8   any contracts or agreements. For despite existing rules and

9   regulations to protect individuals and groups from harassment,

10  discrimination is still alive in the corporate atmosphere, and

11  can have devastating effects on whoever encounters it unawares.

12  Large posters displayed in personnel offices across ^corporate America

13  attest to equal opportunity employment (EOE). EOE has played a

14  powerful role in U.S. labor history. It arose out of the racial

15  battles of the 1960s, a turbulent period of strife and tension

16  as blacks demanded and received recognition from white America.

17  Employment hiring policy came under scrutiny at this time, and,

18  as a result, federal regulations were set down governing hiring

19  procedures. ¶These rulings, commonly referred to today as EOE

20  regulations, state that an individual cannot be denied employ-

21  ment because of " race, color, religion, sex, or national

22  origin." My involvement in the corporate world reveals that

23  while EOE addresses the issue on one level, these regulations

24  ~~are not the complete answer~~ ^fail. They often create another type of

25  discrimination or, through their very existence, create a kind

26  of complacency that will fuel the fires of segregation, assuring

27  powerlessness and disrespect for some groups.

rewrite after the paper or a rough draft has been handed in. After the teacher has evaluated your paper or after you and a classmate have gone over the essay together, you may be called upon to revise the essay based on the comments of a reader. You may even be asked to prepare a port-

**Figure 6-3. Third draft of essay, annotated by writer.**

The Civil Rights Act of 1964 established a special board,   28

the Equal Employment Opportunity Commission (EEOC) to ensure   29

that employers subscribe to EOE regulations. The EEOC requires   30

employers to document hiring procedures and, as a result,   31

~~management is~~ *management* puts in an awkward position X ~~S~~ubject to fine or   *caps*   32

imprisonment if convicted of EOE violations, they have re-   33

sponded by forming "target" groups . This amounts to tracking   34

employees into these categories.¶ ~~This~~ *The* method, while statisti-   35

cally "preventing" discrimination, intensifies it psychologi-   36

cally for those in the targeted groups. Women, minorities, and   37

the handicapped *feel* ~~are~~ isolated; notably absent from the target   38

groups are nonminority males. In the 1990s this absence is a   39

statement of dominance: either they are superior and above   40

categorization or should be the "accepted norm," the standard   41

of measurement for all others. Those placed in special catego-   42

ries—women, minorities, and the handicapped—are made to feel   43

that it is against this norm that they must *demonstrate* ~~be measured and~~   44

~~must prove~~ themselves capable. Worse yet, they must prove their   45

whole group worthy by their performance. Executive women have a   46

reputation for *inflexibility* ~~being hard-nosed~~. Perhaps their attitude arises   47

from the tremendous psychological pressure ~~they feel~~ to act   48

strong in a stereotypical "man's world."   49

¶ ~~The pressure is due largely to the fact that~~ ~~M~~anagement is   *caps*   50

still in the hands of nonminority males, whose experience   51

represents only one of the many groups employed by the corpo-   52

rate world. ~~There is no denying that minorities, for instance,~~   53

*Although* more minorities work in   *now*
~~are more common in the lower ranks of~~ corporations, than ~~they~~   54

~~were~~ ten years ago, ~~but why~~ |haven't| |they|, on the whole, moved   55

up to the top of the corporate ladder X That EOE regulations   56

exist has perhaps quelled the storm. The government offices are   57

(31-35) Vary sentence lengths by breaking up long sentence.

(32) Change passive voice to active.

(35) Topic sentence indicates need for new paragraph.

*Refine What You Have Written*

(38) Revise excessive use of "to be."

(44) Remove deadwood change "prove" to "demon-strate" to avoid repetition.

(47) Rewrite trite phrases.

(48) Remove deadwood.

(50) Remove deadwood.

(53–55) Confusing transition improve sentence combining by adding subordination.

folio of a few revised essays. This assignment may, for a moment, stump you—all those markings on the paper you have already tried to per-

*Refine What You Have Written*

(64) Vary transitions.

(66) Correct grammar.

(68-69) Change passive to active voice.

(71–75) Remove deadwood.

(76) Revise excessive use of "is" ("to be" verb).

(79) Revise excessive use of "to be"

(83–85) Remove deadwood.

**Figure 6-3 (continued).**

58    appeased by statistics, and the general public has little

59    knowledge of what progress has—or should we say hasn't—been

60    made since the 1960s.

61      Unheard on the executive level, minorities form organiza-

62    tions to speak for them. This trend is developing among profes-

63    sional accountants, for instance, the National Association

64    Black Accountants or the Latino CPA's. ~~This~~ forced polarization    *caps*

65    can actually create racial tension because it is based on racial

66    differences rather than ^*on*^ the occupation itself; black accoun-

67    tants do not work any differently than any other accountant.

68    *Discrimination wins out.* ~~This is another case in which the discrimination occurring in~~

69    ~~the workplace has been responded to with more discrimination.~~

70      Even on a daily basis, discrimination can "pass" for

71    "corporate policy." *Recently, the personnel office of a* ~~A recent example in a firm I am familiar~~

72    ~~with occurred one day when one~~ *local firm advised a* black woman ~~showed up for work~~ *who wore her hair in*

73    ~~with a~~ cornrows ~~hairstyle, only to be called in to personnel and~~

74    ~~informed~~ that such a style reflected "ethnic origin," and hence

75    was unsuitable for office attire. ~~What is most revealing about~~

76    ^Ṯhis corporate claim ~~is~~ *reveals* that personnel failed to recognize that    *caps*

77    America's white culture is as much an ethnic group as is black

78    America's. Any hairstyle, a perm or long straight hair, reflects

79    ethnic origin. Once again the ~~assumption was that~~ *company considered* the white

80    style ~~was~~ the "norm."

81      In this case, personnel, by requiring this conformity, acted

82    against EOE: but unless the employee reports the instance, such

83    abuses will recur. Most employees assume that ~~we have~~ laws ~~to~~

84    protect ~~us~~ *them* against discrimination ~~and therefore that it does not~~

85    ~~exist~~ in the workplace. Few employees question the firm's right

86    to determine rules of so-called corporate "professionalism."

87      It is time that corporate America began to respect the

88    differences among people rather than demand an unhealthy

89    conformity to an unspoken norm.

fect may make your previous efforts appear less fruitful than you had expected.

But there is a better way of interpreting these comments. The second revision makes you even more aware of the expectations of your reader, and the resulting essay will naturally be clearer than the first. All writers find it difficult to guess exactly all the reader's responses. Writing alone in your room is equivalent to having a one-way conversation. Thus it is only after sharing your thoughts with someone that you can fully test your effectiveness as a writer. So it is important to look upon reader comments positively and to see the required changes as a challenge in communicating what really matters to you.

---

**Figure 6-4. Final draft of essay.**

Chris Schabow
English 15
September 29, 1989

Discrimination: Legal in the Workplace?

Large posters displayed in personnel offices across corporate America attest to equal opportunity employment (EOE). EOE has played a powerful role in U.S. labor history. It arose out of the racial battles of the 1960s, a turbulent period of strife and tension as blacks demanded and received recognition from white America. Employment hiring policy came under scrutiny at this time, and, as a result, federal regulations were set down governing hiring procedures.

These rulings, commonly referred to today as EOE regulations, state that an individual cannot be denied employment because of "race, color, religion, sex, or national origin" (The Civil Rights Act of 1964). My involvement in the corporate world reveals that while EOE addresses the issue on one level, these regulations fail. They often create another type of discrimination or, through their very existence, create a kind of complacency that will fuel the fires of segregation, assuring powerlessness and disrespect for some groups.

The Civil Rights Act of 1964 established a special board, the Equal Employment Opportunity Commission (EEOC), to ensure that employers subscribe to EOE regulations. The EEOC requires employers to document hiring procedures and as a result, puts management in an awkward position. Subject to fine or imprisonment if convicted of EOE violations, they have responded by forming "target" groups. This amounts to tracking employees into these

---

As you revise you may wish to refer to the list of Twenty-five Questions for the Writer inside the front cover of this book. The questions will perhaps offer clues to some of the concerns of your reader, indicating where you might find helpful suggestions for revising.

## Exercises

Directions: Using the steps described in this chapter, improve the following passages from students' papers.

1. My new life holds so many adventures. College is a time to explore; there are so many ways to be involved. The bare definition of college is taking classes, but to me it is so much more. That is only the beginning. It is an experience. It is activities, new friends, clubs, jobs, etc. My

---

**Figure 6-4 (continued).**

categories. The method, while statistically "preventing" discrimination, intensifies it psychologically for those in the targeted groups. Women, minorities, and the handicapped feel isolated: notably absent from the target groups are nonminority males. In the 1980s this absence is a statement of dominance: either they are superior and above categorization or should be the "accepted norm," the standard of measurement for all others. Those placed in special categories—women, minorities, and the handicapped—are made to feel that it is against this norm that they must demonstrate themselves capable. Worse yet, they must prove their whole group worthy by their performance. Executive women have a reputation for inflexibility. Perhaps their attitude arises from the tremendous psychological pressure to act strong in a stereotypical "man's world."

Management is still in the hands of nonminority males, whose experience represents only one of the many groups employed by the corporate world. Although more minorities work in corporations now than ten years ago, they haven't, on the whole, moved up to the top of the corporate ladder. That EOE regulations exist has perhaps quelled the storm. The government offices are appeased by statistics, and the general public has little knowledge of what progress has—or should we say hasn't—been made since the 1960s.

Unheard on the executive level, minorities form organizations to speak for them. This trend is developing among processional accountants, for mother explained to me that she was envious of my position as a young, healthy college student. She was amazed at how I could function happily day in and day out on so little sleep and how my body maintained its vim and vigor. She was right. The fact is that I love my youth because it allows me to do so many things and still remain flexible. Although I take care of my body, I try to get enough sleep and in return it has allowed me to be active in my school, social and extra curricular life.

2. Orwell expresses extreme amounts of guilt for the killing of the elephant. He continually tries to rationalize in any way possible the circumstances leading up to the event and the event itself. At the beginning, he portrays himself as the victim of an oppressed people, the Burmese, who lash out at him and other Europeans using petty slights against them. For such slights against him he detests the Burmese, but he also sympathizes with them because of the fact that he had decided "that impe-

---

**Figure 6-4 (continued).**

instance, the National Association of Black Accountants or the Latino CPA's. Forced polarization can actually create racial tension because it is based on racial differences rather than on the occupation itself; black accountants do not work differently than any other accountants. Discrimination wins out.

Even on a daily basis, discrimination can "pass" for "corporate policy." Recently, the personnel office of a local firm advised a black woman who wore cornrows that such a style reflected "ethnic origin" and hence was unsuitable for office attire. This corporate claim reveals that personnel failed to recognize that America's white culture is as much an ethnic group as black America's. Any hairstyle, a perm or long straight hair, reflects ethnic origin. Once again the company considered the white style the "norm."

In this case, personnel, by requiring conformity, acted against EOE; but unless the employee reports the instance, such abuses will recur. Most employees assume that laws protect them against discrimination in the workplace. Few employees question the firm's right to determine rules of so-called corporate "professionalism."

It is time that corporate America began to respect the differences among people rather than demand an unhealthy conformity to an unspoken norm.

rialism was an evil thing and the sooner [he] chucked [his] job and got out of it the better" ("Shooting" 11). In making this kind of statement, Orwell presents himself with an internal conflict that eats away at his own sanity. The reader is left to believe that this inner turmoil is one such that it consumes his whole being in its entirety and makes him a pawn in the game of the imperialist British Empire.

3.  Black people have been seen throughout history as an "object of sympathy" and as a "creature who quietly endures and silently listens" (King 16). Although blacks rarely spoke out against their white oppressors, they were constantly reminded of the injustices that they were subjected to by the white supremicist mentality. Instead of blacks responding violently in terms of resisting the harsh abuse of the white oppressors, or acting vengefully, which would have fulfilled the white expectancies of "savagery," black people welcomed it. As stated by King: "Punish me I do not deserve it. But because I do not deserve it I will accept it so that the world will know that I am rightful and you are wrong" (King 30). In this statement King clearly conveys the notion of the strength of his beliefs and of his steadfast devotion in conquering the immoral injustices that black people had to live with in order to survive in white society. The nonviolent stance of the Civil Rights Movement was one which made whites rethink their strategies of retaliation.

4.  The second tool which is an influence in the reliability of this book is the use of the author's personal examples without any supporting citations. All the examples are extrapolated from the author's career as an attorney. By using his profession as a citation, he continues to manipulate the reader because attorneys are most often regarded as the best arguers. Likewise, the author uses the following example: a man is drunk and crosses the street when the sign signaled "walk." The drunk man was hit by a car that ran a red light. The drunk man is suing the man that ran the red light for physical and punitive damages. The author uses this court case as an example of how he was able to argue for a favorable settlement. The author cites additional examples with similar results and concludes that his success relies solely on his ability to argue. However, his assumption is undocumented and discredits the justice system by reducing the system to the whim and talents of the author. This approach appears quite egotistical and exaggerated, subsequently hindering the reliability of the author's own argument.

# WHAT IS A GOOD SENTENCE?

Most of the time you probably don't stop to think about individual sentences and their structure when you write or read. Yet flowing, meaningful sentences are the mark of a mature writing style. Learning to develop such sentences is surprisingly easy and enjoyable. You need to practice two methods: sentence combining and sentence imitation, both of which can give your sentences a professional flair.

The difference between a mediocre sentence and an effective one can be the amount of conscious sentence combining practiced in the revision stage. When you make additions to basic sentences, the sentences take on more texture. For example, both of these sentence groups say the same thing but have different effects on the reader:

> The invasion of American television in Europe has had unforeseen effects. These television shows may have significant effects. The effects of television shows which have been imported show up in strange ways. For instance, a recent news article reported incidents of individuals arrested by the police demanding their right to a phone call. The right to a telephone call is a staple of American crime shows.

> Imported American television shows have affected Europeans in unforeseen, strange, and possibly significant ways; a recent news article reported incidents of individuals arrested by the police demanding their right to a phone call—a staple of American crime shows.

Notice that combining the individual sentences from the first group into one coherent thought has deemphasized certain statements in order to, first, provide a brief background explaining that American television shows affect Europeans and, then, describe one way that effect was evidenced. Joining the example to the main idea with a semicolon also demonstrates that the connection between the two ideas is greater than if they were separate sentences; the second half of the sentence elaborates on the first. Similarly, setting off the appositive "a staple of American crime shows" dramatizes the concept. Also, observe how much smoother the combined sentence sounds when read aloud, whereas the first group of sentences is disjointed and choppy.

There is a real pleasure and sense of creativity to be derived from experimenting with different sentence patterns and discovering the multiple possibilities for expressing any idea. When you begin to juggle the order within your sentences, to experiment with various connective words, and to place emphasis in a variety of positions, it dawns on you that you have the power to convince through your strategies at the sentence level as well as through the content of your argument. You realize that your writing works for you.

## FOLLOWING PATTERNS

Even if you never compose sentences as choppy as the first group above, you can enhance your natural language skills and add precision and variety to your statements by practicing revision of your sentences, a process that makes you conscious of the impact behind your words and that is guaranteed to improve your writing. Notice how many ways the following short sentences can be combined—and these are only a few of the ways!

*Components:*
> The lucrative U.S. diet industry earned $33 billion in 1990.
> The diet industry preys upon many women's and girls' low self-image.

*Results:*
> The lucrative U.S. diet industry may have earned $33 billion in 1990, but it preyed upon many women's and girls' low self-image.
> Because the U.S. diet industry preys upon many women's and girls' low self-image, it earned $33 billion in 1990.
> Though the U.S. diet industry earned $33 billion in 1990, it preyed upon many women's and girls' low self-image.
> The lucrative U.S. diet industry, which earned $33 billion in 1990, preys upon many women's and girls' low self-image.
> The lucrative U.S. diet industry, which preys upon many women's and girls' low self-image, earned $33 billion in 1990.
> After earning $33 billion in 1990, the lucrative U.S. diet industry continues to prey upon many women's and girls' low self-image.
> By preying upon many women's and girls' low self-image, the lucrative U.S. diet industry earned $33 billion in 1990.
> In order to earn $33 billion in 1990, the lucrative U.S. diet industry preyed upon many women's and girls' low self-image.

Certainly there are a number of other possibilities, each demonstrating a slightly different emphasis, a different rhythm, a different relationship between the key ideas.

You may be saying to yourself, "I won't even be able to get out the first word if I have to think of all the possible patterns available!" You would be justified in feeling this way. The clue here is to wait and rephrase your sentences during the revision stage of your paper. First write your rough draft as you usually would and then read through that draft with special attention to the sentence structure. Look at consecutive sentences to see whether by combining, inverting, or embedding parts of them you can clarify the relationships between the ideas in the sentences. See whether you can direct the concentration of your reader to the idea that you most want to emphasize.

Sentences can usually be combined quite naturally by simple imitation of the sentence patterns of other writers. The sentence patterns used by good writers can be categorized into a few basic structures, which can be built by using five devices: coordination, subordination, active or passive voice, reordering, and balance and rhythm.

## USING COORDINATION

Coordination implies setting up a balance. When you balance your sentences, you are really making the decision to give equal emphasis to the sentence parts positioned on both sides of a coordinating conjunction (*and, for, so, but, or, nor, yet, either . . . or, neither . . . nor, both . . . and, not only . . . but also*). Looking back at the sentences on page 176, you find

> The lucrative U.S. diet industry may have earned $33 billion in 1990, but it preyed upon many women's and girls' low self-image.

The use of the coordinating conjunction *but* in this case signals that the $33 billion the diet industry may have earned is equally important as the fact that it continues to prey upon many women's and girls' low self-image. Although the writer wants to signal a contrast and therefore selects "but" to show it, he or she wants neither of the statements to be more important than the other. Here are some more examples of coordination with the different meanings they can suggest:

*And* signals an addition:

> Woodblock printing originated in China in the fourth century B.C.E., and it was introduced to Japan in the sixth century by Chinese and Korean Buddhist missionaries.

*But* indicates a contrast:

> Religion can be a fulfilling, vital force in our lives, but that doesn't mean believers should uncritically accept the edicts of its representatives.

*So* indicates a result:

> Some African Americans believe white society will be changed primarily through economic pressure, so they choose voluntary segregation by supporting African-American-owned businesses and institutions.

*Yet* signals a contrast, much like *but*:

> The United States is supposedly a free country with "equality and justice for all," yet many people have suffered persecution.

*Or* signals an alternative:

> Either China reforms its human rights abuses, or it faces the loss of U.S. trade benefits.

Here are some punctuation pointers for use with coordinating conjunctions:

1. When a coordinating conjunction is used between what would otherwise be two complete sentences, a comma precedes the conjunction.
2. If the coordinating conjunction is removed, coordination is maintained by using a semicolon.
3. Any coordinating link takes a semicolon when the other commas in the clause might confuse or blur the separation between the main ideas.

Another way to coordinate is to combine equally important elements from several sentences. Put them together as a series within one sentence with a coordinating conjunction between the final two elements. For example:

> Ying is one of the three best tennis players on campus.
> Trechelle is one of the three best tennis players on campus.
> Roger is one of the three best tennis players on campus.

becomes

> Ying, Trechelle, and Roger are the best tennis players on campus.

When punctuating a series of words, phrases, or clauses, place commas after all but the last element in the sequence. (For more on punctuation, see Chapter C.) Note the components of the following coordinated sentences:

> Of the 34 percent of film and television roles that go to women, few go to women of color: African Americans play 9.5 percent, Latinas play 3.1 percent, Asian-Pacifics play 2.6 percent, and Native Americans play only 0.1 percent.
> Observant Jews do not eat leavened bread during Passover, do not drive to temple, and do not pierce their bodies, for these activities are forbidden.

American xenophobia towards the Japanese probably arises from fearful ignorance, racist stereotyping, and U.S. economic uncertainty.

The second sentence has two sets of coordination in it. First, there are the two main clauses connected by *for*: *Observant Jews do not eat leavened bread during Passover, do not drive to temple, or pierce their bodies* and *these activities are forbidden.* Second, there is the series that includes *eat unleavened bread during Passover* and *drive to temple* and *pierce their bodies,* each of which is given equal importance as indicated by the coordinating conjunction *or.*

It would be boring to read ideas connected only by simple coordination. You should use coordination precisely and sparingly, as you have at your disposal many other, more sophisticated sentence patterns that point out the exact relationships between any two or three ideas that you may want to link.

## USING SUBORDINATION

Subordination usually requires that one idea be less important than the others. If you are subordinate to your boss, you are dependent on him or her in a sense; if one clause is subordinated to another in a sentence, it is grammatically dependent on it and often is less emphatic. Subordination, then, is a sentence pattern used when two ideas are not to be treated or understood as equal. The subordinated clause is added to a base, or independent, clause. Subordinate clauses may be seen as expansions on an independent clause or on a part of it.

To tilt the balance a bit to one side—to emphasize one idea and to subordinate another—you simply add the appropriate subordinating conjunction (*because, since, whereas, although, when, where, after, before, as, so that, unless*) or a relative pronoun (*who, whose, which, what, whom, that*) to the sentence that you want to deemphasize. Here is an example of this process:

*Components:*
   The FDA subjects each new drug to exhaustive tests before allowing its release onto the market.
   Many new drugs can have dangerous long-term effects.
*Results:*
   Since many new drugs can have dangerous long-term effects, the FDA subjects each new drug to exhaustive tests before allowing its release onto the market.
   The FDA subjects each new drug to exhaustive tests before allowing its release onto the market since many new drugs can have dangerous long-term effects.

In some sentences, the meaning drastically changes if the emphasis pattern is reversed:

*Components:*
    Margaret drank the warm coffee:
    She felt better:
*Results:*
    Margaret drank the warm coffee after she felt better.
    (implies that she couldn't have coffee while she was ill)
    After she drank the warm coffee, Margaret felt better.
    (implies the coffee was the cure)

or look at the difference between

    Because she is beautiful, I love her.

and

    Because I love her, she is beautiful.

Another way to subordinate is to place an idea that you want to deemphasize in a relative pronoun clause. Simply remove repeated nouns and pronouns from the two ideas and attach *who, whose, which, what, whom,* or *that* to the subordinate idea:

    Ara, who is the best runner on the team, is an above-average student.
    The lucrative U.S. diet industry, which earned $33 billion in 1990, preys upon many women's and girls' low self-image.

It is important to place the clause introduced by a relative pronoun next to the word it explains. Some sentences give more trouble than others. Look at the confusion that is caused by a misplaced clause in this sentence:

    Felice gave her sister a check for the sweater, which was quite large.

Does *which was quite large* refer to the sweater or the check? As written, it refers to the sweater; in fact, the student meant it to describe

the generous check. Still, this combining technique is easy to use. Here are some more examples:

*Components:*
> The sounds of all animals have common characteristics.
> These characteristics meet the feeding and mating needs of the particular animal.

*Result:*
> The sounds of all animals have common characteristics that meet the mating and feeding needs of the particular animal.

*Components:*
> Lolita "shipwrecked" Humbert.
> Lolita can be seen as a heartbreaker.

*Result:*
> Lolita, who can be seen as a heartbreaker, "shipwrecked" Humbert.

For variety, make an appositive of a descriptive phrase. An appositive directly follows a noun or pronoun and renames it, as in the following:

> Vincent Van Gogh, a brilliant and original painter, only sold two paintings during his lifetime.

Combine some of your sentences by leaving off the relative pronoun and verb. For example:

> Kate Chopin, who scandalized American society, wrote *The Awakening,* which is a story of a woman's sexual awakening.

becomes

> Kate Chopin, who scandalized American society, wrote *The Awakening,* a story of a woman's sexual awakening.

The writer has chosen to omit the relative pronoun (which) and verb (is) and to place the phrases in apposition. For variety, the writer has maintained the relative pronoun (who) in the first part of the sentence.

## USING ACTIVE VOICE VERSUS PASSIVE VOICE

Verbs in the active voice say what the subject is doing. Verbs in the passive voice say what is being done to the subject.

Subject    Verb

*Active:* Whites terrorized African Americans with widespread lynching after Reconstruction.

Subject      Verb

*Passive:* African Americans were terrorized with widespread lynching after Reconstruction.

Whether you choose to write a sentence in active or passive voice depends on whether you want to emphasize the doer of the action or the receiver of the action. However, you may be cautioned by instructors in some disciplines, such as history, to avoid the passive construction altogether. History is a discipline that emphasizes the doer. Use the passive voice deliberately to achieve an objective stance (for example, to avoid an inessential use of I in a scientific laboratory report) or to emphasize the thing done rather than the doer. This advice does not mean to suggest that the passive voice is any less effective than the active voice; in some instances, it is even more effective. Note the difference in the emphases in these two sentences:

Doer     Active Verb     Receiver of action

*Active:* Copernicus shocked the world of science when he asserted that humanity is not the center of the universe.

Receiver of action     Passive Verb     Doer

*Passive:* The world of science was shocked by Copernicus when he asserted that humanity is not the center of the universe.

Both sentences say approximately the same thing, but the active voice emphasizes who did the shocking, whereas the passive voice construction emphasizes who was shocked.

Be careful not to overuse the passive voice; it is generally more direct to say, "Three gaily dressed, costumed men told the tale," than to say, "The tale was told by three gaily dressed, costumed men." However, if you find the subject of the sentence relatively unimportant, you can feel free to revise the sentence using the passive voice. When vague and indefinite subjects, such as someone or people, weaken a sentence, the passive voice is preferable:

*Weak:* People believe that open-mindedness is the highest virtue.
*Better:* Open-mindedness is considered the highest virtue.
*Weak:* The writer wrote the book in 1909.
*Better:* The book was written in 1909.
*Weak:* Someone has called the shot which killed Crispus Attucks and began the American Revolution "the shot heard round the world."
*Better:* The shot which killed Crispus Attucks and began the American Revolution has been called "the shot heard round the world."

It is important to keep in mind that the use of the passive voice is simply another way for you to direct your emphasis. It is neither all good nor all bad; use it for appropriate occasions, and refrain from adhering to inflexible rules either way.

### REORDERING

Many phrases or clauses can be rearranged so that your sentences are varied and focused. Suppose you have several sentences beginning with *because* or a similar subordinate conjunction. An easy way to achieve variety is to reverse the order of the clauses or to move a phrase to a different part of the sentence. Thus

> Because the U.S. diet industry preys upon many women's and girls' low self-image, it earned $33 billion in 1990.

becomes

> The U.S. diet industry earned $33 billion in 1990 because it preys upon many women's and girls' low self-image.

Here is another example drawn from a paragraph that has four sentences starting with *when*. Certainly, the following one could benefit from reordering:

> When babies first speak, they tend to say nouns such as "mama" or "ball."

The phrase "when babies first speak" can be transposed to the end of the sentence without changing the meaning, and the alteration will add variety to a paragraph that opens too many sentences with *when* or a similar construction:

> Babies tend to say nouns such as "mama" or "ball" when they first speak.

The following sentence has five phrases that might be rearranged to add sentence variety:

> For most people what they do or how much they do for charity is less important than the fact that they have contributed to a worthwhile cause.

The best way to tell whether phrases or clauses can be rearranged more successfully is to try the sentence parts in a number of positions, noting changes in the meaning of the sentence.

Certain sentence parts cannot be rearranged coherently because a phrase must be placed next to the word it modifies. Usually, you can determine whether the new arrangement works by reading your sentence aloud. The flaw in sentence structure illustrated below is very common; it can be not only misleading but also very funny:

Philomela is told of her sister's death *before engaging in a love affair.*

It is unclear to whom the love affair belongs: is it Philomela's or her sister's? Since the italicized phrase in fact applies to Philomela, it must be placed next to her name:

Before engaging in a love affair, Philomela is told that her sister died.

Philomela, before engaging in a love affair, is told that her sister died.

## CREATING BALANCE AND RHYTHM

Well-combined sentences sound pleasant when read aloud partly because we intuitively listen for certain rhythms. These rhythms are signaled by sentence length, parallelism, punctuation, and directional movement.

### Sentence Length

Although the average length of sentences among professional writers is twenty words, there is no ideal sentence length. One of the things that makes for effective writing is variety in sentence length. The most emphatic presentations are those in which a few long sentences are suddenly punctuated by a short one:

When laws are invoked that require sexual perpetrators to announce their presence in a community, the victim is mainly affected by the law. She is engaged in healing mentally as well as physically. For the victim, this law may provide some sense of security in knowing the perpetrator's whereabouts. She may feel "safer" in knowing that the perpetrator is being observed by police. Obviously, not all victims would feel this way. Some might be more threatened by knowing where the perpetrator is; they might imagine seeing him at every corner, develop fears of going outside, and might develop vindictive feelings. Some argue that if the victim deems revenge and retaliation necessary, this law could be potentially very harmful to her. She may even undertake illegal measures and wind up in jail or more debilitated psychologically and physically than when she started. But the chances of a victim coming in contact with the perpetrator are slim if the community is forewarned of his whereabouts. Most likely, the victim will choose to avoid confrontations. Besides, if the victim aims to seek revenge, whether or not the victim does something illegal cannot be blamed on the notification law. The accountability would be complex, involving, but not limited to, an investigation of her psychological state at the time of the retribution. The other kind of victims, those who would feel threatened by the presence of the perpetrator, would more than likely make it a point to move away, in which case the law aids the victim once again.

## Parallelism

When used properly and not to excess, coordination achieves balance and rhythm through parallelism, or uniformity of word and phrase formation. In *I came, I saw, I conquered,* each group of words is parallel, for each is made up of a subject and verb. Notice the parallelism in the following examples:

> My reservation in this matter is due *to my inability* to understand your demands and *to my fear* of the consequences were I to agree.
> Hip hop and rap music are extensions of the African American traditions of *blues, jazz,* and *rhythm and blues.*
> When I get an idea for a poem, I want *to leap into the air, to scream at the moon, to grab history by its collar and shake it.*

To maintain parallelism, you must use the same part of speech (noun, verb, etc.) for each element in the series:

> *Not parallel:* Cesar Chavez organized local workers, activists, and galvanized Chicanos and Mexican-Americans throughout the U.S.
> *Parallel:* Cesar Chavez organized local workers, rallied local activists, and galvanized Chicanos and Mexican-Americans throughout the U.S.

## Punctuation

Your writing can also be improved through judicious use of dashes and semicolons. Both forms of punctuation can make your sentences rhythmic, balanced, and emphatic.

### The Dash

Dashes show special emphasis: parenthetical comments, initial or final focus, interruptions, and illustrative series. To set off a part of a sentence with dashes is to call attention to it. The same phrase could be separated from the rest of the sentence by commas or parentheses, but these devices would deemphasize the phrase. Following are some examples of appropriate ways to use dashes. Read the sentences aloud and observe the rhythm and emphasis in each.

Parenthetical

One example of a group that has made eradicating disease their mission—and a successful one at that—is Amigos de las Americas, which sends teens to Latin America to help develop community sanitation projects in rural towns.

### Final Focus

It sets Americans apart from all other first-world, Western nations; it clearly is not an effective deterrent; it has been called state-sanctioned murder—the death penalty.

### Initial Focus

AIDS—it can strike anyone regardless of gender, color, economic status, or sexual orientation.

### Interruptions

He replied, "Of course—I mean, of course not—why would I do a thing like that?"

### Series Wrap-up

Equal pay for equal work, respect for individuality, recognition in the job market—that's what women want in their careers.

### *The Semicolon*

The semicolon is used to show that the parts of the sentence separated by the semicolon are to be equally emphasized. Two independent clauses separated by a semicolon are therefore coordinated. As perhaps its most important function, the semicolon serves to relate the thoughts in two clauses. The writer might be using a semicolon to show one of three things about the relationship: (1) that the independent clauses are equal and separate but are linked to one idea; (2) that although the clauses could stand alone, the second amplifies the first; or (3) that the second directly contrasts the first. Here are some examples:

### Equivalence in Emphasis

"Diversity" is not difficult to achieve at the college; multiculturalism is a real challenge here.

Note that the emphasis would remain the same even if the order of the ideas were reversed.

### Amplification

Richard III is one of Shakespeare's most memorable villains; he is brilliantly articulate, skillfully manipulative, and morally reprehensible.

### Contrast

Anyone can rewrite a paper; not everyone can rewrite a paper well.

Situated between independent clauses, the semicolon signals a link between complete thoughts. The rhythm is less fluid and slightly more formal than it is with the coordinating conjunctions; for variety, however, and in moderation, semicolons may be used interchangeably with coordinating conjunctions. (Note the use of the semicolon in the preceding sentence.)

Be careful not to place complete independent clauses together without either a coordinating conjunction or a semicolon; to do so creates an error called the comma splice or run-on sentence (see Chapter B).

### Directional Movement

The pattern of movement—backward or forward—you choose for your sentences also affects their rhythm and meaning. You can vary the rhythm and focus of your sentences by varying the direction. Periodic sentences move forward (toward the period) while cumulative sentences move backward (toward the first word of the sentence). The reader's attention is drawn toward the period in the periodic sentence or toward the first part of the sentence in the cumulative sentence.

> Before I had time to refuse, *he had slammed his foot on the accelerator.*
> *She drunkenly made her way across the room,* knocking her hips into tables as she moved, swinging her arms in weird contortions, and singing "Blue Moon" as loudly as she could.

Whether you select forward movement, as in the first example, or backward movement, as in the second example, is simply a decision about effect: the rhythmic, almost poetic sway of the cumulative sentence seems to fit the subject matter in the second sentence. In fact, the high frequency of cumulative sentences in modern essays should encourage you to write them. They so resemble the natural flow of thought that they are often more easily incorporated into a rough draft than periodic sentences, which tend to be assembled from simple sentences during the revision stage.

Cumulative sentences may be developed in much the same way as the paragraphs discussed in Chapter 4. That is, effective cumulative sentences are a logical sequence of clauses and phrases built through coordination and subordination. The particular point of the sentence will, naturally, dictate how you develop it, since certain points require more expansion than others. You might try numbering as you indent your sentence parts to keep track as you write. The base clause, always first in the cumulative sentence, is number 1. The next phrase or clause can be numbered 2 if it expands on (subordinates) the base, or it may be a 1, merely a restatement of the first phrase (any two phrases saying the same thing have the same number and are coordinate). The next element may be another 2 if it expands on the base (subordinate to the first clause and coordinate with the second) or a 3 if it expands on (subordinates) the preceding clause, and so on. Note the numbering for the following sentences:

  (1) He was vigorously telling old war stories,
    (2) his arms flashing about [an expansion on 1]
      (3) as if to keep his enemies at a distance, [an expansion on 2],

(2) his smile wide [an example of 1].
    (3) turning to a snicker now and then. [an expansion of 2]
(1) She was an outgoing young woman,
  (2) with a deep-pitched voice [an expansion on 1]
    (3) that bellowed [expansion on 2]
      (4) when she spoke to strangers, [an expansion on 3]
        (5) especially to men [an expansion on 4]
(1) The nonsmoker has every right to breathe clean air,
  (2) not the smoke-polluted air one finds everywhere these days
    [an expansion on 1]
    (3) in school, [an example of 2]
    (3) in restaurants, [an example of 2]
    (3) in elevators, and [an example of 2]
    (3) especially in doctors' offices [an example of 2]

Cumulative sentences are pleasurable to write, allowing a sense of immediacy, for once the base clause has been written, further details can be added more or less as they occur to you.

Keep in mind, however, that most writers mix patterns of movement as a device to achieve varied stylistic effects. In fact, do not forget the value of short sentences, especially when you want to emphasize a point or pose a climactic remark. Use longer sentences to amplify the shorter ones. Keep your purpose and your audience in mind as you develop sentence strategies. Remember that you are communicating to an audience.

---

### Exercises

A. Combine each group of sentence components in at least two ways and explain your purpose.

1. Because of my age I am stereotyped as a member of Generation X.
   Other than my age, however, I have little in common with the stereotype.
   Besides being politically aware and active, I am working towards a career as a social worker.
   I am tired of being labelled a "slacker."

2. My father had worked for an automobile firm since he came to California in the middle 1940s.
   In about 1953 he decided to go to work for himself.
   He chose to be a landscape gardener.

3. Recycling programs in our cities have been phenomenally successful.
   It's to the point that we have a surplus of certain recyclables.
   We also have difficulty with maintaining the labor force needed to contend with the pickup and depositing of recyclables.
   It is imperative that we reconsider our current practices.

4. Placing an elderly family member in a nursing home is a tricky business.
   Culturally derived beliefs often compound the stress.

African Americans emphasize the importance of taking care of one's own.

This practice often leads to extended families where ties are formed on the basis of need, not blood.

5. Being sick became second nature to me.

The nurses explained to me why I couldn't move and what they were going to do to help me.

However, I was still very upset.

6. Embarking upon a committed relationship during school is difficult.

Besides the distractions of romance, insecurities in one's mate may arise from the necessity of making academic responsibilities the priority.

Open communication and a willing exchange of support are essential.

7. Masako is a strict vegetarian and never lets me forget it.

Each visit to a restaurant is a trial in which she interrogates the server.

What stock is the base for the soup?

Are the tortilla chips fried in animal lard?

When I asked if she enjoyed her vacation in San Francisco, she let slip that she ate fried calamari.

I pounced, demanding, "What, you only abstain from eating cute animals?"

8. Distribution can be the independent's worst enemy.

In the financing stage of a picture, a distribution deal can be a major factor.

9. Some Native Americans were nomadic hunters who followed the buffalo.

Some were primarily farmers who tended peach orchards or raised corn and melons in the fertile river valleys.

10. Chinese immigrants spent years digging and blasting tunnels in the Sierra Nevada mountains.

Then they laid and hammered ties and rails.

They worked from the West towards the East.

At the end of the nineteenth century, the transcontinental railroad was complete.

The Chinese workers were driven away.

B. Combine the sentences in each group below in different ways, each time subordinating different elements.

1. I am 5'11" and weigh 125 pounds.

My legs are deceptively strong.

At the gym, I sometimes ask if I can work in with whoever is doing squats.

Usually I am met with patronizing smirks.

Then I squat 185 pounds.

Most men do not expect a woman to lift as much as them.

Especially when she is feminine and shapely.

2. Dr. Albert Norras is wanted by the FBI.

He is a con-man.

Dr. Norras is a leader of an occult revolutionary group.

He requires his followers to turn over all their belongings to him as proof of their loyalty.

3. The building on the corner lot is for sale.

The lot is in a good location.

The lot is right in the middle of a busy business district.

The district is currently undergoing gentrification.

4. Tyrone ate heavily at the Thanksgiving dinner.

The Thanksgiving dinner was bountiful.

Tyrone cannot control himself.

5. I used to work for Atlantic-Richfield as a paralegal.

The company is sometimes touted as exemplary in its nondiscrimi-
nation policies.

It distressed me that people of color were hired for drudge work like
box inventory and photocopying.

Almost all managerial positions were filled by whites.

Their statistics of numbers of minorities hired probably looks good.

6. Produce in California is unusually large and varied.

This struck me when I traveled in the midwest.

I thought the lemons were kumquats.

The stocker asked me what a kumquat is.

7. During the Civil War, Abraham Lincoln proposed a "black exodus."

He claimed the only solution to the unwillingness of whites to accept African Americans was separation.

He recommended a settlement in Central America for African
Americans.

Lincoln's sentiment was that African Americans were the cause of racism and the Civil War.

For the most part, free African Americans were outraged.

8. Donna Williams' book, *Nobody Nowhere, The Extraordinary Autobiography of an Autistic,* is eye-opening.

Autistic men and women have trouble negotiating what many would
consider basic social skills.

When overstimulated, autistics will often lapse into a catatonic state.

One summer, Williams learned French and German, wrote a book,
composed a musical score for a movie, finished several paintings,
and prepared an instruction manual for teachers of autistic children.

Autistics are designated retarded, but many of their abilities are far
beyond the capabilities of a "normal" individual.

C. Change the active constructions below to passive forms. Describe the difference in meaning or emphasis. When would the active form be more desirable? the passive form?

1. Roger Maris hit 61 home runs in 1961.

2. Only a small number of immigrants survived the long months of hiding until someone secured their passage from Russia to the United States.

3. Despite changing social conventions, some view interracial relationships
with curiosity, or even distaste.

4. This summer Sweden passed a law legalizing same-sex marriages.

5. Republicans and conservative Democrats criticize President Clinton's
proposed national health care plan.

6. Over the past year, the English Anglican church expanded significantly the duties of women in the ministry.

D. Change these passive constructions to active forms. Describe the difference in emphasis between the passive and active versions of each sentence. When would the passive form be most desirable? the active form?

1. A roasted chicken breast was eaten by my father, and it gave him salmonella.

2. The wine was spoiled by someone.

3. The company's earnings were assessed by the tax commissioner and they were found to be substantial.

4. An error was made by the president that the company had to pay for no matter how it was explained away.

5. On October 22, 1962, the United States was informed by President Kennedy that the Soviet Union had begun to build missile bases in Cuba.

6. The Germans were criticized by some for not having sent a representative to the fiftieth anniversary D-Day commemorations in Normandy.

E. Identify the structures by adding numbers to each of these cumulative sentences.

1. It is the vast darkness of a cavern's mouth, the cavern of anterior darkness whence issues the stream of consciousness. (D. H. Lawrence)

2. The pear tree across the road opposite was now in full and frosty bloom, the twigs and branches springing not outward from the limbs but standing motionless and perpendicular above the horizontal boughs like the separate and upstreaming hair of a drowned woman sleeping upon the uttermost floor of the windless and tideless sea. (William Faulkner)

3. He was walking ahead of me along Fifth Avenue in his alert, aggressive way, his hands out a little from his body as if to fight off interference, his head moving sharply here and there, adapting itself to his restless eyes. (F. Scott Fitzgerald)

4. The literature of our society dealing with imprisonment and capital punishment is extensive, including contributions by Tolstoy, Camus, Dostoevsky, and Sartre. (Theodore Roszak)

5. Yet, as I said before, nonviolence has the power of moral suasion, which makes it possible to solicit help from many white and liberal summer soldiers, who would otherwise shrink rapidly from the cause. (J. Oliver Killens)

6. Your fingers must do the releasing, on their own, remotely, like the opening of a flower. (Lewis Thomas)

7. Those last days! There were so many religions in conflict, each ready to save the world with its own dogma, each perfectly intolerant of the other. (E. B. White)

8. "Feeling" as I am using it here covers much more than it does in the technical vocabulary of psychology, where it denotes only pleasure and displeasure, or even in the shifting limits of ordinary discourse, where it sometimes means sensation (as when one says a paralyzed limb has no feeling in it), sometimes sensibility (as we speak of hurting someone's feelings), sometimes emotion (e.g., as a situation is said to harrow your

feelings, or to evoke tender feelings), or a directed emotional attitude (we say we feel strongly about something), or even our general mental or physical condition, feeling well or ill, blue or a bit above ourselves. (Suzanne K. Langer)

9. October 7 began as a commonplace enough day, one of those days that sets the teeth on edge with its tedium, its small frustrations. (Joan Didion)

10. At first I thought it was another party, a wild rout that had resolved itself into "hide-and-seek" or "sardines-in-the-box" with all the house thrown open to the game. (F. Scott Fitzgerald)

## IMITATING SENTENCES

Even with several devices for building sentences now in your repertoire, you may feel that you haven't quite found your own style. One effective way of experimenting with various styles and of broadening your store of sentence patterns is to imitate (or mimic) the style of other good writers, writers you respect. Not all good sentences, not even most, arise out of sentence combining during revision. Having a selection of sentence patterns in your head can ease your drafting process.

The best place to find model patterns is in your reading. The process is simple and enjoyable: pick out sentence structures that you like from the work of professional writers and imitate their patterns, replacing their words and ideas with your own. To assure that you can pick out these patterns accurately, you have to be able to do three things:

1. Identify the base clause.
2. Identify the additions.
3. Identify the connections between the descriptive parts of the sentence and what they describe.

Suppose you have the following sentence:

*Pattern One:* Every child deserves love.

The sentence is only a base clause, made up of a doer (*every child*), a verb (*deserves*), and a thing done (*love*). You could imitate the sentence

by substituting in those same positions other words that would convey different ideas in the same way:

Many children like bugs.

*Children* is the doer, *like* the verb, and *bugs* the thing done. Take a look at the following imitations, noting the form:

Most cats climb drapes.
Some gardeners do landscaping.
Every politician needs support.

The next pattern is a bit more complicated:

*Pattern Two:* Despite what a son or daughter has done to disappoint his or her parents, every child deserves love and understanding.

The base clause is *every child deserves love and understanding.* The base is the same as the base in the first pattern except that now the phrase *love and understanding* serves as the thing done. Also, there is an addition, in this case a subordinate clause: *Despite what a son or daughter has done to disappoint his or her parents.* Its purpose is to tell to what extent every child deserves. An imitation of the base might be:

Many gardeners do landscaping and general maintenance.

An imitation of the addition might be:

Although some do not advertise all their services,

The completed imitation would be:

Although some do not advertise all their services, many gardeners do landscaping and general maintenance.

Here are other imitations of the same pattern:

Because votes are not easy to get, every politician needs support and recognition.
Unless they have been well trained or declawed, most cats climb drapes and furniture legs.

Perhaps these patterns seem too easy. You probably use such structures all the time without consciously imitating them, without giving the bases and additions much thought. However, far more complicated patterns, found in the writing of your favorite authors, can be analyzed and imitated in the same way. Following are examples of more complex patterns.

*Pattern Three:* Although many potted plants thrive in indirect sunlight, a few, including the pothos, can survive in dimly lit environments.

The base clause is *a few can survive in dimly lit environments.* The base clause is interrupted by the phrase *including the pothos,* which describes the word *few.* The additions are *including the pothos* and *Although many potted plants thrive in indirect sunlight* (describing *can survive*). Thus the pattern to imitate is the following:

Although many potted plants thrive in indirect sunlight, a few, including the pothos, can survive in dimly lit environments.

In the imitation a base is needed:

Some individuals can read at a speed of 3,000 words a minute.

Two additions are required, one beginning with an -ing word:

including high school and college students

and one with a subordinating conjunction:

Although many students today are slow readers,

The resulting sentence would be:

Although many students today are slow readers, some individuals, including high school and college students, can read at a speed of 3,000 words a minute.

Here are other imitations of the same pattern:

Despite all the cultural conditioning by the media, some men, including young ones, realize that being a "he-man" is not the best role to play.
Until someone warns them, swarms of teenagers, meaning many of our friends, will mindlessly follow the dictates laid open to them by fanatics.
Because women are entering the workforce at twice the rate of men, women's organizations, bringing large numbers of qualified executives into the business world, are evening out employee rolls for most large companies.

Another pattern might be cumulative.

*Pattern Four:* Working at the wine bottling plant bored me after only two weeks, drove me to counting the minutes left in the day, days filled with small talk, about as meaningful as the incessant droning of the label machine, which I was stationed in front of.

The base clause comes first (*Working at the wine bottling plant bored me*). There are five additions, each expanding on the one before it. An imitation might be:

> Telling my mother that I wanted to drop out of school for a term made me feel small almost immediately, caused me to reevaluate my reasons, reasons that were perhaps irrational, not in line with my usual decisions, which always had to pass rigorous logical tests.

*Telling my mother that I wanted to drop out of school for a term made me feel small* is the base. The first addition tells "when": *almost immediately.* The second addition takes a past tense verb: *caused me to reevaluate my reasons.* The third addition repeats the last word of the second: *reasons that were perhaps irrational.* The fourth addition describes the preceding addition: *not in line with my usual decisions.* The last addition describes the last word of the fourth addition and begins with *which* (*who* might have been substituted, had the sentence called for its use): *which always had to pass rigorous logical tests.*

Whole paragraphs can be imitated in the same fashion. You will be surprised how smoothly some will flow from your fingers. Others may require that you stop to analyze the structures. Sometimes the structures will be familiar and the imitation will serve only to remind you to use them when you write; other times the imitation will cause you to compose sentences that you might never have tried or conceived. An additional benefit, knowing how to disassemble a sentence to analyze its meaning, will help you read complicated passages with ease.

---

### Exercises

A. Imitate the following sentences using your own ideas.
1. Knowledge is always a matter of whole experience, what St. Paul calls knowing in full, and never a matter of mental conception really. (D. H. Lawrence)
2. The Oedipus Complex was a household word, the incest motive a commonplace of tea-table chat. (D. H. Lawrence)
3. One of them, a young dog hound without judgment yet, bayed once, and they ran for a few feet on what seemed to be a trail. Then they stopped, looking back at the men, eager enough, not baffled, merely questioning, as if asking, "Now what?" Then they rushed back to the colt, where Boon, still astride it, slashed at them with a belt. (William Faulkner)

4. When they reached the end of the lane they could see the moon, almost full, tremendous and pale and still lightless in the sky from which day had not quite gone. (William Faulkner)

5. A sure sign of distress: telephone numbers stormed through my head—area codes, digits. I must telephone someone. (Saul Bellow)

6. Some statements are meant to pass, some to echo. (Saul Bellow)

7. Business, sure of its own transcendent powers, got us all to interpret life through its practices. (Saul Bellow)

8. I try to feel proud, but in my heart I know that it was fear of what his friends might do to me that kept me silent, and not the code of the street. (Norman Podhoretz)

9. My son—who is no genius, just an alive young mind—is learning plumbing, electricity, auto mechanics, the joys of sharing. (Judson Jerome)

10. It was an immense crowd, two thousand at the least and growing every minute. (George Orwell)

# WHAT IS THE BEST WORD?

A reporter, apparently expecting a sophisticated, insightful response, once asked Ernest Hemingway what was the single most difficult task he had as a writer. After some careful thought, Hemingway replied that the most difficult task was "finding the right word." It sounds simple enough, but selecting the absolutely right word to convey the exact meaning you intend for a specific situation is no easy task. In this chapter, you will learn several principles that will help you make important decisions about effective word choices.

## MATCH YOUR WORDS TO YOUR PURPOSE

Be natural. Many students feel that when they write they must "sound academic," and inevitably they come up with language that sounds just like the lectures they most hate: stuffy, wordy, excessively formal. Big words can sound impressive, but good lecturers and writers do not stupefy their audiences with them. Their lectures are designed to suit a purpose, and the words are impressive only if chosen with care and used precisely. An excessively formal student paper sounds just as insincere and stiff as a stuffy lecture. For that matter, any piece of writing that is unnecessarily formal for its audience or purpose is drudgery to read.

College writers should select words that would flow naturally in a typical intellectual, friendly discussion with a classmate. A good way to ensure that you have kept your reader in mind is to read your essay aloud. Does your writing sound like you do? Is your writing clear? If the paper discusses a highly technical subject and you had to use new terms to convey your material, have you defined them carefully for the reader? You can follow a simple rule: be yourself. If a phrase you have written doesn't sound like you, revise it.

### Levels of Language

Good writing is natural and consistent. Appropriate word choice is primarily a matter of recognizing and choosing from the various levels of usage. Language can be divided, for the purpose of discussion, into three levels: cultivated, everyday, and informal. Cultivated language is the most formal, made up largely of words that most people do not hear every day but that may be common in academic and professional contexts. Everyday language refers to the middle range of words. Informal language is the least formal; it includes slang and colloquial expressions. The word "question" can be found in just about any context from the most formal to the least formal, but "inquiry" would suggest a cultivated context. The everyday word "alcohol" has its cultivated form, "intoxicant," and its informal form, "booze." The everyday word "children" can be "upgraded" to "offspring" or "progeny" or "downgraded" to "kids."

The range of usage from cultivated to informal is illustrated in Figure 8-1. Most of the writing and speaking encountered in college-level work is cultivated or everyday. Interestingly enough, studies have shown that the more educated a person becomes, the more he or she communicates at the cultivated and everyday levels and the less he or she uses the informal level. Using a language level is neither right nor wrong in itself, but different levels fit different purposes. As you study the graph, think about which level you use most frequently at school: in discussions, in the snack bar, and in papers—from personal essays to research.

### Exercises

A. Place the following words in sentences. Then identify their level of formality as cultivated, everyday, or informal: "guy," "resilient," "lax," "vomit," and "apathy."

B. In the following passage correct any wordiness and stiff expressions so that it will be more readable. Read the passage aloud to hear the problem areas. Note that the excessive formality of the writing causes the passage to sound humorous, whereas the writer intended it to be serious

Left-handed people are a persecuted minority in our society. From the time they reach for their Pablum with the "wrong hand" the idea is infused in their craniums solidly: right is right; left is wrong. A trifle later, when they advance to the lowest level of educational endeavor, they are firmly admonished that they should not use their left digits to learn penmanship. When they also travail to handle a scissors for the purpose of producing a string of paper dolls, they are described with jeers as having clutched the instrument in the very reverse of the normal manner.

This humiliation continues into adulthood. The laughter and scoffing affect different left-handed individuals in different ways. Amid all the embarrassment there is one who is willing to ignore the fuss. In the same room there may be another left-handed person who succumbs to social pressure and uses his right hand in public.

C. List ten words in your everyday vocabulary and try to identify more formal and less formal synonyms (words that mean about the same thing).

D. Write a short dialogue between you and your parents or you and your employer on the subject of an inappropriate use of profanity in public. Can you detect different levels of language usage in the dialogue? What does the level of a person's language say about his or her personality?

E. Analyze the level of language in two advertisements, one from a technical journal and one from a popular magazine. What does the language level tell you about the readers of the periodical?

F. Note the inconsistency in language levels in this passage from a student's research paper. What should the student have done to make her language more acceptable?

The Romans not only imbibed spirits of alcohol when sacrifices were proffered unto the gods, but on great occasions they also had the tendency to "tie one on." On these great occasions and for public entertainment, in ceremonious fashion, the wine was mixed with water

**Figure 8-1. Levels of language.**

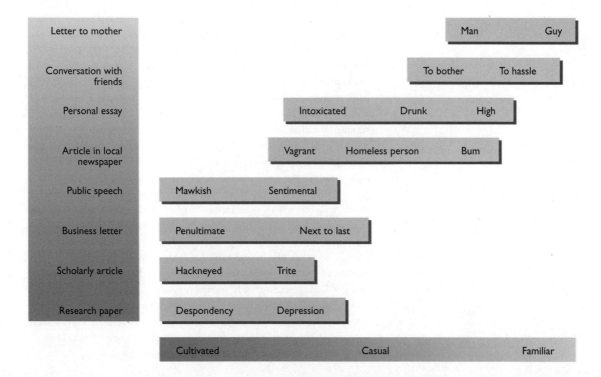

so that the people who partook could return home uninebriated. It was common for people to get loaded, though, to the point that they would consume as much as seven gallons of wine during the festivities. The Romans believed that wine was a very spiritual drink and there was nothing wrong with getting snockered, not morally, anyway. Pliny, a Roman writer, once pointed out something that Romans who drank to excess probably believed: "Wine refreshes the stomach, sharpens the appetite, and conduces to slumber." Thus Romans drank heartily with no reservations, physical or mental.

G. Identify the predominant level of language usage (cultivated, everyday, or informal) in each of the following passages. Which words, in particular, clearly show the level you have indicated?

1. Pastimes occur in social and temporal matrices of varying degrees of complexity, and hence vary in complexity. However, if we use the transaction as the unit of social intercourse, we can dissect out of appropriate situations an entity which may be called a simple pastime. This may be defined as a series of semi-ritualistic, simple, complementary transactions arranged around a single field of material, whose primary object is to structure an interval of time. The beginning and end of the interval are typically signaled by procedures or rituals. The transactions are adaptively programmed so that each party will obtain the maximum gains or advantages during the interval. The better his adaptation, the more he will get out of it. (Eric Berne, *Games People Play*)

2. So the Woodman went at once to the trees and began to work; and he soon made a truck out of the limbs of trees from which he chopped away all the leaves and branches. He fastened it together with wooden pegs and made the four wheels out of short pieces of a big tree trunk. So fast and so well did he work that by the time the mice began to arrive the truck was all ready for them. (L. Frank Baum, *The Wizard of Oz*)

3. We were stuck a whole day in the Suez Canal. A steamer ahead of us ran aground, and had to discharge cargo. Then we passed Sunday at Port Said, which is a hole such as words won't express. Today we are just halfway between Sicily and Corsica. Tomorrow afternoon we hope to reach Marseilles, and by Sunday (11th) we should get to Paris. After four months' steady travel, and fifteen thousand miles of ocean, I ought to be glad to get anywhere; but I don't really feel puffed by the prospect. Our voyage since leaving Brisbane has been so charming that I am spoiled. Never a day when the weather was not fair, and generally quite exquisite; a sea almost motionless for ten thousand miles; constant change, and most of the time near strange and fascinating lands; for the first time in my life I have learned what an ideal journey is. Luckily there is no other like it, and can't be. If there were, I should start on it as soon as I could get my teeth put in order. As there is not, I must first get LaFarge comfortably started for home, and then I will read my letters, and think what next. On reaching Marseilles I shall mail this letter at once so that you may know of my safe arrival. At Paris I shall get something from you, no doubt, and then will start fresh. Love to you all. (Henry Adams, Letter to a Niece, October 8, 1891)

4. Science is enormously disparate—easily the most varied and diverse of human pursuits. The scientific endeavor ranges from the study of animal behavior all the way to particle physics, and from the purest of mathematics back again to the most practical problems of shelter and hunger, sickness and war. Nobody has succeeded in catching all this in one net. And yet the conviction persists—scientists themselves believe, at heart—that behind the diversity lies a unity. In those luminous moments of discovery, in the various approaches and the painful tension required to arrive at them, and then in the community of science, organized worldwide to doubt and criticize, test and exploit discoveries—somewhere in that constellation there are surely constants, to begin with. Deeper is the lure that in the bewildering variety of the world as it is there may be found some astonishing simplicities. (Judson, Introduction, *The Search for Solutions*)

## The Feeling That Your Words Convey

Even if you manage to select language that is both appropriate in level to your topic and natural for you, you haven't limited your choices enough to be sure the words you pick are the best ones. Another important consideration is the feeling attached to your words.

Words have both *denotation* and *connotation*. The *denotation* is the literal definition of the word: the denotation of the word "orphan" is "a child, one or both of whose parents are dead." The *connotation* of a word is the attitude or feeling generated by the word. "Orphan" implies loss, emptiness, lovelessness, and general unhappiness—it has a negative connotation. Although the dictionary frequently gives hints to connotation in the manner it defines a word or through providing a usage of the word in context, it sometimes offers little direct advice about using words with the correct connotation. Under the entry for "nigger," most dictionaries would say that the word is "offensive." But for less apparently negative and positive words, perhaps only a simple definition would occur. Particularly confusing can be a list of synonyms that reflect various connotations with only a vague similarity in their essential meanings. The word "vacillate" is a good example. The dictionary may well tell us that the verb means "to waver in mind or opinion; to be indecisive," but it also provides us with various synonyms such as "hesitate," "oscillate," and "waver," which suggest less negative judgment. In the same way, a word such as "kindred" offers practically no hint of

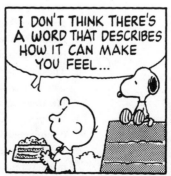

its usual positive connotation when defined as "of the same origin or family." Connotation can become a real issue for a writer looking up a new word; without information on the feeling behind the meaning, a writer cannot use the word accurately.

When you write—especially if you are using new words—it is important to use the right connotation of each word. A man would not walk up to his date and tell her that her perfume has an exotic "odor." Odor is more neutral than a word like "stench" but is still slightly negative; "fragrance," on the other hand, carries a positive connotation.

*"I __am__ a member of the legal profession, but I'm not a lawyer in the pejorative sense."*

## Exercises

A. Suppose you are writing an essay on divorce and the trauma associated with separation. You have written the sentence "Divorce may be such a frightening experience because of the finality it represents that the couple may avoid the experience altogether and settle for separation." You want to substitute something for the word experience, which has already occurred too many times in your essay. You look up experience in your book of synonyms and find the following substitutes: adventure, escapade, lark, ordeal, tribulation, trial. Do any of these words suit the sentence? Analyze the denotations and connotations of each substitute and base your decision on your analysis.

B. The context always coincides with the connotation of your words. In the sentences below, show how the context helps to clarify the connotative meaning of the words. Why would a word with a different connotation be inappropriate?

1. The *girl* who cleans our home comes from a large family who work together weekends. (Compare *woman*.)
2. *Lesbian* mothers are lobbying at the Capitol in order to gain the rights promised to all people in the Constitution. (Compare *queer*.)
3. The defendant was judged not responsible for the crime since he was temporarily *insane*. (Compare *crazy*.)
4. Her *clumsy* girlfriend broke the antique china cup. (Compare *awkward*.)
5. Her boss's *temper tantrums* finally became too stressful for her to endure. (Compare *outbursts*.)
6. Though some clothing appears to be of good quality, it is very *cheaply* made. (Compare *inexpensively*.)

C. Discuss the various connotations that would be conveyed if each of the following words was inserted into the blank: gullibility, innocence, naivete.

> The girl's _____ about sexual matters surprised everyone in her therapy group.

D. What is the difference in denotation in the following pairs of words? In connotation?
1. Aggressive/pushy
2. Reserved/repressed
3. Liberal/permissive
4. Stocky/obese
5. Elderly/old
6. Wealthy/rich
7. Doctrine/policy
8. Request/demand
9. Debt/loan
10. Agreement/compromise
11. Smart/intelligent
12. Independent/alienated
13. Violence/Action (as in a movie)
14. Uninterested/apathetic
15. Prostitute/whore
16. House/home
17. Extensive/exhaustive
18. Long/voluminous
19. Employment/job
20. Reuse/recycle

## SPECIFIC TROUBLE SPOTS

Certain words and phrases tend to give writers trouble. Here are some practical suggestions about their use. Additional usage information is provided in Chapter D.

### I, One, and You

Many students struggle with the problem of how to refer to themselves in their papers. Should they use *I*? The answer depends on the emphasis of the sentence and the purpose of the paper. Some writing, including personal essays, descriptive essays, diaries, letters, and other informal assignments, is rather relaxed and lends itself to use of *I*. To do otherwise would be indirect and unnatural. In the following sentences (from a student's personal essay), the use of *I* seems the natural choice:

> In spite of the fact that I have lived in a large city all of my life, I have always yearned to be part of a community. I found such a group when I moved to a small town in Wisconsin to at-

tend college. There I was not only a part of the college community, but also a part of the town where I served on the Miners' Council and various conservation committees.

Had the student used the more impersonal *one* or the expression *the writer* to refer to himself, this passage would have lost its energy, its intimacy. In this paper the writer wants to show the reader his personal response to being in a community; the *I* is appropriate.

The use of *I* should be avoided, however, if the focus of the sentence does not need to be the writer. Unnecessary reference to yourself only misleads the reader about the content of the passage. Instead of focusing on the *I*, bring forward the real subject of your sentence. Note the difference in emphasis in the following sentences:

> I think that the beach is most beautiful in the winter when the sand is damp and musty and the sky is hazy.
> The beach is most beautiful in winter when the sand is damp and musty and the sky is hazy.

There is no need for the writer's presence in the statement. The reader assumes that all assertions not attributed to another source are statements made by the writer, ones that the writer will then support.

*One* is less personal and more general than *I,* but tedious repetition of *one* can wear on the nerves:

> Whenever *one* tries to correct *one's* own writing, *one* finds *oneself* in a difficult position.

Contemporary usage calls for the simple use of *I* over *one* when you intend to refer to yourself alone. *One* or *the writer of this essay* can get stuffy; on the other hand, unnecessary reference to yourself makes your writing disagreeable in another way. Be as direct as you can in your choice of pronouns, always weighing the relative importance of each questionable pronoun.

Another stickler is the use of *you.* In friendly conversations people often use *you* to mean a group of people. "You get up and the first thing on your mind is coffee," they say. Who is the *you*? It clearly includes the speaker, but it is also a more general reference, probably to the audience. To use *you* in this general sense may be too informal for essays written in some disciplines. Unless you are deliberately addressing the reader, you may wish to avoid the generalized use of you. In this book *you* is used to keep a conversational tone. I am addressing the readers directly.

Try to use "people" instead, or write whatever word the general term refers to—is it politicians? biology students? birth parents? dog owners? Another possibility is of course to use the more formal *one.* Whenever the *you* is not essential to the meaning of the sentence, omit it and bring forward the real subject:

*Too Informal:* When you try to define Existentialism, you realize that there are no definite tenets you can point out.

*Formal:* Because Existentialism has no definite tenets, it is hard to define.

*Too Informal:* Don't think [literally "don't *you* think"] that the government in any way waived the responsibilities of the Puritans.

*Formal:* The government did not, in any way, waive the responsibilities of the Puritans.

---

### Exercises

A. Note the differences in emphasis in the following passages. When would each be appropriate? Which is the most formal and objective?

1. One may stay up all night to study for a physics test, but if he or she misunderstands the concepts he or she will score poorly on the problems. Unfortunately, effort is not a good basis for the grade.

2. Even if I stay up all night to study for a physics test, if I misunderstand the concepts, I will score poorly on the problems. Unfortunately, my effort is not the basis for my grades.

3. Studying all night for a physics test will not help unless the concepts are understood. Unfortunately, effort is not the basis for grades.

B. Make the following sentences formal enough to include in an essay written for one of your classes.

1. Although we often take for granted that our natural resources will survive, the fact is our kids will have a heck of a lot less than we did when we were their age.

2. Dolphins are a lot like people in their family behavior and the way they communicate.

3. After unsuccessfully trying three herbal remedies on my cat, the veterinarian pumped her with antibiotics.

4. When the calendar changed from quarters to semesters, many students found themselves stressed out by the addition of a fifth class.

5. Having a housemate makes you reconsider your habits.

6. Growing up in a gang atmosphere makes you feel that you always have to be ready to crush the next guy because if you don't, he might step on you.

7. Children become rather bothersome when you're trying to get into a good novel.

8. Learning about your body's fat concentration and usage of energy helps you to plan your diet and exercise program.

9. The paint job on my new Precis blew me away..

10. One must recognize that along with the good aspects of providing medical care for all Americans under national health care will come many restrictions we may not be used to confronting

### Contractions

Contractions, such as *"don't"* for *"do not,"* lend an informal quality to writing. They are not necessarily to be avoided altogether, but their overuse should be checked since they affect the tone of your writing (see Chapter 1). Some writers feel that contractions should not be used in formal papers, but many contemporary writers use contractions without interfering with their tone. Even the book reviews and editorials in newspapers, which avoided them in the past as too informal, now contain contractions. In fact, there are times it seems most natural to use a contracted form. For instance, suppose you wrote the following sentence: "Isn't it ridiculous to expect a sixteen-year-old to take care of seven siblings while the parents go on a vacation out of the country?" The sentence would sound less natural if you replaced the contraction with *Is it not.*

### Triteness and Mixed Metaphors

Speakers have little or no chance to go back and revise what they say, but writers are expected to polish their expression. The following passage from a student's paper shows too much resemblance to spoken English. It is highly informal and includes, besides abstractions, many trite phrases:

> As you see, it is almost impossible to remain a Puritan. In other words, you become a little unbalanced from the strain of resisting it all. Every time you experience a little pleasure, you worry yourself sick that you've been living it up too much. So you say, "Forget this trip, man." You cool it considerably and wind up a real deadbeat. How can you keep a level head when everyone is watching you like a hawk night and day? You begin to hate society. But because you are a Puritan, you suppress your hatred, too.

A trite expression, or cliche, is a word or phrase that was once used as an effective image but has since lost its meaning through overuse. No one even thinks about the original "word picture" in any cliche. If words are to be important, they must communicate, and as a writer you should be especially concerned with saying what you mean with vivid, living words. For example, you should avoid expressions like "crowded in an elevator like sardines in a can" because what was once an effective comparison no longer communicates more than a vague sense of crowdedness. You may argue that you know what someone means when he or she says this. The point is that it is not because of the choice of words that you know what "like sardines in a can" means. You don't picture little fish all lined up and smothered in oil. Instead, your reaction is to the word *crowded*. Admittedly, if you had never heard the cliche before, it would seem clever.

It may sometimes be difficult to identify cliches in your own writing. If you can't free your speech and writing of them, at least be aware of them and try whenever possible to avoid using them. Your teachers can help you identify the cliches you don't catch (either because at first they sound good to you or because you do not recognize the prefabricated sense they give your essays). No list could include all the cliches found in speech and writing, but here is a partial list that will help you recognize the types of cliches you should look out for:

| | |
|---|---|
| information superhighway | feast your eyes |
| my right hand | fits like a glove |
| in over your head | happy as a lark |
| greener pastures | head over heels |
| out of the blue | heavy heart |
| like a ton of bricks | horse of a different color |
| snowball in hell | kill two birds with one stone |
| inside scoop | last but not least |
| rock bottom | like it grows on trees |
| cream of the crop | live and let live |
| bottom of the barrel | low blow |
| blink of an eye | mind over matter |
| next to nothing | more or less |
| cool | my cup of tea |
| neat | nip in the bud |
| avoid like the plague | one in a million |
| beat around the bush | pass the buck |
| bite your tongue | put your foot down |
| bored stiff | reading between the lines |
| bright and early | safe and sound |
| budding genius | short and sweet |
| clean as a whistle | sigh of relief |
| cracking up | stiff upper lip |
| crystal clear | that's life |
| deader than a doornail | without rhyme or reason |
| draw to a close | year in and year out |

There are two good ways to revise cliches once you identify them:

1. Rewrite the expression into direct, concrete words.
2. Make up a new phrase that conveys a specific word picture. Make sure that your audience will grasp the implications of the expression you use.

Rewording an expression so that it is more direct is usually the best method. "Our boss really *saved the day* when he let us go home early on Christmas Eve" would become "All the employees appreciated the boss's generosity when he let us go home early on Christmas Eve." "Maria decided that it wasn't worth *eating her heart out* about her broken date for New Year's Eve" would become "Maria decided not to feel depressed about her broken date."

If you choose to be adventuresome and wish to make up an equivalent image to take the place of the worn-out one, be careful to avoid images that do not express just what you mean, even though they sound good to you. If you wish to rewrite "His ideas were as stale as yesterday's news" and come up with "His ideas were as stale as Egypt," your image will not work. Although Egypt is ancient, it is not stale, and consequently the words do not convey a picture. You would be better off just saying that his ideas were "outdated" or even "stale," which is an image in itself. Always try to see the picture your words convey—then your image will usually work.

Also check for mixed metaphors. A *metaphor* makes the informative— yet literally impossible—assertion that one thing is another thing. For example, "Love is a rose," "The heart is a lonely hunter," "Time is a sickle," and so on. *Mixed metaphors* are two or more word pictures that are inconsistent and therefore conflict. As a result, no picture can be formed in the reader's mind; or, if one is formed, it doesn't make sense. If you write, "A diplomat, casting his line far into the troubled sea of his predecessors' blunders, is as courageous as a lion," you have created a mixed metaphor. A diplomat can be a lion. A diplomat can be a brave fisherman. But a lion cannot be a fisherman—and vice versa. Always check the logic of the word pictures you create before you conclude that the words "sound good" in your essay.

## Exercises

A. Identify the cliches in the following passages.

   1. Football tryouts are a blood-and-guts battle, a fight to the finish. Because football is so popular, there are never slim pickings when coaches hold their annual tryouts for the team. There are the brick-wall frontliners who block and push in all their splendor. Also, there appear the statuelike and blue-eyed quarterbacks who want to lead the team on to victory. Last but not least are the monkey-armed defensive backs who are always on hand with their dreams of glory. Each of these prospective team members wages battles against the others. Competition is the name of the game. In the end only the cream of the crop wins the brass ring.

   2. I had not been in a classroom for around twenty years, and going back to college after what seemed an eternity was a trying experience. I must have been a sight for sore eyes the first day of class because I was worried sick for two whole days before. It was necessary to keep a stiff upper lip as I entered the door of Room 212 and found my way to a seat on the left at the back. But then my nerves flared up again. All around me sat young girls, nineteen years old at the most, and younger-looking boys. It was obvious to us all that I was no spring chicken, and the differences in our ages made me feel like last year's model. Even worse, the teacher was nearly young enough to be my daughter. Finally, two minutes before the class began, the door opened and three middle-aged women entered the room. They seemed to feel right at home as they informally greeted a number of the younger students. I gave a big sigh

of relief, sat back in my chair and listened to a very enjoyable lecture about an old man named Robert Penn Warren.

B. Keep a list of your own and friends' cliches for a week. Try to record at least twenty of them.

C. Use four of the phrases on the following cliche list in sentences. Then revise those sentences so that they would be formal enough to include in an essay.

| | |
|---|---|
| part and parcel | blessing in disguise |
| broaden one's scope | sooner or later |
| root of the problem | more or less |
| learning experience | second home |
| problem at hand | stem the tide |
| give undivided attention | rules and regulations |
| undisputed fact | above your head |

## Circumlocutions

Circumlocutions—phrases that travel "roundabout" and get back to where they started—should be cut from your writing. *Circumlocutions* are unconscious redundancies in word choice; many have become cliches. Because they are automatic, they are sometimes hard to spot. But they always have the same effect—they weaken your expression. In the list that follows, words could have been left out of each phrase without losing the meaning of the expression.

| | |
|---|---|
| deciding verdict | part and parcel |
| prior knowledge | period of time |
| countless number | personal friend |
| successful victory | point in time |
| one single thing | regress back to |
| return back | reminisce about past |
| tail end | experiences |
| absolutely empty | return again |
| circle around | strangle to death |
| completely empty | sum total |
| completely finished | tail end |
| distort the meaning of | totally absorbed in |
| final conclusion | true fact |
| if and when | untrue lie |
| in any shape or form | ways and means |
| living incarnation | while at the same time |
| one and the same | |

## Jargon and Slang

*Jargon* is specialized language that has been adopted by people in a certain field (journalism, politics, computers, etc.). Most areas of work and study use some sort of jargon. Jargon can function in your writing if you are exploring a subject employing terms that are new to you and that are essential to an understanding of the subject. In this case, define all jargon so that it makes as much sense to your reader as it does to you. More often, however, jargon should be deleted from your writing whenever the same thought can be expressed in everyday language.

Students often carry over jargon into fields other than the one for which it was intended; consequently, they confuse the average reader. The student who characterizes the narrator of a novel as "id-oriented" instead of saying that the character is "demanding of his wife" may be trapped by the jargon of psychology. A writer who claims that people who "utilize all their potential tend to validate the learning process" is really just saying that students who study hard learn a lot. The student who writes that "attendance at the national convention of chiropractors topped out at 1,500" is borrowing stock-market jargon to say that only 1,500 people attended the convention; if the reader is unfamiliar with the jargon used by stockbrokers, he or she can only guess at the meaning of that sentence. Substitute ordinary English for any unnecessary jargon you find in your writing.

*Slang* is informal vocabulary—often jargonlike—that is used at times by speakers of all levels of education, although less frequently for an educated audience. In your writing for college classes, slang is usually inappropriate (unless it is part of a quotation, is used deliberately to characterize someone's speaking habits, or is consciously employed for some definite and special effect). Some slang is derived from shortening words—*TV*, *photo*, *typo*, *taxi*, *phone*; other slang is specific "code language" that comes from a field or subculture, such as *buff* (from weight lifting) and *wipe out* (from surfing). Other examples of slang are *on my case* (criticizing), *crash* (to sleep), *hot* (very appealing), *high* (intoxicated), and *glitch* (mistake). Slang language is not incorrect or necessarily crude; it simply is too informal for most written college assignments. Unless a teacher specifies the use of spoken English in a paper, try to select more formal, but not stiff, language for your essays.

One reason that slang is inappropriate to academic writing is that it is not a stable form of English. It is always changing. A person can readily show his or her age by using slang from a past decade: consider the expression "far out" so often exclaimed in the 1960's, much the way we say "cool" today, or "diss," used more recently to mean "put down." Perhaps you have noticed this with your parents or with older friends. Slang varies from subculture to subculture, too. When slang does last in the vocabulary, it eventually becomes acceptable as written English; for instance, the slang word *kids* is already popular in journalism, and some linguists believe that it will soon be found in writing of all kinds.

*Take this clear and simple memo of mine and convert it into legalese so it will sound official*

## Abstractions

Words vary in their abstractness, from the concrete to the highly abstract. In everyday life sometimes the same applies; your message is too vague for your own good. You might mention to a friend that you "love to travel." You fail to specify that you only feel comfortable on organized tours and in superior hotels. Before you know it, your friends assume you'd thoroughly enjoy their upcoming trek in Nepal, where they will travel rugged terrain on foot and mountain bike and sleep out in the rain. They figure you in and enthusiastically tell you how much your cut will be. In this situation, you have placed yourself in the awkward position that arises sometimes from vague communication and resulting assumptions held by others about what you mean.

In academic writing the same can happen. The sentence "The 90's Latino male frequently feels torn between the world of his neighborhood and the academic world, sensing that the one offers affiliation and the other promise at a cost." The sentence contains several abstractions with their own implications. Questions are raised in the reader's mind: What is meant by "affiliation"? By "promise at a cost"? Often the puzzling abstraction or abstractions are not conscious on the writer's part; nevertheless, he or she has been a bit careless because the readers may not share the same experience and knowledge that the writer possesses. A revision might explain the abstractions or replace them with specifics: for instance, replacing *affiliation* with "the safety and security of shared community values and cultural practices." He might specify the "cost" as "assimilation to Anglo culture and a loss of the primary culture." In every case when you write, use words that are as specific as possible to convey precisely what you are thinking about. Superficially, it may "sound" more academic to use a great many abstractions, but if you analyze other texts where many abstractions are present, you will find that the use of them is not just to impress or to be vague. Their use depends on whether readers understand them.

Some abstract terms do not add much content to your writing. Words such as *aspects* or *facets* weaken your style and may lead you to be less specific than necessary.

> *Weak:* Many aspects of his work as a fireman were dangerous. (Many of his duties as a fireman . . .)
> *Acceptable:* The new information was presented as a fresh aspect of the defendant's case. (*Aspect* here means a view.)

When you can think only of a generality and you realize that you need something specific, check your book of synonyms; perhaps you will find an entry that fits better.

Abstraction can weaken your evidence. In a paper with the thesis "Urban lower-class children are forced to learn responsibility at an early age," a student cited a case history: "In the Brown family a female member looked after the six younger children every evening when the mother attended night classes to get her high school diploma." Much of the impact is lost because readers don't know who the *female member* is. Is it a sixteen-year-old in charge or is it a seven-year-old girl? Clearly, to be evidence in this essay, the person must be a child, but how young? If it were directly stated that a seven-year-old child was expected to care for six younger children, the information would certainly exemplify the extensive and responsible role played by the ghetto child. But with abstract and general language the connection is loose.

### Euphemisms

*Euphemisms*—seemingly polite ways of saying things that, put more plainly, might be unpleasant or offensive—should usually be avoided in essay writing. In expository writing, and in life, excessive politeness suggests insincerity and evasiveness. To refer to a politician's death as the person's "meeting his maker" or "going to his reward" is clearly hedging when a subject is not too delicate to be discussed.

In some circumstances, use of a euphemism might be quite appropriate. Ask yourself, "Does the evasive term serve a purpose and reflect social change?" For example, recently the insurance industry and others have been referring to couples living together, particularly in the case of gay couples, as "domestic partners." The term is accurate, though it just as easily applies to married and heterosexual unmarried couples sharing a household. "Domestic partners" makes no mention of sexual preference, making it not an issue and avoiding the potential accompanying social stigma. It is true that some readers will dismiss the term as a euphemism. But for others the comfort of not mentioning what might be disagreeable, or indeed in this case irrelevant, outweighs the specificity of the term. As a writer, you would similarly choose the respectful route of "sanitary engineer" over "garbage man." The decision of whether to use a euphemism depends on the subject and the audience as well as on conventional usage. In general, however, they aren't necessary in academic papers with a serious and fairly objective tone.

Just a moment of thought about the manipulation of the truth in euphemistic writing will explain why you should avoid it. Of course, you should not go to the other extreme—obscene or coarse language—

in an effort to avoid euphemism. Use either cultivated or everyday language, and do not assume that unpleasant ideas need to be padded with nice sayings in order to prevent shock.

### Exercises

A. Rephrase the euphemisms or any other unacceptable word choice in the following sentences. In several of the sentences, your rewrite will require you to add specifics because the euphemism is vague.

1. The police officer noted that the man in the car in front of his had had one too many.
2. Overreliance on technology in medicine has impacted doctors' bedside manner.
3. The automobile industry is not without fiscal instability.
4. My father is not as young as he once was and cannot exercise so strenuously.
5. Her intention is to inspire the thought of a nuptial bond in a man of means.
6. The grant from Exxon placed economically challenged students in better equipped high schools.
7. Because Harriet and I wished to speak in private, I suggested that Mark get a bit of air.
8. My father believes that his clients deserve a defense in court even if they have transgressed the law.
9. He procured women of the night for the sailors who had reached port.
10. His strong bond with his family caused others to consider him less than a man.

### Sexist Language

Unnecessary emphasis on gender should be avoided, both in word choice and in thinking, in all writing. Men and women should be treated as people, not as stereotyped members of one or the other sex, each with its place in the family and in the working world. Abuses lie around us everywhere. For instance, the last time you were in a restaurant did you notice the signs on the restroom doors? Often they say "ladies" and "men," which does not contain parallel expressions since "ladies" connotes a type of behavior and "men" only a gender. Using "ladies" and "gentlemen" or "women" and "men," each of which contains parallel expressions, is better.

It is inaccurate to assume that a woman must do the family's shopping and cooking and that a man must be the provider, or that the doctor mentioned in an anecdote or case study is a man. A secretary or nurse is not necessarily a woman, nor is an executive automatically a man. In like manner, all physical and emotional natures belong to all people—crying and experiencing heartbreak are no more natural for a woman than for a man, and physical strength is no more natural for a man than for a woman. Both sexes, when depicted as human beings, have equal capacity for feeling and thinking, productivity and laziness, proficiency and inadequacy in everything they do.

Commonly used expressions that indicate surprise at a woman's role of authority or make clear distinctions in the roles of men and women are offensive and to be avoided. Here are a few of the most abusive expressions and suggested alternatives.

| Avoid | Use |
|---|---|
| gals, girls (referring to adults), ladies, the fair sex, coeds, lady or male as an adjective, as in lady doctor or male nurse | simply use the noun—doctor, nurse |
| my better half, the little lady, the wife | my wife |
| the suffix *ess* or *ette* added to a noun to designate the female, as in Jewess, poetess, heiress, suffragette | Jew, poet, heir, suffragist |
| women's libber | feminist, member of the women's movement |

Many words contain *man* but refer generally to all people. Because many people associate the word *man* with its reference to a person who is male, it is perhaps fairest to use alternative words when people of either gender are referred to in your writing. Of course, if a specific person is being described, it would be permissible to use the appropriate suffix, as in policewoman or policeman. In the following sentences substitutions have been made in an effort to avoid sexist language. Study each sentence until you understand why the change was needed and how the substitution improves the sentence.

*Ineffective:* Manmade lakes are not as exciting as natural ones to most fishermen.

*Effective:* Artificial lakes are not as exciting as natural ones to most people who fish.

*Ineffective:* The manpower needed to build bridges costs the taxpayers millions of dollars each year.

*Effective:* The workforce needed to build bridges costs the taxpayers millions of dollars each year.

You should also watch for more subtle sexist usages of language. Take special care not to imply that the male in the family is always the decision maker and the wife and children his supplicants. For instance, do not unthinkingly write a sentence like this: "Lionel Greer has decided to move his wife and children to a neighborhood that offers many more cultural advantages than where they currently live." The implication is that Mr. Greer makes all the decisions. Instead, convey your idea in this form: "The Greer family has decided to move to a neighborhood that offers many more cultural advantages than where they currently live." Similarly, "Ms. Jordan's husband lets her take night classes at a local community college" offends the ears of those who believe that women are entitled to make their own decisions. Unless you are emphasizing the inequity in the couple's relationship, revise to "Ms. Jordan takes night classes at a local community college."

One of the most problematic uses of language is pronouns, since English does not have a single pronoun to mean *he or she.* Until recently, the masculine forms of pronouns (*he, his, him*) have been used to stand for both sexes, as in the sentence "Everybody should be his own best friend." But such usage has been questioned for the same reason as the suffix *man.* Some writers have tried to dodge sexist language by using the pronoun *one,* as in "One must work hard if one wants to get good grades," but sometimes the result is a string of cumbersome *one*'s, making sentences sound excessively formal. At the other extreme is the informal *you,* as in "You must work hard if you want to get good grades." The problems with this usage were discussed earlier. Since neither of these alternatives presents an especially good solution to the problem, the situation seems to call for the use of plurals whenever possible. In many instances, the singular pronoun can be avoided altogether by making the antecedent (the word the pronoun refers to) plural or by taking out the questionable pronoun:

> *Ineffective:* A person who loves to win will always be disappointed if his team loses.
> *Effective:* People who love to win will always be disappointed if their team loses.
> *Ineffective:* One must work hard if he wants to get good grades.
> *Effective:* One must work hard to get good grades.

The expressions *he or she, him or her,* and *hers or his,* used occasionally, can effectively replace the sexist *his,* but overuse of these long phrases weighs down prose. Some writers alternate *he* with *she.* Some even use combined forms, such as the unpronounceable *s/he,* but because this abbreviation has not yet been adopted by enough users of the language, most readers prefer other forms. It is not effective to use the plural pronoun *their* to modify a singular noun or pronoun. *They* and *their* are gaining some acceptance as singular pronouns and are already popular in speaking, it is true. However, this usage is not generally accepted yet, and it is therefore best avoided in writing, where it is usually perceived as an error in agreement. Thus, if you are writing a sentence with the word *anyone, everyone, somebody,* or *each* and a pronoun is to refer to that word, you might stick with the singular, using the expression *his or her,* or alternating *his* with *her*; better yet, you might change the sentence so that the singular pronoun is not needed:

> *Ineffective:* Everybody in the room did their experiment correctly the first time.

*Effective:* Everybody in the room did his or her experiment correctly the first time.

*Effective:* Everybody in the room did the experiment correctly the first time.

There are many ways to avoid sexist language. Each writer has to decide which way suits a particular sentence. The first step to ridding your language of sexist implications is to look for them.

## Exercises

A. Revise any sexist language in the following sentences, and write a sentence explaining why you made changes or left the wording as is.

1. If the scientist is to feel free to experiment, he must be trusted by the public.
2. Running into bad weather when travelling across country can not only slow down the trip but also break a man's spirit.
3. Bystanders gave the shooting victim a coat to wear since he was in shock.
4. Whereas the Anglo historian would focus on a chronological sequence of events, the Native American might make his focus the setting in which an event took place.
5. Running into debt is not wise for any man.
6. The well-known authoress Sandra Cisneros creates concrete imagery that stirs our emotions.
7. When we formed the university's committee to protect the rights of Internet users from the recent barrage of obscene material on the e-mail system, we never expected girls to volunteer.
8. It's every man for himself on the final examination; no collaboration is permitted.
9. Stewardesses have a hard life because they are constantly travelling and leaving their families.
10. A sign at a busy intersection: "Men Working."

B. Spend no more than 45 minutes on each of the following writing assignments; don't forget to plan.

1. Write a dialogue between two people, one an adamant feminist and another the stereotypical male chauvinist. Your topic is "having a female president of the United States." Which sexist notions contribute most to the use of sexist language?
2. Explain, in an essay of no more than three pages, an experience you had or perceived that you would judge as sexist. Make sure that the details of the event are clear to your reader and that the reader knows why you believe the occasion to have been marked by sexism.
3. For two days keep a list of sexist language in your college environment. Jot down words and phrases as you hear them. Which usages seem to be common? which rare? which controversial?

4. Write a two-page essay about sexist language as a reflection of sexist thinking versus sexist language as a motivator of sexist thinking. Give concrete illustrations of your points.

## INCREASE YOUR ACTIVE VOCABULARY

We have at least two kinds of vocabularies: recognition and active. *Recognition vocabulary is* what we use most when we read and listen. Although we recognize the words in this group, we do not know their exact meanings. We usually do not use these words because, not knowing exactly how they work, we avoid them or they do not occur to us as we are writing. In contrast, our *active vocabulary* comprises all the words we readily use when we write and speak.

As a writer, try to turn much of your recognition vocabulary into active vocabulary. In order to make the switch, you must be certain to observe the context, connotation, and denotation of every word you intend to transfer. Here is one helpful method. First, identify words from your recognition vocabulary by noting those that recur in your reading. Write up an index card for each word you wish to transfer from recognition to active, including the following information:

The word centered at the top of the card.
A notation of the part of speech next to the word.
The sentence in which you found the word.
The definition of the word according to its context in the sentence.

An example is provided in Figure 8-2.

**Figure 8-2. A typical index card for vocabulary words.**

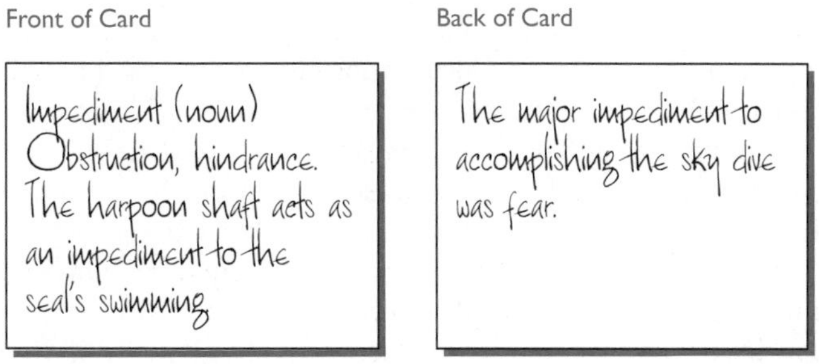

Front of Card

Impediment (noun)
Obstruction, hindrance.
The harpoon shaft acts as an impediment to the seal's swimming.

Back of Card

The major impediment to accomplishing the sky dive was fear.

With a definition, the part of speech, and a sample context for the word, you can fully understand one meaning and one use of it. The word cannot become your own, however, unless you use it yourself.

*"That's right, Dad, I've graduated summa cum laude. What does that mean?"*

Therefore, on the back of the card you should write a sentence of your own using the new word. Imitate the context you wrote down on the front of the card. The next step is to use the word whenever appropriate, making sure that you are adhering to the original context. If at some time you come across other uses of the same word, be sure to make up another card showing the new usage. In this way, you can build up a variety of contextual clues for a single word and increase the number of potential ways that you might use the word.

## USING THE DICTIONARY AND THESAURUS

Every student should own a college-level dictionary and a thesaurus. College, or desk, dictionaries contain about 150,000 entries, among which you should be able to find most of the nontechnical words you will need to check during your undergraduate years. It's handy to access one on your word processing program but also important to own one in book form. As a bonus, collegiate dictionaries in book form usually contain appendixes on grammar, alphabetical lists of colleges and universities, and handy mathematical tables. Thesauruses, either on the computer or in book form, can be helpful reminders of synonyms when you can't think of the exact word you need. But be sure to pick only words you know, not words to impress. Book thesauruses often provide cross indexes to help you identify the correct context for the words they list. By adding these sources to your shelf, you are providing yourself with a small reference library, in addition to a source in which to check definitions and spelling.

### Using the Dictionary

Any dictionary you choose will have invaluable information in its preface; read it to learn about the symbols used, attitudes toward usage, order of definitions, guidelines for pronunciation and syllabication, and placement of variant forms of words. Syllabication, pronunciation, and usage may vary slightly from dictionary to dictionary, but the minor differences are nothing to worry about. If you are really unsure about a matter of usage, it is best to check a dictionary of usage like Wilson Follett's *Modern American Usage,* Bergen and Cornelia Evans's *A Dictionary of Contemporary American Usage,* Roy Copperud's *American Usage and Style: The Consensus,* or the *Harper Dictionary of Contemporary Usage.* For most purposes, the desk dictionary will be adequate.

Although entries in various dictionaries take slightly different forms, all contain much the same information, as is shown in the following sample entry from *The American Heritage Dictionary.*

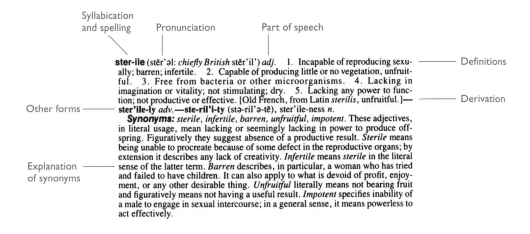

## Syllabication

Check your dictionary whenever you must divide a word because you cannot fit it all on one line. All words should be hyphenated according to dictionary syllabication. Note that some computer programs contain errors in syllabication.

## Spelling

The question "How can I look up a word I can't spell?" has been solved by computer spell checkers, which offer only a few choices. But of course, spell checkers aren't reliable all the time. Some of the words you use frequently may not be in the program and you will have to add them in or remember to check them when they turn up in the spell check. Other incorrect spellings could result from your having written the wrong word but in fact a word that is correctly spelled: *conscious* for *conscience,* for example. Typos are also possible; consider all the times you have typed *the* instead of *they* and it never turned up for the spellcheck session. Until these kinds of errors can be detected by computers, proofreading carefully and dictionaries in book form will not be outdated.

Dictionaries can help you if you have a basic picture of the word and are willing to persevere through trial and error. Sound out the word as best as you can and check the dictionary for that spelling. If you don't find it, substitute different vowels and check those spellings. Say you are trying to check the spelling of *sternum,* the technical word for breastbone. Your first guess is *stirnem,* but since you find no entry under that spelling, you try *sturnem.* Still no luck, so you try *sternem,* from which you locate the correct spelling of *sternum.* It is very important whenever you check a dictionary for spelling that you read the definition of the word so that you can be sure you have located the correct one. If you consider yourself a poor speller, the guidelines beginning on page 389 of this book will be of interest to you.

### Pronunciation

It is important to learn the pronunciation of new words so that you can use them comfortably. Some dictionaries offer British and American pronunciations when the two differ. Accent marks indicate which syllables should be stressed: The syllables marked by heavy accent marks should be emphasized. Pronunciation symbols are explained, in most dictionaries, on each page. If several pronunciations are given for a word, none is more correct than the others. Those listed are alternatives.

### Part of Speech

It makes a considerable difference whether a word is a verb, noun, adjective, or other part of speech if you want to use it well. Many words function as more than one part of speech but have slightly different meanings for each. For example, the word *stew* is both a noun and a verb; so is *advocate.* The part of speech is listed before the respective definition. One abbreviation that you will see pertains only to verbs. *Verb intransitive* (sometimes noted *v.i.* or *i.v.*) means that the verb does not take a direct object. Some verbs have both *transitive* (takes a direct object) and *intransitive* forms, with slightly different meanings for each. Knowing whether a verb takes an object provides an important clue to the use of the word. A good example is *lie* versus *lay*—see page 433.

### Definitions

Different dictionaries place definitions in different orders. The *American Heritage Dictionary* places them in order of "psychological understanding" to show how the various meanings of a word grow out of a central meaning. No one meaning is ever more correct than another, but some other dictionaries use an order based on most common to least common usage.

### Derivation

The derivation is usually placed in brackets. The *American Heritage Dictionary* also makes reference in this space to a special appendix of Indo-European roots that further explains the history of the word.

*Variant Forms*

The spelling of other parts of speech—or other forms of the same part of speech—is given so that the base word may be adapted to your purpose.

*Synonyms*

A list of words that have meanings close to the base word is often given. Because there are distinctions in the shades of meaning conveyed by synonyms, good dictionaries point out distinctions as well as the shared meaning of the words.

*Usage*

Most dictionaries offer usage notes on controversial words. You may have heard somewhere that you shouldn't use *ain't*, because "ain't ain't in the dictionary." In fact, *ain't* is in the dictionary, but it is accompanied by usage notes, as in the following from the *American Heritage Dictionary.*

> **ain't** (ănt). *Nonstandard.* **1.** Am not. **2.** Used also as a contraction of *are not, is not, has not,* and *have not.*
> **Usage:** Even though it would be useful as a contraction for *am not* and as an alternative form for *isn't, aren't, hasn't,* and *haven't, ain't* is still unacceptable in standard usage.

## Using the Thesaurus

The thesaurus is a collection (whether in a book or on the computer) of synonyms that can be useful when you can't think of just the right word to fill a slot or if you feel that your word choice is repetitious. A thesaurus is used to remind you of words you already know. Do not pick words whose meanings you are not sure of. Also pay careful attention to the part of speech of the words you select. The same advice goes for computer thesauruses.

## Learning Word Origins to Expand Your Vocabulary

Affixes (prefixes and suffixes) are parts of words that can give you important clues to the meanings and accurate use of words. The roots in a word offer a basic meaning, the prefixes adjust the meaning, and the suffix tells you the part of speech. All this information can be observed at a glance once you train yourself to pick it out. Suppose you came across the word *recreant* in your reading. You could get a basic idea of its meaning from the root word *cre* from the Latin word *credere* meaning "to believe." Most easily distinguishable is the prefix *re* meaning "back" or "again." The suffix *ant* indicates a noun—the quality of something. Thus the word *recreant* means literally "one who takes back belief" and is used to describe an unfaithful person.

It is easy to see how learning roots and affixes can help you when you come upon an unfamiliar word in reading. But to make words stick in your head, you need more than a vague idea of word origins. When you come upon an unfamiliar word, check its derivation in the dictionary. Take time to see the mechanics behind what makes the word work. What does the root mean? What are the prefixes and suffixes? How has the literal meaning been adapted through usage?

### Exercises

A. Some of the following sentences are inconsistent because they contain a mixture of cultivated and informal words. Replace the familiar diction with more appropriate word choice. Do you think that any of the formal diction is too formal for an essay you would write in class? If so, how would you change the word choice?
  1. Negation of your child's wishes generally leads to tantrums whereas the acceptance of the requests and an explanation for not complying with them might result in a simple "okay."
  2. His tendency to dys his classmates messed up his otherwise pristine morality.
  3. When she could not remedy her faux pas, she simply split—big mistake!
  4. Suffering from a weak will and depression, the character could do no more than drink himself into oblivion over his wife's departure.
  5. Indicative of her propensity for disrespect, Clara kicked her father out of her place.
  6. The heretofore unmentioned factors related to his abandoning the project confirmed that he was a slacker.
  7. He had had it with people who use profanity in public.

B. Change any informal diction in the following sentences to diction more appropriate for a college paper.
  1. She has her act together; she's a role model for others.
  2. Telling his supervisor how bombed out he had been the night before was not too bright.
  3. It was difficult to stay cool about the surprise party.
  4. Shoplifting has been on the rise in the past couple of years.
  5. Drug addicts who live on the street have a number of options for getting clean.
  6. Too many salespeople are fond of hustling customers.
  7. Playing up to the judges only cost her future engagements.
  8. Batman heard about the dangerous liaison and returned to the scene just on time.
  9. When the students in Introductory Sociology found a question about deviance on their final exam, they freaked out.
  10. Unless we begin to take care of our pets, we will have an epidemic kind of like the Plague in Europe.

C. Correct any unnecessary references to the writer, inappropriate uses of *you*, and excessive or unnatural uses of contractions in the following paragraph.

In the current world scientists' biggest fear is being incorrect. They'll do anything to avoid admitting their failures. At a time when little was known in the scientific world it was more common to be wrong than right. Presently the sciences have become so congested with knowledge that there is little room for error. Scientists make a name for themselves by proving other scientists wrong. Ultimately scientists are stereotyped as necessarily infallible thinkers, abnormally intelligent beings incapable of mistakes. The pressure that the field and the public places on scientists makes you not want to take any chances by raising any hypothesis that a later scientist could criticize. It's only human to respond defensively by protecting your research until the absolute last moment it must be revealed. I would too.

D. Correct any errors in word choice and connotations of words in the following sentences.
  1. Korean families stress education so much that their children, though they appreciate what their parents have done for them, may abhor the pressure.
  2. Tunnels under our hallowed halls of learning have leaky storm drains, made even more dangerous to curious student trespassers by high voltage wires and the presence of asbestos in pipes.
  3. Last December all students in our residence hall appointed their doors using the theme of "international Christmas."
  4. Recently a four-year old Native American boy who had been adopted at birth by a loving Anglo family was returned to his tribe by court order; the family is appealing without much success to retrieve the boy.
  5. Claudia's love for Emill was more a reparee than a rapport.
  6. That his father never seemed to grow up had a major impact on all the family's sons, who all entered into a world of blasphemy and irresponsibility.
  7. His fiendish approach to politics caused one to question his most innocent views.
  8. One would hope that an advertiser who embarks on campaigns abroad would cede cultural stereotypes.
  9. Sugar-free snacks aren't necessarily calorie free or healthy because they may have a plethora of bad oils or syrups in them.
  10. When a neat idea plagues you, you must see it through to the end.
E. Correct any cliches, circumlocutions, and euphemisms in the following paragraph.

Part and parcel of a good elementary school learning experience is positive reinforcement from one's teachers. Ms. Glass, my third-grade teacher, just about did me in. One day when I came to class with a hole in the arm of my shirt, she called me to the front of the room to make a spectacle of me. Little did she know (or care) that I had torn the shirt on the way to school when I tried to escape the clutches of Monica, the leader of the 43 Street gang. I'd decided not to make a big deal out of the issue for obvious reasons. Glass was forever calling my name when any trouble was afoot. I was presumed to be "bad" and because I was raised to be submissive to authority, my lack of assertiveness gave her the room to step all over me. She never praised me when I answered a question well, but just moved on to the next victim. There were only one or two children in the class she treated with any amount of respect. Then there were the majority, whom she just ignored. A few of us lucky ones were her targets, and I was the bulls eye. By the end of third grade my self-esteem was so deflated that I could've committed suicide in the blink of an eye. The only thing that kept me going was my faith in God and the knowledge that my sick father needed my help.

F. Rewrite the following paragraph from a college catalog, putting it into more everyday vocabulary an entering freshman would understand. List all the jargon and explain why you think the writer put it in.

Freshmen may be granted credit at the time of entrance for subjects in which they have completed College Entrance Examination Board Advanced Placement examinations with scores of 4 or 5. This credit and resulting placement is subject to review by appropriate departments.

G. Keep a list of the cliches you hear friends use between now and the next class meeting. Collect five of them. Use each in a sentence and then revise the sentences to show a more sophisticated and precise level of usage.

# 4

# WRITING FROM SOURCES

# HOW DO YOU USE THE LIBRARY?

*by Ann Perkins*
*Director of Public Services*
*Oviatt Library*
*California State University,*
*Northridge*

I t has been said that true education lies not so much in knowing large quantities of facts and information as in knowing how to find and evaluate the facts and information you need quickly and efficiently. You can acquire these skills by learning how to use libraries effectively, since most of the information you need to write your papers lies somewhere among the many thousands of books, periodicals, and government documents published each year. This chapter, besides listing reference books and how to use them, provides approaches to research, ideas for getting started, and ways of evaluating information. There are several basic principles to keep in mind as you read.

1. Approach the library in an adventurous frame of mind. You may find yourself changing, refining, or abandoning your original topic as you consult reference sources and move through the research process.
2. Research is not a straight line. You will notice that in different subject sections of this chapter different approaches to research are suggested. This reinforces the idea that you may begin the search process in different ways: sometimes with books, sometimes with encyclopedias, sometimes with journal articles. Using a bibliography at the end of an encyclopedia article may send you to a book, which may refer you to a journal article, which may send you to a dictionary for definitions of terms. The research process is never cut-and-dried, and at its best and most successful, it is not rushed. Exciting ideas and discoveries sometimes evolve slowly.
3. Learn to read critically, picking up clues from the title of the book or article, the intended audience of the book or journal, the length of the material, the currency of the information, and the presence or absence of a bibliography. You can then better determine how or if the information fits in with your argument.
4. Many of the reference books listed in this chapter are examples of types. If your library does not own a particular title, ask the librarian to recommend one which fills the same purpose.

## BOOKS

### The Catalog

Don't be intimidated by the seemingly endless rows of books you see when entering the library. Finding the exact book you want is actually quite easy. Most American libraries arrange their books by assigning call numbers from either the Dewey Decimal System or the Library of Congress System (LC). You don't need to worry about the intricacies of these systems. They are simply number-by-number or letter-by-letter methods of putting books in a logical order. Here are brief outlines of both systems:

*Dewey Decimal Classification*
000 General Works
100 Philosophy
200 Religion
300 Social Sciences
400 Philology
500 Pure Science
600 Technology
700 The Arts
800 Literature
900 Geography, Biography, History

*Library of Congress System (LC)*
A   General
B   Philosophy, Religion
C   History
D   Foreign History and Topography
E-F American History
G   Geography, Anthropology
H   Social Sciences
J   Political Science
K   Law
L   Education
M   Music
N   Fine Arts
P   Language and Literature
Q   Science
R   Medicine
S   Agriculture; Plant and Animal Culture
T   Technology
U   Military Science
V   Naval Science
Z   Bibliography and Library Science

In most libraries, the catalog lets you use three methods for looking up a book: the author, the title, or the subject. Usually, if you are looking for a particular book, you will look under the author's name (last name first, of course). Sometimes you may not know the author's name or be sure of the exact spelling. In such cases, you can look directly under the title. Finally, you can look up a book under the subject or subjects with which it deals. Figure 9–1 provides an example of the information you may find.

Although some libraries still have the conventional form of the catalog, with cards filed in drawers, many are now changing to on line, or computer, catalogs. With these catalogs, you type in the author, title, or subject heading (or possibly key words from the author, title, or subject) and the book or books you want will be listed on the screen. The advantages of these systems are that you can often use key words instead of exact subject headings or titles, and you can see on the screen whether the book you want is checked out, on reserve, or in a special location. There are many variations in on line systems and the way they work, so be sure to read any instructions by the computer terminals or ask at the reference desk for help.

Whether you are using a computer or a conventional card catalog, you will need to become familiar with standardized systems of subject headings. Suppose you are asked to write a paper on violence in the media or on colonial wars and know of no books on the subject. You will quickly realize how useful the subject approach can be. Sometimes, however, you will find what seems to be a gap between the subject headings you have in mind and the headings actually used in the catalog. You might not suspect that books on colonial wars would be listed in the catalog under "United States—History—Colonial period, ca. 1600–1775." How do you bridge this gap? Well, libraries also have systems for assigning subject headings to books. Those who use LC call numbers refer to the *Library of Congress Subject Heading Guide*, and most who use Dewey call numbers refer to the *Sears List of Subject Headings*.

Consulting either the LC or the Sears guides can help you find the headings you want in three ways. To begin with, you will find cross-references. If you look in the LC Guide under the heading "Literature and War," for example, you will be referred to the heading "War and Literature." Secondly, you will find under most of the headings that are used (indicated by dark black print in the subject heading guide) a list of related headings. These will give you ideas for alternate ways to

**Figure 9-1. Example of a library catalog card.**

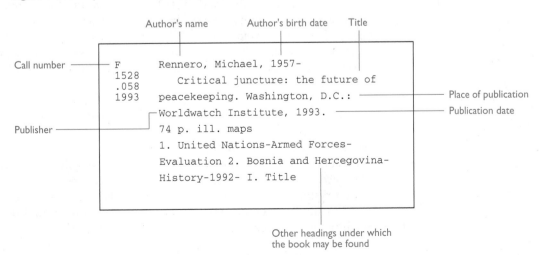

approach your topic. As an example, in the LC Guide, you can find the following:

*Socialism*
UF Marxism
     Social democracy
BT Collectivism
NT Collective settlements
     Mutualism
     Utopias
     Women and socialism

The UF stands for "used for" and means that the headings "Marxism" and "Social democracy" are not used in the catalog. The BT stands for "broader term" and NT stands for "narrower term."

Finally, to help you narrow down a topic to the specific area you are interested in, many useful subheadings are provided. For instance, under the broad heading "Plants," it may be helpful to know of the following subheadings: Identification, Nutrition, Reproduction, and Water requirements. Books about how to teach a particular subject use the subheading "Study and teaching" under that subject, as in "Political Science—Study and teaching." Children's books on a subject come under the subheading "Juvenile literature," as in "Porpoises—Juvenile literature." The subheadings "History" and "Bibliography" appear under many subjects in the guides. Often you may encounter sub-subheadings. How's this for a really long one? "United States—History—Civil War, 1861–65—Personal narratives—Confederate side." As you can see, this heading really does zero in on a specific area of the topic. The point here is that you do not need to settle for the subject heading "Middle Ages" if what you really want is a children's book on the history of the Middle Ages. "Middle Ages—History—Juvenile literature" will take you much closer to what you are looking for.

When you find the entries for the books you want, copy down the entire call number, the author, and the title for each. Most libraries provide maps, directories, or handouts to help you find where in the library various call numbers are located. Still, you may not find a book in its proper place on the shelf. Persistence, you will discover, is one of the keys to successful library use. Circulation departments (where you check books out) maintain lists of missing books and books that have been checked out. If a book you want is not on either of these lists, the staff will usually begin a search procedure and notify you when the book is located.

### Beyond Your Local Library

The catalog will help you to find books in your own college library, but you need not be limited by local resources. There are now several computer systems, such as OCLC, which list books and other materials held in libraries throughout the country. You can often find out which libraries own a particular book.

Another tool that can help you locate the books you need is the *Bibliographic Index* (1937– ), which indexes by subject book-length bibliographies as well as the brief bibliographies that have appeared at the end of books or journal articles.

How can you obtain all these reference sources if your library doesn't have them? First, check the other libraries in your town or immediate area. You can often get borrowing privileges at public libraries or those of neighboring universities. Next, consider interlibrary loan, a procedure by which your library can borrow a book for you from another library. Many libraries are trying to cope with decreasing budgets and increases in the number of books published by expanding their interlibrary loan programs. Be sure to ask at your library's reference desk about this service.

Finally, you may find a particular book so interesting or valuable for your research that you want to buy it. To see whether it is available for purchase, look in *Books in Print* (1948–) or *Subject Guide to Books in Print* (1957–), which are annual author, title, and subject indexes to all the books currently in print in the United States. Here you may obtain the correct author, title, publisher, date of publication, and price and then order the book on your own or through a bookstore.

---

### Exercises

A. Answer the following questions about your library.
   1. Is the card catalog divided into author-title and subject sections? If your library has a computer catalog, what is the system called?
   2. Are books cataloged by the Library of Congress System or the Dewey Decimal System?
   3. Are the bookstacks open, or must you ask for a book you want at the circulation desk?
   4. What special locations for materials, such as a microfilm room or special collections, does your library have?
B. For each of the following topics, find and list four useful subject headings from the subject heading guide your library uses. Use the supplements if necessary.

   evolution                      sex in literature
   energy conservation            world peace
   capital punishment

C. By consulting the *Bibliographic Index*, find out whether a bibliography already exists on any of the topics in exercise B.
D. Compile a minibibliography of your own, listing at least ten books on one of the topics in exercise B. If your library does not have enough books, consult a system such as OCLC or use *Books in Print*.
E. Look up a book in which you are interested, copy the catalog information onto a piece of paper, and identify all the parts of your entry.

## GENERAL REFERENCE WORKS

Reference books are valuable tools for finding specific bits of information about a subject or for locating sources of in-depth information quickly and efficiently. Every library has a special area where they are kept. You should never hesitate to ask the librarian at the reference desk for help or advice. In this section, indexes and fact books of a general nature will be discussed. Those relating to specific areas of study will be covered in later sections.

When approaching a particular reference book for the first time, you should ask yourself several questions. What does the book set out to do? What limitations of time span, geography, or nationality does it have? What kinds of indexes—subject, author, or title—does it have? How up to date is the information in it? Some of these questions will be dealt with in this chapter; others can be answered by scanning the introduction to the book itself. Almost any question you might have, however, can be answered by looking in *A Guide to Reference Books*, 10th ed. 1986 (and supplements), compiled by Eugene P. Sheehy, which gives detailed information on just about every reference work you might want to use.

### Encyclopedias and Dictionaries

Usually, before beginning to search for books, articles, and documents, you will want to more clearly define your topic. Is it so broad that the information available will be overwhelming, or is it so narrow that you will be frustrated in your search? Can it conveniently be broken down into smaller components? A general encyclopedia is an excellent tool for answering these questions. For years, the *Encyclopaedia Britannica* has been considered one of the best English language encyclopedias. The eleventh edition, although published in 1911, was especially well regarded, and contains long, signed articles by specialists in their fields, bibliographies at the end of many of the articles, and detailed indexes. It can still be profitably used for pre-twentieth century topics. With the publication of the fifteenth edition (1974), the format of the encyclopedia was changed and there are now three sections: the *Propedia* (a one-volume outline of knowledge), the *Micropedia* (a ten-volume set of short articles), and the *Macropedia* (a nineteen-volume set of long, detailed articles). Although the fifteenth edition does contain more brief factual information and biographical articles, the lack of a detailed subject index and the sometimes confusing three-part arrangement cause many people to prefer some earlier editions.

The *Encyclopedia Americana* is authoritative and reliable. It has particularly good information on American cities and towns. To get a thorough perspective on a topic, you might find it helpful to read the articles from both the *Americana* and the *Britannica* as well as one from a specialized encyclopedia appropriate to the particular field of study. Suppose you were doing research on the ancient city of Pompeii. Under "Pompeii" in the *Encyclopedia Americana* are photographs, three pages of text, and a bibliography. The *Britannica* includes diagrams and maps rather than photographs and offers a slightly longer text. A specialized subject encyclopedia, the *Encyclopedia of World Art*, which will be introduced later, scatters its references to Pompeii throughout most of its thirteen volumes, giving a total of about ten pages of information along with numerous maps and color plates.

In the process of reading encyclopedia articles, you may run across unfamiliar words, or words you recognize used in unfamiliar ways. A dictionary should help here. Dictionaries can be far from dull. A storm of controversy greeted the publication of *Webster's Third New International Dictionary of the English Language*, unabridged, in 1961. The controversy arose from the dictionary's change to a descriptive mode—reflecting changing speech habits and usage—from its earlier prescriptive mode—decreeing *correct* usage. Offering more direct guidance to traditional usage, *Webster's New International Dictionary of the English Language*, unabridged, 2nd ed. (1934) is still a highly respected dictionary. Another good unabridged dictionary is the *Random House Dictionary of the English Language*, 2nd ed. (1987). Among the many desk dictionaries currently available, *Webster's New World Dictionary of American English* (1988) is highly recommended. If you are unsure of which dictionary to use, compare definitions from various dictionaries.

Many words and phrases currently used are not yet considered to be generally accepted by word experts. To look up expressions like "outfox," "bite the bullet," or "party pooper," you will have to check a dictionary of nonstandard usage such as Chapman's *Thesaurus of American Slang* (1989). Sometimes you may want to find a word that is no longer in common use, see what a word actually meant in the past, or even trace the history of a word. The *Oxford English Dictionary* (2nd ed., 1989), regarded by many as the grandparent of all dictionaries, comes in twenty volumes and can tell you more about most words than you will probably ever need to know.

To add interest and variety to your writing, try using a dictionary that lists synonyms and related words. *Roget's II: The New Thesaurus* (1995) or the *Random House Thesaurus* (1984) can be very helpful.

A quotations dictionary such as Bartlett's *Familiar Quotations*, 16th ed. (1992) or Evans' *Dictionary of Quotations* (1968)—both of which index memorable quotes from prose and poetry by author, first line, and subject—can also help you add color and emphasis to a point you are making. For example, an argument you are presenting against civil disorder might be enhanced by Lincoln's statement: "There is no grievance that is a fit object of redress by mob law."

Once you have a clearer perspective on your subject, perhaps by breaking it down into more workable components and defining any unfamiliar terms, you are ready to begin searching for sources that deal with your topic in greater depth.

### Essay and General Literature Index

Another way to find information contained in books is through the *Essay and General Literature Index*. Often, instead of being a monograph on one subject, a book will consist of a collection of essays, speeches, historical articles, or similar short pieces. One of these may be just the thing you need to back up an important point. How do you find it? Actually, it's quite easy. Suppose you are doing a paper on student rebellion in the 1960s. There is an essay titled "Permanent Campus Revolution?" in *Humanistic Frontiers in American Education*, edited by R. P. Fairfield, that could be very useful. The catalog, however, lists only the main title of the book, not every essay included. You could scan the table of contents, if you were lucky enough to find the book in the first place. Fortunately, there is a better way. Since 1900, the *Essay and General Literature Index* has indexed materials appearing in about 300 anthologies annually by author, subject, and title. The entry for the essay you are interested in looks like this:

"College students—United States—Political activities"
Dixon, J. P. Permanent campus revolution? In Fairfield, R. P., ed.
  *Humanistic frontiers in American education*, pp. 261–68.

Once you have discovered the sources, all you have to do is check the catalog to find out whether your library has the books you want.

### Book Reviews

Normally, you will want the sources you use for a paper to be the best ones possible. Since there is a great deal of material available on most subjects, you don't want to waste your time reading an inaccurate or superficial book. It is sometimes wise, therefore, to first evaluate a book for accuracy and thoroughness. If you are unfamiliar with the subject of executive power, for example, you may wonder whether the book *Human Rights and U.S. Foreign Policy* by David Forsythe (1988) will be a good source of information. The easiest way to find out is to read some reviews of the book.

Book reviews appear in almost every newspaper and magazine. To find the reviews you want quickly, use a reference tool such as the *Book Review Digest*. Every year since 1905, this work has compiled book reviews from about seventy-five periodicals and newspapers, arranged by the author of the book. There is also a title and subject index in the back of each volume. You need to know two things to use this tool: the year the book was published and the correct spelling of the book author's name.

The entries include brief summaries of each review and the name of the periodical or newspaper where the review may be found, along with the volume, page number, and date. In addition, you are given the number of words in each review. This is a helpful clue in deciding which reviews will be the most valuable for you to search out.

A reference tool with slightly broader coverage is *Book Review Index* (1966–). It does not include summaries of the reviews, however. For any book published before 1974, an excellent source is the *Combined Retrospective Index to Book Reviews in Scholarly Journals, 1886–1974*. One hint when searching for reviews: if you don't find one under the year a book was published, look at the following year or years. Reviewers, like college students, sometimes fall behind in their schedules.

### Periodicals and Their Indexes

Most of the reviews you will find appear in periodicals, which are especially valuable sources of current information or information on specific subjects. Don't let yourself be confused by the terminology. Some instructors specify the use of journal articles, by which they mean articles from more scholarly, research-oriented publications; magazines is the term that usually refers to popular, consumer-oriented publications; and libraries often use the terms periodicals or serials. All these terms refer to publications, such as *Sports Illustrated* or *American Journal of Sociology*, that appear regularly (two, four, twelve, or more times a year) for an indefinite period.

Libraries vary widely in how they list and shelve periodicals. Many maintain a separate list of periodical titles, and most have a periodicals room where current, unbound issues are kept. The publications are sometimes arranged by call number, sometimes alphabetically by title. Ask which system your library uses. In most cases, old issues are bound into annual volumes. A useful guide, *Ulrich's International Periodicals Directory*, attempts annually to list every periodical currently being published in the world. The periodicals are grouped by subject so that you can conveniently scan the titles available in the field you are interested in. There is also a comprehensive title index at the end.

A problem you may face is not knowing which periodical you need. You simply know that you need information about a specific topic. This is where the periodical indexes come in. The most general, and the most widely used, is the *Readers' Guide to Periodical Literature*. Along with its predecessor, *Poole's Index*, the *Readers' Guide* indexes the articles in about 150 magazines by subject and author from 1802 to the present. It is published monthly. The magazines included are, for the most part, popular, general-interest magazines such as *Time, New Yorker, Psychology Today*, and *Scientific American*. Thus, the index is a good reference tool for finding articles on newsworthy events, current or historical, and on popular or controversial topics. It also indexes film, theater, and book reviews. As with the catalog, you have to approach the subject headings in the *Readers' Guide* in an adventurous frame of mind. For example, movie reviews are found under the heading "Motion picture reviews—Single works." Articles on busing were listed for years under the roundabout heading "School children—Transportation for integration." Volumes of the *Readers' Guide* are cumulated annually, and, as in any periodical index, the time frame of your search should be determined by your topic.

When you look under a subject heading, such as "Mulching," in the *Readers' Guide*, you will find a citation, or reference, that always gives the following information about an article:

Trashpicker! Using discarded lawn clippings. M. McGrath.
il *Org Gard* v43 p. 3-4 F '96.

First the title of the article is given, then the author (if there is a specific one), then the title of the periodical (usually abbreviated). A list of abbreviations is found at the front of each issue of most periodical indexes. Be sure to verify the full title of the periodical you are looking for; abbreviations can be deceptive. The notation "il" in this citation means that the article is illustrated; here you may also find "por" (portrait), "bibliog" (bibliography), or other informative notes. The numbers in this citation refer to the volume number, the page number, and the date of the article.

Over 100 periodical indexes, covering many fields of study, are currently being published, most of them using a similar form for their citations. Many specific periodical indexes are mentioned in this chapter.

Periodical indexing is also available by computer in many libraries. Such computerized systems allow you to search through several years at once, depending on the size of the database; to search by key words from the title or subject; to combine key words in order to narrow down or broaden your search; and often to print out your citation instead of writing it down.

Combining key words is a technique known as Boolean searching. Suppose you are researching violence in the media. You may ask the computer to retrieve citations that contain both the words violence and media in the title or subject heading. The search might be illustrated in this way:

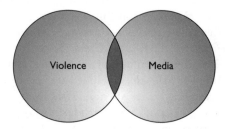

The overlapping area represents citations where both the terms are found. You can also broaden your search by thinking of synonyms for the terms you are interested in. For example, you might want citations that contain the terms violence or war or fighting *and* media or television or journalism or newspapers:

The overlapping area here is likely to be much larger because of the greater choice of terms. Computer systems have various techniques for constructing Boolean searches; be sure to ask the reference librarian for further information.

Many computer indexes are available on CD/ROM. CD/ROM technology provides the information on a self-contained laser disc, similar in appearance to an audio CD. The discs are updated quarterly. CD/ROM indexes are now available in most fields, including education, medicine, literature, business, and psychology. Although in most libraries they are free to the user, there are often sign-up sheets or restrictions on time use, due to their popularity. These indexes are produced by different commercial publishers and thus have varied search systems and instructions. Be sure to read any printed instructions by the computer terminals, or ask at the reference desk for help. A computer equivalent to the *Readers' Guide* is *General Periodicals Index* (also referred to as Infotrac), which is held by many libraries.

With on line computer searching, the user is connected by telephone to a remote database. In some libraries the user pays the telecommunication charges and a prorated amount for on line computer time; sometimes the library covers the charges for some or all of the on line databases. The advantages of on line searching are that a wider variety of databases is available, and the information is updated daily. The Dialog system has available hundreds of databases in all fields; many libraries have some of these available for searching by the librarian, or by the user with librarian assistance. Another on line system that is becoming widely used is OCLC FirstSearch. Among the databases available on this system are WorldCat, which lists books in libraries throughout the world, and Article 1st, which is an index to articles from thousands of journals and magazines.

The Internet, an on line source for information on all topics, is usually accessed through specific "addresses" or through an access service such as the World Wide Web. Many college and university libraries have computer workstations providing Internet access. The advantage of the Internet is the wide variety of information available; the disadvantage is the lack of quality control of the information provided. Still, browsing the Internet can often yield interesting and useful sources. Government publications such as bills and the congressional record, for example, are now available through the Internet. Ask the reference librarian in your library for information about the computer search services available there.

### Newspapers and Their Indexes

Newspapers are also a valuable source of information. A good annual directory of U.S. newspapers is the *Gale Directory of Publications* (1988), which lists newspapers by state and city and has a title index at the end. Many libraries keep older issues of newspapers on microfilm, as they are readily available and much more usable in this form. However, it's difficult to make use of microfilm without an index. That's why well-indexed newspapers tend to be the ones that are well used. The prime example is the *New York Times*, which is indexed from 1851 to the present. In the index, which is cumulated annually, you may look under a subject or person's name and find the titles of articles, often with a brief summary, and the date, the page number, and even the column number. This enables you to turn quickly to the point you want on the reel of microfilm. Researchers looking for a name or a fact often need go no further than the index. Someone wanting to know the U.S. budget for 1974, for example, could find the amount ($277.8 billion) under the heading "United States—Finances—Budget" in the 1974 index. Thus, *The New York Times Index for the Published News* is an important reference tool in its own right. For a more detailed indexing of international news stories, the *London Times Index* (1790–) has long been a major resource. One computer newspaper index is the *National Newspaper Index*, usually available along with the *General Periodicals Index* on the Infotrac system. It indexes the most recent three years of the *New York Times*, the *Los Angeles Times*, *Wall Street Journal*, the *Washington Post*, and the *Christian Science Monitor.*

### Biography

The subject of your research may be a person rather than a topic. You can, of course, look up his or her name in the subject catalog to see whether a book-length biography exists. Relatively few people, however, have entire books written about them, so you must often rely on brief sketches, periodical articles, or news stories. The best place to begin, particularly if you are not sure of the period or the nationality of your subject, is the *Biography Index*. Since 1947, this work has indexed biographical sketches of persons from all occupations, geographical areas, and time periods that have appeared in over 1,500 magazines, newspapers, and biographical dictionaries. It is published by the same company that publishes the *Readers' Guide*, so the citations are in the same convenient form. An interesting feature of this index is the classification by occupation at the back of each volume of all the persons referred to in it. Thus if you are assigned a biographical report on a sociologist or a rabbi and no names spring immediately to mind, you may get some ideas from the *Biography Index*. If your subject is a living American, you may find the *Biography and Genealogy Master Index* (1980, with supplements) very useful. It is a personal name index to the biographical sketches that appear in more than fifty current biography collections, including the *Who's Who* references.

Another reason for obtaining biographical information is to check the background and credentials of an author when you are doing research. Does the person have a degree in the subject on which he or she is writing? Has he or she published many books or articles on the subject? The sources listed above may be used for this purpose, but an especially useful source, with international coverage, for biographies of twentieth-century authors in all fields is *Contemporary Authors*. It includes brief biographies, lists of works published and in progress, and sometimes interviews with the author.

### Government Documents

Government documents are published on almost every conceivable subject. Therefore, they are introduced here as general reference tools rather than under a specific discipline. Although most people think of government publications as including only transcripts of hearings, reports of congressional committees, bills introduced in Congress, or laws passed, almost any topic might be the subject of a government publication. Looking through the *Monthly Catalog of United States Government Publications*, you will find such titles as "Bilingual/Bicultural Education, Privilege or Right?" "Windows and People, Psychological Reaction to Environments With and Without Windows," and "Geological and Geomagnetic Background Noise in Two Areas of the North Atlantic." So, no matter what your research topic is, a look at the *Monthly Catalog* can be fruitful. The catalog, which lists all the publications of the U.S. government, has an annually cumulated subject index. Title and author indexes have been included since 1974. A computerized index to government publications on CD/ROM, covering material published since 1980, is also available. Ask at your library about this index.

### Fact Books and Statistics

After you have located the books, articles, or documents you need for your topic, you may want some hard facts and figures to back up the points you wish to make. Perhaps the most basic type of fact book is a good annual almanac such as the *World Almanac*. An amazing variety of facts and figures, everything from U.S. pollution control expenditures to a list of duckpin bowling champions, is packed into its more than 900 pages. In addition, most general encyclopedias publish yearbooks, which are useful records of each year's progress and events. You may assess, for example, trends in fashion and dress or the most important events in some country, such as China, during a particular year. *Facts on File* is another annual publication that summarizes the news events of each year in chronological order. It has a detailed subject index at the end of each volume.

It seems that almost everything today is measured in one way or another, and people usually tend to be impressed by numbers. You may therefore want to use some statistics to reinforce certain aspects of your research. But a word of caution: when using statistics, you should always do the following.

1. Check the date carefully. Are you sure that the statistics you want to use are not too old for your purpose?
2. Check the size of the sample. Is it large enough to reveal a meaningful trend?
3. Check out the source. How reliable and authoritative is it?
4. Check the size of the number you use. Is it thousands, millions, or maybe even billions? You should always read the notes at the top of a table carefully to find out how many zeros to add to numbers given in the table.

A detailed digest of U.S. statistics may be found in *Statistical Abstracts of the United States*, published annually since 1878. It provides summary tables of statistical surveys made by the government on a wide variety of subjects, from mortgages to museums. *American Statistics Index* (1973–) is a comprehensive guide and index to any statistics that may be contained in government publications; it may lead you to information not contained in *Statistical Abstracts*. For international statistics, look in the *United Nations Statistical Yearbook*, which began publication in 1948. If you are writing a paper about the 1995 rise in coffee prices, for instance, it might be helpful to see the table outlining the world production of coffee, nation by nation, for the past fifteen years.

## Exercises

A. Find out the following information about your library.
   1. Where is the reference desk located?
   2. Is all of the reference collection in the reference room, or are some of the reference tools in other areas or on other floors?
   3. Where are government documents shelved?
   4. Where are current newspapers and periodicals kept?
B. Choose one of the following topics and compare the articles on it from the *Encyclopedia Americana* and *Encyclopaedia Britannica*. List the similarities and the differences. Do you think one is more informative than the other? Why?

| | |
|---|---|
| television | Michelangelo |
| Cincinnati, Ohio | muscles |
| Beijing, China | comic books |

C. Assume you are doing a research paper on one of the topics in B, above. Choose a period of two years and list the citations on your topic (a maximum of ten) from the *Readers' Guide* or a computer index to general periodicals.
D. Using the same time period as for exercise C, check *The New York Times Index* or a computer newspaper index and list a citation, if there is one, appearing there on your topic. If there is not a citation, check for one of the other topics in exercise B. Explain all the parts of the citation.
E. Locate and list a citation to a biographical article on one of the following:

| | |
|---|---|
| Jesse Jackson | Salman Rushdie |
| Joyce Carol Oates | Tonya Harding |
| Bill Clinton | Billy Joel |

F. Find a citation to a review of one of the following books:

| | |
|---|---|
| *The Right Stuff* | *The Accidental Tourist* |
| *A Brief History of Time* | *The Chalice and the Blade* |
| *Satanic Verses* | |

G. Choose one of the following subjects and describe the procedure (search strategy) you would use in finding information about it. List the steps you would take, in order. Describe how you might narrow the topic as you progress.

television censorship          marijuana
solar energy                   euthanasia
organic gardening              computer crimes

## HUMANITIES

People have varying ideas about which areas of study should be included in the humanities. The dictionary definition even includes mathematics. Generally, however, the humanities are thought of as comprising the creative arts (such as literature), the speculative arts (such as philosophy), and the performing arts (such as theater). This section will deal with art, music, languages, literature, the performing arts, religion/philosophy, and history, all of which are considered as areas of the humanities by the majority of colleges and universities.

With the increase of interdisciplinary studies and the complex character of most contemporary problems, it is often difficult to decide which field your topic is most closely related to. For example, if your topic is "The Influence of the Computer on the Arts," you will want to consider art, music, and literature (as well as computer science). A good interdisciplinary periodical index for the humanities is the *Humanities Index* (1974–), formerly part of the *Social Sciences and Humanities Index* (1916–1973). Under the headings "Arts and Computers" and "Computers in Literature" you will find several articles on your topic. The citations are arranged like those in the *Readers' Guide*, but the *Humanities Index* covers more scholarly and research-oriented publications. It is now available on CD/ROM, as are many of the specialized periodical indexes mentioned in this section.

### Art

When you begin research in a specific subject area, you will often find it helpful to first analyze the types of information you will be concerned with in that particular field. Research in art, for example, usually involves the following four aspects of the subject:

Periods, movements, or types of art
Particular artists
Reproductions of artists' works
Critical opinions of artists' works

Suppose you are interested in the general topic "Impressionist Painting." The *Encyclopedia of World Art*, which comes in fifteen volumes with supplements, has a long article with twenty-five color plates. From it, you may get the names of a few major artists in this school and some idea of how you might narrow your topic. The *McGraw-Hill Dictionary of Art* (five volumes) is a shorter but also useful encyclopedia.

Perhaps you decide that you are most interested in the artist Claude Monet. You should then go on to the second part of your research—finding out more about the artist. After checking in the subject catalog to find any book-length biographies, your next resource might be the *Artist Biographies Master Index* (1986), which refers to biographical articles in one or more of seventy different sources.

Your next step may be to look at reproductions of Monet's work. You might want to select a few to concentrate on in your paper. If there is a book-length collection of an artist's work, you will find it listed in the catalog under the artist's name—an artist is the author of paintings just as a novelist is the author of books. Often, however, the works are scattered through various collections of reproductions. To locate them, you can use an index such as Havelice's *World Painting Index* (1977), a guide to reproductions in about 1,100 books and catalogs, or *Index to Reproductions of American Paintings* (1977), an index to reproductions in about 400 books.

After looking at reproductions of Monet's work, you may decide to focus on a series in which Monet painted particular subjects, such as cathedrals and water scenes, during different times of the day. For critical opinions and discussions, your best source would be the *Art Index* (1929–), organized exactly as the *Readers' Guide*, but indexing different journals. Since Monet lived during the nineteenth century, you may want to begin your search with the first volume (1930–1933) of the index and work up to the present in order to find the greatest number of articles. You may find additional biographical information about Monet, more articles on Impressionist painting, or other reproductions included in the journal articles. The following is a typical citation:

> Monet in the 90's: the series paintings. Jan Kear.
> *Art Hist* 14:593–9, Dec. '91
> Waterloo bridge—cloudy weather (col il)

The abbreviations "il" (illustration) and "col" (color illustration) will be of particular significance in the *Art Index. Art Bibliographies Modern* (1973–), formerly *LOMA: Literature on Modern Art*, is another index to articles in art journals. It also includes citations to exhibit and museum catalogs and some books. Its chief advantage is that it includes brief abstracts or summaries of the material indexed. Its limitation is that it covers only "modern" art and artists, which to its editors means beginning in 1800.

In your reading of books and articles on Monet, you may have run across some terms or some contemporaries of Monet that you are not familiar with. To find out something about them, you should consult a good art dictionary, such as the *Oxford Dictionary of Art* (1988). Examples of recent, and very entertaining, dictionaries are *Glossary of Art, Architecture and Design Since 1945* (1977) and Atkins' *Artspeak; a guide to contemporary ideas, movements and buzzwords (1990).* In them you may learn about such terms as "food art" or "lost sculptures" and groups such as the "Hairy Who" and the "Los Angeles Fine Arts Squad." A handy reference book for miscellaneous information is the *American Art Directory*, published annually. It lists art schools, art museums, leading art journals, and contemporary American artists. *Art Museums of the World* (1987) provides articles on the history and collections of major museums, as well as a comprehensive listing of museums. Finally, if your major field is art, you might consult Lois Jones's *Art Research Methods and Sources* (1984), a detailed guide to doing research in this field.

## Music

In music, you may want to investigate a general subject such as musical instruments, a specific musician or composer such as Woody Guthrie, or a particular musical work such as Beethoven's Ninth Symphony. For most general topics, particularly in classical music, the *New Grove Dictionary of Music and Musicians* (1980), which comes in twenty volumes, is the best place to begin. Under the heading "Greece," for example, you will find a twenty-three-page article on Greek music from ancient to modern times, including folk music, with a bibliography at the end. Long biographical articles on composers and musicians are included, and for major composers a useful list of compositions is appended. Suppose you are asked to listen to Haydn's *Military Symphony*. By looking in Grove's, you will find that this is his Symphony No. 100 in G Major, the title under which it is most likely to be classified in library collections. For topics in American music, Grove's has recently been supplemented by the *New Grove Dictionary of American Music* (1986), especially good for modern American music and composers. The *New Grove Dictionary of Musical Instruments* (1984) is now the definitive source of information on musical instruments all over the world. A source with briefer articles is the one-volume *New Harvard Dictionary of Music* (1986). The standard biographical work on musicians is *Baker's Biographical Dictionary of Musicians*, 7th ed. (1984). The almost 7,000 entries cover all periods and nationalities. Again, the emphasis of this work is classical.

For information about persons or groups in recent nonclassical music, you may refer to sources such as the *New Grove History of Jazz* (1988), the *Encyclopedia of Country, Folk, and Western Music* (1983), or the *Rolling Stone Encyclopedia of Rock & Roll* (1983).

The main source for finding articles in music journals is the *Music Index*, which has indexed music journals since 1949. Unfortunately, this index is about five years behind in publishing its cumulative volumes, so for recent years you must look through every monthly issue, one by one. A computer version of the *Music Index* has recently become available, and while its software is not yet as "user-friendly" as some of the other computer indexes, it provides the advantages of searching several years at once and of combining subject terms.

Now let's look at a particular topic. If you have chosen Woody Guthrie, you will find a brief entry in the *New Grove Dictionary of Ameri-*

*can Music.* You may also find book-length biographies of Woody Guthrie in the card catalog, biographical sketches in encyclopedias such as *Encyclopedia of Country, Folk, and Western Music,* or articles about him and his songs through the *Music Index.* Keep in mind the interdisciplinary nature of this and many other topics. You may want to look in the subject catalog under headings such as "Depressions—1929—U.S." You might also look in issues of the *Readers' Guide* during the 1930s to see what the popular magazines were saying about Guthrie then or in more recent issues for reviews of *Bound for Glory,* a film based on his life.

Research in music often includes listening to music. Records, cassettes, and CDs can therefore become a part of your investigation. Find out what your library has and what the borrowing policies are. If you want to evaluate recent recordings of a particular work or a work performed by a particular artist or group, check *Records in Review* (1955–), an annual publication that includes lengthy reviews of classical records by respected music critics, or *Index to Record and Tape Reviews* (1971–1982), which annually indexed reviews appearing in forty different periodicals.

Finally, for the music major, William Brockman's *Music: a Guide to the Reference Literature* (1987) provides a comprehensive guide to research in music.

### Languages

When studying languages, you will usually be either attempting to master the grammar and vocabulary of a particular language or doing research on a general topic in linguistics or the history of language. If you are learning a language, it should be helpful for you to know some of the important catalog subject headings. For vocabulary, the headings "English Language—Dictionaries—Spanish" (or French, German, etc.) can come in handy. For grammar, you might look under the language you are studying with its various subheadings, such as "Spanish Language—Grammar—Orthography—Pronunciation." The *Cambridge Encyclopedia of Language* (1987) contains background essays on major areas in language studies, and Crystal's *Dictionary of Linguistics and Phonetics* (1991) is a good source for definitions of terms.

A good source for finding periodical articles on a specific topic in language, such as speech therapy, is *Linguistics and Language Behavior Abstracts* (1967–). The cumulated subject indexes for each year will refer you to the abstract numbers for that year. Under the abstract number, you will find citations to periodical articles, as in the following example:

9411621
Stubbe, Maria. What's the score? Qualitative analysis in gender
    research. *Int J Appl Ling,* 1994, 4(1), 3–18.

For articles on the history and development of language, check in the Linguistics section (Part III) of the *MLA International Bibliography,* which has been published since 1921 (and is now available both on CD-ROM 1980– and through the FirstSearch on-line computer system 1963–). The articles are arranged by language and by topic (etymology, morphology, phonology, etc.) within the language. You can also use the *Humanities Index*, which indexes many of the most common and generally available language journals.

### Literature

Your research in literature may involve general topics such as novels of the working class, specific authors such as John Steinbeck, or specific works of literature such as *The Grapes of Wrath*. To find brief background material on general topics, brief biographies of authors, or summaries of major literary works, you may first look in a one-volume encyclopedia such as the *Oxford Companion to American Literature*. Oxford also publishes encyclopedias of English, German, French, and Canadian literature. If you are interested in drama, check the *McGraw-Hill Encyclopedia of World Drama* (1984), which includes general topics, brief biographies of dramatists, and brief critiques of plays as literature. For briefer definitions of words and phrases, such as propaganda novel, pathos, or octave, there are several literary dictionaries. Abrams' *A Glossary of Literary Terms* (5th ed., 1988) is one example.

For an extensive history of American literature to about 1970, turn to the two-volume *Literary History of the United States*. The first volume traces movements, influences, and major literary figures from Cotton Mather to Norman Mailer. The second volume is a bibliography of further sources. The British counterparts are the fifteen-volume *Cambridge History of English Literature* and the twelve-volume *Oxford History of English Literature*. Chapters written by specialists cover literature from the earliest times into the twentieth century and also include good bibliographies.

After you have established the scope of the topic and have selected and have defined any terms associated with it, you may want to find out more about a particular author, say John Steinbeck. The first thing to do is check the catalog for a book-length biography. An excellent source for briefer biographies of writers who have worked in the twentieth century is *Contemporary Authors*. This source includes not only literary figures but authors of all types. Brief biographies, lists of works published and in progress, and sometimes interviews with the author are included. You may also be referred to articles in journals and in other reference tools such as the *Dictionary of Literary Biography*. This is a very useful series in progress that provides long, scholarly biographical articles on authors from all time periods, with selected bibliographies.

You may decide at this point that your final topic will be "The Grapes of Wrath: Propaganda or Art?" For critical articles on a particular novel or writer, a valuable source is the *MLA International Bibliography*, an annual publication indexing journal articles and books on the writers of all countries. In the printed index, the articles are grouped by nationality, within nationality by century, and within century under the writers' names, listed alphabetically. Thus, for your topic, you would look for "American Literature—Twentieth Century—Steinbeck, John." In the citations, the abbreviations of periodical titles are particularly cryptic, so it's a good idea to double check the list at the front of each volume. A sample citation is:

Trachtenberg, Stanley. "John Steinbeck: The Fate of Protest,"
*NDQ* 41, ii:5–11.

Notice that the title of this article does not correspond exactly with your topic, but you should usually follow up even those articles whose titles seem only slightly related. The article itself could easily turn out to be very useful. Don't forget the *Humanities Index* at this point; it indexes many literary journals and also provides a good interdisciplinary approach. The *MLA Bibliography* on CD/ROM is particularly useful, as it can provide much more detailed subject indexing than is available in the printed version, and you can cover material from 1980 to the present with one search. *MLA Bibliography* is also now available through the FirstSearch system, 1963–.

A quick way to arrive at critiques of specific novels, poems, plays, or short stories is through using a one-volume index to criticism. Examples of some of these handy tools are *Poetry Explication* (1962, with supplements), *Twentieth Century Short Story Explication* (1967, with supplements), *The American Novel* (1961, with supplements), *English Novel Explication* (1973, with supplements), *The Continental Novel* (1968), and *Drama Criticism* (1966, with supplements). All of the citations are arranged by author and specific work. The drawbacks are that they are less up to date than the indexes that come out every year and they do not cover as many sources or list as many citations.

Finally, you will often want to find the actual works of literature. Novels are not much of a problem, as they are listed in the catalog under the author's name, but what about plays, poetry, and short stories that are often scattered throughout various collections? You may have to consult the *Play Index* (1949–), *Columbia Granger's Index to Poetry* (1994), or the *Short Story Index* (1953–). All are author, title, and subject indexes to works that appear in collections.

To learn more about reference sources for literature, you can consult several good guides, one of which is Michael Marcuse's *A Reference Guide for English Studies* (1990).

### Performing Arts

Performance may be considered common to all the areas so far discussed in this section. Dramas and novels can become plays or films; a gallery exhibition of an artist's works is a "performance," and, of course, the chief communication of music is through performance. Therefore, the *Art Index*, *Music Index*, and *Humanities Index* may all contain articles on the performing arts. In addition, the *Film Literature Index* (1973–) is an author-subject index to about 300 international film periodicals.

Handel's *National Directory for the Performing Arts*, an annual publication, is a good source for information on arts organizations, facilities, and educational institutions.

Reviews of films, plays, TV shows, art exhibits, or concerts may be located through such standard reference tools as the *Readers' Guide*, newspaper indexes, or their computer equivalents, such as Infotrac. *A Guide to Critical Reviews*, 3rd ed. (1984–) is a good source for reviews of staged productions, and the *Film Review Index* indexes reviews of films from 1882 to 1985. *Variety Television Reviews, 1923–1988*, in fifteen volumes, reprints reviews of television shows during these years.

Several good one-volume encyclopedias concentrate on the performing arts. These include the *Cambridge Guide to World Theatre* (1988), the *Oxford Companion to Film* (1976), and *The Filmgoer's Companion*, 8th ed. (1984), a biographical dictionary with numerous illustrations.

### Religion and Philosophy

Religion and philosophy are combined because the terms sometimes overlap and because some of the reference books you will want to use cover the subjects together. Fortunately, there are several encyclopedias to start you on your way. You may want to begin your research by looking in the eight-volume *Encyclopedia of Philosophy* (1967). It provides brief biographies of philosophers from Aristotle to Rousseau, overviews of the philosophies of subjects ranging from tragedy to the social contract, and brief philosophical interpretations of concepts such as ugliness and society. Another interesting encyclopedia, which best fits in this section, is the *Dictionary of the History of Ideas* (1974). In it, topics like "Wisdom of the Fool," "Witchcraft," "Heresy in the Middle Ages," and "Theories of Beauty Since the Mid-Nineteenth Century" are examined and put into historical perspective. For briefer definitions of terms, Lacey's *Dictionary of Philosophy* (1986) is a good, up-to-date source.

The *Encyclopedia of Religion* (1987, 16 volumes) is an excellent source for information about religions and ethical systems from all ages and places. The long articles have good bibliographies at the end. The *Encyclopedia Judaica* (1972) gives detailed information on Jewish customs and is an especially good source for finding out about minor Jewish figures, both biblical and contemporary. Finally, the *New Catholic Encyclopedia* (1967) thoroughly examines matters pertaining to the history, teachings, and activities of the Roman Catholic Church. Particularly useful are its biographies of all the saints, as their names have a way of coming up in many other fields of study. Eerdman's *Bible Dictionary* (1987) is good for briefer references to names and people in the Bible.

If you are studying the Bible, a concordance, or word index to biblical quotations will be most helpful. Nelson's *Complete Concordance of the Revised Standard Version Bible* (1957), compiled by computer, is thorough and reliable. Be sure, however, that the edition of the Bible you are using is the one specified by the concordance. Otherwise, it will do you little good, as different words are used in different editions. Finally, the *Encyclopedia of American Religions* (1987) gives detailed information about religious denominations and sects.

For specific or up-to-date information on religious or philosophical questions and people, there are three useful periodical indexes. The *Religion Index*, 1949– (also available on CD-ROM) is an author and subject index to over 100 journals. Since 1980, this index has covered chapters and essays in books as well as journal articles and has also included brief abstracts. Following is a sample citation under the heading "Euthanasia":

Right to die—Good slogan, fuzzy thinking. Kamisar, John. *First Things* no. 38:6–9 D 1993.

The *Catholic Periodical and Literature Index* (1930–) concentrates on Catholic periodicals and books. It is indexed by author and subject. The *Philosopher's Index* (1967–) is an author and subject index covering international journals. It also includes abstracts.

### History

The study of history involves people, specific events, and general trends or movements. Usually, you will want to begin your research with a brief, rather general description of the area in which you are interested. Therefore, historical dictionaries and encyclopedias will often be the first reference tools you will need. There are so many that it is often difficult to decide which one to use. Only a few of the best ones will be mentioned here, but you can consult your library catalog under the subject heading "U.S. (or Great Britain or France)—History—Dictionaries and Encyclopedias" to find others. You can also browse through the reference collection in your library or consult Ronald Fritze's *Reference Sources in History* (1990), which offers a complete survey of historical reference tools for the student and beginning researcher.

The *Dictionary of American History* (1976), in seven volumes, is a good example of a thorough reference source. For instance, you can look under the Spanish-American War and find a brief summary of the causes and effects, names of important people involved, and dates as well as a bibliography of further sources at the end. For world history, Langer's *New Illustrated Encyclopedia of World History* is a good source. It is arranged chronologically and has a detailed index.

For an overview of historical events or eras, the best place to begin is with one of the multivolume Cambridge series. The *Cambridge Ancient History*, the *Cambridge Medieval History*, and the *Cambridge Modern History* all present essays, written by specialists, offering chronological summaries of the important events in history. Bibliographies of further sources are also included. If you are interested in the Spanish-American War, you might want to find out more about one of the people involved, say, Admiral George Dewey. The standard source for pre-twentieth-century American biographies is *Dictionary of American Biography*

(DAB). The signed articles are well written and usually include a long bibliography of further sources. Under "Dewey, George" there is a seven-page article with a bibliography of six further sources. The DAB does publish supplements for notable twentieth-century figures, but for very recent or less famous people, you may have to turn to the *Biography Index* or one of the *Who's Who* books.

The British counterpart of the DAB is the *Dictionary of National Biography* (DNB), which is, of course, larger since it has more years to cover. Supplements bring it up to 1980. For international biographies, the *McGraw-Hill Encyclopedia of World Biography*, in twelve volumes, is a good reference tool that includes portraits, photographs, illustrations, and bibliographies of further sources for notable world figures throughout history.

When doing research, particularly in history, most of the sources you will use will be of two general kinds: primary and secondary. Primary sources are reports or records of an event as it happens. For instance, suppose that after reading about Dewey you decide that you want to focus on the Philippine Campaign. Your primary sources in this case might be articles from the *New York Times* during the first half of 1898, when this campaign was taking place. There might also be articles in the magazines of the period, possibly written by reporters who were in the actual area. These sources can be found through the supplements to *Poole's Index to Periodical Literature* for the years of the war. Another type of primary source is available in *Documents of American History*. It contains documents ranging from the first charter of Virginia in 1606 to President Kennedy's proclamation calling for the removal of Soviet weapons from Cuba in 1962.

Secondary sources are interpretations of or commentaries on events, usually as seen through the perspective of time. An indispensable secondary source for American history is the American Historical Association's *Guide to Historical Literature* (1995). The best books, articles, government documents, and other materials on American history are listed by broad subject areas. There is a detailed subject index at the end. Looking under "Spanish-American War" in the index, you will be given several sources and referred to the headings "Philippine Campaign" and "Cuban Campaign" and to biographies of Dewey.

A broader reference tool is *Writings on American History* (1948–), published annually and designed to include every book and article of value in the study of American history. The big advantage of this reference is its comprehensive coverage. The disadvantages are that it is a little slow in coming out and that you might be overwhelmed by the amount of material, finding it difficult to select the best sources. The British counterpart, *Writings on British History*, is also extremely comprehensive but slow in coming out—usually about 10 years behind.

For up-to-date international indexing of periodical articles, you should go to the *Social Sciences Index* and the *Humanities Index*. A more specific tool is *Historical Abstracts*. This reference source, which began in 1955, indexes and summarizes articles on history covering the period 1775 to

1945. After 1964, America seceded, so to speak, and the United States and Canada are now covered in an index of their own, *America: History and Life* (1964–, also available on CD-ROM). Beginning with 1971, *Historical Abstracts* comes in two parts: *Modern History Abstracts, 1775–1914* and *Twentieth-Century Abstracts*. Where, then, would you look for recent articles on the Philippine Campaign or the Spanish-American War? Actually, you might find sources in either *Historical Abstracts (Modern History Abstracts, 1775–1914)* or *America: History and Life,* since both the campaign and the war were international issues. All of these abstracts are arranged in broad subject categories and have author and subject indexes at the end.

## Exercises

A. List the relevant subject headings you could use to look for sources for two of the following topics in the library catalog.

the computer and the arts

the hero in the twentieth-century American novel

the rise of religious fundamentalism

popular music and the drug culture

the history of the women's movement in the United States

B. Look up Buddhism in three different encyclopedias. Evaluate and compare the articles you find. Which do you think would be the best starting point if you were assigned to write on this topic? Why?

C. List five works by each of the following authors. Which source or sources of information did you use?

| | |
|---|---|
| B. Traven | Gabriel Garcia Marquez |
| Toni Morrison | Joan Didion |
| Edith Wharton | |

D. Prepare a minibibliography of five articles about one of the following persons. Which sources did you use?

| | |
|---|---|
| Theodore Roosevelt | Mother Teresa |
| Karl Barth | Noam Chomsky |
| Diego Rivera | Harriet Tubman |

E. Locate and give the citation for a biographical sketch or article on each of the following philosophers:

| | |
|---|---|
| Martin Heiddeger | Thomas Dewey |

F. Identify briefly the following people and musical terms. Name your source of information.

| | |
|---|---|
| counterpoint | Branford Marsalis |
| Gustav Holst | Stephen Stills |
| Princess Ida | Amy Beach |

G. Identify briefly the following terms in art. Name your source of information.

| | |
|---|---|
| pantograph | collage |
| Romanesque | pointillism |
| etching | palenque |

H. Identify briefly the following terms in literature. Name your source of information.

| | |
|---|---|
| problem novel | archetype |
| foot | theatre of the absurd |

I. Choose one of the following subjects and describe the procedure (search strategy) you would use in finding information about it. List in order the steps you would take. You should also describe how you might narrow the topic as you progress. Don't forget about the reference tools covered in the section "General Reference Works," as they may be of use here.

| | |
|---|---|
| war protest music | secular humanism |
| performance art | the poetry of Sylvia Plath |

J. Briefly describe the following historical terms or events and give your sources of information.

Federal Emergency Relief Administration
Webster-Hayne debate
Espionage Act of 1917
Treaty of Berlin
Sack of Rome

## SOCIAL SCIENCES

In the humanities, you can usually count on a novel having only one title, a musical piece only one composer, and a work of art only one artist. Similarly, in the physical sciences, the names of plants, animals, and chemical compounds remain fairly constant. But in the social sciences things are different. New words and concepts are coined frequently, and there are sometimes many names for the same thing. Occasionally, you won't even be certain in what field your topic belongs because subjects in the social sciences have a way of spilling over into one another. Is a topic like "The Effects on the Child of the One-Parent Family" in psychology, sociology, or education? In this case, you can probably find useful information under all three.

A well-written and comprehensive reference work that can give you a good background or overview of most social science topics is the *International Encyclopedia of the Social Sciences*, in fifteen volumes with an index. Long signed articles by specialists will give you a thorough background on such broad topics as sleep or human rights as well as clear definitions of more specific terms such as homeostasis or sequential analysis. Recent research is presented in every field, and an extensive bibliography of further sources is given at the end of each article. This reference tool should be considered a starting point for any research you may wish to do on a topic in the social sciences.

Two interdisciplinary periodical indexes, both available on CD/ROM, are also good starting points. The *Social Sciences Index* (1974–) uses broad subject headings such as "War and Society," "Language and Culture," and "Government and the Press." For a paper on the energy crisis, you could look under the heading "Power Resources" and find articles from economic, environmental, and sociological journals, for example:

Energy development in China. Kang Wu.
*Energy Policy.* 23:2, 1995.

The citations take the same form as those in the *Readers' Guide.* Again, remember to look in the front of the volume for a list of abbreviations of journal titles.

A periodical index that is particularly good for economics, sociology, and government is the *Public Affairs Information Services (PAIS)*. It indexes pamphlets, government documents, and books along with periodical articles. Libraries usually have pamphlet collections, which are good sources for current, specific information. If your library does not have the pamphlet you are interested in, you can always order a copy. Many are free or inexpensive.

A unique reference tool that you may find more useful in upper-division courses is the *Social Sciences Citation Index*. Suppose you are doing research in an area where subject headings seem hard to pin down or where little information seems to be available. If you know of one person who has written articles on the subject you are interested in, then the *Social Sciences Citation Index* can be a starting point. By looking in the Citations section of the index under your author's name, you can find a list of articles he or she has written plus a list of other people who have cited or referred to these works in articles of their own. Articles that refer to an article about your topic may themselves have relevant material that you can use.

Finding out about various organized groups is often necessary for research in the social sciences. You may want to find out when the Teamster's Union was founded or its current membership, the names of some professional organizations in psychology, or what exactly the Burlap and Jute Association does. The *Encyclopedia of Associations* gives brief descriptions of more than 16,000 organizations in the United States and Canada. They are grouped by subject but are indexed by name of association and location.

For information about people as individuals, *American Men and Women of Science, Social and Behavioral Sciences* is an excellent source for contemporary figures. Indexes by occupation and birthplace are included at the end, so if, for example, you need to write a biographical sketch of a recreation leader (and few people can think of one offhand), this source will be very useful.

## Anthropology

Anthropology and its closely allied subject archeology are fascinating. Who has not heard of Margaret Mead and her *Coming of Age in Samoa* or Dr. Leakey's discovery of primitive human skeletal remains in Africa? You probably won't have the time or the inclination to live with a primitive tribe or to participate in a "dig" for your research paper, so you will have to rely on secondary sources. These may be less glamorous, but they can still yield interesting topics.

A good place to start looking for information is the *Annual Review of Anthropology*, a collection of bibliographic essays (sources listed in essay form) on current subjects in the field. A typical essay is "New Directions in Ecology and Ecological Anthropology." The *International Encyclopedia of the Social Sciences* will also provide a good background on almost any topic.

Periodical indexing for anthropology is, unfortunately, relatively new on the scene. *Abstracts in Anthropology* began in 1970 and indexes periodicals in archeology, ethnology, and linguistics, with author and subject indexes published annually. Looking under the heading "Kinship" in 1987, you could find:

Kuper, Adam. "Durkheim's theory of primitive kinship,"
*British Journal of Sociology*. 1985, 36(2):224–237.

*Anthropological Literature: An Index to Periodical Articles and Essays* (1979–) includes symposium publications and collected essays as well as journals.

Folklore, which is a part of anthropology, is covered by *Abstracts of Folklore Studies* (1963–). Its indexes are also cumulated annually. The *International Bibliography of Social and Cultural Anthropology* (1955–) is a comprehensive listing of books, pamphlets, and periodical articles in the field, but many of the entries are not in English, which can be a drawback. The author and subject indexes, however, are given in both English and French. Once again, the *Social Sciences Index* and the *Humanities Index* can give you many relevant articles from the more common periodicals.

You can look up terms in anthropology in Seymour-Smith's *Encyclopedia of Anthropology* (1986). Jobes's *Dictionary of Mythology, Folklore, and Symbol*, in three volumes, is a handy key for checking out the significance of certain rites or objects in various cultures. Murdock's *Atlas of World Cultures* (1981) and *Rand McNally's Atlas of Mankind* (1982) list and describe cultures and tribes throughout the world, with topics such as food production, kinship, and taboos. The *Encyclopedia of World Cultures* (1991, in progress) will include, when finished, more than 1,500 cultural groups with their history, cultural relations, and social organization.

## Business and Economics

Topics for most beginning research papers in business or economics are usually fairly specific. You may want to take a look at the advertising of a certain product such as breakfast cereals, do a profile on a particular company such as General Motors, or investigate a particular economic problem such as NAFTA.

The best place to begin searching for current specific topics is a periodical or newspaper index. Business is especially well served by computer indexes, two of which have no print equivalents. *ABI Inform* indexes major business journals and provides lengthy abstracts. *Compact Disclosure* provides financial statements and reports of large corporations. *General Periodicals Index*, previously mentioned, also covers many business journals. One advantage of using a computer index in the field of business is that it can pick up key words from the titles or abstracts of articles that may not yet be used as official subject headings, since terminology in the business world is especially volatile. The *Business Periodicals Index* (1958–), available in both print and CD/ROM, is a subject index to about 170 business periodicals. It is published by the same company as the *Readers' Guide*, so the citations are in the same form. If you are writing about "Ethics in Business," you may want to look under the subject heading "Insider Trading," where you would find the following citation:

> Insider trading: there oughta be a law. S. Crook.
> *Bus Week* p. 82 D12 '94.

*Predicasts F&S Index* (1968–) indexes about 750 financial publications, newspapers, and trade journals. The index, cumulated annually, is divided into two sections: articles on industries and articles on specific companies, so here you could look for information on the cereal industry, for example. More general periodical indexes, such as the *Public Affairs Information Service (PAIS)* and the *Readers' Guide*, may also have articles on this topic.

Another useful index for basic research in business is the *Wall Street Journal Index* (1958–). Many libraries have back issues of the *Wall Street Journal* on microfilm. The index is divided into two sections: corporate news, listed under the names of specific corporations, and general news, listed by subject headings. For example, if you are interested in Quaker Oats, you can find the following citation in the index:

> Probably won't be able to achieve traditional rate of earnings
>     growth in near future, R. D. Stuart, president, told shareholders'
>     meeting. 11/14 25:3

Here you are given not just the title but also an indication of the contents of the article, the date, the page number, and the column number.

Instead of finding bits of information here and there, you may want to locate a summary of the information about a corporation all in one place. If you only want to know the yearly profits, the number of employees, or the name of the president of a company, you can check in a one-volume directory such as *Poor's Register of Corporations, Directors, and Executives*, which is published annually. Dun and Bradstreet and Moody's also publish annual volumes with information about specific companies. If a more complete overview or background is necessary, *Standard and Poor's Corporation Records*, seven volumes of brief histories and financial information about large U.S. corporations, is a good place to look. Mergers and takeovers are a frequent occurrence in corporate America. To keep up with these events, look in the *Directory of Corporate Affiliations*, published annually, where you can find a complete list of the subsidiaries and affiliates of all the large companies in the United States.

Sometimes you will want facts about an industry as a whole. What kinds of profits did the cereal industry make last year? What is the per capita consumption of ready-to-eat cereals? Of course, you can always look under the name of the industry in the *Business Periodical Index* or the *Predicasts F&S Index*. For quick facts, *Standard and Poor's Industry Surveys*, updated periodically, analyzes the leading industries with charts, figures, and brief essays. Industry data, presented in the form of financial ratios, can be found in *Industry Norms and Key Business Ratios* (annual), or *RMA Annual Statement Studies* (annual).

Suppose you run into trouble in your search because you don't understand certain concepts, such as financial ratios, business cycles, or inflation. You can turn to the *International Encyclopedia of the Social Sciences*, which has excellent articles on broad terms and concepts. For briefer definitions of words and phrases like managed currency, Federal Home Loan Bank Act, or Commodity Exchange Commission, check in your library for a recent dictionary such as *A Concise Dictionary of Business* (1990) or *Multinational Enterprise: an Encyclopedic Dictionary* (1987).

Current biographies are well covered by *Who's Who in Finance and Industry*, published every two years. In addition to U.S. business executives, it also includes biographies of the executives of the 1,000 largest corporations in the world.

If you need a particular kind of information in the field of business not covered by the sources mentioned so far, turn to the *Encyclopedia of Business Information Sources* (8th ed., 1991), a detailed two-volume listing of thousands of business-related subjects with references to the publications, organizations, and directories where this information can be found.

### Education
Information in the field of education is well indexed and documented. Once you have decided on a manageable topic, you should have little trouble finding what you will need. It is often difficult, however, to know how much information is actually available on a given topic so, as usual, you should begin with a specialized encyclopedia.

If you are interested in tests, for example, a look at the index to the *Encyclopedia of Education Research* will refer you to many additional subject headings: admissions tests, aptitude tests, achievement tests, and marks. Suppose you decide that marks is the closest to what you want. Under the heading "Marks and Marking Systems" the encyclopedia offers a seven-page article, with a bibliography of other books and articles at the end, describing different systems and reviewing recent research. In the ten-volume *Encyclopedia of Education*, if you look under "Marks" you will be referred to "Grading Systems." There you will find a four-page article with a briefer bibliography. This encyclopedia concentrates on defining and describing subjects rather than on surveying recent research. The *Handbook of Research on Teaching*, 3rd ed. (1986) contains articles with extensive bibliographies on broader topics, such as "teaching functions" and "classroom organization and management."

You may discover that you will need to define some terms and concepts. For example, you may run across terms such as mark-sensing, relative mark, class mark, or admissible mark. All perfectly common English words, but what do they mean in this context? You can find the definitions for these terms in Good's *Dictionary of Education* (1973). It has 681 pages of very small print, so you can be pretty sure of finding the term you're looking for. A later source, although not as detailed, is *Dictionary of Instructional Technology* (1986).

Perhaps you have decided to evaluate the pass/fail grading system in a paper. "Pass/Fail Grading System" is an LC subject heading, so you can find some books on the subject. You can also look under the more general heading "Grading and Marking (Students)" and find certain books that may have sections on the pass/fail system. Remember to also look in the *Essay and General Literature Index*, which indexes essays and sections of books. However, since this is a fairly recent and specific topic, you will probably find that periodical articles are the best source of information.

In the *Education Index* (1929–), an author-subject index to leading periodicals in education, if you look under "Pass/Fail Grading System," you will be referred to "Marking Systems." A sample citation under this heading is:

Wright, Russell G. Don't be a mean teacher.
*The Science Teacher* 56:38–41 Ja '89.

The citations follow the same form as those in the *Readers' Guide*.

Now for a different kind of index. The U.S. government established the Educational Resources Information Center (referred to as ERIC). Its purpose is to collect, index, and publish on microfiche (microfilm on separate sheets rather than on reels) previously unpublished educational information such as conference reports, state government documents, and work done on government grants. To use ERIC, you should start with the *Thesaurus of ERIC Descriptors*, which functions as a subject heading guide to the indexing terms that are used. Under "Marking" you will be referred to "Grading," where you can find a list of related headings and narrower and broader terms to consult, similar to the system in the *LC Subject Heading Guide*. After writing down the subject headings that you think might be helpful, you should go to the index itself.

The index to ERIC is available in both print and CD-ROM formats, but whichever you use, you will find that your citation will have a six digit number , prefaced by "ED" or "EJ". The ED numbers are available on microfiche, and the EJ numbers are journal articles and must be located in the same way as any other journal article. ERIC includes long abstracts of the documents on microfiche, which is a help in deciding whether or not they will be revelant to your research. Many libraries have the ERIC microfiche collection, or if you are starting your research well in advance, you can order most of the documents directly from ERIC in either photocopied or microfiche format.

If you come across a person in your reading whom you want to learn more about, there are several biographical directories. One example is the three-volume *Biographical Dictionary of American Educators* (1978). *American Men and Women of Science, Social and Behavioral Sciences* and *Biography Index* would also be good places to look.

### Geography

The first things people usually associate with geography are maps, so let's begin by talking about some good atlases. After all, if you are going to study geography, you will need a general idea of the lay of the land and need to be able to locate features such as towns, rivers, and mountains. Also, you will need a recently published atlas if you need to keep up with rapidly changing political boundaries.

The *Times Atlas of the World* (1990) is a good basic reference work, very authoritative and detailed, giving as many place names as can be squeezed onto the maps without sacrificing legibility. Other recent and attractive world atlases are the *National Geographic Atlas of the World* (1990) and *Goode's World Atlas*, revised frequently, which contains thematic maps such as the world economic situation. For maps of the United States, you may look at the excellent *National Atlas of the United States of America*, published by the U.S. Geological Survey in 1970. This atlas was in the works for more than twenty years, and the planning shows in the great accuracy and detail of its 765 maps, which give economic, cultural, and historical as well as physical features.

Historical geography, which emphasizes the historical processes of physical and cultural evolution, could be discussed with either history or geography. It is included here because it does rely on maps and atlases. *Shepherd's Historical Atlas* is a standard, frequently used historical atlas. It contains such interesting maps as "The West Indies and Central America, 1492–1525" and "London, 1200–1600."

If you need a specialized or detailed map that you have been unable to find, the American Geographical Society of New York publishes the *Index to Maps in Books and Periodicals*. Entries are alphabetical by subject and geographical-political division.

Most atlases include indexes to geographical features such as cities, towns, and mountains. For more detailed information about a particular place, the source to use is a gazeteer, or dictionary of places. The standard *Columbia Lippincott Gazeteer of the World* (1962) gives the location, altitude, trade, resources, and population (with the date of the census from which figures were taken) for over 130,000 geographical areas. A more up-to-date work, which reflects recent demographic and regional changes, is *Geo-data; the World Geographical Encyclopedia* (1989).

The most specific periodical index for the field of geography is *Geo Abstracts* (1966–). The fragmentation in this work is so great that only a specialist could always know under which category a particular topic would fall. The abstracts are divided into six parts:

A—Landforms and the Quaternary (the Pleistocene era)
B—Biogeography and Climatology
C—Economic Geography
D—Social and Historical Geography
E—Sedimentology
F—Regional and Community Planning

Each part has its own annual subject and author indexes. Thankfully, there is also an annual index that covers all of the parts together, so you don't have to guess which one to look in. This index deserves some special attention. It is what is called a Key-Word-in-Context (KWIC) index. This means that each article is indexed under every word in the title that is considered a significant, or key, word. For example, the title "Food and Population in Historical Perspective" could be found in the index under "Food" as well as the following ways:

Population in historical perspective = Food and
Historical perspective = Food and population in

Another source of articles, books, pamphlets, and government publications is the American Geographical Society of New York's *Current Geographical Publications* (1938–). Its indexes are arranged by author, subject, and region. Also, you will find many geographical journals indexed in the *Social Sciences Index.*

A good dictionary for defining such terms as quaternary and sedimentology is Small's *A Modern Dictionary of Geography* (1989), designed for the beginning student; for further information sources, several research guides such as *Encyclopedia of Geographical Information Sources* (1987) are available.

### Minority and Ethnic Studies

Areas such as African American studies, Hispanic studies, and Women's studies are relatively new and are interdisciplinary by nature. African American studies, for example, can include art, literature, politics, history, music, and many other subjects. The Library of Congress, through its subject headings, and publishers of reference books are acknowledging the presence of minority studies by setting up special headings and reference tools for these areas.

For years, all information about African Americans was entered under the heading "Negro." However, with the eighth edition of its supplement to the *LC Subject Heading Guide*, the Library of Congress changed all headings that used to begin with "Negro" to "Afro-American." Of course, for libraries, changing thousands of cards in the card catalog is an expensive and time-consuming task, so the changeover may not yet be complete in your library. If your library has a computer catalog, however, such changes are relatively easy to make. Similarly, information on Mexican Americans used to be found under the heading "Mexicans in the United States." Now the heading "Mexican Americans" is used. American Indians are still found under "Indians of North America." The more recent term "Native Americans" has not yet found its way into the subject heading guide.

Several useful reference books provide information on minorities as a whole: *Dictionary of Race and Ethnic Relations* (1988) gives information on key events, individuals, and legislation; *World Directory of Minorities* (1990) describes 160 different groups throughout the world; and *We the People: an Atlas of America's Ethnic Diversity* (1988) includes 111 color maps depicting ethnic origins and settlement patterns.

Of all the minority and ethnic studies, Black or African American studies, in one form or another, has been around the longest. For brief factual articles and biographical sketches, there are many sources. The *Negro Almanac*, now in its fourth edition (1983), covers a wide range of topics in the social sciences and has subject and name indexes and bibliographies. The multivolume *Afro-American Encyclopedia* covers topics ranging from a comprehensive list of African tribes to the "Birmingham, Alabama Movement." Another useful handbook is the *Dictionary of Afro-American Slavery* (1988), with signed articles, bibliographies, and a chronology.

For books and articles, the most comprehensive reference tool is the *Dictionary Catalog of the Schomberg Negro History and Literature Collection* at the New York Public Library. This is one of the best collections of African American books, articles, and other materials in the United States, and supplements are published to include additions to the collection. The *Index to Periodical Articles by and About Blacks* provides detailed coverage for periodical articles published since 1960, but it is very slow in coming out. Many of the periodicals indexed here are also covered by the *Readers' Guide* and the *Social Sciences Index* but, by using the more specific indexes, you can zero in on your topic more readily and avoid having to weed out irrelevant material.

*Who's Who Among Black Americans* (1975/76–) provides good coverage for contemporary blacks, and *Black Leaders of the Nineteenth Century* (1988) is a good source for information about earlier figures.

*The Reference Encyclopedia of the American Indian* (1990) is a good source for obtaining information on Native Americans, including organizations, museums, and cultural institutions. A new reference source, still in progress, is *Handbook of North American Indians*; about seven of the planned twenty volumes are now completed. In this work, detailed histories of various tribes and essays on specific aspects of Indian life are presented. The more concise *Atlas of the North American Indian* (1985) includes maps, chronologies, and a classification of Indian languages.

Asian American studies is perhaps the newest of the ethnic studies on the scene and therefore has developed fewer specific reference tools, but the *Dictionary of Asian American History* (1986) contains essays on the historical experience of Asians from all areas of Asia who are now in the United States; for further study, *Asian American Studies: an Annotated Bibliography and Research Guide* (1989) is a good starting point.

The major periodical indexes for Mexican American studies are the *Hispanic American Periodicals Index* (1970–1988, now available on CD-ROM) and *Chicano Periodical Index* (1967 to the present). Several good bibliographies also exist. Among them are *Latinos in the United States: an Historical Bibliography* (1986) and *A Comprehensive Chicano Bibliography, 1960–1972*, by Talbot and Cruz, which includes articles and government documents as well as books. *The Hispanic Almanac* (1990) has socioeconomic, demographic, and linguistic data for the Hispanic population in the United States, presented in maps, graphs, and text. For other reference sources on Mexican Americans, you may look at *Ethnic Information Sources of the United States*, which lists reference books, pamphlets, organizations, agencies, and media sources for many different minority groups, including Mexican Americans.

*Women's Studies Abstracts* (1972–) has proven a valuable guide for locating pertinent information on women from periodicals, books, and pamphlets. As with all publications of abstracts, you have to use the subject index first and then turn to the abstract (or summary) section for the citation. *Women's Studies Index* (1989–) covers 78 periodicals, mainly American in origin.

The *Women's Studies Encyclopedia* (1989, in progress) will include signed articles on all aspects of women's experiences; for example, Chicana writers, osteoporosis, women's colleges, and rape. For biographies of women, you may use any of the standard biography sources already covered. There is also a reference source that covers some relatively minor and otherwise undocumented figures, *Notable American Women, 1607–1950* (with supplements). It reveals an unexpected number of both active and activist women from 1607 on. Most of the women included are not listed in the *Dictionary of American Biography*.

### Psychology

The study of psychology may involve technical terms and concepts unfamiliar to nonexperts. Lulled by the popular approach to psychology of such magazines as *Psychology Today*, you may plunge into an article on "Dream Interpretation" and run into terms such as "psychotropic effects" and "ego modalities" that you do not understand. For a few definitions to help clear things up, you can turn to the excellent *International Encyclopedia of the Social Sciences*, already mentioned, or to the more specific *Encyclopedia of Psychology* (1984). This four-volume set contains about 5,000 brief entries, including a few biographical references. A more specialized source is the *International Encyclopedia of Psychiatry, Psychology, Psychoanalysis, and Neurology* (1977, new edition in progress) in twelve volumes. Articles are written by authorities in the field and include brief bibliographies. An example of a source for brief definitions is the *International Dictionary of Psychology* (1989).

Once you have located some reference aids to bolster your confidence, you should narrow your subject to a workable topic about which there is enough information. One way is to scan a recent issue of the *Social Sciences Index* to see some of the current subject headings. You can find many articles in well-known psychology journals through this index, and they can provide a good starting place for your research. For example, you may decide to write on nightmares. By looking under the more general heading "Dreams," you can find the following citation:

Snoring and nightmares. R. A. Hicks.
*Percept Mot Skills* v. 77 p. 433–434 O '93.

For more technical articles or reports of experiments dealing with your topic, the place to look is *Psychological Abstracts*, 1927– (available on CD-ROM as PsychInfo). The abstracts are arranged by broad subject areas, and there are author and subject indexes for each six-month period. Cumulated indexes are published occasionally. Subject headings are not too specific in *Psychological Abstracts*, so you may want to consult the *Thesaurus of Psychological Index Terms*, a subject heading guide, before beginning. This thesaurus may also help you to develop ideas for a workable topic. For the topic "Nightmares," you can, however, look directly under that heading and find the following:

escape, postescape 8566

This refers you to the following citation:

8566 Cernovsky, Zack Z.
Escape nightmares and postescape stressful events.
*Perceptual and Motor Skills*, 1988(Apr.), v. 66 (2), 551–555.

Since terminology in the field of psychology changes and develops rapidly, and combining terms and concepts is quite helpful, computer searching in this field will be particularly useful.

If your topic falls in the area of psychoanalysis, and many topics in psychology can, another specific index to check is the *Index to Psychoanalytical Writings* (1956–), which covers books, journal articles, and reviews. You can look under the heading "Nightmares" and find a reference to the book *The Nightmare: Psychological and Biological Foundations* (1987). Here you may think, "But I could find books through the catalog." True, but an index such as this covers many books that your library probably doesn't have. Thus, it is a good way for you to find out about the existence of books beyond your local library.

Biographies of contemporary psychologists are covered in the American Psychological Association's *Biographical Directory*, published every three years. Addresses, specialties, degrees, and employment history are given for its members. Important figures in the field who are no longer living may be located through one of the encyclopedias or in the *Biography Index*.

If you find that you need still more information, Bell's *Guide to Library Research in Psychology* is an excellent handbook for locating library sources and doing a research paper in this field. Finally, psychology is one of the subjects with its own rules about bibliography and footnote formats. The APA puts out the *Publication Manual of the American Psychological Association* (1994), and you will probably want to consult it when doing a paper for a psychology class.

### Political Science

In political science, as in any other area, one of the first things to do when beginning your research is to narrow down your topic and identify possibly useful headings. Suppose you are interested in electoral systems. Looking in the LC guide to subject headings, which is always a good place to start, you will find the following:

> *Elections*
> rt Ballot
> Campaign funds
> Presidents—U.S.—Election
> Women—Suffrage

There are many more related references and subdivisions, which should give you some ideas for ways to narrow down your topic. Let's say you decide on campaign funds as a topic. You might want to take a look at the old standby, the *International Encyclopedia of the Social Sciences*. There are over 100 different articles in the area of political science. Looking under "Campaign Funds," you would be referred to the heading "Political Financing," where you would find a six-page article. Don't forget to use the bibliography at the end as a guide to further sources. If you need a dictionary to define any specific terms you may have encountered, good examples are Evans' *Dictionary of World Politics* (1990) and Plano's *American Political Dictionary* (1989).

Next, you will probably want to check the periodical indexes in the field. The major index for political science is *International Political Science Abstracts* (1951–). It selectively indexes over 1,000 journals in many languages, but the abstracts themselves are in either English or French. Under "Elections—Women—Democratic Countries" you can find the following:

> Rule, Wilma. Electoral systems and women's opportunity for election to parliament in twenty-three democracies. *Western Political Quarterly* 40(3), Sept. 87:477–498.

You may notice that in many of the abstracting services, the elements of the citations are presented in a slightly different order than they are in the more common periodical indexes. Still, the basic ingredients are there: the title of the periodical, the volume, the date, and the page numbers. The *International Bibliography of Political Science* (1953–) goes one step further and lists books, pamphlets, and government documents as well as periodical articles.

If you have gone through all the steps mentioned so far and have come up with only foreign language articles or periodicals that your library doesn't have, don't forget the interdisciplinary indexes mentioned at the beginning of the social sciences section. The *Social Science Index* and the *Public Affairs Information Service* index numerous political science publications.

Let's go back even farther, to the section on general reference tools. What could be more pertinent for research in political science than government documents? For example, in 1974 the government held hearings on the campaign practices and finances of the 1972 presidential campaign. These could be very useful for a historical paper on campaign funding.

Political science involves more than theory or history. It is also the study of the ongoing processes of particular governments. One handy reference book for American government is the *Congress A to Z* (1988). It provides information on the history and structure of congress and biographies of outstanding members. Another useful guide is the *U.S. Government Manual*. This publication, updated annually, is a convenient way to keep track of departments and major officials in the government. If you would like to know the names of certain officials in the Defense Department, for example, or how the department is structured, you will find complete information in this manual.

A more specific source for information about Congress is the *Congressional Quarterly Weekly Report,* often referred to as *CQ*. If you ever wonder what Congress did to earn its salary during a particular week, just pick up the issue of *CQ* for that week and you will get a relatively good summary. It also includes a few feature articles on pending legislation.

The same company publishes the *Congressional Quarterly Almanac*, a yearly summary of legislative action and important events in American government. One of the most useful sections is a record of all roll-call votes taken in the House and Senate. You can find out how your congressman or congresswoman voted on key issues and see how well the votes coincide with campaign promises. Also included are transcripts of presidential messages and speeches and an analysis of the presidency. Another reference source, again by the same publisher, gives you longer-term information. It is *Congress and the Nation* (1945–), which is organized at four-year intervals so that you can get a good idea of the developments during a particular presidential term.

The most detailed day-to-day record of what is going on in Congress is the *Congressional Record*. It includes every word that is spoken on the floor, plus a number that aren't. These voluminous records are indexed frequently, and a final index is prepared at the end of each session, so you don't have to wade through thousands of pages looking for a particular speech by a particular member of Congress.

You may not need such a detailed record, however. To keep up with recent developments, such as campaign contributions during a recent election, there are always the *Readers' Guide*, current to within about a month, and *The New York Times Index*, current to within about two months.

Finally, a biographical directory for American politics, which includes local as well as national personalities, is *Who's Who in American Politics* (1967/68–), published every two years.

International relations is another important element of political science. You should know how to find information about the relations between one nation and another in the library catalog. The basic pattern of subject headings you will want is "Country—Foreign Relations—Country." Thus a book on relations between the U.S. and Cuba would be found under "U.S.—Foreign Relations—Cuba." If you then wish to know more about the government of Cuba, one of the best starting points is the *Europa World Yearbook*, published annually. This source gives information about the forms of government and the major officials for nations throughout the world as well as for a selection of international organizations. It also lists major newspapers, languages, and religions and gives statistics on population, finance, trade, production, and so forth. For biographies of international figures, the *International Yearbook and Statesman's Who's Who* (1953–) includes leaders in religion, commerce, industry, and government.

Finally, a well-organized, annotated guide to still more reference tools for students is Holler's *The Information Sources of Political Science* (1986).

### Sociology

Sociology deals with the different types of groups and structures into which people are born or are socialized. It also studies how people may transform these groups or structures. A helpful source to begin with is *Current Sociology* (1958–). Published quarterly, each issue contains a trend report, with a supporting bibliography, on some area in sociology. This publication is a good place to get some ideas for a possible topic for research in the area.

Although there are specific reference tools for sociology, most of the topics in the field are interdisciplinary. Psychology and education are but two of the areas that are often related to sociology. Therefore, it is a good idea to remember the reference works mentioned in the introduction to this section on the social sciences. Many of them can be very helpful in your research in sociology.

Sociology has both its theoretical and its practical aspects. You could choose a theoretical topic such as crowd behavior, or you might be interested in the more practical aspects of social work, such as those involved in family counseling. Suppose you decide to investigate crowd behavior. Looking in the four-volume *Encyclopedia of Sociology* (1992) under "Crowds," you will be referred to "Collective Behavior," "Mass Phenomena," and "Queues." All these articles probably have a bibliography at the end, so you will be off to a good start if you read them and follow up the references. You can find additional books in the library catalog under the subject heading "Crowds." For periodical articles, a useful reference tool is the old standby, *Social Sciences Index*. A new computer index, *Sociofile,* also indexes articles specifically in the field of sociology.

Should you choose a practical topic oriented toward social work, such as family counseling, the *Encyclopedia of Social Work* (1987), which emphasizes the professional practice of social work and welfare institutions, would be a good place to begin. Two abstracting services cover this area specifically. *Social Work Research and Abstracts* (1977–) indexes over 200 journals, and *Human Resources Abstracts* (1966–), formerly called *Poverty and Human Resources Abstracts*, indexes periodical articles, books, pamphlets, and agency reports. It emphasizes research and action programs, legislative and community developments, and policy trends. The subject headings are very general. For instance, under "Family" you will find the following citation:

Armour, M. A. Family life cycle stages.
*J of Fam Social Work* 1(2):27–42, 1995.

If you are investigating a particular state or city and want to get an idea of the services available, the *National Directory of Private Social Agencies* (1964–) can provide valuable information. It is divided into two parts. Part One is classified by services offered, such as homes for delinquents or drug rehabilitation programs. Part Two is a list of agencies arranged by state and city. It is published in a loose-leaf binder so that it can be updated constantly. Also, don't forget another source that may come in handy, the *Encyclopedia of Associations*.

Much of the information in sociology comes from questionnaires and interviews. In fact, most theses and dissertations in sociology are expected to include firsthand information or observations in addition to information gained through searching the literature. Although you may not conduct any personal investigations for a beginning research paper, you should keep the importance of primary sources in mind. You should also be aware of the catalog subject headings—"Questionnaires" and "Social Surveys"—under which you can find books about these information-gathering processes.

Sociology is developing a jargon all its own. This is especially true as the use of statistical methods in research becomes more and more widespread. A reference work such as the *Concise Oxford Dictionary of Sociology* (1994) will be helpful for understanding current usage. There are also encyclopedias covering specific areas of sociology such as the *Encyclopedia of Aging* (1987) and the *Encyclopedia of Adolescence* (1991).

Finally, Pauline Bart's *Student Sociologist's Handbook* (1986) can be a useful aid for finding further sources of information. It includes an introduction to library research as well as a guide to writing research papers involving actual fieldwork.

**Exercises**

A. List three or more subject headings in your library's catalog relevant to the topic of education of African Americans in the United States.

B. List three or more subject headings in your library's catalog relevant to the subject of Mexican American migrant labor in the United States.

C. Give citations for four periodical articles on U.S.–Japanese relations. What sources did you use?

D. Make a minibibliography, including two primary and four secondary sources, on the breakup of the Soviet Union.

E. Write a one-paragraph profile on one of the following corporations. Include what you think to be the most important facts about it. What sources did you use?

    General Motors          Heublein

    Nike                 Revlon

F. Locate by state or province and country the following places:

    Carignan           Golden Hinde

    Pickle Crow       Roxbury

    Narbada River

What source or sources did you use?

G. Look up psychoanalysis in three different encyclopedias. Which do you think provides the best starting point for a paper and why?

H. Locate biographical sketches for the following persons and list the sources you used.

    B. F. Skinner       W.E.B. Dubois

    George Murdock    Mikhail Gorbachev

    Ann Hutchinson    Betty Friedan

I. Outline a search strategy for one of the following topics. You may use any sources you wish, either from this section or from previous sections.

    Nuclear weapons and the future
    Improving the public school system
    Geographical environment and its psychological effects
    The image of Native Americans in the media
    The role of ritual in primitive societies

## SCIENCES

Until you begin to take courses beyond the introductory level in one of the sciences, the library topics you will be investigating will be, for the most part, rather nontechnical. They may deal with areas of general interest, such as pollution problems, alternative sources of energy, or the furor over experiments on recombining DNA molecules. Since many of the indexes, abstracts, and handbooks for specific sciences are quite technical, much of this section will be concerned with the many reference tools that are useful for the sciences in general.

Let's begin by considering a sample topic: solar energy. Many people are interested in this subject. After all, it has been heralded as a solution to many of our future energy problems. As you begin, however, you may not know much about how solar energy works or how feasible it is. Is it expensive? Could it work in such cities as Portland, Oregon, where the annual average rainfall is high? A good starting point for any research in the sciences is the *McGraw-Hill Encyclopedia of Science and Technology* (1992, in twenty volumes). It has well-written articles designed for the non-specialist on many broad scientific topics. It is also illustrated and well indexed, and most of its articles have bibliographies. *The Encyclopedia of Physical Science and Technology* (1987) is a bit more specialized and many of the articles are at a higher technical level. A less specialized but entertaining and informative encyclopedia is *How It Works* (1977), which explains in twenty-two illustrated volumes the workings of inventions, scientific principles, and manufacturing processes.

You may decide, after reading articles and following up some of the bibliographic references in the sources mentioned, that you want to limit your topic to "The Feasibility of Using Solar Energy for Heating Individual Homes." Books can certainly provide additional background information. Going to the catalog, you will find the headings "Solar Energy" and "Architecture, domestic" to be particularly useful. However, science is an area in which many new developments occur every day. Therefore, most important scientific material is first published in journals. To learn of the latest developments in applications of solar energy, you should go to the periodical indexes. Computer databases are also particularly useful in the sciences, where current, up-to-date information is especially important.

For nonspecialist subjects, one good place to look is in the *Readers' Guide*. It indexes such popular journals as *Scientific American*, *Science*, and *Science News*, which offer scientific articles of interest to the general public. There are three other indexes that offer more specific and research-oriented coverage of the sciences but still have many articles that can be read and understood by the nonspecialist. *General Science Index*, 1978– (also available on CD-ROM) is a subject and author index designed to give more thorough coverage of standard science periodicals than the *Readers' Guide*. It's published by the same company, so the format and citations are the same. The *Applied Science and Technology Index*, 1913– (also available on CD-ROM) covers periodicals in such fields as automation, engineering, earth sciences, and transportation. Many of the articles include applications of these fields to energy and the environment. Under "Solar Heating," for instance, you can find the following citation:

Calculating window solar heat gain. J. L. Wright.
*ASHRAF J* v. 37 p. 18–22 Jl '95.

*The Biological and Agricultural Index* (1946–) covers about 200 English-language periodicals. The articles indexed are generally concerned with applying scientific principles to biological research, home economics, and farming. Nevertheless, you might find the following citation under "Solar Heating" interesting:

Sun-heated pond to warm hog house.
*Agricultural Engineering* 69:18 My/Je '88.

The environment is a popular and important subject that makes use of knowledge in many fields of science, including biology, engineering, physics, and chemistry. A reference tool that concentrates on U.S. information in this area is *Environment Abstracts* (1971–). It covers periodical articles, technical reports, and conference proceedings. In addition, each issue contains a review article on the environmental movement for the previous year. The work lists environmental bills that are currently before Congress or pollution control officials. The annual index to the abstracts, *Environment Index*, is published separately.

Another index, a bit more specialized but still with applications for the sciences in general, is *Pollution Abstracts* (1970–). Articles, books, and technical reports on all aspects of pollution—air, water, land, and noise—are covered. The index, of the Key-Word-in-Context variety, can be a little confusing at first. However, since this is the major international service for pollution information, it's a good source to know about. For your paper on solar energy, you might want to use an article on how other types of heating systems can cause pollution.

A great deal of good information on topics in the sciences can be found in U.S. government publications. For instance, on the subject of solar energy, the Energy Research and Development Administration published the "National Plan for Solar Heating and Cooling (Residential and Commercial Applications)." NASA alone puts out hundreds of technical reports yearly. In addition, the government holds numerous hearings each year, with testimony by experts, on many subjects of general scientific interest, from artificial sweeteners to nuclear testing.

The *Social Sciences Citation Index* was briefly discussed in the social sciences section. Its counterpart in the sciences is the *Science Citation Index* (also available on CD-ROM and on line as SCISEARCH). To review briefly what these indexes do, let's suppose that you read an article by R. E. Hartle on solar heating in which he discusses a particular scientific technique or theory that you are interested in. You may want to find some other articles about the same technique or theory, but it is difficult to figure out what subject headings to check under. Using the *SCI*, you would look in the Citation section under "Hartle, R. E.," to find the entry for his article. Under the entry, there will be a list of other articles that have cited or referred to this article. The number of times a particular article has been cited or referred to is also a good indicator of how important or authoritative the article is.

At some point, you may want to consult a biography of an author whose article you have read or a scientist whose work is mentioned in your reading. For biographies of living scientists, *American Men and Women of Science*, updated every four years or so, is a good source. Another good reference is *Who's Who in Technology Today* (1984) in five volumes. It provides an index by discipline. For famous scientists no longer living, the *Dictionary of Scientific Biography* (1980, with supplements) covers all places and periods of history. The articles are by specialists and contain bibliographies of further sources.

In discussing more specific reference sources, the sciences are grouped into three broad categories: the applied sciences, the biological sciences, and the physical sciences. For each of these areas, you should know about at least a few of the major specialized reference tools. When actually doing your research, however, the categories are seldom separated so neatly. Don't be surprised, therefore, if you find that you want to use reference works from all three categories for one topic. Let's begin with the applied sciences, which include such fields as engineering, home economics, agriculture, and computer science. Here, the basic principles of the more theoretical sciences—physics, chemistry, mathematics, and biology—are applied to everyday problems.

### Applied Sciences

A field that is well documented is engineering. *The Engineering Index* (1884–), which now includes abstracts, is among the oldest of the periodical indexes. It also covers books, reports, and lists of patents on all aspects of engineering. You must know something about your subject when you approach this index. The entries are arranged under main subject headings and subheadings with author and subject indexes. For the topic of nuclear fusion, the heading "Nuclear reactors, fusion" is used, and under it you can find a citation such as the following:

Can we recycle fusion materials? Butterworth, G. J.
*Fusion Techol* v. 21, no. 3, May 1992, p. 1994–2000.

In this citation, the title is given first, then the abstract, and then the author, the name of the periodical, the volume, date, and page numbers. Abstracting services often vary in how they arrange their citations, but once you know what elements are necessary in a citation, you can easily sort them out. The computer version of *Engineering Index*, available on line, is COMPENDEX, which is updated monthly. Also, keep in mind the *Applied Science and Technology Index* when looking for articles on engineering topics.

You may run across some puzzling terms as you do your research in engineering. What, for instance, is a phase-advancer? Is it something out of Star Trek? Are fillets some kind of fish? To answer questions like these, a reference tool such as the *McGraw-Hill Encyclopedia of Engineering* (1992) can come in handy. Another useful reference is Eshbach's *Handbook of Engineering Fundamentals* (1990), which includes sections on major topics and types of engineering.

Another applied science, home economics, has several specialized indexes. Two of these are *World Textile Abstracts* (1969–) and *Nutrition*

*Abstracts and Reviews* (1931–). A third, *Food Sciences and Technology Abstracts* (1969–), deals with such consumer-oriented topics as food additives and packaging. These indexes cover rather specialized journals, many of which your library may not own, so it's important to remember the more general indexes such as the *General Science Index* and *Reader's Guide*. Another useful index, which focuses on product evaluations and comparisons, is *Consumers' Index* (1973–). It indexes articles from about 100 periodicals.

Should you choose a topic dealing with foods or nutrition, there are two helpful reference books you might want to take a look at. Articles that present good overviews of topics can be found in the *Encyclopedia of Food Science, Food Technology, and Nutrition* (8 vols., 1993). *Food Values of Portions Commonly Used* (1985) gives the amounts of vitamins, minerals, protein, fat, and other substances in just about everything one might conceivably eat, from fig newtons to armadillo meat.

Although computer science is the newest of the applied sciences, it is one that is already changing our lives. A good place to start exploring this subject might be in the LC subject heading guide. The subject heading guide divides computing machines into two groups. Pre-1945 models are entered under "Calculating Machines" and those coming after 1945 are entered under "Computers." The topic of "Computers" also has some interesting subheadings, such as "Moral and religious aspects," "Caricatures and cartoons," and "Vocational guidance." Some other headings you might want to consult are "Programming languages (electronic computers)" and "Computer programs."

Since this is a rapidly changing field, you will want to check in your library for the most recently published dictionaries if you need definitions of computer terms. Two good examples are the *Macmillan Encyclopedia of Computers* (2 vols., 1992) and Ralston and Reilly's *Computer Sciences* (1992). Computer software programs are also proliferating rapidly, so you may want to take a look at the *Datapro Directory of Microcomputer Software*, updated frequently. The most up-to-date information, however, appears in such on line databases as the *Microcomputer Software Guide*. *Computer Abstracts* (1966–) provides an international index of periodicals, government documents, books, and technical reports in the field. These abstracts will be the most useful if you are researching fairly technical aspects of computer science. The *ACM Guide to Computing Literature* (1978–) also provides an annual index to books, journal articles, conference proceedings, and technical reports. For more general topics, such as the effect of the computer on an individual's right to privacy or computer crimes, other sources would be the *Social Sciences Index*, the *Humanities Index*, or the *General Science Index*.

### Biological and Health Sciences

Since the recognition, description, and classification of plant and animal life is basic to the study of biology, it is important to know which tool can help you do these things. *Grzimek's Animal Life Encyclopedia*,

in thirteen volumes, is an excellent reference tool. It gives the physi-
ological, evolutionary, and behavioral characteristics of animal life all
over the world and has numerous illustrations, many of them in color.
The animals are arranged by broad classifications, but each volume has
a detailed index by both common and scientific names. From the same
publisher there is also *Grzimek's Encyclopedia of Ecology* (1976), which
provides an excellent overview of animal-environment interactions and
current problems, and *Grzimek's Encyclopedia of Mammals* (1990). For
plants, Mabberly's *The Plant Book* (1987) and *Hortus Third* (1981) attempt to present a comprehensive and descriptive list.

For definitions of terms encountered in your reading, works such as
the *Facts on File Dictionary of Biology* (1988) or *Chambers Biology Dictionary* (1989) are good sources. *The Encyclopedia of Human Biology* (8 vol.,
1991) could be useful for topics in either biology or medicine.

A rather overwhelming reference tool but one that is important for
research in biology is *Biological Abstracts* (1926–). A thick volume of
abstracts appears every month, and a three-volume index comes at the
end of each year. Fifteen large volumes per year—now that's a space
problem for a library! Many of the citations are technical, but such titles
as "Criteria for the Diagnosis of Human Alcoholism" and "Crane Populations in a North Florida Sandhill" sound quite readable. In any case,
the abstracts are certainly worth looking at. Coverage of most of *Biological Abstracts* from 1976 to the present is available on CD-ROM as
*Biosis Previews*, updated weekly. Because of the complexity and size of
the printed index, this computer version is much easier to use. Another
index to biological journals, *Cambridge Life Sciences*, is also available on
CD/ROM.

The most comprehensive journal indexing tool for medicine is *Index Medicus* (1960–). Its on-line database, *Medline*, is one of the oldest
of the computer search services, and it is now available in various computerized formats. It occasionally overlaps with *Biological Abstracts* in
areas concerning the human body and how it works. *Index Medicus*, however, emphasizes the practice of medicine and medical research. It also
includes such social concerns of doctors as malpractice insurance. *Index
Medicus* is international in coverage. It indexes only periodical articles
by both author and subject. The first volume for each year includes a
subject heading guide for the headings to be used during that year, with
subheadings and "see also" references. A sample citation under the heading "Natural Childbirth" is:

The alternative birth movement in the United States: history and
current status. Matthers, J. J. et al. *Women Health* 1991;17(1):
39–56.

In looking up articles on natural childbirth, you may run across terms
such as psychoprophylaxis. Good dictionaries for brief definitions of
terms are the *American Medical Association Encyclopedia of Medicine* (1989)

and Miller-Keane's *Encyclopedic Dictionary of Medicine, Nursing, and Allied Health* (1993). Another quick reference work that deals more specifically with diseases and their treatments is the *Merck Manual of Diagnosis and Therapy* (1987). Diseases and their symptoms are grouped according to type, and a list of prescription drugs is included in the back along with an index.

There are many specialized medical encyclopedias, among them the *Encyclopedia of Bioethics* (1978), covering topics such as euthanasia, medical ethics, and drug use; the *Encyclopedia of Drug Abuse* (1992); and the *Encyclopedia of Sleep and Dreaming* (1993). Finally, you can also find information about many topics involving health through such indexes as *Nutrition Abstracts and Reviews* and *Pollution Abstracts*.

### Physical Sciences

Before going on to more specialized reference tools, remember that the *McGraw-Hill Encyclopedia of Science and Technology* and the *General Science Index* are good starting points for many research topics in the fields of chemistry, physics, mathematics, and geology.

There are many dictionaries and encyclopedias in the field of chemistry, but one of the most important to know about is the *CRC Handbook of Chemistry and Physics*, revised annually. It contains tables, formulas, charts, and other quick-reference information. Two of the many encyclopedias covering more specialized aspects of chemistry are *Dictionary of Organic Compounds* (1982), in five volumes, and the twenty-four-volume *Encyclopedia of Chemical Technology* (1978), which provides detailed coverage of applications of chemistry such as air pollution control methods and coal conversion processes. Briefer definitions of terms may be found in a dictionary such as Miall's *Dictionary of Chemistry* (1981). *Chemical Abstracts* (1907–) is one of the most thorough of all the periodical indexes. It provides worldwide coverage of books, periodicals, patent descriptions, dissertations, and government documents. *Chemical Abstracts* appears weekly and offers semiannual indexes by author, subject, patent, and formula. If you are interested in a particular chemical compound, for example, you can use the formula index to find all the ways it has been synthesized and marketed. It is available as a computer database on line as *CA Search*; again, because of the size and complexity of the index, computer searching is desirable if you have access to it.

For research in physics, the *CRC Handbook of Chemistry and Physics*, already mentioned, is indispensable. Good encyclopedias are Besancon's *Encyclopedia of Physics* (1985) and the newer *Encyclopedia of Physics* (1991) by Lerner and Trigg, which is complementary to Besancon. Both include signed articles with bibliographies. The *Dictionary of Physics* (1991) gives brief definitions, many with illustrations, as well as tables and lists such as "Radioactive and Stable Isotopes" and "Nobel Prize Winners in Physics." *Science Abstracts, Section A: Physics Abstracts* (1898–) provides worldwide coverage for journals, books, and other materials, and is available on line as INSPEC.

In mathematics, the *CRC Handbook of Mathematical Sciences*, updated frequently, offers tables, formulas, and theorems and is a good source for quick reference material. Some useful dictionaries and encyclopedias are *Encyclopedic Dictionary of Mathematics* (4 vols., 1987) and James's *Mathematics Dictionary* (1992), which includes brief biographies and a guide to pronunciation, often helpful if you are confronted with a word such as cyclosymmetry. The major index in this field is *Mathematical Reviews* (1940–), which indexes both books and periodicals, but it is quite technical, and for most topics the *Applied Science and Technology Index* and *General Science Index* will work just as well.

Surveys of topics in geology and other earth sciences can be found in the *Encyclopedia of Earth Sciences* (1966–, in progress). About seventeen of twenty-four planned volumes are completed, and all include lengthy articles that begin with simple explanations and expand into more detailed treatments. Briefer definitions of geological terminology can be found in many dictionaries such as the *Concise Oxford Dictionary of Earth Sciences* (1990). The *Bibliography and Index of Geology* (1969–) is the most comprehensive source of information for geological literature. Each volume, published monthly and cumulated annually, consists of a bibliography of books, articles, and government documents on geology and has a detailed index. It is available both on line and on CD-ROM. Geology often tends to intersect with other disciplines, such as archaeology and geography. Therefore, when pursuing the topic of fossil discoveries in Nebraska, don't forget to check *Geo Abstracts* and *Abstracts in Anthropology*.

You may find, in the course of your research, that you would like to know of some additional reference works covering the sciences. For more detailed information on what is available, check a guide such as *Information Sources in Science and Technology* (1988), which gives brief citations and annotations for about 2,000 English language reference works.

---

### Exercises

A. Find three relevant catalog subject headings for the following broad topics:

    the history of science      human factors engineering
    medical ethics      space exploration

B. Briefly identify the following terms and give your sources of information.

    gyrocompass      herbarium
    black hole      Gauss's law

C. Locate a biographical sketch of the following individuals, list their field of study, and name your source of information.

    Robert Oppenheimer      Joseph Priestly
    Henry Gray      Linus Pauling

D. Give citations for four articles on food additives or problems of solid waste disposal and name your sources of information.

E. Give citations for four articles on organ transplants or euthanasia and name your sources of information.

F. Outline a search strategy for one of the following topics. You may make use of reference tools from any of the sections of the chapter.

earthquake prediction        nuclear fusion as a source of energy
transmission of AIDS         hydroponic gardening
saving endangered species

Carefully researching a subject can be one of the most exciting and rewarding activities of your college program. When you research a topic, you become a specialist on that subject. You read extensively what has been written by others, evaluating ideas and comparing and contrasting them; then you synthesize them to develop your own learned opinion. Research writing makes use of all the skills that you have learned for specific writing tasks: effective introductions, clear organization, logical reasoning, and effective expression.

To master research writing, you need to focus attention on three specific new skills:

Finding and using necessary information.
Integrating the ideas of others into your own arguments.
Documenting the sources of your information.

A research paper should not simply be the strung-together ideas of others. You need to use your organizational skills and awareness of logic to go a step further than your sources. You will need to revise the structure of their arguments, add a new idea to their explanation or concept, or reconcile two seemingly opposite views. You will also need to support some opinion—thesis—of your own, which you will develop by reflecting on your own ideas in the context of what has been written by others about the same subject.

Writing the research paper need not intimidate you. The project may be longer than most of your college essays, but you will undoubtedly be given more time to complete it. Having a plan for your work will make the entire process go smoothly. Students use a variety of approaches to note taking. Some highlight their xeroxed sources in different color pens for each topic covered in the texts, taking careful notes in margins or on separate sheets of paper, each sheet keyed to one of the topic colors. One student, for example, writing a paper on outdated Christian views of homosexuality and whether gays should be part of the mainstream church, used four colors to highlight these subtopics:

history of homophobia—pink
for separate church—orange
against separate church—yellow
current happenings in church doctrines—brown

After highlighting a half dozen xeroxed articles, he made four pages of notes, each containing data, quotes, or arguments on one of the subtopics

# HOW DO YOU WRITE A RESEARCH PAPER?

listed. Others take notes on the computer, establishing a separate file for each subtopic of their subject that they want to investigate. Still others simply use highlighters on the xeroxed texts, but this is the weakest of strategies since it is passive, as opposed to taking notes, which is active. Using an active method will not only engage you in the subject more but will help you understand and incorporate into your own thinking what you read. Over the years, most experienced researchers have arrived at the same time-saving approach—a simple, ten-step method. The first five steps prepare you to write, and the remaining five steps help you to write your documented essay. Before you begin, however, you should have a few indispensable materials on hand. You can probably pick them up at your college bookstore. Make it a practice to keep the following items, along with your copy of this text, with you while you are researching:

> 3 × 5 index cards
> 4 × 6 index cards
> a regular pen or pencil
> a red pen or pencil
> scratch paper

## TEN STEPS TO WRITING A RESEARCH PAPER

### Step One: Choosing the Topic

Because you are going to invest a lot of time and energy in your research project, the topic is especially important. In many instances, your instructor will assign a specific topic. If so, you have little choice, but most instructors will permit or even welcome a slight refocusing of a topic when it is supported by interesting critical thinking. In some of your classes, the instructor may present a suggested list of topics from which you can make a choice. In this case, do not simply select the first idea that attracts your attention. It may soon become boring, or it may be difficult to research. Examine all the topics. Try to consider how you might go about developing each of them. When you find one that seems especially interesting and worthwhile, do a bit of preliminary checking in the library to determine whether the basic sources you will need are available.

In some classes, the instructor may require a research paper but permit you to select your own topic. This is the most exciting of all situations, because you can define a subject that particularly interests you. Suppose you are in a psychology class and your teacher asks you to write a paper on "anything you are interested in." If a topic doesn't flash into your mind, go back and do some of the prewriting exercises suggested in Chapter 2. An automatic writing or a word list should help you get started. If you have been keeping a journal, see whether you can find an interesting and workable subject there.

Choosing a good research topic does not necessarily mean finding something that has a lot written about it. Many times you will have to research around a topic to find the most useful information. Exciting and original topics often come to mind by combining two completely different interests. Let's say that you are interested in child psychology and in sports. Perhaps you can combine the two in a paper on the effect that watching violent sports has on children. If there is no material directly available on the subject, you can research the topics individually and, by putting your information together, draw a conclusion.

### Step Two: Becoming Your Own Librarian

The next step takes you to the library. Topics for term papers usually evolve from general ideas broken down into specific areas. Thus, you may start with a general subject like "population problems" and end up looking for specifics such as statistics on the birth rate in South America in 1994. The many information resources of the library are fully discussed in Chapter 9. It is the strategy of searching for information that concerns us here. One strategy is outlined in Figure 10-1.

**Figure 10-1. Strategy for finding information on a topic.**

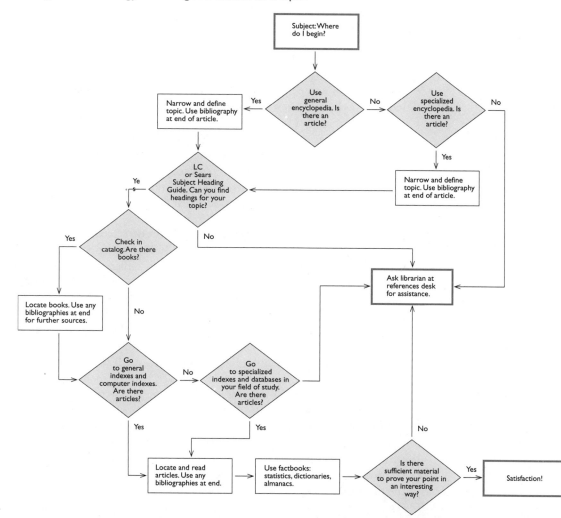

The first phase of the strategy for finding material is to get background on your topic or an overview of it. For this you will want to use a basic reference tool such as a general or subject encyclopedia. Usually, you will also want to make use of the bibliography of further sources found at the end of most encyclopedia articles.

At this point, you may have found some aspects of your topic that interest you. These should be translated into subject headings that will make it easier for you to find books on each subject in the library's catalog. Now you are ready to go on to the second phase of your strategy, consulting the LC or Sears Subject Heading Guide and then looking in the library's catalog. You will note that some libraries' computerized catalogs permit you to search for key words, but even in these cases, it's wise to use the LC or Sears volumes as well, since they are more thorough.

Many of the books you find will probably have bibliographies at the end, similar to those for the encyclopedia articles, and documents. So one reliable source may provide you with the authors and titles of several others, saving you considerable library time. This method is sometimes referred to as "snowballing." From your beginning point, you are directed to a few sources that, in turn, will guide you to more sources. Before you know it, you will have enough material for your paper—maybe even too much.

You will probably still want to go on to the third phase of the strategy. Here you will consult specific reference tools such as computerized indexes, periodical indexes and abstracts, newspaper indexes, dictionaries, and factbooks. Computerized and noncomputerized periodical or newspaper indexes, which are published frequently, can update and supplement the sources you may have found through bibliographies. Dictionaries and factbooks can supply the specifics needed to give your paper interest and authority. After your general search, you will want to turn to Chapter 9 for suggestions on researching your specific subject.

### Step Three: Getting Acquainted with Your Topic

At this point you have selected a subject and have found a few promising books and periodicals. Skim their indexes, tables of contents, and subtitles. Now sit down and quickly read through the ones that seem most important. You do not want to take notes yet. At this stage you are still searching out the limits of your topic. You are not yet compiling information for your paper. Instead, read to find some specific area of the general subject that you might like to develop into a thesis for your paper. Only after reading four or five sources will you want to take pen in hand as you think. Remember, however, that the sooner you commit yourself to a preliminary thesis, the more time you can save for your intensive research.

On the basis of your reading, write down three or four possible thesis statements. Pick the most interesting and list three or four subtopics for it. For example, if your topic is the relationship between fashion consciousness and liberation among contemporary women, you might write the following:

*Tentative Thesis:* Through advertising, women are socialized into roles that insidiously maintain the status quo.

A. The superwoman
B. The man pleaser
C. The mother

Your thesis in this step need not be polished. In fact, you don't want it to be. Your final thesis should evolve as you take notes with the subtopics in mind. The last but most important part of Step Three is to check over your sources to see whether there are enough to do a good job of researching. Many times you will want to go back to the library catalog and indexes to find more specific materials. Note that useful suggestions for further reading often come at the ends of the chapters or articles you have been skimming in this step. Step Three helps you to accomplish three things:

It orients you to the background of your subject.
It directs you to a preliminary thesis.
It leads you to sources for further research.

### Step Four: Writing Bibliography Cards

A bibliography, or "Works Cited" list, is simply a list of books, articles, essays, reviews, or other sources of information. In Step Four, you put together the working bibliography for your paper using either 3 × 5-inch index cards or a separate file on your computer. As you search for information about your thesis, make up a separate entry or card for every source that promises to offer useful material. Each of your bibliography cards should contain all the information shown in Figure 10-2.

The information about each source should be placed on the card in a particular order. The form used should be the same as that you will

Figure 10-2. Sample bibliography cards.

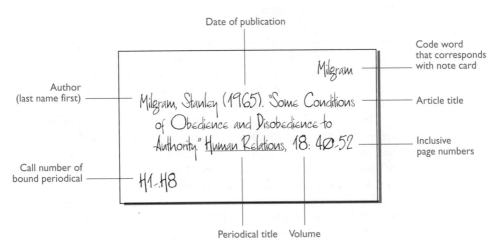

use when you prepare your final "Works Cited" list. You will save time if you get all the necessary information as well as every comma and period in the right place now. Various disciplines require different formats, as we will see later in this chapter in the section on methods of documentation. Unless your instructor specifies the use of a particular form for your bibliography, use the standard format for the discipline.

When you have completed your working bibliography, put the cards in two stacks. Reserve one stack for the sources you have already located and the other for those you have yet to find. The cards will be easy to switch from one stack to the other as you find the sources you need, and, by keeping them separate, you can tell at a glance how well your search is going. Some teachers may want you to hand in an annotated bibliography (see Chapter 11), either with your paper or sometime before the paper itself is due. If so, as you skim each source describe it briefly on its bibliography card. When you have finished your search, you will have almost completed your annotated bibliography as well.

You can also compile your working bibliography on the computer if doing so is convenient for you. The computer can save you from retyping your list of "Works Cited" once you write the paper.

### Step Five: Taking Notes on Cards

Now that you have your working bibliography, your tentative thesis, and some subtopics, you are ready to extract the information you need for your paper from the sources you have found. It is a good idea to use subtopic headings on your note cards or your computer files to help keep all your related ideas together. The more notes you take, the more important it is to use subtopic headings. If you have fifty note cards, for instance, and they are not identified by subtopics, you will have to read through all fifty cards each time you look for evidence to back up one of the subpoints of your thesis.

Note taking is probably the most crucial step in preparing to write your research paper. Naturally, it is necessary to understand a passage before you can take notes on it. Try to take notes only on information that is going to be useful as you develop your thesis. Not all the material you read will be important to your thesis or its subtopics. Be selective, but be sure to write down anything that might be valuable. You will not want to use all your notes in your final paper, yet you cannot tell until your essay begins to take form just which and how much information you will need.

The three techniques used in note taking are paraphrasing, summarizing, and quoting. *Paraphrasing* is putting an author's ideas into your own words while keeping the length about the same as that of the original passage. It is usually used when the style of the passage is notable and would lose something if severely shortened. *Summarizing* is greatly condensing a passage using all your own words. *Quoting* is copying word for word a complete passage, or sometimes even a single significant word or phrase, from someone's writing.

Quotations must always be indicated by quotation marks around both ends of the copied material. But quotation marks are not all you need. In the final paper parentheses containing the page number and often the author or title of the source and sometimes the date must be placed at the end of the idea taken from the source. (Forms vary. See pages 288–290.) Of course, not every word you take from a source needs quotation marks—certainly words like *is* or *these* could appear anywhere and should never be cited for themselves. But any specific word or phrase that is peculiar to an author's argument or style requires quotation marks and a parenthetical citation. If a writer calls the trend of coffee houses a "fad based on the myth that espresso and intellect go hand and hand" and you wish to use the phrase, you must give credit for the specific words as well as for the idea. If an article in a magazine refers to community colleges as "open doors" for immigrants hoping to enter the world of education and you wish to use the phrase, give the writer credit. Remember, even a single word taken from a source, if it is language particular to the author, must be quoted.

Quoting should be held to a minimum. A paper full of quotations jolts the reader, who must constantly adjust to many writing styles even in the same paragraph. It also tends to show a lack of originality. Most of your notes should be summaries of what you have read. Summarizing material forces you to consider the essence of what you read so that you can compare your ideas with those of others who have written on the subject. You may wish to quote a few words that sum up especially important ideas but, whenever possible, you should integrate quotations into your own sentences, not set them off as separate sentences. Your resulting sentences containing the quotations should be smooth and grammatical.

Students who only copy quoted passages onto their note cards or highlight xeroxes of sources without amplifying them with summaries or commentary in their own words often experience difficulty when writing their papers because the ideas from the sources have not been assimilated into their theses. When this happens, it seems especially difficult to meaningfully alter the words from the sources, and the writing in the final essays is frequently less original than it could be. In short, you do not want to be trapped into using the words of others in your final essay when your own would be better.

*Sample Note-Taking Methods*
Let's say that you are writing a paper on executive women—their wins and losses since ERA. You come across the following material in Felice Schwartz's book on management women:

> Men continue to perceive women as the rearers of their children, so they find it understandable, indeed appropriate, that women should renounce their careers to raise families. Edmund Pratt, CEO of Pfizer, once asked me in all sincerity, "Why would any woman choose to be a chief financial officer rather than a full-time mother?" By condoning and taking pleasure in women's tra-

ditional behavior, men reinforce it. Not only do they see parenting as fundamentally female, they see a career as fundamentally male—either an unbroken series of promotions and advancements toward CEOdom or stagnation and disappointment. This attitude serves to legitimize a woman's choice to extend maternity leave and even, for those who can afford it, to leave employment altogether for several years. By the same token, men who might want to take a leave after the birth of a child know that management will see such behavior as a lack of career commitment, even when company policy permits parental leave for men.

Here are some sample notes based on the selection from Schwartz's *Management Women and the New Facts of Life* for you to use as models.

### Paraphrase

Since men still assume women, in general, are responsible for raising children, it isn't surprising that even a male CEO of a large company might be perplexed that a woman would prefer a career like his over motherhood. This attitude reinforces stereotypical sex roles for men and women: parenting is for women, and professional challenge, whether they succeed or not is for men. It also makes reasonable women's choices to take extended leave of absence from jobs if they can handle it financially or to take longer than usual maternity leaves. If a man were to do either, he would be seen as less dedicated to his work than he should be, even if his firm on paper endorses paternity leaves.

### Summary

The male attitude that reinforces sexual stereotypes at home and in the job market pressures men to stay at work rather than take paternity leaves and it "serves to legitimize a woman's choice to extend maternity leave and even, for those who can afford it, to leave employment altogether for several years."

or

Sexual stereotyping in the home and workplace reinforce male attitudes that allow women to take extended maternity leaves or stop working but that stymie any man who "might want to take a leave after the birth of a child [but] know that management will see such behavior as a lack of career commitment, even when company policy permits parental leave for men."

Note that both summaries included direct quotations from the text but placed them in a condensed context.

## Exercises

A. Paraphrase the following selections.

1. But to the Indian there was no such thing as emptiness in the world. There was no object around him that was not alive with spirit, and earth and tree and stone and the wide scope of the heaven were tenanted with numberless supernaturals and the wandering souls of the dead. And it was only in the solitude of remote places and in the sheltering silence of the night that the voices of these spirits might be heard. (Margot Astrov, *American Indian Prose and Poetry*)

2. The superficial adoption of his culture by the African is what the European notices with pride, and is the yardstick by which he measures the African's progress towards civilization. He has been all too unaware of the more significant changes. The fact, for instance, that an urban life not only entirely disrupts the traditional family life of the African, but destroys all the practical economic and political ties that are of any significance to him, resulting in moral and spiritual degeneration. He is also naively unaware of the tremendous intensity of feeling generated by social segregation. The European, particularly in eastern, central and southern Africa, thinks of African hostility and opposition as being founded entirely in political causes. He is so obsessed by the notion that the African wants political equality and equality of economic opportunity, thus challenging white political and economic supremacy, that he has failed to see that a great proportion of the real hostility, the real bitterness and hatred, springs from other causes, trivial to the Europeans but of deepest significance to the African. (Colin M. Turnbull, *The Lonely African*)

B. Summarize the following selections.

1. There are as many different "sub-fields" within bioethics as there are applications of biology; however, those which arouse the greatest emotional response inevitably occupy the largest segments of public consciousness. Recently, genetic ethics has evolved into a significant sub-field within bioethics. Cloning, genetic engineering and gene transplants are fascinating biological procedures and have elicited much public interest. They were first introduced to us in the realm of science fiction, but now have a basis in reality. Although such genetic procedures have yet to be performed upon human beings, genetic counseling is an accepted medical practice. Genetic counseling evolved in response to the perception that genetic disease is a serious health problem. According to the National Genetics Foundations, fifteen million Americans have a genetic problem of one sort or another. One out of every 250 newborn babies has a genetic disorder. One out of every five hospital admissions of infants or children occurs because of a genetic or genetically related problem. Concern about genetic disease has also been stimulated by continuing discoveries of a "genetic predisposition" in many illnesses without previous genetic associations. There is a crucial predisposing factor in some forms of heart disease, cancer, ulcers, and schizophrenia. (Erlaine Bello, "Bioethics and Genetic Counseling")

2. In the early part of this century, mosquitoes got so bad in New Jersey that farmers were unable to farm and industry around Newark had to shut down temporarily on several occasions. To combat the "New Jersey Terror," the state established the first U.S. mosquito control program. They sprayed millions of gallons of undiluted diesel oil on the waters of coastal marshes in amounts of 20 gallons or more an acre. The oil damaged aquatic and plant life, but it killed mosquitoes and brought the Terror under control. Encouraged by these results, other states, including Florida, adopted similar programs. Today, there are some 350 organized mosquito control districts active in the U.S. Altogether, they spend some $50 million a year to kill mosquitoes. But the mosquito has continued to fight back. In 1922, two million people caught dengue fever in Gulf Coast states. In 1933, mosquitoes killed 200 Missourians by infecting them with St. Louis encephalitis. Then, in the 1940s, the world was handed a new weapon so miraculously effective against mosquitoes that some authorities boldly predicted victory in man's battle with the bug. The wonder-weapon was DDT. Dusted, sprayed, or fogged, DDT meant death to both adult and larval mosquitoes. (William Shelton, "Winning the Battle of the Bug." Reprinted with permission of Exxon Company, U.S.A.)

### Mechanics for Note Cards

The mechanics of note taking come easily with a little practice. Note cards are better than full-sized sheets of paper or notebooks because the cards are easier to shuffle and to keep neat. Many students like to use 4 × 6 index cards for notes. The larger cards can be quickly distinguished from the 3 × 5 bibliography cards, and they provide more space. The following suggestions should prove helpful as you write your note cards.

1. Write on only one side of a card or sheet of paper.
2. On each card, take notes on only one subtopic from only one source and indicate the subtopic at the top center of the card.
3. When you quote directly, circle the quotation marks in red ink to remind yourself that the words came from someone else. This practice will protect you from unintentional plagiarism.
4. Write the page number of your source and the abbreviated reference that corresponds with your bibliography card.
5. Make sure that all quotations are copied accurately—double-check the spelling, the punctuation, and the number of words in each quotation. If you find an obvious mistake in spelling or punctuation in your source, you should leave the error in the quoted passage. However, if the error will distract the reader, write [sic] after the word in question. It is a sign to your reader that the error is in the text and not in your copying. For example: The Mayor said he "couldn't recieve [sic] the honor without blushing."

Study the sample note card in Figure 10-3, based on the following extract from Milgram's famous experiment in obedience to authority. Make sure that each of your note cards includes all the essential information written on the sample cards.

**Figure 10-3. Sample note cards.**

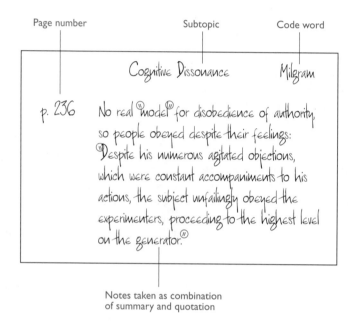

Page number   Subtopic   Code word

Cognitive Dissonance        Milgram

p. 236   No real "model" for disobedience of authority, so people obeyed despite their feelings: "Despite his numerous agitated objections, which were constant accompaniments to his actions, the subject unfailingly obeyed the experimenters, proceeding to the highest level on the generator."

Notes taken as combination of summary and quotation

And here is a transcript from an obedient subject. He began the experiment calmly, but became increasingly tense as the experiment proceeded. After administering the 150-volt shock, he began to address the experimenter in agitated tones:

*150 Volts delivered.* You want me to keep going?

*165 volts delivered.* That guy is hollering in there. There's a lot of them here. He's liable to have heart condition. You want me to go?

*180 volts delivered.* He can't stand it! I'm not going to kill that man in there! You hear him hollering? He's hollering. He can't stand it. What if something happens to him? . . . I'm not going to get that man sick in there. He's hollering in there. You know what I mean? I mean I refuse to take responsibility. He's getting hurt in there. He's in there hollering. Too many left here. Geez, if he gets them wrong. There's too many of them left. I mean who is going to take responsibility if anything happens to that gentleman?

[*The experimenter accepts responsibility.*] All right.

*195 volts delivered.* You see he's hollering. Hear that. Gee, I don't know.

[*The experimenter says: "The experiment requires that you go on."*]—
I know it does, sir, but I mean—hugh—he don't know what he's
in for. He's up to 195 volts.

*210 volts delivered.*

*225 volts delivered.*

*240 volts delivered.* Aw, no. You mean I've got to keep going
up with the scale? No sir. I'm not going to kill that man! I'm
not going to give him 450 volts!

[*The experimenter says: "The experiment requires that you go on."*]—
I know it does, but that man is hollering there, sir . . .

Despite his numerous, agitated objections, which were constant
accompaniments to his actions, the subject unfailingly obeyed the
experimenter, proceeding to the highest shock level on the generator. He displayed a curious dissociation between word and action. Although at the verbal level he had resolved not to go on,
his actions were fully in accord with the experimenter's commands.
This subject did not want to shock the victim, and he found it
an extremely disagreeable task, but he was unable to invent a response that would free him from E's authority. Many subjects cannot find the specific verbal formula that would enable them to
reject the role assigned to them by the experimenter. Perhaps our
culture does not provide adequate models for disobedience.

**Step Six: Devising a Thesis**

By the time you have taken notes from all your sources, you have
probably adjusted your thesis several times. You may have realized that
a slightly different angle on your subject would be more defensible or
that there is a great deal of information on an important point you had
not included at first. In Step Six you are actually working on your thesis, revising and polishing it before setting it into your paper. You may
want to get the thesis in form by using the steps for a good thesis on
page 47. Your subtopics may be tailor-made for the new thesis, but
probably you will want to adjust them, too. Remember that a good
thesis statement covers all the material to be placed in the paper. (See
Chapter 2 for a more complete discussion of theses.) It should be clearly,
concisely, and interestingly stated.

**Step Seven: Constructing the Outline**

Outlining is the step in which you clear a path for using your note
cards. Before you begin working on the paper itself, write a detailed
topic or sentence outline of what you plan to say. Your outline should
be broken down to at least the arabic numeral stage (1, 2, 3, 4) to make
sure that you have developed enough details. If you use a graphic outline (see p. 64), have at least three levels of subtopics for each strand
on the outline. It is particularly important to wrestle with this step
when writing a research paper, since such assignments are usually longer
than unresearched ones. If you find that you have a tendency to digress,

use your outline to help keep track of your thesis. For a thorough review of how to construct an outline, see Chapter 3.

## Step Eight: Writing the Rough Draft

All the following parts of a paper are the same for a research paper as for other types of essays. You may wish to review these sections of the book if you feel unsure of any of them.

Introductions—pages 121–130
Arrangement of middle paragraphs—pages 73-84
Paragraph structure-pages 94–103
Conclusions—pages 133–139

### How to Avoid Plagiarism

Plagiarism is passing off other people's ideas or information as your own. It is dishonest if done deliberately. Plagiarism is more than simply copying someone else's words. It can also occur because of paraphrasing improperly or combining sources incorrectly. Avoid plagiarism by making sure of the following:

1. Carefully mark all notes with source references and page numbers.
2. Identify all quotations by quotation marks. When you type your paper, use the quotation mark symbol, not the apostrophe, which is used only for a quotation within a quotation (in most disciplines).
3. Focus on your own ideas. Never string together the ideas from a number of sources and call the result your research paper.

The two best ways to keep yourself from slipping into plagiarism are to learn all the forms it can take and to document your paper meticulously.

### When to Document

You already know that it is necessary to cite any sources from which you quote and many of those from which you borrow ideas. The general rule for documenting is that every direct quotation and any idea that is not common knowledge must be identified and referenced. The only difficulty with this rule is determining what material is considered to be common knowledge.

Common knowledge does not mean, as many people think at first, only what everyone on the street knows, although that may indeed be included. Instead, it refers to what most authorities on a subject consider to be general information known by most of the writers in the field. General information is "common" enough not to need a reference. For example, the fact that preservatives are added to prepared foods would be hard to pin down to one source and is thus considered to be common knowledge.

The opposite of common knowledge is specific knowledge, the unique view of a particular writer on the subject under study. Specific knowledge is always documented. For example, the statement that the absorption of sodium nitrate, a preservative added to bacon and ham, can cause cancer in humans offers specific information and includes an opinion. It must, therefore, be referenced.

The most reliable way of testing whether a bit of information is common knowledge is to survey what you have read on a subject. If seven out of ten writers mention the same bit of information, you can assume that it is common knowledge.

### When to Quote

Paraphrasing and quoting should be used sparingly. As noted earlier, excessive quoting makes for a poor research paper because the style of the writing will vary so frequently. The reader may, after a while, begin to feel lost. For the most part you should summarize or, if the passage is brief and the style is noteworthy, paraphrase. There are only three instances when quotations should be used:

1. Quote when citing a well-known quotation. You would not want to reword "To be or not to be . . ."
2. Quote when presenting evidence about a particular style or choice of words. In this case, the actual words should be your evidence. For example, if you are doing a study of Faulkner's narrative style, you should quote his writing, not paraphrase it. Similarly, if you are writing a mathematics paper in which you must use a certain equation as evidence, quote the equation directly.
3. Quote when presenting an idea most concisely and effectively requires the use of someone else's words. In some instances, you might wish to quote ideas that are so radical or controversial that your audience needs to see the exact words in order to accept their existence. The direct quote assures your reader that you have not misinterpreted the statement or removed it from the correct context. However, be sure of yourself as a writer—use your own words as much as possible and fit the key words from your sources into your own sentences.

*How to Quote Short Passages*

Short passages can be inserted into your paper to add firm support. It is important, however, to lead up to all quotations and comment on their reason for being in your essay. Quotations should never be "stuck into" your paper as in the following example:

> Many birds are taught to repeat complicated phrases and sentences which sound remarkably like human speech. "One bird was in the habit of saying, 'Hey, who's that guy in back of you with the big, black axe?' The bird's voice was enough to frighten anyone who was brave enough to enter the closet where the bird cage rested on a wooden pedestal" (Johnson 42).

When the quotation begins, the reader, not being prepared to hear from a different writer, gets lost. The preceding passage could have been more smoothly handled in the following way:

> Many birds are taught to repeat complicated phrases and sentences which sound remarkably like human speech. A leading American ornithologist has described a situation in which a Myna bird was trained to repeat, "Hey, who's that guy in back of you with the big, black axe?" As the story goes, the bird's voice frightened anyone "brave enough to enter the closet where the bird cage rested on a wooden pedestal" (Johnson 42).

You should always lead your reader along and give warning when the style is about to shift. Also, extracting the key words from your sources and integrating these quotations into your own ideas makes your paper far more original. Here are a few examples of nicely integrated quotations from some students' research papers:

> Allen characterizes the role of the Coolidge Administration in foreign affairs as "making little effort to persuade the American people that they were not happily isolated" (87).
> During the period flanked by two "limited wars"—the Spanish American and the Korean—the United States is labeled by Allen as "a reluctant world power" (191).
> "Pushed by events," says Allen, Americans "resisted the idea" of greater involvement with "distasteful world politics," but "had no choice"; according to the personal accounts of some Americans, they were stripped of will (76).

*How to Quote Long Passages*

At times you will want to include a longer quotation in your paper. Just as with short quotations, you should lead up to a long quotation. In addition, you should use a special form if the quotation is more than four lines. Long quotations should follow these guidelines:

1. Block off the quotation but continue to double space.
2. Indent ten spaces from the left margin of your paper.
3. Omit quotation marks at the beginning and end of the quoted material: block citations are used only for direct quotations; the form signals word-for-word copying.
4. Do not indent for a one-paragraph quotation, but indent a few more spaces for new paragraphs in quotations of two or more paragraphs.

The following is an example of the use of a long quotation in a student's paper:

> The use of insecticides on our food crops even in the
> 1960s was disturbing to environmentalists for good
> reason. According to Rachel Carson, far too many arsenic
> compounds were used, compounds which have been known to
> be killers:
>
> Despite the competition of a constant stream of new
> chemicals issuing from the laboratories, arsenic com-
> pounds are still liberally used, both as insecticides
> and as weed killers, where they usually take the chemi-
> cal form of sodium arsenite. The history of their use is
> not reassuring. As roadside sprays, they have cost many
> a farmer his cow and killed uncounted numbers of wild
> creatures. As aquatic weed killers in lakes and reser-
> voirs they have made public waters unsuitable for drink-
> ing or even for swimming. As a spray applied to potato
> fields to destroy the vines they have taken a toll of
> human and nonhuman life. (36)

### *How to Quote Poetry*

Two or three lines of poetry can be included in your text. They should be enclosed by quotation marks, with the separation between lines indicated by a slash (/). For example:

> Many writers allude to cats as mysterious creatures of the night or morning. Sandburg compares the fog to a cat, for instance: "The Fog comes/on little cat feet."

Longer quotations from poems (more than three lines) should be separated from your text in a block style and indented 10 spaces. Again, no quotation marks are used at the beginning or the end of a blocked quotation:

> Poe's *Annabel Lee* is a tribute to the intensity of
> childhood love:
> But our love it was stronger by far than the love
>     Of those who were older than we—
>     Of many far wiser than we—

```
And neither the angels in Heaven above,
   Nor the demons down under the sea,
Can ever dissever my soul from the soul
   Of the beautiful Annabel Lee. (92)
```

Note in the above excerpt that the poet's original format is followed. If your line runs over to the next, preserve the format as much as possible by indenting the excess an additional three spaces.

### How to Indicate Omissions from Direct Quotations

You should omit part of a quotation only if what remains can stand by itself and still make sense. An ellipsis (three periods separated by spaces) should be placed where the omission occurs. Usually, no ellipsis is used if the omission comes at the beginning of a quotation. If the omission comes at the end of a sentence, use four dots: one right after the last word (the period for the sentence) and then the three ellipsis dots. Here are some examples:

```
"Three men . . . walked into the cafe, and four men
left . . . at the same time." (Klee 37).
   "There is no point in calling sports-lovers fanatics.
. . . They are . . . advocates of a cause" (Gold 16).
```

To show the deletion of a line or more of poetry or a paragraph or more of prose in a blocked quotation, use an entire line of widely spaced periods:

```
              What Were They Watching?
He'd rise early, he'd leave when the birds sang;
down to the office he'd go without a lark.
She'd rise later, she'd drink coffee slowly,
then plug in the vacuum and collect old dust.

 .  .  .  .  .  .  .  .  .  .  .  .  .  .  .  .  .  .
They never grumbled, living together,
or hoped for some way quicker to pass their time;
when repeat shows stared like sore memories,
their eyes often wavered, glanced down toward
the floor. (S. Robins 94)
```

### How to Punctuate Quotes

Here are some guidelines to keep in mind when punctuating with quotations:

1. When including a quotation in one of your own sentences, punctuate as your sentence requires. Do not place a comma between your sentence and the quotation unless the sentence would call for it anyway. Check the comma rules in Chapter C.
2. Use a colon to introduce lists and passages you have mentioned in the lead-in. Remember that a colon signals an equivalence

between two statements. For a more thorough explanation of the use of the colon, see Chapter C.

3. A basic rule of thumb is to put commas and periods inside quotation marks; always put colons and semicolons outside quotation marks. For use of question marks and exclamation marks with quotes, see Chapter C.

### Exercises

A. Evaluate the use of quoted material in the following excerpts from student essays. Suggest revisions for poorly quoted material.

1. The easiest type of shoplifter to identify is the kleptomaniac, who often has no economic reason to steal. Cleveland police Lt. Frank Corrigan said, "A lot of the poor shoplift because they're poor and can't afford to buy much. But just as many affluent or middle-class people shoplift."

2. Men have never been content to live in a world they cannot understand, so societies have invented religions and promoted investigations of the earth in order to gain that understanding which brings contentment. According to Dr. George Kernalie, "The religious impulse is a reflection of man's need of security," for "man must always know why disasters occur, why death is inevitable, and why rain falls on some days and not on others," even though "man cannot [do] anything to alter these unavoidable facts of life." A gas station attendant I once spoke to informed me that "To know is to control," by which he meant that there is comfort in knowledge, although knowledge may not bring the power to act. One might add, also, that to control is to comfort, for one controls oneself, and so can comfort oneself. This is what W. O. Malid seems to be implying in his fine book which he calls *Nature's Abandoned Children*, which I suggest to all of you. In fact, all of the books I read said that humans have the inherent itch to discover how things work, that they are not satisfied until they can discover the secret of the atom and the composition of the moon's crust. As B. Q. White cogently said, "We all want to know who the murderer is, and what was his motive."

### Step Nine: Revising the Draft

After you have finished writing the rough draft of your paper, let it cool. That is, put it aside for a day or two. If you don't have that much time, at least put it aside for a few hours. When you finish the first draft of your paper, you will probably feel saturated with material. Putting it aside, even for a short while, will help refresh your outlook. When you are ready to get back to it, use the same process you learned for polishing shorter essays (see Chapter 6). Inside the front cover of this book is a checklist you can use to help make sure that you include all the strategic areas. These guidelines also indicate where in this book you can look if you find that you need advice on any of the checkpoints.

### Step Ten: Proofreading

Allow enough time to proofread your paper carefully. This last step is very important. Check your words carefully, especially those you know you tend to misspell; a spelling checker on your computer comes in handy at this stage. A teacher seeing a paper that has not been proofread, one that is spattered with spelling and typing errors, is likely to feel that the errors are evidence of a job done with little care. Also, a paper full of errors is irritating to read. Many teachers will refuse to accept such a paper or will automatically award it a low grade.

## METHODS OF DOCUMENTING YOUR PAPER

The main purpose of citing sources in your paper is to provide your reader with a reference that can supply further information on a particular point you have made. One way of thinking about documentation is to ask yourself whether your reader could go to a particular source to learn more about the idea or information at hand. Your obligation as a writer is to lead your reader directly to the source. When in doubt, put in a citation.

### Forms for Citing Sources

Citing sources is a mechanical process, but one that can differ from field to field, so it is always wise to consult your instructor as to the preferred format. Two main types of documentation are currently used: parenthetical (using parentheses to cite references in the text of your paper) and endnotes. The humanities generally use parentheses to give the author and page number of the idea or quotation being referenced, right in the text, and include a "Works Cited" list that gives full publishing information at the end of the paper. This method of citation was developed in 1984 and slightly revised in 1988 and 1995 by the Modern Language Association. It is commonly referred to as the MLA format. Because this widely accepted technique is an easy, yet thorough, method of noting sources, it is explained in detail in this textbook. Other techniques, including the parenthetical form used most often in the social sciences and the endnote technique used sometimes in both humanities and social sciences, are explained more briefly.

Use of the internet and other on-line information services is becoming a standard part of many students' research process, so this section includes forms for citing such sources.

There are two parts to a citation, the parenthetical note that appears in the text of your paper and the actual reference, which is placed on a list titled "Works Cited" or "Works Consulted" (in the humanities) or "References" (in the social sciences). Take a look at the "Works Consulted" for the sample research paper on page 319 to get a preliminary idea of how such lists are handled. Parenthetical citations should be kept as brief as possible to avoid interference with reading.

*Modern Language Association (MLA) Format*

In deciding what information to include in a parenthetical citation, you must take the context into consideration. Here are a few typical situations to consider:

1. Citing a source that you have not named in the text.

> There are many goals achieved through the use of
> sanctions, and their employments include political or
> economic pressure, or both. In the South African case,
> the goal of sanctions is to reduce the economic and
> social welfare of the country, thereby forcing it to
> withdraw from practicing the policies that other
> nations resent (Porter 581).

2. Citing a source that you have named in the text.

> Not only have sanctions proven to be ineffective in
> paralyzing South Africa's highly developed economy,
> they surprisingly have had a detrimental effect on the
> blacks as well as on those who imposed them. The
> result has become known as the double-edged effect. As
> Ronald Reagan once pointed out, South Africa is like a
> zebra. If the white parts are injured, the black parts
> will die too (1).

This is a reference to a government document, but the form is the same no matter what sort of source is cited. Because this is the only source by Reagan that the student has referred to in his essay, a simple parenthetical reference to the page number from which the quotation comes is adequate. Had the student used several references by the same author, it would have been necessary to give the title of the work, either in the parentheses preceding the page number or incorporated into his sentence.

3. Citing a long quoted passage.

> A report by the Citizens' Board of Inquiry into
> hunger and malnutrition in the United States asked a
> poor woman to describe her life, and this was part of
> her response:
>
> > No food, no meat, no milk—and the children go to
> > bed hungry. Sometimes they cry. There are days
> > without any food—four or five at a time. The parents
> > go hungry and the children may live off powdered milk
> > for a week. At the end of the month when food stamps
> > run out, you mix whatever you have with water. (17)

Note that a long quotation is indented and without quotation marks, whereas shorter quotes are run into the text. Note that there should be no quotation marks around material that is more than four lines and directly quoted. The technique of indenting it from the rest of the text identifies it as a direct quotation. Also, the reference is placed in parentheses outside the final period.

4. Citing a source that quotes another source.

> According to the courts, in 1972 the death penalty was considered illegal, but in 1976 it was constitutional. Oelsner points out that in 1972 the courts considered the death penalty "cruel and unusual punishment," in that it was issued "arbitrarily and capriciously" (18). Speaking for the NAACP, Anthony G. Amsterdam argues that "it is not efficient to execute one man when his two accomplices simply receive life sentences by pleading guilty" (qtd. in Oelsner 21).

Note that for a short quote the citation goes outside the quotation mark but inside the period. The second citation is a quotation found in one of the student's readings. Such a citation is used if the student has not consulted the original source, although going to the original is preferable. For the purposes of this paper, the student needs to cite the source he or she used; however, if the student so desires, he or she may also give a footnote (at the bottom of the page where the quotation occurs) or endnote (at the end of the paper on a separate page placed before the "Works Cited") like the following:

[1]Anthony G. Amsterdam, <u>No Returns</u> (New York, 1987) 218, qtd. in Oelsner 21.

5. Citing literary works.

> It is Chaucer's openness tinged with satire that makes his *Canterbury Tales* so shocking in his time and so complex. For instance, the Wife of Bath tells us that she has moved on from one old husband to the next; she tells us without shame, "As help me God, I laughe when I thinke / How pitously anight I made hem swinke" (lines 208-209). Is this a feminist position or an antifeminist one?

Literary works have often been published in many editions, a fact that may make the particular page reference less important than the act, scene, and line (for a play) or the line numbers for a poem. For a play, separate the act, scene, and line numbers with periods, and use arabic numerals rather than roman, unless you are citing an introduction. For a novel, give the chapter number or title, using the abbreviation *ch.* For a short story, give the title.

6. Citing more than one source at a time. If a point you have made has been generated by two or more sources, list them as usual within parentheses, using a semicolon to separate them. Be careful not to overdo this kind of citation, since long parenthetical interruptions do interfere with reading.

For other examples, see the sample humanities paper and its annotations on pages 319–330.

### American Psychological Association (APA) Format

The parenthetical format used in the social sciences (psychology, sociology, anthropology, education, etc.) differs somewhat from the Modern Language Association format. A commonly used approach is the APA (American Psychological Association) format. The most notable difference from MLA format is that the parenthetical reference in the text contains the author and date. A page reference is included only with direct quotes.

```
Hallucinations, mainly auditory, are often found in
cases of infantile schizophrenia. These hallucinations
usually repeat or anticipate the child's thoughts,
comment on his or her behavior, or, in the case of
thought insertion, instill alien—and usually terrifying—
ideas into his or her mind (Kuhnky & Sikes, 1984, 272).
Delusions are often present as well but are difficult to
distinguish from the normal childhood fantasies (Barker
1983). As Bruno Bettelheim (1950) has emphasized, fanta-
sies play an important role in normal childhood develop-
ment and they are common in most children.
```

### The Sciences' Numbering System

In many of the sciences, the parenthetical citation system is quite different from the previous methods. Each entry in the "References" section is numbered, unlike in the humanities or social sciences. The parenthetical citations in the text give the number of the source from the "Reference" list (usually arranged either alphabetically or by order of occurrence in the paper). For example, for your fourth citation in the paper you would document like this:

```
Lehrmann, in his study of ring doves, found that the
    evolution of beaks defied natural order (4, 471).
```

Each discipline has its own format that permits writers in the field to emphasize what is important to them. For instance, readers (and thus writers) in the social sciences are particularly interested in who did what when, so the citation form emphasizes names and dates. In the humanities it stands to reason that the titles of works would be more important than the dates, and the MLA form permits such an emphasis. Although citing sources is mechanical for the writer, it also allows him or her to express important information in a way that complements thinking in the field. When you use these formats, you are essentially acculturating yourself to the thinking of a specialized community of scholars.

### Forms for Bibliographies

The citations used in the text refer readers to a list of sources at the end of the paper. Like the citations themselves, bibliographic lists vary in format from discipline to discipline. Here we give greatest emphasis to MLA format because it is the one you will most likely be using for English, economics, language, political science, art, music, and history courses. APA is also used frequently: in education, psychology, sociology, anthropology, and other social science disciplines.

#### MLA STYLE: THE "WORKS CITED" LIST

The simplest form for an MLA entry is the book by one author:

```
Martin, Russell. Out of Silence. New York: Henry Holt
    and Company, 1994.
```

For a book with multiple authors, invert only the first author's name and place *and* between the last two names:

```
Belenky, Mary Field, Blythe McVicker Clinchy, Nancy Rule
    Goldberger, and Jill Martuck Tarule. Women's Ways of
    Knowing. New York: Basic B-HarperCollins, 1986.
```

Here is the format for a book in which the "author" is an editor:

```
May, Charles E., ed. Interacting with Essays. Lexington,
    MA: 1996.
```

For more than one editor, place *and* between the names of the last two editors. If the book has an author and editor, place the author before the title and the editor's name after the title:

```
Freud, Sigmund. Moses and Monotheism. Ed. Katherine
    Jones. New York: Vintage, 1967.
```

If a book has more than one volume, list the number of volumes after the title.

```
Gille, Bertrand. The History of Techniques. 2 vols. New
    York: Gordon and Breach Science Publishers, 1986.
```

If the volumes were published in different years, place the inclusive years (e.g., 1969-78) at the end of the entry.

If the book is in a second or later edition, put the book title first, then any editors or translators, and finally the edition number:

Dostoevsky, Feodor. <u>Crime and Punishment.</u> Trans. Jessie
    Coulson. 2nd ed. New York: Norton, 1972.

A government document or a pamphlet published by an association
should have the following format:

United States. National Women's Health Network. <u>AIDS
    AWARENESS. GUIDE 27.</u> Washington: GPO, 1995.

The key here is to give as much information as possible to identify
the publication. If an author is stated, place the name at the beginning of the entry. If the publication is a government document, state
the government first, then the agency. GPO stands for Government
Printing Office, the publisher of most federal documents.

An essay, story, or chapter in a book or any selection from a casebook should be handled as follows:

Oates, Joyce Carol. "Mike Tyson." <u>Woman Writer.</u> New
    York: Dutton, 1988.
Cooper, Bernard, "English as a Second Language." <u>Criti-
    cal Strategies for Academic Thinking and Writing.</u> Ed.
    Malcolm Kiniry and Mike Rose. 2nd ed. New York:
    Bedford-St. Martin's, 1992, 93-102.

Note the inclusive page numbers of the article, chapter, or selection at
the end of the entry.

When citing an introduction, preface, foreword, or afterword, use
this format:

Killingsworth, M. Jimmie. Foreword. <u>Cultural Divide</u>. By
    Valerie M. Balester. Portsmouth, New Hampshire:
    Boynton/Cook, 1993, vii-ix.

Here is the format to follow for a newspaper article:

Sandalow, Marc. "House Votes to End Ban on Assault
    Guns," <u>San Francisco Chronicle</u> 23 Mar. 1996, A-1.

If no author is given, start the entry with the title of the article and
alphabetize by the first letter of the first word in the title, excluding
the articles *a*, *an*, and *the*. Give inclusive section and pages, if possible,
or if the article begins on one page and continues onto others, give the
first page number followed by a plus: 5+, for example.

Here is the format for citing a magazine article or a journal article:

Schneider, James. "A mirror of the World," <u>Careers and
    the Disabled,</u> Fall 1995: 34-40.

```
Vasil, Latika. "Social Process Skills and Career
    Achievement among Male and Female Academics." The
    Journal of Higher Education Jan/Feb 1996: 103-115.
```

Begin the entry with the title of the article if no author's name is
given. Include the inclusive page numbers after the date. If the journal has a volume number, include it after the name of the journal and
put the date in parentheses.

Follow this approach for an encyclopedia article:

```
Hall, Jerome. "American Jurisprudence." Encyclopedia of
    the American Judicial System. Ed. Robert J. Janosik, 3
    vols. New York: Scribner's, 1987.
```

Less familiar encyclopedias require full publishing information, but familiar ones require only the edition and date. If no author is given,
start your entry with the title of the article.

```
"Guggenheim Fellowships." Encyclopedia Americana. 1995 ed.
```

To find the author's name in the *Encyclopaedia Britannica,* note the
initials at the end of the article and check the last sixth of the Outline
of Knowledge, where you will find a list titled "Initials of Contribu-
tors and Consultants." Place the author's full name in the entry.

```
Schwartz, Mischa, "Telecommunications Systems,"
    Encyclopaedia Britannica: Macropaedia, 1989 ed.
```

Here is the reference format for an interview:

```
Coleman, Wanda. Interview with Wanda Coleman. Feminist
    Forum Natl. Public Radio KABC, Los Angeles, 8 Mar. 1994.
Gaz, James. Personal interview. 28 March 1995.
```

To cite a book review, follow this format:

```
Baumgarten, Ralph. "The Life of Philip Roth, or
    Zuckerman's Complaint." Rev. of The Facts: A
    Novelist's Autobiography, by Philip Roth. Los Angeles
    Times Book Review 11 Sept. 1988: 1+.
```

If you need to list a law, use this format:

```
18 California Penal Code. Sec. 42 (A). 1991.
```

The general guideline is to name the case or law, its number or section, and the year. However, note that references to laws can be com-

plex. A good source to check is *A Uniform System of Citation* (Cambridge: Harvard Law Review Association).

To cite a recording, use this approach:

```
Brahms, Johannes. Piano Concerto no. 2 in B Flat Major
    for Piano and Orchestra. Cond. George Szell. The
    Cleveland Orch. CBS, M4T37258, 1982.
```

Do not underline the titles of compositions identified by number, but underline a piece of music given a name.

Here is the format for citing a film:

```
The Big Sleep. Dir. Howard Hawks. Warner Brothers, 1946.
```

If pertinent to the point made in the paper, put actors, writers, or producer after the director. Length of the film can go after the date.

Here is the format for citing art works:

```
Rodin, A. Man Without a Nose. Rodin Museum, Philadelphia.
```

If you use a photograph from a book, include complete publishing information as well.

If you cite letters or Letters to the Editor, use this approach:

```
White, E. B. "To Clarence Day." 18 Nov. 1934. Letters of
    E. B. White. Ed. Dorothy Lobrano Guth. New York:
    Harper, 1976. 121-22.
Snyder, Lawrence. Letter. Newhall Monitor 30 Nov. 1988: 27.
```

To cite a television or radio program, use this method:

```
"Get Real." Sixty Minutes. CBS, WCBS, New York. 24 Mar.
    1996.
```

**MLA STYLE FOR COMPUTER AND ON-LINE SOURCES**

For the citing of computer and on-line sources, a standardized citation is still evolving, but the basic format of a citation is as follows:

Author's last name, First name. "Title of Work" Title of Complete Work. Available [protocol and address] [path] (date of message or visit).

*FTP (File Transfer Protocol) Sites*

To cite files available for downloading via ftp, give the author's name (if known), the full title of the paper in quotation marks, and the address of the ftp site along with the full path to follow to find the paper, and the date of access.

```
Bruckman, Amy. "Approaches to Managing Deviant Behavior
    in Virtual Communities." ftp.media.mit.edupub/asb/
    papers/deviance-chi94 (4 Dec. 1994).
```

### Individual Works

Basic forms, commercial supplier, and using an Internet protocol:

Author/editor. Title of Print Version of Work. Edition statement (if
    given). Place of publication: publisher, date. Title of Electronic
    Work. Medium. Information supplier. File identifier or number.
    Access date.

Author/editor. Title of Print Version of Work. Edition statement (if
    given). Publication information (Place of publication: publisher,
    date), if given. Title of Electronic Work. Medium. Information
    supplier. Available Protocol (e.g., HTTP): Site/Path/File. Access
    date.

Examples:

```
Oxford English Dictionary Computer File: On Compact
    Disc. 2nd ed. CD-ROM. Oxford: Oxford UP, 1992.
Pritzker, Thomas J. An Early Fragment from Central
    Nepal. N.D. Online. Ingress Communications. Available
    HTTP: http://www.ingress.com/—astanart/pritzker/
    pritzker.html. 8 June 1995.
```

These examples are a citation form when the print version is not included in the reference.

### Parts of Works

Basic forms, commercial supplier, and using an Internet protocol:

Author/editor. "Part title." Title of Print Version of Work. Edition
    statement (if given). Place of publication: publisher, date. Title
    of Electronic Work. Medium. Information supplier. File
    identifier or number. Access date.

Author/editor. "Part title." Title of Print Version of Work. Edition
    statement (if given). Publication information (Place of publica-
    tion: publisher, date), if given. Title of Electronic Work. Me-
    dium. Information supplier. Available Protocol (e.g., HTTP):
    Site/Path/File. Access date.

Examples:

```
"Bosnia and Hercegovina." Academic American Encyclope-
    dia. 1995. Academic American Encyclopedia. Online. Dow
    Jones News Retrieval Service. ENCYC. 5 June 1995.
```

This is an encyclopedia article with no author given.

Daniel, Ralph Thomas. "The History of Western Music."
    Britannica Online: Macropaedia. 1995. Online. Encyclo-
    pedia Britannica. Available HTTP: http://www.eb.com:
    180/cgi-bin/g:DocF=macro/5004/45/0.html. 14 June 1995.

Note that it is not necessary to give place of publication and publisher when citing well-known reference sources.

### Journal Articles
Basic forms, commercial supplier, and using an Internet protocol:

> Author. "Article Title." Journal Title. Volume.Issue (Year): paging or indicator or length. Medium. Information supplier. Database Name. File identifier or number. Accession number. Access date.
> Author. "Article Title." Journal Title. Volume.Issue (Year): paging or indicator or length. Medium. Available Protocol (e.g., HTTP): Site/Path/File. Access date.

Examples:

Clark, Jeffrey K. "Complications in Academia: Sexual
    Harassment and the Law." Siecus Report. 21.6 (1993):
    6-10. CD-ROM. 1994 SIRS. SIRS 1993 School. Volume 4.
    Article 93A.

Note that access date is not needed when the medium is a CD-ROM.

Carriveau, Kenneth L., Jr. Rev. of Environmental Haz-
    ards: Marine Pollution, by Marth Gonnan. Environmental
    Green Journal 2.1 (1995): 3 pars. Online. Available
    Gopher: gopher://gopher.uidaho.edu/11/UI_gopher/
    library/egj03/carriv01.html. 21 June 1995.

This is a reference for a book review.
For paging information, substitute number of paragraphs, i.e., "3 pars." for three paragraphs in this reference.

Inada, Kenneth. "A Buddhist Response to the Nature of
    Human Rights." Journal of Buddhist Ethics 2 (1995): 9
    pars. Online. Available HTTP: http://www.cac.psu.edu/
    jbe/twocont.html. 21 June 1995.

### Magazine Articles
Basic forms, commercial supplier, and using an Internet protocol:

Author. "Article Title." Magazine Title. Date: paging or indicator
or length. Medium. Information supplier. Database Name. File
identifier or number. Accession number. Access date.

Author. "Article Title." Magazine Title. Date: paging or indicator
or length. Medium. Available Protocol (e.g., HTTP): Site/Path/
File. Access date.

Examples:

Goodstein, Carol. "Healers from the Deep." American
Health. Sept. 1991: 60-64. CD-ROM. 1994 SIRS. SIRS
1992 Life Science. Article 08A.

Viviano, Frank. "The New Mafia Order." Mother Jones
Magazine May-June 1995: 72 pars. Online. Available
HTTP: http://www.mojones.com/MOTHER_JONES/MJ95/
viviano.html. 17 July 1995.

Newspaper Articles

Basic forms, commercial supplier, and using an Internet protocol:

Author. "Article Title." Newspaper Title. Date, Edition (if given):
paging or indicator or length. Medium. Information supplier.
Database Name. File identifier or number. Accession number.
Access date.

Author. "Article Title." Newspaper Title. Date, Edition (if given):
paging or indicator or length. Medium. Available Protocol (e.g.,
HTTP): Site/Path/File. Access date.

Examples:

Howell, Vicki, and Bob Carlton. "Growing up Tough: New
Generation Fights for Its Life: Inner-city Youths Live
by Rule of Vengeance." Birmingham News. 29 Aug. 1993:
1A+. CD-ROM. 1994 SIRS. SIRS 1993 Youth. Volume 4.
Article 56A.

Johnson, Tim. "Indigenous People Are Now More Combative,
Organized." Miami Herald 5 Dec. 1994: 29SA. Online.
Available Gopher: gopher://summit.fiu.edu/Miami Herald—
Summit-Related Articles/12/05/95—Indigenous People Now
More Combative, Organized. 16 July 1995. 17 July 1995.

Discussion List Messages

Basic forms:

Author. "Subject of Message." Date. Online posting.
Discussion List. Available E-mail: DISCUSSION LIST@e-
mail address. Access date.

*WWW Sites (World Wide Web)*
(Available via Lynx, Netscape, Other Web Browsers)
To cite files available for viewing/downloading via the World Wide Web, give the author's name (if known), the full title of the work in quotation marks, the title of the complete work if applicable in italics, the full http address, and the date of visit.

```
Burka, Lauren P. "A Hypertext History of Multi-User
    Dimensions." MUD History. http://www.ccs.neu.edu/home/
    lpb/mud-history.html (5 Dec. 1994).
```

*Telnet Sites*
(Sites and files available via the telnet protocol)
List the author's name (if known), the title of the work (if shown) in quotation marks, the title of the full work if applicable in italics, and the complete telnet address, along with directions to access the publication, along with the date of visit.

```
Gomes, Lee. "Xerox's On-Line Neighborhood: A Great Place
    to Visit." Mercury News 3 May 1992. telnet
    lambda.parc.xerox.com 8888, @ go #50827, press 13 (5
    Dec. 1994).
```

*Synchronous Communications*
(MOOs, MUDs, IRC, etc.)
Give the name of the speaker(s) and type of communication (i.e., Personal Interview), the address if applicable and the date in parentheses.

```
Pine_Guest. Personal Interview. telnet
    world.sensemedia.net 1234 (12 Dec. 1994).
WorldMOO Christmas Party. telnet world.sensemedia.net
    1234 (24 Dec. 1994).
```

*GOPHER Sites*
(Information available via gopher search protocols)
For information found using gopher search protocols, list the author's name, the title of the paper in quotation marks, any print publication information, and the gopher search path followed to access the information, including the date that the file was accessed.

```
Quittner, Joshua. "Far Out: Welcome to Their World Built
    of MUD." Published in Newsday, 7 Nov. 1993. gopher/
    University of Koeln/About MUDs, MOOs and MUSEs in
    Education/Selected Papers/newsday (5 Dec. 1994).
```

*E-mail, Listserv, and Newslist Citations*
Give the author's name (if known), the subject line from the posting in quotation marks, and the address of the listserv or newslist, along with the date. For personal e-mail listings, the address may be omitted.

Bruckman, Amy S. "MOOSE Crossing Proposal."
    mediamoo@media.mit.edu (20 Dec. 1994).
Seabrook, Richard H. C. "Community and Progress."
    cybermind@jefferson.village.virginia.edu (22 Jan.
    1994).
Thomson, Barry. "Virtual Reality." Personal e-mail (25
    Jan. 1995).
RRECOME. "Top Ten Rules of Film Criticism." 1 Apr. 1995.
    Online posting. Discussions on All Forms of Cinema.
    Available E-mail: LISTSERV@american.edu/Get cinema-1
    log9504A. 1 Aug. 1995.

Note that the author's login name, in uppercase, is given as the first element.

*Personal electronic communications (E-mail)*
Basic forms:

Sender (Sender's E-mail address). "Subject of Message." E-mail to recipient (Recipient's E-mail address). Date of message.

Example:

Day, Martha (MDAY@sage.uvm.edu). "Review of film — Bad
    Lieutenant." E-mail to Xia Li (XLI@moose.uvm.edu). 30
    July 1995.

Much of the preceding list was compiled by Janice R. Walker, Department of English, University of South Florida: MLA<jwalker@chuma .cas.usf.edu>or<xli@moose.uvm.edu>or<ncrane@moose.uvm.edu>. For further information on specific formats, you may access http://www.cas .usf.edu/english/walker/mla.html or others that the World Wide Web refers to for MLA format.

For any questions about how to handle "Works Cited" entries not covered here, see *MLA Handbook for Writers of Research Papers.*

You will, at times, come across materials missing one or more of the bits of information required for your citation. If so, try to find the missing information, and place it in brackets to show that it does not come from the source itself. If you cannot find the information, some of the following abbreviations will help you indicate that it is missing:

    n.p.   no publishing city or state or no publisher
    n.d.   no date
  n. pag.   no page numbers

Place such abbreviations where the information would otherwise fall in the entry.

An example of an MLA-format "Works Consulted" list is provided on page 330 in the sample research paper.

**APA STYLE: THE "REFERENCES" LIST**

Here are some sample entries to give you an idea of how APA references vary from MLA references:

```
Anastasi, A. (1988). Psychological testing (6th ed.).
    New York: Macmillan.
Anzieu, D. (1986). Freud's self-analysis. Madison, CT:
    International Universities.
Arlow, J. A., & Brenner, C. (1988). The future of psy-
    choanalysis. Psychoanalytic Quarterly. 57. 1-14.
Bloom, H. (Ed.) (1987). The interpretation of dreams.
    New York: Chelsea House.
Fosshage, J. L. (1987). New vistas on dream interpreta-
    tion. In M. L. Glucksman & S. L. Warner (Eds.), Dreams
    in new perspective: The royal road revisited. New
    York: Human Sciences.
Freud, S. (1955). Analysis of a phobia in a five-year-old
    boy. In J. Strachey (Ed. and Trans.), The standard
    edition of the complete psychological works of Sigmund
    Freud (Vol. 10). London: Hogarth. (Originally pub-
    lished, 1909.)
Goleman, D. (1988, November 1). Narcissism looming
    larger as root of personality woes. The New York
    Times, pp. C1, C16.
```

Note such features as lack of quotation marks, the use of lowercase in most titles, and the placement of the date immediately following the name. For further details on APA reference style, see *Publication Manual of the American Psychological Association*.

**APA STYLE FOR COMPUTER AND ON-LINE SOURCES**

*Individual Works*
Basic forms, commercial supplier, and using an Internet protocol:

Author/editor. (Year). Title (edition), [Type of medium]. Producer (optional). Available: Supplier/Database identifier or number [Access date].

Author/editor. (Year). title (edition), [Type of medium]. Producer (optional). Available Protocol (e.g., HTTP): Site/Path/File [Access date].

Examples:

```
Oxford English dictionary computer file: On compact disc
    (2nd ed.), [CD-ROM]. (1992). Available: Oxford UP
    [1995, May 27].
```

Pritzker, T. J. (no date). An early fragment from cen-
    tral Nepal [Online]. (1992). Available HTTP: http://
    www.ingress.com/~astanart/pritzker/pritzker.html
    [1995, June 8].

*Parts of Works*

Basic forms, commercial supplier, and using an Internet protocol:

Author/editor. (Year). Title. In Source (edition), [Type of medium].
    Producer (optional). Available: Supplier/Database identifier or
    number [Access date].
Author/editor. (Year). Title. In Source (edition), [Type of medium].
    Producer (optional). Available Protocol (e.g., HTTP): Site/Path/
    File [Access date].

Examples:

Bosnia and Hercegovina. (1995). In Academic American
    Encyclopedia [Online]. Available: Dow Jones News
    Retrieval Service/ENCYC [1995, June 5].
Daniel, R. T. (1995). The history of Western music. In
    Britannica online: Macropaedia [Online]. Available
    HTTP: http://www.eb.com:180/cgi-bin/g:DocF=macro/5004/
    45/0.html [1995, June 14].

*Journal Articles*

Basic forms, commercial supplier, and using an Internet protocol:

Author. (Year). Title. Journal Title [Type of medium], volume
    (issue), paging or indicator of length. Available: Supplier/
    Database name (Database identifier or number, if available)/Item
    or accession number [Access date].
Author. (Year). Title. Journal Title [Type of medium], volume
    (issue), paging or indicator of length. Available Protocol (e.g.,
    HTTP): Site/Path/File [Access date].

Examples:

Clark, J. K. Complications in academia: Sexual harass-
    ment and the law. Siecus Report [CD-ROM] 21(6), 6-10.
    Available: 1994 SIRS/SIRS 1993 School/Volume 4/Article
    93A [1995, June 13].
Carriveau, K. L., Jr. [Review of the book Environmental
    hazards: Marine pollution]. Electronic Green Journal
    [Online], 2(1), 3 paragraphs. Available Gopher:
    gopher://gopher.uidaho.edu/11/UI_gopher/library/egj03/
    carriv01.htl [1995, June 21].

Inada, K. (1995). A Buddhist response to the nature of
    human rights. Journal of Buddhist Ethics [Online], 2,
    9 paragraphs. Available HTTP: http://www.cac.psu.edu/
    jbe/twocont.html [1995, June 21].

*Magazine Articles*
Basic forms, commercial supplier, and using an Internet protocol:

Author. (Year, month day). Title. Magazine Title [Type of me-
    dium], volume (if given), paging or indicator of length. Avail-
    able: Supplier/Database name (Database identifier or number, if
    available)/Item or accession number [Access date].
Author. (Year, month day). Title. Magazine Title [Type of me-
    dium], volume (if given), paging or indicator of length. Avail-
    able Protocol (e.g., HTTP): Site/Path/File [Access date].

Examples:

Goodstein, C. (1991, September). Healers from the deep.
    American Health [CD-ROM], 60-64. Available: 1994 SIRS/
    SIRS 1992 Life Science/Article 08A [1995, June 13].
Viviano, F. (1995, May/June). The new Mafia order. Mother
    Jones Magazine [Online], 72 paragraphs. Available
    HTTP: http://www.mojones.com/MOTHER_JONES/MJ95/
    viviano.html [1995, July 17].

*Newspaper Articles*
Basic forms, commercial supplier, and using an Internet protocol:

Author. (Year, month day). Title. Newspaper Title [Type of me-
    dium], paging or indicator of length. Available: Supplier/
    Database name (Database identifier or number, if available)/Item
    or accession number [Access date].
Author. (Year, month day). Title. Newspaper Title [Type of me-
    dium], paging or indicator of length. Available Protocol (e.g.,
    HTTP): Site/Path/File [Access date].

Examples:

Howell, V., & Carlton, B. (1993, August 29). Growing up
    tough: New generation fights for its life: Inner-city
    youths live by rule of vengeance. Birmingham News [CD-
    ROM], p. 1A(10 pp.). Available: 1994 SIRS/SIRS 1993
    Youth/Volume 4/Article 56A [1995, July 16].
Johnson, T. (1994, December 5). Indigenous people are
    now more combative, organized. Miami Herald [Online],

p. 29SA(22 paragraphs). Available Gopher: gopher://
summit.fiu.edu/Miami Herald—Summit-Related Articles/
12/05/95—Indigenous People Now More Combative, Organized [1995, July 16].

### Discussion List Messages
Basic forms:

Author. (Year, Month day). Subject of message. Discussion List
    [Type of medium]. Available E-mail: DISCUSSION LIST@
    e-mail address [Access date].
Author. (Year, Month day). Subject of message. Discussion List
    [Type of medium]. Available E-mail: LISTSERV@e-mail
    address/Get [Access date].

Examples:

RRECOME. (1995, April 1). Top ten rules of film criticism.
    Discussions on All Forms of Cinema [Online]. Available
    E-mail: CINEMA-L@american.edu [1995, April 1].

(Author's login name, in uppercase, is given as the first element.)

Discussions on All Forms of Cinema [Online]. Available
    E-mail: LISTSERV@american.edu/Get cinema-1 log9504A
    [1995, August 1].

(Reference is obtained by searching the list's archive.)

### Personal electronic communications (E-mail)
Basic forms:

Sender (Sender's E-mail address). (Year, Month day). Subject of
    Message. E-mail to recipient (Recipient's E-mail address).

Examples:

Day, Martha (MDAY@sage.uvm.edu). (1995, July 30). Review
    of film — Bad Lieutenant. E-mail to Xia Li
    (XLI@moose.uvm.edu).

You may access this style sheet on line at http://www.UVM.edu/~xli/
reference/apa.html. Questions may be addressed to the author at
xli@moose.uvm.edu.
    The preceding list of examples was compiled by Philip Dirks, Port-
land State University: APA—<philipd@osa.pdx.edu>

## SPECIALIZED STYLE MANUALS

Every scholarly field has its preferred style, or set of guidelines for writing. MLA style, as presented in this manual, is widely accepted in humanities disciplines. The following manuals describe other styles followed in research disciplines.

### Biology

Council of Biology Editors. *Scientific Style and Format: The CBE Manual for Authors, Editors, and Publishers.* 6th ed. New York: Cambridge UP, 1994.

### Chemistry

American Chemical Society. *The ACS Style Guide: A Manual for Authors and Editors.* Washington: Amer. Chemical Soc., 1986.

### Geology

United States. Geological Survey. *Suggestions to Authors of the Reports of the United States Geological Survey.* 7th ed. Washington: GPO, 1991.

### Linguistics

Linguistic Society of America. *LSA Bulletin,* Dec. issue, annually.

### Mathematics

American Mathematical Society. *A Manual for Authors of Mathematical Papers.* Rev. ed. Providence: Amer. Mathematical Soc., 1990.

### Medicine

American Medical Association. *American Medical Association Manual of Style.* 8th ed. Baltimore: Williams, 1989.

### Physics

American Institute of Physics. *AIP Style Manual.* 4th ed. New York: Amer. Inst. of Physics, 1990.

There are also style manuals that address primarily editors and concern procedures for preparing a manuscript for publication:

*The Chicago Manual of Style.* 14th ed. Chicago: U of Chicago P, 1993.

United States. Government Printing Office. *Style Manual.* Rev. ed. Washington: GPO, 1984.

*Words into Type.* By Marjorie E. Skillin, Robert M. Gay, et al. 4th ed. Englewood Cliffs: Prentice, 1992.

For other style manuals and authors' guides, see John Bruce Howell, *Style Manuals of the English-Speaking World: A Guide* (Phoenix: Oryx, 1983).

## FOOTNOTES AND ENDNOTES

Footnotes and endnotes, both types of source documentation, take up more room than parenthetical notes since they include complete publishing information for each source the first time you make reference to it, in addition to including the same sources in a bibliography. Sometimes use of documentation notes alleviates the need for a full bibliography. Ask your teacher what is preferred in his or her field.

Footnotes are placed on the same page as the information they support. Endnotes, just as their name indicates, come at the end of the text of the paper. Both types of notes, although considered outdated and overly complicated by some scholars, are still used in many different disciplines, from the humanities to the social sciences to mathematics. It's best to check your professor's preference.

Footnotes are used less often than endnotes because they are difficult to type. They do, however, have distinct advantages for the reader, since he or she need not flip to the end of the essay to read notes in context.

In-text citations consist of raised numbers (superscripts) following the cited information in the text. Footnotes use a raised number at the beginning of the note; in some disciplines, endnotes use numbers typed on the same line as the note, not raised. The MLA format used for the most common types of documentation notes is as follows.

For a book by one author:

[1]Russell Martin. <u>Out of Silence</u> (New York: Henry Holt and
    Company), 1944, 47.

For a book by more than one author:

[2]Janice Delaney, Mary Jane Lupton, and Emily Toth, <u>The
    Curse</u> (Urbana: U of Illinois P, 1988) 47.

For a later edition and for a translation:

[3]Feodor Dostoevsky, <u>Crime and Punishment,</u> trans. Jesse
    Coulson, 2nd ed. (New York: Norton, 1972) 321-22.

For a book of more than one volume:

[4]Sigmund Freud, "Splitting of the Ego in the Defensive
    Process," <u>Sigmund Freud: Collected Papers,</u> vol. 5, ed.
    Ernest Jones (New York: Basic Books, 1959), 372-75.

For a government document or a pamphlet published by an association:

[5]Evangelical Lutheran Church in America, Department for
    Studies of the Church in Society. The Church and Human
    Sexuality (Chicago: 1993), 7-9.

[6]John Creswell, Faculty Research Performance, ASHE-ERIC
  Higher Education Report No. 4 (Washington, D.C.: Assn
  for the Study of Higher Education), 1985.

**For an essay, story, or chapter in a book or any selection from a casebook:**

[7]Hope Edelman, "Growth," Motherless Daughters (Reading,
  Mass: Addison-Wesley Publishing Company) 1996, 235–
  259.

**For a newspaper article:**

[8]Jan Breslauer, "A Knight with Noble Intentions," Los
  Angeles Times March 17, 1996, final ed., Calendar, 49.
[9]Marc Sandalow, "House Votes to End Ban on Assault Guns,"
  San Francisco Chronicle 23 Mar. 1996, A-1.

It isn't necessary to give the edition of the paper, but it can be helpful,
since sometimes articles run in one edition are not run in another one.
  **For a journal article:**

[10]Jody Swilky, "Reconsidering Faculty Resistance to
  Writing Reform," WPA: Writing Program Administration
  16. 1-2 (Fall/Winter 1992): 50.

**For an encyclopedia article:**

[11]Mischa Schwartz, "Telecommunications Systems,"
  Encyclopaedia Brittanica: Macropaedia, 1989 ed.

**For an interview:**

[12]Wanda Coleman, interview, Feminist Forum, Natl. Public
  Radio KABC, Los Angeles, March 8, 1996.
[13]Monica Ruiz, personal interview, June 1996.

**For a book review:**

[14]Ralph Baumgarten, "The Life of Philip Roth, or
  Zuckerman's Complaint," rev. of The Facts: A
  Novelist's Autobiography, by Philip Roth, Los Angeles
  Times Book Review 11 Sept. 1988: 6.

If a review has no author, begin the entry with word "Rev."
  **For a lecture:**

[15]Eric, Frank, "The Cleaning of the Sistine Chapel Ceiling." Sixteenth Century Italian Art Lecture, Occidental College (Los Angeles: Jan. 22, 1990.

For a paper:

<sup>16</sup>Joan Fleming, Sol Altschul, Victor Zielinski, and Max
    Forman, "The Influence of Parent Loss in Childhood on
    Personality Development and Ego Structure" (paper
    presented at the annual meeting of the American
    Psychoanalytic Association, San Francisco, Calif., May
    1958.)

For a film:

<sup>17</sup><u>Tetsuo the Iron Man,</u> dir. Shinya Tsukamoto, 1991.

To cite Internet sources:
The basic format for Internet resources is as follows:

    Author's first name, last name. "Title of Work." Title of
        Complete Work. [protocol and address] [path] [date of
        message or visit].

For CD-ROM: Use Internet format, but there is no need to cite date
of visit:

<sup>18</sup>Natalie Angier, "Chemists Learn Why Vegetables Are Good
    for You." <u>New York Times</u> (13 Apr. 1993): C1, New York
    Times Ondisc. CD-ROM. Oct. 1993.

For more complete information see Janice R. Walker, "MLA-Style
Citations of Electronic Sources."

http://www.cas.usf.edu/english/walker/mla.html

For other footnote formats, consult *MLA Handbook for Writers of Research Papers, Fourth Edition.*

You need to spell out all the footnote information only once for each
source. Subsequent references to a source take shortened forms. Latin
terms such as *loc. cit.* and *op. cit.* were previously used for this purpose.
Except for *ibid.*, which is still generally used, these Latin forms are now
outdated. The usual reference to a book that has been cited in previous
notes is as follows:

<sup>19</sup>Mondale 34.

However, if there is more than one author with the same last name or
if an author has contributed more than one source, a fuller reference is
required for clarity:

<sup>20</sup>Richard Mondale 30.
<sup>21</sup>Mondale, <u>The Way Out</u> 28.

Even though Latin abbreviations are becoming less and less common in scholarly works, you may still come across them, particularly if you use older materials. Consequently you should know what they mean. The abbreviations most often used are the following:

op. cit. located in the same source referred to in a recent note but on a different page of that source

loc. cit. located in the same passages referred to in a recent note

ibid. located in the same source referred to in the previous note; when followed by a page number, it means the present reference is to a different page

Other, less frequently used abbreviations include:

cf.   compare
et al. and others, usually used to refer to multiple authors or editors
n.d.  no date
rev.  revised
viz.  consult for information
vol.  volume

## QUESTIONS OFTEN ASKED ABOUT RESEARCH PAPERS

**Do I need a thesis statement for a research paper?**
Yes. You always need an original direction for any essay, and that direction should be clearly set forth in a thesis statement.

**How long should my introduction be?**
The introduction in a research paper may be longer than in shorter essays. Do not delay stating your thesis for too long, however. In a ten-page paper, try to get your thesis in by the second page.

**If I am dealing with a controversial topic, do I have to present both sides of the controversy?**
When writing an essay on any controversial topic, you are obliged to present the opposition and to refute it if you wish to convince the reader of your stand. If you fail to cite the opposition, your reader may judge you as unknowledgeable in the field or feel that your views lack objectivity.

**Since I learned everything about the topic from what I have read, won't my whole paper need to be documented?**
No. First of all you will be organizing your essay around an original premise. Second, most of your topic sentences will be your own ideas and only your support for these ideas will, in most cases, need to be documented.

What if I had a thought about my subject and it turns out that the same idea appears in one of the books I am researching. Do I have to give credit to someone else for something I too considered?

You should give credit whenever an idea of your own occurs in one of your sources. However, if you wish to inform your readers that your idea came first, there is no reason why you shouldn't include an informational footnote such as the one below. Place an asterisk in the text after the idea (following the end-of-sentence punctuation) and write at the bottom of the same page a note to this effect:

> \*My idea is shared by Calvin S. Hall, *A Primer of Freudian Psychology* (New York: World Publishing Co., 1954) 41.

### Does every fact have to be documented?

You should document all information that is not common knowledge. You need not, however, document material noted by most authorities in the field. If seven out of ten sources you read refer to the same information, you can assume that the point is common knowledge and needs no citation. But if a fact is quoted directly from a source or if you use information or opinions presented by a particular writer, you must document them.

### Was the footnote and bibliography form I learned in the past wrong? Why is it different from those in this text?

The main concern that scholars have with documentation is that it be consistent. Don't use a comma for one entry in the same place that you use a period in another. Generally, people in the humanities use the guidelines set by *The MLA Handbook.* Other disciplines may use other style sheets. Unless your instructor asks you to use a specialized format, follow the guidelines in this book.

### Should a bibliography include background reading or just the references cited in the paper?

There is no one answer to this question. It depends on the discipline for which you are writing and on what your professor asks for. If you do not cite background materials, title your bibliography "Works Cited" or "References." If you do cite background readings in the bibliography, call it "Works Consulted."

### Do I need both a bibliography and parenthetical references in every research paper?

The preferred format for the humanities does call for both. However, certain scientific and social science style manuals call for other forms, which include all the bibliographical and footnote references on a page at the back of the paper. It's always best to check with your instructor on this question.

### How many note cards should I have?

You should always have more notes than you need. Having twenty or thirty extra cards for a ten-page research paper is average. Be sure not to throw out your extra cards until you finish your essay—you can never tell when your paper will take an unexpected turn.

### How many sources should I use?

You should use a variety of different types of materials in any research project. Among them should be periodicals, general reference tools, and specialized books. Try to find the classics in the field and read them. In most cases your teacher can suggest primary sources on your subject. An example of a primary source on the study of dreams is Freud's *Interpretation of Dreams*. A secondary source on the same subject would be a discussion of Freud's book. The number of sources will vary with the project, but most teachers agree that two or three are not enough.

### How many citations should I have?

This is a hard one to answer because there aren't any real rules. You should reference whenever necessary. Depending on your topic and the length and breadth of the essay, you will need more or fewer citations. You should not have too many—say, twenty in four pages—as this would indicate that not enough of the thinking in the essay is your own. On the other hand, too few citations might indicate that you did not do enough research.

### When should I paraphrase and when should I quote?

If a quotation is not essential (see the suggestions on p. 281–282), paraphrase the material. It will make your paper easier to read. Since the reader is jolted each time there is a change in the style of writing, unless the shift in style is deliberate or necessary, avoid quoting.

### How many words should a quotation have before I separate it from the body of my text?

Four lines or more of prose and three lines or more of poetry should be placed in block form.

### May I end paragraphs with direct quotations?

It is generally a poor practice to end paragraphs with direct quotations because they tend to just sit there rather than work for you. As a better strategy, lead up to a quotation, include the material, and then comment on it so that your reader knows why it appears in the essay.

## RESEARCH PAPER FORMAT

Your professors may have special format requirements for your research papers, so remember to check with them before setting up your formating commands in the computer or establishing how you will type your essay. Most of the papers you will write in college will conform to the standards explained fully in *The MLA Handbook for Writers of Research Papers.* This reference may be found in your college library and quite possibly in your college's bookstore. You should check it for any format requirements about which you have questions.

Based on the guidelines set forth in *The MLA Handbook,* here are the key specifications you will need to keep in mind for typing or word processing your final draft. For an example of how your paper should look, see the sample humanities paper beginning on page 319.

### Paper and Print

Use a dark ribbon and plain type; avoid script or other fancy type styles. Letter-quality print is preferable to dot matrix.

Use white, twenty-pound, 81/2 × 11 paper, and submit only clear, clean copy. Erasable bond is not acceptable because the type smudges. If you must type on this kind of paper, photocopy it and turn in your copy to the professor. The same is true of papers containing many messy corrections done with Liquid Paper or correction tape.

### Margins and Page Numbers

Use one-inch margins at the top, bottom, and sides of the page. Page numbers are the exception: they are placed at the right-hand margin one-half inch from the top margin, throughout the paper. You should also include your last name as a running head before the page number.

### Spacing and Indentation

Double space all text, quotations, notes, and the "Works Cited" list. Indent new paragraphs five spaces from the left margin and blocked quotations ten spaces from the left margin.

If you use footnotes, single space them and double space between notes. Skip four lines between the last line of text and the beginning of the notes. Indent the first line of a note five spaces. If a note continues onto the next page, do not leave four lines blank between text and note; instead, type one solid line a space below the last line of text and type the note on the next line. The solid line should begin at the left margin and extend about a third of the way across the page.

### Headings

Don't use a separate title page. At the left-hand margin of the first page, type your name, the professor's name, the course title, and the date one inch from the top of the page. Be sure to double space each line.

Double space down from the date and, centered, type the title of the essay. Do not underline, use quotation marks, or place in all caps your original title. Of course, if part of the title is normally to be enclosed in quotation marks (a short story or poem) or underlined (a book), those parts only should be so punctuated.

Quadruple space down to your first line of type.

### Tables and Illustrations

Be sure to place illustrative charts, tables, photographs, and drawings as close as is possible to the material to which they refer. Tables generally are numbered with arabic numerals (1, 2, 3, etc.) and titled, with the source of the table given directly below it. The other types of illustration are usually numbered under the illustration but are called "figures," as in *Fig. 1*, followed by the title and source.

### "Works Cited"

On the first "Works Cited" page, center the title one inch from the top of the page and double space to the first entry. Indent the second and any subsequent lines of each entry five spaces. Double space entries, and do not put extra space between them.

### Binding

Although *The MLA Handbook* recommends securing your essay with a paper clip, which is easily removable and replaceable, professors do not all agree on what constitutes perfect binding. Some become irritated by plastic folders, and others want you to use them. Some insist on staples, and others find them an annoyance. This is definitely an area on which to check with your instructors.

### SAMPLE RESEARCH PAPER

On the following pages is a student research paper which will present you with the correct form for most of the papers you will need to write in the humanities. You will also find annotations on format, citations, and essay development in the MLA style.

**Figure 10-5. Sample research paper.**

1

Uncovering the Truth:

Subjective Analysis Within New Journalism


If reporters detailed the slaughter of innocent Irish-
Catholics by the British Army or the murder of a Black
Panther in a neutral manner, their moral and personal
integrity would certainly be questioned. However,
objectivity and aloofness have long been the keystones of
journalism, confining its professionals to a rigid style
and structure of presentation. Many journalists, like
Gail Sheehy, rebelled against the authoritarianism of the
conventional rules, experimenting with the usage of
literary devices and personal experience to enrich and
extend the content of their articles. Unafraid to take a
position, they employed all writing techniques available
to uncover the actual circumstances behind an incident.
Although critics censure their subjective style of
reporting, these "New" Journalists utilize their own
histories and personal involvement in the material to
extract details that objective reporters often miss,
allowing them to provide a more realistic, and often more
truthful, portrait of the material to the public.

Unlike objective news reporters who strive to recount
only the facts of an event, New Journalists do not
hesitate to use their personal perspectives to gain a
deeper understanding of the material they cover. They
embrace the idea that history shapes all of us, creating

Page numbers go in the upper right-hand corner.

In MLA form there is no cover page.

Although ... public.
Thesis

319

**Figure 10-5 (continued).**                                   2

within each of us a unique background that will always

influence our writing, no matter how impartial we attempt

to be. Unlike newspaper reporters, most New Journalists

openly admit that they filter the material they are

reporting on through the personal lens ground by their

life experiences. In the preface to <u>Panthermania,</u> Gail

Sheehy openly concedes the biases her ethnic background

and childhood exposure to the Black Panthers bring to

material she reports on by acknowledging that "[she] was

painfully aware of my own handicaps as a reporter: my

whiteness, of course, but also my sympathy with the black

radical cause" (xi). By admitting her passionate interest

rather than claiming detachment, Sheehy places the reader

in a position of "critical reader" rather than a passive

recipient of information and creates an interaction

between reader and author: based on honest egalitarian

interchange, there is no arrogance about or excuse for

the presence of interpretations of events.

    New Journalists rely heavily on the use of literary

devices to express their personal interpretations of an

event. By employing tools like symbolism, figurative

language, and metaphors, they can expand upon the short,

straightforward newspaper article and come closer to

uncovering the spirit and emotions of an event. Sheehy

makes extensive use of symbolism in many of her works to

emphasize certain qualities that she notices in events or

subjects. In her 1988 profile of Ronald Reagan, Sheehy

uses his physical near-sightedness to symbolize the

Student incorporates the words of an author into her text by leading in with the word "that" and adjusting the quotation with brackets to fit the context of her essay.

The student eliminates the author's name from citation because it is given in the sentence. Also the book title is mentioned in the citation because Sheehy has more than one entry on the Works Cited list.

**Figure 10-5 (continued).**

3

short-sightedness of his presidential administration
(Character 260). Never concerned about the long-term
impacts of his policies, Reagan did not hesitate to
implement a budget that his advisors warned would amass
an unprecedented deficit or to send soldiers to the
insignificant--but communist--country of Grenada despite
the risk of losing American lives. Sheehy also used
Reagan's blurry vision to signify his ability to create
and to live in his own ideal dream world. By concocting a
perfect American society from the fuzzy images before
him, Reagan was able to overlook the AIDS epidemic, the
growing numbers of poor and homeless, and the human
rights violations of the despotic rulers in the Philip-
pines and Haiti. By using Reagan's eyesight in this
manner, Sheehy reconfigures the news media's image of
Ronald Reagan as a dynamic world leader into one of an
elderly man trying to achieve his vision of the perfect
society but in doing so, neglecting the economic and
social realities of the nation. Her symbolic language
clearly acknowledges and supports the liberal ideology
through which she sees the world, adding a new perspective to the overwhelmingly friendly portrayals of Reagan
by the popular media in the 1980s.

In Panthermania, Sheehy utilizes similar figurative
language to depict the death of a mass social movement.
In the spring of 1970, Sheehy thrust herself into the
middle of a city in turmoil over the murder of a Black
Panther. As evidence began to point to the Black Pan-

The author of the paper now
will refer to the Sheehy books by
title to avoid confusion.

**Figure 10-5 (continued).**

4

thers, themselves, as the killers, and not the white
establishment, disillusionment spread rapidly within the
black radical movement as they started to question the
motives, morality and effectiveness of the leadership.
Sheehy predicted the demise of the black radicals by
dramatically pronouncing "The Movement is eating its last
supper in New Haven" (_Panthermania_ 110). With this
figurative language, she is able to create a double
meaning, emphasizing not only the movement's imminent
death, but also the ability of its spirit to live on as a
martyred symbol of the sixties. Sheehy uses the metaphor
of the closure of New Haven's only coffeehouse, the local
radical hangout, to signify the actual death of the
movement in the area. While an objective newspaper
journalist would only report on the factual events of the
trial and its impact on local politics, with the use of
literary language and her own personal insights, Sheehy
is able to turn the newspapers' simple story into a tale
about the life and death of the black radical movement.

The subjective nature of Sheehy's writing, apparent in
her use of literary devices to advocate certain position,
is an aspect of New Journalism often under critical fire.
Those from the traditional journalistic school quickly
point to the obvious violation of the "reporter's rules"
of objectivity and detachment. By manipulating their
factual knowledge to support a particular position, New
Journalists are presenting biased information to the
public. However, Sheehy claims that reporters like

**Figure 10-5 (continued).**

5

herself have a responsibility to dig behind the statements presented in the popular media because the media
themselves often accept inaccurate statements
uncritically. In <u>Panthermania,</u> she shows how the media's
body count of Black Panthers killed by police, in fact,
mainly contained Panthers killed either by other rival
black militants or by the failure of their own attempts
at robbery (9). She notes that this erroneous number was
widely published throughout the media while the number of
black youths killed in gang-related murders, 699 in the
first nine months of 1970, continued to go unnoticed (9).
Sheehy's example illustrates the necessity of subjective
reporting as a check against propaganda put forward by
big business or government and printed uncritically by
the media.

   A New Journalist's willingness to take a stand on
issues of social concern can be superior to the objective
reporting style, especially when the issue is not morally
neutral. Ronald Weber argues that the issues New Journalists tackle often are not morally neutral and that it
would be unethical to portray them as such (20). Reporting on blatant crimes of racism, sexism or human rights
issues, such as apartheid in South Africa, in an objective manner is morally irresponsible in a country that
places such great worth on individual freedom. Sheehy's
willingness to take a position is present throughout her
works. In <u>Panthermania,</u> she openly admits how difficult it
was to remain neutral in a period like the sixties: "with

The student has already given the book title in the sentence, so she needs only the page number for the idea. Note that nothing is quoted—this is a brief summary all in the student's words.

Only the page number needs to be cited since Weber is mentioned in the text and he has written only one source on the student's Works Consulted list.

**Figure 10-5 (continued).**

6

Panther-baiting on the rise at home and the invasion of Cambodia a bitter truth abroad, one had to take sides," she says (1). However, her personal recollection of the "Bloody Sunday" in British occupied Northern Ireland more vividly illustrates how morally difficult it is to remain neutral, especially when the injustices are occurring right before your eyes.

While researching a story on Irish women, Sheehy found herself in the middle of a spray of British bullets. Without warning, a bullet took the life of the boy she was speaking to as a "steel slug tore into his mouth and ripped up the bridge of his nose and left his face nothing but ground bone meal" (Sheehy, Passages 2). She hid in the closets of Irish Catholics as the British walled the people in and gunned them down. In her description of the event, she depicts the British as unsympathetically brutal, gunning down three boys "like dummies in a shooting gallery," and the priest that followed after them "waving a white handkerchief" (Passages 3). Sheehy subjectively portrays the British soldiers as religiously intolerant and as placing no value on human life. After living through such a horrific incident, it would have been impossible for her to present the actions of the British impartially. Instead, Sheehy is able to use that personal experience to draw a graphic image of life as a Catholic in Northern Ireland, revealing the cruelty of our British allies to the uninformed American Public.

The first time the student refers to another book of Sheehy's, she gives a full citation, including author, title, and page number. Later in the paragraph, only the title is needed.

Transition comes at the end of the paragraph, raising the subject to be discussed next and connecting it to the ideas that precede it.

**Figure 10-5 (continued).** 7

Besides allowing their own histories and personal experiences to enhance the material on which they report, New Journalists can also gain unique angles on stories by penetrating the minds of people involved, bringing their thoughts and emotions to the surface. A person's naked words and outward appearance may be quite different from internal feelings; and any journalist determined to flesh out all nuances of a story must accurately depict their subject's state of mind. Besides simply providing a person's words, New Journalists also describe the subject's speech pattern, appearance and mannerisms, providing their readers with the visual and emotional context in which the words were said. By breaking the constrictions of "old" journalism and diving into the minds of people, a New Journalist can portray the entire range of physical and mental details hiding behind an event or within person, giving the readers a comprehensive picture from which they can draw their own conclusions.

Although Gail Sheehy was not able to interview then-President Ronald Reagan for her biographical essay of him, she used information from numerous books and articles on the president, as well as interviews with those who worked with him, to sketch a unique and revealing image of Reagan's consciousness. Drawing together the details of his childhood as the son of an alcoholic, his love affair with the magic of the movies, and his severe near-sightedness, Sheehy depicts a man

The quotes around "old" are placed there to point out the term the student has given to objective reporting. These quotation marks do not indicate use of a source. Note also use of quoting around "rapping" on p. 10 of paper.

**Figure 10-5 (continued).**

8

The writer of this paper selects the key phrase "continued to believe his own fiction" from her source, surrounding it with her own words and ideas.

One writer is quoting another in a source used by the student who wrote the paper. The student explains this use of sources right in her sentence and cites the page number from the *secondary* source.

The student writer uses brackets to explain and ellipses (three dots) to make an omission in the middle of quoting.

The student gives the title as well as the author in the citation since more than one book by the author is listed in her bibliography.

Here the student writer is using a *quotation*, given in a source, that is one author (Sheehy) quoting another. The same occurs later, with the Weber citation; p. 9.

hopelessly lost in a make-believe world, who, throughout his presidency, "continued to believe his own fiction" (<u>Character</u> 269). She supports her critical representation with a detailed look at the painful moments of his life that shaped his mental state. His father's alcoholism initially steered Reagan into a fictional world that Anne Edwards observed in her biography, <u>Early Reagan,</u> and that Sheehy quoted in <u>Character:</u> "'Dutch [Ronald Reagan] developed two worlds--public and private--and was acutely alert to the dangers of Jack's benders so that when they came he could cope with them, a feat that took a tremendous amount of self-control. . . . Nell [his mother] worried about Dutch's . . . ability to block out such things as Jack's binges'" (259). His love of acting and the movies further instilled within him the idea that with a little money and the right words he could recreate the mythological ideal America and provide all citizens with a happy ending. These qualities enabled him to believe that he was implementing spending reductions and cutting waste during his presidency when, in fact, he sent the budget deficit to record numbers. David Stockman, the inventor of "Reaganomics," noted Reagan's denial of reality: "When you sit there going over the deficit projections, the man's eyes glaze over" (Sheehy, <u>Character</u> 276). By the end of the essay, Sheehy's extensive use of commentary from Reagan's advisors and from biographical works allows her to present what she interpreted to be his thought process and mindset, convincingly charac-

**Figure 10-5 (continued).** 9

terizing this man, greatly revered at the time, as "The
Great Pretender," a man who would simply block out the
country's biggest problems in favor of his imagined
reality (qtd. in <u>Character</u> 256).

The attempts of New Journalists to probe the minds of
their subjects has drawn substantial criticism from those
who believe it is impossible to depict what someone is
actually thinking and feeling. Critics have called this
method of journalism "creative writing" because they
contend the author is only guessing about the subject's
internal character (qtd. in Weber 15). To vanquish these
accusations, New Journalists load their articles with
verifiable "hard" facts, as well as utilizing a rigorous
interview process. In order to achieve the complete
awareness of a person necessary to justify interpreting
their thought patterns and emotions, New Journalists
often spend weeks or months observing and questioning
their subject about every facet of their life. This
information is then processed through the author's
acknowledged subjective consciousness and presented in
often dramatic fashion. While the abundance of criticism
is understandable, New Journalists' intensive research
methods and open acknowledgment of their biases usually
ensures that the readers are presented with a genuine
depiction that often reveals something new about the
subject.

Gail Sheehy's research for <u>Panthermania</u> exemplifies the
intensive technique of the New Journalists as she scoured

**Figure 10-5 (continued).**

10

New Haven to uncover the truth behind the murder of a
Black Panther. She spent nine months in Connecticut with
her partner, David Parks, a young black photographer,
whom she hoped would help counterbalance her white
perspective. During this period, the two of them be-
friended many of the families and friends of the defen-
dants of the trial and community leaders in the ghettos
surrounding Yale University, spent many hours "rapping"
on street corners and absorbed the atmosphere at the local
coffee shop. By immersing herself in the local culture,
Sheehy was able to feel the pulse of the black community,
epitomized by the change she observed in the young
radical, Mentor Jones. During one of her first meetings
with Mentor and his father, she listens to him making a
"Tip-tick, tip-tick" noise in the basement which turned
out to be him jamming his pen into one of the holes in his
revolutionary notebook (<u>Panthermania</u> 30). After spending
many hours getting to know Mentor, she could report that
he spent those hours in the basement, "untying his mind,"
writing down his revolutionary ideology. By the end of the
summer, Sheehy illustrates the transformation the events
surrounding the Panthers created within Mentor by
reporting that the "Tip-tick" noise no longer came from a
pen but from a rifle in Mentor's hand (<u>Panthermania</u> 124).
Sheehy observes that within his consciousness, "the
Shift," had occurred, changing Mentor from a "docile
Negro" to a revolutionary black (<u>Panthermania</u> 33). In the
final chapter of <u>Panthermania</u>, the puzzle that was

The author puts "rapping" in quotes to acknowledge its slang usage so that her readers do not think she is unaware of her mixed tone by inclusion of slang.

**Figure 10-5 (continued).**                                           11

Mentor's mind finally becomes clear to her as she declares this his "mask begins to crumble like papier-mâché. For an instant his face is stripped raw of poses, theories, words, defenses and pretense—everything falls away except the loneliness of being fifteen and black in New Haven, Connecticut (124).

While the interpretive statement above would never be printed in a newspaper because of its subjective nature, New Journalists revel in the style and expression it represents. Sheehy allowed her mind, with all of its preconceived biases, to filter the images she saw and words she heard, a method that enabled her to present a fresh perspective of her subjects. Literary devices are often an important tool for New Journalists trying to capture the novelty and vitality of their vision, providing them with the style and images necessary to move beyond the empty words of the newspaper articles. The resulting dramatic presentation of their work vividly conveys, not only the authors' opinions and interpretations, but also the naked thoughts and feelings and of their subject. While the New Journalists' lack of objectivity will always vex conventional critics, their ability to dig beneath the surface of a story and reveal the deeper truth underneath is invaluable to those who seek the complexity and honesty that are missing in the dispassionate popular press. New Journalism is like a gourmet meal at an excellent restaurant that pays attention to every detail; the popular media is more like

The final paragraph summarizes the main arguments of the essay, draws an analogy, and asserts the significance of what she has said.

Works Consulted refers to a list of works including background reading and citations. Works Cited would be used to list only sources cited in the student's paper.

Ask your professors which they prefer.

**Figure 10-5 (continued).**

12

fast food. It is the sensitivity of palate that determines whom one should read, but one thing remains certain: the whole experience provided by New Journalists is worth entertaining, at least some of the time if one is to be fully aware of the news.

Works Consulted

Lounsberry, Barbara. _The Art of Fact: Contemporary Artists of Nonfiction._ New York: Greenwood Press, 1990.

Sheehy, Gail. "Madness and Method." _Passages: Predictable Crises of Adult Life._ New York: Dutton & Co., Inc., 1974. 2-19.

Sheehy, Gail. _Panthermania._ New York: Harper & Row, Publishers, 1971.

Sheehy, Gail. "Refusal to Change" and "Ronald Reagan: Who _Was_ that Masked Man?" _Character: America's Search for Leadership._ New York: William Morrow and Company, Inc., 1988. 252-303.

Weber, Ronald, ed. _The Reporter as Artist: A Look at the New Journalism Controversy._ New York: Hastings House, Publishers, 1974.

Most of the writing assignments you will encounter as a student, such as doing book reviews, preparing abstracts of articles, or answering in-class essay examinations, will use the writing skills you have already learned. But many of these assignments will require special formats. They are best approached by using the step-by-step processes explained in this chapter. The guidelines presented are those commonly and successfully used by most students. In Figure 11-1 you will find a successful in-class essay. Read it over to see its strengths: a clear thesis, a logically progressing argument, and strong topic sentences in the body paragraphs. Observing the practices on the following pages will help you, too, to succeed.

# WHAT IF YOU HAVE A SPECIAL ASSIGNMENT OR TASK?

## WRITING TIMED ESSAY EXAMINATIONS

Usually, in-class essay examinations require some analysis, not just repetition of a bunch of memorized facts. It is therefore important to do more than just leaf through your notes the night before the test. Thinking of possible test questions can be a fruitful way to spend your study time. After reviewing the chapters from the texts and your class notes, make up some questions your teacher might ask. Try to invent questions that relate various facts to one another. You might base them on the following:

Points that your teacher has emphasized in class.
Points that "sum up" the meaning behind what you are studying.
Points that relate the current information to that studied during previous weeks.
Points that compare with or contrast to other points in the same chapters or units.

Without looking at the texts or your notes, develop a thesis sentence that responds to each question. For every thesis, outline in your head or better yet jot down on paper all the information you need to support it. When you have done so, go back and look up any facts that you were unsure of or did not know. Naturally, the number of questions you should think of depends on the type and amount of material to be covered by the test. Keep at it until you are satisfied. Just remember that knowing a lot of facts will not help you very much unless you also know how to use them.

**Figure 11-1**

```
                                                        Timed Essay
                                                           1 hr.

                                                      Cameron Cooper
                                                        English 201
                                                      Professor Robins


     Question: How does Wilson develop the theme of conservation throughout
Biophilia? Cite relevant passages.


                               "Constant Advance"


  In Biophilia, Edward Wilson offers his extended definition of

"biophilia." In the body of the book, however, Wilson presents a new facet

of biophilia with each chapter. He expands the traditional definition from

being a simple "innate tendency" to an evolution of thought that brings

humanity to an understanding of nature and how humanity relates to nature,

or should: the conservation ethic.

     In the prologue, Wilson defines "biophilia" as the "innate tendency to

focus on life and lifelike processes." The first chapter focuses on Wilson's

own experience of and reason for studying nature. Wilson is intrigued by

the wonder of nature and what it has to offer. From Wilson's scrutinizing

eye, nature is seen as a "biological maelstrom of which only the surface

could be scanned by the naked eye." As a scientist, Wilson longs for a

feeling of "constant advance" in his quest for understanding nature. Nature

gives Wilson a mystery to solve and an infinite number of questions to

answer. In the tradition of Star Trek, it is the final frontier.

     Through Wilson's quest for an understanding of nature, several realiza-

tions have resulted, which he reflects in the later chapters of Biophilia.

His study of individual organisms has begun to encompass a more global
```

Considering possible questions can help you in more ways than one. While trying to "psych out" what may be on the test, you will also be learning the material and, more important, gaining an understanding of it. This preparation should lessen your anxiety about the examination, since you will be sure that you know how to answer some of the questions you might be asked. It should also make you confident that you can rearrange the information you have studied in any new combinations that might be required. Besides, you may be lucky and think of a question that actually is on the test.

**Figure 11-1 (continued).**

meaning. An ant is no longer an individual ant; rather, it is a vital part of a "superorganism": an ant colony which relies upon the effort of every ant to survive. This interlocked relationship, however, is not limited to a single species. Rather, this dependent relationship transcends species boundaries and creates an interdependent sphere called "nature." Wilson finds that "a few of the species were locked together in forms of symbiosis so intricate that to pull out one would bring others spiraling to extinction." It is this connection that people must recognize with nature, though the links appear more distant than they might between certain other species.

In realizing the interdependent relationship of species, Wilson elevates the value of nature. No scientist can truly predict what the continual degradation of species will eventually lead to. Wilson does know, however, that "deep mines of biological diversity will have been dug out and carelessly discarded." Each time a species is lost, a question is left unanswered and a piece of the genetic pool is forgotten. Finally this leads Wilson to say: "The phylogenetic continuity of life with humanity seems an adequate reason by itself to tolerate the continued existence of apes and other organisms. This does not diminish humanity—it raises the status of nonhuman creatures. We should at least hesitate before treating them as disposable matter."

Wilson brings "biophilia" up from an "innate tendency" to a realization of the conservation ethic through observation and respect of nature. "Biophilia" can be described as an evolution of thought. Through observation and reflection, "the natural world [becomes a] refuge of the spirit, remote, static, richer even than human imagination."

## Studying in Groups of Students

Collaboration at this point—once each student has reviewed the material—is generally a good idea. Classmates can divide up the material with you (make sure you do so in a manner that requires all students to at least skim all the materials before the test) so that not everything will need to be read as thoroughly. In the case of "sharing" the material this way, be sure that the student who leads the discussion brings questions to the group and elicits feedback from them rather than just reporting to them and having everybody copy down what is said. Group study is most effective when it is based on true collaboration, including discussion and debate. The value of group work is the multiple perspectives that can arise to clarify what's being studied. Working with well-prepared friends can strengthen your critical reading skills and boost your ability to respond effectively to challenging test questions.

### Approaching the Test

Prewriting is important in all writing assignments, but it is especially necessary for in-class essays, during which you rarely have enough time to recopy. The secret to doing well on essay examinations is to budget your time carefully. Up to about one-third of the time allotted for the examination should be spent in prewriting. Save five or, at the most, ten minutes at the end for proofreading and correcting errors, and spend the remaining time actually writing.

For an exam that requires one essay to be written in an hour, allow fifteen to twenty minutes of preparation and prewriting. Some tests may include a passage that you are supposed to read; others may ask you to select your topic from two or more alternatives. Include the time needed for reading or for deciding on a topic in your prewriting allowance. As soon as you have devised your thesis and a scratch outline, get to work on the essay. You should spend about half an hour writing the essay, making sure to leave five or ten minutes for proofreading. If the exam is longer than an hour, allow more time for writing the essay.

For an exam that requires several short essays, you may want to allot time for each according to its relative importance. Often the instructor indicates the importance of specific questions by mentioning the number of possible points awarded for each essay or the amount of time that should be spent on it. If not, you may need to estimate for yourself the relative importance of each question by gauging just how much you will have to write in order to answer it fully. Naturally, you would not want to spend forty minutes answering a rather limited question only to find that you have left yourself only twenty minutes to answer two questions that demand greater probing. If you think all the questions will be scored equally, allow equal time for each answer. Spend the bulk of your time on writing out the answers to the questions, but still give five minutes or

**Every high school student's worst enemy: the essay question.**

so to jotting down notes before you begin working on especially complex questions.

Remember, you should aim for only one draft during any timed essay examination.

### Writing the Test

*Step One*

The first step in writing an essay examination should always be to read the question carefully. What does it ask you to do? To find out exactly, underline the key words in the directions. These will give you clues as to:

The *arrangement* of your answer (discuss, analyze, criticize, tell, explain, trace, outline, cite evidence for, justify, clarify, exemplify, and so on).

The *content* of your answer (why, what, which, how, when, the effects of, the causes of, the value of, the significance of, the reasons for, and so forth).

Next, underline the key words dealing with the subject matter of the question. These will help ensure that your answer includes all the aspects of the topic the question asks for. Take a look at the following test question:

Tell about the three effects of urbanization on Latin American politics during the industrial revolution.

The key words in the directions are *tell* (the arrangement the question asks for) and *three effects* (the content the question asks for). The key words about the subject matter are *urbanization on Latin American politics* during the *industrial revolution.*

Not all questions are so easily underlined. Many are made up of several sentences. Check out the following example. All the key words are underlined. Notice that most of them occur in the last sentence.

*Ayn Rand's conception* of the *value of selfishness* has met with considerable *criticism* not only *from socialist theorists* but from *conservatives* as well. *In light of these criticisms* and *contemporary international economic* and *political affairs, discuss* what you consider to be the *principal inaccuracies* in Rand's philosophy.

*Step Two*

Next, form a question from the key words you have underlined. If the test topic is already a one-sentence question, you will not need Step Two. However, for longer test questions, use all of the key words to compose a one-sentence question. Doing so will probably remind you of the steps for forming thesis statements explained in Chapter 2. Actually, the process is very much the same. From the limited subject defined by the key words, you compose a focused question that you will later phrase into a thesis. The preceding test topic might become the following question:

> In light of the criticisms of both socialist and conservative theorists, can the principal inaccuracies in Ayn Rand's conception of the value of selfishness be demonstrated through current international political and economic affairs?

### Step Three

The third step is to turn the question formed from the key words into a thesis statement:

> In light of the criticisms of both socialist and conservative theorists, the principal inaccuracies in Ayn Rand's conception of the value of selfishness can be demonstrated through current political and economic affairs.

### Step Four

Now you can write the body of your essay. You may be able to organize the essay in your head, or you may want to jot down a scratch outline. Begin writing by placing your thesis statement as the first sentence. Then present your first point. After making the first point, go on to the second. After the second, make the third. It's that simple to be organized.

The most important parts of an in-class essay are a strong and relevant thesis and good topic sentences with plenty of supporting examples. Transitions, while still important, are not as vital as in writing in which your time is not so limited. Most of the coherence of your essay will depend on appropriate paragraphing and a logical presentation of your ideas. Usually, the introduction should be pared down to a concise statement of your thesis, and your conclusion should be merely a quick summary.

Good in-class writing should always be concise. Padded answers are detectable right away. They contain vague, wordy sentences supported by only a few concrete examples, and they may even contain irrelevant information. Here are some suggestions for making your answers concise:

Avoid digressions. Make sure everything you say clearly supports
your thesis or one of the points proving it.
Avoid unsupported generalizations. Make specific statements you
can back up with examples and analysis of examples; avoid
relying only on feelings.

If you absolutely do not know the answer to a question on a test, blame your failure on inadequate studying, fate, or whatever seems likely and

MOVE ON to the next question. There is no reason to waste time on what you don't know when you could be using the time to do an excellent job on another part of the exam. Nevertheless, if you know part of the answer to a question, do your best to present what you do know. Many teachers will give partial credit for such answers, especially if they are well written.

*Step Five*

Spend the last five minutes or so reading over what you have written and making any minor corrections you find necessary. Grammatical consistency, correct spelling, and proper mechanics are, of course, important, but occasional slips of the pen are usually judged less harshly in impromptu writing than in out-of-class essays.

Well-written answers to in-class essay examinations look like and sound like any other essay you would write. The transitions may not be as smooth and the overall structure may seem more mechanical, but your general writing abilities will suffice. Just remember to budget your time and respond directly to the question.

### Short-Answer Essay Examinations

Sometimes an essay examination will be made up of several short questions that ask you to define specific terms, to tell the function of characters in a literary work, or to identify people in history. To answer these questions, compose a well-developed paragraph for each one. Following the same five steps as you would for longer essay questions will ensure that your answers are complete.

---

### Exercises

A. Underline the key words in the questions below and state how the contents of a good thesis sentence would reflect them.

1. Compare and contrast the role of women in Reconquest Spain and Aztec Mexico. What is the significance of the similarities and differences in the way they were treated.

2. Ancient Athenian democracy is often described as "participatory," whereas modern democracies (such as the ones found in the United States, Canada, or Britain) are often described as "representative." What are the crucial differences between these two types of democracy? Which type is more faithful to the literal meaning of "democracy"? Explain.

3. "A lover must desire immortality along with the good, if what we agreed earlier was right, that Love wants to possess the good forever. It follows from our argument that Love must desire immortality" (Symposium 207a). What do you think Socrates and Diotima mean when they agree that a lover wants to possess the good forever and hence that a lover must desire immortality? Can you find examples in modern life to support their views or do you think their views are unpersuasive?

4. Trace the development of the medieval conception of the universe.

5. The conflict between Hebraism and Hellenism, as Matthew Arnold has defined these terms, is the great and basic conflict shaping the histories of art, of governments, and of religions. Analyze the actions of the principal American participants in the Cuban Missile Crisis as an example of this struggle. Explain which influence—the Hebrew or the Hellenic—offered the soundest course toward relieving tense conditions and securing peaceful relations with the Communist nations.

6. What is the relation of the statement "Good fences make good neighbors" to the central meaning of Frost's "Mending Wall"?

7. Describe the innovations in composition that appeared in paintings of the Italian Renaissance.

8. Is modern war all out or can St. Thomas Aquinas's precepts for a "just war" be approximated today?

9. Many rumors are circulated about the spread of AIDS. Name one way in which the disease can be transmitted and three ways in which people falsely believe it to be passed on. How can the misinformation be accounted for?

10. Historically, what has been the role of the mother in the Asian family? Is this role applicable today or is it outdated? Why?

B. Explain how a change in the key words in the directions for the following questions would change the structure of the essay you would write in response to the question.

1. Identify the significant events of antiwar protests that led to the United States's withdrawal from the Vietnam War, and explain the importance of each.

2. Why did the movement for racial equality become especially prominent among the white middle class during the sixties?

3. Porpoises were once land animals. Supposing Darwin's theories of evolution to be valid, calculate what the porpoise's adaptation for life in the sea explains about the environment.

4. In his essay "How to Size Up a Man," David Reuben says that people are constantly exposing their deepest secrets through gestures and dress. Would Sigmund Freud have agreed with this view? Support your answers with pertinent case studies and the discussion of specific theories.

## KEEPING UP WITH THE READING WORK LOAD

Probably the most common concern among students is keeping up. They universally feel swamped! There are times that it seems every teacher is requiring a paper due and times when the length of just one reading assignment is overwhelming, and—given the amount of work required in one's other classes—it seems just plain hopeless. What does one do to keep up? Many students have approached me for "speed-reading" techniques. Usually, what I work on with them is reading flexibility and efficiency. That's different from, and far superior to, "speeding" through a work and retaining relatively little so that when the test comes around one has to start over. The key concepts to master for reading effectively and quickly are framing your reading and reading different materials at different rates.

*Framing the reading* means to set goals, not just for time management, but for what you want to get out of reading a particular assignment. For instance, if you are assigned 40 pages in a history text about the legacy of Reconquest Spain, you should probably try to establish what its legacy is, why Spain is so rich and diverse a society under the rule of certain leaders and not under others. If you are assigned a novel to read, ask yourself how the theme of work is reflected in certain characters or symbols. And so on. But that is easy to say; how do you know what to look for? There are clues all around. In the classroom the professor may have actually given some details about the upcoming reading or a list of study questions. Of course that is ideal. But if your professor chooses to have you do all the discovering as you read, you will have to think about the progression of topics in the course, the material studied up to the point of the assignment, and the context of previous discussions and lectures in the class. The syllabus is a source of many clues. When is the next writing assignment due? What will it likely cover? You can read the work in the light of the eventual writing assignment. How has the book been broken down into units by the professor? If it is a series of articles that must be read, what are the titles? How do they seem connected? Framing the reading is your way of "getting a grip" on the purpose of the reading material. Try to create a question or a list of topics you expect to find information about. But don't start reading yet!

Most students read too soon. They start at word one and go until the end (if there's time!) of the article or chapter assigned. But that is not at all efficient. It's uninformed reading that hasn't given the reader a chance to establish a framework for comprehending what is being read. There's an axiom that good learners connect the old with the new— this means that it is important to make a connection for yourself between what you already know and what you are about to learn. Trained educators refer to this concept as creating "schema."

Here's a practical method of achieving an adequate knowledge base before reading, in order to speed up the actual time it takes you to pass your eyes across the page and to make the memory of what you have read last longer.

After creating a basic framework by looking at the syllabus, recent notes, and any study questions handed out by your teacher, read over very quickly the subtitles or titles of the material. Are there any charts? If so, read them over. Are there any photos or cartoons with captions? Study them quickly. Get a sense of the structure of the piece. Is it divided into chapters with multiple subheads? Are there questions starting out sections? Are there a pro and a con? About how many pages is each subsection? The whole process of previewing should take only a few minutes. They are minutes well invested.

Now when you begin to read, try to use the subtitles to make up a question for yourself. If the subtitle is "Aztec Women," ask yourself "What was the role of women in Aztec Mexico?" As you read the section, look for the answers and underline or highlight the material. You will be directed in your reading and therefore will not read every word or sentence at the same speed. After you complete a section, go back and write in the margins in your own words what the highlighted or underlined material suggests to you. Marginal notes of this sort will be invaluable to you in class discussions and in preparing material for future papers. Highlighting alone does not make the material your own in the same way, and you will be more likely to forget it and to have to read it again thoroughly in order to recall it. When you have finished jotting marginal notes, proceed to the next subtitle and make up a question. And continue the process throughout the reading. Students have sometimes become concerned that they might make up the "wrong" questions. It's not likely this will happen if you keep them simple and linked to the subtitle, but if you get halfway through a section and your reading seems to be taking you in another direction, simply re-phrase your question and take a moment to recap for yourself what you have just read, placing it in the new context.

Being flexible in your rate of reading is a part of the previously de-scribed process, but it is also a goal by itself. Consider the variety of materials you will be assigned: movies with guides for viewing, maga-zine articles, journal articles, textbooks, and other books. Some will be fiction and some nonfiction; some will contain a lot of technical or new information whereas some will be more familiar and less technical. As you assess each task, you need to keep in mind that you must "hurry" on some of the reading, if it's not as difficult as other parts of the as-signment, and "slow down" on some parts. Which to read quickly and which to read slowly is highly individual to you and depends on all the framing strategies you have applied. This "advice" to get moving or to hit the brakes you can give yourself as you read a whole piece or sections of it. For example, if you note that the structure of a book is that the first third of it contains a general overview and that the last two thirds of it repeat that information more succinctly and go into more detail on it, you can give yourself permission to skim the first third and thus leave more time to read the second two-thirds closely and slowly. The same general rule applies to leisure reading. You should not read the newspaper for entertainment at the same rate you read a novel for a literature class. And you should not read a popular self-help book at the same rate that you read a scientific article for your biology paper. Your reading in and out of study time will affect your ability to keep up with your class reading, so keep as a priority a range of read-ing rates to apply when appropriate; such flexibility will help you com-plete assignments more efficiently.

## EVALUATING NONFICTION

Every day, you are required to make a number of evaluations. Friends tell you of the injustices they have suffered and expect you to take their side, but you evaluate their stories and try to determine for yourself which side is more supportable. Advertisers try to sell you a product and you must assess the reliability of their claims. The media bombard you with editorialized news from which you must decipher the facts as objectively as possible before taking a stand. It is equally important to examine and evaluate the nonfiction books and articles you read in college.

### Maintaining a Critical Attitude

Not everything in print is reliable. The argument set forth in one article may be well supported, while an argument in another article on the same subject may lack proper evidence or adequate discussion. Also, an author's bias may interfere with the authenticity or completeness of the information presented. You should remember that all writers are capable of misevaluating information or of presenting it in ways that distort its meaning. To determine whether a particular argument is sound, you must be able to look closely at what the author both says and implies. Then, when you do accept what a writer has to say, your acceptance will be meaningful because it will have come from critically analyzing what you have read. To feel comfortable making judgments about what you read, you need to adopt a critical attitude. You must come to realize that there is nothing sacred about what is printed. Published books and articles may be well written or they may be poorly written. Don't be afraid to pass judgment. Every time you read something, you should be able to assess the performance of the author and to support your evaluation.

Evaluating what you read requires more than a vague sense that something appeals or does not appeal to you. Knowing something is more important than simply "feeling" it. Appeal based only on identification with an experience or agreement with an idea is not valid. You should appraise what you read using the standards normally expected of good writing. Then the "why" that gives your judgment support will be well thought out.

### Using the T.A.P.S. System

The "why" can be determined only after you have figured out for yourself "what" an essay intends to accomplish and "how" it proceeds. Understanding the thesis, the intended audience, the supports, and the conclusion of an essay or book is necessary for crystallizing your opinion. Finding this information and writing it down as you read something should aid you in evaluating it. The following step-by-step T.A.P.S. system offers the structure to help you tap the important material in whatever nonfiction you may read and also gives you the means to express a sound personal opinion. It can also help you to balance your emotional and intellectual responses to what you read.

Before you start to read a piece of nonfiction, take out a clean piece of paper and set it up for a T.A.P.S. evaluation. To do so, simply write the letters T, A, P, and S in the left-hand margin, allowing about a quarter of the page for material to go with each letter.

*Step One: Record the Thesis*

As you read, keep alert for the author's thesis. This information usually occurs in the early part of what you are reading, although it may not be in the introduction. Note that while in your essays you try to state the thesis in one sentence, professional writers sometimes use a thesis made up of several sentences. Still, you should be able to extract the writer's assertion and state it concisely.

*Step Two: Identify the Audience*

After looking at the level of the language and considering the attitudes expressed in the essay, decide what sort of audience the essay was written for. What is the expected age and educational background of the average reader of the piece? Can you conjecture about the values of the average reader? (This question is tricky. Do not assume that an attitude or value expressed in the essay is automatically shared by the reader. After all, the writer may be trying to change the reader's mind.) By identifying and assessing the audience, you can better judge whether the author has succeeded in presenting effective arguments. For example, has the writer used the best possible strategies for influencing the intended audience, or has that audience been unnecessarily offended?

*Step Three: Isolate and Record the Points of Support*

In your own words, describe and enumerate the author's subtheses, the points used to support the major assertion. Ask yourself whether each supporting point directly furthers the thesis. Is each point well enough developed to be clear and convincing?

*Step Four: Record Suggested Insights*

As you read, try to relate the author's ideas to your own experience, both personal and intellectual. The best form for recording these suggested insights is to make a list of questions. Aspects noted in this step may well become the core of essays or classroom discussions on what you have read. Try to record at least ten questions dealing with both form and content.

After you have completed the T.A.P.S. process, ask yourself whether you feel that the essay is a good one. You should be able to find material in your T.A.P.S. that would support your opinion if you were ever asked to defend it.

The T.A.P.S. in Figure 11-2 was written by a student. Look it over carefully to see how the system works.

## WRITING BOOK REVIEWS ON NONFICTION

Although book reviews, or "critical analyses" as some teachers label them, may be any length, they usually contain some of the same basic information:

An attention-getting device to open.

A statement about the problem or thesis presented in the book.

A discussion of the perspective into which the thesis of the book fits, which might include a key passage.

An evaluation of the form and content.

An analysis of the importance of the book in relation to its field or to the coursework you are studying.

One way to get a good idea of what constitutes an effective book review is to read the *New York Times Book Review*. Generally of high quality, the articles in it might present some structures that could be use-

---

**Figure 11-2. Sample of a T.A.P.S. evaluation.**

T.A.P.S. on "Why I Want a Wife" by Judy Syfers

T.   Through implication (discussing women's needs), Syfers defines the typical male view of a wife. By asserting, rather shockingly, that everyone should have a wife (someone who caters to him or her), Syfers is attempting to force husbands to reassess their definitions of wives. Wives are not, as they seem to think, women who exist solely to satisfy their spouse's needs. Syfers offers her thesis in two ways: by the repetition of the line I want a wife who will . . . and by the line My God, who wouldn't want a wife? What she is saying, in effect, is that people should realize that a spouse is a partner, not a slave.

A.   There are two main audiences for the essay: men and women who would assert along with Syfers that marriage is a partnership. A secondary audience is the male who holds to the stereotype of the wife that Syfers is trying to dispel. Since Syfers treats the point of view of the typical wife, another secondary audience is the wife who is just beginning to tire of male expectations, of being a superhuman. Syfers's sarcastic tone shows that she is talking to all these groups, but she is directing her article more at the first two groups than at the others.

P. 1. A wife is designated to perform certain duties so that her husband can be concerned only with earning a living (husband's need for economic independence). The wife often supports the husband while he is in school.

   While this point is interesting, and often true, Syfers forgets that often the favor is reciprocated later when the wife quits work.

2. A wife takes care of her husband's physical needs including food, keeping up the house, and so forth.

   Good point. Many husbands automatically expect this from their wives. The point supports Syfers's argument perfectly.

3. A wife takes care of the details of social life—babysitters, parties at home (plays hostess); still she gives her husband the freedom of having a night out with the boys.

   A weak point. Many husbands and wives both take time off. Syfers is being too sarcastic and one-sided about the matter. What about other details of social life—who decides to go to restaurants and movies, for instance?

ful to you. Try to evaluate what makes a professional book review interesting and well thought out. Then see whether you can incorporate those elements into your own reviews.

When writing book reviews:

Do not use outside sources in your discussion of the concepts in the book.
Do not quote from the book without clearly showing the importance of the quotation.

Sometimes you will want to write a comparison of two books in review form. Reviews of this nature are similar in format to other book reviews. Be sure, however, to select books that have a strong basis for comparison or contrast. Handle a comparison and contrast in the following way:

Give a clear statement of the thesis or hypothesis of each book.
Place each thesis or hypothesis in perspective with other works on the subject.
Devise your own thesis stating the comparison that the rest of your paper will make.

---

**Figure 11-2 (continued).**

4. A wife is sensitive to her husband's sexual needs. This includes the responsibility for birth control, responsiveness, and being understanding about extramarital sexual involvements.

> I'll accept all but the last point. Culturally the woman is supposed to be responsive and even understanding but who says she is supposed to accept whatever the husband does? What are Syfers's sources of this information?

5. A wife assumes the responsibility for children in the event a husband wants a divorce. Laws are changing. Is Syfers correct? If so, she has a good point.

S. 1. Is woman trapped into this stereotype through her own ignorance? Does she want to neglect her own individuality?
2. Is it possible that the role of wife is biologically determined? What about for animals other than humans?
3. Do any women really have wives in the sense Syfers means? Aren't all men and all women sometimes in this role? When a man is the wife, what is the woman?
4. Why do some men believe women don't have sex drives like they do?
5. Does a happy marriage depend upon one mate having less individuality?
6. Does having a role automatically mean that one is trapped and has no real sense of self? Do I have a set role in my relationship with Jim?
7. Even if women are treated equally to their husbands, won't the relationship eventually define new roles for each partner? Will there be any difference?
8. Can an androgynous woman (Jung) really survive in a role-dominated society? Whom would she have to marry?
9. Is it wrong for a woman not to want children—biologically a mutation? Is it wrong for a woman to support a man?
10. Do more men divorce women or vice versa?

If possible, use the alternating pattern (see p. 78) to compare or
contrast the two books.

Conclude with an evaluation of the two books in relation to your
field of study. Is one superior in form or content? Why?

## WRITING RÉSUMÉS

Most professions require that job applicants submit a résumé describing their personal and educational background, employment record, honors received, and extracurricular activities. Even if a job announcement does not ask for one, a well-composed résumé can often enhance your application. Résumés indicate professionalism and, in today's competitive job market, anything that makes an application more attractive is definitely worth the effort.

There are many convenient formats for résumés, but most of them share two qualities: they are brief and they are positive. A résumé should rarely exceed two pages and, except for one written by someone with several decades of employment history, can usually be handled in a single page. Attitude is also important. A positive attitude is best shown by careful selection of words. A résumé should not carry any hint of insecurity about your ability to do the job for which you are applying. Seemingly small matters of word choice, such as using "collaborated with" over "helped," can keep the prospective employer on your side.

Although it would be ideal for both the prospective employee and the employer if a new résumé could be drawn up for each job application, doing so would be impractical. Aware of this, most employers will accept well-reproduced copies. Today, computers can produce a typeset look with a variety of print options. The best way to reproduce your résumé is to have it either photocopied or printed on offset. Because a résumé may have to serve for several similar job applications, be careful to keep the material specific enough to show your background but general enough to submit for different positions.

Still, in certain cases, it is necessary to prepare more than one résumé. Let's say you were applying for two types of jobs, one editing a local publication and the other teaching English at the high school level. It would be important to emphasize your writing skills and background in English for the editing job, but it would be more important to focus on your teaching skills and tutoring experience for the teaching job. Since your résumé is your first chance to convince an employer that you can handle the job you want, it should demonstrate competence in the particular type of employment you are seeking. Always keep in mind that, although employers do not expect you to draw up a special résumé for every job, the applicants with a background closest to what is required by the positions will be the ones interviewed. Therefore, you should prepare a new résumé if you feel that it will better meet the job requirements than would your old résumé.

You should not be afraid to show some originality in your résumé. Do not follow the standard résumé format so doggedly that you put yourself in a bad light. Leave out information that you consider unnecessary and put other material in its place. Try to be flexible. Some career and placement centers suggest innovations such as including a photograph on a particularly short résumé or using brightly colored paper. Most experts in business, however, say that a well-produced, error-free typed résumé on white paper is more impressive. Career counselors at most colleges are willing to look over student résumes to suggest revisions and various techniques for adding spark to the presentation. Do not hesitate to check whether your school offers this service.

Figures 11-3 and 11-4 provide a couple of alternative sample résumés to provide you with guidelines for preparing your own. Which format you use for subtitles depends on your experience and education; you will want to choose the headings that highlight your strengths.

---

**Figure 11.3**

```
                                              1600 Campus Rd. #709
                                              Los Angeles, CA 90041
                                                  (213) 341-4447

OBJECTIVE
Entry level management position.

EDUCATION
Bachelor of Arts in Russian Studies at Occidental College 1990-1995
Yaroslavl' State University (Occidental Abroad Program)
University of California at Berkeley (Summer of 1992)
University of Washington (Summer of 1993)

EXPERIENCE
DIRECTOR OF INTERNATIONAL SALES, Globimex USA, Ltd., New York 1994
Duties: Researched products, compiled information, and prepared proposals for
    prospective buyers in Russia, which culminated in a two-week trip to
    Moscow to broaden clientele base in Russia. August - December 1994.

AMERICAN REPRESENTATIVE, Rose Vetrov, Moscow 1994
Duties: Translated administrative meetings for Moscow based tourist company
    during World Cup 1994.

LEGAL ASSISTANT, Law Offices of John M. Kaman, San Francisco 1990
Duties: Data entry and data management.

EXTRACURRICULAR ACTIVITIES
Lacrosse Team 1991-1993, 1995. President 1993
Member Sigma Alpha Epsilon Fraternity 1991-1995. Internal Vice-President 1993
Cacophony 1993, 1995. Co-President Cacophony 1995
Occidental College Glee Club 1991

PHILANTHROPICAL EVENTS
Tutored underprivileged children in Highland Park
Built housing for a family in Mexico
Participated in La Tunga Canyon clean-up
Cleaned graffiti in South-Central L.A.

SKILLS
Fluent in Russian, most proficient in conversation
Familiar with "WordPerfect" for the IBM, and windows applications for
    Macintosh

REFERENCES
All references will be provided upon request.
```

Keep the following hints in mind while writing your résumé:

Be positive in your choice of words. Use energetic verbs.
Be only as specific as necessary. For a particular position, do not
explain in detail what duties you had in the same capacity for
another employer. For instance, if you were a teacher's aide, you
would not want to list grading papers as part of your job. Instead,
you would want to emphasize the broad range of your skills.
Be informative and brief. A reader should be able to skim your
résumé easily.
Be original enough to show your personality.
Design a readable format: Type style, white space, and headings all
contribute to the overall picture.

---

**Figure 11-4**

```
Campus Address                                    Permanent Address
1600 Campus Road
Los Angeles, CA 90041
(213) 259-2701


EDUCATION    OCCIDENTAL COLLEGE, Los Angeles, California.
             Major in Political Science with minor in Economics, knowledge of
                computer usage. B.A. expected June 1987. GPA 3.2/4.0 in major.

EXPERIENCE   CREW SUPERVISOR, Nevada Power Company, Las Vegas, Nevada; Summer
             1984-86.
             • Supervised nine full-time student workers.
             • Reduced average time spent on a job by 20%

             STUDENT SPEAKER: Articulated liberal arts program to educators,
             parents and students; 1985-86.

             HEAD INTERN, Pasadena Neighborhood Housing Service, Pasadena,
             California; academic year 1985-86.
             • Coordinated a Resident Attitude Survey of 5,000 households,
               targeting community needs.
             • Compiled and analyzed data.
             • Presented a subsequent report on data to the Board of Directors.

             PEER COUNSELOR, Upward Bound Program, University of Nevada, Las
             Vegas; Summer 1985.
             • Planned and supervised youth activities for 50 high school
               students.

             CREW CHIEF, McDonald's Restaurant, Las Vegas, Nevada; Summer
             1981-84.
             • Cited by management for outstanding sales and efficiency.
             • Interacted effectively with 35-40 subordinates and shift
               supervisors.

ACTIVITIES   Coordinated fundraisers for various organizations at Occidental
                College, 1984-87.
             Volunteer Scout Leader at local elementary school, 1984-86.
             Active in dorm council activities.
             Four years on the Varsity Basketball Team, 1983-87;
             TEAM CAPTAIN for 1986-87 season.

AWARDS       Awarded Distinction on Political Science Comprehensive Exams.
             Occidental College Scholarship.
             All-League Varsity Basketball honors, 1984-85.
```

## WRITING ANNOTATED BIBLIOGRAPHIES

While doing research, you may have discovered the usefulness of annotated bibliographies, which are simply final bibliographies that include summaries of the information contained in each source and evaluations of that information. The annotations, which are generally written
in block form, may contain standard abbreviations and incomplete sentences, as long as the point gets across to the reader. Key quotations are
also often included. When writing annotations, try to be as concise and
informative as possible. The bibliography entries themselves follow the
standard guidelines for bibliographies for the particular discipline.

Some teachers may ask you to include an annotated bibliography at
the end of a research paper in place of the regular bibliography. Others
may request that you prepare an annotated bibliography on a certain
subject without actually writing a paper. In either case, you may use
the format of the sample annotated bibliography entry that follows:

Wender, Paul H. (1987). *The Hyperactive Child, Adolescent, and
Adult.* New York: Oxford University Press.
Wender examines from a pro-pharmacological perspective the
symptoms, treatment, and socialization of both attention-deficit
disorder and that disorder complicated by hyperactivity. He es-
tablishes that the disorders are not adequately treated by counseling and require medical intervention and supervision. Part of
what Wender tries to do is to tear down the myth that attention-
deficit is a response to a lack of stability in the home. He sees
this not as causation but as a complication of the already existing chemical imbalance in the child or adult, going so far as to
say that the instability in the home is often the result rather than
the cause of the disorder. Wender analyzes the various drug treatments, giving the advantages and disadvantages of each. He suggests social conditioning at home, with parents being "firm," "consistent," and "explicit." Immediate rewards and punishment are
recommended; punishments are to be handled without negative
reinforcement, which, though effective in extinguishing the
specific behavior, leads to neurotic behaviors that magnify the
problem. The text is eminently readable by the educated adult
and is useful for parents who suspect that they or their loved ones
suffer from the disorder.

Annotations should give a quick synopsis and a reference to the audience for whom the work is most effective.

Sources should be numbered and the text of your synopsis should
begin a new line after the bibliography entry.

The heading on the paper is standard for your discipline and class.
Simply title the document "Annotated Bibliography."

You should use these guidelines for any annotations and the bibliography format for the field you are writing in (sciences, social sciences,
or humanities) unless your teacher prefers that you use an alternate form.

## WRITING SCIENTIFIC REPORTS

Much of the writing done for science classes is in the form of scientific reports. In these reports, which mainly convey data, clarity and good organization are especially important. Most authorities agree that scientific papers should deliver their data as plainly as possible, avoiding flamboyant style or poetic words. Still, the value of good and varied sentences should not be underestimated. After all, anything you write, regardless of its subject, should be readable. Scientific writing should not be made up of boring, one-idea, one-clause sentences, nor should it be a jumble of excessively complicated sentences. As in all your writing, you should use active verbs whenever possible in scientific essays. Give your writing punch, but avoid fussy touches.

Two types of scientific reports are most often assigned. Research reports are in-depth discussions of a term project. They usually run ten to twenty pages. Laboratory reports, which are considerably shorter, are detailed discussions of an experiment. They normally run four to ten pages.

### Research Reports

Research reports should be carefully planned because they are usually long and complex. Most writers of scientific research papers use a four-part structure with the following subtitles:

Introduction
Methods and Results
Discussion
Literature Cited

#### Introduction

In the introduction to your report, you should specify the scientific problem you are investigating and give a brief summary of any current related research. The simplest method to use in arranging this survey is to place the related research in chronological order. You may, however, wish to develop a different arrangement based on the ideas, procedures, or results shown in the literature or on some other logical principle. Next, state the method you used for your investigation and present the principal findings—all in summary. Since this statement serves as the thesis of your paper, it should not be put off too far into the text. In addition, be sure to define any specialized language you may have used so that classmates on your level will be sure to understand what you write.

#### Methods and Results

Some instructors may want you to have a "Methods" section followed by a separate "Results" section, but others will prefer that you combine the two into one section. Whichever format you use (you will probably want to check this out with your instructor), you should generally present the methods or procedures you used to solve your scientific problem before you present the results. The methods should be explained so clearly and so thoroughly that another individual could repeat them almost exactly. You should start by describing all of the materials you used, being sure to include any important technical specifications. Then outline the procedures you followed, step by step.

Your results, which are the most important data offered in your report, should be clearly, but briefly, stated. You do not want to interrupt your results by giving any analysis of them here. The next section is for that.

### *Discussion*

The "Discussion" is where you tell what your results mean. You do not want to repeat your results in this section. Here you want to discuss, interpret, and analyze what you have discovered. You should give the implications of your findings and show how your work agrees or disagrees with previous studies in the field. You will also want to assess any inconsistencies or unresolved matters and indicate what directions future research might take. Suggestions for future work might include the ideas you would explore if you had more time. Keep in mind that information suggesting specific directions open to future research might inspire those who read your report to carry on the study or to investigate related problems. You should therefore present the ideas logically, making sure that you have evidence to back up the suggestions.

### *Literature Cited*

The last section is where you cite the published sources you used in solving your scientific problem. Most instructors, and also journals that publish scientific reports, prefer that you list only your primary sources. In addition, many fields, particularly those in the sciences, use specialized formats for footnotes and bibliographic entries. You should find out the forms most appropriate for your report.

### **Laboratory Experiment Reports**

Many introductory science classes require reports on experiments. These reports usually follow the format of a report from a respected journal in the particular field of science you are studying. In writing experiment reports, as in writing many types of papers, it is important to realize that your audience is not made up of specialists. That is, assume that they are hearing this information for the first time. You should conceive of your readers as your fellow science students. The typical experiment report follows a straightforward, seven-part format.

### *Abstract*

The abstract is a concise summary of your experiment. You should try to keep it brief, no more than 250 words.

### *Title*

The title of your report should be brief and informative.

### Introduction

The introduction should include a summary of the historical development of the method you used in the experiment, a general description of the current method, possible comparisons with other models, and any limitations or advantages of the method you used.

### Theory

The theory should be a few pages of discussion of the concepts that stand behind the methods and goal of your experiment. Included should be specific information about the chemistry and physics or other field of study relating to the particular experiment.

### Experimental Techniques and Apparatus

The techniques section, also known as the methods section, is a detailed description of the process and the apparatuses used in the experiment. Be sure to give specific details, including the specific settings used to obtain your data.

### Results and Discussion

The results section is a detailed discussion of what you found, how precise the results were, and any problems you encountered. Criticism of your method should be included. All calculated data should be presented, along with any important graphs or plots.

### References

At the end of the report, references should be listed alphabetically by the last name of the author. It is usual to include only the sources cited in the report.

Keep in mind that directness is important to communication in technical writing. You should use a simple style, free of complicated terminology and fancy sentence structure. You may wish to ask your instructor to show you an example of a good report written by a former student.

## WRITING SOCIAL SCIENCE REPORTS AND THEORETICAL PAPERS

In psychology and other classes in the social sciences, you will be called on to do either reports or papers that incorporate research, original thinking about theories, and sometimes field work. The format used in the humanities, MLA (see Chapter 10), generally cannot be used for these essays because dates are important; the date of the studies in your secondary research can be crucial to the understanding of and the accuracy of the text of your paper. Therefore, unlike scholars in the humanities, social science writers employ a name-date format inserted in parentheses in the text of the paper. Page numbers are given for quotations only. Social science papers commonly also require abstracts, 100-

150-word summaries of the paper. In Figure 11-5, you will find sample pages from a psychology field work/ research paper on Attention Deficit Hyperactivity Disorder. The student, Jeff, volunteered in a clinic and combined his experience with his background research on the origins and symptoms of the disorder. As you skim the pages provided, note the citation form, the placement of parenthetical documentation, the location of punctuation in citations and bibliography entries, and the heading on the bibliography.

---

**Figure 11-5. Psychology research paper**

Casey
1

Field Work at Pacific Clinics, Pasadena
Attention-Deficit Hyperactivity Disorder
and Oppositional Defiant Disorder
Applied to Two Case Studies
Jeff Casey

Professor Schell
Field Work
June 9, 1993

Running head: Pacific Clinics

Prevalence of Attention-Deficit Hyperactivity Disorder accounts for about 3% of the general population (APA, 1987). Males are anywhere from two to ten times more likely to be diagnosed with ADHD, with epidemiological studies reporting a 3:1 ratio of males to females (Mash & Barkley, 1989). Anderson (1987) reports that 6.7% of boys have ADHD.

It is widely agreed upon that ADHD has a multiple etiology (Campbell, 1986). Genetic factors, brain damage, neurotransmitter disfunctions and imbalances, decreased central brain functioning, central nervous system failure, environmental factors such as disfunctional family structures, and unhealthy prenatal diet have all been correlated with disorder (Weiss, 1986). Marshall (1989) has suggested the possibility of a biological explanation of an allergic reaction to food dyes. Psychosocial studies of parental style report that the parents of hyperactive children are more punitive than normal, but it is difficult to tell if the parent is reacting to the child or the child to the parent, an interaction between the two being likely (Weiss, 1986). Barkley (1985) suggests that the parents' negativity may be in reaction to the child's behavior. The topic is open

## WRITING BUSINESS LETTERS

Many occasions call for writing business letters—applying for jobs, appealing to your congressperson to change an unjust law, bringing consumer complaints to the attention of companies, asking for information from agencies. Technically, any letter addressed to people you do not know is a business letter. When composing a business letter, you should be as direct as possible and follow a standard form. At the same time,

---

**Figure 11-5 (continued).**

for debate on a conceptual level, but in reality each family system must be individually assessed in its own right. As for a general etiology, Carson (1992) reports that there is "no compelling evidence for a biological basis" (539), nor is there strong support for a specific psychosocial cause. However, other research does point to a biological predisposition with severity determined by environmental factors (Mash, 1989).

The available treatment of children with ADHD includes both psychotherapeutic and psychopharmacological therapies. Cognitive behavioral therapy (CBT) and strict behavioral therapy (BT) are widely used. In CBT, the main components focus on self-instruction and self-reinforcement; while in BT, the use of time constraints and contingency programs are central. BT is the method of choice since it uses less time and labor than CBT with similar results (Bloomquist, 1991).

**References**

American Psychiatric Association. (1987). *Diagnostic and Statistical Manual of Mental Disorders (3rd ed. rev.)*. Washington, DC: Author.

Anderson, J. C., Williams, S., McGee, R., & Silva, P. A. (1987). DSM III Disorders in Preadolescent Children. *Archives of General Psychiatry, 44*, 69-80.

Barkley, R. A. (1985). The Social Interactions of Hyperactive Children: Developmental Changes, Drug Effects, and Situational Variation. In R. McMahon & R. Peters (Eds.), *Childhood Disorders: Behavioral-Developmental Approaches*. New York: Brunner/Mazel.

Bloomquist, M. L., & Lillienfeld, S. O. (1991). Diagnostic Efficiency of Symptoms for Oppositional Defiant Disorder and Attention-Deficit Hyperac-

**Figure 11-5 (continued).**

tivity Disorder. *Journal of Consulting and Clinical Psychology, 59,*

    732-738.

Carson, R. C., & Butcher, J. N. (Eds.). (1992). *Abnormal Psychology and*

    *Modern Life, Ninth Edition.* New York: HarperCollins.

Marshall, P. (1989). Attention Deficit Disorder and Allergy: A Neurochemical

    Model of the Relation Between the Illnesses. *Psychological Bulletin,*

    *106,* 613-616.

Mash, E. J., & Barkley, R. A. (Eds.). (1989). *Treatment of Childhood*

    *Disorders.* New York: Guilford Press.

Weiss, G., & Hechtman, L. T. (1986). *Hyperactive Children Grown-Up:*

    *Empirical Findings and Theoretical Considerations.* New York: Guilford

    Press.

you should try to inject your personality into your writing. Also, you should try to avoid outdated phrases like "enclosed please find" and "see attached." Figure 11-6 presents an annotated sample business letter. The annotations indicate the correct forms, but notice that they can be varied to suit the purpose of the particular letter you are writing.

When writing a business letter, always use 8 1/2-inch × 11-inch paper, preferably good bond. Center the letter on the page. Set the typewriter or computer on single spacing with 1 1/2-inch margins. Type on only one side of the sheet. Here is the usual format for typing a business letter.

### Step One

Type your return address, single-spaced, at the upper left margin. Type the date on the next line. If you are using a printed letterhead, space down a few lines from the printing and put only the date at the left margin. You should not abbreviate.

### Step Two

Insert at least two lines of space and then type the name of the person to whom you are writing, his or her title, and the address at the left-hand margin. This part of the letter is called the inside address.

### Step Three

Insert one line of space and type the greeting followed by a colon. The person's title should be included. For example, you might write "Dear Ms. Johnson," "Dear Mr. Simpson," or "Dear Dr. Wing." For the special abbreviations of clergy and high officials, check your desk dictionary. When writing to a special group or company of people you may write "Dear Sirs" or "To Whom It May Concern," the second choice to avoid sexist implications. Or you may choose to leave out the greeting and skip to the next step.

### Step Four

Now you are ready to write the body of the letter. Space down two lines from the greeting and begin the first paragraph at the left-hand margin. Continue to block (line up at the left margin) all new paragraphs. Leave a line of space between paragraphs for easy identification.

An alternate form for the body, used infrequently, is to indent each new paragraph five spaces and single-space the entire body of the letter without spacing between paragraphs.

Notice the structure of the letter of application in Figure 11-6.

---

**Figure 11-6. Example of a business letter.**

```
343 Mill Dale Lane ————— Return address
Meadowbrook, CA 91325
February 13, 1989 ————— Date


Arthur Weinar
Personnel Director
Bay Area Regional Planning Commission ————— Inside address
P.O. Box 702
San Francisco, CA 94501

              ————————— Double space

Dear Mr. Weinar:

              ————————— Double space

   I am writing in response to your Los Angeles Times advertisement for an
Assistant to the Transportation Planner.

   With my double major in urban studies and economics, I am able to
approach urban planning from both perspectives. As for practical experi-
ence, I can offer my two summers during my sophomore and junior years when
I worked as an assistant to James Soverign, a planner for an urban renewal
project in the Denver area. My primary interest is in urban reconstruction,
and I believe I can bring some innovative ideas to your projects.

   The transportation needs of urban centers have been aggravated by
financial cutbacks. Despite these setbacks, I continue to be impressed with
the programs implemented through your department. It would please me to be
able to work with you.

   Enclosed is a résumé. After you have had a chance to evaluate my
background, I hope you will contact me so that we may arrange a personal
interview.

              ————————— Double space

Sincerely yours, ————— Closing

              ————————— Double space

Richard B. Albany ————— Writer's typewritten name


encl.: résumé ————— Indication of enclosure
```

Paragraph one indicates the purpose of the letter.
Paragraph two quickly reinforces the résumé by pointing out important background.
Paragraph three discusses why the applicant wants the job.
Paragraph four encourages the employer to contact the applicant. The letter ends on a positive note, setting out the next action the writer would like the reader to take.

### Step Five

Double-space from the last line of the body and type a closing followed by a comma. Here are a few examples.

Yours truly,                          Very truly yours,
Sincerely,                            Sincerely yours,

Considering the formality of the letter, pick the closing that feels the most natural and conveys your attitude.

### Step Six

Space four lines down and type your name. It is usual to include your middle initial. If you have a title, type it a single space below your name.

### Step Seven

If you have mentioned individuals' names and you want to call their attention to that fact, you will want to send them a copy of the letter. To record that you have sent out copies, write at the bottom left of the letter the names of the people you have sent them to. For example:

Sincerely yours,

John C. Smith
cc: Mr. Tony Grant
Ms. Linda Maruyama

### Step Eight

Sign the letter in the space above your name.

### Step Nine

Note any enclosures or attachments to your letter, as shown in Figure 11-6. Don't forget to put them in the letter before you mail it!

### Step Ten

Prepare the envelope as shown in Figure 11-7. For both the inside and outside addresses, use proper U.S. Postal Service abbreviations. A list of the standard abbreviations for states can be obtained from the post office in your community. These abbreviations are always two capital letters followed by no punctuation, two spaces, and then the zip code.

## KEEPING A JOURNAL OF READINGS OR A FIELD NOTEBOOK

Journals can be used in every sort of class for many purposes. In an English class, you might wish to keep a journal as you read a novel. One evening, your journal entry might deal with what you believe to be the major theme of the book thus far, even though by the time you read fifty pages more you may have changed your mind. You could then note in a second entry that your first perception of the theme of the novel was only a partial understanding of the theme found in later pages. Such reflections on former entries are what make good journals. Keeping a journal as you read can help to improve your interaction with books, a necessary step in becoming a good reader. Instead of letting your thoughts escape you, record your impressions. Later, take the time to observe the changes in your thoughts. You will probably find that this process will give you valuable insights concerning both the book and yourself.

Many science classes include lab work for which a field notebook is essential. In an archaeology class, your discovery of a fragment of pottery one day could lead to the discovery of the rest of the pot the next, and your original insights about the origin of the fragment can strongly influence your later conclusion about the date and purpose of the pot. Your field notes in geology class will reflect your growing awareness of

**Figure 11-7**

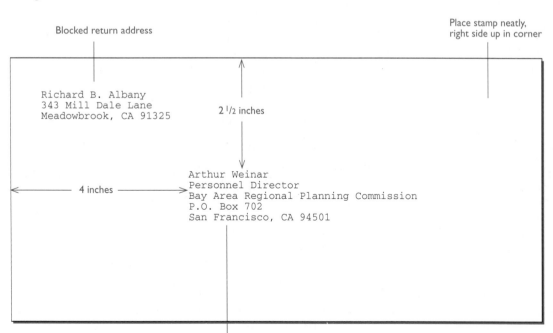

Blocked return address

Place stamp neatly, right side up in corner

Richard B. Albany
343 Mill Dale Lane
Meadowbrook, CA 91325

2 1/2 inches

4 inches

Arthur Weinar
Personnel Director
Bay Area Regional Planning Commission
P.O. Box 702
San Francisco, CA 94501

Blocked mailing address
(same as inside address on letter)

rock and soil excavations and help you to draw conclusions about your project. In fact what you record, including how accurately you draw the diagrams of your findings, will later influence how accurately you think about what you have found; your findings, as reflected in the field notebook, are as important to your intellectual development as the specimen itself.

Both personal and intellectual satisfaction can be derived from journal writing while you study a certain subject or unit in class. Most journals allow you to evaluate and explore ideas in a loose format. You might even want to examine subjects you do not like in order to try to understand why. Journals offer good preparation for class discussions, in-class essays, and papers. The medium is equally valuable for the shy person, who wants to "try out" ideas before taking the chance of presenting them in class, and the more extroverted student, who simply hasn't had enough time to explore all the good ideas thought of during a regular class period. Journals are good, too, for recording those ideas that occur at odd hours, when you haven't the heart to wake up your roommate to join you in a meaty discussion. In fact, many a student has been known to sneak around a dark room in search of a pen and a flashlight in order to make a journal entry.

## THE PERSONAL STATEMENT

If you are applying to a graduate school or to a medical or veterinary science school or for a fellowship, you will need to write a statement about your interest in the field of study. In many cases, since personal interviews may not be extended for a desired program or school, the personal statement serves as your only chance to convince an admission or selection committee that your application deserves special consideration. It is the one chance you will have to show who you are as a person, not as just the collection of statistics about G.P.A. and honors received but as a whole human being with interests and abilities that show you to be among the most desired applicants. In your personal statement you should always tell the truth and should always convey a positive attitude, without being flamboyant or insincere in your tone. You want to give the committee reviewing your statement a chance to know you.

Some preliminary questions you might ask yourself in writing the personal statement include (we will use a medical school applicant's statement as an example) the following:

1. Why do you want to go to medical school?
2. Who has been an important influence in your life?
3. What are your values?
4. What would you like said of you at your death?
5. Describe what your professional and personal situation might be in ten years. In twenty?
6. What has been important to you about your research and volunteering experience?

7. Can you cite specific incidents that were turning points in your career planning or your perception of medicine?
8. Who is a role model for you? Why?
9. What do you do to relax?
10. If there are any "unusual" circumstances concerning your academic progress (say you had a really bad year because of family problems and having to take on an extra job), try to explain the situation and its impact on you.

Answering such questions can set you in the right direction on compiling information for your statement. Sometimes a limit on number of pages is prescribed and sometimes not (for medicine it is one page). In either case, you will need to explore your ideas fully before considering the product that you will actually print or type onto your application form. This process usually takes several drafts and much cutting and refocusing. Give yourself a matter of months for the whole process, if possible.

After answering the kinds of questions above, you will have a wealth of information to write about—do it, paying no attention to length. Then read what you have and condense, condense, condense. Your final draft will produce a picture of you that you will be pleased to share with an admission committee, one that says, "I have given this a great deal of thought and take this matter very seriously."

The personal statement in Figure 11-8 can serve as a model, but it is by no means the only way to go about writing a statement. Some statements are chronological, others ordered by concept. Read over Jean's statement and study the annotations which accompany it; you will be able to identify the strengths.

---

**Figure 11-8**

Personal Statement

    Witnessing death, suicide, and rape during my boat escape out of Vietnam left a precociousness that has endured throughout my life.

    At five years old, I knew my division and times tables and even worked as a vendor, selling my mother's mung-bean cakes at the local bazaar in our refugee camp. After a year in the United States, the media proclaimed me as the nation's youngest published writer at eight years of age. At sixteen, graduating with honors, I was the first in my family to go to college. While my friends were on dates and at dances, maturity and responsibility kept me

Jean starts out the essay with a dramatic and sincere account of her journey to the United States.

**Figure 11-8 (continued).**

at my mother's nail station doing manicures and pedicures all throughout my teenage and college years. At times, I resented my precociousness and envied other people's carefree childhoods. But the memories of my terrifying escape from communism quickly replaced the resentment, driving me to work hard and to make the most out of life.

Due to necessity, I began working at an early age. Dubbed by my family as a "Jack of all trades," I have done everything from being a well-known freelance writer to a minimum-wage switchboard operator answering two hundred phone lines to a "perspiring" actress, who recently appeared in an MCI commercial. As a former refugee, I volunteer to help ease the hardships of Vietnamese asylum seekers still living in detention camps. Advocating for their human rights, I have represented both the Los Angeles and the San Diego Vietnamese communities on a national delegation to Washington, D. C. In addition, directing the 1996 Vietnamese culture show for the Vietnamese Club at UCLA also enables me to develop my leadership abilities as I help promote cultural awareness and unity within the community.

I believe my personal qualities and my biology major prepare me well for Public Health studies, after which I hope to help other striving immigrants. Thank you for your consideration.

Jean has incorporated an explanation of what her experience means to her, not just given the concrete experience.

Jean ends with a polite gesture, generally looked upon favorably by readers of hundreds of such statements.

**THE HANDBOOK**

As you work on your own writing assignments, you will become increasingly aware that some things just do not sound right; certainly, too, there will be times when your instructor marks something on your paper as an error in usage or grammar. You might be surprised to know that you do not need sophisticated knowledge to write correctly. Actually, you probably need only some brushing up on a few important terms and principles with which you are already generally familiar.

# A REVIEW OF GRAMMAR AND SPELLING

## THE PARTS OF SPEECH

Every word in every sentence is a part of speech. However, the same word does not always function as the same part of speech. For example, the word *piece* can serve as a noun, a verb, or an adjective. In one context the word may function as a different part of speech than it will in another context:

The piece of tape stuck to the envelope. (noun)
They can piece a puzzle together in one afternoon. (verb)
Factory workers at the turn of the century were paid a piece rate.
    (adjective)

You must not assume that because a word is used as a noun, it cannot also be used as a verb. For instance, the word *silence* is usually thought of as a noun, but in the sentence "The police silenced the crowd" it is used as a verb. To analyze the part of speech of words you find in a particular sentence, you must be able to identify each of the eight parts of speech. Then you can determine the function of each word in the sentence.

### Nouns

Nouns name persons, places, things, or ideas. They do a variety of things in sentences. Most nouns have different forms to show whether they are singular or plural:

| | |
|---|---|
| relationship | relationships |
| ethnicity | ethnicities |
| Martinez | Martinezes |

Others, however, have the same form whether they are singular or plural:

series                    sheep                    species

Nouns can also be made possessive:

the boy's shirt                    the foxes' den
a culture's paradigms              an hour's work

Nouns are often preceded by the words (articles) *a, an,* and *the.* Be careful, however, not to be thrown off track by an intervening word:

a wicker chair                    an inexpensive suit
the Smiths' address

**Pronouns**

Another kind of word that sometimes functions in the same ways as a noun is the pronoun. Pronouns can stand for nouns. They help writers to avoid producing sentences full of repetition.

> *Weak:* Rasta gave Rasta's brother a resentful look when Rasta's brother told Rasta to keep quiet.
> *Effective:* Rasta gave her brother a resentful look when he told her to keep quiet.

The second version is a lot smoother.

Not all pronouns take the place of nouns. In the following sentences, the pronouns are not substitutes for nouns:

> Tomorrow is the third Monday of this month.
> Anything John does is okay with Mary.

*This,* in the first sentence, is a demonstrative pronoun. *Anything,* in the second sentence, is an indefinite pronoun.

The best way to become familiar with pronouns and their uses is to notice them in what you read and write. Following are descriptions of the main types of pronouns. For more information about the distinctive features of pronouns, turn to page 448.

*Personal Pronoun*

Personal pronouns usually take the place of nouns:

I                    you                    he, she, it, we
they, me             her, him, us          them

> The state's population is dissatisfied—*we* want a more responsive governor.
> Margaret was always pointing out conflicts; it's no surprise that the last item on the agenda upset *her.*

*Relative Pronouns*

Relative pronouns link subordinate clauses (p. 376) to other parts
of a sentence:

who(m), which, that, whoever, whose

The sociologist *who* for a year in 1994 lived in the streets with
homeless women will discuss his study on Friday in Alumni Hall.

(Note that *where* is not a relative pronoun.)

*Interrogative Pronouns*

Interrogative pronouns begin direct and indirect questions (p. 520):

who, what, which, whom, whose

*Who* will be able to attend the baseball game?

*Demonstrative Pronouns*

Demonstrative pronouns point out what they refer to:

this
any, these
every, that, those, such

*These* volunteers have donated over one hundred hours to the
Heart Fund.

*Indefinite Pronouns*

Indefinite pronouns represent undefined or loosely defined numbers
of things:

| | | | |
|---|---|---|---|
| few | both | neither | several |
| each | all | other | anyone |
| another | none | anybody | most |
| such | somebody | many | some |

*None* of us could attend the lecture, so it was canceled.

*Reflexive Pronouns*

Intensive pronouns and reflexive pronouns refer to or stress the doer
of the action in a sentence:

| | | | |
|---|---|---|---|
| myself | ourselves | yourself | yourselves |
| himself | themselves | herself | |

## Verbs

Verbs are words that indicate actions or states of being. Those that
indicate actions are called action verbs; those that indicate states of be-

ing are called linking verbs. The term verb is used both for the particular part of speech and for its sentence part (also known as the simple predicate). But not every verb can be spotted easily. Remember that a word that looks like a noun can function as a verb. Some examples are *handcuff, sleep, dress,* and *snow.* All verbs have certain qualities, however, that make them stand apart from nouns. There are four characteristics of verbs you should know about.

### Types of Verbs

There are two types of verbs: transitive and intransitive (noted as v.t. and v.i. in most dictionaries). These labels can help you to understand how to use a new word that happens to be a verb. An intransitive verb acts without needing any person or thing to act upon. A transitive verb, on the other hand, must act on something or someone in order to make sense. The verb *go,* for example, is intransitive, but *convey* is transitive:

> We go to museums whenever we can.
> We conveyed our warmest wishes to Mary's mother.

You do not *go* something. You do *convey* something. It would make little sense to say or write *I convey.* The thought is not complete. Some verbs are transitive in one context and intransitive in another. An example is the word *run.* You can run things, such as vacuum cleaners or businesses. In either case the verb would be transitive. But what about the sentence "I run every day"? Nothing is being run, and the verb is thus intransitive.

Verbs that indicate states of being (linking verbs) are always intransitive. Most people choose to memorize the list of common linking verbs rather than try to recognize them by their function in sentences. The following list covers most that you will need to know:

| | | | |
|---|---|---|---|
| to be | to seem | to become | to appear |
| to look | to act | to sound | to remain |
| to feel | to taste | to smell | |

### Tense and Number

Tense indicates time. Number indicates whether the verb is singular or plural. The past and present are the two most basic tenses. The present tense is used to refer to things that happen now. The past is used to refer to things that happened before. But by no means is a writer restricted to these two forms. Helping verbs (such as *has, have, may, might, will, would, must, ought to, does, do,* and *be*) blend with these simple tenses to make verb phrases that can express many more time sequences than could be expressed by the past and present tenses alone.

All verbs have principal parts (you can find the principal parts of a verb immediately after each entry word in your dictionary). Once you can find the principal parts of a verb, you can conjugate the verb—

that is, name all its forms in all tenses in both singular and plural. The principal parts are the first person singular in the present tense, the first person singular in the past tense, and the past participle (the form used with *is, have,* or *has*). The principal parts for the verb *talk* are *talk, talked, talked.* All writers use a variety of tenses. Here are the tenses most commonly used and some examples:

| | |
|---:|:---|
| *Present:* | I give money to charities. |
| *Present Progressive:* | I am giving money to charities. |
| *Present Perfect:* | I have given money to charities. |
| *Past:* | I gave money to charities. |
| *Past Progressive:* | I was giving money to charities. |
| *Past Perfect:* | I had given money to charities. |
| *Future:* | I will give money to charities. |
| *Future Progressive:* | I will be giving money to charities. |
| *Future Perfect:* | I will have given money to charities by then. |

### Voice

Verbs may be either active or passive. In the active voice, the doer of the action usually comes first:

Julius ran the mile.

In passive constructions, the doer of the action either is not stated or is in a phrase beginning with *by,* and the verb includes a form of *to be* with the past participle of the verb:

The mile was run by Julius.

In the passive voice, the thing done is emphasized over the doer (see p. 181).

### Mood

Verbs, in some instances, change their forms to show mood. The most common usages of mood convey the nature of an expression.

The indicative mood is used to make a statement:

Last Friday's earthquake measured 4.2 on the Richter Scale.

The interrogative mood is used to ask a question:

Why are women less frequently called on in class than men?

The imperative mood is used to give a command. The understood subject of *do* and *kiss* in the following sentences is *you*:

Do your homework.
Kiss me, you fool.

The subjunctive mood is used to convey a condition that is contrary to fact or a suggestion or request introduced by a clause beginning with *that:*

> If I were angry with you, I would not be so affectionate.
> Our neighbors asked that we be considerate of them and not let our dog dig up their flowers.

The various rules for the use of subjunctives can be found on pages 437–439.

### Adjectives

Adjectives modify nouns or pronouns, adding meaning to them, limiting or specifying something about them. They tell which, what kind, or how many. The articles *a*, *an*, and *the* are special adjectives. The possessive pronouns (*my, your, his, her, its, our, their*) are adjectives in many sentences. The possessive forms of nouns are often adjectives; for example, in the sentence "The president's speech raised the consciousness of even the greatest cynic," the word *president's* acts as an adjective; *greatest* is also an adjective.

Adjectives frequently come before their nouns but may also follow the words they modify:

> The *supermarket* checker, *unable* to deviate from *store* policy, could not comply with *my* request for a *single bottled* drink from the *six* pack.
> A mule is sometimes *reluctant* to move along the trail, and a person could be *stuck* for *an* hour in a *single* spot.

### Adverbs

Adverbs modify verbs, adjectives, or other adverbs. They tell how, when, to what extent, or where:

> They did *well* on their exam.

Here the adverb *well* modifies the verb *did*. (How did they do?)

> Mr. Logan is the *most* sincere person I have *ever* known.

The adverb *most* modifies the adjective *sincere*. (How sincere?) The adverb *ever* modifies the verb *have known*. (When have you known?)

> Even though English was not her native language, she was learning to speak it *very* well.

The adverb *very* modifies the adverb *well*. (To what extent?) *Well* is an adverb because it modifies the verb *was learning*. (How was she learning?) It is a good idea to memorize that *not*, *too*, and *very* are always adverbs. You can see that they answer the question "To what extent?"

Many adverbs end in *ly*:

hungrily, hopefully, hatefully

But don't assume a word is an adverb solely by the ending: a friendly ghost (*friendly* is an adjective).

### Prepositions

Alone, many prepositions are hard to describe. For instance, if some-one were to ask you what *for* means, you would probably have a hard time answering. In general, prepositions are structure words that tie parts of sentences together. But they also contribute meaning to sentences. Think of how *before*, *after*, *under*, and *over* have different mean-ings from each other and how often you use them to clarify what you are saying. Quite often, prepositions show direction. However you choose to define prepositions, they are easy to spot. Read over the fol-lowing list and try to develop a "feel" for picking them out. There is no need to attempt to memorize the list because, first of all, not all prepositions are included here. Second, this page will be handy when-ever you wish to check a particular word.

| | | |
|---|---|---|
| above | but (meaning | outside |
| across | except) | over |
| after | contrary to | owing to |
| ahead of | down | past |
| along | due to | rather than |
| among | during | save (meaning |
| apart from | except | except) |
| around | for | since |
| as well as | for the sake of | through |
| aside from | from | to |
| at | in | together with |
| because of | in terms of | toward |
| before | inside | under |
| behind | into | underneath |
| below | like (meaning | until |
| beside | similar to) | up |
| besides | near | up at |
| between | of | with |
| beyond | off | with regard to |
| by | on | within |
| by means of | out of | without |

Prepositions introduce prepositional phrases. The phrases are made up of the preposition and usually the closest noun or pronoun to the right of it along with all the noun's or pronoun's modifiers. In two in-stances, though, finding the whole phrase can be a bit tricky. Not a noun but a nounlike element may end the phrase, as in *of what I mean* or *for his smiling.* The second case is situations in which the word *and* or *or* is used between two or more nouns or pronouns: *inside the Senate and the House.* Keep on the lookout for *and* and *or* so that you will remember to identify the whole prepositional phrase.

You can be sure that any word on the list is a preposition in a particular sentence only if it has an object—the label given to the noun, pronoun, or nounlike element that ends or completes the prepositional phrase. In the following sentences, the words in italics are not prepositions:

> The party was *over.* (*Over* is an adjective here.)
> They searched the house *inside* and *outside.* (*Inside* and *outside* are adverbs here.)
> Thomas shut *off* the engine. (*Off* is part of the verb *shut off.*)

In the following prepositional phrases, the objects are italicized:

> under the *auspices*
> without *sympathy*
> as well as *swimming* and *tennis*
> beyond *what had been expected*

One last point about prepositions is that they sometimes come at the ends of sentences. There they may seem to have no object when in fact the object is earlier in the sentence, if only you will take a minute to think through the meaning of the sentence. In such sentences splitting the preposition from the object sounds more natural than keeping the preposition and object together. For example, read aloud the following sentences:

> What is it for?
> For what is it?

The first sentence sounds smoother than the second. You can see that the object of the preposition in the first sentence is still *what,* just as it is in the second sentence. The actual prepositional phrase is *for what.*

### Conjunctions

Like prepositions, conjunctions join words or groups of words to express a relationship between them. Some of the same words, in fact—*but, for, after, before,* and *until*—are prepositions in certain sentences and conjunctions in others. Whether a particular word is one or the other depends on just which words it joins. Conjunctions are mere joiners of words and groups of words; they never take objects and they do not come at the ends of sentences. Of course, prepositions always have objects. This distinction is clear-cut:

> CONJ
> I am hungry, *but* I can wait until lunchtime, I am sure.

I ate everything in the refrigerator *but* the last *piece* of American cheese.

There are two kinds of conjunctions: coordinating and subordinating. Coordinating conjunctions connect sentence parts that are grammatically equal. The following list includes all the coordinating conjunctions:

| | | | |
|---|---|---|---|
| and | for | but | yet |
| nor | so | or | |

Correlative conjunctions that come in pairs are also coordinating:

| | |
|---|---|
| either . . . or | both . . . and |
| neither . . . nor | not only . . . but also |

Subordinating conjunctions introduce grammatically dependent clauses, connecting them and setting them up as modifiers to the main part of the sentence. The following list includes many of the subordinating conjunctions:

| | | | |
|---|---|---|---|
| because | where | unless | since |
| after | in order to | whereas | before |
| although | as | whether | when |
| so that | | | |

Take a look at how the coordinating and subordinating conjunctions in the following sentences connect words or groups of words:

COORD
Jim asked for some good advice, *and* he got it.
SUBORD
*When* Jim asked for some good advice, he got it.

Sometimes coordinating conjunctions start out complete sentences:

COORD
Jim did not ask anyone for advice. *But* he got it.

### Interjections

Interjections are grammatically independent words that usually convey emotion and seem thrown into the sentence, interrupting its flow. Adverbs, adjectives, and other parts of speech can serve as interjections on their own when used as exclamations—outbursts of emotion. The interjections in the following sentences are italicized:

During the revision stage, a writer might discover that, *oh no*, too many sentences are splattered with "and's."

*Well,* the time has come to pay what is owed.
*Well!* Look who finally showed up.
I thought you would do well on your Spanish test, and you did. *Good!*

### Verbals

Verbals are not, strictly speaking, a part of speech. Instead, they are a hybrid form of verbs and certain other parts of speech. There are three kinds of verbals: infinitives, gerunds, and participles.

*Infinitives*

An infinitive is the base form of a verb. Infinitives are usually preceded by *to: to hope, to ski, to know, to be felt, to have been.* Infinitives may come with subjects, objects, and complements. Together the subject, object, infinitive, and any modifiers intervening are called an *infinitive phrase.*

Infinitives are not always preceded by *to.* The form of the base word (the one that does not have any special ending attached indicating tense and number) is the strongest clue to finding these infinitives. Also, they are usually found after certain helping verbs:

should *interest*          will *pertain*          did *show*

The italicized words in the following sentences are examples of infinitives without their *to* signposts:

Don't you dare *tell* the new owners of the house that it is infested with termites.
With his friends coming, he need not *play* the game alone.

Infinitives may look much like verbs. Both may have subjects and objects or complements. However, infinitives never function as verbs. The infinitive phrase acts as a noun, adjective, or adverb.

He wanted *to go fishing.*
She always plays *to win.*
I'm happy *to be here.*

*Gerunds*

Gerunds end in *ing* and act as nouns. They can occur by themselves:

*Loving* him was like no other *loving.*

The first *loving* acts as the subject of the sentence. The second *loving* acts as the object of the preposition *like.*

*Running* is my favorite form of exercise because I do not like to compete with others.

*Running* is the subject of the sentence. Gerunds can also occur as the first word of gerund phrases.

*Running up a high bill at the grocery store* is, for him, unusual.

### Participles

Participles act as adjectives. The present participle form, in most instances, looks like the verb with an *ing* ending added to it:

| *Verb* | *Participle* |
| --- | --- |
| go | going |
| say | saying |

Many participles look just like gerunds and can be distinguished only by their function in a sentence:

Her *unflagging* belief in her abilities always motivated her to complete assignments on time and well.

The past participle may be formed in two ways. The first way is by adding a special ending, usually *ed*, *en*, *t*, or *n*. Some examples of past participles with these endings are *played*, *broken*, *spent*, and *torn*. The second way to form a past participle is by changing a vowel. The usual pattern is illustrated by the following words:

| *Verb* | *Participle* |
| --- | --- |
| fling | flung |
| sing | sung |

## SENTENCE STRUCTURE

As you already know, not every combination of words can make a sentence. "Fence brown," for instance, is not a sentence. Neither is "In conclusion" or "Running to the market." For a string of words to be a sentence, the words must be specific parts of speech arranged in proper sequence, and when read together, the words must make a complete thought.

The most basic form for a complete sentence has a subject and simple predicate. You are already familiar with the parts of speech that function as these sentence parts: nouns, pronouns, and groups of words can function as subjects; verbs function as simple predicates. In the following sentences the simple predicates are italicized and the subjects are labeled with an S.

S
John *thinks*.

S

Dogs *bite*.

S            S

Books and movies *entertain*.

In the first sentence, *John*, a noun, functions as subject; *thinks*, a verb, functions as the simple predicate. In the second sentence, *dogs* is the subject, and *bite* is the simple predicate. In the third sentence, *books* and *movies* are the subjects and *entertain* is the simple predicate. Each sentence is a complete thought.

You can look at this basic sentence structure in another way. In the above examples, the subject and simple predicate relate to each other in the same way. The subjects state what the sentences are about (someone named John, dogs, books and movies), and the simple predicates say something about the subjects (John is someone who thinks, dogs have a tendency to bite, and books and movies are sources of entertainment).

### Simple Sentences

The subject/simple predicate structure is called a *simple sentence.* Either or both parts of the simple sentence may be compound: have more than one part. For instance, the following sentences have a compound subject or compound simple predicate. They are, though, still simple sentences.

John and Laurie think.
Dogs bite and bark.

Five simple sentence patterns can be built from the subject/simple predicate base. Each of the following sentences represents one of these five patterns:

1. Gloria drinks milk.
2. She gave me the milk.
3. I was given the milk.
4. She is generous.
5. She is a friend.

Sentence 1 begins with subject and simple predicate but adds a new part: a direct object. Direct objects are those parts of sentences to which subjects do something. Gloria does something to the milk—she drinks it. The direct object receives the action of the simple predicate. In the following sentences, direct objects are italicized:

I brought the *cake*.
Grover ate *it*.
I spanked *him*.

Sentence 2—"She gave me the milk"—has a direct object, milk, but also has another sentence part, called an indirect object. Not all sentences with direct objects have indirect objects, but all sentences with indirect objects must include direct objects that are either stated or implied. Indirect objects are the beneficiaries in sentences. When subjects give away, teach, offer, bring, or do some such action to direct objects, it is the indirect objects that receive the direct object. Sentence 2 then includes the indirect object, *me*, for it is the *me* in the sentence that gets the milk. You may find it helpful to remember that indirect objects must come before direct objects. In the following sentences, indirect objects are italicized.

> Grover offered *me* the cake.
> I gave *Grover* a hard time.
> He told *me* the news.
> Sharon told *me.*

In the last sentence the direct object—news, a story, or whatever it was that Sharon said—is implied. In the context within which this sentence would have been written, the direct object would be clear, even though implied.

Sentences 1 and 2 are both written in the active voice. That is, the subject of the sentence is doing the action. Gloria is drinking and she is giving. Sentence 3, however, is written in the passive voice; the subject, *I,* does not do the giving. Instead, the subject receives what would be the direct object if the sentence were written in active voice: "Someone gave me the milk." When the verb of a sentence with objects is in the passive voice, either of the potential objects becomes the subject of the passive construction. The remaining object is called the retained object. In sentence 3 *milk* is the retained object. Retained objects are italicized in the following sentences written in the passive voice:

> *Passive:* We were given high *grades.*
> *Active:* Someone gave us high grades.
> *Passive:* They were shown the *exhibit.*
> *Active:* Someone showed them the exhibit.
> *Passive:* The team was awarded a *trophy.*
> *Active:* Someone awarded the team a trophy.

Sentence 4—"She is generous"—has neither a direct object nor an indirect one. Rather, it has a *predicate adjective.* Predicate adjectives are adjectives that follow the simple predicate and describe the subject. *Generous* describes the subject of the sentence and is the predicate adjective. Predicate adjectives in the following sentences are italicized:

> Two-year-olds are *dogmatic.*
> Grover is *hungry.*
> Lamb chops are *fatty.*

*Hungry, dogmatic,* and *fatty* are all adjectives that describe their respective subjects.

Because predicate adjectives follow the simple predicate and can be said to "complete" it, they are called complements. When sentences include complements, the simple predicates always are linking verbs (*is*, *seems*, *appears*, and so forth), never an action verb (*hit*, *run*, *stir*, and so forth). Another kind of complement is contained in the fifth sentence, "She is a friend." Notice that *friend* is not an adjective describing the subject but instead a noun that renames the subject. Nouns, pronouns, and groups of words that function as nouns are called *predicate nouns* when they follow the simple predicate and rename the subject. Predicate nouns are the second kind of complement. Note the predicate nouns italicized in the following sentences:

> Gloria is a *student.*
> Antelope Valley College is an *institution.*
> She is an *executive* and a *mother.*

*Student, institution,* and *executive* and *mother* are all nouns that rename their respective subjects.

One last comment is needed regarding simple sentences. Thus far, in talking about predicates, we have discussed simple predicates (verbs) and complements of simple predicates, or predicate adjectives and nouns. Complete predicates include the simple predicate and any predicate adjectives, predicate nouns, direct objects, or indirect objects that accompany the simple predicate. Complete predicates are italicized in the following sentences:

> She *is an executive and a mother.*
> This year's first-year students *seem smart and inquisitive.*
> Mr. Muldare *wrote five books.*
> She *gave me her last dime.*

Simple sentences are made up of subjects and complete predicates. If a sentence has only a subject and simple predicate—as in the sentence "John thinks"—then the simple predicate is considered to be the complete predicate, too.

### Clauses

Clauses are any groups of words that include both a subject and a simple predicate. Thus, we can say that simple sentences are also clauses. Not every clause, however, is a simple sentence. Those clauses that have been called simple sentences here (i.e., clauses that are complete thoughts) are *main clauses.* Every sentence must include at least one main clause.

Sentences may also contain one or more *subordinate clauses*—clauses that are not complete thoughts. You can usually identify subordinate clauses by the words that begin them. Relative pronouns (*who, which, that*), relative adverbs (*when, where,* and so forth), and subordinating conjunctions (*because, since, although,* and so forth) indicate that the clauses following them are subordinate. Note the italicized subordinate clauses in the following sentences:

> I went to the store *because I needed some bread.*
> The boy *who served me* was quite young.
> *Although I kept quiet,* I felt like singing.

Each of the subordinate clauses is an incomplete thought, one that needs the other part of the sentence, the main clause, in order to make sense.

Subordinate clauses that function as nouns are called noun clauses and are often introduced by pronouns such as *who, whoever, what, which,* and *that.* Words such as *why, whether,* and *how* may also begin noun clauses. Like nouns, noun clauses can become part of another clause or group of words and can function as subjects of main clauses, as objects, or in any other way that nouns function. The following sentences include noun clauses functioning as subjects of main clauses:

> *Whoever ate the cake* was hungry.
> *What the book said* was interesting.

You can see how easily noun clauses might also be made to function as direct objects:

> I envy *whoever ate the cake.*
> They discussed *what the book said.*
> Mary knows *why I left.*

Noun clauses function as indirect objects in the following sentences:

> I gave *whoever was hungry* the cake.
> They told *whoever was listening* the story.

Noun clauses function as predicate nouns in the following sentences:

> His friendship was *what I wanted.*
> The question was *whether we would win or lose.*

Noun clauses also function as appositives. Appositives define or rename nouns (rather than add detail to them, as do adjectives):

> The newly diagnosed AIDS patient spoke to my concerns: *what would happen to his partner?*

The italicized portion of the sentence is the equivalent of *concerns,* the noun it defines.

Subordinate clauses can also be used like adjectives and adverbs. Those clauses that describe nouns or pronouns are said to be *adjective clauses.* Adjective clauses are usually introduced by relative pronouns (*who*, *that*, *which*), but they can also be introduced by relative adverbs (*where*, *when*, and so forth). It is important to remember that relative adverbs can introduce subordinate clauses that function as nouns, as adjectives, or as adverbs. Consequently, you must determine the kind of subordinate clause you are faced with by noting its function in the sentence. The following italicized clauses are adjective clauses:

The student *who works hard* will succeed.

The adjective clause describes *student*.

I lost the book *that you gave me*.

The adjective clause describes *book*.

Adverb clauses are subordinate clauses used to describe verbs, adjectives, or other adverbs. Adverb clauses are introduced by subordinating conjunctions that indicate time, purpose or reason, a condition or stipulation, or a conflict between information in the adverb clause and information in some other part of the sentence. Adverb clauses in the following sentences are italicized.

I left *when I became tired*.

The adverb clause describes the verb *left*, indicating a time.

It will rain *if we go to the beach*.

The adverb clause describes the verb *will rain*, indicating a stipulation.

We were pleased *because we did well*.

The adverb clause describes the adjective *pleased*, indicating a reason.

*Although we were present*, we did not see you.

The adverb clause describes the verb *did see* (*not* is another adverb). The adverb clause points out a conflict.

When subordinate clauses are adjective or adverb clauses, they describe some part of the sentence. By describing, they change or modify what they describe. You can easily see the difference between the sentence "The boy was my friend" and the same sentence with a modifying clause added: "The boy who punched me was my friend." The parts of sentences that function as adjectives or adverbs, describing other parts of sentences, are called *modifiers*.

You can see, then, that modifiers are often subordinate clauses. Modifiers may also be single words. For instance, *heavy* modifies *automobile* in the following sentence:

She owns a *heavy* automobile.

The sentence could have been written with an adjective clause:

She owns an automobile *that is heavy.*

### Phrases

The sentence "She owns an automobile that is heavy" might also have been written like this:

Her Ford is an automobile *of considerable weight.*

You will notice that *of considerable weight* is neither a single word, such as *heavy,* nor a clause, such as *that is heavy. Of considerable weight* cannot be a clause because it does not have a subject and a predicate. Instead, it is a phrase, a group of words that seem related, that form a functioning unit within a sentence, and yet that do not include both a subject and a predicate.

Phrases can function in the same ways that nouns, adjectives, verbs, and adverbs do. Note the functions of the phrases in the following sentences:

He is the chairman *of our committee.*

The adjective phrase modifies *chairman.*

She lives *without a care.*

The adverb phrase modifies *lives.*

*Studying Latin* has helped me write English.

The noun phrase functions as the subject of the sentence.

Ms. Williams, *the club treasurer,* has been married for forty years.

The noun phrase renames *Ms. Williams,* the subject of the sentence.

We enjoyed *working on our research papers.*

The noun phrase functions as the direct object.

*To lie in the sun* is what I want to do.

The noun phrase functions as the subject of the sentence.

*Forgotten by his mother,* the infant began crying.

The adjective phrase modifies *infant.*

*Wanting desperately to win,* the coach played his best team.

The adjective phrase modifies *coach.*

The lake was *too pretty to describe.*

The adjective phrase *too pretty* modifies lake. The adverb phrase *to describe* modifies the adjective phrase.

Phrases may sometimes function independently, not fitting into the structure of the rest of the sentence. Such phrases, which do not modify any particular part of the sentences but modify the whole sentence in a general way, are called *absolute phrases.* In the following sentences, the absolute phrases are italicized:

> *The room being in a mess,* I decided to leave for a while.
> *Time running out,* there wasn't much we could do.

In both examples, the absolute phrase modifies the entire sentence.

Often verbals—participles, gerunds, or infinitives—combine with other words to make verbal phrases. The three kinds of verbal phrases—participial phrases, gerund phrases, and infinitive phrases—function in sentences in the same ways that their verbal counterparts do:

| *Verbal Phrase* | *Function* |
|---|---|
| participial phrase | adjective |
| gerund phrase | noun |
| infinitive phrase | noun, adjective, or adverb |

Notice the types and the functions of the verbal phrases in the following sentences:

> *Leaving by the back door,* he tripped on a loose floorboard.

The participial phrase, begun with the participle *leaving,* modifies the subject of the sentence—*he.*

> When we learned that Judy, *wanting some privacy,* had locked herself in the bathroom, we thought it best to let her stay there until she was ready to come out.

The participial phrase, begun with the participle *wanting,* modifies the subject of the subordinate clause—*Judy.*

> *Thinking about vacation* does not help me finish my papers.

The gerund phrase, introduced by the gerund *thinking,* functions as the subject of the sentence.

> Coach Kleinbaur loved *eating apples during halftime.*

Here the gerund phrase functions as a direct object. And notice that within the gerund phrase is another phrase—*during halftime*—that modifies the gerund.

*To enrich one's life* is a worthy goal.

The infinitive phrase, begun with the infinitive *to enrich,* functions as the subject of the sentence.

Right now I want *to rest quietly.*

The infinitive phrase, begun with the infinitive *to rest,* functions as a direct object.

That is a book *to read again and again.*

The infinitive phrase acts as an adjective, modifying *book.*

By the time we reached them, the opportunity *to strike fear in their hearts* had passed.

The infinitive phrase acts as an adjective, modifying *opportunity.*

I always read *to discover motives of characters.*

The infinitive phrase functions as an adverb, modifying the verb *read.*

I wish I were small enough *to wear children's sizes.*

The infinitive phrase functions as an adverb, modifying the adverb *enough.*

Prepositional phrases function most often as adjectives or adverbs. You will remember that prepositional phrases include a preposition, an object (noun, pronoun, noun phrase, or noun clause), and any modifiers of the object:

```
PREP    ADJ  OBJ
to the new store
```

Note the prepositional phrases in the following sentences and what they modify:

My goals *for the future* were not formed then.

The prepositional phrase acts as an adjective, modifying *goals.*

We went *to the lighthouse.*

The prepositional phrase acts as an adverb, modifying the verb *went*.

That man looks like a person *without a care.*

The prepositional phrase acts as an adjective, modifying *person.*

Friends are helpful *in times of distress.*

This sentence has two prepositional phrases. The first, *in times,* acts as an adverb, modifying the adjective *helpful.* The second prepositional phrase, *of distress,* modifies *times,* the object of the first phrase, and acts as an adjective.

### Kinds of Sentences

As you know, a simple sentence is the subject/predicate structure, or a single main clause. The simple sentence is one of the four kinds of English sentences. By adding subordinate clauses or additional main clauses to the simple sentence, other kinds of sentences can be formed. Plainly stated, a sentence with one main clause and one or more subordinate clauses is called a complex sentence. A sentence with two or more main clauses and one or more subordinate clauses is called a compound sentence. And a sentence with two main clauses and one or more subordinate clauses is called a compound-complex sentence. The number of phrases that a sentence has does not determine the kind (simple, compound, complex, compound-complex) of sentence it is. Nor does the function of subordinate clauses determine the kind of sentences in which the subordinate clauses are found. Instead, it is only a matter of numbers: the number of main and subordinate clauses in particular sentences.

In the following sentences, main clauses are italicized and subordinate clauses are indicated by brackets.

1. They spoke to the convocation. (simple sentence)
2. They left {when they were ready.} (complex sentence)
3. {Although I waited at the station for an hour,} I saw only strangers. (complex sentence)
4. {Whoever wants to see the show} can go with us. (complex sentence in which a subordinate clause functions as the subject of the main clause)
5. Alvina {, who was really a sensible person,} could not live {as her parents did.} (complex sentence}
6. The horse {that won the race} was my father's favorite. (complex sentence)
7. I waited at the station, but I saw only strangers. (compound sentence)
8. I was there; he was elsewhere. (compound sentence)
9. {That he was lonely} was no excuse, and I told him so. (compound-complex sentence in which a subordinate clause functions as the subject of one main clause)

Notice the manner in which clauses are joined. When, in a complex sentence, the subordinate clause follows the main clause (as in sentence 2), no comma is needed to separate one clause from the other. However, when the subordinate clause precedes the main clause in a complex sentence (as in sentence 3), a comma separates the two clauses. Of course, when the subordinate clause is part of the main clause (as in sentence 4 or sentence 9), no punctuation is needed to join the clauses.

An important distinction exists between the two ways that clauses interrupting main clauses are treated. When the subordinate clause is a nonessential modifier (as in sentence 5), commas set it apart from the main clause. When the subordinate clause is an essential modifier, no commas surround it (as in sentence 6). For definitions of essential and nonessential modifiers, see page 496.

The ways in which clauses in compound sentences are joined are easily understood and applied. If a coordinating conjunction joins the two main clauses of a compound sentence (as in sentence 7), a comma precedes the conjunction. If the two main clauses are not separated by a coordinating conjunction (as in sentence 8), a semicolon divides them. The same applies to main clauses in compound-complex sentences. Commas are not used preceding a coordinating conjunction if the words following the conjunction constitute a subordinate clause or a phrase rather than a clause:

He knew that the money had been discovered *and* that the jig was up.

Note the lack of commas in the above sentences.

## GRAMMAR, DIALECT, AND LANGUAGE

You have been unconsciously using grammar since you first began speaking in sentences. Since then, you have been creating complex, intelligent sentences without having to pay much attention to their grammar. You may think, "Oh, but I talk in such bad grammar all the time." Actually, you shouldn't assume so, because you are probably talking quite effectively in a variety of grammars that suit the group with whom you are conversing. Many people automatically associate the word grammar with correctness—good or bad grammar. But those who do may well be unaware of what grammar really is. A grammar is an underlying system used by a closely associated group of people who wish to communicate. Grammar includes word order, word endings, and word forms. As Kenneth Oliver puts it in his pamphlet, *A Sound Curriculum in English Grammar,* "Grammar is what distinguishes a sentence from a list of words randomly ordered." Thus, grammar contributes to meaning.

Those who limit their idea of grammar to correctness or incorrectness fail to recognize that grammar must contribute meaning within a context. The context is usually the regional or social group of the speaker and the speaker's audience. Many people who are concerned with correctness in grammar are automatically, but inappropriately, using one standard to judge all communication. The standard commonly used is not based on whether a statement is grammatical (in the sense that it has a grammar), or even meaningful, but whether it conforms to standard English, which is one variety, or dialect, of English.

A dialect is a system for use of vocabulary, grammar, and pronunciation that occurs within a language. People who live in a certain region and who, in turn, belong to certain social groups within a region share certain habits of language. You yourself may have observed that certain sounds or expressions are typical of New Yorkers, Southerners, or Midwesterners, or you may speak a different dialect in your home than in school. Nobody speaks strictly standard English, although some dialects are more like standard English than others. Perhaps the most obvious signals that people speak a different dialect than yours are what appears to be their "strange" use of words and pronunciations. Roger Shuy, a prominent researcher in the study of dialects, compares the first impressions of a person hearing someone speak a different dialect to an American going to England and finding that Londoners drive on "the wrong side of the road." Well, it may be a different side of the road, but it isn't the "wrong" side. Other dialects than one's own sound different and may even be momentarily confusing, but they are not inferior. A dialect is more than one person's idiosyncrasies of speaking; it is a recognized system.

Here are just a few of the many examples of regional and social dialects in the United States. First, vocabulary varies. The animal called a "polecat" in the North is called a "skunk" in the South. What is called a "bag" in the North is called a "sack" in the South and in regions between North and South (the Midland). Most people are familiar with the food "cottage cheese"; however, in the North it is also known as "Dutch cheese," in the South it is also known as "clabbercheese," and in the regions between is also known as "smearcase."

Pronunciation differences between dialects can be marked. Southerners would say bacon is *greazy,* but Northerners would say it is *greacy.* People in the Midwest might add an r to the middle of words, such as *worsh* for wash or *gorsh* for gosh. A Southerner might pronounce the words time and Tom or oil and all almost the same way. Even within the broad regions of North, South, and Midwest states there are pronunciation differences. You may have noticed that people in New England say *cah* when other Northerners say *car,* or *pahk* when other Northerners would say *park.* Social groups vary in pronunciation as well. For instance, certain social groups within the Midwest would be more likely to say *gorsh* than would others.

Grammar also varies. In the North people are more likely to say, "It's a quarter of (or to) five" than "It's a quarter till five," which is common in the Midwest. Likewise, in the North people often say, "I had four bushel apples," but in the South people often say, "I had four bushels apples." Certain social groups are likely to say, "He Jim father," but others are more likely to say, "He's Jim's father." Some regional and social dialects would say the past tense of *to dive* is *dove*, others would say it is *dived*.

The differences between dialects of the same language do not usually undermine communication, because dialects of a language tend to share basic features of the language. All dialects of English share features (e.g., sentence patterns) that make them distinctively English. It is true, however, that some of the nuances may be lost among speakers of different dialects because of the combined specialized features of vocabulary, pronunciation, and grammar. Also, because there are so many factors contributing to the speech of two individuals, including levels of formality within the dialects, communication might be difficult. Even with the special flavor of the regional or social group, the dialects are, overall, similar enough to be mutually intelligible.

Dialects differ from languages in this way. Even though languages can have common roots, they are not mutually intelligible because among languages not only do underlying grammatical systems differ, but vocabulary differs as well. Languages, then, do not overlap, a fact that is reflected in great barriers to communication. Therefore, it is unwise to perceive the distinctions among dialects of the same language as being like distinctions among languages. Other dialect speakers are not talking a language foreign to you. Learning other dialects than your own is much easier than learning a foreign language, and speakers of other dialects than your own are relatively easy to understand. The person who says, "Ain't nobody care 'bout 'im" usually has no trouble understanding the person who says, "There isn't a soul who cares about him," and vice versa.

### Standard English

Standard English is the dialect used by members of the most prestigious groups in our society: lawyers, doctors, broadcasters, writers, politicians and educators. It is a shared, public form of English used whenever and wherever speakers of many dialects come together. However, it should not be considered superior to other dialects, as other dialects of English have their own sets of grammatical rules, are equally logical, and are equally expressive, although they perhaps appeal to a more limited audience. Realistically, people should recognize the value and effectiveness of the many dialects of English, not see any one as the only proper or elegant way to communicate. (Certainly, those speaking in other dialects have been communicating.) Instead, people should try to view dialects in the context of varying social situations.

In itself, whether a statement conforms to one dialect or another does not make it grammatical or ungrammatical. An ungrammatical statement in English would have to be one that did not conform to any dialectical patterns of English. "I bit into the apple green" is not grammatical because it does not conform to the basic sentence patterns of English. *Green* should come before *apple;* then it becomes meaningful in English.

Dialects other than the standard may be more appropriate in certain situations, while in other situations standard English would be more appropriate. Still, appropriateness is the issue, not the presence or absence of grammar, not correctness without a context. Using one dialect in one situation and another in another situation is often compared to dressing one way for one occasion and another way for a different one. The analogy works because people often shift back and forth between dialects as they find themselves in different social situations.

### Recognizing Interference from Nonstandard Dialects

Americans grow up speaking various dialects of English, many with grammatical features that differ from standard English dialect. Because a great deal of shifting between dialects is required of those who use nonstandard dialects in their communities and standard dialect for writing and other school activities, both dialects must be constantly present in their minds. The result is that sometimes the dialects get mixed up. The person makes a perfectly logical analogy between usages in the two dialects, but the idiosyncrasies of one dialect make the analogy imprecise. Most of a student's paper could conform to standard English, but the rest could be sprinkled with inconsistencies based on these poor analogies. These inconsistencies are considered "errors" by most careful readers. However, they are not careless mistakes. They may represent gaps in understanding how the standard dialect differs from the nonstandard dialect the writer is used to. Such errors are called *interference errors*.

The first step for writers struggling with the problem of interference is to learn the major contrasts between their home dialect and the standard dialect. It is important to see both the overlapping grammatical features and the distinguishing grammatical features. Here the contrasts will be emphasized, since they are what most people tend to forget. Of course, understanding the source of interference between dialects is only the beginning. Meticulous dialect shifting comes with patience and practice.

Although it is impossible to classify or explain briefly all the variations within nonstandard dialects, some generalizations can be useful. The following discussion includes many of the common interference errors found in students' papers. Not all of them apply to all dialects of Americans, but among them you should be able to find a few that apply to you.

*Verbs*

The greatest contrast between standard and nonstandard English occurs in the formation of verbs.

1. Some nonstandard dialects do not usually use the verbs *is* and *are* in simple sentences, whereas standard dialect does.

   ***Nonstandard:*** She over there.
   ***Standard:*** She is over there.

Nonstandard users have a special use for *is* and *are*—emphasis:

*Nonstandard:* She *is* hungry. (emphasized)
*Nonstandard:* She hungry. (not emphasized)
*Standard:* She is hungry.

2. Many nonstandard dialects do not consistently add an *s* to the third person singular verb, but standard dialect always does in the indicative mood (see p. 367).

   *Nonstandard:* She cry every time her daddy leave.
   *Standard:* She cries every time her daddy leaves.
   *Nonstandard:* She know him from last term.
   *Standard:* She knows him from last term.

3. Often, even when the forms of *to be* are used in nonstandard dialects, they do not necessarily follow the subject-verb agreement rules that standard dialect follows. The choice of singular or plural can depend on context.

   *Nonstandard:* They was on time.
   *Nonstandard:* They were on time.
   *Standard:* They were on time.

4. The verb *to be* has a special form in some nonstandard dialects. For instance, black English makes the distinction not present in standard English that the *be* added to a statement indicates that the action is habitual.

   *Nonstandard:* They be in trouble when their mama not
      around.
   *Standard:* They were frequently in trouble when their mama
      was not around.

These statements are different from the following, which do not indicate habit:

   *Nonstandard:* He working.
   *Standard:* He is working.

5. The past tense of irregular verbs is often different in nonstandard dialects than in standard dialects. The standard dialect forms are listed in the dictionary after the infinitive form of the verb. The commonly confused verbs are listed on pages 440–441.

   *Nonstandard:* They run down to the store a few minutes ago.
   *Standard:* They ran down to the store a few minutes ago.
   *Nonstandard:* She give me a B.
   *Standard:* She gave me a B.

6. Many nonstandard dialects do not end certain past tense regular verbs with *ed.* The same verbs in standard dialect do have an *ed* ending. In the nonstandard dialects, whether the *ed* is added is usually decided by sound.

   > *Nonstandard:* I ask him to tell me what happen.
   > *Standard:* I asked him to tell me what happened.

7. Many nonstandard dialects do not use a *to be* verb as part of the progressive verb and thus have only one signal for it (the *ing* ending) instead of two as in standard dialect (*to be* and the *ing* ending).

   > *Nonstandard:* They telling the same story.
   > *Standard:* They are telling the same story.

8. Many nonstandard dialects use one of two signals (*have* and the *ed* ending) for perfect verb tenses, but standard dialect uses both.

   > *Nonstandard:* I have talk with you before.
   > *Nonstandard:* I talked with you before.
   > *Standard:* I have talked with you before.

9. Some nonstandard dialects use *get* or *got* to form the passive voice (see p. 181), but standard dialect uses a form of *to be.*

   > *Nonstandard:* The young man got hurt by his friends.
   > *Standard:* The young man was hurt by his friends.

   In addition to the *got,* a nonstandard dialect may use the past tense form of the verb or may omit the *got* and use only the past tense form.

   > *Nonstandard:* All the meat got ate by the hunters.
   > *Nonstandard:* All the meat ate by the hunters.
   > *Standard:* All the meat was eaten by the hunters.

*Nouns*

1. Some nonstandard dialects do not add *s* or *es* to form plural nouns, especially if the meaning is already clear from the context, but standard dialect always takes the *s* or *es* on regular nouns.

   > *Nonstandard:* twenty book
   > *Standard:* twenty books
   > *Nonstandard:* many desk
   > *Standard:* many desks

   Some nonstandard dialects add the *s* or *es* to what would already be considered plural forms of irregular nouns in standard dialect.

*Nonstandard:* the childrens
*Standard:* the children

2. Some nonstandard dialects do not use *'s* in forming the possessive and rely on context instead, but standard dialect requires the
ending on the noun to show possession.

   *Nonstandard:* Over there is Steve girl.
   *Standard:* Over there is Steve's girl.

3. Nouns formed from verbs (verbals) often have the same form as
the infinitive, but in standard dialect they take an *ing* ending.

   *Nonstandard:* Arnetta thanked James for try to help.
   *Standard:* Arnetta thanked James for trying to help.
   *Nonstandard:* In the begin the class was easy.
   *Standard:* In the beginning the class was easy.

*Pronouns*

1. In some nonstandard dialects *which* is the most common pronoun
and it may be used in the same places that standard dialect uses
*which*, *that*, or *who*. But standard dialect differentiates between the
meanings of *which* (nonrestrictive), *that* (restrictive—see p. 497),
and *who* (used only for people and animals, not things.)

   *Nonstandard:* The motor belongs to the man which came
      into the station yesterday.
   *Standard:* The motor belongs to the man who came into
      the station yesterday.

2. In some nonstandard dialects the subjective or objective pronoun
is used as a possessive pronoun. In standard dialect only possessive pronouns may be used.

   *Nonstandard:* Yesterday was they big chance.
   *Standard:* Yesterday was their big chance.

3. The same rules apply for reflexive pronouns as for possessives (see
rule 2).

   *Nonstandard:* You just let youself go.
   *Standard:* You just let yourself go.

4. Some nonstandard dialects use a form such as *that there* or *these
here,* where standard dialect would use only *that* or *those*.

   *Nonstandard:* That there book is old.
   *Standard:* That book is old.

5. Some nonstandard dialects use *them* where standard dialect uses *these* or *those*.

> *Nonstandard:* Them books weigh a ton.
> *Standard:* These books weigh a ton.

*Adjectives and Adverbs*

1. Nonstandard dialects may form adjectives by using the infinitive, whereas standard dialect adds an *ed* or *ing* ending.

> *Nonstandard:* They just love boil potatoes.
> *Standard:* They just love boiled potatoes.
> *Nonstandard:* I am use to hard work.
> *Standard:* I am used to hard work.

2. To show comparisons, some nonstandard dialects use two signals (the *er* or *est* ending and the word *more* or *most*), but standard dialect uses only one or the other of the signals.

> *Nonstandard:* He is the most fastest gun in the West.
> *Standard:* He is the fastest gun in the West.

3. The same rules apply for adverb comparisons as for adjective comparisons (see rule 2).

> *Nonstandard:* They talk more quicker in New York than in South Carolina.
> *Nonstandard:* They talk more quick in New York than in South Carolina.
> *Standard:* They talk more quickly in New York than in South Carolina.

4. In many nonstandard dialects the adjective form may also be used as an adverb. This rule applies to certain adjective forms used with action verbs (see p. 366) and to the word *good* used instead of *well*. In standard dialect the *ly* ending is most often used to distinguish adverbs from adjectives, and *well* is used as an adverb.

> *Nonstandard:* They fix cars good.
> *Standard:* They fix cars well.
> *Nonstandard:* Run quiet in the corridor.
> *Standard:* Run quietly in the corridor.

*Conjunctions*

Nonstandard dialects may use two signals (the conjunction and the word plus) to show a connection between phrases or clauses, but standard dialects use only one.

*Nonstandard:* She drank three glasses of milk and plus a cup of tea.

*Standard:* She drank three glasses of milk and a cup of tea.

### Negatives

Many nonstandard dialects use two signals for negatives (a *not* with the verb and a *no* modifying the noun), but standard dialect uses only one signal.

*Nonstandard:* Tom didn't want no money for it.
*Standard:* Tom didn't want any money for it.
*Standard:* Tom wanted no money for it.

### Articles

Some nonstandard dialects do not make any distinction between the use of *a* and *an*, but standard dialect uses *an*, not *a*, before a word beginning with a vowel sound.

*Nonstandard:* A automatic transmission on a car is convenient.
*Standard:* An automatic transmission on a car is convenient.

## Recognizing Interference Between Languages

The difference between standard English and another language can be great, more marked, of course, than the differences among various dialects of the same language. Many college students today have learned English as a second language. They may continue to speak their first language at home and in their community and English at school. But because languages differ so significantly in idioms, pronunciation, and grammar, strict translation from one to the other is rarely effective. With both languages available to the mind of the bilingual speaker, transference of some of the conventions of the first language into written English is quite common. Of course, these half-English constructions are considered errors by readers: they do not conform to the standards of written English. Sometimes the writers have used a perfectly logical structure in their first language, generalizing it to a principle of English, but the result is considered wrong. It is important to realize that this kind of error is not merely a careless mistake. The thought that has gone into the analogy between the two languages needs to be re-channeled into recognizing the contrasts in the two languages. Once aware of some basic contrasts, any writer can look out for cases in which they would be likely to occur. By reinforcing the distinctions between the languages through observation and practice, the writer learns to separate the languages.

All speakers of second languages could benefit from learning the contrasts between their first and second languages. In this section Spanish will be used to illustrate some of the kinds of contrasts that might be noted and reinforced. Of course, college students who speak Spanish as a first language come from many ethnic backgrounds. The form of Spanish they speak reflects their social status and where they come from. Their family may be from Cuba, South America, Mexico, or Puerto Rico. How much formal Spanish the students know and how often they speak it also contribute to the frequency and kinds of interference from Spanish they will find in their written English. And the social level of the people with whom they most often communicate in Spanish will influence vocabulary and grammar, the two most common types of interference from first languages. Despite differences in the backgrounds, some general contrasts and common interference errors are worth noting because they are the source of confusion in the English of many bilingual students.

*Verbs*

1. In Spanish, questions do not include the emphatic *do*, but in standard English the *do* is needed at the beginning of many questions.

    *Spanish:* You see what I mean?
    *English:* Do you see what I mean?

2. In Spanish, a final *d* on a word is not pronounced as distinctly as it is in English, so many speakers of Spanish tend not to hear the *ed* at the end of a past tense verb or past participle. Because English speakers commonly drop the sound, too, it is not reinforced in the Spanish speaker's listening. Thus, the *ed* is sometimes left off in error. A Spanish speaker hears the following:

    I listen to him for the last time.

    In English, the *ed* is needed on many verbs in the past tense and in perfect tenses:

    I listened to him for the last time.
    I have listened to him for the last time.

3. Because contractions are not used in Spanish, many Spanish speakers avoid the use of contractions or may misspell them when trying to write them. The best way to learn contractions is to memorize them and to notice whenever using them that the apostrophe replaces particular letters.

    *Spanish:* I am not home in the mornings.
    *English:* I'm not home in the mornings. (the apostrophe marks the missing *a* in *am*)

*Nouns*

1. In Spanish, possessives of nouns are shown by a phrase beginning with *of*. In English this structure is not incorrect, but it may be excessively formal or awkward when something is possessed by a

person. English uses an apostrophe and s ('*s*) to show possession. Because the structure is strange to speakers of Spanish, they may avoid it even though it would make their sentences more fluent, or they may have trouble placing the apostrophe, tending to leave it out. In standard English the apostrophe must be present and in the appropriate place to convey the writer's meaning. See page 480 for the rules.

> *Spanish:* The house of Mary is very small.
> *English:* Mary's house is very small.

2. In Spanish, nouns have gender (masculine or feminine) expressed in the noun endings, but in English noun endings are the same for most nouns. In English, too, plurals are formed without regard to gender: *s* or *es* is usually added to the singular form of the noun (see p. 410).

> *Spanish:* los rios (indicates masculine by *o* ending)
> *English:* the rivers (makes no reference to gender by *s* ending only)

*Pronouns*

1. In Spanish, the pronoun is combined with the verb form and may otherwise be omitted in a sentence, but in English the pronoun is always used in addition to the proper verb form.

> *Spanish:* The reason she did it is has nothing else.
> *English:* The reason she did it is she has nothing else.

2. In Spanish, a phrase beginning with *of* is used to show the possessive pronoun, but in English specific words are used alone as the possessive pronouns (see p. 450).

> *Spanish:* The book of her is on the table.
> *English:* Her book is on the table.

3. In Spanish, the relative pronouns *that*, *which*, *who*, and *whom* are all one word, *que*, but in English each of the words has a slightly different function.

> *Spanish:* The man which sold me the radio is friendly.
> *English:* The man who sold me the radio is friendly.

4. In Spanish, the pronoun used in front of a question will often be *which*, but the corresponding question in English would require *what*.

> *Spanish:* Which is your name?
> *English:* What is your name?

*Adjectives and Adverbs*

1. In Spanish, adjectives agree in number with their nouns, but in English the adjective form remains the same whether the noun is singular or plural.

> *Spanish:* in differents classes
> *English:* in different classes

2. In Spanish, adjectives agree in gender with the nouns they modify, but in English noun endings do not show gender, so neither do their adjectives.

3. In Spanish, only one word, *mucho*, is used to mean much and many, but in English the two words are used differently. *Much* is used in English to describe quantities, and *many* is used to describe items that could be counted.

> *Spanish:* A person who lives on county money has much problems in these days of high inflation.
> *English:* A person who lives on county money has many problems in these days of high inflation.

4. In Spanish, adjectives are placed after the nouns they modify, but in English adjectives often precede nouns.

> *Spanish:* The house white looks beautiful.
> *English:* The white house looks beautiful.

*Negatives*

In Spanish, two signals are used to show negatives, but in standard English only one is acceptable.

> *Spanish:* She does not want nothing today.
> *English:* She does not want anything today.
> *English:* She wants nothing today.

*Articles*

1. There is no equivalent in Spanish for the article *an*. Many Spanish speakers therefore tend to use *a* all the time, not realizing that before a noun with a pronounced vowel, *an*, not *a*, is used in English.

> *Spanish:* A amateur does something for the love of it.
> *English:* An amateur does something for the love of it.

2. In Spanish, the article may be used with an adjective to form a noun, but in English the word *one* must be added to the phrase to achieve the same effect.

*Spanish:* the ugly (meaning the one who is ugly)
*English:* the ugly one
*Spanish:* the great
*English:* the great one

3. In Spanish, an article is used before a generalized noun, but in English the article is not usually present.

   *Spanish:* the humanity
   *English:* humanity
   *Spanish:* the love
   *English:* love

## Prepositions

Prepositions are perhaps the stickiest problem for Spanish speakers, as many idioms in Spanish cannot translate directly into English because different prepositions are used. Unfortunately, the Spanish speaker must simply memorize or refer to a list of common English expressions that take prepositions. With practice and recognition of which phrases tend to be confusing a writer can reduce the interference. Here is a common example of this kind of interference.

*Spanish:* I was married with Julio last May.
*English:* I was married to Julio last May

The following list of idiomatic expressions shows the way prepositions should be used in English. Reading it over and practicing with the expressions can help many. It can also be used as a reference.

### Idiomatic Prepositional Expressions

abstain *from* something
abundance *of* something
acceptable *to* someone
access *to* someone or some place
accuse someone *of* something
acquaint *with* someone or something
adapt *to* something
adhere *to* something
affection *for* someone
afraid *of* something
agree *to* something
agree *with* someone about something
amazed *at* something
analogy *between* two things

angry *at* something
angry *with* someone
apply *to* someone *for* something
appropriate *to* something
ashamed *of* something
ask someone *for* something
ask something *of* someone
assure someone *of* something
*at* the top *of*
attraction *to* or *toward* someone or something
aversion *to* someone or something
aware *of* someone or something
because *of* something or someone
blame someone *for* something

call *on* someone
call *to* someone
capable *of* something
certain *of* something
characteristic *of* someone
characterized *by* something
communicate something *to* someone
communicate *with* someone *on* something
comparable *to* something
complain *to* someone *about* something
composed *of* something
concerned *about* someone or something
confess *to* someone or something
confident *of* something
conform *to* something
congratulate someone *on* something
conscious *of* something
consistent *with* something
consult *with* someone *about* or *on* something
count *on* someone or something
cure *for* something
demand something *of* someone
depend *on* someone or something
destined *for* something
die *from* a cause other than disease
die *of* a disease
disgusted *with* someone or something
distrust *of* someone or something
doubtful *of* someone or something
dream *of* or *about* someone or something
engaged *in* some activity
engaged *to* someone
equality *with* something

escape *from* something
excel *in* something
exception *to* something
explain something *to* someone
failure *of* someone *in* something
faithful *to* someone or something
fall in love *with* someone
fond *of* someone
*for* fear *of*
*for* the purpose *of*
*for* the sake *of*
free *from* someone or something
full *of* something
guess *at* something
hear *of* something
hinder someone *from* doing something
hint *at* something
hope *for* something
*in* accordance *with*
*in* case *of*
*in* defense *of*
*in* favor *of*
*in* opposition *to*
*in* spite *of*
*in* the event *of*
inform someone *of* something
insist *on* something
intent *on* something
interested *in* someone or something
interfere *with* someone
introduce someone *to* someone else
irrelevant *to* something
knock *at* or *on* the door
laugh *at* something or someone
lecture *on* some subject
listen *to* someone or something
look *at* someone or something
look *for* someone or something
look *up* someone or something
motive *for* something

need *for* something

opportunity *for* someone or something

opposed *to* something or someone

pity *for* someone

prefer something *to* something else

prejudice *against* someone or something

previous *to* some event

proficient *in* something

protect someone *from* something

quarrel *with* someone *over* or *about* something

reason *for* something

reason *with* someone *about* something

recover *from* something (an illness)

refrain *from* something

regardless *of* something

rely *on* someone or something

reply *to* someone or something

require something *of* someone

research *in* a field

reverence *for* someone or something

run *into* debt

similar *to* someone or something

subscribe *to* something

surrender *to* someone

sympathy *with* or *for* someone or something

take advantage *of* someone or something

talk *over* something *with* someone

thankful *for* something

tired *of* something

wait *for* someone or something

wait *on* someone (customer)

*with* reference *to*

work *for* something or someone

When in doubt as to the correct preposition to be used with a word, always consult your dictionary. Also, try to note how idioms are used in your readings and imitate them in similar contexts.

## PRINCIPLES OF SPELLING

Research on what good spellers do reveals that spelling well is not an inborn talent or just a matter of confidence. The best spellers, as they write, use strategies for remembering how to spell difficult words. Many of them pronounce a word the way it is spelled rather than the way it is actually said (only in their heads, of course). So *definite* becomes *dee-finite* and *separate* becomes *sep-a-rate*.

You can develop your own system. The pressure to spell well has lessened somewhat with the use of computer spell checkers, but that does not lessen the anxiety associated with proper spelling when a handwritten note is required. Just as you are expected to use the commonly accepted practices for grammar, punctuation, and mechanics, so are you expected to use conventionally correct spelling. To do otherwise, either through error or simple carelessness, slows your reader and detracts from your message. In the time it takes your reader to realize that you meant *they're* and not *their*, he or she may have lost the flow of your thoughts.

For some, spelling seems an easy task; for others, it is always difficult. You know which category you fit into. Even those individuals who find spelling simple usually write with a dictionary close at hand to check words they may not be familiar with. But if you are one of those for whom spelling is always a problem, a review of some of the most effective ways of improving will be beneficial.

### Use a Dictionary

Disciplining yourself to check a dictionary whenever you have doubts about a word's spelling is one of the most important writing habits you can develop. Using the dictionary to correct your rough draft, or using the spelling checker on your word processor in conjunction with a dictionary, can help you check spelling and, at the same time, ensure that you have the right word.

The rest of the guidelines presented in this chapter are designed to save you time by reducing the number of words you should have to look up. None of them, however, should be thought of as a substitute for using a dictionary.

### Learn to Correct Your Pronunciation

Many people misspell words because they mispronounce them. Usually, the closer you come to pronouncing a word correctly, the closer you are to spelling it correctly. As you have already discovered, having some idea of how a word is pronounced is helpful when looking for that word in your dictionary. Therefore, it is worthwhile to learn a few basic principles of correct pronunciation. These principles fall into three general categories: the letters themselves, the syllables, and the symbols for sound and stress.

#### Letters

Every letter is either a vowel or a consonant. The letters *a*, *e*, *i*, *o*, and *u* are always vowels. The letter *y* behaves less consistently. Sometimes it is a vowel, as in the word *sky*, and sometimes it is a consonant, as in the word *yes*. All the other letters are always consonants. Thus, in the word *placard*, there are two vowels—the two *a*'s—and five consonants—*p*, *l*, *c*, *r*, and *d*. Similarly, in the word *restraint* there are three vowels—*e*, *a*, and *i*—and six consonants—*r*, *s*, *t*, *r*, *n*, and *t*.

#### Syllables

Recognizing words as a whole can often lead to mispronunciation and later to misspelling. Sounding words out, on the other hand, can often improve spelling. Every word is made up of units of sound called syllables. Each syllable always contains at least one vowel. When you first pronounce a word, begin by saying each syllable separately:

in-scru-ta-ble
pop-u-la-tion

Then say all of the syllables together. Make sure that you do not add a syllable that is not there or skip one that is. Such errors in pronunciation can often lead to spelling mistakes. For instance, a commonly misspelled word is athlete. Although the word has only two syllables, *ath-lete*, many people tend to pronounce the word with an extra syllable, *ath-e-lete*, which is incorrect. Those who add the extra syllable are misreading and mispronouncing the word and will probably misspell it later.

*Emphasis*

Every dictionary uses symbols to show how the various letters in a word should sound and which syllable in a word should be stressed. You will find a list of these symbols in the front of your dictionary. Two of the most common symbols are ˘ and ¯. They are used to indicate some of the sounds for vowels. A ˘ above a vowel means that its sound should be short:

ăpple          lĕt          lĭttle          ŏn          ŭp

A bar above a vowel means that the sound of that vowel should be long:

āpe          mēēt          īce          nō          ūse

Another common symbol is the stress, or accent, mark (´). It indicates which syllable in a word should receive the most stress.

re-tir´                              glit´-ter

Thus, in the word *retire* the second syllable should be stressed, whereas in *glitter* the first syllable should be stressed.

Although correct pronunciation can be very helpful in spelling, you must be careful not to rely on it to too great an extent. Sometimes spelling a word according to the way it is pronounced can get you into trouble. For instance, the last syllable of the word *proceed* is pronounced exactly as is the last syllable of both *supersede* and *precede*, but the spelling of the sound is different for each word. Similarly, English has many letter combinations that are pronounced differently in different words. For example, the *ough* in *tough* is not pronounced the same as the *ough* in *through* or *ought*. Therefore, as good a guideline as pronunciation can be, it is a guideline that must be used with caution.

**Learn the Nine Major Spelling Rules**

There are many different spelling rules, and each rule has a number of exceptions. It would be nearly impossible to memorize all of them. For this reason, only the nine major rules are given here. They cover the spelling problems that most frequently bother the largest number of writers. You should learn these rules well. It would even be a good idea to memorize the first four along with their exceptions. Learning these rules may not solve all of your spelling problems, but once you know them, you will be well on your way to becoming a better speller.

*Putting I Before E*

When *i* and *e* appear together in a word, the *i* normally comes before the *e*. The *e* comes before the *i*, however, when the combination is sounded like a long *a* or when it follows a *c*. The *ie* and *ei* rule can be mastered by learning the following jingle:

I before E
Except after C
Or when sounded like A
As in neighbor and weigh.

*Examples:*
| | | | |
|---|---|---|---|
| sleigh | neighbor | weight | feign |
| receive | conceit | receipt | conceive |

*Exceptions:*
| | | | |
|---|---|---|---|
| either | neither | height | leisure |
| seize | weird | seizure | counterfeit |
| financier | species | | |

*Doubling the Final Consonant When Adding a Suffix*

Double the final consonant before adding a suffix beginning with a vowel when the final consonant is preceded by a vowel and the word is accented on the last syllable or is composed of only one syllable.

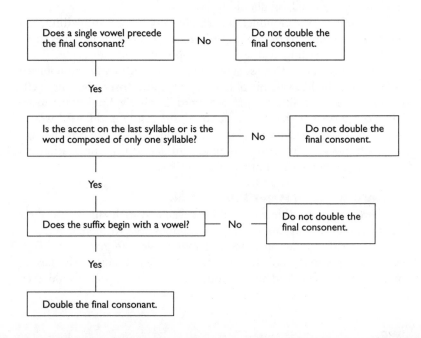

*Examples:*

| | | | |
|---|---|---|---|
| occurred | batter | omitted | stopped |
| occurrence | madden | recurring | running |

There are no exceptions to this rule.

*Adding a Suffix to Words Ending with an Unpronounced E*

Leave out the final unpronounced *e* before adding a suffix that begins with a vowel, but keep the *e* before adding a suffix that begins with a consonant.

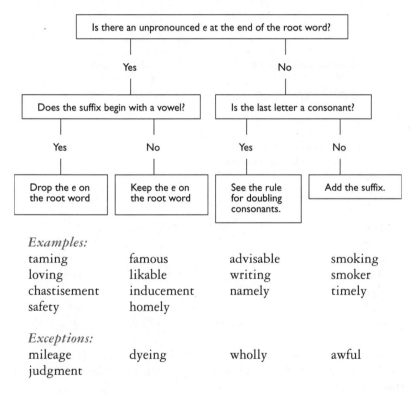

*Examples:*

| | | | |
|---|---|---|---|
| taming | famous | advisable | smoking |
| loving | likable | writing | smoker |
| chastisement | inducement | namely | timely |
| safety | homely | | |

*Exceptions:*

| | | | |
|---|---|---|---|
| mileage | dyeing | wholly | awful |
| judgment | | | |

Many of the exceptions to this rule have their own rule.

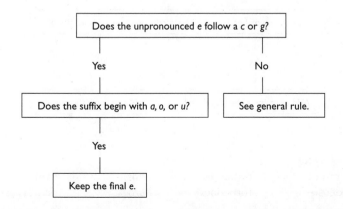

*Examples:*

| | | | |
|---|---|---|---|
| changeable | arrangeable | courageous | replaceable |

### Changing Y to I When Adding a Suffix

If the root word ends in a *y* that is preceded by a consonant, change the *y* to *i* before adding any suffix that does not begin with *i*.

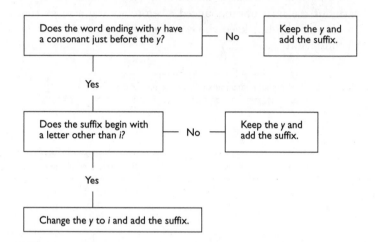

*Examples:*

| | | | |
|---|---|---|---|
| cried | tries | implying | reliable |
| cries | tried | relies | studies |
| crying | trying | relied | studied |
| flies | implies | relying | studying |
| flying | implied | | |

There are no exceptions to this rule.

### Forming Plurals of Words Ending in O

Add *es* to form the plural of words ending in *o* when a consonant precedes the *o*.

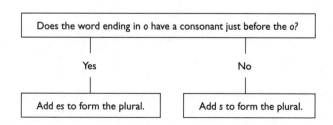

*Examples:*

| | | | |
|---|---|---|---|
| potatoes | tomatoes | trios | vetoes |
| rodeos | torpedoes | heroes | embryos |

*Exceptions:*

autos                    solos                    bassos                    altos

## *Changing C to CK When Adding ED, Y, or ING as a Suffix*

When a word ends with a *c* that is pronounced as a *k*, change the *c*
to *ck* before adding *ed*, *y*, or *ing* as a suffix.

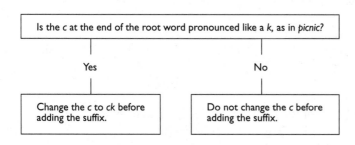

*Examples:*

politicking         picnicking         frolicked           mimicked
colicky             mimicking          sarcastically       caustically

*Exceptions:*

mimicry             arced

## *Adding DIS, UN, or MIS as a Prefix*

Do not change the root word when the prefix *dis*, *un*, or *mis* is added
to it. This rule applies even if the root begins with the same letter that
the prefix ends with.

*Examples:*

disappoint          dissolve            misspell            unnatural
dissuade            misrelated          unnecessary         unnerve
dissatisfy

There are no exceptions to this rule.

## *Adding LY to Words Ending in L*

When adding the suffix *ly* to a root word ending in *l*, keep the *l* on
the root.

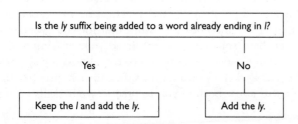

*Examples:*

finally            incidentally        cynically           imperially

There are no exceptions to this rule.

*Handling Words Ending in CEDE, CEED, and SEDE*
Use the ending *cede* for most English words with the sound "seed" as the last syllable.

*Examples:*

concede            precede             secede              intercede
recede

*Exceptions:*
Three words end in *ceed*: succeed, proceed, exceed
One word ends in *sede*: supersede

### Learn to Proofread Effectively

Effective proofreading can save you a number of spelling errors on each paper. Unfortunately, proofreading is not always as easy as it may first appear. Frequently, writers are too familiar with what they have written and become blind to mistakes they may have made. When reading over their papers, they tend to see what they meant to write rather than what actually appears on the page. For this reason, it is always a good idea to let a paper or essay "cool" before checking it for errors.

Spelling checkers can go a long way in helping you to proofread. But remember, they only catch typos that do not match the words listed in the program's dictionary. Many errors writers make do conform to English words; in many cases the writer has typed a legitimate but inappropriate word, such as *to* for *too* or *be* for *by*. For these reasons, spelling checkers can aid you in the proofreading process, but they should not replace proofreading your work.

When you proofread, try to concentrate on the individual words. Depending on sight recognition alone will seldom be effective. Instead, actually spell out each word to yourself. One way to help focus your efforts is to keep in mind the types of errors you most often make. As you proofread, try to find a set number of these errors, say three or four, on each page. You may also find that it helps to read aloud. Some writers find it easier to concentrate on the spelling of each word if they read each line of their papers backward, from right to left. Although the context is missing, you can easily note any words for which this might cause a problem and quickly check them by reading forward.

Becoming a good proofreader takes practice. As you gain experience, you will discover the methods that work best for you. Whenever possible, however, have someone else proofread your writing also. Talk a friend into trading papers. The fresh eye can almost always detect errors that the overworked eye would miss. In addition, proofreading each other's work will allow both of you to practice your skills on unfamiliar material. Frequently, finding errors in someone else's writing will help you to find similar errors in your own.

## Commonly Misspelled and Confused Words

The following is a list of words that students and writers often misspell or confuse. Although a dictionary is always the best place to check the spelling of a word, some writers prefer word lists because they are so easy to refer to. The problem is that the lists usually do not include definitions. Therefore, anyone using a list must be very careful not to choose the wrong word simply because it looks or sounds like another word. If you decide to use the following list, be sure that you do not make mistakes such as using *accept* for *except* or *device* for *devise*.

| | | |
|---|---|---|
| abbreviate | awkward | compliment/ |
| absence | bankruptcy | complement |
| absorption | bargain | compromise |
| absurd | basically | conceit |
| accept/except | becoming | conceive |
| access/excess | beginning | condemn |
| accidentally | believe | conference |
| accommodate | beneficial | confidence |
| accumulate | biscuit | conscience/ |
| achievement | breathe/breath | conscious |
| across | bulletin | conscientious |
| actually | bureaucracy | consensus |
| address | burglar | considerably |
| adequately | calendar | consistent |
| adolescence | camouflage | controlling |
| adopt | candidate | controversial |
| advise/advice | carburetor | convenient |
| aggressive | careful | correspondence |
| all right | category | courageous |
| alleys/allies | caucus | crises/crisis |
| a lot/allot | cautious | criticism |
| alter/altar | cellar/seller | curriculum |
| amateur | cemetery | decimal |
| analyze | choose/chose | defense |
| angle/angel | circuit | definite |
| annual | circular | delicious |
| apparatus | circumference | dependence |
| appropriate | clause | descent |
| arctic | coarse/course | describe |
| article | coincidence | desert/dessert |
| ascent | college/collage | desirable |
| assassinate | coming | desperate |
| athlete | commission | destroy |
| attendance | committee | deterrence |
| audience | competent | develop |

| | | |
|---|---|---|
| development | harass | muscle |
| device/devise | hear/here | naturalization |
| dictionary | height | Negroes |
| difference | hereditary | nickel |
| dilemma | heroes | ninety |
| disappoint | hindrance | observance |
| disdain | holiness | occasion |
| dissent | hoping | occurred |
| divine | humorous | omission |
| dominance | hypocrisy | opportunity |
| dropped | illegible | panicked |
| dying/dyeing | illogical | paragraph |
| echoes | impostor | parallel |
| eighth | incidentally | parentheses/ |
| eligible | incredible | parenthesis |
| embarrass | independent | passed/past |
| eminence | indict | peculiar |
| environment | inherent | pedal/peddle |
| equivalent | inoculate | perceive |
| exaggerate | insistent | permanent |
| exceed/accede | instance | permissible |
| excellent | intelligible | perseverance |
| excess/access | interruptions | personnel/personal |
| exercise | irrelevance | pertain |
| existence | irresistible | Philippines |
| expense | irreverent | physical |
| extremely | its/it's | physician |
| exuberance | jam/jamb | pickle |
| facetious | judicial | piece/peace |
| fantasies | knead/need | plagiarize |
| fascinate | knot | playwright |
| feasible | laboratory | polar |
| February | leisure | politician |
| fictitious | library | poll/pole |
| finally | license | possess |
| flexible | likely | practical |
| foreign | liquefy | presence/presents |
| formally/formerly | literature | principle/principal |
| frantically | loneliness | privilege |
| friend | lose/loose | probably |
| frolicking | maneuver | proceed |
| fulfill | marriage | professor |
| fundamentally | medieval | pronunciation |
| further/farther | mediocre | psychology |
| goddess | merely | purl/pearl |
| grammar | mimicking | quandary |
| grievous | miniature | quantity |
| guarantee | misspell | quiet/quite/quit |

quotation
radioactive
receipt
receive
recognize
recommend
reference
relief
reminisce
repetition
representative
residence
responsible
rhythm
scarcity
schedule
scissors
secede
seize
sentence
separate
September
sergeant
severely
shepherd
siege
silence
simultaneous
sincerely
slimy
solely
solemn

sonnet
sophomore
souvenir
species
stationary/
   stationery
statue/statute
straight/strait
strength
studying
subsequent
subtle
suburbia
succeed
success
summary/
   summery
superfluous
supersede
supplement
symbolize
tawdry
technique
temperament
tenant
tendency
than/then
there/they're/their
theses/thesis
thorough/through
though/thought
to/too/two

toeing
tragedy
tranquillity
tried
truly
twelfth
tyranny
unanimous
unnecessary
usually
vacuum
vetoes
villain
vinegar
violence
visibility
volume
waste/waist
watt
weather/whether
Wednesday
weight
weird
where/wear
wholly/holy
whose/who's
wintry
woman/women
wondrous
writing
written

When you write, it is normal to make a few grammatical errors. After all, you are concentrating on the content of your paper. However, you will want to find these errors before you turn your paper in. The best way to do so is to sift through your paper several times, directing your attention toward each potential error in turn. In effect, you want to treat your writing as if it were an exercise. By going quickly through your paper five times, you can cover the seven most common trouble spots.

As thorough as this method is, it is also time consuming. Of course, the amount of time needed will depend on the length of the paper. Because you will not always have as long as you would like to correct your writing, two plans are included here. The first is for those times when you have thirty minutes to an hour to check for errors. The second is a briefer plan for those occasions when you have less than half an hour.

# THE EDITING PROCESS: CORRECTING COMMON ERRORS

## ADOPTING A PLAN

This chapter is designed to be of use both before you submit a paper and after the paper is returned. Before handing in a paper, you should use the guidelines to edit your writing for any grammatical inconsistencies. As doctors say, prevention is the best medicine. After the paper is returned, you should review any errors that you may have let slip by but that were caught by your teacher. Try to analyze your errors by figuring out why you made them. This will help you to keep from making the same ones next time. On the inside front cover is a list of questions that cover the major areas in the text.

### Plan One

Go through your paper five times. On each pass answer one of the following questions, making sure that you correct any errors you discover:

1. Do your subjects agree with their verbs? Do your predicates match their subjects?
2. Are there any sentence fragments or run-on sentences?
3. Are all your verbs and verbals formed accurately?
4. Do all your pronouns fit their references and functions?
5. Is your syntax correct?

## Plan Two

The second plan, designed for when the amount of time you have to look over your writing is brief, is an abbreviated version of the first. It makes use of the most recent paper returned by your teacher.

1. Identify the three grammatical errors that occurred the most frequently in the last essay you wrote.
2. Categorize these errors according to the following numbers.

| | |
|---|---|
| verb agreement—1 | sentence fragments—2 |
| pronoun agreement—4 | pronoun case—4 |
| pronoun reference—4 | modifiers—5 |
| parallelism—5 | run-on sentences—2 |
| verb tenses—3 | subjunctive verbs—3 |
| predication—1 | syntax—5 |
| irregular verbs—3 | confusing modifiers—5 |

3. Go through your paper for each of the three problems you are having the most trouble with. If many of your errors were in word choice, check Chapter D, "A Glossary of Usage." For errors in spelling or punctuation, see Chapters A and C.

The rest of this chapter helps you sift for errors in your work following the steps in Plan One.

## I. DO YOUR SUBJECTS AGREE WITH THEIR VERBS? DO YOUR PREDICATES MATCH THEIR SUBJECTS?

If you already know how to pick out a singular verb and a singular noun, you may want to skip to the section called "Check Verbs and Subjects for Number" on the next page. If you sometimes have trouble identifying singulars and plurals, you will want to study this section carefully.

### Distinguish Singular from Plural

Recognizing whether your simple predicates (also called verbs) and subjects are singular or plural is not complicated. The same endings mean different things on nouns and verbs.

- Most singular nouns do not end in *s*: *car, dog, tomato.*
- Most plural nouns end in *s* or *es*: *cars, dogs, tomatoes.*
- Most singular verbs end in *s* or *es*: *says, runs, takes, smokes.*
- Most plural verbs do not end in *s*: *say, run, take, smoke.*

Usually, then, both the subject—when it is a noun—and the verb in a sentence will not end in *s*. Of course, there are a few exceptions to forming both the plurals of nouns and the plurals of verbs. Keep in mind the following irregular nouns:

1. Words like *people* and *children:* Some nouns become plural by changing their forms, not by adding an *s* or *es* ending. *Person* becomes *people; child* becomes *children.*
2. Words like *species* and *deer* and names: Some nouns have the same forms for their singular and plural meanings. Also, a person's name may end in *s,* but the *s* ending does not mean the noun is plural. *Charles* and *James* are singular, despite their last letter.

Simple predicates that include helping verbs reflect the number of the simple predicate only by the helping verb, and the other verb never ends in *s.* Thus, just looking at a verb that has a helper you cannot expect to see an *s* ending, which would ordinarily reveal at a glance that the verb is singular. Usually, a present tense verb will not end in *s* if any of the following conditions exist:

1. The verb has a helper (*might go*).
2. The subject ends in *s,* except for names or special words that have the same form in the singular and plural.
3. The subject of the clause has been made plural by changing the form of the word.
4. The subject of the clause is *I* or *you.*
5. The verb is a form of *to be* other than *is.*

When pronouns are the subjects of clauses you can figure out whether they are singular or plural very easily. Only with indefinite pronouns like *everyone* and *none* should you even question the number. Otherwise, the number for pronouns is consistently as the following chart points out:

| *Singular* | *Plural* |
|---|---|
| I | we |
| you (ask yourself: Do I mean one person?) | you (ask yourself: Do I mean more than one person?) |
| he, she, it | they |

### Check Verbs and Subjects for Number

The point of checking the number of subjects and verbs is to make sure they agree: a singular subject should go with a singular verb and a plural subject with a plural verb. For example, in the following sentence the subject, *authorities,* is plural. Therefore, the verb for this subject should also be plural.

The *authorities* consider all the evidence before suspending a student.

But if the subject is singular, the verb must be singular.

> The final *authority* is the president.

This rule may seem almost too easy. With most subjects and verbs, agreement is just as clear-cut as in these examples. However, in some sentences, the rules are more complicated, and it is harder to tell whether the subject is singular or plural.

A prepositional phrase coming between the subject and the verb does not influence the number of the verb. In the following examples, the prepositional phrases are indicated by brackets:

> *One* [of the interviewers] *knows* just the right questions to ask.
> The *impact* [of all the meetings] [with the union leaders] *was* hardly felt [by the employees].
> The *flu* [as well as the common cold] *is* a threat to every student.

When the word *it* begins a sentence, the verb following is always singular.

> *It* sometimes *seems* as if I will never be able to get an A in French.
> *It is* the three girls over there who have volunteered to serve on the screening committee.

When the word *there* begins a sentence, the verb depends on what comes next. If what follows is plural, the verb should be plural; if what follows is singular, the verb should be singular.

> *There are ways* of adjusting an overdrawn checking account.
> *There is one joke* that always makes me laugh—the one about nearsightedness.

When a sentence begins with a verbal, the subject sometimes comes after the verb. Nevertheless, the subject and the verb should still agree in number.

> Splashed on the ground *was* the *blood* of the defeated men.
> Wandering around the golf course *were* two *children* who had run away from home.

When a sentence contains a linking verb and a complement, the subject, not the complement, determines the number of the verb.

> *Mothers are* a wonderful breed.
> *It is* my grades that will suffer from all my frivolity.

Two subjects joined by *and* usually take a plural verb.

*Scrabble and Hearts are* my favorite games.

Exception: When two subjects connected by *and* really represent parts of the same unit—when they are actually inseparable—the verb is singular.

> *Bacon and eggs is* a satisfying meal any time.
> *There is time and money enough* for an extensive study.

When *each* or *every* comes before singular subjects joined by and, the verb is singular.

> *Every* man and woman *has* a vote.
> *Each* owner and renter *receives* a different tax credit.

If *who, which,* or *that* is the subject, the only way to determine the correct number of the verb is to discover what the pronoun stands for (the antecedent). The simple predicate should take the singular form if the word that *who, which,* or *that* stands for is singular and the plural form if that word is plural.

> The person *who sells* pretzels in the shopping plaza is not here today.

Sometimes the antecedent is found in a prepositional phrase. Nevertheless, the rule remains the same.

> He is *one of those people who go* to midnight horror movies.

When *or* or *nor* separates two subjects, the number of the verb should agree with the number of the subject closest to it.

> Jim *or his parents walk* and *feed* our dog when we are on vacation.
> Either Eddie *or his sisters are* responsible for the debt.
> Tomorrow is the anniversary of the day neither the unions *nor labor wants* to remember.

With indefinite pronouns such as *each, everyone, anybody, nobody, none, either,* and *neither* as subjects, use singular verbs.

> *Each* of us *is* doing his or her share to clean up the air.
> *Anybody* who *comes* late to a surprise party is inconsiderate.
> *Everyone has* a vote.

Collective nouns such as *family, class, number, public,* and *orchestra* may be considered either singular or plural in a particular context. If the collective noun refers to the whole, a singular verb should be used.

> The *committee votes* at noon.

The committee is treated as a whole group who will vote together.

"The *public wants* more for its tax dollars than run-down and poorly staffed hospitals," said the president of the nurses' association.

The *public* is one whole group that wants more.

However, if the collective noun emphasizes the parts of the whole, a plural verb should be used.

A *number* of my friends *have expressed* interest in joining the Peace Corps.

The number is made up of several individuals, each expressing interest.

*Half* of the people in the afternoon crew *want* to work for overtime.

The *half* is made up of several individuals each wanting to work overtime.

Some words indicating quantities take singular verbs to show a lump sum and plural verbs to emphasize the individual units.

*Fifty years* of marriage *were* not easy.
*Four blocks was* not too far to walk.
*Three hundred words is* a short essay.
*Four hundred words are* on each page.

Sometimes an entire phrase is treated as a unit. When such phrases serve as a subject, they take singular verbs.

*"All men are created equal" is* a statement much in question.
*Down and Out in Paris and London is* a good book, but *Dubliners is* my favorite.
*"The American people" is* a common term in speeches.

When words end in *s,* they usually take plural verbs, but there are some special cases. When a word ends in *ics,* apply a special test: ask yourself if the word in context describes a field of study. If it does, the verb is usually singular. Otherwise, it's plural.

*Athletics is* a required activity.
*Athletics are* good for people.
*Ethics is* a major branch of philosophy.
His *ethics are* questionable.

Certain words, such as *scissors, riches, pants,* and *hopes,* are always considered as plural even though they seem to convey singular concepts.

These *pants do* not fit.
The *scissors are* in the drawer.

Some words ending in *s* take singular verbs.

The *news is* all happy.
*Mumps is* a childhood disease.

---

### Exercises

A. In the following sentences, correct any errors in subject-verb agreement.
   1. The buildings with red painted panels along their sides seems to fit an elementary school better than they fit a college.
   2. If a pair of pants have holes, they should be sewn.
   3. Nineteen of the windows in the house was blown out by the high winds.
   4. The scissors has always been kept in one place, under a blanket, in the hallway closet.
   5. If, as they say, there are not one place—much less two places—to stay in the town, then why is it called a tourist spot?
   6. Neither Joseph nor the authorities knows why he speaks as he does.
   7. Both the fishing and the skiing is excellent on Lake Isabella.
   8. One among many are required to do extra work for no extra pay.
   9. Either worldwide starvation of poor people or the redistribution of wealth are in store for us in the next thirty years.
   10. The United States of America are a great place for people who have drive.
   11. Because every one of the Bengals play as if his life depends on the game, I must conclude that the coach instills in his players a sense of competition and the knowledge of what it means to succeed.
   12. The members of that group is so different from each other that I'm amazed to find them all still friendly.
   13. People's style of talking is individualistic because no two people think alike.
   14. Whether one person or a dozen people tells me to do something, I will refuse if I do not want to do it.
   15. The mass media is not very responsible, surely not as responsible as the intellectuals are.

B. Correct any errors in subject-verb agreement in the following sentences and state the rule that you apply to correct each error.
   1. Either a refund or four new tires is in order for the customer whose new car had defective tires.
   2. One of the many reasons a person should not suddenly undertake a strenuous program of exercise is that the heart cannot adjust to the excessive activity and must build up to it slowly.
   3. There are a wealth of opportunities awaiting any adult who wishes to return to school.

4. The failure of the drug rehabilitation programs make current problems in the inner city seem even more difficult to overcome.

5. ESP are, surprisingly enough, to be found in everyday experiences.

6. The depiction of ethnic groups on television shows are misleading.

7. It isn't easy to cook for six people who has different tastes from one another.

8. There are no reason a man and a woman cannot get along if they really try.

9. All the setbacks in a person's life adds up to nothing if that person succeeds at the one thing that matters to him or her.

10. On top of the dead man's dresser was found a woman's wedding ring, two tickets to a Ram's game, and a note addressed to Suzanne.

11. Near the train tracks live a group of tramps who survives on the heat of the sun and the food distributed by the mission on Main Street.

12. According to some sociologists, rivalry between gangs are expected and provide reinforcement of identity for urban youths.

13. White-collar workers who use their heads to keep the "system" going are just as dehumanized as blue-collar workers who are tied to the master-slave relationship of assembly line work.

14. The only troublemaker in the group of children attending the concert is David.

15. The lack of concentration among poorly fed children are to be expected because their bodies cannot stop telling their minds how hungry they feel.

16. The delicate, restrained, and collected manner in which some women like to think of themselves are not in keeping with the sensibilities of today's women.

17. The ability to understand and react to other people and their ideas are essential to personal happiness.

18. There are usually a combination of reasons for any war.

C. In the following paragraph, correct any subjects and verbs that do not agree.

Financial aids is not fairly given out to students whose parents are in certain income brackets. The government look at the money going into the homes of the students, but they fail to see how much of it must leave the homes because of special financial circumstances. A student with parents who earn over $60,000 a year may find it harder to get a job or a loan for school than will a student whose parents makes $30,000. It would seem that the parents who earn $60,000 have a lot more money than the ones earning only $30,000. But suppose that the family earning $60,000 supports a sick relative or has to pay for the college education of three children, whereas the family who earns $30,000 has only one child to support. If both students are applying for college, the $60,000 family is actually in worse financial condition to bear the burden of a college education.

D. When a sentence begins with the word *there,* what is the special rule for deciding whether the verb is singular or plural? Write three sentences beginning with *there* and explain why the verbs you use are singular or plural.

E. Write four sentences that contain collective nouns as the subjects. What is the general rule for subject-verb agreement with collective nouns, and how does it apply to each sentence you have written?

F. Do you think that informal conversation should require strict adherence to rules of subject-verb agreement? Why or why not? Write a paragraph that explains your view and gives at least two examples of how the rules should be used in conversation.

G. Correct any errors in subject-verb agreement found in the following brief paragraph.

> Descending from the sky high above, a sea gull swoop down for a piece of bread left on the ground by a sixth grader. Trees swaying left and right from the force of the north wind, flowers adding their sweet smell to the air, and children rushing to play on the swings also makes up this pleasant environment. These are just a few of the beautiful scenes one might see. Riding a bicycle is one of the best ways to feel and enjoy a lovely environment.

H. Which sentences below contain errors in subject-verb agreement? What caused the writer to make whatever errors you find?

1. Even the best of people forget the social graces taught them in childhood.
2. Either administrative priorities or concern for individuals seems to be the most important consideration of many of our current leaders.
3. Neither I nor my neighbors are in a position to buy fencing, so their dog continues to run freely about my yard.
4. Yesterday the neighbor's dog, along with another mangy stray I'd never noticed before, knocked over my trash cans; today I, with all my gumption, are in an argumentative mood.
5. Pages of clean paper and a pencil are things I always seem to forget.
6. Strings tied in bows around index fingers is a clumsy and foolish technique for remembering something.
7. The first thing I was told was that the barracks are no place to keep private property.
8. Dickens, Melville, and Shakespeare, the greats of literature, are the writers I choose from when I want to enjoy a story.
9. The drivers who travels on our highways has a responsibility to drive safely.
10. The assembly were not clear whether one position or the other was best, so the vote was split.
11. Posters on walls are funny when they are inappropriate to the setting, when they are as out of place as candy would be at a dieters' convention.
12. A pack of dogs don't have animosity toward each other unless food or mating are involved.
13. The alumni from this college is very successful.
14. Without being too harsh, I had to say that the kind of ideas he had were not those I'd care to share.
15. They sometimes play at those nightclubs in the area that gives them all the free food they want.

I. Write a paragraph that explains the main ideas of one of your beliefs. After you write the paragraph, underline all the verbs and circle their subjects. Are there any errors in agreement?

### Check Your Predication

While checking your sentences for subject-verb agreement, make sure that the predicates of your sentences actually say something about their subjects. An equation is set up in sentences, especially when the simple predicate is a form of *to be*. It is easy to slip into the habit of faulty predication. The result is that your sentences do not say what you intended, although, with a little trouble, the reader can sometimes untangle the mess. Look at the following sentence:

> Seventeen doctors on the staff of Rivers Hospital refused to perform the new operation, considering it too dangerous.

The predicate—*refused to perform the new operation, considering it too dangerous*—does say something about the subject—*seventeen doctors on the staff of Rivers Hospital*. The sentence is clear and correct. But now take a look at this sentence:

> Whatever the cause, the cure for bad behavior has to be patient, kind, and responsive.

The predicate—*has to be patient, kind, and responsive*—does not say something about the subject—*the cure for bad behavior*. How can a cure be patient or kind? The writer has lost sight of what the sentence was originally supposed to say. Patience can be attributed to a person or an animal, but not to a thing like a cure. Probably the writer means that *parents* need to be patient and kind in order to cure their children of bad behavior.

When you check the predicates of your sentences, you are really asking yourself, "What did I set out to say here, and what did I actually end up saying?" If you haven't said what you mean, you need to reword the sentence.

---

### Exercises

A. Check each predicate in the sentences below, making sure that it says something about the subject. Make any necessary corrections by rewording sentences with faulty predication. Which sentences are made especially confusing by the faulty predication?

1. The life of a professional swimmer gets very little time off to relax.
2. The food served in most college snack bars is not a wide enough selection to satisfy discriminating eaters.
3. His restraint failed to answer the teacher's questions quickly enough.

4. A tragic man's mind must be a paradox, his pride must be strong, and his suffering must be without reason.

5. My roommate, Rosemary, was a prime example of wish fulfillment the other day.

6. Senator Price has been a man of many positions, including the power of secretary of state.

7. Friendship between men and women can be an uncomfortable role.

8. The drinks would be a small donation.

9. The Anglo ideal of beauty is fashion and femininity.

10. Since I was a child, the most disagreeable place for me was in the waiting room of a hospital.

11. Detachment was his ideal man in society.

12. Drugs are an escape from reality.

13. A comparison of the bike would be the car.

14. The child may interpret failure in class as lacking what most students have mentally.

15. The main function of a mixed bar is the transition from straight to gay and back to straight.

16. Conversations at a dance can range from gossip to pickups.

17. An early morning class is hard to get out of bed.

18. For the insecure person, the role of rebellion and its cause are a chance to find a place in the world and identity.

## 2. ARE THERE ANY SENTENCE FRAGMENTS OR RUN-ON SENTENCES?

### How to Detect and Correct Fragments

Fragments are incomplete sentences. Here are some common examples:

> When we go shopping.
> Being in the insurance business.
> Of course.

Although they may have subjects and verbs, fragments are not complete thoughts that can stand alone. In most writing, they should be avoided.

### *Looking for Fragments*

Many patterns, phrases, and clauses that begin with certain words tend to be mistaken for complete sentences. Once you familiarize yourself with these fragment patterns, you will be on your way to distinguishing incomplete sentences from complete ones. Then you can correct many of the fragments simply by incorporating them into adjacent sentences. Others will require, as you will see, converting the fragment into a complete sentence in its own right.

A fragment can occur because a helping verb is needed to complete the main verb in a sentence. The following is a list of helping verbs. Check page 366 if you do not know their functions.

| | | |
|---|---|---|
| am | does | were |
| should be | are | had |
| was | will be | can |
| has | will | can be |
| could | have | must |
| did | is | have been |
| might have been | | |

Of the following sentence pairs, one is complete and the other is a fragment. Looking at them closely, you will notice that the only difference between the two is the addition of a helping verb. The fragment (italicized) lacks the helping verb. In the complete sentence the helping verb is in italics.

*Jose counting the votes.* Jose *will* be counting the votes.
*The dogs barking because they feel hungry.* The dogs *are* barking because they feel hungry.
*Aunt Hilda gone to work early today.* Aunt Hilda *has* gone to work early today.

A fragment may simply be a phrase, or it may be a clause. A clause, although it has both a subject and a verb, still may not be a complete thought. The following words often begin clauses that are fragments:

| | | | |
|---|---|---|---|
| that | who | to whom | where |
| whose | | | |

Of course, not all sentences starting with these words are fragments; the clause may be connected to a main clause. When a clause beginning with the words just listed is connected to a main clause, the result is a complete sentence.

In each of the following examples, one sentence is only a clause that cannot stand on its own. It is italicized. It is a fragment that must depend on the main clause. The other sentence is a main clause.

It was the Superintendent of Schools in the Lakeland District. *Who voted against the new program for distributing condoms at the health office.*
Participating in an alcohol rehabilitation program made one thing clear to him. *That for him drinking could not be a recreational activity.*

Here are some other words that often indicate fragments:

| because | as if | though | if |
| although | by | even though | unless |
| as | since | in order to | so that |

In each of the following examples, one sentence (italicized) is a fragment and could not stand alone. The other sentence is a main clause and could stand on its own. The fragment could be attached to the main clause to create one complete sentence.

> Massive reconstruction is underway as a result of earthquake damage in Los Angeles. *Because the public has finally been able to collect on claims for federal assistance.*
> *Although she was tired of his excuses.* She listened to one last explanation.

Some fragments begin with certain words that indicate time and place:

| before | when | whenever | while |
| after | until | wherever | |

In the following examples, one sentence (in italics) is a fragment beginning with a word that indicates time or place. The other is a main clause. The italicized fragment could be attached to the main clause to create one complete sentence.

> My parents like to invite the entire family over for a reunion. *Whenever I come home on vacation from school.*
> She learned that her husband was blind in one eye. *After living with him for fourteen years.*

Prepositional phrases are often mistaken for complete sentences. (See page 369 for a list of prepositions.) Just think of how often this type of fragment appears in advertising. In the following examples, the fragments are all prepositional phrases. Each fragment is italicized. Attached to the main clauses adjacent to them, they would be correct. They cannot, however, stand alone as complete sentences.

> When midterm arrives, coursework places great demands on students, so they often form study groups to help each other prepare for tests. *Outside of required review sessions.*
> *Between the unions' demands for better conditions and the employers' demands for greater productivity.* Very little change can occur.

Verbals that act as adjectives often end in *ing*, *en*, or *ed*. As you recall, these verbals are called participles. A sentence having a participle but no verb is always a fragment. In the following examples, the incomplete sentences begin with participles, and the phrases that contain the participles have no other verbs. These phrases (italicized) are, therefore, fragments. Connected to the main clauses that stand next to them, the participles would begin phrases that help to make up complete sentences. Still, you can see how incomplete the phrases are alone.

Late last night three girls saw two young men. *Running stark naked across campus.*

*Called to jury duty at the end of the school year, just as vacation started.* I complained that it was a waste of time.

If the only verb in a sentence is an infinitive, the sentence is a fragment. Infinitives cannot function as sentence verbs. Remember that all sentences must have both subjects and verbs. In the following examples, the fragments are introduced by infinitives. Each fragment is italicized. You will notice that there is no other verb form in the fragments. The fragments could be incorporated into the main clauses that come before or after them to make complete sentences. But as they stand, you can see why the phrases beginning with infinitives are not complete sentences.

I worked in a drug rehabilitation program at the Marlborough Home. *To learn more about problems in the inner city and to understand current theories about intervention.*

Ms. Corman tried to do her best. *To motivate her students to want to learn.*

Appositives are words or groups of words that rename a noun. They are usually set off by commas. Take a look at the following sentence:

Jim Drugel, a baker at the Seventh Street Bakery, is coming to dinner.

The words *a baker at the Seventh Street Bakery* are an appositive renaming the noun Jim Drugel. An appositive used by itself is a fragment. Such fragments are particularly common when the appositive comes before or after the main clause containing the noun it renames. In the following examples, appositives alone (italicized) are mistaken for complete sentences when, in fact, they are only fragments. Incorporating the appositives into main clauses would create complete sentences. But you can see that the appositives, as they stand, are incomplete.

It is difficult to explain all the meaning Cesar Chavez holds for laborers. *A group who had little to look forward to until he raised their pride and self-esteem.*

Since I constantly made long-distance telephone calls and got tired of feeding quarters to the black box on the wall, I decided to get my own telephone. *A convenience I have learned to regret.*

Up until now we have been looking at pairs of sentences so that the relationships between fragment patterns and main clauses could be shown. Now let's look at a paragraph from a student's paper. As you read along, try to identify the type of fragment pattern each of the italicized clauses and phrases represents. Also notice how the meaning of many of the fragments seems incomplete or confusing without the meaning of an adjacent main clause.

A tarantula is an easy pet to get to know as long as you know how to handle one. Once your pet is settled in its new environment in your home and seems calm, move your hand slowly. *Across the line of vision.* If it remains calm, it is ready to be handled. If you are unsure of yourself or of your spider, you may feel better wearing close-fitting gloves. *Like a snake.* A tarantula cannot bite through cloth. Slowly try to put your hand into your spider's box. *In front of its head.* Resting your hand there for a few minutes gives the spider a chance to take the initiative and climb onto your hand. *If after a short time it hasn't moved toward you.* Reach over with one hand slowly. Pick it up. *Gently grasping the body of the spider and placing it in the palm of your hand. If it puts itself in a squatting position with its stomach making contact with your skin or gloves.* It is trying to bite. Its mouth is located on its stomach. If you find instead that it sits quietly, leave it for a minute, and then pet its back softly. *Whenever it acts jumpy.* Leave it alone for a few minutes. *To let it get better acquainted with its environment. Once your spider will sit quietly.* In your hand. You can do anything with it. The key words to remember are "calm," "careful," and "slow." *Which is how you should act with it.*

The types of fragments named in this section on "Looking for Fragments" are the most common. You may find others, too. However, if you can isolate all the fragments that fit the patterns discussed here, you will be able to make great improvements in your writing.

### Correcting Fragments

There are two reliable ways to correct fragments. The best method to use depends on the particular sentences you are trying to correct.

The first method is to incorporate the fragment pattern into a main clause that comes before or after the fragment. This method often works smoothly because many of the sentences you broke up into fragments and main clauses on paper were actually linked in your mind. The result is a kind of postscript fragment, one that tags along with the idea just stated. Once you have found a fragment, look at the closest main clauses that come before and after it. You may want to connect the fragment to one of these complete sentences, either at one end or at some appropriate point inside the sentence. Let's take a look at how the process works.

*Fragment:* Like a snake.
*Main clause:* A tarantula cannot bite through cloth.
*Complete sentence:* A tarantula, like a snake, cannot bite through cloth.

How about another?

*Main clause:* To June, a husband must be a perfect person.
*Fragment:* Understanding in every way.
*Complete sentence:* To June, a husband must be a perfect person, understanding in every way.

Of course, each time you want to combine a fragment with a main clause, you must really think through what you are trying to say. What is the best possible way to get across what you mean? Haphazardly combining a fragment and main clause just because they are close to each other may cause you to write awkward, wordy, and even confusing sentences. Keep in mind that when you combine, you are combining ideas, not just words. You may need to change a word here and there to avoid repetition or add clarity. For instance, in the following combination the pronoun *he* is substituted for the name Winston to avoid repetition of the name:

*Main clause:* Winston tried his best in all sports, including baseball.
*Fragment:* Which Winston had never played very well.
*Complete sentence:* Winston tried his best in all sports, including baseball, which he had never played very well.

The second method of correcting fragments is to remove the fragment pattern by changing a word or creating a complete subject and verb sequence. The point of these changes is to leave the sentence able to stand on its own. This method is easiest for sentences lacking helping verbs.

*Fragment:* Jim having a hard time with calculus but doing well in geology.
*Complete sentence:* Jim is having a hard time with calculus but is doing well in geology.

How about another kind of sentence fragment?

*Main clause:* Jinny knew she would be elected to serve as the chairperson of the finance committee.
*Fragment:* Being the most experienced fund-raiser in the group.
*Complete sentence:* Jinny knew she would be elected to serve as the chairperson of the finance committee. She was the most experienced fund-raiser in the group.

Of course, the fragment could also be incorporated according to the first method: "Jinny, being the most experienced fund-raiser in the group, knew she would be elected to serve as the chairperson of the finance committee." In this group of sentences about Jinny, it is impossible to leave the two sentences and simply drop the fragment pattern *being,* since the result is also a fragment. But adding a subject (*she*) and changing the participle to a verb (*being* to *was*) works well. In other sentences dropping the key word in the fragment pattern is an easy way to make the fragment into a sentence in its own right.

> *Main clause:* Everyone was surprised to hear the news.
> *Fragment:* That Bottleneck had been awarded the first prize.
> *Complete sentence:* Everyone was surprised to hear the news.
> Bottleneck had been awarded the first prize.

Of course, a less wordy version would be "Everyone was surprised to learn that Bottleneck had been awarded the first prize." The first method would have worked well here, too: "Everyone was surprised to learn the news that Bottleneck had been awarded the first prize." The method you choose for correcting fragments will be influenced by your personal writing style and the effectiveness of the possible combinations.

### How to Detect and Correct Run-On Sentences

Run-on sentences are main clauses connected with a comma (an error also called the comma splice) or simply run together without any punctuation. Instead, the sentences should be separated by a semicolon or by a period and a capital letter. The following examples contain two main clauses incorrectly joined by commas:

> Making scrambled eggs is harder than most people think, it takes careful planning and a lot of concentration.
> The kitchen in our new apartment was old and dingy, however, we have brightened it up with red-checked curtains and a new coat of paint.

The following example is a run-together type of run-on sentence, the kind containing two main clauses without any punctuation between them:

> The sales personnel at Grandy's is very efficient they always know where to find the item a customer wants.

Two sentences may be closely linked in meaning. If each is a main clause, each generally must stand alone as a complete thought. Occasionally, however, you may find run-on sentences that are deliberately used for effect in a piece of writing. Generally, the main clauses are short and connected by commas. The point of connecting the sentences instead of leaving them separate is to show how one idea quickly leads to the next.

The stream gushed down the gully, it whooshed through the fallen trees.

It is quite a different story to connect complete sentences unknowingly. Only experienced writers who can tell the difference between an effective run-on and an ineffective one should even try to use run-on sentences for effect. In most of your writing, you will want to avoid run-on sentences and stick to the more conventional structures instead.

*Looking for Run-On Sentences*

Many writers who tend to run their sentences together have trouble telling a correct sentence from a run-on. The most common way of trying to do it, reading the sentences aloud, often doesn't help because most readers normally pause for commas, just as they do for periods. As a result, a sentence that actually requires a period or semicolon may sound just fine when read with a comma. If you have a tendency to write run-on sentences, the best way to find them is to study your sentences carefully, one by one, after you have completed drafting a paper.

As you read through your paper, you can quickly eliminate from run-on status any sentence that is a single main clause.

Today is hot.

You should also be able to recognize as correct those sentences composed of two main clauses joined by a comma and a coordinating conjunction (*and, or, for, but, yet,* or *so*) or by a semicolon.

Today is hot, but last night was cool.
Today is hot; last night was cool.

You should then check the rest of your sentences one at a time, looking at them part by part. Let's use an example. Suppose you have the following sentence:

In the darkness, the two men saw the gunfighter, his face tensing with expectation.

Consider the first part, up to the first comma. By itself, does this look like a complete sentence, or would it be a fragment? If it would be a fragment, place an F above it.

F
In the darkness

The second part of the sentence, which in this case is a main clause, would obviously be a complete sentence were it to appear alone. Therefore, put an S above it.

S
the two men saw the gunfighter

Now, what about the last part of the sentence? Since it has only an *ing* form of a verb and no actual verb, it is another fragment. Put an F above it also.

       F
his face tensing with expectation.

The final sentence should look like this:

    F                S                F
In the darkness, the two men saw the gunfighter, his face tensing with expectation.

Since there is only one *S,* the sentence is not a run-on. Here are two more examples of sentences that have been analyzed using this procedure.

           F                                 S
When the swimming season is in full swing, there is hardly a spot to be found on a local beach.

   S                        F
Harold, who is the most businesslike person I have ever met, keeps his room a mess.

Notice that in the second example, the subject and verb are split up by the fragment. When the subject and verb are united, the clause stands as a complete thought.

Each time you reach the end of a sentence, look back over it to check the combination of its parts. If the combination is a main clause with one or more fragments, the sentence is probably correct and complete. If the combination is two main clauses connected by a comma or having no punctuation, you have a run-on. All of the examples so far have been composed of a main clause plus a fragment. This combination is typical. Let's look at two more examples, one a correct sentence and one a run-on:

                          F
*Correct:* Whenever there is a gathering of students over some
          S                      F
cause, there are bound to be those who call the protestors "radicals." (fragments + main clause = sentence)
                                S
*Run-on:* People have little choice about what they pay for gro-
                          S
ceries, they just go shopping and pay the prices. (main clause + main clause = run-on)

One kind of run-on that occurs frequently is caused by the confusion of transitional expressions such as *however, consequently,* and *therefore* with coordinating conjunctions such as *and* and *but.* When preceded by commas, coordinating conjunctions can connect main clauses. Transitional expressions between main clauses, however, must be preceded by a semicolon, not a comma. They may also begin new sentences.

S　　　　　　　　+　　　　　　S
I cannot stay in town all day, nevertheless, it has been a pleasant afternoon. (a run-on sentence)

S　　　　　　　　+　　　　　　S
I cannot stay in town all day; nevertheless, it has been a pleasant afternoon. (a correct sentence)

S　　　　　　　　+　　　　　　S
I cannot stay in town all day. Nevertheless, it has been a pleasant afternoon. (two correct sentences)

The following list includes most of the common transitional expressions you should look for when checking for run-on sentences:

| | | |
|---|---|---|
| therefore | consequently | indeed |
| however | for example | still |
| thus | nevertheless | of course |
| instead | besides | next |
| for instance | then | on the other hand |

Some of the following examples are run-on sentences and some are correct. Note how the transitional word (italicized) comes between the two main clauses. The examples that are main clauses connected by commas or that are run together without punctuation are run-on sentences. The main clauses connected by semicolons or made into two separate sentences are correct.

S
Condominium complexes should not have the right to encroach
+　　　　　　　　　　　　S
on neighborhoods of single-family dwellings, *instead,* homeowners should form associations and petition the city to maintain the current quality of life by keeping population density low. (a run-on sentence)

S　　　　　　+　　　　　S
Many fish are hard to see in the water, *for instance,* the brown trout hides itself among the rocks at the bottom of streams. (a run-on sentence)

S
The government should not treat minorities unfairly merely
+　　　　　　　　　　　　S
because they have little power *nevertheless,* the rights of the majority must not be forgotten. (a run-together sentence)

S             +             F
There are no longer any heroes in baseball, because baseball
players have become businessmen concerned only with money;
      +                      S
besides, modern players are not as skillful as the old-timers were.
(a correct sentence).

S             +             S
The president spent the afternoon with his cabinet. Then he
took a walk on the White House lawn. (two correct sentences)

Many run-on sentences occur because a writer merges two related
ideas improperly, not realizing that each idea forms a complete sentence
on its own. In the following examples, some of the related ideas are
joined correctly and some are joined incorrectly. Note that both halves
of each sentence are main clauses, meaning that they should either stand
alone as separate sentences or be joined with a semicolon. They should
never be joined with a comma. The main clauses connected by commas are run-on sentences.

F             +             S
In the early days of New England settlements, the life of
Americans would have been considered rough by modern stan-
      +                      S
dards, it was "rough" in more than the sense that pioneers had
no electric blankets, toasters, or televisions. (a run-on sentence)

                        S
Jobs that had been done by hand were taken over by machines,
      +             S
this revolution drastically altered the lifestyles of those Americans who lived in cities. (a run-on sentence)

S             +             S
Parents give up much of their own lives for their children; this
is the way parenthood has always been and always will be. (a correct
sentence)

                        S
The depiction of figures on Russian icons was a serious matter;
      +             S
the iconographers had very strict rules about the poses of figures
and the surroundings used for each scene. (a correct sentence)

F             +             S
In the schools of Peyrane, children are taught never to express
      +             S
their feelings; they are told to keep what is inside them constantly
under control. (a correct sentence)

THE EDITING
PROCESS:
CORRECTING
COMMON ERRORS

*429*

*Correcting Run-On Sentences*

Once you have isolated the run-on sentences in the essay, you have several options for correcting them. For each method, a corrected version of the following run-on sentence is given:

Jeanie is your friend, Susan is only your neighbor.

1. Place a period at the end of one main clause and capitalize the first word of the second main clause.

    Jeanie is your friend. Susan is only your neighbor.

2. Place a semicolon between the main clauses. Semicolons are not interchangeable with commas. To use a semicolon correctly, each main clause must be able to stand on its own as a complete sentence. The semicolon indicates a close connection between the two ideas.

    Jeanie is your friend; Susan is only your neighbor.

3. Connect the two main clauses with a comma and a coordinating conjunction.

    Jeanie is your friend, but Susan is only your neighbor.

4. Subordinate one of the main clauses. This can often be done by adding *because, since, while,* or some other subordinating conjunction (see page 371).

    Although Jeanie is your friend, Susan is only your neighbor.

---

**Exercises**

A. Mark each sentence in the following pairs with an F for a fragment or an S for a main clause. Make any fragments into complete sentences.
   1. The Puerto Rican is subjected to the unfortunate racial discriminations against two groups of people. Which he is often mistaken for, blacks and Chicanos.
   2. Many students are so relieved to finish final exams that all they want to do is either go out and celebrate or fall into bed and sleep. Because finally the pressure on them has been lifted and there is a chance to breathe.
   3. The Forest Service was formed as a result of concern over the devastation of forests. Because of the movement west, the railroads, and the timber industries.
   4. Politics attracts people who desire power and popularity. Who at heart do not really care about serving the public.

5. Enhancing the parent-teenager relationship through better communication can help a great deal. In eliminating some of the reasons teenagers want to run away from home.

6. America wants the Supreme Court to maintain the principles our government operates on. Perceiving the court in idealistic terms.

7. People who plan to marry have to think about their future. Where they plan to live. Whether they will have children.

8. The feeling of alienation known to anyone who grows up on the streets. He or she just doesn't seem to fit in like other guests at a party.

9. In South Africa, blacks were refused many of the rights and freedoms of citizenship. Despite their being natives by birth.

10. The main concern of the Truman administration was to achieve a smooth transition from a wartime to a peacetime economy. With the immediate objective being to ensure full employment.

11. Based on the careful observation of two distinct populations of sparrows. The study lasted for ten years.

12. In 1884, William LeBaron Jenney designed the first ten-story "skyscraper." The Home Insurance Company of Chicago.

13. De facto segregation occurs even in schools that have "racial balance." Counteracting the value of integration programs.

14. Due to the constant threat of urban renewal and other possible government projects. We are losing the sense of neighborhood that once united the community.

15. If I agree to protect you and you agree to protect me. We will not need police everywhere on campus.

B. The following paragraph contains six sentence fragments. Find and correct them by writing the correct sentences on a piece of paper. Do you think that any of the fragments is effective as a fragment? Which? Why?

   A runaway teenager can be symptomatic of deep family problems. Some parents, for instance, are overly intent on their children's success in school. Often, the children are under such pressure to get good grades that they do just the opposite. Fail. Failure in school is a way to get back at parents. The children cannot stand the parents' pressure. Nor the prospect of failure. Which makes them feel inferior to other students. One answer to the frustrations of either route is to avoid everything. To run away from what seems to be the source of the problem— home. Other family problems are apparent in the runaway who has been abused or neglected. Parents sometimes cannot cope with their own problems and may take them out on the children. Who at these times seem nothing but a burden to them. Perhaps deep inside they resent the children for limiting what they wanted to do in life. No matter what the reason is, the child who is abused over a period of years gets to the point where he or she can't take any more mistreatment or indifference. The child develops an emotional wound. That may never heal, one that seems especially painful when the parents are around. For many, the only answer to the problems of home is escape.

C. Indicate which of the following are run-on sentences. Give two possible ways of correcting each run-on.

1. We are arriving at the time when human beings will no longer have to be able to analyze, they will only have to learn to program computers.

2. This question is disturbing, will people survive all this industrialization?

3. There is at least one compensation to getting old. Half-price movie tickets.

4. One major obstacle in changing from single-sex to coed dorms is the fear that it might encourage a decline in students' morality, however several studies have shown this fear to be unjustified.

5. An important question must be asked, has technology caused people to lose their individuality?

6. Today more and more people are disregarding the need for marriage, many people are just living together.

7. There are two factors that help explain why so many young people begin to smoke, one is the desire to imitate adults and peers.

8. About one-half of all persons living in the United States die of arteriosclerosis, consequently, concerned physicians are recommending that adults minimize milk and dairy products in their diets.

9. It is people's nature to create, creativity comes from a desire to communicate.

10. The beginning of the scientific revolution occurred during the seventeenth century; for this reason the period is known as the "dawn of modern science."

11. Culture is not static, to cling to the ideas of the distant past does not preserve it.

12. Filling in the "personal questions" on my registration computer cards, I came to the question of race, although my family is mixed, as usual I checked the box marked "African American."

13. The parent is the key to a child's development, that parent can mold the child into either a criminal or an angel.

14. One of Manet's most controversial paintings was banned in Solano until 1863. People thought its subject matter was immoral.

15. The young should not take jobs from the aged; the elderly may lack the physical energy and productiveness of youth, but they often offer more dedication and knowledge.

16. Many people conclude that those who speak a different dialect are less educated or less intelligent than themselves, this attitude is a product of ignorance.

17. Over-the-counter and prescription drugs are abused just as often as those drugs that are considered "dangerous," therefore even people who are not using illegal drugs may have a drug problem.

18. Gang members who leave the community may not have the chance to change their roles completely, back in the old neighborhood everyone remembers them as they were.

D. Correct any fragments or run-on sentences in the following paragraphs.

1. In starting your search for a job. You will probably want to rely more on personal contacts than on the classified section of a newspaper. Thousands of people begin by looking at the want ads; that is why the odds are against you right away. There is too much competition. Seeking interviews through personal contacts; you will already have an "in"

Whereas applying for jobs as a total stranger puts you in a more difficult position. Sometimes you can learn of possibilities while in your present job by speaking with other employees, they may have information about openings at other firms. Openings that may not even be advertised. Of course, you have to be discreet so you do not offend your present employer. Always remember that the more personal contacts you cultivate, the better chance you have of hearing about good opportunities.

2. Being considerate of one's spouse is a vital part of marriage, the awareness of each other's needs and feelings makes for a close relationship. Also helping in the raising of children. The opportunities to explain situations or problems and to settle them fairly become easier to find. The couple enjoy one another more than do people in relationships that are full of pent-up feelings. All people should try to be honest with their mates. Not an easy task but it can be done.

E. There are several fragments or run-on sentences in the following paragraph. Find and correct each of them.

Why do well-mannered house pets suddenly begin to chew pillows and upholstery, steal shoes, and wet the carpet? The problem may be physical, that possibility should always be considered. More likely, though, the problem is an emotional disturbance. A problem you should look into. There are certain things that might have happened, in such circumstances, what was going on in the house when the behavior first started? Did an unfamiliar visitor upset your house pets? For example, a strange pet in the house or a newly born child? Maybe a piling up of many events caused this bad behavior. Not necessarily one recognizable incident. Such as you moved, left your pets at a kennel, and then took them to a new home. Retraining pets will not work. If all you want to do is scold them. You should calm yourself down, try to understand their emotional environment, then you can attempt to get your pets to respond properly. Without doing things behind your back.

## 3. ARE ALL YOUR VERBS AND VERBALS FORMED ACCURATELY?

Read through your paper once to check all verbs and verbals for accuracy and consistency.

### Verbs

You will recall that verbs change their form to show tense and mood. Because the forms of verbs are so essential to communicating exactly what you mean, you will want to double check to make sure you have selected the most accurate tense and mood. Tense shows time. The interaction of verbs creates a sequence of time frames within each sentence and between sentences. Mood shows how close your meaning is to being a simple statement. The mood of a particular verb shows whether it makes a statement of assertion, sets forth an idea to ponder, or presents a condition or consequences. A more thorough discussion of the basics of verb forms is in Chapter A. If you feel unfamiliar with the concepts of tense or mood, you will probably want to review the basics before you continue reading this section.

### Use the Right Tense

You should use the verb tenses that convey the exact meaning you want.

### The Perfect Tenses

The perfect tenses are used to show the relationships of verbs in time. The past perfect tense expresses an action that occurred before the action expressed by another verb in the past tense. It uses the helping verb *had.* For instance, study the following sentence:

> The judge asked the defendant if he had wanted to confess.

There are two actions in the sentence: *asked* and *had wanted.* Which action occurred first? Using the past perfect tense shows that the *wanting* came first. It puts the verb *wanted* into its proper relation to the verb *asked.* Suppose this had been the sentence:

> The judge had asked the defendant if he wanted to confess.

Here, the sequence is reversed. Had the writer wanted both actions to occur at the same time, the past perfect tense would have been omitted:

> The judge asked the defendant if he wanted to confess.

Let's look at another example:

> Sarah had known Joe for two years before she realized he was a liar.

The two actions are *had known* and *realized.* Which happened first? She *knew* him and then she *realized.* The first action to occur is always the one placed in the past perfect tense.

The present perfect tense is used to express an action that occurred just before the present. It uses *have* or *has* as a helper. Here is an example:

> Although Sarah has known Joe for two years, she now realizes he is a liar.

Sarah realizes right now (present tense), after knowing Joe for a while (present perfect tense), that he is a liar. Observe the similar sequences in the following sentences:

> Unless the group has already decided otherwise, we can go to Florida for a vacation.

Once he has apologized to her, she wants nothing more than to be his friend.

Another use of the present perfect tense is to indicate something happening up through the present. *Always* and *never* may serve as clues that *has* or *have* may be needed as a helper.

> Norbert *has always been* a tolerant individual.
> I *have never drawn* such a large check on my account.
> His life *has been* full of disappointments.

The future perfect tense is used to express the completion of some future action. The tense is formed by using *will have* along with the past participle of a verb. Take a look at the time expressed in the following sentence:

> By the time we will have graduated, there may be many more teaching jobs available.

Which is the action that already will have been completed? The clause *we will have graduated* expresses what will already have been done before *there may be many more teaching jobs available.* Here is another example:

> How many criminals will have been rehabilitated when they are released from prison?

Using the future perfect tense, the writer questions whether a completed action will have occurred (the rehabilitation) by the time another future action (release from prison) occurs. Thus, the future perfect tense tells the reader to look ahead to a time when a future action will have been completed.

### The Future Conditional

If the verb is in the past tense and you want to express an action in the future, use the helper *would* with your verb.

> As a new employee, Pat understood that he would not be permitted to have keys to the locked jewelry cases.
> Linda Davett knew that she would have to act hurt in order to convince her employer to give her a raise.

### Tenses in Discussing Literature

The present tense is used to write about the actions that occur in literature. Although you may have read a particular book a month ago, and although it may have been written over two hundred years ago, the work is still considered to be alive. In a sense, it remains living forever. Consistency with the rest of your essay is most easily achieved if all discussion of the work is placed in the present. Below is a sample from a student's literary discussion. Note the careful attention to tenses.

In *Henry V*, Shakespeare portrays King Henry as an ideal Christian king. Through his every action, Henry rules according to the guidelines for a Christian king as set forth in Erasmus's *Institution Principis.* When he is contemplating war on France, Henry checks with the Church to be sure England has the right to the French throne, and he proceeds to France only after being assured that England can remain safe in his absence. Once in France, he maintains his unspotted conduct, tolerating no abuse of the French or of their countryside. Henry judiciously hangs Bardolph and Nym for violating a French church.

Even when quoting passages written in the past tense, your own tenses should be in the present.

In "The Princess" by D. H. Lawrence, the descent from mountainous heights to cavernous depths becomes a journey into Dollie's unconscious. It is a descent that she, in the ebb and flow of her consciousness, is able to make when Romero unveils "some unrealized part of her wish which she never wished to realize."

Because it is part of a quotation, *wished* remains in the past tense while the rest of the discussion is in the present tense.

### Make Tenses Consistent

Events that occur at the same time should be written about in the same tense. A common error, especially when telling about a sequence of events, is to slip back and forth between the past tense and the present. This error is demonstrated by the following passage from a student's essay:

I was walking down Laurel Canyon one day when a strange-looking man crossed my path. He said, "Howdy," and I respond with a hello. But I am quite reserved and suspicious of his motives. What is this guy all about, I wonder. Then, before I can resist, he pushed me down on the sidewalk, grabbed my purse, and ran away. The whole incident changed my opinion of taking an afternoon stroll in my own neighborhood.

The writer first goes wrong in the middle of the second sentence. Up to that point, all the verbs have been in the past tense. *Respond* begins the use of the present tense but then, in the middle of the fifth sentence, the writer shifts back to the past tense with the word *pushed.* Since all of these events happened in a sequence, there is no reason to shift tenses. The writer probably wanted to use the present tense, as many storytellers do, to make the events sound immediate. This method would have been effective if it had been employed throughout the passage:

I am walking down Laurel Canyon one day when a strange-looking man crosses my path. He says, "Howdy," and I respond with a hello. But I am quite reserved and suspicious of his motives. What is this guy all about, I wonder. Then, before I can resist, he pushes me down on the sidewalk, grabs my purse, and runs away. The whole incident has changed my opinion of taking an afternoon stroll in my own neighborhood.

Of course, the passage could also have been written completely in the past tense.

Being consistent does not mean that you must always use the same tense throughout an essay, a paragraph, or even a sentence. Sometimes you will want to express two or more different time frames, and the only way to do so is to use different tenses. In many of these cases, you will also use the other words as clues to the various time frames in your sentences.

Thirteen years ago he embezzled one hundred thousand dollars from the company and now he is asking the same firm for a job.

Besides the verbs, there are two clues to time in this sentence. *Thirteen years ago* obviously refers to the past, and *now* just as obviously refers to the present.

They were good friends a long time ago, but these days they never speak to one another.

In this sentence, there are again two clues in addition to the verbs. The past is indicated by *a long time ago,* and the present is indicated by *these days.* As helpful as these types of clues can be, they are not always present, nor are they always needed.

I used to like mathematics, but the more I study the humanities, the more I am impressed with them.

Although this sentence includes no extra clues, the tenses of the verbs make the meaning clear.

Clear writing makes understandable connections between the time sequences. Because the reader can comprehend any time shifts built into the sentences and because each verb represents an accurate time frame, the writing is meaningful and still considered consistent when tenses are shifted deliberately.

### Use The Subjunctive Correctly
The subjunctive mood is used either to show conditions contrary to fact or to show requests or demands.

### Conditions Contrary to Fact

A conditional statement is a sentence stating that something would happen if something else were to occur first. The conditional word *would* is used in one part of the sentence, and the subjunctive form of the verb is used in the other part. The subjunctive verb often follows the word *if.* Present tense subjunctives seem to give writers the most problems.

> If tea *were* as expensive as coffee, most Americans, a recent survey shows, *would select* coffee as their morning beverage. (present)
> If New Yorkers *had been* more prepared than they were for the 1977 blackout, they *would have suffered* less than they did. (past)

Be careful, however, not to place *would* in both parts of the sentence:

> *Incorrect:* If he *would* have asked, he *would* have found out the answer.
> *Correct: Had* he *asked*, he *would* have found out the answer. (*If he had asked* is also correct. )

A statement including a subjunctive verb is often described as being contrary to fact. In the previous examples, for instance, tea is not as expensive as coffee and New Yorkers were not prepared. Conditional statements that are not contrary to fact are not in the subjunctive mood, even when the word *if* is used in the sentence. You should never substitute *would* for *will* or *can* in statements such as the following:

> If we take umbrellas, we will not care whether it rains.
> If we arrive at six-thirty. we can be on time for dinner.

### Requests or Demands

The subjunctive is used with requests or demands introduced by the word *that.* Regular uses of *that,* without the tone of demand or request, do not take the subjunctive.

> I saw a car *that* reminds me of yours.

The following sentences, which are requests or demands, do require the subjunctive.

> The airlines require that travelers *make* reservations thirty days in advance in order to get the reduced rates.
> I ask only that you *understand* the position I am in.

The subjunctive is also used for a few commands that are common expressions.

> Heaven *forbid.*
> Let it *be* known.
> God *bless* you.

### Correct Subjunctive Form

For conditional statements that are contrary to fact, the present tense subjunctive for all verbs, with the exception of *to be,* is the same as the past tense of that verb.

> If he *asked* me, I would feel flattered to accept the invitation.

The present tense subjunctive for requests or demands introduced by *that* for all verbs, including *to be,* is formed by using the infinitive without the *to.*

> He asks only that I *act* with understanding.
> He asks only that you *act* with understanding.
> He asks only that she *act* with understanding.
> He asks only that we *act* with understanding.
> He asks only that they *act* with understanding.

The past tense of the subjunctive takes the same form as the past perfect tense.

> *Had* he *asked* me, I would have accepted.
> If he *had asked* me, I would have accepted.

The subjunctive forms of the verb *to be* are especially puzzling to many writers. In the present tense, *were* and *be* are used. With *if, were* is used, never *was.*

> If he *were* my friend, I would help his mother fix her car.

*Be* should be used with *that.*

> I demand *that* he *be* fired.

In the past tense, the subjunctive form of *to be* is *had been.*

> If I *had been* there, the accident would not have happened.
> *Had* I *been* there, the accident would not have happened.

### Form Irregular Verbs Correctly

Basically, a verb is irregular if its past tense is not formed by simply adding *d* or *ed.* Variations in forming the present participle (the *ing* form used as an adjective with *is* or *was*) and the past participle (used with *has, have,* or *had*) also make a verb irregular. Whenever you are unsure of the correct form for a particular verb, check the dictionary. The listings for verbs always include the infinitive, the past tense, and the past participle. You can also refer to the partial list of irregular verbs in Table B-1. It gives the correct forms for most of the troublesome verbs you are likely to run across.

**Table B-I. Common Irregular Verbs**

| Infinitive | Present Participle | Past Tense | Past Participle |
|---|---|---|---|
| be | being | was, were | been |
| bear | bearing | bore | borne |
| beat | beating | beat | beaten |
| become | becoming | became | become |
| begin | beginning | began | begun |
| bend | bending | bent | bent |
| break | breaking | broke | broken |
| bring | bringing | brought | brought |
| build | building | built | built |
| burst (never bust) | bursting | burst | burst |
| choose | choosing | chose | chosen |
| cling | clinging | clung | clung |
| dive | diving | dived, dove | dived |
| do | doing | did | done |
| draw | drawing | drew | drawn |
| dream | dreaming | dreamed, dreamt | dreamed, dreamt |
| drink | drinking | drank | drunk |
| eat | eating | ate | eaten |
| fall | falling | fell | fallen |
| fling | flinging | flung | flung |
| fly | flying | flew | flown |
| freeze | freezing | froze | frozen |
| get | getting | got | gotten, got |
| give | giving | gave | given |
| go | going | went | gone |
| grow | growing | grew | grown |
| hang (on the wall) | hanging | hung | hung |
| have | having | had | had |
| keep | keeping | kept | kept |
| know | knowing | knew | knew |
| lay (to place) | laying | laid | laid |
| lead | leading | led | led |
| lie (to recline) | lying | lay | lain |
| make | making | made | made |
| put | putting | put | put |
| raise (to lift up) | raising | raised | raised |
| ride | riding | rode | ridden |
| ring | ringing | rang | rung |
| rise (to go up) | rising | rose | risen |
| run | running | ran | run |
| set | setting | set | set |
| sew | sewing | sewed | sewed, sewn |
| shine (to glow) | shining | shone | shone |
| shine (to polish) | shining | shined | shined |
| show | showing | showed | shown |
| shrink | shrinking | shrank, shrunk | shrunk |

| Infinitive | Present Participle | Past Tense | Past Participle |
|---|---|---|---|
| sink | sinking | sank, sunk | sunk, sunken |
| sing | singing | sang | sung |
| sit | sitting | sat | sat |
| slay | slaying | slew | slain |
| speak | speaking | spoke | spoken |
| steal | stealing | stole | stolen |
| strive | striving | strove | striven |
| swim | swimming | swam | swum |
| take | taking | took | taken |
| wake | waking | waked, woke | waked, woken |
| wear | wearing | wore | worn |
| weave | weaving | wove | woven |
| weep | weeping | wept | wept |
| write | writing | wrote | written |

Are you always sure when to use *lay* and when to use *lie*? What about *set* or *sit*, *raised* or *rose*, *hanged* or *hung*? These irregular verbs are often confused by writers, who use one when they mean the other.

Lay/Lie
*Lay* means to place.

> You *lay* the glass on the table.
> Yesterday, you *laid* the glass on the table.
> You *have laid* the glass on the table.

Notice that *lay* is always a transitive verb. Each time you use it, *lay* must have a direct object.

*Lie* means to recline.

> I *lie* down every afternoon.
> I *lay* down yesterday afternoon.
> I *have lain* down today already.
> *Lie* down right now.

The past tense of *lie* can be tricky. It is spelled the same as the present tense of *lay*. A good way not to mistake the two is to remember that *lie* is always intransitive. It never takes a direct object.

Raise/Rise
*Raise* means to lift up.

> I *raise* my hand in class.
> I *raised* my hand in class yesterday.
> I *have raised* my hand several times this week.

*Raise* is a transitive verb and always takes a direct object.

*Rise* means to go up or to get up.

The prices *rise* every week.
The prices *rose* last week.
The prices *have risen* constantly for a month now.

*Rise* is an intransitive verb and never takes a direct object.

Many things—prices, grades, people (she *rose* from her chair)—can either *rise* or *be raised.* The important clue is whether the verb takes a direct object.

### Set/Sit
*Set* means to place or arrange.

> The students *set* their books on the table every afternoon before they go to recess.
> The children *set* the table for their mother.
> Anyone who has *set* his or her hopes on becoming wealthy eventually becomes disenchanted.

*Set* is usually transitive and takes a direct object. The only exceptions are when it means "is situated," refers to the sun, or is synonymous with *hardens.*

> The house *is set* high on a hill overlooking the city.
> The sun *set* at 5:05 today.
> Once the cement *sets,* we can finish the job.

*Sit* means to occupy a seat.

> The people who work at the bank *sit* all day.
> The student who *sat* in this chair last week is absent.
> I *have sat* here long enough.

*Sit* is intransitive and never takes a direct object.

A common mistake is to write something like "It's so hot. Let's just set awhile." The correct form is *sit.*

### Hanged/Hung
The past tense of the verb *to hang,* meaning to execute, is *hanged.*

> They *hanged* Tom Dooley.

The past tense of the verb *to hang,* meaning to put up on the wall or to attach to a line, is *hung.*

> We *hung* out the wash yesterday because it was sunny.

### Verbals
Verbals function as parts of verbs (with helpers) and as other parts of speech: nouns, adjectives, and adverbs. They are not the verbs that

distinguish main clauses, being in themselves only half-verbs. In fact, as you recall, any sentence having only a verbal and no other sentence verb is incomplete, a fragment. The verbals are infinitives, gerunds, and participles. Each verbal has tense and voice as Tables B-2 and B-3 show.

**Table B-2. Infinitives**

|  | Present | Present Perfect | Ongoing Present |
|---|---|---|---|
| *Active* *voice* | to show | to have shown | to be showing |
| *Passive* *voice* | to be shown | to have been shown | — |

**Table B-3. Gerunds and Participles**

|  | Present | Past | Present Perfect |
|---|---|---|---|
| *Active* *voice* | showing | — | have shown |
| *Passive* *voice* | being shown | shown (participles only) | — |

More information on the basics of verbals can be found in Chapter A. You may wish to review that section before continuing to read the section at hand.

### Infinitives

If the time expressed by the infinitive is not before the time expressed by the main verb, use the simple infinitive—*to go, to sew, to speak, to shun*—for all tenses of the main verb.

> I want to know when you're free for lunch.
> It has been nice to meet you.
> He needed to say what he felt.
> We will need to make airline reservations before Sunday.

If the infinitive expresses a time before the time of the main verb, insert *have* after the *to* and use the past participle to form the infinitive.

> For them *to have begun* on time is unusual.
> We believed that they had *to have been* licensed physicians since they were listed in the phone book.

Often it is clearer to shift the main verb to another tense in order to keep the simple infinitive.

It is nice *to have met* you.
It has been nice *to meet* you.
There is no reason *to have gone* to so much trouble.
There was no reason *to go* to so much trouble.

*Verbals Ending in* ing: *Gerunds and Participles*
If the time expressed by the verbal is not before the time expressed by the main verb, the simple verbal should be used, no matter what the tense of the main verb:

Needing attention from everyone around him is Norman's problem, not mine.
Knowing that Michael would be pleased, Felicia chose a simple gray dress to wear to his parents' house.

If the action of the verbal expresses a time before that of the main verb, *having* plus the past participle is used to form the verbal.

*Having worked* for a lawyer for the past two years was not enough to get Lydia a position on the district attorney's staff.
*Having known* David for five years, Marcia could guess what he would say on most subjects.

*Verbals Ending in ed, t, or n: Participles*
If the participle follows a linking verb (*is, are, was, were, seem, seems, appear, appears, become, becomes,* etc. ), the past participle is used. You will recall that complements after linking verbs often act as adjectives that describe the subject of the clause. In such constructions the participle, not the infinitive without the *to,* is used.

*Ineffective:* He is prejudice against tall people.
*Effective:* He is prejudiced against tall people.
*Ineffective:* He is use to being successful.
*Effective:* He is used to being successful.

Similar guidelines might be set up for verbs with forms of *be* or *have* as helpers. Even though the past participle ending is often hard to hear in speaking the words, the *be* or *have* helper must be joined by the verb with its *ed, en, t,* or *n* ending if the simple predicate is to be formed properly. Do not use the infinitive without *to* instead.

*Ineffective:* She has listen to this recording before.
*Effective:* She has listened to this recording before.
*Ineffective:* The canvas is wash and laid out to dry.
*Effective:* The canvas is washed and laid out to dry.

Even without the helping verb, a participle (a verbal used as an adjective) often takes the *ed, en, t,* or *n* ending.

*Ineffective:* Stretch out on the couch, Bob fell asleep.
*Effective:* Stretched out on the couch, Bob fell asleep.
*Ineffective:* Bias in favor of the team, Jill expected them to win.
*Effective:* Biased in favor of the team, Jill expected them to win.

### Exercises

A. Correct any errors in verb tense in the following sentences.

1. Traveling in a car brings me closer to scenery and is better for distinguishing details, but the plane gave me a new perspective of the landscape.

2. 1 always had a negative view of my marriage, but yesterday my encounter group made me realize how much my marriage really means to me.

3. I develop a fear of writing what I think, so I wrote what I thought my teacher wanted to hear.

4. Every night I turn on my television to hear the news, and every night I heard the same thing with only the names and the statistics slightly changed.

5. It was not until Ricardo telephone me to say he learned of my mother's remarriage that I really had to tell anyone my feelings about the event.

6. Many Americans are so disgusted with politics that they wanted to never vote again.

7. Living in the city all my life, I didn't have the opportunity to see many of the country's natural wonders.

8. In the novel, the minister suddenly decides early in his career that there is no supernatural being, so he left the church.

9. This community is integrated. It was integrated for as long as I can remember.

10. Admitting his tendency to get angry at the smallest disturbance, my father told my boyfriend Charles that he was not welcome in our house because Charles had slammed the front door.

11. The most embarrassing moment I can remember is the time I planned a meeting for the Student Committee on Equality and forget to attend.

12. Before I told my parents the truth, I had hoped they would discover it by themselves.

13. A big problem in the last presidential election is voter apathy.

14. Up until this year, I played on the women's volleyball team and served as manager for the men's track team, but now I must quit and concentrate more on my studies.

15. As the over-the-counter drug industry grows, so did our reliance on it; we began to take nonprescription pills for the slightest discomfort, telling ourselves that they can't harm us since they are weak enough to get without prescriptions.

B. Identify the tense of each italicized verb and check its accuracy.

1. It *has* always *been* difficult for me to speak with strangers.

2. Although the term "senior citizen" somehow *did* not *seem* appropriate to me, I prefer it to "old man."

3. Before I knew a real actor, I *think* their lives were charmed.

4. Last on my list of chores for today *was* washing the windows of my room.

5. The high cost of food *has* practically *assured* malnutrition for the nation's poor.

6. Racial and ethnic jokes *can promote* stereotyped thinking.

7. Platonic friendships between the sexes *can be* more fulfilling than friendships between members of the same sex.

8. In *Lady Chatterley's Lover* Connie's values *conflict* with the values of most aristocrats, yet her relationships with others seem to be healthy.

9. The conquest of Mexico *was accomplished* by Spaniards from many different social classes.

10. Unless the legislature does decide to give the residents in our area a tax break, many *will have been forced* to sell their homes.

C. Correct the verbs that have inaccurate endings or confusing shifts in tense.

1. When students look back at all the years they spend in high school, they sometimes wonder why they learn so much faster in college.

2. I wanted to have understood everything we studied by the time I took the examination, so I got a tutor.

3. During my years as a student, art classes were always a relaxing way to end the otherwise hectic days.

4. If the three of us had more sense, we would have shopped around for a place to live instead of taking the first apartment we saw.

5. The state capital was where I had to sent the letter for my teaching credentials.

6. Unless I am marry, I will not have children.

7. In our culture, there is a constant battle between the sexes for who gets the upper hand. Neither men nor women can be happy as long as they have allowed this battle to continue.

8. At first glance, this group of college students may seem to have nothing in common. One was from as far away as Egypt or Iran, and another could be from the all-American San Fernando Valley. Some spoke in foreign tongues, and others speak in English.

9. Restrictive policies against ethnic minorities have been illegal for a long time and should be, but until recently the law could not stop private clubs from skirting the issue through cleverly worded phrases on contracts and brochures.

10. A common type of date is the "joking session." I found this type of constant teasing and kidding very frustrating because it gets nowhere. All the fooling around makes it impossible to have an honest conversation or get to know each other.

D. Correct any tense errors in the following paragraphs.

The other day, when my sisters and I were in a department store looking for a gift for my mother, we discovered how it feels to be subjected to racial prejudice. After a long search, we finally found what we thought would be a nice present. Then we went to stand in line to pay for it. The line seems especially long, and forty-five minutes pass before we reach the cashier. As we stand in line, we happen to notice how nice and pleasant the cashier is to all the customers. She always smiles and offers a friendly hello to each one. I finally get up to the counter and placed the present on it. I said hello to the cashier, but she did not answer. At first I thought she did not hear me. I want an answer, so I waited a minute until I got her attention and repeat my hello. Still she doesn't answer. In fact, she looked and yelled, "Is there anyone else?" It was as if I did not exist. I tried to show her that I was next, but she continued to ignore me.

The realization of the clerk's motives made me so hurt and angry that I knew I had to insist. When I still did not get service, my sisters moved to another line but I stayed put. Finally, after helping a few customers who had been behind me, the clerk turned to me impatiently and said, "Yes?" I looked her straight in the eye and smiled. Somehow, I expected my insistence to feel more rewarding than it did, and I still wish I had the nerve to give that woman a piece of my mind.

E. Identify which of the conditional statements below are contrary to fact and require the subjunctive.
   1. If I were a Martian, I would find the marriage ceremony on Earth a very strange celebration.
   2. If two and two are four, what is two squared?
   3. Were you a patron in the days of the Renaissance, what type of art would you support?
   4. If young ghetto children want to succeed, they have to overcome their fear of failure.
   5. If a man and a woman are compatible, they still are not necessarily in love and should think twice before getting married.
   6. Television would be better if the shows were about people like you and me and not about stereotyped characters.
   7. The need for relaxation away from the pressures of the office would be less apparent if a shorter workweek were the rule instead of the exception.
   8. What is the safest method to use if you have to jump from the sixth floor of a burning building?
   9. I thought I would make my demands only if my boss did not offer me a big raise.
   10. When times are difficult, I always say to myself, "You are really lucky. What if you were in a situation like Jim's or Mary's?" I always pick a situation that is much worse than my own, so I don't feel so bad.
F. Correct any errors in the use of the subjunctive in the following sentences.
   1. If I were in his situation, not wanting to insult an important client but feeling unable to accept a valuable gift, I would simply explain my policy about such matters.
   2. The coach asks that all members of the track team work out every day if they are serious about running.
   3. If it were Molly who just telephoned, we can leave now.
   4. His attitude that all men be equal is admirable, but he doesn't practice what he preaches.
   5. If we are supposed to be your best friends, why must you ask that we leave?

6. Students who attend a college near home often want to stay close to their parents.

7. If interracial marriages were more accepted in our society, there is no doubt that I would date members of other races.

8. If I would always have all the money I would need, my values would be less developed than they are now.

9. Were the voters to demand an explanation for our President's actions with regard to foreign policy, the country would be in a lot better shape today.

10. When Jeffrey Thomas was three years old, his mother taught him how to read, and now, in third grade, Jeffrey has an eighth-grade reading level.

G. Correct any mistakes in verb usage in the following sentences.

1. Before long it became apparent that everyone at the party had drank more than anyone who wants to drive home should.

2. The self-hypnosis class offered by Balley College begin last Thursday in Bungalow 32, and the turnout was enormous.

3. The crew should have took the day off if the weather report said it would rain.

4. Despite studies that have show a trend toward equality in the distribution of family income, we still have many people who are poor.

5. A machine can get things did faster than a person can.

6. We have build entire cities that could not function without the automobile.

7. My roommate's telephone had just rang when someone knocked at our door.

8. My sister wrote a long letter to the Hilton Hotel in which she complimented their services, but few people ever do this kind of thing.

9. Whenever I really need to lay down, my eyes begin to feel heavy.

10. Knowing that most species had flew south already, we wondered what a little bluebird was doing on our snow-covered lawn.

11. They hanged criminals in France in those days for the same things we fine people for today.

H. In the following paragraph, identify all the irregular verbs and tell the tense of each.

> After completing our swimming drills, we swam back to shore, shook the water from our bodies in the cold morning air, and set out to find waters more suited for skin diving. During the short drive to the other shore, the sun shone brightly and the temperature rose. By the time we found a good place, the day had become lovely. I looked across the glistening lagoon at the many sailing boats, and I prepared to dive.

## 4. DO ALL YOUR PRONOUNS FIT THEIR REFERENCES AND FUNCTIONS?

The fourth time you sift through your paper, if you're using the first plan, you should concentrate on the pronouns. For each one you find, ask yourself the following questions:

Have I used the proper case?
Is the pronoun's reference obvious?
Does the pronoun agree with its reference?

Checking these areas will ensure that every pronoun does exactly what you want it to. For a review of pronouns, see Chapter A.

### Case

The case of a pronoun is determined by the way it is used in a sentence. There are three cases: subjective, objective, and possessive. Each one has its own group of pronouns.

#### Subjective Pronouns

A pronoun that acts as the subject of the verb or as a subject complement (except for possessive pronouns like *his, hers,* and *ours*) is in the subjective case. Here is a list of the subjective pronouns:

| | | |
|---|---|---|
| 1 | we | you |
| they | he, she, it | |

The following sentences include subjective pronouns used correctly:

*He* and *I* are best friends.

*He* and *I* are the subjects of the sentence.

*They* asked the minister for advice.

*They* is the subject of the sentence.

It is *she* who borrowed my typewriter.

*She* is the subject complement.

If *I* were *he*, I'd be honest about the situation.

*He* is the subject complement. *I* is the subject of the main clause.
In informal writing and speaking, the use of the subjective pronoun for the subject complement is no longer popular. For instance, in the last sentence, most people would use *him,* not *he.* If you were to answer the telephone, would you say, "This is me" or would you say, "This is I"? Usage seems to call for the *me,* even though strict grammarians say it should be *I.* In formal assignments, it is best to stick to the subjective case of the pronoun.

#### Objective Pronouns

A pronoun that serves as the direct or indirect object of a verb or as the object of a preposition is in the objective case. (The object of a preposition, you will remember, is the end word or words of a prepositional phrase.) Here is a list of the objective pronouns:

me                  us                  you
them                him, her, it

Learning about the objective case can help you with some common problems. For instance, many writers have trouble deciding whether to use *I* or *me* in the phrase *between you and me*. *Between* is a preposition, so the final word in the phrase is the object of a preposition. As you have just seen, the object of a preposition is always in the objective case. Therefore, *me* is the pronoun that should be used. In the following sentences, the italicized pronouns are all in the objective case:

Mr. Brown gave John and *me* the highest grades in all of his intermediate Spanish classes.

*Me* is one of the indirect objects.

The solution to the problem I had been thinking about for days finally struck *me.*

*Me* is the direct object.

My father lent Joe and *her* the car for the evening.

*Her* is an indirect object.

The police officer told *them* which traffic laws were and were not enforced.

*Them* is the indirect object.

Campus security officers explained the misunderstanding to *us* students.

*Us* modifies the object of the preposition *to.*

To Joe and *her,* nothing could be more pleasant than a quiet evening at home.

*Her* is one of the objects of the preposition.

*Possessive Pronouns*
A pronoun that shows ownership or that modifies a word ending in *ing* is in the possessive case. Here is a list of possessive pronouns:

my, mine            our, ours           your, yours
their, theirs       his, her, hers, its

Notice that possessive pronouns do not have apostrophes. Apostrophes are unnecessary since the words are possessive to begin with. All of the possessive pronouns in the following sentences are italicized:

> The book is *ours*.

The pronoun *ours* shows ownership. Therefore, even though it is a subject complement, it is possessive.

> *Your* studying late may disturb your roommate.

It is your *studying*, not *you* studying, that might be disturbing.

> *His* ability to win tennis matches arouses envy in us all.
> *Their* constant nagging about the money they lent me makes me want to scream.
> *Our* knowing Bill influenced the company's decision to hire him.

In sentences such as the following, however, you should not use possessive pronouns:

> I could hardly stand to watch *you* fawning all over the professor.

It was *you* that the writer could hardly stand to watch, not the fawning.

> We wanted to see *him* doing his act at the Bitters Box.

They wanted to see *him*, not the doing of the act.

### Special Problem Pronouns

*Who and Whom*

Many writers have problems when trying to decide whether to use *who* or *whom* in a sentence. Knowing the following rules can help you avoid this difficulty in your own writing.

*Who* is a subjective pronoun. It should be used as the subject of a verb. The same rule applies to *whoever*.

> *Who* asked the president whether he really believed in the Equal Rights Amendment?

*Who* is the subject of the verb *asked*.

> *Who* is it?

*Who* is the subject of the verb *is*.

*Whom* is an objective pronoun. It should be used as a direct or indirect object of a verb or as the object of a preposition. The same rule applies to *whomever*.

He is the person with *whom* Dr. Sabin travels.

*Whom* is the object of the preposition *with*.

*Whom* did you speak with?

*Whom* is again the object of the preposition *with*.

*Who* and *whom* or *whoever* and *whomever* can also cause what may appear to be another type of problem. Take a look at the following sentence:

You may give a check to *whoever* needs the money.

At first glance, you might think that *whomever* should be used because the pronoun seems to be the object of the preposition *to*. Notice, however that there is a verb following the pronoun. Every verb must have a subject. Therefore, *whoever* has to be the subject of the verb *needs,* and the entire clause, *whoever needs the money,* acts as the object of the preposition *to.* Situations such as this may be a bit more difficult to figure out, but the rules still apply.

*Whose*
*Whose* is a possessive pronoun.

*Whose* handwriting is this?

Be careful not to confuse *whose* with *who's. Who's* is the contraction for *who is.*

*Reflexives and Intensifiers*
A reflexive pronoun is an objective pronoun that renames the subject of the clause. Here is a list of reflexives:

| | |
|---|---|
| myself | ourselves |
| yourself | yourselves |
| himself, herself, itself | themselves |

Note that there are no such words in standard English as *ourself, them-self, theirself,* or *theirselves.* Correct formation of words that end with *self* or *selves* requires that both halves of the word be either singular or plural.

| *singular* | + *singular* | = *singular* |
|---|---|---|
| him | + self | = himself |
| *plural* | + *plural* | = *plural* |
| them | + selves | = themselves |

Reflexives should never be used as the subject of a sentence. They never, in the subject position, make the writer seem polite or modest. If you slip into putting a reflexive into a subject position, your sentence can easily be corrected by replacing the reflexive with a subjective pronoun.

> *Ineffective:* Joseph and myself have done our art project
>    together.
> *Effective:* Joseph and I have done our art project together.
> *Ineffective:* It was myself and Judy who were responsible.
> *Effective:* It was Judy and I who were responsible (or Judy and I
>    were responsible).

Reflexives should be used only if the subject of the clause is the same as the object. Otherwise, substitute the correct objective pronoun.

> *Ineffective:* I was surprised that they voted for *myself* on both
>    occasions.
> *Effective:* I was surprised that they voted for *me* on both occasions.

*They* is the subject of the clause. The object *me* does not refer to the same person.

> *Ineffective:* We knew *us* better than anybody did.
> *Effective:* We knew *ourselves* better than anybody did.

*We* is the subject of the clause. The object *ourselves* refers to the same people.

> *Ineffective:* I asked them to give their donations to Henry or
>    *myself.*
> *Effective:* I asked them to give their donations to Henry or *me.*

The object, *Henry or me*, is not identical to the subject of the clause; *I* is the subject of the clause, not *Henry and I.*

Try not to confuse the functions of reflexives with the functions of intensifiers, which look exactly like them. An intensive pronoun emphasizes the word it reflects, whether the word is a subject or object in the sentence.

> *Effective:* The Pope *himself* will speak on television this evening.
> *Effective:* I want to write this essay *myself.*

Note that there is no such word in standard English as *hiself* or *hisself.* The word is *himself.*

### Pronoun Reference

Personal, possessive, relative, and demonstrative pronouns all stand for nouns or other pronouns. The word that a pronoun stands for is called the pronoun reference (or antecedent). This reference should always be clear to your reader. As you check over your paper, make sure that the reference for every pronoun is easy to find.

Look at the following sentence:

They tell us that the solar system is several billion years old.

How many times have you said something like this, only to be asked, "Who is they?" You were asked this question because you had not provided a pronoun reference. In your writing, take extra care not to make the same mistake. Try to ensure that all of your pronoun references are obvious, whether they refer to a noun or to another pronoun. Most of your pronouns should appear in the same sentence as their reference or in the one immediately following. Even the clearest reference should never be separated from the pronoun by more than two or three sentences. If you find that you have used a number of pronouns in a row, it is probably time to repeat the reference. Also, when you use two or more pronouns having different references, make sure that the referencing is clear. Finally, avoid starting a paragraph with a pronoun. References are hard to carry from paragraph to paragraph.

In the following sentences, the pronouns that require references and the words that they refer to are both italicized.

*People* who smoke should make sure that *their* smoking does not bother others.

Frozen yogurt *parlors* are currently popular because *their* product is considered healthful.

*Everyone* who had intended to go to the concert should return *his* or *her* ticket for a refund.

Most private *colleges* in the United States are restructuring *their* *programs* to make *them* more responsive to the needs of today.

Sentences having pronouns with no references may sound correct, but often they do not communicate exactly what the writer intends.

*Ineffective:* In restaurants I often order fish dinners, but sometimes I wonder whether *it* is fresh.

The writer wants *it* to refer to *fish*. *Fish*, however, serves as an adjective in this sentence. Since pronouns should refer to nouns or other pronouns, the sentence would work better if expressed in either of the following ways:

*Effective:* In restaurants I often order fish dinners, but sometimes I wonder whether the fish is fresh.
*Effective:* In restaurants I often order fish for dinner, but sometimes I wonder whether it is fresh.

Here is another example:

*Ineffective:* Robert's arms were a mess of grease and suds by the time *he* finished cleaning the oven.

The writer wants *he* to refer to *Robert.* But in this sentence, the word *Robert's* acts to describe *arms.* The word *Robert* is not even in the sentence. The word *Robert's* is there, but it would be imprecise if used to replace *he.* The writer could correct the sentence easily in either of the following ways:

> *Effective:* Robert's arms were a mess of grease and suds by the time Robert finished cleaning the oven.
> *Effective:* By the time Robert finished cleaning the oven, his arms were a mess of grease and suds.

In some sentences, it is difficult to tell which reference a pronoun refers to. Even if the meaning can be figured out from the context, it is best to avoid any possibility of confusing your reader. If a pronoun can possibly refer to more than one noun or pronoun, you should repeat the reference or reword the sentence rather than leave the sentence ambiguous. Let's look at an example.

> Candy and Joyce talked for a long time about the trip *she* was planning to take.

Who was planning to take a trip? Was it Candy, Joyce, or maybe even someone else? The way the sentence is worded, these questions cannot be answered. Repeating the appropriate name, however, makes the sentence clear.

> Candy and Joyce talked for a long time about the trip Candy was planning to take.

References for pronouns should be explicit whenever possible. The pronouns *that, which, it,* and *this* are often used to refer to a complete statement that precedes them. The result of this practice is that sometimes the connection between the pronoun and its reference is too subtle. Some statements are perfectly clear, and you can use one of these pronouns to refer to them. Others, especially those that contain multiple nouns that could be possible references, are confusing. Let's take a look at a few examples.

> *Effective:* Human beings reason. This is the difference between them and other animals.
> *Ineffective:* My brother has always liked reading, but I am different. This annoys me.

What annoys the person in the second example? Is it that his brother likes to read, is it reading itself, or is it the fact that he and his brother are different? The *this* does not specify. Here's another example:

> *Ineffective:* We often go for a drive in the city late at night. It is so interesting.

What exactly is interesting? The late hour? The city? The whole idea—going for a drive in the city late at night? The *it* confuses the reader.

The best solution to avoiding ambiguity is to try, as often as possible, to use clear, distinct references. Whenever you want to use a *this,* a *which,* an *it,* or a *that* to stand for an entire preceding statement, be prepared to defend the usage on the grounds of absolute clarity, or recast the sentence, as did the writers of the following sentences:

*Original version:* Many artists' work is so entwined with values that there is no separation between the artists' life and their work. This almost makes art into a religion.

*Recast version:* Many artists' work is so entwined with values that there is no separation between the artists' life and their work. This intense involvement with their artwork almost makes art into a religion.

*Original version:* Last week my friend won a raffle with a $1,000 prize. It has changed his attitude about entering contests.

*Recast version:* Last week my friend won a raffle with a $1,000 prize. This stroke of luck has changed his attitude about entering contests.

### Pronoun Agreement

In your writing, you should make sure that every pronoun agrees with its reference. Agreement simply means that a pronoun and the word it stands for have the same gender, number, and person. The following sentences are all examples of correct pronoun agreement:

Anita was upset with *her* mother.

*Her* is correct because it is a feminine singular third person pronoun and therefore agrees with *Anita.*

You should receive *your* grades tomorrow.

*Your* is correct because it is a second person pronoun and therefore agrees with *you.* It is impossible to tell whether you is singular or plural from its form alone. Context provides the number of the reference.

*Everybody* has *his* or *her* own way of telling a story, and the same story told by two separate people will seem very different.

*His or her* is correct because it is a singular third person pronoun and therefore agrees with *everybody.* Note that the expression *his or her* indicates no gender, and its use avoids the sexist connotations of using only *his.*

The chickens ran around in the yard, never knowing that any minute the butcher would chop off *their* heads.

*Their* is correct because it is a plural third person pronoun and therefore agrees with *chickens.*

Many of the errors in pronoun agreement (and in reference) are simply caused by writers' becoming too rushed to pay enough attention to what they are putting on paper. These errors are usually easy to find and correct when you look for them. There are a few specific areas, in fact, that you will want to watch for because problems in agreement seem to occur there with some frequency.

### *Either . . . Or and Neither . . . Nor*

When *either . . . or* or *neither . . . nor* serves to connect the words that are references for a pronoun, use the noun or pronoun closest to the verb of the sentence to determine the number of the pronoun. The following sentence is correct:

Neither Ms. Karr nor her students could simply explain their school's policies on attendance.

*Their* is correct because it is a plural third person pronoun that agrees with *students.*

### *Each*

Use the singular pronoun to refer to *each.*

Each of the members of the class has completed *his or her* assignment.

*His or her* is correct because it is a singular third person pronoun that agrees with *each.* See page 213 for a discussion on how to avoid sexist language.

### *Everyone, Everybody, Nobody, Anyone*

Use the singular pronoun to refer to *one, everyone, everybody, nobody, no one, anybody, anyone, somebody,* and *someone.* The word *one* or *body* contained within each word is the indication that references to these words should, as much as possible, retain the singular meaning. In current informal usage, people often ignore the rule, preferring the plural *their* or *they;* the main point of avoiding the singular in speaking is to avoid sexist language. But the use of the singular expression *his or her* or the avoidance of singular concepts such as those expressed by *someone* and *anybody* is preferred to mixing plural pronouns with singular references. The sentences below illustrate informal and formal usage:

**Informal:** *Everybody* believes that *they* have the right answers.
**Formal:** *Everybody* believes that *he or she* has the right answers.

If the meaning you are trying to convey is clearly plural and could not be singular, the plural pronoun is appropriate.

*Everybody* thanked me for the gift, which meant so much to *them*. (clearly not singular)

### A Person

Use the singular to refer to the word *person*. The sentences below are formal and correct:

A *person* should investigate for *himself or herself* what jobs seem most rewarding.

*People* should investigate for *themselves* what jobs seem most rewarding.

### Collective Nouns

Use the singular to refer to a collective noun treated as one whole unit and the plural to refer to a collective noun emphasizing the separate individuals that make up the unit, though there may be many of them.

The *team* plays *its* best when feeling confident.

*Its* is correct because it is a third person singular pronoun that agrees with *team,* treated as a unit.

The *committee* did *their* best to convince the governor to reconsider the antiquated law.

*Their* is correct because it is a plural third person pronoun referring to *committee*; the meaning of the sentence emphasizes the many individuals who make up the committee.

### References Joined by And

Use the plural pronoun for most references joined by *and.* If the words are treated as a unit, however, the singular pronoun seems more appropriate.

*Karen and Martin* do *their* calculus homework together.

*Their* is correct because Karen and Martin are two separate people.

Love and affection brings *its* own rewards.

*Its* is correct because *love and affection* are not intended to be separate, as far as the meaning of the sentence shows.

### Any, None, All, Some

Use either the singular or plural pronoun to refer to *any, none, all, some, most,* and *more.* The pronoun should reflect the meaning, as in the following sentences:

If *any* of the turkey is left, *it* should be frozen.

*Most* of the story is as good as *it* can be.

*None*, which contains the word *one*, should be singular when its meaning in the sentence is *not one*. You should be careful to use the singular pronoun with *none* whenever possible, reserving the plural pronoun only for instances in which you can clearly justify it.

> *None* of the wild animal parks in California is as scenic as *it* is described in the advertisements.

The writer is stressing that not one of the parks is as scenic as the advertisements promise. *It* is correct because *none* emphasizes the singular.

> *None* of the orchestra's members played well tonight for *their* opening show.

In this case, the implication is plural.

### Who, Which, That

Use the singular pronoun if the word that *who, which,* or *that* refers to is singular, and use the plural if the reference is plural.

> Professor Miles is the kind of *person who* makes up *her* own mind on issues.

*Her* is correct because it is a third person singular pronoun that refers to *who,* and *who* refers to the singular word *person*.

> Professor Miles is one of those *people who* make up *their* own minds on issues.

*Their* is correct because it is a third person plural pronoun that refers to *who*, and here *who* refers to the plural word *people*.

---

**Exercises**

A. Correct any pronoun errors in the following sentences.
1. There are very few secrets between my boyfriend and 1.
2. Orwell's *1984* is a book that predicts what we will do to ourself if we continue to be apathetic to our surroundings.
3. Knowing that my grandfather was happy when he died helped myself accept the loss more easily.
4. Only a pessimist like he would say that a glass is half empty when it's obvious that it is half full.
5. The grades the students gave theirself were surprisingly fair.

6. Natural philosophy comes from looking around you and finding the truths in your own existence.

7. For most students, final exams are the natural completion to a semester; it sums up all the information studied during the term.

8. Myself and many other economics majors protested the question on the midterm because we felt it was sexist.

9. When we were children, the smell of freshly baked cookies was enough to drive we children wild.

10. John asked whether him or me will do the work.

B. Correct any errors in pronoun usage in the following sentences.

1. A light bar, which is a deluxe feature in many cars, is a bar of lights that will light to different sounds from the car's stereo. They are placed on the dash on the passenger side.

2. What makes the adult student special is that they are often very motivated and have many life experiences to bring to what they study.

3. A car club provides a cruiser with a common group of friends and provides him or her with social events in which they are able to participate: dances, parties, and picnics.

4. The average person thinks that they can derive increased pleasure from life by depending on time-saving devices.

5. Anybody who wants to increase their tolerance should practice sharpening a pencil with broken lead in it.

6. It is common for the college graduate to be hired for jobs requiring specialized skills because they feel a college graduate can quickly be trained in almost any field.

7. For some people, low carbohydrate diets are dangerous because it drastically reduces the amount of sugar the body gets, though sugar still may be needed by the body.

8. It is hard enough for a freshman to decide what courses to take for the term during the first few days of the semester, but for them to decide courses for a whole year is an unreasonable demand.

9. Confucianism sets out to reform people, for they believe change and discipline to be very important.

10. Two areas of concern to psychology majors are physiology and mathematics. It is an important course for a psychology major because of all the computations required in surveys and experiments.

C. Correct any errors in pronoun references in the following sentences.

1. Once you are in a car club, they care for their own people.

2. In California, repeated attempts by public officials to ease traffic problems by setting up special lanes for car poolers have failed. Most of them want "the other guy" to give up his car.

3. The world is evolving to a point where thinking is less important than it used to be. They have computers to do thinking of all kinds.

4. Many times, a dieter consumes too much of one food. This results in an unbalanced diet and is just as fattening as eating small amounts of very fattening food.

5. Although I knew my friends were behind me, I could not get up enough nerve to invite the president to dinner. It didn't seem my place.

6. For the first time in my life I realized that if I wanted to play football I would have to work for it.
7. In the book about the theologian Lao Tzu, it explains the way the sage is to conduct his government.
8. In the selection from Whitman's *Passage to India,* he describes the terrifying search for satisfaction that most Americans experience at some time in their lives.

D. Correct any mistakes in pronoun agreement or reference in the following paragraph.

Some members of the "cruiser" culture belong to car clubs. There are many car clubs in Los Angeles, and it serves a social and political function for this subculture. The car clubs provide cruisers with a group of common friends that are all interested in cars. It also provides him or her with social events in which they are able to participate: dances, parties, and picnics. Politically, the car club is a source of prestige, demanding respect within the cruiser subculture. The cruiser who is a member has no worries about trouble from others. In a way, the cruiser subculture could be viewed as a clan and the different clubs as a lineage. Once you are in, they care for their own people.

E. Correct any errors in the use of pronouns in the following sentences.
1. Anyone who could prove something was wrong with them was excluded from service in the Army.
2. The lecture hall looks like a long and narrow tunnel. This makes for too great a distance between the speaker and their audience.
3. Since my roommate's mother lives nearby, she goes home more often than I can.
4. I do not like to study in the library, though it is fine for locating books I need for classes.
5. Many companies make electric heaters, but most of them are small.
6. Even though love involves a longer involvement with other people than infatuation does, they seem to occur at the same time.
7. Christmas is a joyous time in a child's life. The thought of getting a present makes them all excited. I can remember times when my brother and I would be awake all night waiting for Santa Claus. It wasn't that Santa was a special figure in our life. We knew Mom and Dad put presents under the tree for us. We just couldn't wait for morning to celebrate the holiday in all their warm spirit.

F. Correct the pronoun usage in the following paragraph. The writer has used the informal *you.* Would the type of audience for whom the paragraph is intended make a difference as to whether the use of *you* is acceptable?

Hypnotizing yourself is a simple routine of progressive relaxation. The first step is physical. Start with your feet. Stretch them and relax them two or three times. Next, move up to your calves. Tense and relax them. Progressing up the body to your thighs, do the same tensing and relaxing, tensing and relaxing. Then one must continue to move upward until you have relaxed every part of your body. The second step requires you to use your imagination. Picture yourself slowly walking down a flight of stairs. It helps if one can think of a specific staircase. You see yourself stepping down with one foot, then the other, then the first again, until you reach the bottom of the stairs. At the bottom, you imagine that you have come to a beautiful, peaceful place. This is an ideal spot that has whatever environment you consider most desirable. In fact, thinking of a real place oneself has been helps to make the experience vivid. You want to linger at that place until you feel worry-free and wonderfully relaxed. Then you are ready to place positive suggestions into your mind.

## 5. IS YOUR SYNTAX CORRECT?

Syntax is the arrangement of words and groups of words in sentences. You should read through your essay to make sure that sentence parts are arranged in the best possible way so that they do not sound awkward. Although keeping your reader interested is also important, the best arrangement is, of course, the one that produces the clearest statements. Because most errors in syntax sound wrong when you hear them, it is helpful to read your paper aloud as you listen for placement of modifiers, parallelism, use of negatives and comparisons, and positioning of emphasis.

### Modifiers

Modifiers are words or groups of words that describe nouns, pronouns, verbs, or other modifiers. They may function, as you recall, as adjectives that answer the questions *what, which,* or *what kind* about a noun, or as adverbs that answer the questions *how, why, when,* or *to what extent* about a verb, adjective, or other adverb. Modifiers should be placed as close as possible to what they modify. Sometimes no special effort is needed to make clear the connections between modifiers and what they describe, but some structures can be a bit tricky. Knowing what to look out for will help you recognize and correct errors in the placement of modifiers.

#### Misplaced Modifiers

In good sentences, the proper placement of modifiers is important. Misplaced modifiers can make what you intend to say hard to understand. Sometimes, they may even cause the sentence to seem nonsensical. *Whenever possible, a modifier should come immediately before or after the word or phrase it modifies.* When this close relationship is not practical, you should take extra care to ensure that it is perfectly clear which modifier is associated with which word or phrase.

One of the best ways to detect misplaced modifiers is to read what you have written aloud. Misplaced modifiers usually sound misplaced. Try this procedure on the following sentence:

*Weak:* The young girl skipped down the street and bumped into an elderly gentlemen with bells on her shoes.

Did the phrase *with bells on her shoes* surprise you? You probably expected it to tell you something about the elderly gentleman. Then you ran into the pronoun *her,* so you knew the phrase had to refer to the young girl. The momentary confusion you likely experienced could have been avoided if the writer had put the phrase next to *young girl,* where it belongs.

Here are two more examples of sentences with misplaced modifiers, each followed by a corrected version. Notice how much better the sentences sound when the modifiers come where they are supposed to.

> **Weak:** Next week my cousin whom I haven't seen in eight years
>    will be visiting our family from Oregon.
> **Effective:** Next week my cousin from Oregon whom I haven't seen
>    in eight years will be visiting our family.
> **Weak:** I made a beautiful blanket for my bed that was made of
>    wool.
> **Effective:** I made a beautiful wool blanket for my bed.

A slightly different problem occurs when a modifier could modify either of two different words or phrases. If the writer is careless in the placement of such a modifier, the intended meaning may be unclear.

> **Weak:** Her ability to dance quickly affected her career.

Does *quickly* refer to the way she dances or to the way her career was affected? Logically, *quickly* would be more likely to modify *affected.* See how much clearer this would have been if the writer had been more careful.

> **Effective:** Her ability to dance affected her career *quickly.*
> **Effective:** Her career was *quickly* affected by her ability to dance.

### Dangling Modifiers

A dangling modifier is a modifier that has no word or phrase to modify. It is an error that often occurs because a writer begins a sentence with one idea in mind and then has another idea before the sentence is completed. Check over your writing to make sure that you have not allowed any dangling modifiers to creep into your sentences. Pay special attention to participle phrases that begin sentences. This type of modifier tends to dangle the most often.

> Being almost eighteen, my little brother was born.

This sentence does not make much sense, does it? The phrase *being almost eighteen* has nothing to modify. It obviously does not refer to *brother.* The following might be what the writer meant to say:

> Being almost eighteen, I was surprised when my little brother was born.

When you find a dangling modifier in your writing, the best way to correct it is to rewrite the sentence so that the word meant to be modified is included. Check your understanding of dangling modifiers and how they should be corrected by looking over the following examples:

> *Incorrect:* Tired and looking forward to a rest, the day dragged on.
> *Correct:* Tired and looking forward to a rest, he felt that the day dragged on.
> *Correct:* Because he was tired and looking forward to a rest, the day seemed to drag on.
> *Incorrect:* Speaking for the committee, the president's decision is appropriate and fair.
> *Correct:* Speaking for the committee, I think that the president's decision is appropriate and fair.
> *Correct:* I speak for the committee in saying that the president's decision is appropriate and fair.

### Parallelism

In a sentence, words or groups of words that express similar thoughts should be similar in form. This similarity is called *parallelism*. Elements in a series should be parallel. So should words joined by *and, or, but, as well as*, and sometimes *is*. Grammatical structures used with comparative pairs of words such as *neither . . . nor, not only . . . but also*, and *if . . . then* should also be parallel. A lack of parallelism is shown in the following sentence:

> I like not only swimming but also to run and to jump rope.

The use of *not only . . . but also* should serve as a clue that the elements being compared should be similar. Rewording the sentence in either of the following ways makes the structures parallel.

> *Effective:* I like not only swimming but also running and jumping rope.
> *Effective:* I like not only to swim but also to run and to jump rope.

The lack of parallelism occurs most frequently with verbs and verbals. Nouns, prepositions, and adjectives, however, can all cause problems as well. The best way to detect elements that do not have parallel structures is to read sentences aloud. You should try this method with the following examples:

> *Incorrect:* Eating well, exercising, and enough sleep are part of healthful living.
> *Correct:* Eating well, exercising, and getting enough sleep are part of healthful living.

*Incorrect:* My math teacher makes every effort to encourage, instruct, and to praise her students.

*Correct:* My math teacher makes every effort to encourage, to instruct, and to praise her students.

*Correct:* My math teacher makes every effort to encourage, instruct, and praise her students.

*Incorrect:* All my work paid off, not only because I learned a lot about a subject I was interested in, but also got an A on the paper.

*Correct:* All my efforts paid off, not only because I learned a lot about a subject I was interested in but also because I got an A on the paper.

See how much better a sentence sounds when the elements are parallel? Here are some more examples of effective parallelism taken from students' papers:

> Other proposals by gun control advocates include a ban on handguns, registration of all firearms, and control over the manufacture of guns.

> Alexander Phillips maintained his contract labor force by a yearly recruitment of poor whites from nearby towns and villages. On roads that were too far from towns for anyone to commute there, he not only set up work camps but also provided wholesome food for these people.

> If a forest is cut down, earth is removed, coal is extracted, and earth is replenished with new plants, in about fifty years the location will look the same as it did before strip-mining.

> Mourning is dying. To mourn is to express the death wish.

### Comparisons

Comparisons are used to show differences or similarities. They tell how things are alike or how they are not alike. Many writers run into difficulties when making comparisons. Their mistakes generally fall into two categories: incomplete comparisons and inappropriate comparisons. As you read through your paper, make sure that all your comparisons are complete and accurate.

*Incomplete Comparisons*

A comparison may be incomplete because only part of it is given. Such incomplete comparisons are particularly common in advertising.

> Learning to read with Eve Woodhue is more fun.
> Smoke Choker's 100's, a longer low tar cigarette.

These advertisements promise a comparison, but only one thing is mentioned. What is "learning to read with Eve" more fun than? What are Choker's longer than? The advertisements are incomplete. The thing the product is compared to is left to the imagination. Although such comparisons may serve the purposes of ad agencies, they should be carefully avoided in your own writing. At best, they can only lead to confusion.

Even when all of the things being compared are included, a comparison may still be incomplete because necessary words or punctuation is missing. In some cases, the omissions simply cause confusion. In others, the sentences may be nonsensical.

> Chicago has a skyscraper that is taller than any building in the world.
> My mother is kinder than any woman.

According to the wording of the first example, a skyscraper is not a building. In the second, a mother is not considered to be a woman. Adding the word *other* to both would make the intended meaning of the sentences clear.

> Chicago has a skyscraper that is taller than any other building in the world.
> My mother is kinder than any other woman.

A word you should be particularly careful to include when it is needed is *as*.

> *Weak:* Rosa is *as* strong, if not stronger than, Mike.
> *Effective:* Rosa is *as* strong *as,* if not stronger than, Mike.

Perhaps an even better way of writing this sentence is:

> Rosa is *as* strong *as* Mike, if not stronger.

Here are some more examples in which missing words make the comparisons incomplete:

> *Weak:* John has lived in the building longer than anyone.
> *Effective:* John has lived in the building longer than anyone else.
> *Weak:* I like Fred more than Mary.
> *Effective:* I like Fred more than I like Mary.
> *Effective:* I like Fred more than Mary does.
> *Weak:* Larry used to seem much younger.
> *Effective:* Larry used to seem much younger than he was.
> *Effective:* Larry used to seem much younger than Margaret.

*Inappropriate Comparisons*

An inappropriate comparison has no sound basis and reflects a problem in thinking. A comparison may be inappropriate either because a form of the word *compare* is used too loosely or because the two or more ideas being related are not expressed in a form that makes them comparable. Inappropriate comparisons always sound awkward when read aloud. They also make no sense when they are analyzed. The following sentence illustrates the first kind:

> In comparison to people, the song shows people's inability to cope with social problems.

Such statements promise a comparison, but no comparison is made. The writer probably does not understand the exact meaning of the word comparison. In this example there are no similarities and differences to discuss. It is likely that the writer wanted to lead into the point with a sentence like:

> The song reflects people's struggles with social problems.
> *or*
> The song is about people's struggles.

After one of these sentences, the writer could expand on the point.

> It reveals ways in which people have difficulty coping.

Even when two ideas or things are present in a sentence and they are to be compared, the comparison may be inappropriate because the basis is not clearly stated or thought out. You cannot compare the incomparable. All comparisons and contrasts are based on some likeness between ideas or things. For instance, you could show comparisons and contrasts between two chairs, one modern and the other old fashioned. Although the chairs are different, both are still chairs, so there is a logical basis for comparison. The same would be true of a comparison of two writers from the same period who had similar influences and similar ideas but radically different styles. The form of a sound comparison, then, makes clear the basis of the comparison or contrast. In the following comparative statements, the basis for comparison is italicized:

> The *personality* of my French teacher is similar to the *personality* of my Aunt Essie.

The statement is correct because the basis of comparison is the personality of each person.

> The *color* of her eyes is similar to the *color* of mine.

The statement is correct because the basis of comparison is the color of each person's eyes.

You can see why the following sentence winds up trying to compare the incomparable simply because the writer fails to state the basis for comparison.

> The embarrassment I felt when I realized that I was wearing two completely different shoes was like the time I mistakenly wore my pajamas to school in fourth grade.

According to the wording of this example, embarrassment can be compared to a *time*. Of course, such a statement is nonsense. What the writer probably means to compare is the embarrassment he felt on both occasions. An effective revision would be written as follows:

> The embarrassment I felt when I realized that I was wearing two completely different shoes was like the embarrassment I had experienced back in the fourth grade when I mistakenly wore my pajamas to school.

Some inappropriate comparisons are less obvious than this one. They may even sound correct if you aren't listening closely. Here are two examples:

> My hat is bigger than Jan.
> Their old VW is in better condition than Alec.

The bases for comparison, *hats* in the first sentence and *old VWs* in the second, are not stated. The result is that the first sentence compares a *hat* to *Jan* and the second sentence compares an *old VW* to *Alec*. It doesn't make much sense to compare hats or cars to people. The following sentences are correct:

> My hat is bigger than Jan's hat.
>    *or*
> My hat is bigger than Jan's.
> Their old VW is in better condition than Alec's old VW.
>    *or*
> Their old VW is in better condition than Alec's.

Let's look at one more example. The following comparison is incorrect:

> In France, like the United States, and unlike Sweden, any driver can refuse to take a test for drunk driving.

On a quick reading, you might think the sentence sounds correct. But the basis for comparison is not stated. The writer is not comparing France, the United States, and Sweden with each other generally but is, instead, comparing the drunk driving laws in the three countries. The writer could rework the sentence as follows:

In France, like in the United States, and unlike in Sweden, any driver can refuse to take a test for drunk driving.

### Double Negatives

Words such as *no, not,* and *nothing* are useful for making negative statements:

> This relationship is *nothing* like my last.
> I do *not* like him.
> She has *no* friends.

Nevertheless, these simple little words often cause problems when more than one is used for the same idea. This usage is called a double negative. All double negatives should be avoided. Using two negatives is not more emphatic than using just one. If you wish to be technical, the negatives actually cancel each other out and make the statement positive. Suppose someone has written the following:

> I *can't* do *nothing* about it.

What the writer probably meant to say was:

> I *cannot* do *anything* about it.

But what the sentence actually states is the opposite:

> I can do something about it.

As you read through your paper, make sure that any time you have used a negative you have used only one. Remembering that the following words should usually be used together may help you to avoid double negatives in your own writing:

| | | |
|---|---|---|
| Not . . . anything | Not . . . anybody | Do not . . . any |
| Does not . . . any | Hardly . . . any | Scarcely . . . any |

Also remember that *hardly* and *scarcely* should never be preceded by a negative.

> *Incorrect:* He *cannot hardly* realize how rich he has become.
> *Correct:* He can *hardly* realize how rich he has become.

Several types of negative expressions seem to cause problems for many writers. If you use expressions such as the following in your writing, be sure not to accidentally make them double negatives.

> *Incorrect:* I should not wonder if he did not make a fool of himself.
> *Correct:* I should not wonder if he made a fool of himself.

*Incorrect:* I cannot help but wonder whether the fuel crisis will get worse.

*Correct:* I cannot help wondering whether the fuel crisis will get worse.

*Incorrect:* I doubt but what the team will win.

*Correct:* I doubt that the team will win.

### Mixed Syntax

As you read through your paper, make sure that you do not have any sentences in which the syntax is mixed. Mixed syntax is the blurring together of two related but distinctly different sentence patterns. These mistakes are often hard to spot. The beginning sounds right and the ending sounds right, but the two parts together sound awkward and are incorrect:

*Incorrect:* The reason for the general's anger is because some young officers did not behave properly at his garden party.

The writer of this sentence probably had both of the following sentence patterns in mind and allowed them to become mixed.

*Correct:* The reason for the general's anger is that some young officers did not behave properly at his garden party.

*Correct:* The general is angry because some young officers did not behave properly at his garden party.

Either sentence is fine, but mixing the two is incorrect. Here is another example:

*Incorrect:* Janie has serious learning disabilities, but she tries her best as she can.

Again, the writer was probably thinking of two different sentence patterns.

*Correct:* Janie has serious learning disabilities, but she tries her best.

*Correct:* Janie has serious learning disabilities, but she tries as hard as she can.

As before, either pattern is acceptable, but a mixture is not.

There are generally two causes for mixed syntax. The writer may begin a sentence and then get a related idea but forget to go back and change the first part accordingly. Such errors are easily eliminated by carefully rereading what one has written. The other cause of mixed syntax is a lack of familiarity with particular expressions. Writers can avoid mistakes of this type by noticing how these expressions are used in what they read and by looking closely at any sentences that might seem strange. Writing sentences in imitation of good prose, as covered on page 192, can also be helpful. In addition, writers should take special care when using any expressions with which they are not totally at ease.

**Exercises**

A. Correct any confusing or misplaced modifiers in the following sentences.
  1. She'd be the one to recognize the house, as a native of the area and a friend of the past owners.
  2. The decision to give up my future for her which was so promising was a difficult one.
  3. Not pretty and no conversationalist, I still cared more for her than I did for any model or social jabberer.
  4. Steaming so comfortingly in the mug, I sometimes think that hot chocolate offers even more companionship than a friendly dog.
  5. Schools and prisons, which are both institutions, are often similarly designed.
  6. It is where the road narrows that cars speed through the curves like lightning.
  7. So that no one would get them confused, large signs were placed on the machines made of cardboard.
  8. Given the open classroom approach to education, I think there could be some improvement made by teachers of most subject areas.
  9. My car was returned after a few days by the police all dirty and scratched.
  10. I should mention now that some people will be given more time than others so that there will be no confusion.
B. Underline all the modifiers and draw arrows to the words they modify in the following sentences. Correct any dangling or misplaced modifiers.
  1. When young, the id is the dominant part of the personality.
  2. As a child, all needs are felt intensely.
  3. Sitting in the classroom, the time to give my speech grew near.
  4. Looking at the boring art exhibit, each minute went by so slowly I thought the tour would never end.
  5. Trying to be friendly but assertive, the subject of conversation was a bad one.
  6. Full of thoughts of winning, the game seemed to pass quickly.
  7. Knowing that the jockey was not too happy about his record, the win was a surprise to the audience.
  8. Being an advocate of preserving endangered species, lions and tigers should be kept on animal reserves.
  9. Glued to the counter, they laughed at him as he tried to hide what he was doing.
  10. Without a cent, traveling would be difficult but not impossible.
C. Correct any dangling or misplaced modifiers in the following sentences.
  1. Moving on to the days of Malcolm X, young blacks at that time had very little to do.

2. Eating only a few bites, my lunch was unfinished.

3. When looking at the pencil's diameter, lead forms a circle about half the way across the instrument.

4. The unique vocabulary and syntax of the *Old Testament* helps to disprove the theory of cultism.

5. After a year of frequent use, I found myself unable to do certain math problems without a calculator.

6. Out of habit, I waited in the long line at the bank until the teller recognized me.

7. Speaking to an expert on teaching reading to young children, he told me that using phonetics is the best method.

8. In speaking to a successful motion picture director, the movie industry is losing hundreds of thousands of dollars each year.

9. In keeping with the cosmic cycles of the universe, the Chinese thought that the human body had 365 parts, corresponding to the number of days in a year.

10. Driving down the freeway, the mattress in the middle lane caught me by surprise.

D. Underline the parallel structures in the following sentences.

1. Although nobody knew it then, we were ashamed of ourselves and our families.

2. He said that I was usually cheerful and always trying to see the best in a situation.

3. People without mates, without self-respect, and without foundation are also without happiness.

4. A life spent with well-defined goals will be a life that brings clearly defined successes.

5. Going out on the town often results in the same sort of fatigue one feels after reading from a book for a long time.

6. In case of a fire, or in the event of an earthquake, a person should not worry about saving a few bits of clothing or a handful of jewelry.

7. Working on a farm, one learns much about the land on which one labors and the seasons that change the land.

8. "If there isn't a pail by the door or a basin in the farm house, I'll let the cow's milk soak into the ground," he said.

9. Even though the senator is an important political figure, she is not a popular one.

10. I never met a person who enjoyed eating, fishing, and sleeping more than my brother does.

E. Correct any errors in parallelism in the following sentences.

1. I enjoy arguing and yelling, but I don't like to fight.

2. There was a building that I thought would look good in New York City and cause a stir there, too.

3. If, as is sometimes the case, a bride hasn't met the father of her fiancé or his mother, a meeting of them all during the wedding will be very emotional, to say the least.

4. But it's true that a day with a friend's company seems brief and full.

5. Although there are many attaché cases on the market, there is none I would like to have, to use, or even enjoy carrying as much as I did the one I lost.
6. Summer is a time for swimming and to relax.
7. Right now I want rest and to stop working so hard.
8. Everyone is invited to an evening of singing, to dance, and to feast.
9. The architecture of the office building is too stilted, cold, and without any grace.
10. 1 am looking for a man who is intelligent, understanding, and a good friend in times of stress.

F. Underline all the parallel elements in the following introductory paragraph from a student's essay.

Dull, lifeless, and metallic, the machine may one day replace people's best friends. People will have robot friends to talk to and to confide in. It will be perfectly acceptable to invite a robot home for dinner. Every robot, just like every person, will have an address and telephone number and maybe even a social security card. If all these possibilities seem farfetched or undesirable, one has only to consider the advantages of an automated relationship. First, robots can be turned off whenever he or she desires peace and quiet. Robots tend to be servile and are willing to do anything to please. Also, many people will program their robot's topics for conversation in order to assure themselves that they will never be bored. Having a robot as a companion might be a little hard to get used to, but in the end it might offer more privacy, better schedules, and more stimulating talk than the conventional person-to-person relationship.

G. Correct any faulty comparisons in the following sentences.
1. The chief of the Navajo tribe is more powerful than any Navajo.
2. Having a better English teacher in college helped me improve my writing skills.
3. A beginning police officer has to undertake fewer risks.
4. A racquetball player has a faster response to the ball than in tennis.
5. When I was younger, people used to think I looked older.
6. In a competitive situation, the runner is much more nervous.
7. The writer's role in making a film is not as demanding as the producer.
8. Drawing inferences from the stories a person tells can make them more interesting.
9. The president's response to the bill was more like a child.
10. Eating TV dinners instead of home-cooked meals is like single people.

As a writer, you have an obligation to assist your reader in every way possible to get the intended meaning from what you write. One way that you accomplish this goal is by using generally accepted practices regarding punctuation and mechanics. Because most writers have agreed on basic concepts of usage, your ability to use punctuation and mechanics correctly will bring your own writing into line with other writing with which your reader is probably familiar. For instance, your reader is already accustomed to other writers helping him or her through a passage by marking off units of thought into sentences. Certainly, then, you should also punctuate your sentences to provide this same assistance.

Standard guidelines for mechanics, if applied, will also help you to make certain that your essay will be properly received and interpreted by your reader. After all, a reader who finds "individualized" mechanics in an essay is likely to find his or her attention drawn not to what the writer intends but to the nonstandard method of presentation.

Entries in this glossary are arranged alphabetically so that information regarding particular topics can be easily located. Although this chapter is intended as an easy reference, a source of answers to questions that occur as you write, you can benefit by giving it a close reading from start to finish. By reading all entries carefully, you can discover new ways to present your ideas. You might also discover that some of your old methods should be replaced.

Keep in mind that many of the "rules" presented here are simply guidelines. Handling of such things as numbers and capitalization often varies from discipline to discipline. To check the recommended uses for a particular subject matter, consult the appropriate style manual (MLA, APA, AMA, etc.).

# A GLOSSARY OF PUNCTUATION AND MECHANICS

## ABBREVIATIONS

Abbreviations are space-saving devices. They are especially helpful in footnotes, in bibliographic entries, within parentheses, and on charts or graphs. A few abbreviations are acceptable in all forms of writing. Most, however, should be avoided in papers and essays.

### Forms of Address

Titles or forms of address such as Ms., Mrs., Mmes. (plural of Mrs.), Mr., Messrs. (plural of Mr.), St. (Saint), Jr., Sr., Dr., Ph.D., and M.D.

should be abbreviated only when they come before or after names. Used alone they should be spelled out.

> Ramon R. Alba, Ph.D., and Mr. James S. Wright are the junior members of the committee.

Mr., Ms., Mrs., and Dr. are dropped if Ph.D., M.D., or D.D.S. follows the name.

### Time

Indicators of time such as B.C., A.D., P.M., and A.M. are used with dates and times. A.D. precedes the date, but B.C. comes after it.

> The manuscripts dated A.D. 900 were an amazing find.
> Aristotle wrote the *Poetics* in the fourth century B.C.

### Organizations and Agencies

The abbreviations for well-known organizations and agencies such as UNESCO, NATO, the CIA, the VFW, and NOW are usually written without periods. It is a good practice to spell out the full name of an organization the first time it is used in your essay and to place the abbreviation after the name in parentheses. Doing so will assure that the reader recognizes what the abbreviation stands for when it appears again.

> The American Civil Liberties Union (ACLU) took on the controversial affirmative action case.

### Money

Symbols for dollars and cents may be used if spelling out the figure would take several words, if the figure is to be compared to several other figures in the sentence or paragraph, or if using them lends special clarity to what you are saying. Otherwise, spell out the numbers.

> Last summer my brother earned twelve hundred dollars working for a moving company.
> Including tax and license, the car cost $14,026.37.
> A dinner that cost six dollars a few years ago now costs twelve.
> I paid $157 for the stove, $140 for the refrigerator, $1,400 for the first and last months' rent, and $35 for a cleaning fee. That means I have exactly $47.29 left to live on this month.

### Technical Terms

In technical papers, terms such as mpg and BTUs are common and correct. Note that these terms are used with figures, not alone.

> How many miles per gallon does your car get?
> The estimated consumption by the energy-saving devices was 1,000 BTUs.

### Percent

Spell out the word percent unless it is used in a comparison. Most comparative uses of percent symbols are obvious because the percents are used frequently throughout a sentence or paragraph. Using the symbol in these instances not only saves space but makes for consistency. Always spell out percent or percentage when the term is not preceded by a figure.

> The percentage of smokers in the crowd was unusually high.
> I am not talking about 10% cutbacks in hospitalization payments or even 20%—I'm talking about a whole 60%.

### Measurements

Standard abbreviations such as the following should be used in technical or scientific writing only. In your other writing, spell out the word.

| | |
|---|---|
| in. | inch or inches |
| ft. | foot or feet |
| cm. | centimeter or centimeters |
| lb. | pound or pounds |
| yd. | yard or yards |

Except in tables, you should avoid using the symbols " to mean inches and ′ to mean feet, since they are easily confused with punctuation.

### Latin Terms

Latin terms are sometimes abbreviated in footnotes, bibliographies, and parenthetical references. Terms such as i.e. (that is), e.g. (for example), c. (circa—means "about" and is always used with a specific year), cf. (compare), etc. (and so forth), and et al. (and others, always referring to people) are most effectively saved for places in a paper where space is at a premium. To use them in the text of the paper, where an everyday English word would serve just as well or better, is unnecessary, not to mention a bit pretentious.

### Publication Data

Publication data are also abbreviated in notes, bibliographies, and parentheses. Terms such as vol., ed., trans., col., p., and pp. are commonly used instead of the full words.

### Business Terms

Abbreviations of business terms such as Co., Inc., Corp., and Ltd. are used in notes and bibliographies to conserve space.

### Abbreviations Inappropriate to the Text of a Paper

Many abbreviations should not be used in the running text of your papers. There are two reasons for this rule of thumb. First, in the text of the paper you have plenty of room to spell out the words you mean. Second, the tone of abbreviations in the text may conflict with the tone you want to maintain. Abbreviations seem out of place because they are too casual. The most common mistakes in this area occur because the etiquette of writing letters permits the use of many of the following abbreviations. Since most of them are fine to use in the addresses of letters, continue to use them there. For your essays, however, either use the suggested rewordings that follow or make up your own.

### Place Names
**Weak:** She lives on Macapa Dr. in a huge house.
**Effective:** She lives on Macapa Drive in a huge house.

On envelopes and in letters this abbreviation is acceptable. The same is true of the following: St., Ave., Blvd., Ct., Pl., Ln., Rd., and so forth.

### Ampersand
**Weak:** Crankson & his undefeated team play our team next week.
**Effective:** Crankson and his undefeated team play our team next week.

### Ranks
**Weak:** My prof. had already assigned us fifty pages of reading when he decided to add a thousand-word essay for next week, too.
**Effective:** My professor had already assigned us fifty pages of reading when he decided to add a thousand-word essay for next week, too.

### Places
**Weak:** After attending college in N.Y. City for one term, I decided to transfer to a university in L.A.
**Effective:** After attending college in New York City for one term, I decided to transfer to a university in Los Angeles.

### Names
**Weak:** The letter of recommendation was sent to Jas. Mitchell on Thompson Street.
**Effective:** The letter of recommendation was sent to James Mitchell on Thompson Street.

### Days or Months
**Weak:** Last Mon. the Senate met to discuss funding for the proposed energy plan.
**Effective:** Last Monday the Senate met to discuss funding for the proposed energy plan.
**Weak:** Is Sept. or April the beginning of the new fiscal year?
**Effective:** Is September or April the beginning of the new fiscal year?

## Exercises

A. Correct any abbreviation errors in the following sentences. Assume that the sentences are from an informal essay you might write for a class.

1. Never has there been a president of the U.S. of A. who was younger than J.F.K. when he was president.

2. All the pp. in the novel are filled with witty dialogue, fast action, pathos, etc.

3. Stat. and econ. are courses worth taking even though one's major makes it unnecessary to do so.

4. Nobody around here ever believes me when I say that I do not own a t.v.

5. By the time I reach my Jr. year, I will be taking only those classes I need for my major.

6. When she looked at me that way, I said, "Well, how many lbs. do you think I've gained?"

7. Pretense is not respected where I come from: Chicago, Ill.

8. There's no place like Frisco for a night out on the town.

9. Outpost Dr. is so steep that bike riders have to push their ten speeds up it.

10. I never get upset by anything that anyone over six ft. tall says to me, even though I'm only four ft. tall.

## THE APOSTROPHE

The apostrophe is used to form possessives, contractions, and certain plurals.

### Possessives

Possession indicates that a thing or person belongs to or is closely associated with another. A simple test usually shows whether a word will require an apostrophe because it is possessive. Can you say "the \_\_\_\_\_ of (a or the \_\_\_\_\_)"? In this test you insert in the blanks any combination of the nouns or indefinite pronouns that come next to each other in your sentence. If the word following *of* or *of the* needs an apostrophe, the phrase will make perfect sense. Otherwise, it usually will not make sense. Let's look at an example:

A person's life is what he or she makes of it.

Suppose you wanted to check the relationship between *person* and *life.* You would insert it in the test phrase:

the life of a person.

The phrase makes sense; it says what you mean. Therefore, you are correct in including the apostrophe: *person's life.* Similarly, you could say that the phrase *Mary's hat* can be thought of as *the hat of Mary* or that *anyone's guess* could be thought of as *the guess of anyone*. Every now and then, however, you will find a phrase that sounds better with the "of." Follow your ear in such cases. For example, *the roar of the crowd* sounds better than *the crowd's roar*, and *the height of the bookcase* sounds better than *the bookcase's height*.

Placement of apostrophes becomes automatic once you get the hang of it. One of the main distinctions you have to make is whether a possessive word is singular or plural. Regular singular words take *'s*, and regular plural words take *s'*.

| *Singular* | *Plural* |
| --- | --- |
| the girl's grades | the girls' grades |
| the student's attitude | the students' attitude |

If the singular noun ends in *s*, the singular possessive usually adds *'s*. It is true that whether to add the apostrophe alone or to add the apostrophe and the s is up to the writer. However, most people form the possessive according to how they say the word. Since they would pronounce the possessive of *Jones* as *Jonesus,* they would write *Jones's.* Plural possessives that end in *s* take the *es'* ending. Take a look at the following examples of how nouns ending in *s* form the possessive:

| *Singular* | *Plural* |
| --- | --- |
| Mr. Jones's cat | the Joneses' cat |
| one boss's orders | the bosses' orders |

When a noun has a special plural form, such as when *man* becomes *men,* the possessive of the plural is formed by adding *'s*.

| *Singular* | *Plural* |
| --- | --- |
| a woman's liberation | women's liberation |
| the child's toy | children's toys |

When a word ends in *z,* the singular form of the possessive is *z's* and the plural is *zes'*.

| *Singular* | *Plural* |
| --- | --- |
| Mr. Gonzalez's son | the Gonzalezes' house |
| Chavez's campaign | the Chavezes' dedication |

Compound words or groups of words take the *'s* on the last word only.

my father-in-law's house
someone else's paper
the Secretary of Defense's office

Individual ownership is shown by placing the *'s* at the end of each person's name.

Jane's and Mary's business ventures

Joint ownership is shown by adding the *'s* only to the last name.

Jack and Jill's dog Spot

Double possessives use both the *'s* and the *of* phrase. Using them is perfectly correct; they serve to indicate one possessive relationship among many. Note how the possessives are formed in the following examples:

a remark of my Aunt Esther's

This phrase refers to one remark of Aunt Esther's, among many other such remarks.

a friend of my sister's

This phrase refers to one friend among my sister's many friends.

### Contractions

A contraction is a word, number, or group of words that has been shortened by omitting certain letters or numbers. The apostrophe is used to indicate the omission and is placed where the original letters or numbers occurred. Contractions tend to be informal and should be used when you wish to give a conversational tone to your writing. Placing a few contractions in your essays when you would naturally use them in speaking can increase the flow and make the writing lively. But make sure they blend with your tone. For instance, the following sentence would be rather stiff:

*Do* they *not* realize the important implications of this decision?

It would be much more natural to use the contracted form of *do not:*

*Don't* they realize the important implications of this decision?

Here are some other commonly used contractions and their full forms:

| | | |
|---|---|---|
| would not | may be contracted to | wouldn't |
| could not | may be contracted to | couldn't |
| you would | may be contracted to | you'd |
| I would | may be contracted to | I'd |
| it is | may be contracted to | it's |
| are not | may be contracted to | aren't |
| they are | may be contracted to | they're |
| will not | may be contracted to | won't |

Do not confuse the contractions *who's* (*who is*), *they're* (*they are*), and *it's* (*it is*) with the possessive pronouns *whose, their,* and *its.*

Contractions of numbers are treated in the same way: the apostrophe is placed where numbers are left out. For example, *1955* may be contracted to *'55*. Contracted numbers are commonly used in phrases such as the *class of '91* or *back in '74*.

### Plurals

An apostrophe and *s* (*'s*) may be used to form the plurals of certain letters, numbers, symbols, abbreviations, and words used as words. But it is also correct to form many of these plurals by simply adding an *s*, as long as no confusion results. Here are examples that could be written either way.

> I asked my little brother if he had studied the three Rs yet.
> I asked my little brother if he had studied the three R's yet.
> By the early *90s* nonfat dairy products had become an established part of the food industry.
> By the early *90's* nonfat dairy products had become an established part of the food industry.

Now, here are examples that require the apostrophe to avoid confusion.

> The first paragraph of my essay had seven *I's* in it.

The apostrophe prevents any confusion between the plural of *I* (*I's*) and the word *Is*.

> I have always figured out problems in terms of *x's* and *y's*.

The apostrophe clearly shows that the plurals of *x* and *y* are to be treated as nouns.

> How many M.A.'s and how many Ph.D.'s applied for the job?

The apostrophe clarifies that the abbreviations end with a period.

---

### Exercises

A. Correct any mistakes in the use of apostrophes or formation of possessives and contractions in the following.
   1. There aren't any good old beer halls anymore where people can laugh, sing, and generally have a good time.
   2. A cat is considered a calico only if it's fur is of three or more colors.
   3. The room's air seemed unusually stuffy, but we couldn't open the tightly locked windows.
   4. Most people's impressions of the lives led by Hollywood stars are very naive.

5. A woman's need for companionship is no greater than a man's.
6. We were surprised to find so many old toy's still in the attic, abandoned so many years ago when we stopped playing there.
7. With as many colds' as I have suffered through in my life, I really don't believe vitamin C helps very much.
8. The surface of the plants' leaves was tinged with brown spots, which indicated a fungus.
9. Even though my cousin childrens' are not of elementary school age yet, they often go with her to activities held at the school where she is a teacher.
10. Wonderful opportunities' present themselves at the parties' held by the Martinez family.

## BRACKETS

Square brackets are used when a writer wishes to clarify or comment on certain parts of a quotation. They set apart the writer's words from the material being quoted. Brackets can be used in one of four ways.

### Further Identification

Brackets are used to clarify or explain words or ideas that may not be perfectly clear from the quoted material given. Here are a few examples:

They [the existential psychologists] were willing to respond directly and humanely to people's problems.

According to Jones, "That man [D. H. Lawrence] was simply childish."

### Addition of a Personal Comment

A personal comment may be added when it shows your interpretation of the quotation and can help lend support to the thesis at hand. Personal comments should be used sparingly, however.

A typical example of glossing over the problem came from Smithson's report to the State Referral Board: "We are not aware of [that is, they never investigate] any mistreatment of mental patients in California's hospitals."

### Editorial Correction

Occasionally you will find an error in spelling, tense, pronoun reference, or word choice in the quotation you wish to use. The usual way to note that the error is not your fault is to use the Latin word *sic,* which means "thus" or "so." The *sic,* in brackets and italics, or underlined to indicate italics, is placed next to the incorrect word. Note how the *sic* is placed in the following example:

The group complained that "protestors were siezed [*sic*] by police without first being asked to leave the site."

### Parentheses Within Parentheses

Parentheses that come within parentheses are marked with brackets.

A thorough discussion of problems with syntax may be found in one of the classics on the subject (see Mina P. Shaughnessy, *Errors and Expectations* [New York: Oxford University Press, 1977], 49-50).

## CAPITALIZATION

Capitalization is one of those areas in which we all know some rules, but we have all probably come upon a puzzling instance at one time or another. Most people would agree that capitalization is a matter of some importance. After all, it helps readers to see the point of what they read. For example, the message the brain receives differs when the eye sees *Turkey* and when it sees *turkey*. Also, the eye refocuses itself on the signal of a capital letter at the beginning of the sentence. Even though there is agreement about the value of capitalizing words, there is controversy as to exactly what should be capitalized. Modern publishers in the United States would like writers to use the lowercase instead of capitals whenever a controversial word is clear and unchanged by doing so. They feel that, basically, nothing is lost.

Most of the rules here are drawn from those in *The Chicago Manual of Style,* Fourteenth Edition, published by the University of Chicago Press. That source may be turned to for further assistance with any rule included in the following section on capitalization.

### Beginning of a Sentence

Capitalize the first letter of the first word of every sentence. This rule also applies to the first letter of the first word of a direct quotation that could stand alone as a sentence within a sentence.

Connors asked, "Why in the world should I be accused of murder?"

Oscar Wilde once commented, "Divorces are made in heaven."

### Beginnings of Lines of Poetry

Capitalize the first letter of the first word of each line of poetry if the original is capitalized.

Let me not to the marriage of true minds
Admit impediments; love is not love
Which alters when it alteration finds,
Or bends with the remover to remove.

## Titles of Books, Records, Stories, Essays, Plays, and Poems

Always capitalize the first and last word of a title or subtitle. Articles (*the, an,* and *a*) and *to* infinitives are usually not capitalized when they appear inside a title. Prepositions, regardless of length, should not be capitalized.* Coordinating conjunctions (*and, or, nor, for, but, yet,* and *so*) are not capitalized, but subordinating conjunctions such as *because, since,* and *when* are.

> *An American Dream*
> *You Know I Can't Hear You When the Water's Running*
> "Ode on a Grecian Urn"
> "A Tent That Families Can Live In"

Do not capitalize references to a publication's introduction, preface, foreword, contents, appendix, glossary, bibliography, index, or chapter (when used with an arabic numeral). The same rule applies to the words *edition* and *series* when not part of a title.

> The introduction to the novel is an essay by Lionel Trilling.
> In chapter 4 of *Secret Agent,* Conrad introduces a new symbol.
> The hardcover Modern Library edition is usually more attractive
>     than the paperback copy.

### Names

Capitalize the names of specific people, places, monuments, artworks, organizations, schools, buildings, companies, and movements in history.

| | |
|---|---|
| *The Lovers* by Picasso | Watson Hall |
| Kennedy Airport | Statue of Liberty |
| the Russian Revolution | Rutgers University |
| the Industrial Revolution | Mexico |
| Procter & Gamble | |

Do not capitalize words such as university, college, or company when they appear alone unless they are used as a proper name.

> My university is highly thought of.
> I go to the University of Texas.

Do not capitalize nouns and adjectives derived from names but used to refer to common objects.

| | |
|---|---|
| chinaware | roman numerals |
| baked alaska | dutch oven |

*Some style manuals allow for prepositions of five or more letters to be capitalized. That rule has been used in this textbook.

Capitalize the names of people and countries and the nouns and adjectives derived from those names.

| Freud | Freudians | Freudian |
| Orient | Orientals | Oriental |
| Brooklyn | Brooklynites | Brooklynese |

### Groups of People
Capitalize the names of most racial, linguistic, religious, and tribal groups of people and their adjectives.

| Magyar | Mormon | Nordic |
| African American | Indo-European | Caucasian |

However, do not capitalize groupings by color, size, or common expressions.

| redneck | black | white |
| pygmy | small people | gays |

### Titles of People
Capitalize a title or an office if it precedes a person's name.

| President Slaughter | General Eisenhower | Pope John Paul |

Titles following a name or used alone in place of a name are not capitalized. The following examples show how to treat some common titles.

> General John M. Shalikashvili, chairman of the U.S. Joint Chiefs of Staff
> the chairman
> Bill Clinton, president of the United States
> President Clinton
> the president

In England certain high offices and forms of address are still capitalized.

| Queen Mother | the Prince of Wales |
| Your Royal Highness | His Majesty |

Do not capitalize epithets that indicate a role.

> The outspoken talk show host Oprah Winfrey
> the brilliant new comedian Jim Wise
> the singer Tevin Campbell

Do not capitalize terms that indicate a person's year in school.

| freshman | sophomore | junior | senior |

### Relatives

Capitalize a relationship when it is used as a name or when the person is spoken to directly.

> It was fun to go fishing with Grandpa.
> Mother, why did you marry Dad?

Likewise, you should capitalize a relationship when it is used as a part of a person's name.

> Ask Aunt Emma whether she wants to go out to dinner tonight.

Do not capitalize a relationship when it is preceded by *my*.

| my uncle | my uncle Al | my brother Bill |
|----------|-------------|-----------------|

### Time

Capitalize the days of the week, the months, and the names of holidays (except for any prepositions, articles, or conjunctions). Never capitalize the names of the seasons.

| Monday | July | Mother's Day |
|--------|------|--------------|
| Memorial Day | the Fourth of July | spring |
| winter | | |

Do not capitalize words that refer to general periods of time.

| the nineteenth century | the fifties |
|------------------------|-------------|
| the space age | the romantic age |

Many established historical periods, however, should be capitalized.

| the Middle Ages | the Roaring Twenties |
|-----------------|----------------------|
| the Christian Era | the Industrial Revolution |
| the Stone Age | the Age of Reason |

Do not capitalize most philosophical or artistic schools or movements unless derived from words that are capitalized.

| Aristotelian | Cartesian | naturalism |
|--------------|-----------|------------|
| romanticism | pop art | surrealism |

### Places

Capitalize the abbreviated forms of time and time zones, but do not capitalize the words when they are spelled out.

> daylight saving time (DST)
> eastern standard time (EST)
> central daylight time (CDT)

Capitalize words that show political divisions, such as empire, state, county, city, and territory, when they are part of a name.

> New York City is fun to visit.
> The District of Columbia is sixty-nine square miles in area.

Do not capitalize such divisions when they are alone in a sentence or when they come before the name.

> The city of New York has many exciting museums.
> The whole province was colorful.

Capitalize geographical terms such as lake, stream, river, delta, mountain, or valley if they are used as part of a name.

> Vassar Mountain is a good place to ski.
> The Channel Islands are not as isolated as they seem.
> The White Hills are lovely in summer.

Do not capitalize the terms when they are not part of a name.

> I love the mountains in the deep of winter.
> My father has moved to the desert.

Do not capitalize such geographic terms when they are used collectively for several similar places.

> Between Blue and Carson lakes is a vast mountain range.

### School Courses

Capitalize the names of specific courses, but do not capitalize general subject areas. Exception: Capitalize the names of language courses.

> I liked Math 91, but that isn't surprising since I usually like math classes.
> My physics class has a two-hour lab each week.
> We study short stories in English.

### Directions

Capitalize directions only when they are generally considered to be the name or a part of the name of a specific geographical area.

| | |
|---|---|
| the East | the West Coast |
| the South | Southeast Asia |

Words that indicate directions or points of the compass should not be capitalized.

> Turn left at Cahuenga Boulevard and then travel east.

Do not capitalize words such as northward, southward, eastward, or westward.

### Religious Words

Capitalize the names of religions and their derivatives.

| | |
|---|---|
| Christianity | Christian |
| Seventh-Day Adventists | Adventist |
| Buddhism | Buddhist |
| Shinto, Shintoism | Shintoist |
| Islam | Islamic |

Capitalize sects, orders, and movements along with their derivatives.

| | |
|---|---|
| the Baptist church | Baptists |
| Christian Science | a Christian Scientist |
| Gnosticism | a Gnostic |
| Jehovah's Witnesses | a Jehovah's Witness |

Religious contexts often contain the capitalized forms of ideals.

| | | | |
|---|---|---|---|
| Truth | Beauty | Goodness | Charity |

Do not capitalize words like church, synagogue, or temple unless they are part of a name.

| | |
|---|---|
| the Church of England | the Universal Church of Love |
| the church on the corner | the beautiful temple |

Capitalize the titles of religious books.

| | | |
|---|---|---|
| the Koran | the Bible | the Talmud |

Do not capitalize the word *god* if referring to other than the one God of Judeo-Christian religions.

The Greek *gods* often interfered in the lives of humans.

### Diseases

Unless the name of the disease is based on a capitalized noun, do not capitalize it.

| | |
|---|---|
| mumps | influenza |
| Asian flu | Alzheimer's disease |
| Parkinson's disease | diabetes |

### Products

Unless known by a brand name, do not capitalize the names of food products or cosmetics.

| Häagen Dazs ice cream | Coca-Cola |
|---|---|
| cantaloupe | pizza |
| Magic Eyes makeup | Chanel No. 5 perfume |

### Professions

Do not capitalize the names of professions unless they are a person's title coming before a name.

| attorney | professor |
|---|---|
| surgeon | Doctor Jimenez |

### Earth

Do not capitalize the word *earth* unless it is listed along with the other planets, which are always capitalized.

> On this earth, is there any place without air pollution?
> The Earth, Mars, and Venus are relatively small planets.

---

### Exercises

A. Add capital letters to any words that require them and remove capitals from those that do not. State the rule for every capital letter you add or delete.

1. Professor Bedrosian, who works for the federal government, said that he had to spend more time with his family.
2. When archbishop frandee decides to do something, he usually does it.
3. Some would say that politics is filled with fawning lobbyists and snooty senators.
4. I was surprised to discover that the lady biscuit, my friend's yacht, has been to the galapagos islands.
5. Her vacation in the east was uneventful, but the united airlines flight was, at least, a pleasant one.
6. Father tried to stop smoking; my sister, at the same time, was trying to learn how.
7. a black woman I know said she had no patience with "jive artists" of any race.
8. The capital gains tax does not help the "common Man" put bread on the table or braces on his children's teeth.
9. The Moon has always intrigued Dreamers; it is a symbol of the quest for a new life in a new eden.
10. I wanted to take an english class, but the counselor insisted that a mathematics course would be more useful.

B. The paragraph below, from a student's essay, is missing some essential capital letters. Change any incorrect lowercase letters to capitals. Also correct any capitals that should be lowercase.

Until the Amnesty Law passed in 1987, Mexicans were the second largest Group of undocumented workers in the united states for understandable reasons. Because of the united states' curtailment of the bracero program for migrant workers in 1964, there had been a sharp increase in the number of workers coming from mexico. Figures show that 800,000 to 1 million were in the United States; 500,000 of these were mexicans. Many came from mexico because they were looking for a Better Life in the united states, where a week's salary was equivalent to a month's salary in Mexico.

## THE COLON

In a sentence, the colon normally follows some sort of introductory main clause. The colon is also used as a separator.

### The Colon as Introducer

*Introducing a List or Series*

The colon frequently signals that a list or series of items, ideas, or explanations that illustrate the clause preceding it will follow.

> General McNally was divorced by his wife for three reasons: his affair with an associate's sister, his violent manner, and his disturbing habit of gnashing his teeth while sleeping.
> The results of this year's election are the following: 17 votes for Grand, 117 for Connelly, and 84 for Bogden.

Any number of elements can be in the list as long as there are at least two. A colon is not usually used after *for example*. The colon should follow only a main clause; it should never be used between a *to be* verb and the complement or a verb and its direct object.

*Introducing a Related Statement*

The colon prepares the reader for an expansion on the idea in the main clause that precedes it. What follows the colon may or may not be a grammatically complete clause.

> Helene possesses a fine gift for music: she has won many awards for her performance.

Note that the main clause that follows the colon is not necessarily capitalized. It would also be correct, and more common today, to place a semicolon between the two closely related main clauses.

> Helene possesses a fine gift for music; she has won many awards for her performances.

The colon may also expand on the introductory clause by explaining a word or phrase that comes at the end of the clause.

We have only one concern: your safety.

The information after the colon explains the word *concern*.

### *Introducing a Quotation*
The colon should be used to introduce long quotations. It may also be used in place of a comma to introduce short quotations. The colon is simply a little more formal than the comma. It creates more distance between the statement that leads up to the quotation and the quotation than the comma does.

It was Buddha who stated the idea best: "The thoughtless are dead already. The thoughtful live forever."
Chan restated his position on open admissions: "Everyone should have a chance to get an education, even though some will prove unworthy."

### The Colon as Separator
Use a colon for openings of formal letters.

Dear Mr. Simpson:
Dear Ms. Jones:

Use colons for expressions of time.

10:30
11:00

Use colons to separate titles from subtitles.

*The Way of the Land: Our Last Domain*
*The Doll: The Mystery of Childhood*

Using a colon now and then can add sparkle to your style. Be careful to add the colon only in places that would require a stop in the reading. The mechanics of the colon are simple. In most cases one space should be left after a colon. With expressions of time, no space is left between the colon and the numbers on either side. When a colon is used with other punctuation, such as parentheses and quotation marks, the colon falls outside the other punctuation.

When students are unsure of a term their teacher uses, there is only one thing to do (no matter how silly they may feel): raise their hand and ask about it.

There are at least two possible interpretations of the phrase "personal relations": one stressing "personal" and the other stressing "relations."

### Exercises

A. Correct the misused colons in the following sentences. Write the correct punctuation, if any, in place of the errors.

1. Jorge had only one complaint to direct to the teacher: two hours is not enough time to answer all the questions on the exam.
2. His only response was: that two hours is not sufficient time to finish the exam.
3. By tomorrow or Friday, there will be initiated industry-wide controls on waste seepage that will include: dumping schedules, use of improved filtering systems, and independent pollution surveillance.
4. English 255, Introduction to Literature, has recently become popular with students since it: introduces students to famous literary works, teaches students how to read critically, and is relevant to the cultural interests so prevalent at most colleges.
5. Cultural anthropologists use the results of studies made by: sociologists, psychologists, and linguists.
6. Variety in the growth patterns of vegetables is considerable: radishes grow quickly in observable spurts, tomatoes develop gradually, and squash starts slow but suddenly races out in all directions.
7. He believed that children were a plague on adults: and that dogs were even worse.
8. Listen to me: you're the ones who are being taken advantage of.
9. She recently told me that most men are: selfish, insecure, spoiled, and crude.
10. She recently told me that she thought men were sad creatures: selfish, insecure, spoiled, and crude.

## THE COMMA

Commas make reading easier. The comma interrupts a sentence to clarify its grammatical structure and its meaning. It is therefore important to familiarize yourself with the established rules for comma usage. Combining a knowledge of the rules with your own common sense will give you a feel for those places where the use of commas will make your writing more readable.

### Main Clauses Joined by Coordinating Conjunctions

Use commas to separate most main clauses that could stand as individual sentences but are connected by *and, or, for, nor, but, yet,* or *so.* The comma should precede the coordinating conjunction. If the clause or phrase on one side of the conjunction is a subordinate clause, do not connect the two parts of the sentence with a comma. Note the effective use of commas in the following sentences:

> There are times when fights are unavoidable, but to go out looking for them is quite another matter.
>
> The political climate in most Midwestern towns has been solidly conservative for a long time, and it does not look as if it will change.
>
> We were perplexed by the finding that nearly all the subjects in the sociology experiment had very low incomes, but the people involved had high self-esteem and considered themselves successful.
>
> Only a few of the students in our class are taking photography for credit, so our teacher is very relaxed about attendance.

When the main clauses are brief, the comma may be omitted.

> I may be hungry but I can't eat.
> He left and she stayed.

### Following Introductory Groups of Words

Many introductory groups of words are followed by commas. Some contemporary writers omit the comma if the clause or phrase is brief and is clear without it. However, it is wise to include a comma if you are not sure how clear a particular sentence might be without the comma.

*Clauses*

Introductory subordinate clauses are usually followed by a comma.

> When our basketball team concentrates on teamwork, we usually win.
>
> If the weather is as cold this January as it was last year, I will need warmer clothes.

Even when introduced by a short clause, some sentences might be misread if the comma after the clause were left out.

> If he tells, somebody might feel hurt.

Without the comma, a reader might perceive the beginning of the sentence as *If he tells somebody.* The comma makes the reading clear. If even for a moment a sentence might be confusing to the reader because you have left out the comma after the introductory clause, you should put the comma in.

*Phrases*

Introductory phrases are usually followed by a comma, unless they are immediately followed by a verb.

> After hearing the news, everybody celebrated.
> To surprise her parents, neighbors, and friends, Karen had not told anyone that she was coming home for vacation.
> Knowing his own motives had become important.
> Going to school at night is stimulating.

Even a short phrase sometimes needs to be set off from the rest of the sentence so that the meaning will be clear.

> To help, his friends pooled their money and lent it to him.

Without the comma, a reader might perceive the beginning of the sentence as *To help his friends.* Use commas in any sentence that could cause a reader even momentary confusion.

Also use commas with short phrases to indicate a distinct pause.

> Before today, I never realized how much I like the rain.
> Without a doubt, my dog is bigger than your dog.

## Transitions

Transitional words and phrases such as *nevertheless, however, therefore, besides,* and *on the other hand* are usually followed by a comma when they appear in a sentence, are set off by commas when they occur in the middle of a sentence, and are preceded by a comma when they are at the end of a sentence.

> Because of alcohol addiction, he did not succeed in business. Then too, he did not succeed in other less demanding areas of his life either.
> Herman doesn't like formal occasions. He felt very pleased, however, to be at my wedding.
> Judy wants to wait until tomorrow morning, but we are leaving tonight, nevertheless.

The comma should be omitted, however, when the transitional word is obviously a part of the sentence, not an addition to it, and requires no pause.

> The best-qualified applicant was therefore Montoya.

## Interjections

Interjections and short phrases inserted in a sentence to create a conversational tone are set off by commas.

Well, there doesn't seem to be any complaint.
I think, by George, that the time has come!
You realize, of course, that the situation isn't serious.

### Elements in a Series

Use commas to separate the elements in a series. A series is a listing of three or more words, phrases, or clauses in a row, such as *apples, bananas, and peaches.*

Bees, mosquitoes, and flies are plentiful food for jumping fish.
Most of the salesmen, all of the managers, and a few of the clerical staff came to work early today to attend a meeting.
I wanted to please my mother, I wanted to shock my father, and I wanted to convince myself.

Although some authorities say the comma before the conjunction in a series is optional, you should develop the habit of putting it in, simply for clarity. You never know when you might be writing a sentence that would be ambiguous without it. For example:

Boredom, jealousy, anger, guilt, a need for reward, and fatigue are some of the psychological reasons for overeating.

If the last comma had been left out, the final element would have read "a need for reward and fatigue." This is not what the writer had in mind, we can be sure.

### Adjectives Before Nouns

Use commas to separate two or more coordinate adjectives. Coordinate adjectives independently modify the same noun. The order of these adjectives is reversible without changing the meaning of the sentence. A reliable test for this type of adjective group is to insert the word *and* between the adjectives. If you still have a fluent sentence and the adjectives still say what you mean, the adjectives are coordinate.

The tarnished, worn-thin fork gave the food a metallic taste.

The fork has two qualities. It is tarnished and worn thin.

A dedicated, humane, concerned veterinarian from Denver saved my dog's life.

The veterinarian has three qualities. He is dedicated, humane, and concerned.

### Unessential Elements

Use commas to set off unessential modifiers and appositives in a sentence. A modifier or appositive is unessential if what it modifies is fully identified without it. A modifier is essential if it limits the scope or meaning of what it modifies.

Note the function of modifiers and appositives in the following sentences:

> Commander Michilen, *who conducted the inspection of the barracks,* found no unauthorized weapons.

Commas are placed around the unessential clause. There is only one Commander Michilen. The title and the name fully identify him for the reader.

> The commander *who conducted the inspection of the barracks* found no unauthorized weapons.

Since a reader can identify which commander is meant only by the information in the *who* clause, that clause is essential to the sentence and therefore is not set off by commas.

> His attention to detail, *it is known,* was compulsive and undesirable.

The italicized phrase could be removed without changing the meaning of the sentence. Therefore it is not essential.

> The Spanish poet *Lorca* wrote a lovely piece of verse about his guitarra.

*Lorca* is not set off with commas because it is necessary in order to understand that the writer is speaking about that particular Spanish poet, not all.

### Contrasts

Use commas to set off contrasted elements.

> Their grandmother, not mine, is standing on the porch.
> I want to proceed toward, rather than away from, my intended goal.

### Direct Address

When people are directly addressed by their names, the names are set off from the rest of the sentence by commas.

> I wonder, John, when your dental appointment is.
> Ladies and Gentlemen, may I present Mr. Rhodes?
> It's later than you think, Sally.

### Omissions

Use commas to show omissions from parallel statements.

Mary got an A; John, a B.
To err is human; to forgive, divine.

### Quotations

Use commas to set off a quotation from the rest of the sentence, unless the quotation is integrated into the grammar of the surrounding phrases.

My best friend looked at my girlfriend and said, "Glad to meet you."
Mark said, "Can you tell me where to find Mr. Johnson?"
According to my mother, my fiancée is "one girl in a million."

### Cumulative Sentences

In a cumulative sentence, the main clause comes first and is followed by additional modifiers, expanding the base idea. Commas should separate the modifiers from each other and from the initial clause.

People streaked down Main Street, trying with all their might to escape the flames from the burning buildings, their legs flying in front of them, their arms propelling them.
No woman should apply for a job she is incapable of doing, hungry, liberated, and adaptable as she might be.

### Numerals

Commas are used to set off every three digits of a number.

42,319                   2,350                   1,275,500

They are not used, however, when writing years or zip codes.

1990                   77011

For telephone numbers, parentheses and hyphens are used, not commas.

(213) 555-1212

### Dates

Dates are usually written in one of two ways.

July 7, 1988          7 July 1988

When just the month and the year are used, a comma is not required.

August 1985 was the hottest month I can remember.

### Addresses

Commas are used to separate the elements of an address when it is included in a sentence.

Send the letter to Daniel Speigelman, Attorney, 24 Drury Lane, Oswego, IL 54041.

Notice that no comma is used between the state abbreviation and the zip code.

### Statistics
Commas are used to show divisions within statistics.

Her mother is five feet, eleven inches tall.
Read page 26, line 5 aloud.
Act IV, scene 3 is the climax.

### Excessive Use of Commas
If an extra comma seems necessary to clarify your meaning, you should not hesitate to put it in. At the same time, you should be aware that most established writers today avoid using a lot of commas. Using commas only where they are needed makes for the most clarity. A sentence with too many commas confuses readers more than it helps them. There are a few places in sentences where you might tend to overuse commas. As you read through the following guidelines, note how the use of excessive commas actually obscures the meaning of the sentences. Each incorrect sentence that follows would be correct if the comma were left out.

Commas never come between the subject of the sentence and the verb, unless they are setting off unessential elements.

*Incorrect:* The issue I have been trying to get on the June ballot, is property tax relief.

Do not confuse a pause in this sentence with the need for a comma. No comma is needed.

*Incorrect:* "To teach in a public school, is a difficult position," admitted the Superintendent of Schools.

Naturally, a pause comes after a long subject with modifiers, but no comma is needed.

Commas should never come between the verb and the direct object or subject complement except to separate unessential elements from the rest of the sentence.

*Incorrect:* The reason the power company has been waiting so long to begin construction is, that the people of the town requested a hearing on the project.
*Incorrect:* The three ingredients of old-fashioned ice cream as we knew it were, cream, butter, and sweetener. (A colon after *were* would also be incorrect.)
*Incorrect:* I told the officer, that, had she come an hour earlier, we might have been able to contribute to the fireman's ball.

**Exercises**

A. Remove any unnecessary commas and insert any that are missing.

1. A man, who told neighbors that he saw the murder committed, later was too frightened to testify.

2. Having many sisters and brothers living with you in your youth, makes you feel secure.

3. Even, if I had studied for that math test I wouldn't have known the answers to the questions the teacher asked.

4. The last person in the world I thought would show up on graduation day was, my uncle.

5. Intramural sports are fun, but not as much fun as intermural.

6. The reason over half my friends wanted to watch the movie on television, was, it was filmed in our neighborhood.

7. Neighborhood parties brighten up the block, and can even make friends of enemies.

8. My youngest brother, who was elected president of his eighth-grade class, lost all his popularity when he started to associate with the wrong crowd in high school.

9. The Robertses who introduced my wife to her current employer were at our party on Christmas Day.

10. Registration to vote is a necessary system, because, otherwise, everybody would show up at the same polling place and other places would be left empty.

11. I lost my place in the book I was reading, when the telephone rang.

12. Street violence is at its height, in the hot, summer months.

13. Unless we try to change the new law that allows adult book stores to open, in any neighborhood, we could find our children bringing home pornographic pictures. Maybe that's an exaggeration but the situation could get serious.

14. On the one hand we expect political candidates to be honest. On the other hand we want them to be shrewd.

15. Therefore we have concluded that young children are not harmed by television violence. But are we right?

## THE DASH

Writers use the dash to indicate a break in the thought expressed in a sentence. The dash, like commas and parentheses, separates part of a sentence from the main clause. The dash is different from these other marks of punctuation, however, because the break in thought that it creates is greater than the break introduced by the comma and less than the break introduced by the parentheses. Furthermore, the dash creates a sudden shift of thought. In other words, what dashes set apart is more important to the sense of the sentence than what the parentheses set apart, and less important—though more dramatically presented—

than what commas set apart. When what is to be set off has punctuation within itself—as does the series "Fred, Mary, and Jorge," for instance—dashes rather than commas work well.

Dashes may set off a word, a phrase, or a clause and may do so at the beginning, middle, or end of a sentence.

Try to add liveliness to your writing by using dashes, but remember that you should use them sparingly. An essay sprinkled with dashes is like a highway with too many stop signs—annoying. The overuse of dashes makes them ineffective. Note the effective use of dashes in the following sentences:

> The phenomenon of "precognition"—perhaps the most often reported extrasensory perceptual experience—offers an explanation for many dreams.
>
> All the men—William, James, Arthur, and Ted—arrived at ten in order to get a volleyball court by eleven.

Be careful when you use dashes in the middle of a sentence. The rest of the sentence must be grammatically complete without the portion set off by dashes. The tendency to fit the end of the sentence to the part of the sentence in dashes leads many to write incorrect sentences.

> *Ineffective:* Although she hoped for her children to attend the best possible school—she wanted one with excellent teachers and supplies—but she did not want to live in an expensive neighborhood to buy the privilege of education.

The writer goes wrong by inserting the *but,* which shows she has lost sight of the first word in her sentence. Make sure you do not slip into this error. Read over the sentence without the portion in dashes to make sure it could stand alone grammatically.

The dash is effectively used in certain specific situations.

### Setting Off a Climactic Phrase

The dash can be used to emphasize a phrase or word at the end of a sentence.

> Swimming was the best event of the day—the only event that was really fun.
>
> At the end of the trip, there was only one thing left to do—sleep.

### Setting Off a Summary

The dash can focus the meaning of an involved sentence.

> People who will give you their last dollar, who will comfort you even when they are depressed, who will listen to your plans and dreams as if they were their own, who will dare to criticize

you to help you, who will remain loyal at all cost—these are the ideal friends we carry around in our minds.

### Expanding on the Main Clause

Use the dash to expand on a word or phrase in the main clause.

Shelley's moods—happiness one moment, depression the next—were difficult to judge.

Harriet had decided to leave early—why, no one knew.

The high school diploma—that essential piece of paper—was worth studying for at night.

### Inserting an Appositive or Parenthetical Element

The man—the one in purple sneakers—must have been more than seventy, and he arrived on a bicycle.

Before we knew it, Alicia—that sensitive girl!—had phoned the chaplain.

### Inserting One Sentence into Another

A dash may be used to insert a complete sentence next to the word it explains or expands on.

Maria—she was the second person to arrive—slowly pressed the door buzzer.

The mission was to be a difficult one—three men would have to travel on foot across the frozen lake—and not many were willing to take the chance.

### Setting Off Modifiers with Internal Punctuation

Use a dash to make the separation from the rest of the sentence clear when the phrase enclosed in dashes has its own special punctuation.

All the volunteers—Rita, Ted, Linda, Carole, and Jack—had grown up in the inner city and were used to many of the problems faced by the people in the county program.

### Setting Off a List from a Conclusion

Games, dolls, puzzles—these are the accompaniments of an affluent childhood. But are they good for the child?

A dash is typed as two unspaced hyphens. No space should be left before or after the dash. In handwriting, draw a line twice as long as that for a hyphen.

Elements set off by dashes should be separated grammatically from the rest of the sentence. When the idea set off in dashes occurs in the middle of the sentence, be sure to place dashes on both sides of it—at the beginning and at the end. When a dash is used where a comma would normally fall, the comma is omitted.

When I reported the incident—the burning car, the bolt of flames, the odd visitor—the police looked at me as if they thought I had dreamed it.

Do not set off more than one part of a sentence with dashes; your readers will become confused as to which dashes represent beginnings and which represent endings.

---

### Exercises

A. Insert dashes where appropriate into the following sentences.
1. The people who attended our party, Mike, Joe, and Christopher, were considerate enough to help us clean up.
2. Dogs, cats, goldfish: they would all be a drain on my schedule, and that is why I have no pets.
3. My aunt bought me the pair of boots, a sturdy pair that look like the kind cowboys wear that I had wanted for months.
4. There is one thing I demand from every friend: consideration for the feelings of others.
5. During the filming of the movie *Some Prefer Nettles* an earthquake struck, but much to everyone's relief, nothing was damaged.
6. The train, the last one to leave Oakland this year, departs from the terminal at 11:15.
7. The medical supplies, desperately needed to keep the victims of the accident alive, arrived by helicopter before they were expected.
8. The best kind of hero, the only kind I can take seriously, is the hero who does not try to be one.
9. It wasn't his life he ended up fighting for in that war; it was his philosophy of living.
10. Preferring to be known as Dr. Stone, Ellaine Doople, daughter of the man who invented carrot peelers, was hired as chief of nutrition for our local hospital.

### ELLIPSES

Ellipses, or ellipsis points, are used to indicate omissions from quoted material. They are handy for removing those parts of a quotation that do not add to the point you wish to make. These omissions may range from a single word to entire paragraphs.

When using ellipses, you should keep several things in mind. First, make sure that your omissions do not change the meaning or intent of the quoted passage. Second, all of the sentences in the quotation must still be grammatically correct even though you have left out some of the original words. The same guidelines apply to sentences that are a combination of your own words and quoted material.

Finally, ellipses should be used only when quoting the work of others. You should not use them in your own writing.

## Quoting Prose

### Midsentence

Three spaced periods can be used to note omissions in the middle of a sentence. Compare the original quotation with the student's use of it in this example:

> That budget can be drawn up in no time with everyone in mind, not with just a few top officials in the company getting all the benefits.
>
> Michael Conrad, the union leader, disapproves of the proposed budget: "That budget can be drawn up . . . with everyone in mind, not with just a few top officials in the company getting all the benefits.

### Ends and Beginnings of Sentences

Four spaced periods—the period marking the end of the sentence added to the three ellipsis points—show that a full sentence in a quotation has been omitted or that the beginning of a sentence is missing. Again, note the original quotation and the student's use of it.

> It can be disastrous to continue our operation before a thorough investigation of each department's safety standards. We need an agreement on the part of everyone that safety on the job is what counts. Unless we agree to carry this procedure forward, we might as well expect to be closed down by the county.
>
> Mr. Cohen says, "It can be disastrous to continue our operation before a thorough investigation of each department's safety standards. . . . Unless we agree to carry this procedure forward, we might as well expect to be closed down by the county."

Ellipsis points are rarely used at the beginning of a quotation. Most quoted material is extracted from a passage, and it is therefore already obvious to most readers that passages often begin before the section extracted for quotation. In the rare instances in which the use of ellipses will clarify the meaning of the quoted passage, you may use three spaced periods before the first word of the quotation. The quotation marks, if needed, would come before the ellipsis points.

### Other Punctuation

Punctuation may be retained from the original quoted passage and placed on either side of the ellipses if doing so will help retain the meaning of the passage.

### Quoting Poetry

A line or more omitted from poetry is shown by an entire line of spaced periods.

## THE EXCLAMATION POINT

The exclamation point is used with strong imperatives or to show intense emotion.

Watch out!                    Help!                    She loves me!

Exclamation points should rarely be used in essays written for classes. Rather than relying on them, you should try to make sure that your choice of words reveals any emotion you wish to convey.

### Quoting Dialogue, and Appeals

When quoting, writing dialogue, or trying to move an audience through an appeal to action, you may find that an exclamation point is either required or appropriate. Remember, however, that exclamation points should be used sparingly. Using too many of them lessens their effect.

> *Weak:* If abortion is not paid for by welfare, mothers and children will starve, and the populace will be overrun by poor, unhealthy children!

No exclamation point is needed. The language is emotive enough, perhaps too emotive for expository writing.

> *Effective:* Women of the United States, get off your rump roasts!
> *Effective:* "I can't believe it. All my money—gone!" screamed Hillary.

### Interjections

Interjections—expressions such as *well, ah, oh, whew, too bad,* and *darn it all*—are used to interrupt the normal flow of sentences in order to express emotion. An interjection is usually set off from the main clause by commas. If the sentence is meant to convey strong emotion, an exclamation point may be used for the entire sentence.

> I am late again, darn it all!
> Ah, look at that view!

Milder interjections, of course, take a period at the end.

> Oh, that's too bad.

In some rare cases, where the emotion is particularly strong, both the interjection and the sentence will take an exclamation point.

Whew! That was a close one!

## THE HYPHEN
The hyphen is used to divide words at the end of a line, to separate some prefixes from their base words, and to form compound words.

### Dividing Words at the End of a Line
You may wish to avoid the problem of hyphenating words at the end of a line by always taking care to end lines with complete words. But most writers, at one time or another, wish to hyphenate words out of convenience—they have already begun to type or write a word before they realize they are at the right-hand margin. To maintain the margin, they choose to divide the word. Words must be divided between their syllables. Some words are easier to divide than others because the syllabication is obvious. Words with prefixes or suffixes are usually divided between the prefix or suffix and the base word.

| | | |
|---|---|---|
| pre-fix | pro-vide | re-tire |
| com-fort-ing-ly | use-ful | in-spir-ing |

Words with double consonants are usually divided between the two consonants.

| | | |
|---|---|---|
| bab-ble | em-bel-lish | cun-ning |

Syllable divisions can often be guessed at by the pronunciation of a word, but, whenever you are in doubt of the proper place to divide a word, it is best to look it up in the dictionary. Here are a few rules for dividing words at the end of a line, even when you already know the syllables:

One-syllable words can never be broken.
Proper names of people, places, or things should not be broken.
A one-letter syllable should not be used either at the end of one
    line or the beginning of the next.
Two-letter syllables should not begin a line.
Words should not be divided in a way that causes even momentary
    confusion.
Hyphenated words should be divided at the existing hyphen only.
The last word on a page should not be divided.

### Hyphenating Words in the Text
Whether you are using a regular typewriter or an elaborate computer, you will have to think about the use of hyphens in your essays. Spell

checking systems are not always perfect, so it is important to look up the rules if you sense a possible error.

*Prefixes*

The hyphenation of words with prefixes is a tricky area in the mechanics of grammar. Some of these words are hyphenated and some are not. To make matters even more confusing, some words that used to be hyphenated are now written without the hyphen. The following general rules can serve as good guidelines, but for specific words you may be unsure about, you should always check your dictionary.

When the last letter of the prefix and the first letter of the base word are the same, the word is normally hyphenated.

pre-existing          de-emphasize          anti-intellectual

However, a word is not usually hyphenated when the consonants are the same.

unnecessary          nonnegotiable

There are also words like *cooperation,* where the hyphen has been dropped as a result of the trend away from hyphenation. Again, when in doubt, check your dictionary.

The prefix *ex,* meaning former, is usually hyphenated.

ex-officio          ex-husband          ex-ball player

The prefix *self* is usually hyphenated.

self-starting          self-involved

However, be careful not to confuse the prefix *self* with the base *self. Selfish* and *selfless,* for example, are both composed of the base *self* plus a suffix. There is no prefix in either word, and there are no hyphens.

When confusion would occur from combining a prefix with the base word, the word is usually hyphenated.

re-collect (to pick up again)          recollect (to remember)
co-op (a cooperative)          coop (a home for chickens)

Hyphenate when joining a prefix to a proper noun.

Un-American          Anti-Marxist          Anti-Darwinism

Sometimes, however, the words are not hyphenated in current usage.

Unchristian          Antichrist

Prefixes such as *ultra, pseudo,* and *co* should be checked in the dictionary; their usage varies greatly. Most dictionaries use a dot between syllables and a hyphen between hyphenated parts of a word.

### Compound Words: Nouns

When two or more words act as a single noun, the way they are written varies greatly. Some that were originally hyphenated are now combined.

bookkeeper          basketball

In other cases, the words remain separate.

boot camp          problem solving

In still others, the words are hyphenated.

vice-president          mayor-elect          mother-in-law
know-it-all

Unless you are familiar with the particular words, the only way you can be sure whether they should be hyphenated, remain separate, or be combined is to look them up in your dictionary.

### Compound Words: Adjectives

When two or more words act as a single adjective, they are connected by a hyphen if they precede the noun they modify.

the all-in-one automatic cooker          a soft-spoken person
the well-designed house          a mass-produced toy

When the words follow the noun, they are not hyphenated.

The man was soft spoken.
The house was well designed.

Also, if one of the modifiers ends in *-ly,* the combination of words is not hyphenated.

a firmly drawn decision          the perfectly executed crime

A special rule operates with compound adjectives that include the word *all.* Words formed using *all* are hyphenated wherever they appear in a sentence.

all-purpose paragraph          all-around fellow

Sometimes you want to join two separate prefixes or words to the same noun. Normally, you would hyphenate each prefix. In combination, they are still hyphenated. Remember to place a hyphen and a space after the prefix that precedes the conjunction.

Second- and third-grade students
short- and long-term memory

### Numbers

Numbers between twenty and one hundred are hyphenated when written out no matter where they appear in a sentence. Fractions are also always hyphenated.

seventy-nine      thirty-four      one-third      one-half

---

**Exercises**

A. From the dictionary, copy out the following words, showing the syllable breaks where each might be divided. If the word is only one syllable, write "one."
1. loosely
2. apparent
3. infinite
4. tryst
5. caution
6. apologetic
7. knowledge
8. recently
9. international
10. reclusive
11. reputation
12. accidental
13. restoration
14. opportunity
15. reforestation
16. pliant
17. pronunciation
18. children
19. anxious
20. deliberate

B. Add hyphens where needed in the italicized words in the following sentences.
1. The *infant mortality rate* has decreased greatly in the past ten years among children born to mothers in their thirties.
2. Julia was a *self reliant woman* who did not need others to make her life complete.
3. That *pseudo intellectual* is not worth considering as a candidate for office.
4. She is the most *self centered* person I have ever known.
5. One of her *co workers* is married to an actor who makes a lot of money.

6. *Try as you will* to get there on time, the stores always seem to close just before you arrive.
7. Suzanne was an outgoing individual, but she was *nevertheless* often lonely.
8. Their *ex football coach* left teaching to become an advertising executive.
9. His views are strongly *anti business and taxes.*
10. My *ex boyfriend and employee* recently got a new job.
11. A *by product* of inflation is *unemployment.*
12. As part of a sociological experiment, three people on Market Street were stopped by a *passerby* and each was given a *thousand dollar bill.*
13. The *tenth and eleventh grade students* at Hoover High were instructed in self-defense measures.
14. The *who done it movie* playing around the corner is worth seeing.
15. This is the *eighth or ninth time* I have seen *Gone with the Wind,* and I would still go again.

## ITALICS

See Underlining.

## MULTIPLE END PUNCTUATION

Avoid the use of multiple punctuation for the purpose of emphasis. Instead, decide which mark of punctuation is most fitting.

*Weak:* The conditions in Mexican prisons are terrible!
*Effective:* The conditions in Mexican prisons are terrible.
*Weak:* And just why should women accept lower salaries than men for the same work?!
*Effective:* And just why should women accept lower salaries than men for the same work?

Of course, it is correct to use parentheses, quotation marks, and ellipses along with other punctuation without violating the rules.

## NUMBERS

### Numbers Within Sentences

As a general rule, numbers that do not require more than two words should be spelled out in a sentence.

When Jeremy was thirty-three, he was married for the third time.

My grandmother lived to be one hundred years old.

Numbers that would require more than two words should be written in numerals.*

154 5,423 22,324

Numbers in short lists should be spelled out, but numerals should be used for long lists or for comparisons among several numbers, especially if they contain fractions.

> My uncle has three dogs, four cats, and one parakeet.
> The stock for the Johnson and Meyers Corporation has fluctuated quite a bit over the past three months: starting at 18 1/2, it dropped to 11, rose again to 17, and is now back down to 16 1/4.

However, if any number in a paragraph referring to a particular category is written in numerals, all of the numbers referring to that category should also be placed in numerals, even though some of them could be spelled out in one or two words.

> My grandfather has 5 horses and 125 cows.
> Of the three buildings built in the past two years, one has 60 stories, one has 75, and the tallest has 105.

### Numbers Beginning Sentences

Numbers at the beginning of sentences should always be spelled out, even if other numbers in the same category are written in numerals. If spelling out the number would be awkward or if you wish to avoid spelling out one number and writing another in numerals, the sentence should be rearranged so that the number does not come first.

> *Incorrect:* 125 men and 132 women were in my graduating class.
> *Effective:* There were 125 men and 132 women in my graduating class.

### Time

The time of day should usually be spelled out.

> My biology class begins at eight in the morning.
> Some people eat supper as early as five o'clock.
> We should be finished by half past three.

However, numerals should be used when you wish to emphasize the exact moment or when using A.M. or P.M.

*The *Chicago Manual* recommends spelling out whole numbers one through ninety-nine but points out that newspapers and journals often spell out only one through nine and use figures for all higher numbers.

The movie starts at 6:25.
We got home at 5:30 A.M.
There are two buses a day to Cincinnati, one at 10:00 A.M. and the other at 4:36 P.M.
Last night, I studied from 8 P.M. until 2 A.M.

You should never use *morning* after A.M. or *evening* after P.M. Also, you should never use *o'clock* with A.M., P.M., or with figures.

### Dates

The year should always be placed in figures unless it comes at the beginning of a sentence.

The first award was made in 1995.
Nineteen eight-five was not so very long ago.

There are several ways to write dates, all of them acceptable.

May 6, 1978          6 May 1978               the sixth of May
May sixth

According to the *Chicago Manual, st, d,* and *th* should not be used with numerals. Thus, *May 6* is preferred over *May 6th.*
Ordinarily, you should spell out the names of centuries in the text of a paper. The names of decades are also spelled out.

twentieth century        the thirties and forties

### Roads

Use arabic numerals with highways.

Interstate 90          Texas 291               Route 66

However, spell out the numbers of street names.

Fifth Avenue            Eighty-fourth Street

### Parts of Books

Always use arabic numerals to refer to pages.

page 55                 page 385

Chapter numbers may be indicated either with an arabic numeral and a lower-case *c* in the word *chapter* or with the number spelled out and capitalized along with the capitalized word *Chapter.* The guidelines are the same for *part* and *exercise.* You should, however, decide on one way and use it consistently within a particular paper.

### Large Round Numbers

Numerals may be used for emphasis or for comparison with other figures, but they should be avoided if the number of zeros becomes cumbersome. All the following usages are correct.

two million people      2 million people      2,000,000 people

### Currency

Most units of currency that include whole dollar amounts should be spelled out.

> My gloves cost eighteen dollars.
> Bus fare has gone up fifty cents since 1992.

Fractional amounts should be placed in numerals.

> They are on sale for $4.99.

When whole dollar amounts appear in the same sentence as fractional amounts, you should place all the amounts in numerals.

> One usually costs $4.00, but you can buy three for $10.25.

There are various forms for very large amounts of money. All are correct, and you should pick the one you like. Then use that form throughout the paper.

three million dollars      $3 million      $3,000,000

### Fractions and Percents

Fractions should be spelled out when they require no more than two words.

> The man was able to pay only a third of the costs incurred in his accident.
> Two-thirds of the group arrived early.

Whole numbers mixed with fractions should usually be written as figures.

> Of the couple's assets, only 66 2/3 percent could be used as collateral on the loan for the new building.

However, certain commonly used mixed numbers are spelled out.

My bill was one and a half times as much as yours.
Five and a quarter percent interest on savings adds up.

Except in common usages, as in the preceding example, percentages should usually be written in arabic numerals. The percent symbol, %, should only be used in technical or scientific writing or in tables. In other types of writing, the word *percent* should be spelled out.

### Numbers in Parentheses
In legal documents, numbers are sometimes spelled out and then repeated as an arabic numeral in parentheses.

The fee should not exceed seventy-five (75) dollars.

In all other types of writing, this usage should be avoided.

### Plurals of Numbers
You may form the plurals of arabic numerals by adding either an *'s* or an *s*. Either way is correct, but making sure that you are consistent throughout the paper.

| | | |
|---|---|---|
| 5's | 10's | 40's |
| 5s | 10s | 40s |

When numbers are spelled out, their plurals are formed just as they would be for any other nouns.

| | | |
|---|---|---|
| fives | tens | forties |

---

### Exercises

A. Assuming that the following phrases appear in a paragraph without any other numbers in it, indicate which of the numbers and symbols should be spelled out.
   1. 153 couples
   2. 97 days
   3. $200
   4. 1,000 people
   5. 84 percent
   6. 666 letters
   7. 308 books
   8. $100,000
   9. 32 guests
   10. 21 months
   11. 18 men
   12. 454 dollars

13. 1/3 of the pie

14. 10.2%

15. 75%

16. 40 individuals

17. 4,024 contestants

18. 12 P.M.

19. 20 women

20. 3.44 liters

B. Correct any errors in the writing of numbers in the following sentences.

1. When my uncle was 37, he married a countess in Spain.

2. The year 2000 is expected to raise eyebrows.

3. 19 1/2 percent of the company's revenue went to charity last year.

4. Joseph is 3, his sister Marce is 12, and little Karen is two months old.

5. As corny as it may sound, I love films from the 40's.

6. If 15 or more people sign up for the class, it will not be dropped.

7. 3 of our guests were from Montana.

8. 1,333 was the answer to the math problem.

9. The budget was for nearly 1,000,000 dollars.

10. Chapter 5 is the hardest one in my math book.

## PARENTHESES

Parentheses are used to include extra information, such as explanations, amplifications, or digressions that you consider important but not quite important enough to interrupt the flow of your writing. The material inside parentheses, then, is a sort of aside that adds meaning to your discussion but does not exactly fit into it.

The entire family (Mary, Karen, Bob, Mom, Dad, and I) are the token intellectuals on our block.

H. G. Wells (1866–1946) was more than a simple science fiction writer.

I told her that I was unsure (I actually did know) and that I would find out the answer to her question the next morning.

### Cross References

Cross references are often enclosed in parentheses and placed next to the word or phrase that the cross reference expands on.

The predicate adjective (see chapter 13) should take the participle form of the verb.

### Enclosed Letters or Numbers

Parentheses should be used to enclose letters or numbers in the running text of a paper. This type of enumeration is most common in papers written for the sciences, social sciences, and other technical fields such as mathematics.

The main types of wooden joints are (a) dovetail, (b) mortise and tenon, (c) miter, (d) oblique, (e) square butt, (f) housed, and (g) rabbet.

Before a juvenile is placed behind bars, he or she is screened closely by the staff of the Kirkby Institute and the case is judged (1) approved, (2) approved with reservation, (3) approved with strong reservation, or (4) rejected.

Be sure not to confuse parentheses with brackets. Brackets are used for interior comments in quotations or for parentheses within parentheses.

Parentheses, dashes, and commas can all be effectively used to set off parenthetical expressions. Commas are used when the parenthetical elements are closely related to the rest of the sentence. Dashes usually emphasize the elements, but parentheses de-emphasize them. Used sparingly, parentheses are interesting and lively. Overused, they are constant interruptions in the flow of thought and thus annoying to the reader.

### Punctuation with Parentheses

A sentence containing parenthetical elements must be grammatically correct when the parenthetical elements are excluded. This requirement makes the use of punctuation with parentheses a bit tricky at times. A few cases require special use of punctuation. If a remark in parentheses is independent of other sentences and is a full sentence on its own, the parenthetical sentence is capitalized and the period is contained within the end parenthesis.

> When it was ready, Laura refused to eat the lasagne I had just spent an hour and a half preparing because she had said she was in the mood for it. (This annoying habit of changing her mind was nothing new.)

If the parentheses contain a complete sentence that is inserted into another sentence, the remark in parentheses does not begin with a capital letter (unless the word is always capitalized) nor does it end with a period. The period comes at the end of the sentence into which the parenthetical remarks have been inserted.

> Sheilah Graham depicts F. Scott Fitzgerald (he was a close friend) as a person full of tenderness.

A comma should never precede a remark in parentheses; if a comma would normally have followed the material before the parentheses, place it after the closing parenthesis.

> If students can get as far as their junior year in college (six out of ten can), they have already mastered the academic formula and should have no trouble with the last two years of college.

Often no punctuation is needed after the parentheses.

Did you ever wonder what draws people (men, women, and children) to nude beaches?

---

### Exercises

A. Correct any errors in the use of parentheses and correct the punctuation used with them in the following sentences.
  1. The act of writing an essay, (a short expository piece), is as creative as writing fiction.
  2. Their astonishment at the beauty of the snowy mountain roads reminded us that they were from sunny (and warm) California.
  3. Most of the members of the band had rehearsed all week for the one-evening performance. (Only a few had missed rehearsals because this was the really big night for the troupe.) and they were tense and exhilarated as the curtain was drawn.
  4. The security officers were too worn out (they had been working all day) to help us carry our parcels, but it was nice to have their company.
  5. Mary knew her way around Memphis (a point of pride with someone like her); she led us up alleys, using all sorts of shortcuts, so that we would get to the restaurant in time for our reservations.
  6. Louise Acker (my great aunt) was a suffragist.
  7. Guinea pigs, (I was surprised to learn,) are intelligent pets, considering how little they are and how people always laugh at them.
  8. In the end, no knowledge can hurt. (Even when it is the painful truth, knowing is better than not knowing). The doctors are morally obligated to tell people what their conditions really are so that they can plan their lives accordingly.

### THE PERIOD

#### End Punctuation

Of the three types of end punctuation—the period, the question mark, and the exclamation point—the period is the most common. It is used to indicate the end of many sentences.

> I hope to go to Florida on my vacation.
> Wait a minute.

Sentence fragments used deliberately for effect are also usually followed by a period.

> Ice and snow. Freezing cold. Will winter ever be over?

You should remember, however, to be very careful when using sentence fragments. For the most part, they should be avoided.

A period is also used to mark the end of an indirect question, which is a statement about a question.

> She asked me if I would go with her.
> The senator wondered whether he would be reelected.

Sometimes one can use either a period or a question mark.

> Would you try to be on time tomorrow.

Although this statement is worded as a question, it is actually more of a command than it is a request, so the period is appropriate. However, a question mark would also be correct.

### With Other Punctuation
The period is used in conjunction with only three other types of punctuation: quotation marks, parentheses, and brackets.

*Quotation Marks*
The period should be placed inside both quotation marks and double quotation marks.

> My favorite short story is "The Dead."
> She said, "My mother told me there would be days like this."
> John complained, "I have always had trouble defining words like 'love.'"

*Parentheses and Brackets*
The period is used in the same way with both parentheses and brackets. If the enclosed expression comes at the end of a sentence, the period goes on the outside.

> Jackie was there (as usual).
> One of the protesters carried a sign that read: "Save Amerika [sic]. Leave now."

If the expression is a complete and independent sentence, the period is placed inside the parentheses or brackets.

> Every fifteen minutes or so, I checked the locks on the doors and windows. (I have never liked being alone.)
> The president stated: "Our most important possessions are *freedom* and *dignity*. [The italics are mine.] Without them, we can never be happy."

However, if a complete sentence is inserted as a parenthetical expression into another sentence, the period should be omitted.

Once upon a time (I hope this does not sound too familiar), two young children were playing in the park.

## Abbreviations

Periods are often used in abbreviations.

| e.g. | N.A.S.A. | N.O.W. | m.p.h. |
|------|----------|--------|--------|
| A.M. | P.M. | A.I.D.S. | |

Some of these terms could also be abbreviated without the periods.

| NASA | NOW | mph | AIDS |
|------|-----|-----|------|

Neither method is more correct than the other, but you should try to be consistent in a particular paper. Scientific and technical writing usually calls for the use of certain abbreviations without the periods. Good indicators of the appropriate form are the sources you use for the papers you write. For instance, you may wish to check whether journals in the field use or omit periods.

When an abbreviation comes at the end of a sentence, the period for the abbreviation also stands as end punctuation. When the abbreviation is the last word in the parentheses, the period may also stand as the end punctuation.

### As a Decimal Point

Periods are used as decimal points in figures.

| 11.25% | $25.95 | 2.5 acres |
|--------|--------|-----------|

### As an Ellipsis Point

Three spaced periods are used to signal that something has been left out of a quotation.

## THE QUESTION MARK

### Direct Questions

All direct questions should end with question marks.

Why would a doctor become a politician?
Is it possible to learn how to spell in ten days?
I read that the bank was sued for a million dollars—is it true?

Many questions begin with interrogative words such as *what, which, who, when,* and so forth.

### Indirect Questions

Indirect questions are statements about questions. They are not actually questions themselves. Therefore, an indirect question should end with a period instead of a question mark.

He kept asking himself what he had done wrong.

The preceding sentence is not a question even though the word *asking* appears. However, notice how easily the statement may be turned into a question.

He kept asking himself, "What have I done wrong?"

One of the best ways to tell whether a sentence is a direct question or an indirect question is to figure out whether it asks for a response. If it does, it is probably a direct question. If it does not, you can be almost sure that it is an indirect question. Here are some more examples of indirect questions.

I wonder if it will rain today.
They asked me how they might find the library.
The committee wanted to know whether the motion had been passed.
I asked him when the assignment was due.

For some more information about indirect questions, see page 518.

### Interior Questions

Direct questions that are inserted into a sentence and are set off from the rest of it usually take question marks. Basically, the question is set into a statement and the end punctuation for the sentence is usually a period or another question mark standing for the entire statement.

It was only two weeks ago—wasn't it?—that I met you.
George Chapman (1559?–1634) was a British poet, translator, and dramatist.

The question mark should not be used to indicate sarcasm. Instead, the diction and discussion should show your attitude.

*Incorrect:* Ms. Baker's beauty (?) was only skin deep.
*Correct:* Ms. Baker's beauty was only skin deep.

### With Other Punctuation

Question marks with quotations are a little tricky. If the entire statement is a question, place the question mark outside the quotation mark at the end of the sentence.

Do you like the sound of the word "iconographic"?

If just the quoted material is a question, place the question mark inside the closing quotation mark.

Last night my boyfriend asked me to sing "What Now, My Love?"

Because the quotation ends the sentence and the quotation requires the question mark at the end, the sentence period is unnecessary.

There are also special rules for the use of question marks with parentheses. If the whole question is in parentheses and is independent of other sentences, place the question mark inside the closing parenthesis.

We could attempt to solve the problem by May. (But do we dare?)

---

### Exercises

A. In the following sentences, correct any flaws in the position or use of periods and question marks.
  1. We all tried not to laugh, but we couldn't hold back when my grandfather said in his Russian accent. "So vat".
  2. Last New Year's Eve, I went to see a movie by Woody Allen.
  3. The policemen who were helping us find our way were very kind, and one of them suggested, "You both ought to get some sleep before you drive much farther."
  4. We had a flat just after we passed a sign that said, "Seven miles to Stuckey's."
  5. Stores that accept food stamps are cautious about what products they allow to be purchased with them. No wonder. They are audited by the federal government.
  6. I have often questioned myself about my own motives when I do something excessively honest, such as tell a checker at a store that he or she has given me too much change.
  7. Many Americans are beginning to question whether living together is as popular as some advocates of cohabitation claim?
  8. Why would the president want to change his energy policy in midstream?
  9. Have you ever known a person who thinks everything is "beautiful?"
  10. I have gone to see *To Have and Have Not* so many times that I know Bogart's lines by heart.
  11. If there are any questions concerning the homework, we are supposed to ask our professor before we do it, not guess at what she means. But I often wonder if she will think we are "dumb" if we ask her.
  12. What should we do if we can't get in to see *Water World?* asked the leader of our group.

13. Sometimes it is hard to determine what people are thinking if they do not want to communicate with you; at other times, they are very easy to "read."

14. "Isn't this the same restaurant we ate at on the day we were married" asked his wife?

15. The dieffenbachia, a common house plant, contains a white liquid which, if it is ingested, affects the vocal apparatus and "can make a person temporarily mute even if only a few drops are eaten". says an article in a weekly magazine.

## QUOTATION MARKS

There are two kinds of quotation marks: the double quotation mark (") and the single quotation mark ('). Although you may sometimes come across books, particularly novels, that use only single quotation marks, you should avoid this usage in the papers you write. Single quotation marks should be used only when quotation marks are needed inside of other quotation marks. In all other situations where quotation marks are required, you should use double quotation marks.

### Direct Quotations

Words taken from another source and dialogue should be placed in quotation marks.

> Dr. Johnson sums up his argument by stating that "far too many individuals are not aware of the almost limitless possibilities for self-improvement."
>
> The professor asked, "How many people have not read the assignment?"

When you are quoting dialogue, only the words actually spoken should be placed in quotation marks. For material from a source, only the words actually taken from that source should be placed in quotation marks. Remember, though, that sometimes even one word taken from someone else can require quotation marks.

> The article deals with the "sexploitation" present in many television commercials.

### Quotations Within Quotations

When quotation marks are needed inside of other quotation marks, single quotation marks should be used.

> Professor Peterson explained, "The line 'And sawdust restaurants with oyster-shells' is not a reference to Cape Cod resorts."
>
> Jane Shahan, literary critic for Channel Seven, said, "A close look at Comrack's newest short story, 'Daddy's Mother,' reveals it to be just another sentimental love story."

### Words as Words

When a word is used as a word instead of for its meaning, it may be placed in quotation marks.

> Try not to have too many "and's" in your sentence.
> In the jargon, "cherry" means "fantastic."
> For me, all those "if's" hindered growth in our relationship.

However, italics or underlining is more often used for this purpose (see p. 531).

### Titles

Titles of short stories, essays, articles, parts of books, short poems, songs, and television shows are placed in quotation marks. The titles of long poems, published separately, are usually underlined.

> In the story "The Peaches," Dylan Thomas mixes autobiography with fantasy.
> Ciancio's article, "The Sweetness of the Twisted Apples," explains Sherwood Anderson's view of the grotesque.

You should not put quotation marks around your own title for a paper or essay. If that title happens to include the name of a poem, short story, or some other work that would normally require quotation marks, place quotation marks around those words only.

Fantasy and Fact in Dylan Thomas's Poetry
"The Peaches": An Autobiographical Sketch

### Special Uses

Quotation marks are an effective way to call attention to an uncommon use of a word or phrase. This usage is particularly appropriate when you are using a technical term in a nontechnical context. For instance, in the following example terms from computer science are applied to the field of writing.

> Your "hardware" is a pen and a piece of paper, and your "software" is everything you know about good writing.

Writers sometimes use quotation marks to show that they know that a particular word or expression they are using is slang or a cliché. Although this usage may occasionally be effective, most often it should be avoided. The quotation marks are unnecessary if the word or expression works well in your sentence. If it does not work well, you should find a better way of expressing the thought instead of using quotation marks.

Some writers also use quotation marks to add a note of disparagement or to indicate irony. This usage should almost always be avoided.

*Weak:* The Queen's address was typically "proper" and boring.
*Effective:* The Queen's address was typically proper and boring.

### Placement of Quotation Marks

Placement of quotation marks follows certain standards established by American printers. The rules differ slightly in England, and you may have learned the British method from a teacher schooled by others who have learned the British way. The American method, which is a bit less complicated than the British, is the one you should use.

#### For Direct Quotation

Fit the quotation into your sentence. Punctuate the sentence as your own. Usually, periods from the original passage are dropped unless the quotation also ends your sentence.

> "There's a type of intense personality that drives me wild," Senator Wilard has been quoted as saying.

#### With Parenthetical Citations

When you use a parenthetical citation for a quotation, omit the end punctuation for the quotation unless it is a question mark or an exclamation point. The parenthetical reference, which is considered to be a part of the sentence, should follow the closing quotation mark and should in turn be followed by a period.

> "During the sixties, protest was at such a height that often five or six prisoners a day in a single cell block would go on starvation diets" (Anderson 17).
>
> H. L. Mencken, talking about his experience as a reporter, said that though he had never covered a lynching, he "had rather better luck with revolutions" (*The Vintage Mencken* 57).

Parenthetical citations for block quotations are slightly different. The reference is placed in parentheses after the quotation, which retains its own end punctuation. Remember that quotation marks are not used with block quotations. For examples, see Chapter 10.

### With Other Punctuation

#### Periods and Commas

The rule for using quotes with periods and commas couldn't be simpler. Periods and commas always go inside quotation marks.

> His reserved nature made us nickname him "Mole."
> The officer remarked, "Hot days like this one can bring out the anger and violence in people."
> "The hot days can bring out the anger and violence in people," remarked the officer.

*Semicolons and Colons*

Semicolons and colons always go outside quotation marks.

> There is one thing I have always liked about reading "Dover Beach": the mood it puts me in.
>
> It is not unusual for a consumer to argue with a store manager that an item he or she purchased was advertised as complete, "not a bunch of rubber and plastic scraps with a few washers"; the important question raised by such complaints is whether a manufacturer should be required to advertise items as "unassembled."

*All Other Marks of Punctuation*

Other marks of punctuation are sometimes placed inside and sometimes placed outside quotation marks. You must determine how the other punctuation relates to the group of words enclosed in quotation marks. Question marks, exclamation points, and dashes go inside quotation marks when they are part of the quotation. Otherwise, they go outside the quotation marks.

> Did he say, "Your teeth are like pearls"?

The whole sentence is a question.

> I was the one who asked, "What time is it?"

Only the question is a question. Note that the period for this writer's sentence is dropped because the question mark acts as ending punctuation.

---

**Exercises**

A. In the following sentences, make any needed corrections in the use of quotation marks or in the punctuation used with them.

1. Yesterday three men, according to a local report, 'were herded into a pick-up truck on Vineland Avenue, abducted to a beautiful forest, and given the time of their lives.' This is a new kind of "personsnatching" that is spreading across the country.

2. It is "the American Way" to try to outdo your neighbors.

3. According to Fromm's essay, "Where Are We Now and Where Are We Headed?" we can have a 'humane' technological society!.

4. Even in ordinary conversation, some people cannot resist the temptation to quote what they are reading or to drop lines from their favorite authors, a practice that can get rather foolish: "You look beautiful today, my dear, and 'that is all ye know on earth and all ye need to know'".

5. Many people get into the annoying habit of saying "you know" after almost every other word.

6. If writers get "hung up" on personal experiences, they may not be able to relate to a broad audience.

7. Phrases like "the fact that" and "in my opinion" make sentences wordy and can be chopped off without changing the meaning.

8. In my contract for automobile insurance is a line I had not noticed before that says, "Only the undersigned is protected under the aforesaid conditions".

9. The best essay I ever read by Joan Didion is "Some Dreamers of the Golden Dream".

10. When I read Twain's "The Storm", I was struck by how he uses the senses in his descriptions.

## THE SEMICOLON

The functions of the semicolon are less like those of the colon than they are like those of a combination of a period and a comma. The semicolon has three uses.

### Joining Main Clauses

Semicolons can join two related main clauses. A grammatical balance is set up between the clauses. Sometimes the second clause expands on the first; sometimes it does not.

Farmworkers often do not demand their rights; the fear of deportation makes them afraid to speak up.

She is hasty when making decisions; he takes too long.

The Supreme Court unites and transcends the separate denominational religions and groups; the Court is far more powerful than any of these sects and can serve as an impartial judge.

### With Transitional Words

Semicolons are used before words like *however* and *therefore* when they join main clauses. Other transitional words include *nevertheless, consequently, thus, instead,* and *on the other hand.* Note that the use of a comma instead of a semicolon would create a run-on sentence.

Energy supplies are not getting any more plentiful; therefore, Americans will probably have to give up many of the luxuries they have become so used to.

### For Clarity

Semicolons can help clarify the meaning of a sentence. They may be used in place of commas to join the elements of a series when the elements themselves contain commas.

Some people picture a rural school as a one-room schoolhouse with a fatherly principal who caters to every student's needs; a motherly teacher, who knows all the answers and imparts them with tact and grace; and sisterly and brotherly students, who teach each other important values in life. Those who picture this heavenly family scene have obviously never gone to school in a small town.

The semicolons make the sentence easier to read than if commas had been used between the elements of the series.

The semicolon can also be used in place of the comma when a coordinating conjunction (*and, or, but, nor, for, yet,* or *so*) is used to join two long or complex independent clauses that contain a number of commas.

> Leash laws must be drawn up, enforced, and respected by all citizens; and everyone must realize, once and for all, that the problems the city faces with stray animals are serious and not merely "hogwash," as one councilman has called them.

Notice that, even for the sake of clarity, the semicolon is still only used between elements that are grammatically equal.

### With Other Punctuation

Semicolons always fall outside quotation marks and parentheses.

> Mr. James suggests that if in one week we could attend all the movies shown in New York City, we would become "saturated with a mish-mash of mediocre entertainment"; the chances are, however, that nobody will prove James to be right or wrong. The argument is academic.
>
> The meeting was rescheduled for the noon hour (it had originally been set for 10 A.M.); the chairperson realized that the turnout would be better on everyone's lunch hour.

---

### Exercises

A. Correct any errors in the use of semicolons or commas in the following sentences.

1. I have tried all my life to overcome my fear of water; and in the past two years I have made progress.
2. New artwork for one's house is always fun to frame and hang up; even if finding a place for it can be frustrating.
3. It is often not easy for people who have grown up in the city to adapt to country life; rural lifestyles seem slow to them.
4. When we first moved to the city from a small town in Iowa; we were shocked at how impersonal the people in the stores were.
5. The need to find approval for everything he does makes Jeffrey frustrating to deal with; at the same time, we people at the clinic understand his needs and do our best to help him.

6. Scientists who have studied the causes for earthquakes claim; within twenty years we will be able to predict them well enough to avoid fatalities.
7. Tea is supposedly as bad for one's health as coffee if it is consumed in very large quantities; nevertheless, I can drink tea all day without it upsetting my stomach, while just a little coffee bothers me a lot.
8. Its coat is like a rabbit's its voice is like a cat's; so it's called a "rabicat."
9. I am not the kind of person who wants to work all her life; neither do I want to stay at home and have children.
10. I love to build furniture from oak, its hard texture is a challenge to work with.

## THE SLASH

The slash has five basic uses. Only two of these are commonly found in essays, but the others are often seen in technical writing and scientific reports.

### Poetry Quotations

The slash is used to mark the separation between lines of poetry when they are quoted in the text of an essay or paper. This is the use of the slash that most frequently occurs in essays.

> Erica Jong may be describing the feelings of women dissatisfied with their roles as mothers and wives; alienated "by quarrels, baby bottles, charge accounts of guilt / the sour smell of money," they want a way out of the marriage trap.
>
> The common theme that the world is a stage and life is a mere play can be found in "What Is Our Life?" by Sir Walter Raleigh: "What is our life? A play of passion, / Our mirth the music of division."

The slash is necessary only for short poetry quotations. Longer quotations are normally put in block form. The slash is not necessary in blocked quotations because the lines of poetry appear as they do in the original.

### Options or Alternatives

The slash is used to show options. It is rarely used in essays except in cases such as the following.

the that/who controversy          male/female roles

The legalistic term and/or should be avoided in essay writing.

### Instead of Per

The slash is used to stand for *per,* which means "each" and is commonly used in technical and scientific writing.

20 mi./hr. (miles per hour)
33 mi./gal. (miles per gallon)
30 min./person (minutes per person)

### Line Fractions

The slash separates the numerator and denominator of line fractions, which are commonly used in technical papers.

2/3                                        3/4

Line fractions are also used in essays when a fraction would have to be written out in more than two words.

Because I kept track of distances, I knew that 21/62 of the trip had not yet been completed.

### Abbreviation of Dates

The slash may be used to abbreviate dates in much the same way as the hyphen. Usually abbreviations of this sort are not used in essays. Instead, the date is normally spelled out.

April 11, 1995          4-11-95                    4/11/95

It may also be used to indicate that a period spans parts of two consecutive years.

The 1995/96 school year          Fiscal year 1995/96

## UNDERLINING (ITALICS)

In print, *italics* (this kind of print) are commonly used to distinguish certain words, such as book titles, foreign words, and words used as words. Italics are also used for emphasis. In your papers, indicate that a word should be italicized by underlining it. When underlining several words that come together, either underline each word individually or underline the entire group together. The rules for when to use italics are fairly simple and straightforward. Notice that in a few cases you may either italicize a word or place it within quotation marks.

### Titles

Italics are used for the titles of independently published works. These include books, plays, long poems, musical compositions, newspapers, and periodicals. The titles of movies are italicized, as are the names of ships, aircraft, trains, and works of art. Here are some examples.

*My Life As a Man* (a novel)
*Hamlet* (a play)

*The Waste Land* (a long poem)
*The Planets* (a musical composition)
*The Los Angeles Times* or the *Los Angeles Times* (a newspaper)
*Newsweek* (a periodical)
*Top Gun* (a movie)
the *Amsterdam* (a ship)
the *Spirit of St. Louis* (an aircraft)
the *Orient Express* (a train)
Brancusi's *The Kiss* (a work of art)

Common usage requires that some titles not be italicized. These include holy books as well as a few other well-known works. You should not italicize titles such as the following. Notice that when an article is used with the title, it is not capitalized.

the Bible
the New Testament
the Koran
the Book of Common Prayer
the Declaration of Independence
the Gettysburg Address
the Constitution (of the United States)

### Foreign Words

Foreign words and abbreviations that are not commonly used in English are usually italicized. Foreign words and abbreviations that are common in English writing need not be italicized. Dictionaries may indicate that particular words have become sufficiently common so as not to require italicizing. A general rule, though, is that when you are in doubt, do not italicize foreign words or abbreviations.

*Foreign Words or Abbreviations That Require No Italics*

| | | |
|---|---|---|
| ad infinitum | berserk | vice versa |
| alter ego | bourgeoisie | et al. |
| apropos | fiancé | etc. |
| aria | petite | e.g. |
| baccarat | placebo | i.e. |
| baguette | pimento | ibid. |
| ballerina | salon | op. cit. |
| barrage | status quo | ad hoc |
| barette | | |

*Foreign Terms That Require Italics*
*bon marché* (a bargain)
*coup de grace* (death blow)
*objet d'art* (art work)
*pièce de résistance* (the main dish, item, or event)

## Words as Words

Words used as words instead of for their meaning are generally italicized.

Is *fitted* the past tense of *fit?*
*Love* and *happiness* are both hard words to define.

You may also use quotation marks instead of italics to indicate that a word is used as a word, although italics are used more often. Whichever form you decide on, make sure that you are consistent throughout the essay.

## Emphasis

Italics are also used in prose to emphasize words or ideas. This practice is helpful in textbooks for pointing out those words or phrases that students should be sure to take note of. As a general rule, however, the use of italics in papers and essays should be kept to a minimum. There are times when using italics can be effective, particularly when they help to clarify what you are trying to say. At such times, do not hesitate to use them. Make sure, though, that you are not using them simply to prop up ineffective words. You should depend on your choice of words for your meaning and emphasis. Relying on italics not only diverts your reader's attention but also lessens the effectiveness of italics when they are appropriate.

## Exercises

A. In the following sentences, underline any words that should be italicized.

1. Of all our textbooks, Encountering Biology is the most costly.
2. The concise use of language in the poem The Red Wheelbarrow makes it challenging.
3. It is surprising how accurate Ibsen was in A Doll's House, a play about women's frustrations with the role of the perfect little wife.
4. One of the challenges of making Peter Pan was how to make him fly without the props showing on the screen.
5. Elle magazine attracts a selective audience.
6. Before I took an introduction to literature class, I didn't know how to find the symbols in a novel or short story, but now I can read a book as hard as Moby Dick and see beyond the basic adventure story.
7. Georgia O'Keefe's paintings are full of mysteries, especially the Ladder to the Moon.
8. When my dad goes to Las Vegas, he likes to stand around and watch the wealthy people play baccarat.
9. Because of their political connections, the Smiths were asked to serve as ad hoc members of the book selection committee at our school.
10. The Bible is one work of literature I have never studied as carefully as I should have.

# A GLOSSARY OF USAGE

Good writing is made up of those words that convey the writer's message to the intended audience as clearly as possible. Sometimes, however, the best words are not easy to find. A word or phrase that means one thing to one person may mean something entirely different to someone else. This difficulty is partly overcome through the use of standard English, which you will remember is that form of English accepted and used by the largest number of educated people. But standard English is not frozen. Its usages are mostly habits, not hard and fast rules, and these habits are constantly changing. Words and phrases that were frowned on in the past are now accepted, and many current usages will undoubtedly become obsolete in the future. Still, the standards of the times determine what is good writing. For this reason, every writer should learn what is currently acceptable and what is not.

Good usage is also determined by the intended audience and by the level of formality of what is being written. An expression that is well suited to a specialized paper may be jargonistic in something aimed at a general audience. Similarly, a phrase that is perfect for a formal essay may be stuffy or obscure in one that is informal. It is up to you, the writer, to decide what works in each specific case. To help you make the best possible choice, this chapter not only distinguishes between poor and effective usages but also indicates levels of usage. *Nonstandard* means that a usage should be avoided in relatively formal speaking and writing. *Colloquial* indicates that a usage is fine for speaking but should usually be avoided when writing. *Formal* and *informal* mean just what they say. The one to use depends on the needs of the paper, and only you can decide which is best suited for your purposes.

### Absolutely No

The phrase *absolutely no* is wordy (see circumlocution, p. 209) and should be avoided.

### Acquiesce In

Use *acquiesce in* instead of *acquiesce to.*

Jim acquiesced in his parents' demands.

### Ad, Exam

The word *ad* is a shortened form of the word *advertisement. Ad* should be used only informally and is best avoided in papers.

An advertisement in the *Times* led to my current job.

533

The word *exam* is a shortened form of the word *examination. Exam* should be used only informally and is best avoided in papers.

> To become certified by the state, one has to take an examination.

### Adverse, Averse
*Adverse* means "unfavorable."

> The adverse circumstances of her youth in Harlem permitted her to develop enormous empathy for those in underserved communities.

*Averse to* means "opposed to."

> I am not averse to eating raw onion.

### Advice, Advise
*Advice* is a noun.

> His mother's advice was to finish college before getting married.

*Advise* is a verb.

> His mother advised him to finish college before getting married.

### Affect, Effect
Except in psychology, where it has a specialized meaning, *affect* is always a verb meaning "to influence" or "to put on or pretend."

> The write-in votes affected the outcome of the election.
> He affected sophistication.

*Effect* is usually a noun meaning "a result."

> The law did not have the effect that was intended.

But *effect* can also be used as a verb meaning "to bring about."

> The employer effected changes that angered her employees.

### Aftereffect
The word *aftereffect* is redundant, since an effect always comes after its cause. The word *effect,* by itself, is all that is necessary.

### Aggravate
*Aggravate* means "to make worse."

> Her insistence aggravated his bad mood.

The colloquial use of the word, meaning "to bother or annoy," is acceptable in informal writing but should be avoided in most papers or essays.

*Weak:* You aggravate me.
*Effective:* You annoy me.

### All Ready, Already

*All ready* and *already* mean two different things. *All ready* means either "completely prepared" or "all are prepared."

If we are all ready, we can leave.
Is the equipment all ready?

*Already* is an adverb meaning "before an indicated time" or "previously."

Since I have already completed the requirements for basic Spanish classes, I will now take a more advanced class.

### All Right

*All right* is correct. *Alright* is a misspelling.

### All Together, Altogether

*All together* and *altogether* mean two different things. *All together* means "physically or spiritually close together."

This Christmas, my family will be all together for the first time in over three years.

*Altogether* means "completely, thoroughly, or when all is said and done."

The evening seemed altogether too brief.
Altogether, it was the best show to open this year.

### Almost Always, Most Always

*Almost always* is more acceptable than *most always,* which is generally considered to be nonstandard English. However, you are probably better off using *usually* instead of either of these expressions.

### Also

*Also* should not be used as a coordinating conjunction. It cannot be used in place of *and. Also* may occur at the beginning of a sentence as a transitional word or may follow a semicolon that separates two main clauses. However, if what follows the *also* is a main clause and what precedes it is also a main clause, you will want to replace the *also* with a coordinating conjunction from the following list: *and, or, nor, for, but, yet,* or *so.* Make sure that the one you choose fits the context of your sentence.

*Weak:* I like painting, also singing is fun.
*Effective:* I like painting; also, singing is fun.
*Effective:* I like painting, and singing is fun.

When there is no main clause before and after the *also,* you should change the *also* to *and.*

*Weak:* Ted needs new shoes, also socks.
*Effective:* Ted needs new shoes and socks.

### Although, Though
*Although* and *though* can be used interchangeably.

### Alumnus, Alumna
An *alumnus* is a male graduate. *Alumni* is the plural of *alumnus,* but it is also generally used when referring to groups that include both male and female graduates. An *alumna* is a female graduate. The plural of *alumna* is *alumnae.*

### Ambiance
Avoid using *ambiance* to mean "atmosphere." This usage sounds pretentious.

*Weak:* The ambiance of luxury at the hotel suited the queen's tastes.

Use *atmosphere* instead.

### Among
See *Between, among.*

### Amount, Number
*Amount* refers to a quantity.

He left a small amount of milk in his glass.

*Number* refers to items that are countable.

The number of people who demand the right to free speech is increasing every year.

### Analyzation
*Analyzation* is not a word. It is a mistake some writers make when the word they intend is *analysis.*

### And Etc.
Omit *and* before *etc.*

### And/Or

Although sometimes effective in legal or commercial writing, *and/or* is distracting to readers and should be avoided in most papers and essays.

### Anticipate, Expect

Do not use *anticipate* to mean *expect*. *Anticipate* conveys the added meaning of "to prepare for what is to come."

> We anticipated his arrival by phoning the station.
> We expect interest rates to rise this year.

### Anyways

*Anyways* is a colloquial usage that should be avoided in papers and essays. Use *anyway* instead.

### Apropos Of

Be careful not to write *apropos to*. *Apropos of* is the current usage.

> My point is apropos of the remark you made a few minutes ago.

### Aspect

Although it actually refers to "a particular side or view of something," *aspect* is too often used to mean part or element. When you use the word, be careful to retain the original meaning.

> She views the problem from a different aspect than her father does.

### Assure, Ensure, Insure

*Assure, ensure,* and *insure* are similar in pronunciation but different in usage. *Assure* means "to engender trust in a person by encouraging him or her to believe in the truth of something."

> Ivan assured us that the party could not go on without us.

*Ensure* means "to make certain."

> Getting a real estate license does not ensure a successful career.

*Insure* means the same thing as *ensure* but is most often used in the context of the insurance business.

> The jewelry was insured for $100,000.

### At This Point in Time

Always wordy for *now.*

### A While, Awhile

*A while* and *awhile* sound alike, but they are quite different. *A while* is made up of the noun *while* and the adjective *a.* Use it in phrases beginning with *in* or *for.*

I told him I would see him in a while.

*Awhile,* on the other hand, is an adverb meaning "for a time."

We walked awhile instead of going right home after dinner.

### Basically

Even though it is sometimes appropriate, the adverb *basically* is often overused. Be careful not to allow it to become deadwood in your sentences.

*Weak:* He is basically a man who exploits women.
*Effective:* He is the kind of man who exploits women.

### Between, Among

Generally, *between* is used when referring to two people or things and *among* is used with more than two.

Saturday's game was between the Sea Hawks and the Brass Bells.
Is there anyone among us who will stand up to the mayor?

### Between You and I

The usage should be *between you and me* because *me* is the object of the preposition *between* (see p. 450). *Between you and I* is incorrect.

### Broke

The word *broke* meaning "out of money" is colloquial and should not be used in papers.

*Weak:* Martin was broke, so he couldn't afford to buy a hamburger.
*Effective:* Martin had no money, so he couldn't afford to buy a hamburger.

### Can, May

Often used interchangeably, *can* and *may* have different meanings. *Can* indicates the ability to do something.

I can touch my toes.

*May* indicates the permission to do something.

May I go with you?

### Cannot, Can Not

Either *cannot* or *can not* is acceptable. The form *can not* emphasizes the *not*.

### Cite

See the entry *Sight, Site, Cite.*

### Climactic, Climatic

*Climactic* is an adjective that means "referring to or constituting a climax."

> The story ends following the climactic meeting between the two brothers.

*Climatic* is an adjective that means "referring to the weather or climate."

> Scientists are studying the climatic effects of sunspots.

### Compose, Comprise

The words *compose* and *comprise* are often used to mean the same thing, but they are actually opposites. Compose means "to form by putting together." The parts *compose* the whole.

> The organization is composed of dedicated men and women.

*Comprise* means "to be made up of" or "to consist of." The whole *comprises* the parts.

> My chemistry course comprises both class meetings and laboratory sessions.

The phrase *is comprised of* should be avoided.

### Consist of, Consist In

*Consist of* means "to be made up of." The whole *consists of* the parts.

> The play consists of three acts.

*Consist in* means "to exist in" or "to have a basis in."

> Their relationship consists in mutual dependency.

### Contemporary

The word *contemporary* occasionally causes problems because some writers think that it always refers to the present. Actually, *contemporary* refers to the period being discussed. For example, if a writer is speaking of the late eighteenth century in one sentence and uses the word *contemporary* in the next, then *contemporary* refers to the late eighteenth century. In the same way, if the writer is talking about the 1960s, *contemporary* refers to that period.

### Correspond To, Correspond With
*Correspond to* means "to be in close agreement with" or "to match."

> The line on the right of the graph corresponds to the number of heartbeats per minute.

*Correspond with* means "to communicate with through an exchange of letters."

> I correspond with my aunt who lives in Connecticut.

### Could Of
See the entry *Should of, Could of, Would of.*

### Council, Counsel, Consul
A *council* is a group of people, usually formed to give advice.

> The students formed a council to consider student-faculty relations.

*Counsel* is advice or, particularly in a legal sense, a person who gives advice.

> My friend's counsel was sound, so I followed it.

A *consul* is a government official who lives in a foreign city.

> Her uncle is the American consul in Sidney.

### Credible, Credulous
*Credible* means "believable" or "worthy of belief."

> Some stories about flying saucers are surprisingly credible.

*Credulous* means "gullible" or "believing too readily."

> The man was credulous in his dealings with the pawnbroker.

### Criteria, Criterion
*Criteria* is always plural. It should be followed by *are* or another plural verb.

> The criteria for the proper evaluation of each new product are many.

*Criterion* is the singular form of the word. It should be followed by *is* or some other singular verb.

The only criterion Ms. Gage has set for hiring a new secretary is the ability to organize a schedule.

### Data
*Data* is the plural form.

The data are available.

### Dilemma
*Dilemma* should not be used interchangeably with *problem*. A *dilemma* is a special kind of problem, one for which there seems to be no satisfactory solution or one having two solutions that are equally unattractive.

The city faced the dilemma of raising taxes or going without adequate garbage collection.

### Discreet, Discrete
*Discreet* and *discrete* sound the same but mean two different things. *Discreet* means "acting in good taste" or "tactful."

Senator Corey had to be discreet about the information he had received that afternoon.

*Discrete* means "entirely separate."

The scene has two discrete functions in the play.

### Disinterested, Uninterested
In recent years, *disinterested* and *uninterested* have come to be used interchangeably. Their original meanings, however, supplied useful distinctions, and to some extent the words still have the following connotations.

*Disinterested* implies an unbiased attitude or a lack of selfishness. A disinterested person is usually the best judge.

*Uninterested* implies a lack of interest.

Irene is uninterested in the sciences.

### Drink, Drank, Drunk
The forms of *drink* that give the most trouble are the past tense and those with *have, has,* and *had.* The correct usage of these forms is as follows:

She drank too much wine.
She has [had] drunk too much wine.
They have drunk too much wine.

*Have drank,* a common mistake, is a nonstandard usage.

### Due To

*Due to* is always acceptable after *to be* (*is, are, was, were,* etc.) verbs.

> His poor writing was partly due to his lack of reading experience.

In most other cases, it is better to use *because of.*

> **Weak:** Due to his negligence, we had to pay a lot of money to fix the car.
> **Effective:** Because of his negligence, we had to pay a lot of money to fix the car.

### Due to the Fact That

The phrase *due to the fact that* is overworked. Try to do without it or replace it with *because.*

> **Weak:** I was late to work due to the fact that I missed my bus.
> **Effective:** I was late for work because I missed my bus.

### During the Course Of

The phrase *during the course of* is wordy. Leave out *the course of.*

### Effect

See *Affect, Effect.*

### E.g.

See *I.e., E.g.*

### Eminent, Imminent

*Eminent* means "notable."

> Her eminent professor received an invitation to speak to a group of accountants about corporate change.

*Imminent* means "very soon."

> His greatest fear was that an earthquake was imminent.

### Emphasis, Emphasize

*Emphasis* and *emphasize* are similar in meaning, but they are different parts of speech. *Emphasis* is a noun.

> The main emphasis in most writing should be the orderly arrangement of ideas.

*Emphasize* is a verb.

> Many women feel that there is a need to emphasize equality between the sexes.

**Ensure**

See the entry *Assure, Ensure, Insure.*

**Enter Into**

*Enter into* should be used only when referring to nonphysical things such as agreements, contracts, and discussions.

> He finally entered into the discussion.
> They entered into a partnership.

*Enter* should not be followed by *into* when referring to a physical structure.

> She entered the room.

**Equally As**

*Equally as* is a nonstandard usage that mixes *equally* with terms such as *as good as.* In your writing, use one term or the other but not the combination.

> John's essay is as good as Marsha's.
> John's and Marsha's essays are equally good.

**Et al., Etc.**

*Et al.* and etc. are abbreviations for Latin words meaning "and others." *Et al.* is used for people; *etc.* is used for things. These abbreviations should be used in footnotes, bibliographic entries, and other places where space is at a premium. Normally, they are not italicized. In the text of a paper, such abbreviations should usually be avoided and words such as *and others* used instead.

> *Weak:* Many poets of the period—Wordsworth, Keats, Shelley, et al.—wrote about nature.
> *Effective:* Many poets of the period—Wordsworth, Keats, Shelley, and others—wrote about nature.

**Etc.**

See *And etc.; Et al., Etc.*

**Ethics, Morals**

The two words are not interchangeable. *Ethics* means "a system of moral principles" and is theoretical.

> His business ethics were questionable.

*Morals* refer to behavior based on ethics. *Moral code* usually refers to sexual behavior.

> The closed-minded young man believed that anyone who dated more than one woman was immoral.

### Exam
See *Ad, Exam.*

### Excess Verbiage
Using *excess* with *verbiage* is redundant. *Verbiage* by itself means "wordiness" or "an excess of words." Thus, you could say that the phrase *excess verbiage* is *verbiage.*

### Expect
See *Anticipate, Expect.*

### Facet
The word *facet* is often misused. It is not interchangeable with the word *part.* A *facet* is technically the plane surface of a cut gem. Try as much as possible to retain the original meaning by using the word only in reference to a new or unexpected consideration or aspect of a subject. Otherwise use *part.*

> *Weak:* There are four facets to doing original research.
> *Effective:* The most shocking facet of the testimony by Ms. Conroy was her involvement with child pornography.

### Factor
The word *factor* is greatly overused. Try to do without it.

> *Weak:* Good eating habits are an important factor for good health.
> *Effective:* Good eating habits are important for good health.

### Farther, Further
Although the words are often used interchangeably, *farther* is generally used to refer to physical distance.

> He lived farther away than we thought.

*Further* is used to refer to a greater degree or extent in a more abstract sense.

> Taking his argument a step further shows why it is illogical.

### Fellow
The word *fellow* is colloquial. *Man* or *person* should be substituted in your papers.

> *Weak:* He is a fellow who likes to win arguments.
> *Effective:* He is a person who likes to win arguments,

### Fewer, Less
*Fewer* refers to items that can be counted.

Fewer dignitaries than ever attended the convention this year.

In the fraternity, fewer men like to play cards than like to play chess.

*Less* refers to quantities or amounts.

There is less time left to register for voting than I had thought. Less money was found in the old box than had been expected.

### Fictitious Novel

Novels are a type of fiction. Therefore, the phrase *fictitious novel* is redundant. Use only the word *novel.* Works that are not fiction are called *nonfiction.* A historical novel is a fictionalized account of an event in history.

### Flaunt, Flout

*Flaunt* and *flout* sound similar and are sometimes used in the same context, but they mean different things. Flaunt means "to show off" or "to display oneself."

He flaunted his wealth.

*Flout,* however, means "to condemn" or "to scorn."

He flouted the convention of removing one's hat in public buildings.

Both words could be used to describe someone's behavior, but the words are not synonymous.

Must they flaunt their immorality and flout the upstanding values of the respectable citizens in this town?

### Flunk

*Flunk* meaning "to fail" is colloquial. Do not use it in papers.

*Weak:* He flunked the eye test for his driver's license.
*Effective:* He failed the eye test for his driver's license,

### Former, Latter

See *Latter, Former.*

### Fun

*Fun* is sometimes used informally as an adjective before a noun. In papers, however, this usage is inappropriate. *Fun* should be considered a noun.

*Weak:* My friend Tom is a fun person to be with.
*Effective:* My friend Tom is a lot of fun to be with.

### Funny

You should use *funny* only when referring to something that is humorous. Avoid using it to mean "strange" or "unusual."

*Weak:* A funny feeling came over me.
*Effective:* A strange feeling came over me.

### Further

See *Farther, Further.*

### Generally, In General, Obviously

Try to do without these words. They are overworked. Nevertheless, they may be valuable to you in one way. In your rough draft, they may be clues that you are tending to think in too general a way or are making obvious statements. In such cases, you will want to omit, or at least revise, the sentences and ideas these words point out.

### General Public

*General public* is wordy and overused. *Public,* alone, will serve the purpose.

### Geographical Location

The term *geographical location* is redundant and should be avoided. Instead, use *location.*

### Good, Well

*Good* should always be used as an adjective. Notice that it frequently follows linking verbs (see p. 365) such as *to be* and *to feel.*

> He feels unusually good today.
> She looks good in brown.
> Carla is a good driver.

*Well* is used as an adjective only when referring to physical health.

> Michael is not well.

Otherwise, *well* should be used as an adverb that tells "how" about a verb.

> Carla drives well.
> Most college students do not write as well on in-class exams as on take-home papers.

### Great Deal

The phrase *a great deal* is often a wordy way of writing *much* or *many.*

### He/She, His/Her

You should avoid using constructions such as *he/she* and *his/her.* Instead, use *he or she, his or her.*

Each student was asked to write about a subject he or she found interesting.

Each of us was expected to do his or her own laundry.

Some writers feel that using *he or she* is awkward, yet they do not like the implications of using *he* by itself. An easy way to avoid this problem is to make the noun referred to plural.

The students were asked to write about subjects they found interesting.

We were expected to do our own laundry.

### Healthful, Healthy

*Healthful* and *healthy* are both adjectives, but they have different meanings. *Healthful* means "good for the health."

Walking is a healthful exercise.

*Healthy* means "in good health."

Jacques is a healthy man.

### Heap of, Heaps of

Although they are frequently heard, the phrases *heap of* and *heaps of* are too informal for most essays. In papers, use either *many* or *a large number of.*

### Height, Heighth

*Height* is the correct spelling. Be careful not to confuse the spelling of *height* with that of *length,* which should end in *th.*

### Hisself, Theirselves

*Hisself* and *theirselves* are not standard usages. *Himself* and *themselves* are the accepted forms.

### Hopefully

Literally, *hopefully* means "full of hope."

Janice looked at her doctor hopefully as he told her the results of her laboratory tests.

In conversation, *hopefully* is often used to mean "it is hoped." In papers and essays, however, it is best to avoid this usage unless you are writing informally.

### Idea, Ideal

The two words are confused because they sound similar. An *idea* is a thought in the mind.

His idea is worth considering if it can save time.

An *ideal* is a state of perfection to be striven for. The same word acts as an adjective meaning "perfect."

His ideal of a good parent is a good friend.
An ideal arrangement would be driving to work together.

### I.e., E.g.

An abbreviation of a Latin term, *i.e.* means "that is." It is used to explain or restate a preceding word or phrase. The abbreviation should not normally be italicized and should be used primarily in places where space is at a premium, such as in footnotes and tables. You should usually avoid using it in the text of an essay. Another abbreviation of a Latin term, *e.g.* means "for example" and is used to introduce one or several examples of a preceding word or phrase. It should normally not be italicized. The abbreviation is frequently used in footnotes and other places where space is at a premium but should usually be avoided in the text of a paper.

### If, Whether

*If* and *whether* both convey the sense of something conditional, doubtful, or uncertain. *Whether* is generally used to introduce a noun clause.

I wonder whether we will have to wait on line.

However, *if* is generally acceptable in such constructions as well. *If* is sometimes used with then. This usage, however, is not effective, since the sentence the expression is contained in makes perfect sense without the *then.*

*Weak:* If my intentions appear good, then you must trust me.
*Effective:* If my intentions appear good, you must trust me.

Likewise, it is not effective to write *if* and *when.* In speaking, some people feel that the combination of the words emphasizes their point. Actually, the combination, at least in writing, would weaken the point, since either *if* or *when* alone would do the job.

### Imminent

See *Eminent, Imminent.*

### Imply, Infer

*Imply* and *infer* are often confused. In a sense, these two words can be thought of as the opposite sides of a single coin. *Imply* means "to indicate without stating" or "to express indirectly." *Infer* means "to draw a conclusion." Thus, what a writer may *imply,* a reader may *infer.*

The writer of the article implies that the mayor is incompetent.

I infer from the article that the author believes the mayor to be incompetent.

## In Regard to
See *Regards, In Regard to.*

## In Terms of
*In terms of* is a vague phrase that is seldom necessary. Usually, a sentence is more effective without it.

*Weak:* In terms of money, Terry is very frugal.
*Effective:* Terry is very frugal.

## Incident, Incidence
The words *incident* and *incidence* are often confused because of the similarity in their pronunciation. An *incident* is an occurrence or happening.

One senator has been involved in a number of embarrassing incidents.

*Incidence* means "the rate of occurrence."

Surprisingly, the incidence of polio in the United States is once again increasing.

## Incredible
*Incredible* is frequently misused. Too often, writers use it as a catch-all intensifier. Actually, *incredible* means "too improbable or extraordinary to be readily believed." Use of the word should be reserved for this meaning.

*Weak:* Nuclear accidents represent an incredible hazard to human life.
*Weak:* He is an incredible person.
*Effective:* Her story about the ordeals of the survivors of the airplane crash was incredible but true.
*Effective:* The jury felt that his testimony was incredible.

## Insure
See the entry *Assure, Ensure, Insure.*

## Ironic, Irony
The words *ironic* and *irony* are often used imprecisely. You should not use these words to point out just any contrast or change of events. For something to be *ironic,* it must contrast dramatically with what the reader would normally expect.

*Weak:* The irony is that she always forgot something even though she went to the market every day.

*Effective:* It is ironic that many bank tellers are unable to balance their own checkbooks.

### Irregardless

*Irregardless* is nonstandard. This form of the word is redundant, as both the prefix *ir* and the suffix *less* mean "without." Use *regardless* instead.

### It Must Be Noted Here

Phrases such as *it must be noted here* are usually deadwood and should be avoided.

### Its, It's

The words *its* and *it's* are often confused because the possessive one (its) does not take an apostrophe.

> The cat played with its tail.

*It's* is the contraction for "it is" or "it has." The omitted letters are marked by an apostrophe.

> It's been years since I've gone to a baseball game.
> It's not fair to the rest of the team for you to show up late.

### Kids

*Kids* is a colloquial term. It should be avoided in most essay writing. Use children or a similar word instead.

### Kind Of

*Kind of* is colloquial. In most papers, the word *somewhat* would be more appropriate. Either expression should be avoided if it does not add information to your sentence but is, instead, used as a catchall.

*Weak:* Herman Core is kind of outspoken for somebody who calls himself a "diplomat."

*Weak:* Herman Core is somewhat outspoken for somebody who calls himself a "diplomat."

*Effective:* Herman Core is outspoken for somebody who calls himself a "diplomat."

*Effective:* My father is not angry but somewhat disturbed by my decision.

### Latter, Former

*Latter* and *former* should be used only to single out one of two previously mentioned items. These terms sound very formal. Instead of using them, it is often more effective to repeat the particular word you are referring to.

### Lay, Lie

Confusion between *lay* and *lie* is the cause of a large number of errors in speaking and writing. Most of the difficulty seems to stem from the forms of these words in the past tense.

> Yesterday I laid the magazine right here, and now I can't find it.
> Yesterday I lay down at around the same time as I did today.

See page 441 for a complete discussion of these two verbs.

### Lend, Loan

*Lend* is always a verb.

> Please lend me a cup of sugar.

*Loan* is normally used as a noun, but it can also be used as a verb.

> I am going to the bank to ask for a loan.
> James loaned Elizabeth his class notes.

### Less

See *Fewer, Less.*

### Less, Least

*Less* and *least* are both comparative words. *Less* means "not as much" or "smaller" and is used when comparing two things. It is usually followed by *than. Least* means "smallest" or "the minimum amount" and is used when comparing more than two things.

> He is less friendly than she is.
> Burt is the least interesting person I know.

### May

See *Can, May.*

### Media

*Media* is always the plural form. *Medium* is singular.

> The medium of television alone is not responsible for students' difficulty with writing.
> The media have promoted sexist values.

### Morals

See *Ethics, Morals.*

### More

When using the word *more,* be careful not to form an incomplete comparison. *More* should usually be followed by *than.*

*Weak:* He is more willing to work.
*Effective:* He is more willing to work than we expected.

## More Preferable

When you state that one thing is *preferable* to another, you have made an appropriate comparison. Adding the word *more* is therefore redundant and should be avoided.

## Most Always

See *Almost Always, Most Always.*

## Neither . . . Nor

*Neither* should always be followed by *nor;* never by *or.*

Neither Jan nor David was in class today.

## Nice

The word *nice* is greatly overused. It is also imprecise. How can your reader know exactly what you mean by *nice?* Whenever possible, you should replace *nice* with a more specific word or phrase.

*Weak:* Marsha is a nice person.
*Effective:* Marsha is a friendly and considerate person.

## Nowhere Near, Not Nearly

*Nowhere near* is colloquial. For essays, *not nearly* is preferred.

*Weak:* He was nowhere near as strong as Atlas, but sometimes he felt that the whole world was on his shoulders.
*Effective:* He was not nearly as strong as Alice, but sometimes he felt that his family expected him to be the one in charge of difficult decisions.

## Number

See *Amount, Number.*

## Off, Off from, Off of; Out, Out from, Out Of

Avoid using either *from* or *of* with *off* or *out.*

They jumped off the wagon.
The Robinses put the cat out the door before going to bed.

## One

See *You, One.*

## On the Basis of

The phrase *on the basis of* is greatly overworked. It is seldom necessary and should usually be eliminated from your sentences.

### Oriented, Orientated

*Orientated* is usually a mistake for oriented.

The Puritans were a God-oriented society.

*Orientation* is the noun form of the word.

### Owing to the Fact That

Phrases such as *owing to the fact that* are almost always wordy. Use *because* or *since* instead.

### Pecuniary Reimbursement, Remuneration

Avoid these highly formal phrases for *pay*.

### Phenomena, Phenomenon

*Phenomenon* is the singular form of the word.

An eclipse of the moon is an impressive phenomenon.

*Phenomena* is always plural.

Many phenomena in nature are still unexplained.

### Prefer . . . to

*Prefer* should be followed by *to,* never by *than*.

*Weak:* I prefer talking on the telephone than writing letters.
*Effective:* I prefer talking on the telephone to writing letters.
*Prefer* may also be followed by *instead of*.

I prefer talking on the telephone instead of writing letters.

### Prejudice, Prejudiced

*Prejudice* can be either a noun or a verb.

His prejudice against recent immigrants reveals his intolerance.
The judge was accused of trying to prejudice the jury in favor of the defendant.

*Prejudice,* however, should never be used as an adjective. The correct adjective form of the word is *prejudiced*.

Jim is a prejudiced man.

Of course, *prejudiced* can also be used as a verb.

Betty Jo's attitude prejudiced the committee against her.

Notice that *prejudice* and *prejudiced* can be used in either a positive or a negative sense.

### Pretty

*Pretty* is sometimes used colloquially to mean "rather" or "quite." This usage should be avoided in papers or essays.

*Weak:* She reads Spanish pretty well.
*Effective:* She reads Spanish rather well.

### Prior to

In most cases, it is better to use *before* instead of *prior to.*

### Pseudo-intellectuals

Do not use this term for people who you think are lacking intellect. Call them *nonintellectuals. Pseudo-intellectuals* applies to people who pretend to be more intellectual than they actually are.

### Put Across

*Put across* is a wordy and often confusing phrase. More appropriate is either *expressed* or simply *said.*

### Raise, Rise

*Raise* and *rise* are often confused, especially in the past tense. *Raise (raised, raised)* means "to lift up."

The girl raised her hand.

*Rise (rose, risen)* means "to go up" or "to get up."

The company's stock rose over eight points last Thursday.
He rises before seven every morning.

### Rare, Scarce

Both *rare* and *scarce* mean "infrequently found." *Rare,* however, usually connotes a permanent lack of availability.

The prize of my collection is a rare Egyptian gold piece.

*Scarce,* on the other hand, usually connotes a temporary lack of availability.

When commodities are scarce, their prices rise.

### Real, Really, Very

*Real* is often used colloquially to mean *very.* Unless you are writing informally, you should avoid this usage in papers and essays. *Really* will work, but *very* or a word that is even more descriptive is better.

*Weak:* Mary is real happy about her new job.
*Effective:* Mary is really happy about her new job.
*Effective:* Mary is very happy about her new job.
*Effective:* Mary is ecstatic about her new job.

### Reason, Rationalize

*To reason* is to think rationally.

Her reasoning led her to the correct solution of the complex math problem.

*To rationalize,* however, has the connotation of providing reasons for conduct that are plausible but untrue.

He rationalized his mother's drinking problems by telling himself that she had lived a difficult life.

### Regards, In Regard to

It is never acceptable to say *in regards to* or *with regards to.* Correct idioms for the phrase include *in regard to, with regard to, regarding,* and *concerning.* The word *regards* means "good wishes" and is used as in the following sentence:

Give my regards to Emma.

*Regard* is also a verb used to mean "refer to."

My concern regards a disturbance you initiated in class the other day, Jim.

### Scarce

See *Rare, Scarce.*

### Self-Concept

Adding words such as "of herself" to the term *self-concept* is redundant. You should use either *her concept of herself* or *her self-concept,* but be careful not to combine the two.

### Sensual, Sensuous

*Sensual* and *sensuous* both refer to satisfaction of the senses. However, the two words are usually used with different connotations. *Sensual* implies indulgence in one's appetites for pleasure and often suggests sexuality.

Lord Byron was known as a sensual man.

*Sensuous,* on the other hand, implies taking enjoyment from more aesthetic delights such as those of nature or the arts.

Concerts under the stars appealed to her sensuous nature.

### Set, Sit

*Set* and *sit* are often confused. *To set* means "to place."

She set her glasses down on the table.

*To sit* means "to rest the body upright" or "to be situated."

They sit in the same seats at every concert.
Our house sits on a hill overlooking a golf course.

For a more detailed coverage of these words, see page 442.

### Should of, Could of, Would of

*Should of, could of,* and *would of* are sometimes incorrectly written for *should have, could have,* and *would have.* The confusion probably arises from what is heard when someone speaks quickly. A good way to avoid this mistake is to remember that in the contractions of these words—*should've, could've,* and *would've*—the *ve* is a shortened form of have.

### Sight, Site, Cite

*Sight, site,* and *cite* all sound the same, but their meanings are very different. *Sight* is a noun meaning "something seen."

The sight of my grandmother working in her garden lives in my memory.

*Site* is a noun meaning "the location of something."

The site of their next film is a small ranch in Mexico.

*Cite* is a verb meaning "to refer to" or "to quote in order to offer an example, establish authority, or provide proof."

To back up her argument, she cited the opinions of several noted experts.

### So

Using *so* as the first word of a sentence is highly informal. Use a transitional word such as *therefore* instead in papers.

*Weak:* Our new neighborhood was well integrated. So, our high school offered all the advantages of multicultural experiences.
*Effective:* Our new neighborhood was well integrated. Thus our high school offered all the advantages of multicultural experiences.

### Some Time, Sometime, Sometimes

*Some time, sometime,* and *sometimes* have different meanings and are often confused. *Some time* is made up of an adjective and a noun and means "an amount of time."

> Whenever you have some time to chat, feel free to visit me.
> Some time has passed since our last conversation.

*Sometime* is an adverb. It means "an unspecified time."

> No one is sure when, but the dog will have to eat sometime.

*Sometimes* is also an adverb, but it means "now and then."

> Sometimes I feel so clever that I could do anything.

### Stationary, Stationery

*Stationary* is an adjective meaning "not moving" or "not changing in condition."

> The flight was so smooth that the airplane seemed to be stationary.

*Stationery* is a noun meaning "paper used for writing letters."

> John writes his letters in dark brown ink on light brown stationery.

A good way to avoid confusing these two words is to remember that stationery and paper both contain *er.*

### Subconscious

See *Unconscious, Subconscious.*

### Such As

When you introduce a list or series with the term *such as,* be sure that you do not use the phrase *to name a few* to conclude the list or series.

> *Weak:* At the party there were many refreshments, such as fruit, cheese, homemade candies, ice cream, soft drinks, and coffee to name a few.
> *Effective:* At the party there were many refreshments, such as fruit, cheese, homemade candies, ice cream, soft drinks, and coffee.

### Such That

*Such that* is a term that usually introduces a formal description. It often follows a linking verb, usually a form of *to be* (*is, are, was, were,* etc). What comes after the *that* is a further explanation or description of the subject under discussion in the sentence.

> The behavior of the two men was such that none of the rest of us wanted to admit to knowing them.

### Summary, Summation
A summary is an abstract or a concise condensation used by writers to present the substance of something they do not wish to quote directly.

> Our teacher warned us not to give a summary of the plot in our book reviews.

A *summation* is the final part of an argument that reviews the points previously made and offers conclusions.

> The prosecuting attorney presented an emotional summation of the state's case.

### Super
The use of *super* as an intensifier is colloquial and should be avoided in most papers and essays.

> *Weak:* She is super intelligent.
> *Effective:* She is very intelligent.

### Suspect, Suppose
*Suspect* usually has negative connotations. Avoid using it when what you really mean is *suppose.*

> *Weak:* We suspect that all the members of the committee will attend the luncheon.
> *Effective:* We suppose that all the members of the committee will attend the luncheon.

### Terrific
*Terrific* is overused. Try to substitute a more specific word for it.

> *Weak:* All in all, he was a terrific friend.
> *Effective:* All in all, he was a loyal friend.

### That
*That* should be used to connect a subordinate clause to a main clause if you feel the word sounds natural. Keep in mind that it is acceptable and correct to omit the *that* whenever the subordinate clause following it is clearly subordinate. Both of the following sentences are acceptable.

> I felt he was less qualified than I was.
> I felt that he was less qualified than I was.

However, when the clause introduced by *that* comes before the main verb in the sentence, be sure to use the *that*.

> That I had run the mile in record time was a surprise to me.
> That she could be fooled I had to question.

### That That

Sometimes the phrase *that that* is present in a sentence. Even though the two *that's* appear next to each other, they are not redundant and are acceptable. They each have different functions. If you wish, you may leave out the first *that,* which acts as a subordinate conjunction (see entry for *that*). Either of the following sentences would be acceptable.

> It would surprise me to learn that that house is for sale.
> It would surprise me to learn that house is for sale.

### That, Which, Who

Although the preferred usage of *that, which,* and *who* is less rigid than it once was, *that* is normally used to refer to people, animals, and things. *Which* usually refers to things or animals, and *who* generally refers only to people. *That* is used to introduce essential clauses. Remember that essential clauses (those which cannot be removed from the sentence without changing the meaning of the noun they follow) are never set off by commas. *Who* and *which* can introduce either essential or unessential clauses, but many writers use *which* only for unessential clauses. Unessential clauses should be set off by commas. (See Chapter C for more information on the use of commas.)

### Theirselves
See *Hisself, Theirselves.*

### This

When the word *this* is used it should have an obvious referent in preceding sentences or the word following it should be a noun specifying exactly what *this* refers to.

> *Weak:* It was three in the morning when this knock came at my door.
> *Effective:* It was three in the morning when a knock came at my door.
> *Weak:* This was the turning point in the war.
> *Effective:* This battle was the turning point in the war.

### Though
See *Although, though.*

### Thusly

The word *thusly* is not used by careful speakers or writers. Use *thus* instead. *Thus* is already an adverb and does not benefit by the *ly* ending. The *ly* is thus unnecessary and a bit pretentious.

### To, Two, Too

*To, two,* and *too* are often confused. Each is set into a different context. *To* is used as part of an infinitive or a prepositional phrase.

> I want to know the answer.
> They went to college.

*Two* is the number.

> Two hours is hardly enough time to study for a final examination.

*Too* means "also" or "excessive."

> John played very well. I did well, too.
> Labor unions require too much dues of their members.

Be careful to use intensifiers like *too, very,* and *really* only when they add meaning to your statements.

> *Weak:* I was too thrilled when I found a letter from my sister in the mailbox.
> *Effective:* I was thrilled when I found a letter from my sister in the mailbox.

### Today's Society

The expression *today's society* is trite and should be avoided, especially in the introduction to an essay.

> *Weak:* Prejudice against minorities is surprisingly widespread in today's society.
> *Effective:* Prejudice against minorities is surprisingly widespread.

### Toward, Towards

*Toward* is more common in the United States while *towards* is more common in England. For formal writing, stick with American usage.

### Try And, Try To

*Try and* is colloquial. Most often, *try to* should be used instead. The phrase *to try and learn* actually indicates two distinct actions—trying and learning. Avoid the *and* unless you really mean it,

> *Weak:* I always try and help my friends when I can.
> *Effective:* I always try to help my friends when I can.

### Type

When the word *type* is used as a noun, it should usually be followed by *of.*

*Weak:* This type person should not be trusted.
*Effective:* This type of person should not be trusted.

## Unconscious, Subconscious

The adjectives *unconscious* and *subconscious* are often confused. *Unconscious,* in popular usage, means "lacking awareness" or "not intentional."

> His unconscious slip of the tongue was funny.
> He was unconscious for a few seconds after the fight.

*Subconscious,* in popular usage, means "not fully aware of" or "working in the mind beneath the level of consciousness."

> Luckily, some subconscious conservatism in my nature told me to return to my home town instead of venturing into strange places.

Each of these words has a slightly different meaning in psychology than in popular usage.

## Uninterested

See *Disinterested, Uninterested.*

## Unique

Technically, *unique* means "one of a kind." The use of *unique* to mean "rare" has become generally accepted, but you should be careful when using the word for this purpose. Avoid using *unique* to mean "appealing" or "not very common." You should also avoid using adverbs such as *more, very,* and *most* with unique. Such intensifiers corrupt the meaning of the word.

> *Weak:* He has a unique personality.
> *Effective:* He has a warm and outgoing personality.
> *Effective:* Gerald Wilson's photography is uniquely displayed.

## Use to, Used To

*Use to* is a mistake for *used to.* Confusion between the two occurs because of the way the words are pronounced. When you are writing, make sure you include the *d.*

> He used to be my friend
> She is used to getting A's.

## Variance

The term *at variance* should always be followed by *with,* not by *from.*

> The majority of the committee is at variance with the mayor's ideas about how to curb street violence.

**Very**
See *Real, Really, Very.*

**Vested Interest**
The term *vested interest* does not necessarily have a negative connotation. The use of the term in each of the following sentences can be negative or positive, depending on the context.

> An executive has a vested interest in every project the company undertakes.
> The gardener has a vested interest in keeping the yard in order.

**Wait on, Wait for**
Although it is sometimes used colloquially to mean "wait for," *wait on* should be used only to mean "to serve."

> The young man who waited on us at the restaurant was studying to be an actor.
> We had to wait for John almost an hour.

**Wander, Wonder**
*Wander* means "to travel about without a fixed course" or "to stray in thought."

> I like to wander around the country.
> During the spring, my mind often wanders, and I find it difficult to concentrate.

*Wonder* means "to feel curiosity or doubt about something."

> I wonder what Jim is doing.

Since *to wonder* is a mental activity, the expression *wonder in my mind* is redundant.

**Well**
See *Good, Well.*

**Where**
*Where* should be used only to refer to location. Using *where* in place of *that* is colloquial and should be avoided in most papers and essays.

> *Weak:* I read in a report where many high school students have trouble doing simple math problems.
> *Effective:* I read in a report that many high school students have trouble doing simple math problems.

## Where . . . at, Where . . . to

Avoid adding *at* or *to* to the ends of sentences or phrases beginning with *where.*

*Weak:* Where do you suppose John is at?
*Effective:* Where do you suppose John is?
*Weak:* Where are you going to?
*Effective:* Where are you going?

## Whether

See *If, Whether.*

## Which

See the entry *That, Which, Who.*

## While

Technically, *while* refers to a span of time and is used to indicate that two or more things occur at the same time.

> While I recite the poem, you read along in the book.

*While* is also used in two other ways, although they are not as generally accepted and can sometimes lead to confusion. Often, *while* is used to mean *even though.*

> While he is my best friend, I will not lie to help him.

Less frequently, *while* is used to mean *and.*

> I like coffee, while she prefers tea.

This usage is not accepted by some in academic writing, and it should be avoided if there is any chance that it will cause ambiguity.

*Weak:* I fixed dinner, while she washed the dishes.

The use of *while* is confusing. It seems to indicate that the two actions—fixing dinner and washing dishes—are taking place at the same time. Since dishes are usually washed after the dinner is fixed and eaten, *and* would be more effective.

> Effective: I fixed dinner, and she washed the dishes.

## Who's, Whose

*Who's* and *whose* sound alike but are quite different. *Who's* is a contraction for "who is" or "who has."

Who's responsible for this mess?
It is Jim who's pulling his car into the driveway.

*Whose* is a possessive pronoun.

The parents whose children acted in the play were proud.
Whose book is it?

### Wise

Coining new words by adding *wise* as a suffix to existing words has become a fad in recent years. These manufactured words—contrarywise, friendshipwise, and selectionwise, for example—should not appear in academic essays.

### Would of

See *Should of, Could of, Would of*

### You, One

Both *you* and *one* can be used to refer to people in general. *You* is more informal than *one.* In an informal situation it would be fine to write the following:

The Grand Canyon and the Carlsbad Caverns are two of the most impressive creations of nature you could ever hope to see.

However, in academic papers, *one* is most often used to refer to people in general and *you* is reserved for occasions when the writer wishes to speak directly to the audience.

The Grand Canyon and the Carlsbad Caverns are two of the most impressive creations of nature one could ever hope to see.
You, the students in this school, must speak up to make the educational needs in our community clear to the school board.
Did you ever wonder what caused you to forget something?

Whichever level of formality you choose, be sure to remain consistent throughout a particular essay.

# INDEX

567 | 🌺

568